CONSTELLATIONS

CONSTELLATIONS

A Contextual Reader for Writers

JOHN SCHILB
University of Maryland

ELIZABETH A. FLYNN
Michigan Technological University

JOHN CLIFFORD
University of North Carolina at Wilmington

HarperCollins*Publishers*

Sponsoring Editor: Patricia A. Rossi
Development Editor: Marisa L'Heureux
Project Coordination and Cover Design: York Production Services
Cover Art: Wright, Frank Lloyd. *Window from the Coonley Playhouse*,
     Riverside, Illinois, 1912. Leaded clear and cased glass,
     18⅝" × 34¾₆". Collection, The Museum of Modern Art, New
     York. Joseph H. Heil Fund. Photograph © 1991, The Museum of
     Modern Art, New York.
Production Manager: Michael Weinstein
Compositor: York Production Services
Printer and Binder: R.R. Donnelley & Sons Company
Cover Printer: The Lehigh Press, Inc.

Constellations: A Contextual Reader for Writers

Library of Congress Cataloging-in-Publication Data

Constellations: a contextual reader for writers / [edited by] John
   L. Schilb, Elizabeth A. Flynn, John Clifford.
       p.   cm.
     ISBN 0-673-46427-X
     1. College readers.   2. English language—Rhetoric.   I. Schilb,
John, 1952– . II. Flynn, Elizabeth A., 1944– .   III. Clifford,
John.
PE1417.C6518   1992
808'.0427—dc20   91-29698
                                                                       CIP

91 92 93 94 9 8 7 6 5 4 3 2 1

Contents

CHAPTER 8   Language   510

CHAPTER 9   Science and Cultural Values   574

Preface

*C*onstellations: A Contextual Reader for Writers is designed to stimulate critical reading, discussion, and writing in composition courses. Its 93 selections, chiefly essays, enable students to examine a variety of perspectives on issues relevant to their lives. Organized by theme, the ten chapters present various approaches to such important contemporary topics as personal identity, family relationships, education, gender, race relations, mass culture, science, and ethics. Instructors will find here venerable writers such as E.B. White, George Orwell, Loren Eiseley, and Joan Didion, but they will also discover more new voices and greater diversity than in most such collections. Over half the selections were written since 1980. Over half are by women. Nearly 30 percent are by authors from ethnic minorities, including 17 African-Americans. The modes of writing presented are also diverse. They include argument, exposition, reportage, personal narrative, description, speculation, and fiction.

The term *constellations* refers to a distinctive feature of the book's structure. We believe that students respond most thoughtfully to a text when they can compare it to another. Too often, anthologies for composition fail to relate their selections much, thus leaving students without any real context for the texts they encounter and the texts they are supposed to produce. Throughout the book, we juxtapose selections, explicitly inviting students to consider the different ideas and rhetorical strategies that writers can bring to a topic. As our term for these groupings, we have borrowed the word *constellations* from Walter Benjamin, a perceptive observer of European culture during the 1920s and 1930s. He used the German equivalent of the word to describe the thought-provoking patterns that can emerge when one juxtaposes historical periods, technological developments, or texts. We think our own constellations of texts will engage students' interest and help them achieve a higher level of inquiry because they will see that a topic can have various dimensions and that writers can take various approaches to it.

Most of the constellations are pairs of texts. We include four in each chapter, and they focus in turn on various aspects of the chapter's theme. The constellations themselves are organized according to various principles. Often, we present multiple viewpoints on a common subject. For example, both Marianna De Marco Torgovnick and Barbara Grizzuti Harrison ponder the implications of a racial killing in their native community of Bensonhurst, New York. Sometimes we present starkly opposing views on a contemporary issue, such as rap music, affirmative action, abortion, euthanasia, calls for "cultural literacy," and the treatment of people who have AIDS. Sometimes we present texts that convey similar ideas, but through different forms. For example, both James Baldwin and Geneva Smitherman defend Black English, but they use different styles in doing so. In certain other constellations, the authors convey parallel experiences, although they may bring different perspectives or backgrounds to them. George Orwell and Richard Rodriguez recall what it was like to be a "scholarship boy"; N. Scott Momaday and Maxine Hong Kingston describe their efforts to understand their ancestors; Brent Staples, Arturo Madrid, and Mitsuye Yamada explain their feelings of "invisibility" as a member of a minority group in America. On occasion, we bring together a long-admired text with a more recent one. Students are invited, for example, to compare Joan Didion's portrayal of Las Vegas in "Marrying Absurd" with Michael Ventura's depiction of it in "Report From El Dorado." They can better understand how E.B. White treats family, time, and place in "Once More to the Lake" when they see how Kathleen Stocking handles these themes in "The Dunes, My Father." They can better evaluate James Agee's portrait of a rural, working-class woman in *Let Us Now Praise Famous Men* by turning to the account she herself gave of her life many years later. In one way or another, many of the constellations bring up issues of gender, class, and race. Yet we do not press students to adopt particular positions on these issues or any others. Instead, we encourage them to cultivate open-ended inquiry as they read the selections, discuss them with one another, and compose texts of their own.

In addition to its method of organization, other aspects of the book help students develop a context for the readings. Some current anthologies for composition provide only a few instructional aids. We continue to believe that students appreciate background information and suggestions for inquiry if they also feel encouraged to develop their own thoughts. We offer such an apparatus here. Its specific features:

- An introduction to the whole book explains the process of critical reading and writing, identifies the book's format, and shows how a particular student analyzed a sample constellation of essays.
- Introductions to each chapter and to each constellation identify the readings to come and some of the issues that will emerge.
- Biographical headnotes for all selections provide important background information on the authors.
- "Reflections Before Reading," a set of questions before each selection, invite students to review their prior knowledge about a selection's content before they read it. Instructors can use these questions to stimulate not only class discussion but also freewriting or similar composing activities.

- Questions after each selection, divided into "Rhetorical Focus" and "Thematic Focus," allow students to analyze the rhetorical strategies that writers use, as well as their ideas. These questions not only deal with the particular text, but also encourage comparisons with any other texts that have preceded it in the constellation.
- "Suggestions for Writing," three possible assignments after each constellation, ask students to continue pursuing issues that the constellation has raised. Just as the book's selections exemplify various modes of writing, these assignments call for students to use them. Usually, at least one asks students to continue comparing the texts in the form of a scholarly argument, while at least one other has them incorporate ideas or rhetorical strategies from the texts into an essay analyzing their personal experience.

Acknowledgments

We are deeply grateful to Ted Simpson, our original editor, who invited us to undertake this project and helped us to conceptualize it. Patricia Rossi, our present editor, has provided us with sound and friendly guidance. We have benefited, too, from the continual wit, intelligence, sympathy, and patience of our developmental editor, Marisa L'Heureux. Robert Schwegler from the University of Rhode Island aided us significantly at a number of stages.

We thank several colleagues and students at our home universities. Many of the selections were class-tested by Nancy Shapiro from the University of Maryland at College Park, as well as by Wendy Gwathmey and Pam Hurley from the University of North Carolina at Wilmington. We appreciate the advice we received from them, from their students, and from students of our own. Janet Ellerby from Wilmington also made useful suggestions, as did John Flynn and Nettie Jones from Michigan Technological University. At Michigan Tech, Linda Reinhardt provided helpful secretarial assistance and Diane Molleson and Jim Cichoracki designed and produced the instructors' manual. Although an innocent bystander, Wendy Elliot contributed an important sense of perspective and key moral support.

Finally, we thank our reviewers for their insights, suggestions, and general encouragement: Dana Beckelman, University of Wisconsin, Milwaukee; Wendy Bishop, Florida State University; Patrick A. Bizzaro, East Carolina University; Patricia A. Bridges, Grand Valley State University; Carol David, Iowa State University; Donald Gray, Indiana University; Barbara G. Ladd, University of North Carolina, Chapel Hill; Sarah Liggett, Lousiana State University; Karen Rodis, Dartmouth College; John Ruszkiewicz, University of Texas; Jeff Schiff, Columbia College; Craig S. Smith, University of Northern Colorado; and Richard J. Zbaracki, Iowa State University.

John Schilb
Elizabeth A. Flynn
John Clifford

Introduction

*L*earning to read is frequently thought of as a childhood skill that is mastered early in grade school and, like swimming or riding a bicycle, does not need to be relearned, certainly not in college. If this is true, then our notion of reading might seem a bit odd. We think reading can never be completely mastered; it can never be just a series of skills that one learns regardless of the reading material. There are, of course, basic decoding skills that are learned in the first years of school and that grow over time, but our notion of college reading is more advanced than that, more complicated, more intellectually challenging.

Reading is not a passive activity in which you simply sit back and let the sentences flow over you. Instead, reading in college should be an active transaction with a text, a kind of vigorous conversation not only with the voice of the writer of the text, but also with the voices of your own experiences, values, assumptions, and ideas. And that is just the beginning, because no reading means very much in isolation from other readings that deal with comparable issues. A reading on gender roles, for example, cannot be progressive or reactionary, cannot be original or thoughtful unless we read it in relation to other literature that also focuses on gender, on the values of the dominant culture we live in at the moment, and on our own values. Of course, that might mean we would have to read and compare everything ever written about gender roles to respond perfectly to that text. Although that might be true, it is also highly impractical. We simply cannot read all, or even a significant amount, of the interesting material on gender. However, that should not be reason for pessimism. Actually, one way to look at it is that we have a responsibility to read what we can carefully because our response matters.

We can still read a given essay in an enriched environment, a constellation of voices: those we hear in the text, those that come from our own experiences and ideas, as well as those from other texts. This is why we have divided *Constellations* into chapters with eight or so pieces on the same broad topic, and why we have grouped readings that can usefully be compared to each other. Reading essays, writing responses, and then discussing these responses with others is the best way we know to create a literate environment where intelligent and critical writing can flourish. When reading, discussion, and writing all interact with each other, they can deepen the intensity and range of ideas. They can create a constellation of ideas and questions that did not and could not exist before. That is why we think every act of reading and writing you do will be uniquely yours.

To many students this idea probably seems unusual, especially when we are talking about reading nonfiction. Because essays are usually thought of simply as a vehicle for information, a group of readers might be expected to extract the same meaning. However, this is only partially true. We certainly hope you will comprehend the relevant information in the readings, but we are also interested in the significance they have for you. We want you to grapple with a reading, to wonder about its assumptions, to be suspicious, to be a difficult reader and a hard critic. We expect that there will be considerable agreement about the factual nature of the reading and considerable disagreement about the significance of it. We also expect that your classroom discussions will not necessarily lead to consensus, but to a clarification of why you are responding this way and your classmates that. The reasons probably have as much to do with your family background, education, experience, gender, race, or religious affiliations as with the actual readings. Learning why you think a certain way is as crucial as learning what you think.

An important part of the format of *Constellations* is learning to share your perspective on important issues. We have put together a selection of essays that will allow you to read, discuss, and write about the current dynamics of our culture. Ethics, education, language, science, gender, community, and family are important to us all. We need to know what thoughtful writers say about these matters, but we also need to clarify our own thinking in the give-and-take of intellectual discussion. Perhaps the best way to think through your own ideas about issues such as gender or science is to write about them yourself. By engaging in a writing process that moves from reading, responding, discussing, and other prewriting activities such as freewriting or brainstorming to drafting, revising, editing, and proofreading, you will be adding yet another informed voice to the various constellations of meaning that emerge from intellectual sites such as a college classroom.

We want to underscore the importance of thinking of reading and writing as ways of both finding and making meaning. Both matter. An essay on gender will change your ideas on the issues, if only slightly. It has to if you have read the essay with an open mind, looking for the author's ideas and attitudes. If nothing else, you had to engage the voice of the writer. You might have been surprised or disappointed; you might have been angered or intrigued. Regardless, you were moved, changed by the experience. Your ideas will be altered as you confront the meaning you find in the text. However, this is only half the story. Because you have special experiences and ideas, the essay will, in a manner of speaking, be changed also. For you, its meaning will be altered. No one can give you the meaning of any given text. That would be like borrowing someone else's mind, temporarily renting someone else's experiences, using another person's eyes to see with. You are the only one who can read a text as you, and in the process, both you and the text will be affected. That does not mean that once you have read an essay, you should stick to your guns no matter what. The exciting part of a college education is that you are always being challenged to grow, to risk, to change. It is through such a dialogue between a writer and you as a reader and then between you as a writer and your classmates as readers that knowledge can grow. That is the exciting and difficult challenge *Constellations* offers you: the opportunity to make a difference in the way others think, and, more exciting, to make a difference in the way you read and write and think.

A STUDENT'S RESPONSE

To introduce you more specifically to the concept of *Constellations*, we have included in the following pages two essays on sports, a topic not included in our collection. Before we get to them, however, we want to explain how the text is organized. We follow the same format in each chapter. We begin with a brief essay that introduces the chapter topic. Then, each of the four sections within the chapter is also introduced with a more specific introduction. Chapter 9 on "Science and Cultural Values," for example, has four sections: Science and the Unknown, Animal Rights, AIDS and Politics, and Science and Gender. There are two or three readings in each section. We have included a brief biographical sketch for each writer, followed by a series of questions called "Reflections Before Reading." We hope you will simply respond to these questions openly and quickly. Your instructor might ask you to give an oral or a written reaction. Both are fine, but if you write, be sure to jot down what you really feel, not what you think your instructor expects. Our purpose is to prime the pump—that is, to alert you to your own thinking or memories about a particular topic. That way, your consciousness will be engaged before you encounter the essay. Then comes the essay itself, followed by two sets of questions: "Rhetorical Focus" and "Thematic Focus." The former tries to alert you to some of the writing devices the writer used, such as the tone, how arguments are supported, or how evidence is arranged. The thematic questions hone in on ideas, on your evaluation of the evidence, on the strength of the logic. Finally, at the end of each section of essays, we make three "Suggestions for Writing." Depending on the advice of your instructor, you should feel free to modify these suggestions to meet your own plans.

To be clearer about what we have in mind, we have chosen two essays on sports to illustrate the sequence we have just outlined. We asked a student, David Allen, to go through parts of the sequence, answering questions and responding in his journal. He began with these questions from "Reflections Before Reading": Do you enjoy playing in competitive sports? Can you recall your feelings about winning or losing in sports when you were young? Does competition bring out the best in you? Are males taught a different set of values about sports than females?

> I enjoyed sports when I was young more than school, more than anything I can think of. I ran track from about the seventh grade on: dashes, the long jump and the high jump. I was lucky to be fast since I certainly enjoyed running. Maybe it's the other way around: I enjoyed running because I was fast. I still play softball once in a while and I still enjoy the competition. I have to admit that I do get angry when everybody in my

dorm gets to play regardless of ability. "It's just for fun," they say, which is true I guess but I'd rather play hard and seriously. That's more fun for me. Maybe I'm too competitive.

I can recall a couple of things. I can remember being about 10 or 11 and racing everyone around my age in the neighborhood. It was a hot summer night and it seemed as if everyone was there, even older brothers and sisters. I can remember running as fast as I'd ever run before and beating everyone in a race from one street light to the next. It felt good. I can still remember my heart racing and my face pounding. I can also remember a softball game when I was about fourteen. I was in a summer league, playing on a team with kids sixteen and seventeen. I was about average on the team but one night everything went wrong. I dropped a fly ball in center field that I still can't understand. It just happened. I wanted to scream that there was some mistake; I never dropped flies. But it happened, and I can never take it back. It kind of hurts to remember.

I'm not sure about what sports brings out in me. It changes me, I think. I'm not as competitive in school or in my relationships with people. When I'm running, though, I want to win, and I take delight in it. I guess if you looked at all the hard work I did like the training in the morning before school and then the long work-outs into the dark, that would be positive. That was hard, so I guess doing all that took discipline. So, yes, I guess training did bring out my potential to work hard and to reach a goal and I'm proud of that.

On the track team, males and females trained about the same and were expected to work as hard. I'm not sure though about males getting different values. Maybe track isn't a good example since it is really the same for both sexes, like swimming I guess. Maybe the lack of contact in running makes the values more equal. In football or boxing or hockey the violence is not something females can relate to. I would accept it where females wouldn't, so I think different values are involved but maybe they are already there before the sport or maybe the particular sport reinforces what society thinks is right for each sex.

After David Allen wrote these honest responses in his journal, he read Pete Hamill's essay, "Winning Isn't Everything." His instructor had asked the class first to annotate the piece by underlining interesting phrases and writing comments in the margins. They were then asked to read the piece again and to do five minutes of freewriting. Here is Hamill's essay, with David's annotations and freewriting.

WINNING ISN'T EVERYTHING

Pete Hamill

One of the more widely accepted maxims of modern   1
American life was uttered on a frozen winter afternoon
during the early sixties. The late Vince Lombardi, who
coached the Green Bay Packers when they were the great-
est team in football, said it. "Winning isn't everything," he   *theme?*
declared. "It's the only thing."

Vince Lombardi's notion was immediately appropri-   2
ated by an extraordinary variety of American males: presi-

dents and lesser politicians, generals, broadcasters, political columnists, Little League coaches, heads of corporations, and probably millions of others. In fact, it sometimes seems that Lombardi's words have had greater impact than any sentence uttered by an American since Stephen Decatur's "our country, right or wrong."

don't agree with this

That's surprising on many levels, beginning with the obvious: It's a deceptively simple premise. Winning *isn't* "the only thing." Such an idea muddles the idea of competition, not simply in sports, but in all aspects of our lives. We've learned the hard way in this century that the world is a complex place; it's certainly not the National Football League. Winning isn't the only thing in love, art, marriage, commerce, or politics; it's not even the only thing in sports.

3

real theme

In sports, as in so many other areas of our national life, we've always cherished gallant losers. I remember one afternoon in the fall of 1956 when Sal Maglie was pitching for the Brooklyn Dodgers against the hated Yankees. Maglie was an old man that year, as age is measured in sports. But this was the World Series, and he hauled his thirty-nine-year-old body to the mound, inning after inning, gave everything he had, held the Yankees to a few scattered hits and two runs—and lost. That day Don Larsen pitched his perfect game: no runs, no hits, no errors. Yet, to me, the afternoon belonged to Maglie—tough, gallant, and a loser.

4

my father's team

There was an evening in Manila when Joe Frazier went up against Muhammad Ali for the third and final time. That night, Frazier brought his workman's skills into combat against the magic of the artist, called on his vast reservoir of courage and will, and came up empty at the end of fourteen rounds. Frazier was the loser, but that evening, nobody really lost. Because of that fight, Joe Frazier can always boast with honor that he made Muhammad Ali a great fighter. He was the test, the impactable force who made Ali summon all of his own considerable reserves of skill, heart, and endurance for a final effort. The contest consumed them both. Neither was ever again a good fighter. But during their violent confrontation, winning or losing was, in the end, a marginal concern; that all-consuming effort was everything.

5

There are hundreds of similar examples of losers who showed us how to be more human, and their performances make the wide acceptance of Lombardi's notions even more mystifying. Lombardi's thesis, in fact, represented something of a shift in the nation's popular thought. Americans had been the people who remembered the Alamo or

6

courage not winning

Pearl Harbor; we blew taps over the graves of those who lost at the Battle of the Bulge or Anzio or the Yalu Basin. Those soldiers had all been defeated, but we honored them for their display of a critical human quality: courage.

Ernest Hemingway once defined courage as grace un- [7] der pressure, and that's always struck me as an eminently useful definition. The best professional athletes not only possess that kind of courage but, more important, are willing to display it to strangers. Baseball's Reggie Jackson or Richard ("Goose") Gossage, for instance, function most completely as athletes and as men when appearing before gigantic crowds under pressure: bases loaded, late innings, a big game. They come to their tasks with gladness and absolute focus, neither whimpering, complaining nor shirking when doing their job; they just try their best to get that job done. And, of course, sometimes they fail. Gossage gives up a single and his team loses. Jackson strikes out. No matter. The important thing is that such men keep their appointments with confidence and grace. Courage has become so deep a part of their character that they don't even think about it. (They certainly *want* to win. Sometimes they absolutely lust for victory. But they know that winning isn't everything. All a man can do is his best.)

really? is this courage?

Competition isn't really a problem for Americans. All [8] sports, in one way or another, are competitive. But an individual's primary competition is with himself and all his attendant weaknesses. That's obviously true of boxing, where fear must be dominated and made to work to the fighter's benefit. Yet it's also true for team sports, as well as such solitary endeavors as golf, where a player must learn control before anything else. The problem isn't competition, which is a part of life; it's in the notion of the necessity of triumph. A man can lose but still win. And the point of competition in sports is an old and not very fashionable one: It builds character.

sound good!

emphasis still on winning

That's especially true of prizefighters, the athletes I've [9] known best. Outside the ring, almost all fighters are the gentlest of men. They carry themselves with the dignity of those who have little to prove, either to others or themselves. They're never bullies, rarely use their dangerous skills against ordinary citizens and avoid pointless confrontations. When a fighter hears that a colleague has been involved in a bar brawl or a swingout with a cop, he dismisses that fighter as a cowardly bum. Most of the boxers I know are honest, generous, funny. Yet they also know that as good as they are, there might be someone down the line who has their number. Again, they would prefer to be winners. But they're aware that losing, if a courageous effort is made, is never a disgrace. The highest compliment one fighter can pay another is to say that he has "heart."

really?

There are lessons to be learned from such athletes that   10
can be applied to how we live our lives. In the long run, we'll all come up losers because there's no greater loss than death. And since primitive man first began to think, we humans have devised strategies to deal with dying. Religion is the most obvious one, usually demanding that we adhere to a moral code on earth in exchange for a serene existence after death. Ideologies offer secular versions of the same instinct, insisting that we sacrifice now, directing our lives toward the ideal of a better future, with each man becoming an architect of his own utopia. Patriotism and nationalism carry some of the same fearful baggage.

An athlete's goals are less cosmic, his field of struggle   11
less grandiose and therefore more applicable to ordinary citizens. Great athletes teach us that life is a series of struggles, not one giant effort. Just when we appear to have triumphed, we must stop like Sisyphus and again begin rolling the boulder up that mountain. The true athlete teaches us that winning isn't everything, but struggle is—the struggle to simply get up in the morning or to see hope through the minefields of despair.

is this true

extreme attitude

Viewed that way, a marriage, or any relationship with   12
another human being, is an ongoing struggle. The mastering of a skill or craft doesn't end with the granting of a diploma; it goes on for life. The relationship between parents and children doesn't end when the children turn eighteen. The running of a corporation isn't a one-shot affair, measured by a single year's statements of profits and losses; it's a continuing process, accomplished by human beings who learn from mistakes, plunge fearlessly into the struggle, take risks and prepare for the future.

It's probably no accident that American capitalism,   13
with its often permanently infantile male executives, experienced a decline that coincided with the period when Vince Lombardi's values received their widest acceptance. The results are visible everywhere. Sit on a plane with American businessmen and they'll be chattering about the Pittsburgh Steelers. Join a group of Japanese businessmen and they'll be discussing twenty-first-century technology. One group is trapped in a philosophy that demands win-

he seems angry

ning as its goal; the other cares more about patient, long-term growth—and for the moment at least, the latter is winning.

Another great maxim of the years of America's triumphs also came from the sports pages via the writer Grantland Rice. "It matters not who won or lost," declared the esteemed chonicler of the prewar years, "but how they played the game." By the time Vince Lombardi came along, such sentiments were being sneered at. We had then become a superpower, capable of blowing up the world. The man of grace, courage, endurance, and compassion was replaced in the public imagination by the swaggering macho blowhard; Humphrey Bogart gave way to John Wayne. With such attitudes dominating the landscape, we were certain to get into trouble, and we did. Vietnam and Watergate underscored the idea of winning at all costs. Yet today we seem incapable of admitting that an obsession with winning often leads to the most squalid of defeats.

Still winning is the point?   14

good phrase

interesting! examples?

Solid marriages are often built upon the experience of disastrous ones. Politicians who lose elections become tempered for the contests that follow, sometimes going on to solid, useful careers. Painters, playwrights, novelists, and other artists often learn as much from their failures as they do from those rare moments when vision, craft, and ambition come together to produce masterpieces. It's also that way in sports.

15

I remember a night when my friend José Torres, then a middleweight, was boxing Florentino Fernandez in Puerto Rico. I couldn't go to the fight, so I spent the night tuning in and out of the all-news radio stations, anxious about the result because Florentino was a great puncher. About three in the morning, Torres called.

16

"Oh, Pete," he said, close to tears. "I'm so sorry."   17

"What happened?"   18

"I got knocked out," Torres replied, his voice brimming with emotion, since he'd never lost as a professional. We started discussing what had happened. Emotions cooled; the talk became technical. Torres explained that he had learned some things about himself, about boxing. He now understood some of his flaws, and thought he could correct them. We talked for an hour. Then I asked what he was going to do next.

19

macho? attitude

"Go to the gym," he said. "I'm going to be champion of the world."   20

Two years later, Torres _was_ the world's light-heavy-   21

But isn't it?

weight champion. He didn't quit after his first defeat. That night in San Juan he didn't say winning was the only thing, that it was time to pack it in. He had learned something from defeat, and knew that one violent night, somewhere down the line, he would show the world what he had learned. And that was precisely what he did. But he was aware of something else too: Sooner or later, someone might come along who was better than he was, for at least one evening. After all, even champions are human. Even champions eventually lose. *and die* That happened to José Torres as well. But then it didn't really matter. José Torres, like the rest of us, had learned that winning wasn't everything. Living was all, and in life, defeat and victory are inseparable brothers.

   David Allen's freewrite: I really liked the part about building character. I think that's true for me. Running did do that as far as making me do things I didn't think I could. I had to get up early, especially in the winter. So running around the track at 8 in the morning now seems to be an act of strength or of character. I was surprised by his idea that great athletes can teach us lessons like "life is a series of struggles." I never saw it like that, and I wonder if it's true. I can see the point about trying hard all the time, but I was thrown by the "mine fields of despair." That sounded like Hamill was too depressed. But the point about playing the game being more important seemed important. I lost plenty of races and felt badly, but not when I had run well. I felt as if I had done as well as I could have and had the bad luck to have run against faster people, so all you can do is the best you can do. I was a little confused by the Torres story. If winning was everything, why did he need to come back to win after the defeat? Maybe winning was too important. I think Hamill exaggerates winning as an American character trait because even the fastest man in the world will someday just be an average runner.

   David then answered the questions we posed in both "Rhetorical Focus" and "Thematic Focus."

Rhetorical Focus

1. Hamill begins with a thesis he goes against in the first two sentences of the third paragraph. Is this a device worth imitating in writing your own arguments? What are its benefits and risks?
2. As part of his evidence for his thesis, Hamill gives several examples. What is the purpose of these, especially those involving boxing?
3. Hamill ends his essay with the Torres anecdote. How do the last two sentences relate to this story? How do they relate to the opening paragraph?

Thematic Focus

1. Are there possible contradictions in Hamill's argument that winning isn't everything? Examine, for example, paragraphs 13 and 15, as well as the last paragraph?
2. Hamill claims that Lombardi's statement was accepted by a large number of American males. Did he leave out females on purpose? Why does he use only males in his examples? Do the ideas Hamill develops only apply to males?
3. Do you think different people would have conflicting ideas on how the game should be played—that is, might Torres have retired after his emotional defeat; might he have run away to become a recluse? What values are involved in Hamill's approval of Torre's choice?

Here are David Allen's brief notebook replies.

Responses to Rhetorical Focus

1. I remember that in high school my English teacher said that we should treat the opposition in an argument paper fairly, but I don't remember if you are supposed to present their point of view before or after your own. I guess Hamill's idea is fine if you think Lombardi's quote is off-base. The problem might be that you would agree with it and then might not want to backtrack.
2. He is trying to show that the struggle to win is more important than winning or maybe that just struggling is the chief thing. But I don't understand how Jackson and Gossage are courageous. Isn't it just their job? What else could they do, hide in the clubhouse?
3. I guess that Torres finally learned that there are more important values in life than winning. But after he lost that is all he could think of—how to win. The last sentence seems too obvious. We all know that you have to lose (die?) sometime. And ideas on the best way to live are relative. I guess he means living the way he thinks is right, which means struggle and courage. It looks as if in the conclusion he repeats the opening theme and then adds a little something new.

Responses to Thematic Focus

1. I didn't think there were contradictions, but it seems as if Hamill is putting American businessmen down for not beating the Japanese. The Japanese are winning, and I guess Hamill is blaming the Americans for talking about football. You could also say this was a healthy diversion. And the point of the failures he mentions in politics and such seems to be that they came back to win. The same seems to hold for Torres. Maybe Hamill needs to define winning.
2. I thought he was talking about everybody but he does specifically say males. I am surprised now by all the references only to men. I don't think Hamill is sexist, but I guess he should have included women since they do struggle and, from the female runners I know, show courage and "grace under pressure." Maybe Hamill didn't know many women athletes. That seems like a poor excuse now. And now I notice that he ends with "brothers." He does make fun of John Wayne however, so he can't really be a male chauvinist. Maybe feminism wasn't so popular in 1983.

3. I guess so. Now I think that one way of looking at Torres was that he was obsessed with revenge. And the Hemingway idea of grace under pressure just seems like one way to act. There were a lot of Italians in my neighborhood when I was growing up and they seemed very different in the way they handled stress or arguments. They got very emotional and demonstrative. Maybe Hamill wouldn't have liked that, but it seems fine to me, just a different way to live.

David's comment seemed thoughtful to us, especially as freewriting entries in his journal. He combined his own experience, values, and cultural baggage with an attempt to see the other point of view, and that's a good beginning. In a college classroom discussion filled with diverse reactions to this essay, we are confident David would both influence and be influenced by other authentic responses from men and women, from athletes and couch potatoes. However, as we suggested earlier in this introduction, essays cannot really be read in isolation. Other perspectives exist, many of which are at variance with our own view of the world. We read in part to discover those other visions and in part to adjust our own inherited perspectives. We have paired the Hamill essay with a brief selection from Joyce Carol Oates's *On Boxing*. David Allen read the essay and wrote another five-minute response, but this time with the experience of Hamill's piece fresh in his mind. We think he makes some interesting connections:

IN PLACE OF WOMAN

Joyce Carol Oates

What time is it?—"Macho Time"!

—Hector "Macho Man" Camacho
WBC Lightweight Champion

I don't want to knock my opponent out. I want to hit him, step away, and watch him hurt. I want his heart.

—Joe Frazier,
Former Heavyweight Champion of the World

1   A fairy-tale proposition: <u>the heavyweight champion</u> is the most dangerous man on earth: the most feared, <u>the most manly</u>. His proper mate is very likely the fairy-tale princess whom the mirrors declare the fairest woman on earth.

Hamill would agree

2   <u>Boxing is a purely masculine activity and it inhabits a purely masculine world</u>. Which is not to suggest that most men are defined by it: clearly, most men are not. And though there are female boxers—a fact that seems to surprise, alarm, <u>amuse</u>—women's role in the sport has always been extremely marginal. (At the time of this writing the most famous American woman boxer is the black cham-

pion Lady Tyger Trimiar with her shaved head and theatrical tiger-striped attire.) At boxing matches women's role is
limited to that of card girl and occasional National Anthem
singer: stereotypical functions usually performed in stereotypically zestful feminine ways—for women have no natural place in the spectacle otherwise. The card girls in their
bathing suits and spike heels, glamour girls of the 1950s,
complement the boxers in their trunks and gym shoes but
are not to be taken seriously: their public exhibition of
themselves involves no risk and is purely decorative. Boxing is for men, and is about men, and *is* men. A celebration
of the lost religion of masculinity all the more trenchant for
its being lost.

true!

In this world, strength of a certain kind—matched of
course with intelligence and tirelessly developed skills—
determines masculinity. Just as a boxer is his body, a man's
masculinity is his use of his body. But it is also his triumph
over another's use of his body. The Opponent is always
male, the Opponent is the rival for one's own masculinity,
most fully and combatively realized. Sugar Ray Leonard
speaks of coming out of retirement to fight one man, Marvin Hagler: "I want Hagler. I need that man." Thomas
Hearns, decisively beaten by Hagler, speaks of having been
obsessed with him: "I want the rematch badly . . . there
hasn't been a minute or an hour in any day that I haven't
thought about it." Hence women's characteristic repug-
nance for boxing per se coupled with an intense interest in
and curiosity about men's fascination with it. Men fighting
men to determine worth (i.e., masculinity) excludes
women as completely as the female experience of childbirth excludes men. And is there, perhaps, some connection?

can be with his head?

3

In any case, raw aggression is thought to be the peculiar province of men, as nurturing is the peculiar province
of women. (The female boxer violates this stereotype and
cannot be taken seriously—she is parody, she is cartoon,
she is monstrous. Had she an ideology, she is likely to be a
feminist.) The psychologist Erik Erikson discovered that,
while little girls playing with blocks generally create pleasant interior spaces and attractive entrances, little boys are
inclined to pile up the blocks as high as they can and then
watch them fall down: "the contemplation of ruins," Erikson observes, "is a masculine specialty." No matter the
mesmerizing grace and beauty of a great boxing match, it is
the catastrophic finale for which everyone waits, and
hopes: the blocks piled as high as they can possibly be

true

good point

I hated guys who did that

4

piled, then brought spectacularly down. Women, watching a boxing match, are likely to identify with the losing, or hurt, boxer; men are likely to identify with the winning boxer. There is a point at which male spectators are able to identify with the fight itself as, it might be said, a Platonic experience abstracted from its particulars; if they have favored one boxer over the other, and that boxer is losing, they can shift their loyalty to the winner—or, rather, "loyalty" shifts, apart from conscious volition. In that way the ritual of fighting is always honored. The high worth of combat is always affirmed.

seems true!

Boxing's very vocabulary suggests a patriarchal world taken over by adolescents. This world is young. Its focus is youth. Its focus is of course *macho*—*machismo* raised beyond parody. To enter the claustrophobic world of professional boxing even as a spectator is to enter what appears to be a distillation of the masculine world, empty now of women, its fantasies, hopes, and strategems magnified as in a distorting mirror, or a dream.

5 *immature?*

the opposite of female — which is ??

Here, we find ourselves through the looking-glass. Values are reversed, evaginated: a boxer is valued not for his humanity but for being a "killer," a "mauler," a "hitman," an "animal," for being "savage," "merciless," "devastating," "ferocious," "vicious," "murderous." Opponents are not merely defeated as in a game but are "decked," "stiffed," "starched," "iced," "destroyed," "annihilated." Even the veteran sportwriters of so respectable a publication as *The Ring* are likely to be pitiless toward a boxer who has been beaten. Much of the appeal of Roberto Durán for intellectual boxing *aficionados* no less than for those whom one might suppose his natural constituency was that he seemed truly to want to kill his opponents: in his prime he was the "baby-faced assassin" with the "dead eyes" and "deadpan" expression who once said, having knocked out an opponent named Ray Lampkin, that he hadn't trained for the fight—next time he would kill the man. (According to legend Durán once felled a horse with a single blow.) Sonny Liston was another champion lauded for his menace, so different in spirit from Floyd Patterson as to seem to belong to another subspecies; to watch Liston overcome Patterson in tapes of their fights in the early 1960s is to watch the defeat of "civilization" by something so elemental and primitive it cannot be named. Masculinity in these terms is strictly hierarchical—two men cannot occupy the same space at the same time.

6

really?

At the present time twenty-year-old Mike Tyson, Cus   7

D'Amato's much-vaunted protégé, is being groomed as the most dangerous man in the heavyweight division. He is spoken of with awe as a "young bull"; his strength is prodigious, at least as demonstrated against fairly hapless, stationary opponents; he enters the arena robeless—"I feel more like a warrior"—and gleaming with sweat. He does not even wear socks. His boxing model is not Muhammad Ali, the most brilliant heavyweight of modern times, but Rocky Marciano, graceless, heavy-footed, indomitable, the man with the massive right-hand punch who was willing to absorb five blows in the hope of landing one. It was after having broken Jesse Ferguson's nose in a recent match that Tyson told reporters that it was his strategy to try to drive the bone back into the brain. . . .

David Allen's freewrite: I noticed right away that she says that boxing is totally masculine. That might explain why Hamill didn't say anything about women. I wonder if he realizes that the only women in boxing are so obviously there to be whistled at by "the boys." I am interested in boxing, but I don't know any women who are. It is very masculine which I guess means violent and competitive. But what if you never boxed? Does that mean you aren't a man? I think boxing illustrates an old-fashioned idea of masculinity that most people my age don't share any more. Masculinity can change, just as femininity does. Women today can look good and still be competitive and aggressive. But I don't like the idea that boys are naturally aggressive since birth. I think it is learned from our society and from peers in games—like in "King of the Hill." John Wayne was an extreme type and he would probably like boxing and Rambo. It seems true that women are not brought up to think violence is acceptable. Even in the Israeli army where all women are drafted, they are not in combat roles. Boxing seems a throw-back to a primitive idea of men. I think its a valid sport, but it probably should fade away like the gladiators.

David made some connections with the Hamill piece that helped him put both essays into a new perspective. That new constellation can offer rich possibilities for writing about sports, about the values it teaches, about particular sports, about the specific notions of winning and losing that they promote, about the ways men and women are socialized to think of themselves in relation to competition, violence, and winning. We hope you will read the pieces in each section with an active intelligence, comparing your responses to those of others, juxtaposing this essay with that, all the while writing about ideas that engage you. In short, we invite you to join in an ongoing intellectual conversation at the university, one that needs your voice to endure, and one that will reward your efforts to be a reader and writer who matters.

CONSTELLATIONS

Chapter
1
Identity

We begin this book with a series of constellations that show ways of using personal identity as a source and subject matter for writing. Of course, not everything you write explicitly deals with your life. Throughout your college education, you will get assignments that ask you to concentrate on other people or phenomena. Sometimes they will require you to avoid the word *I*. Yet even writing meant to be impersonal, objective, and outward-looking reflects in some way the personal interests, assumptions, and background of the writer. In fact, whatever the particular context and demands of the assignment, poor writing is often poor because in one way or another it seems disconnected from what the writer has actually experienced, valued, and believed. Directly writing about your life enables you, therefore, to sense how it may influence other kinds of writing you do. Also, your life can provide you with innumerable topics for writing. Although various assignments in college will compel you to investigate areas that you do not know much about yet, the experiences you have already had can often inform and inspire you. In addition, writing about your life can help you understand crucial elements of your identity. It can enable you not only to communicate with others, but also to learn about yourself.

Writing about your life does not mean simply conveying indisputable facts about it. When they turn to personal narratives, writers interpret their experience and shape it for particular aims. They may use such writing to determine the forces influencing them, to understand people they have met, to show the human effects of social structures, and to argue the lessons of their experience for particular audiences. Often, they strive for the compelling narratives, colorful descriptions, and memorable characters found in great fiction. When you set out to write about your life, you need to decide why and for whom you are recalling it in the first place. You need to decide what events you will relate and what meaning you will give

1

them, bearing in mind that you can interpret your past in all sorts of ways. You need to decide what organization of these events will prove most appropriate to your purpose. You need to determine what aspects of your personality you will emphasize, both in your content and in the tone you will use. Some of the most interesting personal writing presents the self as multiple voices or beings. Indeed, writing can help you learn a great deal about yourself when you use it to explore your inner conflicts.

As you write about your personal identity, also try to bear in mind its social context. Your sense of self emerges from and contributes to your interactions with other people and larger forces. To emphasize this point, we present here selections on the ways that gender, ethnicity, class, and region affect concepts of identity. In the first constellation, Carolyn Heilbrun draws on her own experience to analyze how women have repressed certain aspects of their identity, while Trip Gabriel examines how a "wildman" retreat addressed what men have denied about themselves. The second constellation touches on gender dynamics by dealing with mother–daughter relationships, but it also concerns ethnicity, for it details the efforts of some Asian-Americans to determine how their cultural background should figure in their sense of identity. In an essay, Kesaya E. Noda reflects on her heritage as a third-generation Japanese-American, including her relation to her mother; then, in a short story, Amy Tan presents a Chinese immigrant's thoughts on her relationship to her American daughter. The third constellation brings up issues of class as well as gender, presenting James Agee's 1941 account of a poor rural woman, followed by the account she gave many years later of Agee's visit and her whole life. This constellation gives you the opportunity to see whether and how social differences between the observer and the observed are illuminated when they switch roles. Finally, we present a male and a female writer who view identity within the context of time and place. E.B. White uses his return to the summer vacation place of his childhood to reflect on the course his life is taking, whereas Kathleen Stocking locates her personal history within the larger history of her native region. With each of these constellations, we encourage you to analyze the similarities and differences between the writers' examinations of identity. We also encourage you to think about the experiences in your own life you can turn to and the rhetorical strategies you can employ as you use writing to explore your own identity.

GENDERED IDENTITY

Consciously or not, gender is for most people a crucial aspect of their identity. Indeed, we consider the subject of gender so important that we later devote a whole unit to it. Note what the term implies, especially compared with the term *sex*. When in this book we distinguish between male and female experience, we follow several contemporary scholars by emphasizing differences in *gender* rather than in *sex*. We do so because we want to emphasize that male and female identity reflect, to a significant extent, cultural interpretations rather than biological givens. Of course, there continues to be much debate over whether and how biological sex differences figure in the development of human identity. Yet a culture's notions of gender—its own ideas about how sex differences matter—greatly influence the ways it socializes children, organizes work, provides services, distributes rewards, and values other activities. To be sure, gender is not the only element shaping people's lives. As many constellations in this book suggest, factors such as race and social class often matter as well. Also bear in mind that gender differences themselves have varied with time and place; they have not always taken the same form or had the same power. Yet they continue to play key roles in our societies and others. They still pervade even our everyday lives, including our very notions of what constitutes an appropriate identity for ourselves.

In examining gender and identity, the selections here raise a more specific issue: To what extent do society's gender distinctions force women and men to adopt identities that actually repress important parts of themselves? Examining how and why she decided to write mysteries under a pseudonym, Carolyn Heilbrun suggests that women have often concealed images of themselves that for one reason or another they felt unable to reveal in public. Trip Gabriel reports on a weekend retreat that encourages men to recover their lost "wildman" self and understand how they have been physically wounded. As you read these texts about gender, note the visions of men and women that emerge. Do they correspond to your own experience? Consider, too, the ways each author relates personal experience to larger social developments. When, in Carolyn Heilbrun's words, you try to "write your own life," do you think social forces affect your sense of its past and future shapes? Also consider why, when, and how people adopt multiple identities. Have you had different ones, perhaps even at the same time? Do women and men differ in the aspects of themselves they keep secret? Finally, take this constellation and others in this unit as opportunities to explore issues you have personally faced because of your gender and other aspects of your identity.

Writing a Woman's Life

Carolyn Heilbrun

Carolyn Heilbrun (b. 1926) graduated from Wellesley College in 1947. She
then attended Columbia University, earning a master's degree there in 1951
and the doctorate in 1959. The following year she began a long and
distinguished career teaching at Columbia, where presently she is Avalon
Foundation Professor of the Humanities. As a scholar, Heilbrun has been
known chiefly for her work in nineteenth- and twentieth-century British
literature as well as feminist theory. Her books include *The Garnett Family,
Christopher Isherwood, Toward a Recognition of Androgyny: Aspects of
Male and Female in Literature, Reinventing Womanhood, Hamlet's Mother
and Other Women*, and *Writing a Woman's Life*, a 1988 book from which
the following is an excerpt. Explaining the title of her book in her
introduction to it, Heilbrun points out, "There are four ways to write a
woman's life: the woman herself may tell it, in what she chooses to call an
autobiography; she may tell it in what she chooses to call fiction; a
biographer, woman or man, may write the woman's life in what is called a
biography; or the woman may write her own life in advance of living it,
unconsciously, and without recognizing or naming the process." Heilbrun
proceeds to explore these various meanings in seven chapters. We reprint
her next to last one, where she analyzes how and why she began in 1964 to
write mysteries under the pseudonym "Amanda Cross." By now she has
produced several popular volumes in this series, including *In the Last
Analysis, The James Joyce Murder, Poetic Justice, The Theban Mysteries*,
and *Death in a Tenured Position*. A few years ago, Heilbrun revealed
"Amanda Cross"'s secret identity. As she reviews the history of it here, she
puts it in the context of other women's efforts to write their own lives in
some sense.

Reflections Before Reading

Did earlier teachers of yours emphasize or discourage personal writing? If
so, how did you feel about their practice? Have you thought about using
writing, either in college or outside it, to explore issues of personal identity?
Why or why not? Here Carolyn Heilbrun explores not only how people
literally write about their lives, but also how they metaphorically write their
lives by imagining a particular narrative for them. What general themes
would you emphasize if you told the story of your life so far? Heilbrun refers

mostly to women's efforts at writing their own lives. In your experience, do women and men take different things into account when they refer to the basic story of their lives?

[Marilyn Monroe] was a female impersonator; we are all trained to be female impersonators.

Gloria Steinem

We must recognize what the past suggests: women are well beyond youth when they begin, often unconsciously, to create another story. Not even then do they recognize it as another story. Usually they believe that the obvious reasons for what they are doing are the only ones; only in hindsight, or through a biographer's imaginative eyes, can the concealed story be surmised. I have decided, in order to illustrate the way such a story might be uncovered, to use myself as an example, analyzing the reasons why I adopted and for years kept wholly secret the pseudonym of Amanda Cross, under which, beginning in 1964, I published detective stories. Not until I had been asked repeatedly to account publicly for my decision to write detective novels under a pseudonym did I realize that the explanation I had always offered, and believed, was perhaps insufficient.   1

I have the impression—and I want to emphasize that it is no more than an impression—that, despite a few famous male exceptions, women write under an assumed name far more often than do men, and have done so since the early nineteenth century. Women write under pseudonums for profound reasons that require scrupulous examination. As Gilbert and Gubar put it, "the [woman's] pseudonym began to function more prominently as a name of power, the mark of a private christening into a second self, a rebirth into linguistic primacy" (1987, 241).   2

Certainly I was not without coldly practical reasons when I decided to write detective novels as Amanda Cross. There was no question in my mind then, nor is there any now, that had those responsible for my promotion to tenure in the English department of the university where I teach known of the novels, they would have counted them heavily against me; I would probably have been rejected. As it happens, the professor who came up for tenure before me had written several novels—serious ones, not items of "popular culture"—and was turned down, as he supposed then, for being a novelist. I don't intend to analyze the motives behind this harsh response to English professors' forays into fiction, but harsh it is. So the practical reasons for writing under a pseudonym were clear. One had one's "real" identity, and if one chose to indulge in frivolities, however skillful, one did it under another name than that reserved for proper scholarship.   3

I no longer think that this was the whole explanation. I think now that there are layers within layers of significance to a woman's decision to write under a pseudonym, but the most important reason for her doing so is that the woman author is, consciously or not, creating an alter ego as she writes, another possibility   4 of female destiny. So full of anxiety were women, before the current women's movement, when imagining alternate destinies that they wished to hide their authorial identity from prying eyes.

Charlotte Brontë, after writing to her publisher that she was "neither man nor woman," went on to say, "I come before you as an author only. It is the sole standard by which you have a right to judge me—the sole ground on which I accept your judgment." She felt, correctly no doubt, that certain scenes she had created that were considered "unfeminine" had been judged so only because she was a woman; a man would have been able to "get away with it." She wished to bring *Villette* out under what Margot Peters calls "the sheltering shadow of an incognito" (Peters, 256, 352). She had, in fact, an overwhelming desire for anonymity. And, indeed, even her best friends secretly, or not so secretly, found her novels "coarse" and unbecoming in their presentation of passion. When Matthew Arnold disliked *Villette* because it was so full of hunger, rebellion, rage, he was at the same time identifying its strengths, but these were unbearably presumptuous in a woman writer.

George Sand, too, chose a name other than her own, but, as we have seen, before the pseudonym came male impersonation, the freedom of moving like a boy. George Eliot, too, as we know, sought the safety of anonymity.

But what has all this to do with an assistant professor of English in 1964 who was hardly as restricted as those three literary giants? What does a woman setting out in the early 1960s to write a detective story have to do with the problems of women in the nineteenth century, before women had any legal identity or, indeed, any rights at all? How could someone worried about promotion in a profession, enjoying all the freedoms of action by then won for women, if not quite all the liberties of dress and movement the next decade would bring, compare herself to these women so constrained, so much the prisoners of powerful convention, so lacking a tradition of female accomplishment?

I believe that women have long searched, and continue to search, for an identity "other" than their own. Caught in the conventions of their sex, they have sought an escape from gender. A woman author who was not content to expound the titillations of romance, or to live out Freud's family romance, had two means of escape. One was to hide her identity as an author within the shelter of anonymity, the safety of secrecy, to write while protecting the quotidian self leading her appropriate life. The other way was to create in her writings women characters, and sometimes male characters, who might openly enact the dangerous adventures of a woman's life, unconstrained by female propriety. Some, like Charlotte Brontë, did both. George Eliot, whose "significant other," George Henry Lewes, protected her from all assaults from public, publisher, or reviewer, did not re-create new female destinies, but examined with genius and wisdom the life of her times. Willa Cather lived a private life meticulously protected from scrutiny, and, in the words of Louise Bogan, when she was awarded Princeton's first honorary degree to a woman, Cather "well knew that she had accomplished, in the last decade or so, a miracle which would cause any university now extant to forget and forgive her sex" (Schroeter, 126). We know, however, that she dressed as a boy when in college, and was able so successfully to ghostwrite S.S. McClure's autobiography, with its account of male adventures, that not even his family suspected that he had not written it himself. She could neither fit, within the expectations for her sex, into a life that allowed the enactment of her dreams, nor discover in the public sphere a place where she could be wholly herself.

We return from this account of great names to the life of a woman in her late thirties in the year 1963. Why did she determine to write a detective novel? It certainly was not because time was hanging heavy on her hands: she had three children under the age of eight, a large dog, newly acquired, a husband who had gone back for his Ph.D. in economics, and a full-time job. Her motives were both clear and clouded. She "knew" then what her "single" motive was: she had run out of English detective novels, having read them all many times. She felt an enormous need to enter the world of fiction that the English detective-novel writers were no longer providing, or were unable to provide in sufficient numbers. Why not try to write one?

Many people have had the same thought; few enough have acted on it, for the very good reason that writing a detective novel is a lot of work, much easier to conceive than to carry through, to abandon than to complete. Only recently have I asked myself whether the urge to write them instead of reading them is, after all, a sufficient explanation, given the circumstances.

I believe now that I must have wanted, with extraordinary fervor, to create a space for myself. This was, physically, almost impossible. The cost of renting an apartment in New York City was certainly insignificant then compared to now, but for us the need for each child to have a room took precedence over my needs. I used to notice, visiting in the suburbs where so many of my contemporaries lived in those days (and from which our holdout was considered almost as eccentric as my working), that there would be a den, and a finished basement, and a laundry, and, in fact, a room for everyone but the wife/mother, who, it was assumed, had the whole house. Anne Sexton has written a very good poem about this point, which shocked many people at the time:

Housewife

Some women marry houses.
It's another kind of skin; it has a heart,
a mouth, a liver and bowel movements.
The walls are permanent and pink.
See how she sits on her knees all day,
faithfully washing herself down.
Men enter by force, drawn back like Jonah
into their fleshy mothers.
A woman *is* her mother.
That's the main thing.[1]

If there was no space for a woman in the suburban dream house, how unlikely that there would be space in a small city apartment. So I sought, I now guess, psychic space.

But I also sought another identity, another role. I sought to create an individ-

---

[1] From ALL MY PRETTY ONES by Anne Sexton. Copyright © 1962 by Anne Sexton. Reprinted by permission of Houghton Mifflin Company.

ual whose destiny offered more possibility than I could comfortably imagine for my-self. Charlotte Brontë, that genius, in creating Jane Eyre, was not more hungry or re-bellious than I. Our talents are not comparable, but our impulses are. Writing even the most minor of novels, formula fiction as it is called, nonetheless teaches one a great deal about the ways of genius. (It has often occurred to me that all teachers of literature ought to have written and published a work of fiction in order to under-stand something fundamental about what they teach, but that is another matter.)

Many women writers used a male protagonist in their first novels: George Eliot,   13
Charlotte Brontë, Willa Cather, May Sarton, to name a few; and among the famous women who wrote detective stories in what have come to be called the golden twenties, all featured male detectives. Some, later, created women sleuths to act with their male detectives, or instead of them—Christie's Miss Marple, Tey's Miss Pym, Sayers's Harriet Vane; indeed, a number of male detective writers also had temporary female sleuths—and the logical thing for me to have done, looking back, would have been to create a male detective. I do remember trying, very briefly, to do so, and abandoning the attempt with great haste. Here again we have a good sur-face reason: I simply didn't know enough about how men thought, as opposed to spoke, and I had read enough modern novels written by women but with male pro-tagonists—Nadine Gordimer had recently written one—to know that male sexual-ity, to go no further, was a problem. And one did not create detectives, even in the dreary 1950s and early 1960s, wholly without sexual thoughts or experience. (Wo-men writers in the nineteenth century had certain minor advantages.) But there was more to it than that. In our post-Freudian days—and mine was a generation that bowed down before Freud and paid constant homage—abandoning one's womanhood fictionally meant exposing oneself to terrible accusations and suspi-cions, far too risky for one working as hard as I was to maintain a proper wife, mother, role-playing mask. These days, when, I am glad to say, there are many wo-men mystery writers creating sexually active women detectives, both lesbian and hetero, it is hard to think oneself back to that situation, but it was very real indeed.

I created a fantasy. Without children, unmarried, unconstrained by the opin-   14
ions of others, rich and beautiful, the newly created Kate Fansler now appears to me a figure out of never-never land. That she seems less a fantasy figure these days—when she is mainly criticized for drinking and smoking too much, and for having married—says more about the changing mores, and my talents as prophet, than about my intentions at the time. I wanted to give her everything and see what she could do with it. Of course, she set out on a quest (the male plot), she became a knight (the male role), she rescued a (male) princess. Later I found Denise Le-vertov's lines:

> In childhood dream-play I was always
> the knight or squire, not
> the lady:
> quester, petitioner, win or lose, not
> she who was sought.[2]

---

[2] Denise Levertov: "Relearning the Alphabet" (excerpt) from POEMS 1968–1972. Copyright © 1970 by Denise Levertov. Reprinted by permission of New Directions Publishing Corporation.

(That Kate had the help of a man is neither here nor there. We all need help. She was dependent not on any male individual but on the New York police force and the D.A.'s office, without which action was impossible.) Kate was gutsy. She also held a few opinions I now consider retrograde (such as her faith in Freud's conviction that the complaints of sexual abuse on the part of his women patients were all fantasy), but she has changed with time, she's learned, and that's all one can ask of anybody.

The question I am most often asked is how and why I chose the name "Amanda Cross." This was, or seemed at the time, a matter of no significance. My husband and I had once been stranded in a deserted part of Nova Scotia; while we awaited rescue, we contemplated a road sign reading "MacCharles Cross." My husband, attempting cheer, remarked that if either of us ever wanted a pseudonym, that would be a good one. I remembered that moment in 1963 when I finished my first detective novel, but was told that my book had obviously been written by a woman and that I should use a woman's first name. I chose "Amanda," under the (as it turned out, entirely mistaken) impression that no one since Noel Coward's early plays had had that name. In recent years, I have heard many other explanations of my choice of pseudonym: that I stole Agatha Christie's initials; that the word *cross* carries many meanings of conflict, tension, and choice, which I wanted; that the phrase *a-man-da-cross* is not without significance, and so on. I accept all of them, even the one claiming it was after Katherine Hepburn's role of Amanda in *Adam's Rib*. I didn't see that movie until a few years ago, on television. Certainly if I had, the name would have appealed to me for that reason. A word or name must bear, I agree with Coleridge, all the meanings that connotations attach to it. 15

I had a very good reason for secrecy, but as I now perceive, the secrecy itself was wonderfully attractive. Secrecy is power. True, one gives up recognition and publicity and fame, should any be coming one's way, but for me that was not difficult. I do not care for publicity and, because I have a regular paying job, I can afford, as a writer of detective novels, to avoid it. I think that secrecy gave me a sense of control over my destiny that nothing else in my life, in those pre-tenure, pre-women's-movement days, afforded. 16

(I might mention, in passing, that the secret was easily kept, because I told no one other than my husband, my agent, and my publisher. Doris Lessing, in her recent stunt of publishing novels under a pseudonym, the motives for which I shall abjure examining, found that her secret was easily kept because she did not tell any friends or acquaintances; so my instincts were proved right. But there was one awful moment. My first novel was nominated for the Edgar, awarded annually by the Mystery Writers of America for the best first novel. As E.B. White has said, it is a very satisfactory thing to win a prize before a large group of people. But winning would have blown my cover, and I prayed to lose: I was absolutely unambivalent. As it turned out, the prize was won by the first of the Rabbi novels, which was a vast relief to me.) 17

Meanwhile, creating Kate Fansler and her quests, I was recreating myself. Women come to writing, I believe, simultaneously with self-creation. Sand went to Paris and dressed as a boy. Colette was locked in a room by her husband to become his ghostwriter; that was what her self demanded to take the terrible risk of 18 writing. Even when the writing self was strengthened, only after great trouble could she leave her husband and find her own name, a single name, peculiarly marked by both feminine and—because it was her father's name—patriarchal significance.

Let me add that for female writers this act of self-creation comes later in life   19
than for such a one as Keats. George Eliot was thirty-eight at the time her first fiction was published. So was Willa Cather. Virginia Woolf was in her thirties. This is by no means a universal rule with women writers, but it is frequent enough to be worth noticing. Acting to confront society's expectations for oneself requires either the mad daring of youth, or the colder determination of middle age. Men tend to move on a fairly predictable path to achievement; women transform themselves only after an awakening. And that awakening is identifiable only in hindsight.

There were aspects of my double life that were fun. Before the Amanda Cross   20
secret was out, I found myself corresponding under both identities and, in one instance, writing different letters to the same person under both names. James Sandoe, well-known professor of drama and critic of mystery stories, decided on different occasions to write to Amanda Cross about her novels and to Carolyn Heilbrun about androgyny and her essay on Dorothy Sayers. Eventually I admitted to him the identity of his two correspondents.

We are only just beginning, I think, to understand the way autobiography   21
works in fiction, and fiction in autobiography. Consider, for example, the question of mothers in novels. Florence Nightingale, writing of her despair at a life without occupation or purpose, commented on how young women pass their time by reading novels in which "the heroine has generally no family ties (almost invariably no mother), or, if she has, they do not interfere with her entire independence." The heroines of most novels by women have either no mothers, or mothers who are ineffectual and unsatisfactory. Think of George Eliot; think of Jane Austen; think of the Brontës. As a rule, the women in these novels are very lonely; they have no women friends, though they sometimes have a sister who is a friend.

What was the function of mothers toward daughters before the current wom-   22
en's movement, before, let us say, 1970? Whatever the drawbacks, whatever the frustrations or satisfactions of the mother's life, her mission was to prepare the daughter to take her place in the patriarchal succession, that is, to marry, to bear children (preferably sons), and to encourage her husband to succeed in the world. But for many women, mothers and daughters alike, there moved in their imaginations dreams of some other life: of personal accomplishment, of the understanding and control of hard facts and complex problems, of a place in a community where women were in sufficient numbers to render the accomplished woman neither lonely nor an anomaly. Above all, the dream of taking control of one's life without the intrusion of a mother's patriarchal wishes for her daughter, without the danger of injuring the much loved and pitied mother.

When, safely hidden behind anonymity, I invented Kate Fansler, I gave her   23
parents, already dead, whom she could freely dislike, and create herself against, although they had been good enough to leave her with a comfortable income. (So Samuel Butler, writing *The Way of All Flesh*, recommended that all children be deserted at birth, wrapped in a generous portion of pound notes.) Carolyn Heil-

brun had, in fact, great affection for her parents, great admiration for her father and a sense of affectionate protectiveness toward her mother. But they were conservative people; they could not understand her wish to remake the world and discover the possibility of different destinies for women within it. Amanda Cross could write, in the popular, unimportant form of detective fiction, the destiny she hoped for women, if not exactly, any longer, for herself: the alternate life she wished to inscribe upon the female imagination.

It is of the very first importance to realize, however, that Carolyn Heilbrun in 1963 was not dissatisfied with her life. She was not, like Florence Nightingale, or Charlotte Brontë isolated at Haworth, dreaming of some event to rescue her. She believed then, as now, that her life was a full and satisfactory one, with every promise of becoming more so. When she sought psychic space, it was not from personal frustration but rather from a wish, characteristic of almost every woman writer who did not write erotic romances, for more space, less interruption, more possibility of adventure and the companionship of wiser women through these adventures, greater risk and a more fearless affronting of destiny than seemed possible in the 1950s and early 1960s.

How much of this wish to transform female destiny was conscious? None of it. I suspect that if I had been told then that my depriving Kate Fansler of parents indicated any ambivalence on my part toward my parents, I would have disputed that conclusion with vigor. All the conscious reasons for writing were good ones; they operated, they were sufficient to explain my actions. Yet the real reasons permitted me, as other women have found ways to permit themselves, to write my own life on a level far below consciousness, making it possible for me to experience what I would not have had the courage to undertake in full awareness. I think Virginia Woolf, for example, early realized, deeply if unconsciously, that the narratives provided for women were insufficient for her needs. Her life and her works, the equal to any by her contemporaries, have been until recently less studied academically because we quite literally did not have the language, the theory, or the perceptions with which to analyze them. All her novels struggle against narrative and the old perceptions of the world. She felt in herself a powerful need for a love we have come to call maternal, a love that few men are able to offer (outside of romance) and that women have been carefully trained not to seek in other women. Virginia Woolf found a nurturing man to live with, and she found women to love her. She needed to be loved, and she knew it. Most of us women, I think, transform our need to be loved into a need to love, expecting, therefore, of men and of children, more than they, caught in their own lives, can give us. But Woolf, whether from need or genius, or both, knew that when Chloe and Olivia worked side by side in a laboratory, when women had a room of their own and money of their own (which is power), the old story of woman's destiny, the old marriage plot, would give way to another story for women, a quest plot.

So women like Carolyn Heilbrun in 1963, and writers of an earlier time, seeking some place outside Freud's family romance, wrote out, under other names or in hidden stories, their revolutionary hopes.

Women have long been nameless. They have not been persons. Handed by a father to another man, the husband, they have been objects of circulation, exchanging one name for another. That is why the story of Persephone and Demeter is the story of all women who marry: why death and marriage, as Nancy Miller pointed out in *The Heroine's Text*, were the only two possible ends for women in novels, and were, frequently, the same end. For the young woman died as a subject, ceased as an entity. For this reason, then, women who began to write another story often wrote it under another name. They were inventing something so daring that they could not risk, in their own person, the frightful consequences.

Let me return, after these grand statements about famous women and female destiny, to my two names adopted so cavalierly twenty-five years ago. Something happened to both Carolyn and Amanda: the women's movement. Carolyn began writing in a more personal, for her more courageous, manner, recognizing that women could not speak to other women as men had always spoken, as though from on high. She wrote of herself, she told her own story, she risked exposure; going public was still a chancy thing for a woman, but not as chancy as it had been, because there were more women doing it. 28

And Amanda became more openly courageous too: she wrote of feminist matters, and let her heroine continue to smoke and drink, despite frequent protests from readers. I think too much drinking is a fearful affliction, and I don't smoke, but Kate Fansler has stuck to her martinis and cigarettes as a sort of camouflage for her more revolutionary opinions and actions. For some reason, I was reluctant to reform her, to tell her how to behave. My hope, of course, is that younger women will imitate her, not in smoking and drinking, not necessarily in marrying or declining to have children, but rather in daring to use her security in order to be brave on behalf of other women, and to discover new stories for women. She is, oddly, no longer a fantasy figure but an aging woman who battles despair and, one hopes with a degree of wit and humor, finds in the constant analysis of our ancient patriarchal ways, and in sheer effrontery, a reason to endure. 29

Kate Fansler has aged less rapidly than do mortals, but inexorably. And it is she, rather than the persona "Amanda Cross," who has come to be a presence in my life. When I have not written about her for a while, she makes her presence known. Biographers have sometimes written, as have fiction writers, of the palpable existence of their subjects. I remember reading once that Simenon, when he had ignored Maigret for many months, would find him waiting around corners, silently confronting his creator, demanding incarnation, or at least attention. So it has been with Kate. And when I recently promised not to begin a new detective novel until I had finished another, different kind of book, she would not let me be. So for the first time I wrote short stories about her, told by her niece Leighton Fansler as a kind of Watson. Though I have often thought in the past that I would write no more detective novels, I now think that I shall probably be forced to write them as long as Kate is there to nudge me. 30

Kate Fansler has taught me many things. About marriage, first of all. I could see no reason for her to marry: there was no question of children. But, insisting upon marrying, she taught me that a relationship has a momentum, it must change and develop, and will tend to move toward the point of greatest commitment. I don't wholly understand this, but I accept it, learning that the commitment of marriage, which I had taken for granted, has its unique force. But it is about aging 31 that she has taught me most. She is still attractive, but no longer beautiful, and unconcerned with her looks. Her clothes she regards as a costume one dons for the role one will play in the public sphere. Her beauty was the only attribute I regreted bestowing, and age has tempered that, although, unlike her creator, she is still a fantasy figure in being eternally slim. But most important, she has become braver as she has aged, less interested in the opinions of those she does not cherish, and has come to realize that she has little to lose, little any longer to risk, that age above all, both for those with children and those without them, is the time when there is very little "they" can do for you, very little reason to fear, or hide, or not attempt brave and important things. Lear said, "I will do such things, what they are yet I know not, but they shall be the terrors of the earth." He said this in impotent rage in his old age, but Kate Fansler has taught me to say it in the bravery and power of age.

Rhetorical Focus

1. What does Heilbrun apparently assume that her audience is curious to know? Note, in particular, the questions she raises. Does she satisfy your own curiosity? Why or why not?
2. At several moments, Heilbrun refers to herself in the third person (paragraphs 7, 9, 23, 24, 26, 28). Why do you think she resorts to this device? Is it rhetorically effective? Why or why not?
3. Twice, Heilbrun shifts from prose to poetry, apparently to give her points greater force (paragraphs 11 and 14). Is this shift effective, or should she have stayed with straightforward expository language? Explain.

Thematic Focus

1. According to Heilbrun, in what ways does her present reasoning differ from the understanding she had of her motives when she started writing mysteries as Amanda Cross?
2. What are the various forms of Carolyn Heilbrun's identity that she deals with in this selection? Does she succeed in helping you realize why her identity took various forms? Explain.
3. In what ways does Heilbrun relate her own life to the lives of other women? What does she acknowledge as particular to her own circumstances? Do you think society now enables younger women to experience the sense of freedom that Heilbrun and her heroine Kate Fansler have come to enjoy? Why or why not?

Call of the Wildmen

Trip Gabriel

Trip Gabriel (b. 1955) graduated from Middlebury College in Vermont with a degree in philosophy. He now lives in New York City, where he not only serves as a contributing editor for *Rolling Stone* and a correspondent for *Outside* magazine but also does free-lance journalism. In his reporting, Gabriel has covered a wide range of topics, including the film industry, true crime stories, subjects having to do with the outdoors, and various social trends, including ones that bear in particular on men's lives. The following essay appeared in *The New York Times Magazine* on October 14, 1990 and was also widely syndicated. It deals with the Wildman Gathering, a weekend retreat that promotes ideas of a burgeoning men's movement. The article was unusual for Gabriel, in that it reports an event by featuring himself as a witness. Note that he also refers to the "forefather" of the new men's movement, Robert Bly. Subsequently, Bly's own book *Iron John* became a number one bestseller for several weeks.

Reflections Before Reading

Recall the quotation from Gloria Steinem that Carolyn Heilbrun uses to begin her chapter: "[Marilyn Monroe] was a female impersonator; we are all trained to be female impersonators." Do you think men are often trained to be male impersonators—that is, trained to assume an identity that in some sense is not really theirs? Explain. In the following essay, Trip Gabriel reports his visit to the Wildman Gathering, a weekend retreat where men are supposed to discover their so-called deep masculinity. Do you think such a retreat can be a good idea? Why or why not? What kinds of experiences do you think it may feature?

It was spring in the Emerald Hill country of North Texas, a region of rolling fields   1
clotted with purple asters, mustard and black-eyed Susans. Signs that hung beside the white-rail fences of prosperous-looking ranches boasted of the breeds of cattle raised there, Brangus and Herefords and Santa Gertrudis. One sign, as vast as a billboard, said, "Polled Herefords: the Big Bold Breed." At a freshly plowed field, I turned off the blacktop onto a muddy ranch road, following directions to some-

thing called the Wildman Gathering, a weekend of outdoor living that, the brochure promised, would put me in touch with my "deep masculinity."

Around the nation, increasing numbers of men have been gathering at similar   2
retreats to discover an earthier, more self-assured version of themselves. The workshops are part of a loosely organized but rapidly growing phenomenon known as the men's movement. Adherents claim that there is a gruff, elemental "wildman" lying deep inside every regular guy. This wildman, who can be freed by such activities as drumming and dancing around bonfires, has long been suppressed by industrialization, the corporate culture and 20 years of feminism.

Certainly, I was in the right place to shuck off civilization. I was 50 miles south   3
of Fort Worth, in the heart of Texas, home of that masculine icon, the cowboy. Arriving at the Bosque Creek Ranch, a scrub-covered spread with a modest cabin and corral, I parked my car alongside many others. A man checked me off a registration list that included more than 130 names. He turned out to be Marvin Allen, the weekend's organizer and director of the Austin Men's Center. When Allen helped start the center in 1988, he noted, Austin had more than a dozen resource centers for women, but not one for men. Today the men's center offers a support group for new and expectant fathers, a Men's Codependency and Emotional Release Therapy Group, men's poetry evenings and the Wildman Gathering, which takes place here three times a year and is so popular it is booked up months in advance with participants from many states.

The growing men's movement has spawned magazines like Wingspan and   4
Man!, and workshops along the lines of Allen's, some lasting a day and others as long as a week, have been held in Boston, Seattle, Minneapolis, Mendocino, Calif., and the mountains of New Mexico. By one estimate, the gatherings have attracted 50,000 men. Situated at the intersection of the personal growth movement and the new age, the phenomenon for years was known almost exclusively to adherents of holistic healing or crystal collecting. But recently it has come up from underground and is attracting mainstream attention. Interest was stirred this year by a 90-minute Bill Moyers television program on the poet Robert Bly, the grand-daddy, so to speak, of the men's movement.

Marvin Allen created the Wildman Gathering so males could come together in   5
semiwilderness, apart from women, to get in tune with their bodies and their feelings. Or, as he had told me on the phone, "We work on joy and exuberance and fierceness." Now he said I could set up my tent wherever I chose. Beside some brushy trees, I pounded in the tent stakes, while from a short distance away I heard the clang of pitched horseshoes.

At dusk came a steady drumbeat from a wooded grove a few hundred yards   6
away. Though no one had told us ahead of time, we all seemed to understand this was a signal to head toward the trees with the drums we'd each been asked to bring. A drum not being the sort of thing one has lying around the house, before flying down from New York I'd hastily visited a 48th Street music store, where I was persuaded to buy a dusty silver instrument lying forgotten in a corner. It was a type of drum used by old mambo bands, and for the next two days, whenever I thumped it, I could not remove the image from my mind of Ricky Ricardo leading his band at the Tropicana nightclub.

Inside a grove of Spanish oaks, we assembled. Hay bales were arranged in a large circle, and a fire burned at the center. Soon we would learn to call this the Sacred Grove. Tribal masks hung in trees to inspire us with their fierce, primitive maleness. The mask closest to me was a scowling African face with slit eyes, cow horns and a fringe of snakeskin. 7

The drumming ended with a burst of whistles and cheers. At the center of the circle, Marvin Allen asked us to introduce ourselves to our immediate neighbors, and to "tell them if you were afraid to come tonight." The man to my left, Jim, who was from Houston, confided at length and with much feeling that he'd been fearful of showing up. 8

Allen turned over the proceeding to his co-leader for the weekend, John Lee, the author of one of the best-selling books of the new masculinity, "The Flying Boy." In the book Lee relates how he once "overvalued the feminine" side of himself, cultivating a sensitive nature and wearing his hair long like a girl. He became a Peter Pan-like figure unable to make commitments to women or begin a career. To get on in life, he had to embrace the "deep masculine" side of his personality. 9

Striding around the grove in calf-high mud boots, Lee indeed cut a rugged profile. He wore jeans and a denim shirt. He had a salt-and-pepper beard and he now wore his hair in a Marine cut. He spoke confidently in a rich Southern accent. 10

Lee told us his father, a machinist, was a "tough s.o.b." who would think what we were doing this weekend was "a crock." Lee said his dad had been an angry alcoholic who was always emotionally and physically absent. He never taught his son how to have close male friends, and he never showed him that it was all right to express his feelings "And," Lee said, drawing out the words for effect, "he never taught me how to cry." 11

"Ho," said many men, uttering the American Indian word we'd been told to use to signal our assent or understanding. 12

Lee told us to close our eyes and imagine our fathers standing 100 yards behind us outside the circle. "They're mad at us," Lee said. "They're scared we're leaving them out." He said he was going to try something. He told us to take slow deep breaths. Then, as if intoning a mantra, he said, "Dad." He repeated it "Dad." Then he said, "Father." He paused, "Father. Daddy." 13

Remarkable, men began to break down. At first, with eyes closed, I didn't recognize the sound. How often had I heard men weep? Almost never. It began like a strangled cry, as if the men were gargling. Then their anguish burst forth in heaving sobs that rolled through the grove. Beside me, Jim cried freely. A couple of places to my right, a man gasped, "Hug me!" and he was embraced by the man next to him. 14

I was surprised and somewhat confused. What depths of sorrow did these men feel, what scars could they be carrying associated with their fathers? Furthermore, who were they who could, at the incantatory mention of a parent, spill over in such showy, if nonetheless sincere, emotions? I felt distant from the public expression of grief. Dry-eyed, I returned to my tent. That night I slept restlessly and had vivid, disquieting dreams. 15

The concept of the wildman was introduced by Robert Bly, a National Book Award-winning poet, about 10 years ago. Bly looked around in the early 80's and 16 decided the nation was populated by many wimpified men, whom he labeled "soft males." These soft men, influenced by the cultural upheaval of the women's movement, could read poetry and talk to their wives and girlfriends. But they lacked energy, assertiveness and the ability to make commitments. Bly did not believe that men should look to John Wayne or Arnold Schwarzenegger as role models. He spurned these caricatures of masculinity. Rather, he noted that almost every pre-industrial culture, from ancient Greece to the Middle Ages, projected in its myths and poetry an image of an ideal man as a forceful, spontaneous, primal being. "What I'm proposing," Bly once said, "is that every modern male has, lying at the bottom of his psyche, a large, primitive man covered with hair down to his feet. Making contact with this wildman is the step the 70's man has not yet taken: this is the process that still hasn't taken place in contemporary culture."

The men's movement says it's not a reactionary response to feminism. Rather, it sees itself as a parallel development. While feminism has often dealt with politics and the outward conditions of women's lives, the men's movement is about internal issues, about men's psyches. At the Wildman Gathering I figured I'd hear a lot of grousing about wives and mothers, but in two full days women were hardly mentioned. Men were too busy talking about themselves.

Bly, 63 years old, is a white-haired paterfamilias whom many in the men's movement regard as a guru. They buy his audio tapes and his volumes of poetry, and invariably, whether they've met him or not, refer to him as "Robert." At one point in our weekend someone mentioned that Bly was lecturing in Portland, Ore., at that very moment, whereupon John Lee encouraged everyone to shout over the tops of the trees, "Hello, Robert!"

A stirring storyteller and poetry reader, Bly has spread his message in week-long workshops and weekend lectures that draw huge crowds (and earn him up to $20,000 a pop). One event in San Francisco in May attracted 700 men, plus a waiting list of 700. Bly bars TV cameras from these gatherings and has been known to tell members of the audience not to take photographs or make recordings. The reason, a participant says, is that these are intrusions into the "ritual space" of the gatherings.

A major theme of Bly's is that men feel a great sense of grief and loss, often unacknowledged. On the subject of what, specifically, men have to grieve over, Bly can be vague. "It's as if grief is impersonal with men," he told Bill Moyers. "Its always present. You don't know if it's about the absence from their father, or it may be about all of the animals that we were in touch with all the millions of years we were hunters, and all the animals that died. . . . Men have lived for centuries out there, and they feel that terrific grief of nature and the out-of-doors and pine trees."

John Lee and Marvin Allen, who are both trained psychotherapists, are much more specific: the grief men feel is for the wounds inflicted on them by their fathers. Men feel a sense of loss that their fathers were never the kind of fathers they wished them to be, or needed.

Saturday morning in the Sacred Grove, Allen said: "Probably every way a man could be wounded by his father is represented here. Fathers have shamed us and criticized us. Some of our fathers have whipped us."

Quietly, several men answered, "Ho."

Allen told of his own father, a fighter pilot, and the image that came to mind   24
was of the swaggering Robert Duvall in "The Great Santini." Allen's father
sounded distant and disapproving, and he passed onto his son the image of a man
as someone who never felt pain or fear.

Allen is slight, with blue eyes and a neatly trimmed, professorial beard. He has   25
a gentle, unthreatening manner. If one were to picture him as a high-school athlete, the last sports that would come to mind are football and boxing. Yet to win his
father's approval, Allen said, those are the sports he took up. "I got into Golden
Gloves boxing, and I never lost because I had a burning desire to win," he told us.
"But never once did he come to watch or tell me he was proud."

"Ho," responded many men.   26

"So I got into high-school football, and I was the skinniest guy on the team,   27
125 pounds. Every time I got tackled I got hurt." Once, he said, he tried extra hard
because his father was attending a game. He made a couple of big plays and heard
his name announced on the loudspeaker. "I knew he was up there hearing my
name, which was his name too: Allen." The son came home thinking that now,
certainly, his father would give him the love and praise he thirsted for. But the
father only grunted as the son entered the house. "Out of all the times he beat me
and criticized me, that was the worst," Allen said in a voice thickening with emotion. "I realized seven or eight years ago that I spent most of my life trying to get
him to appreciate me and validate me. Later he was able to. But it didn't mean that
much by then. The little boy had already grown up."

Around the grove, several men were sniffling sympathetically. Others had put   28
their arms around one another as they listened. If there was concern the wildman
would turn out to be just another male brute, unable to express his feelings or to
nurture, it was not in evidence here.

It seemed that many men listening to Allen had heard their own stories told.   29
Indeed, over the weekend, I heard a surprising number of accounts of men who'd
had outstanding athletic careers, primarily, they said, to win the love of distant
fathers. It may have been that because we were in Texas, home of overvalued
college and high-school sports, that father–son dynamics had worked themselves
out this way. One burly man, who said he'd been a state-champion wrestler, said:
"My father instilled a competitive fierceness in me. Somehow it wasn't good
enough to be second. I loved him and he loved me, but that's not all there is to it."

Another man, whose dad, like Allen's was a fighter pilot, recalled: "My father   30
always told me of all the things I could do in this world, if I didn't fly a fighter, I'd
failed. But I never flew a fighter and I don't want to."

The men were largely in their 30's and 40's, healthy and presentable-looking   31
guys. With only a few exceptions, they didn't strike me as life's losers. Most had
weathered the traditional rites of passage for American males—college or the military, marriage, a successful career—but these passages left them somehow uncertain of their masculine identity. A Vietnam veteran, a survivor of the hoariest tradition of all for forging men, said, "I went to Vietnam a boy, and I came back an
emotional baby."

There was a minister present, two judges, psychologists and entrepreneurs   32
with their own businesses. The gathering included many lawyers. One confessed a

desire to switch careers because, after 20 years of adversarial dickering, he realized he'd only been "re-enacting the kind of abusive relationship I've always had with my father."

What men were saying was that the traditional images of masculinity had failed them, especially as represented by a hard-boiled figure who might be a football coach, a litigator or a fighter pilot. Many men spoke of having had distant fathers like Allen's, prone to wound themselves and their families with alcohol or workaholism. A surprising number of men indicated they had received frequent beatings.   33

Allen said he wanted everyone to go off by himself for a while. "Go and draw a circle, get inside it, and invite your father in," he said. "Tell him what you've always wanted to, the fear, the anger."   34

We left the grove and headed to the far corners of the ranch. I walked a few hundred yards and sat down in front of a half circle of pine trees, with a view of a marshy frog pond. Behind me, I heard a man's tormented voice shouting at an imaginary father, "I hate your violence!" Another man, below me near the pond, whacked the trunk of a tree over and over with a branch.   35

I tried to zap some hostility onto an image of my dad. Although there'd been plenty of times I'd been angry in his presence, I found that in such a warm, sunny spot, with crickets and frogs making a chirpy racket, it was impossible to feel bitter about much of anything. My father had not hit or neglected me, and if he was sometimes insensitive and unable to express his feelings, I could be equally insensitive and mute around him. I did not think he'd wounded me to the degree that other men described in moving terms.   36

I was uncertain what to grieve over. I tried to sense the more general "grief of pine trees" that Bly referred to. The problem was, I've always felt upbeat around pine trees. I have always liked the outdoors. I'd sometimes wished for a more outdoorsy father, one who might have taught me to identify trees and animal tracks and to survive in the wilderness. As it happened, his back-country lore was pretty much limited to barbecuing in our suburban yard. One of the few nature skills he did teach me was how to blow on a blade of grass to make a whistle. Thinking of my father, I yanked a blade from the ground, stretched it between my thumbs, and blew into them to make the blade vibrate in a low, mournful whistle.   37

People in the men's movement believe there was once a golden age of masculinity, when strong men hugged, expressed their feelings, honored their elders and served as mentors to younger men. This era is sometimes said to have existed during Arthurian times, when kings, warriors and wise magicians served as role models. These ancient societies offered men clear road maps of how they ought to behave through myths, legends and poetry. There were ceremonies to show respect, and rites to initiate adolescents into adulthood.   38

In modern times, rites and myths no longer exist to set men right, and thus many are deeply confused. A major focus at men's retreats is to enact latter-day rituals to replace the old ones. Saturday afternoon and evening was to be our time to recover the rituals our post-industrial age denied us. I came to think of it as our time of Dungeons and Dragons.   39

After a lunch of rabbit stew, we returned to the Sacred Grove, where Allen   40
and Lee had spread an inner circle of dry hay around the fire. "I'd like to take this
time to bring up and honor the elders." Lee said. He invited all the men over 50,
about 15 in all, to step forward and be seated on the dry hay. "These men know
secrets, mysteries, truths," Lee said solemnly. "I bet if you ask them over the weekend they'll share some things we in our 30's and 40's don't know." He paused.
"We're going to drum for these men. And drum for the lost fathers."

We pounded our drums. After many minutes the drumming had a lulling ef-   41
fect that lent a kind of gravity to what struck me as a frivolous ritual. When we
stopped, it was determined the oldest man present was 73. He was helped to his
feet by the others. "We honor the eldest of the eldest," Lee said. We drummed
furiously.

Our co-leaders spoke often of the wildman inside us, but they regularly in-   42
sisted that the wildman is not hostile, insensitive or full of rage. That creature, Lee
and Allen said, is known as the savageman. The savageman represents the macho,
aggressive side of masculinity, which is what women and others may fear is what
the men's movement has in mind when it speaks of getting in touch with "deep
masculinity." This fear is erroneous, say the men. In order to feel the difference
between the savageman and the wildman, we were to act them out in a pair of
improvisational dances.

We paraded from the Sacred Grove to a large pasture doing the "king walk,"   43
striding with chests puffed out, expressing pride without arrogance. Once in the
pasture, we were encouraged to do a savageman dance. At first most men stood
looking embarrassed, a perfectly normal reaction to being told to express oneself
spontaneously. When Allen suggested "you might want to growl to express the
savagery within" more than 100 men suddenly began running through the field
snarling like rabid dogs. Most were enthusiastic savages. My own snarling left me
hoarse the rest of the day.

Then it was time to dance like wildmen, and here many seemed at a loss. One   44
man skipped. Another jumped from side to side across a tractor rut. I picked up
heavy rocks and threw them into the next pasture, thinking the gist of the wildman
might lie in the primitive expression of strength and control. When Allen suggested we might wish to raise our arms in praise of the rosy sunset, many men took
his suggestion. Whatever this wildman was, I thought, he still seemed to be an
abstraction. We'd been far more convincing as savages.

All day, two mysterious structures had been taking shape beyond the ranch   45
corral. They were built of wood boughs bent in the skeletons of Indian lodges,
which were heavily covered with blankets. The structures were sweat lodges, natural saunas that in some American Indian tribes are used for rituals of renewal and
rebirth.

As night fell, we stripped off our clothes and lined up to enter the lodges. A   46
smoldering fire heated rocks for our natural saunas. A man named Lance conducted the ceremony in the lodge I entered. He compared the cave-dark enclo-
sure to the womb of Mother Earth. Inside, we were squeezed together shoulder to
shoulder and hip to hip, the great sweaty brotherhood of naked men that stretched
back ritualistically, if not to a golden age, at least to the locker rooms of junior high.

Lance ordered the glowing rocks to be shoveled in. He sprinkled them with   47
water and cedar chips, and lung-scalding steam boiled up. Soon it was hot and
claustrophobic. Earlier Lance had warned us that the sweat lodge could be an
ordeal. "Pain is a powerful teacher," he said. "In a way, in the lodge we suffer a
little bit. It takes that to open us up."

Lance, who is part Sac and Fox Indian, sang Indian prayers in a fine, soft   48
voice. I scooped up cool mud from the ground to smear across my face, as a cricket
crawled over my bare leg. After 40 minutes or so, the ceremony was over. I stumbled out beneath a brilliant starry sky and immediately found a cattle trough to use
as a cold plunge. When I emerged, I indeed felt very good. But was I spiritually
cleansed? Was I now a born-again wildman? I wasn't sure. My body hummed all
over, but I've felt a similar uplift after a day's skiing and a hot tub.

It seemed to me there is a problem with the search for latter-day rituals by the   49
men's movement. In themselves, rituals performed outside a cultural context don't
mean very much. The power of a rite, be it a Christmas Mass or an Indian sweat
lodge, comes from what the participants bring to it, which is a result of a long
history of beliefs and expectations. It may be that American culture fails to respect
the earned wisdom of its elderly, but 10 minutes of drumming isn't going to redress the hurt feelings of the oldsters. Enacted without a pre-existing system of
beliefs, the drumming, dancing and vision-questing of the new masculinity feel
pretty silly—at least they do to this camper.

The rituals were only part of our weekend, however. They provided a rough   50
structure, but in between times, in what seemed to me ultimately a subtle subversion of the wildman's agenda, men would stand up spontaneously in the grove and
tell chapters from their life stories. That's what these men apparently wanted to do
most, just talk. The format derived from self-help groups where participants identify themselves by first names only and share their experiences. Many of the men
were veterans of A.A. or groups for adult children of alcoholics or child-abuse
victims, so they knew the program. The others got with it pretty quickly.

What emerged in the testimonies of men was a deep confusion at having to   51
live up to conventional expectations of masculinity. Men said they'd tried to be
fearless, invulnerable, all-knowing. Their fathers and their culture had taught
them this was the way to act manly. But no one had prepared them for real life, for
the breakup of a marriage and the sadness they would be unable to express. No one
had prepared them for the emptiness of growing old without having gained maturity and wisdom. No one had showed them how to face death.

On Sunday morning, with a sense that time was running out, various men   52
stood up to address the group. One took a step into the circle, an athletic-looking
man in his mid-30's who was bare-chested in the sun. "I'm Randy," he said in a
deep Southern accent. His voice was shaky but he held himself rigidly erect, as if
hoping to control powerful emotions through his posture. "I buried my father
about a week ago," he said, choking out the words. "Before he died, I saw a scared
old man. And I don't want to die that way."

"Ho," a few men said very softly.   53

"And like a lot of y'all," he went on, "I have the fear that I don't know   54
what's. . . . I don't know how. . . . I don't know what to do with it. He didn't know
a damn thing about feelings. See, I don't know if I grieved enough. It was all so

fast. He died Wednesday. We bought the coffin Thursday. And we buried him Friday. Come Saturday I shut the hell down. Sunday I wished I was here. The rest of the week I was scared I wasn't going to come.

Randy paused to take several breaths. All around the circle, men had inhaled sharply when he began to speak of burying his father only the week before. Now there was silence.   55

He struggled to continue. Tears were running freely down his cheeks. "Now I don't want what he gave me. I still remember him walking like a child among men. *I don't want to walk like a child among men.* I want to stand up and walk. . . . I don't remember feeling this feeling before. . . . Yeah, I think I was alone all of my damn life."   56

"Ho." Many others had been moved to tears.   57

"Thank you," Randy said in conclusion.   58

Lee commanded him, "Walk around the fire." Randy did so, his posture as rod-straight as when he had begun to speak.   59

The Wildman Gathering was at an end, and for me it was ending on a note of pitched emotion and some confusion. On the one hand, there seemed a patent foolishness in the rituals we enacted—the drumming and dancing. But on the other hand, who could not be moved by stories like Randy's? The men around the fire had seemed at times ridiculous, but they were ridiculous and real. Many were struggling to overcome the image of a man, passed down by their fathers, as someone who is miserly with his feelings and in whom any sign of vulnerability is a sign of weakness. They had bought into this code of masculinity, and in all cases, they said, it had stunted them.   60

I didn't know how the concept of a fierce, elemental wildman fit into this realization. Nor, I suspect, did many others. The wildman weekend hadn't made men fierce so much as it had tenderized them. The men's movement hardly needs its sweat lodges and sacred groves. What most men seem to want are more forums in which they can talk directly to one another, a kind of recovery program for victims of errant notions of masculinity, a sort of Men's Anonymous.   61

Around the fire, there was applause and drumming in support of Randy, and then Lee said: "Look at this man. God. When he was standing there, you just saw it, a man feeling his feelings. As strong as the goddamn Rock of Gibraltar with tears running down his face."   62

He embraced Randy, and then, one after another, other men got up to join in, until almost the entire group was standing in a kind of huddle around the man, swaying slowly like a rugby scrum, or a many-legged amoeba, while wood smoke rose through the sunlight in the grove.   63

Rhetorical Focus

1. In what places, if any, does Gabriel seem to address a question, concern, or attitude that his audience may have? Does he seem to anticipate the reactions you have as you read his essay? Explain.

2. As he describes his experiences at the retreat, how does Gabriel position himself with respect to the other men who were there? For example, does he closely identify with them as he writes about them? Does he seem to detach himself from them? Or does he alternate his stance? Refer to specific passages in the text.

3. Both Gabriel and Heilbrun alternate paragraphs emphasizing their personal experience with ones reporting larger events or social developments. Does each author manage smoothly to integrate these two kinds of paragraphs? Where does Gabriel choose to reveal his personal feelings and judgments? Where, if anywhere, does he basically just describe what is going on? Should he have done more of one or the other? Explain.

Thematic Focus

1. On the basis of what Gabriel reports, what aspects of the Wildman Gathering, if any, do you think are all right? What aspects, if any, make you uneasy? Explain your reasoning.

2. Again going by what Gabriel reports, what in your own words would you say are the main ideas of the Wildman Gathering? Do you think your summary would differ from the participants'? If so, in what ways? If there were a Wildwoman Gathering, in what ways do you think it might differ from the Wildman Gathering?

3. After reading Gabriel's and Heilbrun's selections, do you find yourself thinking that the men's movement and the women's movement are up to radically different things? Why or why not?

Suggestions for Writing

1. Write an essay explaining the ways in which both of these selections deal with the subject of repression—that is, the idea that people repress certain aspects of their identity or express them only indirectly. In your essay, identify the extent to which these texts suggest that women and men engage in different forms of repression. Also indicate what course of action Heilbrun seems to recommend for women and Gabriel for men. Keep in mind that even though Gabriel reports what the Wildmen say, he doesn't necessarily share all of their views.

2. When Heilbrun reviews her decision to write as Amanda Cross, she attributes to herself other motives than she was aware of at the time. Think of an action you undertook for a particular reason, only to realize later that you really had another motive. Write an essay identifying this action, the motive you were conscious of at the time, and the process by which you came to see that another motive was operating.

3. Gabriel describes a set of rituals in which a group of men try to learn more about their personal identity. Describe an occasion in which being part of a group's ritual or ceremony helped you develop a sense of identity. What

specific details of this ritual or ceremony proved helpful or inspiring to you? Would you be pleased to go through the same ritual or ceremony today? Are you the same person now that you were then?

ETHNIC IDENTITY

In addition to gender, people's identities are often affected by their belonging to a particular ethnic group or race. Sometimes, this situation is less one of their own choosing than one imposed upon them by another culture disposed to look at them in a certain way because of their apparent ethnic affiliations. For example, people's skin color can trigger stereotypical responses that hardly take into account the sorts of persons they really are. Because many white Americans still consider their skin color the norm—and perhaps not even a color at all—they are apt to see other races as distinctly marginal.

At other times, however, people actively seek to define themselves in the context of a native ethnic or racial community, in effect questioning the age-old notion of America as a "melting pot." Members of certain groups affirm their solidarity in order to meet challenges they continue to face in American society, from subtle differences in culture to outright discrimination. Other people seek to renew ethnic ties because they see them as a means of preserving identity amidst the increasing fragmentation of modern American life. In a variety of ways, therefore, ethnicity is less a fixed, clear aspect of people's nature than a process of identification that they find themselves pushed into, or wish to undergo, or both.

This constellation examines such possibilities by presenting two works on Asian-American women reflecting on their identity, especially in relation to the country of their heritage as to well as the American culture in which they now find themselves. The first work is an essay by the Japanese-American writer Kesaya E. Noda; the second is a short story by the Chinese-American writer Amy Tan. Because different genres are at work here, you should consider whether and how they produce different effects. Be careful, too, not to lump Japanese-Americans and Chinese-Americans together; these ethnic groups have endured similar responses from Americans, but their histories differ significantly. We have put Noda's and Tan's works together, however, because they do involve some common themes. Both analyze ethnic identity by looking at interactions between generations, especially the dynamics of mother–daughter relationships. Both examine the role that facial features can play in shaping other people's attitudes toward an ethnic group and the ways that its members define themselves. Both situate the self in the context of history, culture, and geography.

Perhaps the biggest difference between these texts lies with point of view: Noda writes from her own perspective as a third-generation Japanese-American, while Tan's short story emphasizes the perspective of a woman who immigrated from China years ago and now confronts her American daughter. As you read, consider whether this difference in narrative strategy produces different insights, or whether the texts wind up asserting much the same thing about ethnicity and identity. Also think about the role of ethnicity in your own life, along with the rhetorical strategies you would use to analyze it.

Growing Up Asian in America

Kesaya E. Noda

Kesaya E. Noda (b. 1950) is a *sansei*—that is, the American-born grandchild of Japanese immigrants to the United States. Although she studied for a year and a half in Japan, she was born in California and grew up in New Hampshire. Noda earned a master's degree from Harvard Divinity School and is now pursuing a doctorate in religious studies at Harvard. She has also published a book entitled *The Yamato Colony* (1981), in which she relates the history of the California community where her grandparents settled and her parents grew up. The following essay comes from the 1989 collection *Making Waves: An Anthology of Writings By and About Asian and American Women*, published by Asian Women United of California.

Reflections Before Reading

In the following essay, Kesaya E. Noda analyzes the extent to which her identity has been shaped from outside rather than inside. To what extent do you think your identity has been shaped from outside—that is, by other people or social forces? In what ways, if any, do you believe your identity has been affected by your belonging to a particular race or ethnic group? Again, think not only of how groups define themselves, but also of how other people define them. Ultimately, do you consider ethnic identity something to embrace, resist, ignore? Noda discusses in particular the history of Japanese-Americans. What, if anything, do you associate with their history?

Sometimes when I was growing up, my identity seemed to hurtle toward me and paste itself right to my face. I felt that way, encountering the stereotypes of my race perpetuated by non-Japanese people (primarily white) who may or may not have had contact with other Japanese in America. "You don't like cheese, do you?" someone would ask. "I know your people don't like cheese." Sometimes questions came making allusions to history. That was another aspect of the identity. Events that had happened quite apart from the me who stood silent in that moment connected my face with an incomprehensible past. "Your parents were in California? Were they in those camps during the war?" And sometimes there were phrases or nicknames: "Lotus Blossom." I was sometimes addressed or referred to as racially Japanese, sometimes as Japanese American, and sometimes as an Asian woman. Confusions and distortions abounded.   1

How is one to know and define oneself? From the inside—within a context that is self defined, from a grounding in community and a connection with culture and history that are comfortably accepted? Or from the outside—in terms of messages received from the media and people who are often ignorant? Even as an adult I can still see two sides of my face and past. I can see from the inside out, in freedom. And I can see from the outside in, driven by the old voices of childhood and lost in anger and fear.   2

I Am Racially Japanese

A voice from my childhood says: "You are other. You are less than. You are unalterably alien." This voice has its own history. We have indeed been seen as other and alien since the early years of our arrival in the United States. The very first immigrants were welcomed and sought as laborers to replace the dwindling numbers of Chinese, whose influx had been cut off by the Chinese Exclusion Act of 1882. The Japanese fell natural heir to the same anti-Asian prejudice that had arisen against the Chinese. As soon as they began striking for better wages, they were no longer welcomed.   3

I can see myself today as a person historically defined by law and custom as being forever alien. Being neither "free white," nor "African," our people in California were deemed "aliens, ineligible for citizenship," no matter how long they intended to stay here. Aliens ineligible for citizenship were prohibited from owning, buying, or leasing land. They did not and could not belong here. The voice in me remembers that I am always a *Japanese* American in the eyes of many. A third-generation German American is an American. A third-generation Japanese American is a Japanese American. Being Japanese means being a danger to the country during the war and knowing how to use chopsticks. I wear this history on my face.   4

I move to the other side. I see a different light and claim a different context.   5
My race is a line that stretches across ocean and time to link me to the shrine where my grandmother was raised. Two high, white banners lift in the wind at the top of the stone steps leading to the shrine. It is time for the summer festival. Black characters are written against the sky as boldly as the clouds, as lightly as kites, as sharply as the big black crows I used to see above the fields in New Hampshire. At festival time there is liquor and food, ritual, discipline, and abandonment. There is music and drunkenness and invocation. There is hope. Another season has come. Another season has gone.

I am racially Japanese. I have a certain claim to this crazy place where the   6
prayers intoned by a neighboring Shinto priest (standing in for my grandmother's nephew who is sick) are drowned out by the rehearsals for the pop singing contest in which most of the villagers will compete later that night. The village elders, the priest, and I stand respectfully upon the immaculate, shining wooden floor of the outer shrine, bowing our heads before the hidden powers. During the patchy intervals when I can hear him, I notice the priest has a stutter. His voice flutters up to my ears only occasionally because two men and a woman are singing gustily into a microphone in the compound, testing the sound system. A prerecorded tape of guitars, samisens, and drums accompanies them. Rock music and Shinto prayers. That night, to loud applause and cheers, a young man is given the award for the most *netsuretsu*—passionate, burning—rendition of a song. We roar our approval of the reward. Never mind that his voice had wandered and slid, now slightly above, now slightly below the given line of the melody. Netsuretsu. Netsuretsu.

In the morning, my grandmother's sister kneels at the foot of the stone stairs   7
to offer her morning prayers. She is too crippled to climb the stairs, so each morning she kneels here upon the path. She shuts her eyes for a few seconds, her motions as matter of fact as when she washes rice. I linger longer than she does, so reluctant to leave, savoring the connection I feel with my grandmother in America, the past, and the power that lives and shines in the morning sun.

Our family has served this shrine for generations. The family's need to protect   8
this claim to identity and place outweighs any individual claim to any individual hope. I am Japanese.

I Am a Japanese American

"Weak." I hear the voice from my childhood years. "Passive," I hear. Our parents   9
and grandparents were the ones who were put into those camps. They went without resistance; they offered cooperation as proof of loyalty to America. "Victim," I hear. And, "Silent."

Our parents are painted as hard workers who were socially uncomfortable and   10
had difficulty expressing even the smallest opinion. Clean, quiet, motivated, and determined to match the American way; that is us, and that is the story of our time here.

"Why did you go into those camps," I raged at my parents, frightened by my   11
own inner silence and timidity. "Why didn't you do anything to resist? Why didn't

you name it the injustice it was?" Couldn't our parents even think? Couldn't they? Why were we so passive?

I shift my vision and my stance. I am in California. My uncle is in the midst of   12
the sweet potato harvest. He is pressed, trying to get the harvesting crews onto the field as quickly as possible, worried about the flow of equipment and people. His big pickup is pulled off to the side, motor running, door ajar. I see two tractors in the yard in front of an old shed; the flat bed harvesting platform on which the workers will stand has already been brought over from the other field. It's early morning. The workers stand loosely grouped and at ease, but my uncle looks as harried and tense as a police officer trying to unsnarl a New York City traffic jam. Driving toward the shed, I pull my car off the road to make way for an approaching tractor. The front wheels of the car sink luxuriously into the soft, white sand by the roadside and the car slides to a dreamy halt, tail still on the road. I try to move forward. I try to move back. The front bites contentedly into the sand, the back lifts itself at a jaunty angle. My uncle sees me and storms down the road, running: He is shouting before he is even near me.

"What's the matter with you," he screams. "What the hell are you doing?" In   13
his frenzy, he grabs his hat off his head and slashes it through the air across his knee. He is beside himself. "Don't you know how to drive in sand? What's the matter with you? You've blocked the whole roadway. How am I supposed to get my tractors out of here? Can't you use your head? You've cut off the whole road-way, and we've got to get out of here."

I stand on the road before him helplessly thinking, "No, I don't know how to   14
drive in sand. I've never driven in sand."

"I'm sorry, uncle," I say, burying a smile beneath a look of sincere apology. I   15
notice my deep amusement and my affection for him with great curiosity. I am usually devastated by anger. Not this time.

During the several years that follow I learn about the people and the place,   16
and much more about what has happened in this California village where my par-ents grew up. The issei, our grandparents, made this settlement in the desert. Their first crops were eaten by rabbits and ravaged by insects. The land was so barren that men walking from house to house sometimes got lost. Women came here too. They bore children in 114 degree heat, then carried the babies with them into the fields to nurse when they reached the end of each row of grapes or other truck farm crops.

I had had no idea what it meant to buy this kind of land and make it grow   17
green. Or how, when the war came, there was no space at all for the subtlety of being who we were—Japanese Americans. Either/or was the way. I hadn't under-stood that people were literally afraid for their lives then, that their money had been frozen in banks; that there was a five-mile travel limit; that when the early evening curfew came and they were inside their houses, some of them watched helplessly as people they knew went into their barns to steal their belongings. The police were patrolling the road, interested only in violators of curfew. There was no help for them in the face of thievery. I had not been able to imagine before what it must have felt like to be an American—to know absolutely that one is an Ameri-can—and yet to have almost everyone else deny it. Not only deny it, but challenge

that identity with machine guns and troops of white American soldiers. In those circumstances it was difficult to say, "I'm a Japanese American." "American" had to do.

But now I can say that I am a Japanese American. It means I have a place here in this country, too. I have a place here on the East Coast, where our neighbor is so much a part of our family that my mother never passes her house at night without glancing at the lights to see if she is home and safe; where my parents have hauled hundreds of pounds of rocks from fields and arduously planted Christmas trees and blueberries, lilacs, asparagus, and crab apples; where my father still dreams of angling a stream to a new bed so that he can dig a pond in the field and fill it with water and fish. "The neighbors already came for their Christmas tree?" he asks in December. "Did they like it? Did they like it?"   18

I have a place on the West Coast where my relatives still farm, where I heard the stories of feuds and backbiting, and where I saw that people survived and flourished because fundamentally they trusted and relied upon one another. A death in the family is not just a death in a family, it is a death in the community. I saw people help each other with money, materials, labor, attention, and time. I saw men gather once a year, without fail, to clean the grounds of a ninety-year-old woman who had helped the community before, during, and after the war. I saw her remembering them with birthday cards sent to each of their children.   19

I come from a people with a long memory and a distinctive grace. We live our thanks. And we are Americans. Japanese Americans.   20

I Am a Japanese American Woman

Woman. The last piece of my identity. It has been easier by far for me to know myself in Japan and to see my place in America than it has been to accept my line of connection with my own mother. She was my dark self, a figure in whom I thought I saw all that I feared most in myself. Growing into womanhood and looking for some model of strength, I turned away from her. Of course, I could not find what I sought. I was looking for a black feminist or a white feminist. My mother is neither white nor black.   21

My mother is a woman who speaks with her life as much as with her tongue. I think of her with her own mother. Grandmother had Parkinson's disease and it had frozen her gait and set her fingers, tongue, and feet jerking and trembling in a terrible dance. My aunts and uncles wanted her to be able to live in her own home. They fed her, bathed her, dressed her, awoke at midnight to take her for one last trip to the bathroom. My aunts (her daughters-in-law) did most of the care, but my mother went from New Hampshire to California each summer to spend a month living with grandmother, because she wanted to and because she wanted to give my aunts at least a small rest. During those hot summer days, mother lay on the couch watching the television or reading, cooking foods that grandmother liked, and speaking little. Grandmother thrived under her care.   22

The time finally came when it was too dangerous for grandmother to live alone. My relatives kept finding her on the floor beside her bed when they went to wake her in the mornings. My mother flew to California to help clean the house   23 and make arrangements for grandmother to enter a local nursing home. On her last day at home, while grandmother was sitting in her big, overstuffed armchair, hair combed and wearing a green summer dress, my mother went to her and knelt at her feet. "Here, Mamma," she said. "I've polished your shoes." She lifted grand-mother's legs and helped her into the shiny black shoes. My grandmother looked down and smiled slightly. She left her house walking, supported by her children, carrying her pocket book, and wearing her polished black shoes. "Look, Mamma," my mom had said, kneeling. "I've polished your shoes."

Just the other day, my mother came to Boston to visit. She had recently lost a lot of weight and was pleased with her new shape and her feeling of good health. "Look at me, Kes," she exclaimed, turning toward me, front and back, as naked as the day she was born. I saw her small breasts and the wide, brown scar, belly button to pubic hair, that marked her because my brother and I were both born by Caesarean section. Her hips were small. I was not a large baby, but there was so little room for me in her that when she was carrying me she could not even begin to bend over toward the floor. She hated it, she said.

"Don't I look good? Don't you think I look good?"

I looked at my mother, smiling and as happy as she, thinking of all the times I have seen her naked. I have seen both my parents naked throughout my life, as they have seen me. From childhood through adulthood we've had our naked mo-ments, sharing baths, idle conversations picked up as we moved between showers and closets, hurried moments at the beginning of days, quiet moments at the end of days.

I know this to be Japanese, this ease with the physical, and it makes me think of an old, Japanese folk song. A young nursemaid, a fifteen-year-old girl, is singing a lullaby to a baby who is strapped to her back. The nursemaid has been sent as a servant to a place far from her own home. "We're the beggars," she says, "and they are the nice people. Nice people wear fine sashes. Nice clothes."

If I should drop dead,
bury me by the roadside!
I'll give a flower
to everyone who passes.

What kind of flower?
The cam-cam-camellia [tsun-tsun-tsubaki]
watered by Heaven:
alms water.

The nursemaid is the intersection of heaven and earth, the intersection of the human, the natural world, the body, and the soul. In this song, with clear eyes, she looks steadily at life, which is sometimes so very terrible and sad. I think of her while looking at my mother, who is standing on the red and purple carpet before me, laughing, without any clothes.

I am my mother's daughter. And I am myself.

I am a Japanese American woman.

Epilogue

I recently heard a man from West Africa share some memories of his childhood.   31
He was raised Muslim, but when he was a young man, he found himself deeply
drawn to Christianity. He struggled against his inner impulse for years, trying to
avoid the church yet feeling pushed to return to it again and again. "I would have
done *anything* to avoid the change," he said. At last, he became Christian. Afterwards he was afraid to go home, fearing that he would not be accepted. The fear
was groundless, he discovered, when at last he returned—he had separated himself, but his family and friends (all Muslim) had not separated themselves from
him.

The man, who is now a professor of religion, said that in the Africa he knew as   32
a child and a young man, pluralism was embraced rather than feared. There was "a
kind of tolerance that did not deny your particularity," he said. He alluded to zestful, spontaneous debates that would sometimes loudly erupt between Muslims and
Christians in the village's public spaces. His memories of an atheist who harangued
the villagers when he came to visit them once a week moved me deeply. Perhaps
the man was an agricultural advisor or inspector. He harrassed the women. He
would say:

> "Don't go to the fields! Don't even bother to go to the fields. Let God take care of you.
> He'll send you the food. If you believe in God, why do you need to work? You don't
> need to work! Let God put the seeds in the ground. Stay home."

The professor said, "The women laughed, you know? They just laughed. Their   33
attitude was, 'Here is a child of God. When will he come home?' "

The storyteller, the professor of religion, smiled a most fantastic, tender smile   34
as he told this story. "In my country, there is a deep affirmation of the oneness of
God," he said. "The atheist and the women were having quite different experiences in their encounter, though the atheist did not know this. He saw himself as
quite separate from the women. But the women did not see themselves as being
separate from him. 'Here is a child of God,' they said. 'When will he come
home?' "

Rhetorical Focus

1. What purpose does Noda's title serve, considering that she was not born in
    Asia? Refer to details in her essay that you think relate to its title.
2. Noda chooses to divide her essay into a number of subsections. Does the
    order in which she puts them seem to matter? Why or why not? What, if
    anything, do they have or do in common? Ultimately, which strikes you
    more, the individual points they make or the relations between them? Ex-
    plain.
3. Noda resorts to both telling and showing in this essay. Where does she
    straightforwardly report her thinking? Where does she basically rely on
    scene and anecdote to make her points? Do you find the proportion of
    telling and showing here appropriate? Why or why not?

Thematic Focus

1. With what about her identity do you see Noda trying to come to terms in this essay? In what ways is she trying to determine the proper relation between the outside and the inside? Do you get the sense that she succeeds? Explain with details from the text.
2. Identify what you take to be the main point of each episode that Noda presents. For example, what do you think is the main idea of the shrine episode? Of the incident where Noda's car became stuck in sand? Of the scenes involving her mother? Of the epilogue?
3. Trace the references to voices, speaking, and singing in this essay. How, ultimately, do they relate?

Double Face

Amy Tan

Amy Tan was born in Oakland, California in 1952, her parents having emigrated from China 2½ years previously. She herself ultimately visited China 35 years later. After working as a consultant to programs for disabled children and as a free-lance business writer, Tan began writing fiction in 1985. In 1991 she published a novel, *The Kitchen God's Wife*. The following is from her first book, *The Joy Luck Club*, a collection of interrelated short stories that became a surprise bestseller in 1989. The title refers to a mah-jongg club made up of Chinese women who immigrated to America. Tan alternates stories told by these women with ones told by their American daughters. She thereby conveys the differences and similarities between two generations of Chinese-Americans. "Double Face" presents Lindo Jong's reflections on her immigrant past and her present relationship with her daughter Waverly.

Reflections Before Reading

Tan presents an immigrant mother trying to understand her American daughter's life. What sorts of things do you think the mother may focus on, as opposed to the daughter? Do you know of situations where immigrants and their children revealed different interests? If so, what were the issues involved? Tan refers specifically to the history of Chinese-Americans. What, if anything, do you associate with their history? Have you assumed that it is very similar to that of Japanese-Americans? Why or why not?

My daughter wanted to go to China for her second honeymoon, but now she is afraid. 1

"What if I blend in so well they think I'm one of them?" Waverly asked me. 2 "What if they don't let me come back to the United States?"

"When you go to China," I told her, "you don't even need to open your mouth. 3 They already know you are an outsider."

"What are you talking about?" she asked. My daughter likes to speak back. She 4 likes to question what I say.

"Aii-ya," I said. "Even if you put on their clothes, even if you take off your 5 makeup and hide your fancy jewelry, they know. They know just watching the way you walk, the way you carry your face. They know you do not belong."

My daughter did not look pleased when I told her this, that she didn't look 6 Chinese. She had a sour American look on her face. Oh, maybe ten years ago, she would have clapped her hands—hurray!—as if this were good news. But now she wants to be Chinese, it is so fashionable. And I know it is too late. All those years I tried to teach her! She followed my Chinese ways only until she learned how to walk out the door by herself and go to school. So now the only Chinese words she can say are *sh-sh, houche, chr fan,* and *gwan deng shweijyau.* How can she talk to people in China with these words? Pee-pee, choo-choo train, eat, close light sleep. How can she think she can blend in? Only her skin and her hair are Chinese. Inside—she is all American-made.

It's my fault she is this way. I wanted my children to have the best combina- 7 tion: American circumstances and Chinese character. How could I know these two things do not mix?

I taught her how American circumstances work. If you are born poor here, it's 8 no lasting shame. You are first in line for a scholarship. If the roof crashes on your head, no need to cry over this bad luck. You can sue anybody, make the landlord fix it. You do not have to sit like a Buddha under a tree letting pigeons drop their dirty business on your head. You can buy an umbrella. Or go inside a Catholic church. In America, nobody says you have to keep the circumstances somebody else gives you.

She learned these things, but I couldn't teach her about Chinese character. 9 How to obey parents and listen to your mother's mind. How not to show your own thoughts, to put your feelings behind your face so you can take advantage of hidden opportunities. Why easy things are not worth pursuing. How to know your own worth and polish it, never flashing it around like a cheap ring. Why Chinese thinking is best.

No, this kind of thinking didn't stick to her. She was too busy chewing gum,   10
blowing bubbles bigger than her cheeks. Only that kind of thinking stuck.

"Finish your coffee," I told her yesterday. "Don't throw your blessings away."   11

"Don't be so old-fashioned, Ma," she told me, finishing her coffee down the   12
sink. "I'm my own person."

And I think, How can she be her own person? When did I give her up?   13

My daughter is getting married a second time. So she asked me to go to her   14
beauty parlor, her famous Mr. Rory. I know her meaning. She is ashamed of my
looks. What will her husband's parents and his important lawyer friends think of
this backward old Chinese woman?

"Auntie An-mei can cut me," I say.   15

"Rory is famous," says my daughter, as if she had no ears. "He does fabulous   16
work."

So I sit in Mr. Rory's chair. He pumps me up and down until I am the right   17
height. Then my daughter criticizes me as if I were not there. "See how it's flat on
one side," she accuses my head. "She needs a cut and a perm. And this purple tint
in her hair, she's been doing it at home. She's never had anything professionally
done."

She is looking at Mr. Rory in the mirror. He is looking at me in the mirror. I   18
have seen this professional look before. Americans don't really look at one another
when talking. They talk to their reflections. They look at others or themselves only
when they think nobody is watching. So they never see how they really look. They
see themselves smiling without their mouth open, or turned to the side where they
cannot see their faults.

"How does she want it?" asked Mr. Rory. He thinks I do not understand En-   19
glish. He is floating his fingers through my hair. He is showing how his magic can
make my hair thicker and longer.

"Ma, how do you want it?" Why does my daughter think she is translating   20
English for me? Before I can even speak, she explains my thoughts: "She wants a
soft wave. We probably shouldn't cut it too short. Otherwise it'll be too tight for the
wedding. She doesn't want it to look kinky or weird."

And now she says to me in a loud voice, as if I had lost my hearing, "Isn't that   21
right, Ma? Not too tight?"

I smile. I use my American face. That's the face Americans think is Chinese,   22
the one they cannot understand. But inside I am becoming ashamed. I am
ashamed she is ashamed. Because she is my daughter and I am proud of her, and I
am her mother but she is not proud of me.

Mr. Rory pats my hair more. He looks at me. He looks at my daughter. Then   23
he says something to my daughter that really displeases her: "It's uncanny how
much you two look alike!"

I smile, this time with my Chinese face. But my daughter's eyes and her smile   24
become very narrow, the way a cat pulls itself small just before it bites. Now Mr.

Rory goes away so we can think about this. I hear him snap his fingers. "Wash! Mrs. Jong is next!"

So my daughter and I are alone in this crowded beauty parlor. She is frowning   25
at herself in the mirror. She sees me looking at her.

"The same cheeks," she says. She points to mine and then pokes her cheeks.   26
She sucks them outside in to look like a starved person. She puts her face next to mine, side by side, and we look at each other in the mirror.

"You can see your character in your face," I say to my daughter without think-   27
ing. "You can see your future."

"What do you mean?" she says.   28

And now I have to fight back my feelings. These two faces, I think, so much   29
the same! The same happiness, the same sadness, the same good fortune, the same faults.

I am seeing myself and my mother, back in China, when I was a young girl.   30

My mother—your grandmother—once told me my fortune, how my character   31
could lead to good and bad circumstances. She was sitting at her table with the big mirror. I was standing behind her, my chin resting on her shoulder. The next day was the start of the new year. I would be ten years by my Chinese age, so it was an important birthday for me. For this reason maybe she did not criticize me too much. She was looking at my face.

She touched my ear. "You are lucky," she said. "You have my ears, a big thick   32
lobe, lots of meat at the bottom, full of blessings. Some people are born so poor. Their ears are so thin, so close to their head, they can never hear luck calling to them. You have the right ears, but you must listen to your opportunities."

She ran her thin finger down my nose. "You have my nose. The hole is not too   33
big, so your money will not be running out. The nose is straight and smooth, a good sign. A girl with a crooked nose is bound for misfortune. She is always following the wrong things, the wrong people, the worst luck."

She tapped my chin and then hers. "Not too short, not too long. Our longevity   34
will be adequate, not cut off too soon, not so long we become a burden."

She pushed my hair away from my forehead. "We are the same," concluded   35
my mother. "Perhaps your forehead is wider, so you will be even more clever. And your hair is thick, the hairline is low on your forehead. This means you will have some hardships in your early life. This happened to me. But look at my hairline now. High! Such a blessing for my old age. Later you will learn to worry and lose your hair, too."

She took my chin in her hand. She turned my face toward her, eyes facing   36
eyes. She moved my face to one side, then the other. "The eyes are honest, eager," she said. "They follow me and show respect. They do not look down in shame. They do not resist and turn the opposite way. You will be a good wife, mother, and daughter-in-law."

When my mother told me these things, I was still so young. And even though   37
she said we looked the same, I wanted to look more the same. If her eye went up and looked surprised, I wanted my eye to do the same. If her mouth fell down and was unhappy, I too wanted to feel unhappy.

I was so much like my mother. This was before our circumstances separated 38
us: a flood that caused my family to leave me behind, my first marriage to a family
that did not want me, a war from all sides, and later, an ocean that took me to a new
country. She did not see how my face changed over the years. How my mouth
began to droop. How I began to worry but still did not lose my hair. How my eyes
began to follow the American way. She did not see that I twisted my nose bouncing
forward on a crowded bus in San Francisco. Your father and I, we were on our way
to church to give many thanks to God for all our blessings, but I had to subtract
some for my nose.

It's hard to keep your Chinese face in America. At the beginning, before I 39
even arrived, I had to hide my true self. I paid an American-raised Chinese girl in
Peking to show me how.

"In America," she said, "you cannot say you want to live there forever. If you 40
are Chinese, you must say you admire their schools, their ways of thinking. You
must say you want to be a scholar and come back to teach Chinese people what you
have learned."

"What should I say I want to learn?" I asked. "If they ask me questions, if I 41
cannot answer . . ."

"Religion, you must say you want to study religion," said this smart girl. 42
"Americans all have different ideas about religion, so there are no right and wrong
answers. Say to them, I'm going for God's sake, and they will respect you."

For another sum of money, this girl gave me a form filled out with English 43
words. I had to copy these words over and over again as if they were English words
formed from my own head. Next to the word NAME, I wrote *Lindo Sun*. Next to the
word BIRTHDATE, I wrote *May 11, 1918*, which this girl insisted was the same as
three months after the Chinese lunar new year. Next to the word BIRTHPLACE, I put
down *Taiyuan, China*. And next to the word OCCUPATION, I wrote *student of theology*.

I gave the girl even more money for a list of addresses in San Francisco, peo- 44
ple with big connections. And finally, this girl gave me, free of charge, instructions
for changing my circumstances. "First," she said, "you must find a husband. An
American citizen is best."

She saw my surprise and quickly added, "Chinese! Of course, he must be 45
Chinese. 'Citizen' does not mean Caucasian. But if he is not a citizen, you should
immediately do number two. See here, you should have a baby. Boy or girl, it
doesn't matter in the United States. Neither will take care of you in your old age,
isn't that true?" And we both laughed.

"Be careful, though," she said. "The authorities there will ask you if you have 46
children now or if you are thinking of having some. You must say no. You should
look sincere and say you are not married, you are religious, you know it is wrong to
have a baby."

I must have looked puzzled, because she explained further: "Look here now, 47
how can an unborn baby know what it is not supposed to do? And once it has
arrived, it is an American citizen and can do anything it wants. It can ask its mother
to stay. Isn't that true?"

But that is not the reason I was puzzled. I wondered why she said I should look   48
sincere. How could I look any other way when telling the truth?

See how truthful my face still looks. Why didn't I give this look to you? Why do   49
you always tell your friends that I arrived in the United States on a slow boat from
China? This is not true. I was not that poor. I took a plane. I had saved the money
my first husband's family gave me when they sent me away. And I had saved
money from my twelve years' work as a telephone operator. But it is true I did not
take the fastest plane. The plane took three weeks. It stopped everywhere: Hong
Kong, Vietnam, the Philippines, Hawaii. So by the time I arrived, I did not look
sincerely glad to be here.

Why do you always tell people that I met your father in the Cathay House, that   50
I broke open a fortune cookie and it said I would marry a dark, handsome stranger,
and that when I looked up, there he was, the waiter, your father. Why do you make
this joke? This is not sincere. This was not true! Your father was not a waiter, I
never ate in that restaurant. The Cathay House had a sign that said "Chinese
Food," so only Americans went there before it was torn down. Now it is a McDon-
ald's restaurant with a big Chinese sign that says *mai dong lou*—"wheat," "east,"
"building." All nonsense. Why are you attracted only to Chinese nonsense? You
must understand my real circumstances, how I arrived, how I married, how I lost
my Chinese face, why you are the way you are.

When I arrived, nobody asked me questions. The authorities looked at my   51
papers and stamped me in. I decided to go first to a San Francisco address given to
me by this girl in Peking. The bus put me down on a wide street with cable cars.
This was California Street. I walked up this hill and then I saw a tall building. This
was Old St. Mary's. Under the church sign, in handwritten Chinese characters,
someone had added: "A Chinese Ceremony to Save Ghosts from Spiritual Unrest 7
A.M. and 8:30 A.M." I memorized this information in case the authorities asked me
where I worshipped my religion. And then I saw another sign across the street. It
was painted on the outside of a short building: "Save Today for Tomorrow, at Bank
of America." And I thought to myself, This is where American people worship.
See, even then I was not so dumb! Today that church is the same size, but where
that short bank used to be, now there is a tall building, fifty stories high, where you
and your husband-to-be work and look down on everybody.

My daughter laughed when I said this. Her mother can make a good joke.   52

So I kept walking up this hill. I saw two pagodas, one on each side of the street,   53
as though they were the entrance to a great Buddha temple. But when I looked
carefully, I saw the pagoda was really just a building topped with stacks of tile
roofs, no walls, nothing else under its head. I was surprised how they tried to make
everything look like an old imperial city or an emperor's tomb. But if you looked on
either side of these pretend-pagodas, you could see the streets became narrow and
crowded, dark, and dirty. I thought to myself, Why did they choose only the worst
Chinese parts for the inside? Why didn't they build gardens and ponds instead?
Oh, here and there was the look of a famous ancient cave or a Chinese opera. But
inside it was always the same cheap stuff.

So by the time I found the address the girl in Peking gave me, I knew not to   54
expect too much. The address was a large green building, so noisy, children run-

ning up and down the outside stairs and hallways. Inside number 402, I found an old woman who told me right away she had wasted her time waiting for me all week. She quickly wrote down some addresses and gave them to me, keeping her hand out after I took the paper. So I gave her an American dollar and she looked at it and said, "*Syaujye*"—Miss—"we are in America now. Even a beggar can starve on this dollar." So I gave her another dollar and she said, "Aii, you think it is so easy getting this information?" So I gave her another and she closed her hand and her mouth.

With the addresses this old woman gave me, I found a cheap apartment on Washington Street. It was like all the other places, sitting on top of a little store. And through this three-dollar list, I found a terrible job paying me seventy-five cents an hour. Oh, I tried to get a job as a salesgirl, but you had to know English for that. I tried for another job as a Chinese hostess, but they also wanted me to rub my hands up and down foreign men, and I knew right away this was as bad as fourth-class prostitutes in China! So I rubbed that address out with black ink. And some of the other jobs required you to have a special relationship. They were jobs held by families from Canton and Toishan and the Four Districts, southern people who had come many years ago to make their fortune and were still holding on to them with the hands of their great-grandchildren. [55]

So my mother was right about my hardships. This job in the cookie factory was one of the worst. Big black machines worked all day and night pouring little pancakes onto moving round griddles. The other woman and I sat on high stools, and as the little pancakes went by, we had to grab them off the hot griddle just as they turned golden. We would put a strip of paper in the center, then fold the cookie in half and bend its arms back just as it turned hard. If you grabbed the pancake too soon, you would burn your fingers on the hot, wet dough. But if you grabbed too late, the cookie would harden before you could even complete the first bend. And then you had to throw these mistakes in a barrel, which counted againt you because the owner could sell those only as scraps. [56]

After the first day, I suffered ten red fingers. This was not a job for a stupid person. You had to learn fast or your fingers would turn into fried sausages. So the next day only my eyes burned, from never taking them off the pancakes. And the day after that, my arms ached from holding them out ready to catch the pancakes at just the right moment. But by the end of my first week, it became mindless work and I could relax enough to notice who else was working on each side of me. One was an older woman who never smiled and spoke to herself in Cantonese when she was angry. She talked like a crazy person. On my other side was a woman around my age. Her barrel contained very few mistakes. But I suspected she ate them. She was quite plump. [57]

"Eh, *Syaujye*," she called to me over the loud noise of the machines. I was grateful to hear her voice, to discover we both spoke Mandarin, although her dialect was coarse-sounding. "Did you ever think you would be so powerful you could determine someone else's fortune? she asked. [58]

I didn't understand what she meant. So she picked up one of the strips of paper and read it aloud, first in English: "Do not fight and air your dirty laundry in public. To the victor go the soils." Then she translated in Chinese: "You shouldn't fight and do your laundry at the same time. If you win, your clothes will get dirty." [59]

I still did not know what she meant. So she picked up another one and read in   60
English: "Money is the root of all evil. Look around you and dig deep." And then in
Chinese: "Money is a bad influence. You become restless and rob graves."

"What is this nonsense?" I asked her, putting the strips of paper in my pocket,   61
thinking I should study these classical American sayings.

"They are fortunes," she explained. "American people think Chinese people   62
write these sayings."

"But we never say such things!" I said. "These things don't make sense. These   63
are not fortunes, they are bad instructions."

"No, Miss," she said, laughing, "it is our bad fortune to be here making these   64
and somebody else's bad fortune to pay to get them."

So that is how I met An-mei Hsu. Yes, yes, Auntie An-mei, now so old-fash-   65
ioned. An-mei and I still laugh over those bad fortunes and how they later became
quite useful in helping me catch a husband.

"Eh, Lindo," An-mei said to me one day at our workplace. "Come to my   66
church this Sunday. My husband has a friend who is looking for a good Chinese
wife. He is not a citizen, but I'm sure he knows how to make one." So that is how I
first heard about Tin Jong, your father. It was not like my first marriage, where
everything was arranged. I had a choice. I could choose to marry your father, or I
could choose not to marry him and go back to China.

I knew something was not right when I saw him: He was Cantonese! How   67
could An-mei think I could marry such a person? But she just said: "We are not in
China anymore. You don't have to marry the village boy. Here everybody is now
from the same village even if they come from different parts of China." See how
changed Auntie An-mei is from those old days.

So we were shy at first, your father and I, neither of us able to speak to each   68
other in our Chinese dialects. We went to English class together, speaking to each
other in those new words and sometimes taking out a piece of paper to write a
Chinese character to show what we meant. At least we had that, a piece of paper to
hold us together. But it's hard to tell someone's marriage intentions when you can't
say things aloud. All those little signs—the teasing, the bossy, scolding words—
that's how you know if it is serious. But we could talk only in the manner of our
English teacher. I see cat. I see rat. I see hat.

But I saw soon enough how much your father liked me. He would pretend he   69
was in a Chinese play to show me what he meant. He ran back and forth, jumped
up and down, pulling his fingers through his hair, so I knew—*mangjile!*—what a
busy, exciting place this Pacific Telephone was, this place where he worked. You
didn't know this about your father—that he could be such a good actor? You didn't
know your father had so much hair?

Oh, I found out later his job was not the way he described it. It was not so   70
good. Even today, now that I can speak Cantonese to your father, I always ask him
why he doesn't find a better situation. But he acts as if we were in those old days,
when he couldn't understand anything I said.

Sometimes I wonder why I wanted to catch a marriage with your father. I   71
think An-mei put the thought in my mind. She said, "In the movies, boys and girls

are always passing notes in class. That's how they fall into trouble. You need to start trouble to get this man to realize his intentions. Otherwise, you will be an old lady before it comes to his mind."

That evening An-mei and I went to work and searched through strips of for- 72
tune cookie papers, trying to find the right instructions to give to your father. An-mei read them aloud, putting aside ones that might work: "Diamonds are a girl's best friend. Don't ever settle for a pal." "If such thoughts are in your head, it's time to be wed." "Confucius say a woman is worth a thousand words. Tell your wife she's used up her total."

We laughed over those. But I knew the right one when I read it. It said: "A 73
house is not home when a spouse is not at home." I did not laugh. I wrapped up this saying in a pancake, bending the cookie with all my heart.

After school the next afternoon, I put my hand in my purse and then made a 74
look, as if a mouse had bitten my hand. "What's this?" I cried. Then I pulled out the cookie and handed it to your father. "Eh! So many cookies, just to see them makes me sick. You take this cookie."

I knew even then he had a nature that did not waste anything. He opened the 75
cookie and he crunched it in his mouth, and then read the piece of paper.

"What does it say?" I asked. I tried to act as if it did not matter. And when he 76
still did not speak, I said, "Translate, please."

We were walking in Portsmouth Square and already the fog had blown in and 77
I was very cold in my thin coat. So I hoped your father would hurry and ask me to marry him. But instead, he kept his serious look and said, "I don't know this word 'spouse.' Tonight I will look in my dictionary. Then I can tell you the meaning tomorrow."

The next day he asked me in English, "Lindo, can you spouse me?" And I 78
laughed at him and said he used that word incorrectly. So he came back and made a Confucius joke, that if the words were wrong, then his intentions must also be wrong. We scolded and joked with each other all day long like this, and that is how we decided to get married.

One month later we had a ceremony in the First Chinese Baptist Church, 79
where we met. And nine months later your father and I had our proof of citizen-ship, a baby boy, your big brother Winston. I named him Winston because I liked the meaning of those two words "wins ton." I wanted to raise a son who would win many things, praise, money, a good life. Back then, I thought to myself, At last I have everything I wanted. I was so happy, I didn't see we were poor. I saw only what we had. How did I know Winston would die later in a car accident? So young! Only sixteen!

Two years after Winston was born, I had your other brother, Vincent. I named 80
him Vincent, which sounds like "win cent," the sound of making money, because I was beginning to think we did not have enough. And then I bumped my nose riding on the bus. Soon after that you were born.

I don't know what caused me to change. Maybe it was my crooked nose that 81
damaged my thinking. Maybe it was seeing you as a baby, how you looked so much like me, and this made me dissatisfied with my life. I wanted everything for you to be better. I wanted you to have the best circumstances, the best character. I didn't

want you to regret anything. And that's why I named you Waverly. It was the name of the street we lived on. And I wanted you to think, This is where I belong. But I also knew if I named you after this street, soon you would grow up, leave this place, and take a piece of me with you.

Mr. Rory is brushing my hair. Everything is soft. Everything is black. 82

"You look great, Ma," says my daughter. "Everyone at the wedding will think 83 you're my sister."

I look at my face in the beauty parlor mirror. I see my reflection. I cannot see 84 my faults, but I know they are there. I gave my daughter these faults. The same eyes, the same cheeks, the same chin. Her character, it came from my circumstances. I look at my daughter and now it is the first time I have seen it.

"Ai-ya! What happened to your nose?" 85

She looks in the mirror. She sees nothing wrong. "What do you mean? Noth- 86 ing happened," she says. "It's just the same nose."

"But how did you get it crooked?" I ask. One side of her nose is bending lower, 87 dragging her cheek with it.

"What do you mean?" she asks. "It's your nose. You gave me this nose." 88

"How can that be? It's drooping. You must get plastic surgery and correct it." 89

But my daughter has no ears for my words. She puts her smiling face next to 90 my worried one. "Don't be silly. Our nose isn't so bad," she says. "It makes us look devious." She looks pleased.

"What is this word, 'devious,' " I ask. 91

"It means we're looking one way, while following another. We're for one side 92 and also the other. We mean what we say, but our intentions are different."

"People can see this in our face?" 93

My daughter laughs. "Well, not everything that we're thinking. They just know 94 we're two-faced."

"This is good?" 95

"This is good if you get what you want." 96

I think about our two faces. I think about my intentions. Which one is Ameri- 97 can? Which one is Chinese? Which one is better? If you show one, you must always sacrifice the other.

It is like what happened when I went back to China last year, after I had not 98 been there for almost forty years. I had taken off my fancy jewelry. I did not wear loud colors. I spoke their language. I used their local money. But still, they knew. They knew my face was not one hundred percent Chinese. They still charged me high foreign prices.

So now I think, What did I lose? What did I get back in return? I will ask my 99 daughter what she thinks.

Rhetorical Focus

1. Why do you think Tan describes the visit to Mr. Rory, instead of using some other kind of scene to reveal the present relationship of mother and daughter?

2. With the long middle of this story, Tan flashes back to Lindo Jong's past. What does the reader gain from this narrative strategy? Do Lindo Jong's recollections and the present circumstances that frame them strike you as having equal importance? Why or why not?

3. Tan presents the story from the immigrant mother's point of view. What does this technique enable? How reliable is Lindo Jong as a narrator? Are there any places where you question what she says? Recall that Noda writes from the point of view of an American-born daughter. Is this difference in narrative method related to other important differences in the texts? Explain.

Thematic Focus

1. Summarize in your own words the main points that emerge from Lindo Jong's recounting of her past. What aspects of her identity, if any, does she seem certain about by the end of the story? What, if anything, about her identity is she still trying to figure out?

2. Trace the references to faces in Tan's story and in Noda's essay. Do these references take on the same meaning(s) in both? Support your answer with details from both texts.

3. Reading Tan's story and Noda's essay, what differences do you sense between Chinese-American and Japanese-American experiences, if any? What similarities do you sense, if any?

Suggestions for Writing

1. At one point in Amy Tan's story, Waverly Jong says, " 'I'm my own person' " (paragraph 12). Her mother thinks, "How can she be her own person? When did I give her up?" (paragraph 13). Write an essay in which you explain the ways in which Waverly Jong's and Kesaya E. Noda's quest for identity involves their relationships with their mothers. To what extent does each text leave mother and daughter identified with each other, sharing characteristics and values? To what extent does each text leave the daughter "her own person"? In what ways, if any, does it matter that these mothers and daughter are from particular ethnic groups?

2. Describe an occasion when you grew more conscious of your own ethnic identity or that of someone you knew. Besides giving details of this occasion, identify what your thoughts and feelings were then, and any subsequent reflections you had. Was the experience ultimately positive for you? Negative? Both?

3. In examining ethnic identity, Noda writes from a daughter's point of view, Tan from a mother's. In a few paragraphs, describe from your own point of view an incident in which you were involved. Then, again in a few paragraphs, describe the incident from the point of view of someone else who was involved; try, in fact, to write as this person. Finally, write a paragraph

in which you identify what you learned about point of view from this exercise. You may want to write about an incident you and your mother or another family member experienced together.

OBSERVING SELF AND OTHER

Even when you write about people other than yourself, your personal experiences and assumptions can influence how you perceive them. Indeed, the process of exploring another's identity can at the same time be an opportunity to explore your own. In a number of instances, your perspective can genuinely illuminate the other person's life. You need to keep in mind, however, that you may be projecting an image of your own onto the person rather than truly struggling to understand what he or she is like. In particular, you need to consider how your perspective may be limited if you do not share the other person's social situation—if, that is, the two of you differ in gender, race, social class, culture, sexual preference, or some other respect. To be sure, it is not always immediately clear just what difference such differences make. For example, someone of another gender than yours may still agree with you on a wide range of issues. Nonetheless, if you commit yourself to acknowledging human differences when you observe another person, you can situate yourself in the world better than you would if you simply assumed that everyone resembles one another.

This constellation examines what the observer and the observed may or may not learn from each other about their identities. It emphasizes this topic by bringing together two texts about the same person, one by an observer of her and the other originating with the person herself. The first text comes from *Let Us Now Praise Famous Men*, James Agee and Walker Evans's celebrated 1941 report on the plight of tenant farmers in America during the Great Depression. In the excerpt here, Agee describes a woman he calls "Emma McCloud." The second account is Emma McCloud's own story of her life, produced almost 40 years later, with the assistance of an interviewer–editor. Among other events, Emma recalls her encounter with Agee. As you read this pair of texts, note the extent to which each is self-reflective. Does Agee write with sufficient consciousness of the ways that his own background may influence his view of Emma? Does Emma seem to grasp her whole life history and Agee's standpoint on it? Also note what happens when the observer and the observed trade places as narrators. Is Agee able to predict in general the sort of direction Emma's life indeed takes? Are his rhetorical techniques appropriate for analyzing her? Does she challenge his account through the language, experiences, and ideas she puts forth in hers? Consider, too, whether and how their differences in gender and social class affect their perspectives. Finally, think what this juxtaposition of texts implies about the issues and techniques you as a writer should consider if you are to analyze well both yourself and other people.

Emma's Story I

James Agee

James Agee (1909–1955) wrote in many genres, including film criticism, screenplays (such as *The African Queen*), poetry, and novels (such as *A Death in the Family*, an autobiographical work that was published after his death and won the Pulitzer Prize in 1958). We reprint here an excerpt from his 1941 book *Let Us Now Praise Famous Men*, which can be described as lyrical but nevertheless hard-hitting journalism. It emerged from a journey through Alabama that Agee and the photographer Walker Evans took in 1936, in the midst of the Great Depression. The two men focused on the lives of sharecroppers, farmers who had to rent the land they worked. In writing the book's prose, Agee wondered how best to represent the people he came to know. He hoped to depict them as vividly as Evans did in the photographs accompanying the text; at the same time, he was self-conscious about presuming to interpret their lives, given that he himself lived in better material circumstances. Although the book is now praised for exposing harsh social conditions, its concerns prevented its being published for several years.

Just before this excerpt begins, Agee depicts himself writing alone at night in the Gudger family house, where he and Walker Evans are staying. This family of sharecroppers includes George Gudger, his wife Annie Mae, and their four children. Agee now writes about another visitor to the household, Annie Mae's sister Emma. (Note that Agee changed his subjects' names to protect their privacy.) You will notice right away that Agee's sentences are often long, meditative, and almost poetic as they switch their attention back and forth from the Gudger family to Agee himself. Agee recommended reading his text aloud, and you may want to try doing this to savor more fully his language, as well as his powers of observation.

Reflections Before Reading

What limitations, if any, do you think middle- or upper-class people face when they try to understand poor people's lives? How can they overcome these limitations? Do you think their materially better situation can actually give them insight into poor people that the latter may not achieve? Explain. In the following selection, James Agee writes for a presumably middle- to

upper-class audience about poor sharecroppers he is visiting during the
Great Depression. What, if anything, do you associate with this period in
American history? What sorts of information would you like Agee to obtain?
What things might he do to evoke his subjects' lives? What precautions, if
any, do you want him to bear in mind as he writes about these people?

I am fond of Emma, and very sorry for her, and I shall probably never see her again   1
after a few hours from now. I want to tell you what I can about her.

She is a big girl, almost as big as her sister is wiry, though she is not at all fat: 2
her build is rather that of a young queen of a child's magic story who throughout
has been coarsened by peasant and earth living and work, and that of her eyes and
her demeanor, too, kind, not fully formed, resolute, bewildered, and sad. Her soft
abundant slightly curling brown hair is cut in a square bob which on her large fine
head is particularly childish, and indeed Emma is rather a big child, sexual beyond
propriety to its years, than a young woman; and this can be seen in a kind of dim-
ness of definition in her features, her skin, and the shape of her body, which will be
lost in a few more years. She wears a ten cent store necklace and a sunday cotton
print dress because she is visiting, and is from town, but she took off her slippers as
soon as she came, and worked with Annie Mae. According to her father she is the
spitn image of her mother when her mother was young; Annie Mae favors her
father and his people, who were all small and lightly built.

Emma is very fond of her father and very sorry for him, as her sister is, and   3
neither of them can stand his second wife. I have an idea that his marrying her had
a lot to do with Emma's own marriage, which her father so strongly advised her
against. He married the second time when Emma was thirteen, and for a long
while they lived almost insanely, as I will tell you of later, far back in a swamp: and
when Emma was sixteen she married a man her father's age, a carpenter in Cherokee City. She has been married to him two years; they have no children. Emma
loves good times, and towns, and people her own age, and he is jealous and mean
to her and suspicious of her. He has given her no pretty dresses nor the money to
buy cloth to make them. Every minute he is in the house he keeps his eye right on
her as if she was up to something, and when he goes out, which is as seldom as he
can, he locks her in: so that twice already she has left him and come home to stay,
and then after a while he has come down begging, and crying, and swearing he'll
treat her good, and give her anything she asks for, and that he'll take to drink or kill
himself if she leaves him, and she has gone back: for it isn't any fun at home, hating
that woman the way she does, and she can't have fun with anyone else because she
is married and nobody will have fun with her that way: and now (and I think it may
be not only through the depression but through staying in the house because of
jealousy and through fear of living in a town with her, and so near a home she can
return to), her husband can no longer get a living in Cherokee City; he has heard of
a farm on a plantation over in the red hills in Mississippi and has already gone, and
taken it, and he has sent word to Emma that she is to come in a truck in which a
man he knows, who has business to drive out that way, is moving their furniture;

and this truck is leaving tomorrow. She doesn't want to go at all, and during the past two days she has been withdrawing into rooms with her sister and crying a good deal, almost tearlessly and almost without voice, as if she knew no more how to cry than how to take care for her life; and Annie Mae is strong against her going, all that distance, to a man who leaves her behind and then just sends for her, saying, Come on along, now; and George too is as committal over it as he feels will appear any right or business of his to be, he a man, and married, to the wife of another man, who is no kin to him, but only the sister of his wife, and to whom he is himself unconcealably attracted: but she is going all the same, without at all under-standing why. Annie Mae is sure she won't stay out there long, not all alone in the country away from her kinfolks with that man; that is what she keeps saying, to Emma, and to George, and even to me; but actually she is surer than not that she may never see her young sister again, and she grieves for her, and for the loss of her to her own loneliness, for she loves her, both for herself and her dependence and for that softness of youth which already is drawn so deep into the trap, and in which Annie Mae can perceive herself as she was ten years past; and she gives no appear-ance of noticing the clumsy and shamefaced would-be-subtle demeanors of flirta-tion which George is stupid enough to believe she does not understand for what they are: for George would only be shocked should she give him open permission, and Emma could not be too well trusted either. So this sad comedy has been going on without comment from anyone, which will come to nothing: and another sort has been going on with us, of a kind fully as helpless. Each of us is attractive to Emma, both in sexual immediacy and as symbols or embodiments of a life she wants and knows she will never have; and each of us is fond of her, and attracted toward her. We are not only strangers to her, but we are strange, unexplainable, beyond what I can begin yet fully to realize. We have acted toward her with the greatest possible care and shyness and quiet, yet we have been open or 'clear' as well, so that she knows we understand her and like her and care for her almost intimately. She is puzzled by this and yet not at all troubled, but excited; but there is nothing to do about it on either side. There is tenderness and sweetness and mutual pleasure in such a 'flirtation' which one would not for the world restrain or cancel, yet there is also an essential cruelty, about which nothing can be done, and strong possibility of cruelty through misunderstanding, and inhibition, and impos-sibility, which can be restrained, and which one would rather die than cause any of: but it is a cruel and ridiculous and restricted situation, and everyone to some extent realizes it. Everyone realizes it, I think, to such a degree even as this: supposing even that nothing can be helped about the marriage, supposing she is going away and on with it, which she shouldn't, then if only Emma could spend her last few days alive having a gigantic good time in bed, with George, a kind of man she is best used to, and with Walker and with me, whom she is curious about and at-tracted to, and who are at the same moment tangible and friendly and not at all to be feared, and on the other hand have for her the mystery or glamour almost of mythological creatures. This has a good many times in the past couple of days come very clearly through between all of us except the children, and without fear, in sudden and subtle but unmistakable expressions of the eyes, or ways of smiling: yet not one of us would be capable of trusting ourselves to it unless beyond any doubt each knew all the others to be thus capable: and even then how crazily the conditioned and inferior parts of each of our beings would rush in, and take revenge. But this is just a minute specialization of a general brutal pity: almost any person, no matter how damaged and poisoned and blinded, is infinitely more capable of intelligence and of joy than he can let himself be or than he usually knows; and even if he had no reason to fear his own poisons, he has those that are in others to fear, to assume and take care for, if he would not hurt both himself and that other person and the pure act itself beyond cure.

But here I am going to shift ahead of where I am writing, to a thing which is to   4
happen, or which happened, the next morning (you mustn't be puzzled by this, I'm writing in a continuum), and say what came of it.

The next morning was full of the disorganized, half listless, yet very busy mo-   5
tions of ordinary life broken by an event: Emma's going away. I was going to take her and Annie Mae to her brother Gallatin's house near Cookstown, where she was to meet the man with his truck, and I was waiting around on the front porch in the cool-hot increasing morning sunlight, working out my notes, while the morning housework was done up in special speed. (George was gone an hour or more ago, immediately after the breakfast they had all sat through, not talking much. There had been a sort of lingering in eating and in silences, and a little when the food was done, broken by talk to keep the silences from becoming too frightening; I had let the breakfast start late by telling him I would take him in the car; then abruptly he got up saying, 'Well, Jimmy, if you—' Whether he would kiss Emma goodbye, as a sort of relative, was on everybody's mind. He came clumsily near it: she half got from her chair, and their bodies were suddenly and sharply drawn toward each other a few inches: but he was much too shy, and did not even touch her with the hand he reached out to shake hers. Annie Mae drawled, smiling, What's wrong with ye George; she ain't agoin' to bite ye; and everyone laughed, and Emma stood up and they embraced, laughing, and he kissed her on her suddenly turned cheek, a little the way a father and an adolescent son kiss, and told her goodbye and wished her good luck, and I took him to work in the car, and came back. And now here I was, as I have said, on the porch.) Here I was on the porch, diddling around in a notebook and hearing the sounds of work and the changing patterns of voices inside, and the unaccustomed noise of shoeleather on the floor, because someone was dressed up for travel; and a hen thudded among dried watermelon seeds on the oak floor, looking, as they usually do, like a nearsighted professor; and down hill beyond the open field a little wind laid itself in a wall against the glistening leaves of the high forest and lay through with a long sweet granular noise of rustling water; and the hen dropped from the ledge of the porch to the turded dirt with a sodden bounce, and an involuntary cluck as her heaviness hit the ground on her sprung legs; and the long lithe little wind released the trees and was gone on, wandering the fringed earth in its affairs like a saturday schoolchild in the sun, and the leaves hung troubling in the aftermath; and I heard footsteps in the hall and Emma appeared, all dressed to go, looking somehow as if she had come to report a decision that had been made in a conference, for which I, without knowing it, seemed to have been waiting. She spoke in that same way, too, not wasting any roundabout time or waiting for an appropriate rhythm, yet not in haste, looking me

steadily and sweetly in the eyes, and said, I want you and Mr. Walker to know how much we all like you, because you make us feel easy with you; we don't have to act any different from what it comes natural to act, and we don't have to worry what you're thinking about us, it's just like you was our own people and had always lived here with us, you all are so kind, and nice, and quiet, and easygoing, and we wisht you wasn't never going to go away but stay on here with us, and I just want to tell you how much we all keer about you; Annie Mae says the same, and you please tell Mr. Walker, too, if I don't see him afore I go. (I knew she could never say it over again, and I swore I certainly would tell him.)

What's the use trying to say what I felt. It took her a long time to say what she wanted so much to say, and it was hard for her, but there she stood looking straight into my eyes, and I straight into hers, longer than you'd think it would be possible to stand it. I would have done anything in the world for her (that is always characteristic, I guess, of the seizure of the strongest love you can feel: pity, and the wish to die for a person, because there isn't anything you can do for them that is at all measurable to your love), and all I could do, the very most, for this girl who was so soon going on out of my existence into so hopeless a one of hers, the very most I could do was not to show all I cared for her and for what she was saying, and not to even try to do, or to indicate the good I wished I might do her and was so utterly helpless to do. I had such tenderness and such gratitude toward her that while she spoke I very strongly, as something steadier than an 'impulse,' wanted in answer to take her large body in my arms and smooth the damp hair back from her forehead and to kiss and comfort and shelter her like a child, and I can swear that I now as then almost believe that in that moment she would have so well understood this, and so purely and quietly met it, that now as then I only wish to God I had done it; but instead the most I did was to stand facing her, and to keep looking into her eyes (doing her the honor at least of knowing that she did not want relief from this), and, managing to keep the tears from running down my face, to smile to her and say that there was nothing in my whole life that I had cared so much to be told, and had been so grateful for (and I believe this is so); and that I wanted her to know how much I liked them, too, and her herself, and that I certainly felt that they were my own people, and wanted them to be, more than any other kind of people in the world, and that if they felt that of me, and that I belonged with them, and we all felt right and easy with each other and fond of each other, then there wasn't anything in the world I could be happier over, or be more glad to know (and this is so, too); and that I knew I could say all of the same of Walker (and this, too, I know I was true in saying). I had stood up, almost without realizing I was doing it, the moment she appeared and began to speak, as though facing some formal, or royal, or ritual action, and we stayed thus standing, not leaning against or touching anything, about three feet apart, facing each other. I went on to say that whatever might happen to her or that she might do in all her life I wished her the best luck anyone could think of, and not ever to forget it, that nobody has a right to be unhappy, or to live in a way that makes them unhappy, for the sake of being afraid, or what people will think of them, or for the sake of anyone else, if there is any way they can possibly do better, that won't hurt other people too much. She slowly and lightly blushed while I spoke and her eyes became damp and bright, and said that she

6

sure did wish me the same. Then we had nothing to say, unless we should invent something, and nothing to do, and quite suddenly and at the same instant we smiled, and she said well, she reckoned she'd better git on in and help Annie Mae, and I nodded, and she went, and a half-hour later I was driving her, and Annie Mae, and her father, and Louise, and Junior, and Burt, and the baby, to her brother's house near Cookstown. The children were silent and intent with the excitement of riding in the car, stacked on top of each other around their mother on the back seat and looking out of the windows like dogs, except Louise, whose terrible gray eyes met mine whenever I glanced from them in the car mirror. Emma rode between me and her father, her round sleeveless arms cramped a little in front of her. My own sleeves were rolled high, so that in the crowding our flesh touched. Each of us at the first few of these contacts drew quietly away, then later she relaxed her arms, and her body and thighs as well, and so did I, and for perhaps fifteen minutes we lay quietly and closely side to side, and intimately communicated also in our thoughts. Our bodies were very hot, and the car was packed with hot and sweating bodies, and with a fine salt and rank odor like that of crushed grass; and thus in a short while, though I knew speed was not in the mood of anyone and was going as slowly as I felt I could with propriety, we covered the short seven mileage of clay, then slag, to Cookstown, and slowed through the town (eyes, eyes on us, of men, from beneath hatbrims), and down the meandering now sandy road to where her brother lived. I had seen him once before, a man in his thirties with a bitter, intelligent, skull-formed face; and his sour wife, and their gold skinned children: and now here also was another man, forty or so, leathery-strong, blackshaven, black-hatted, booted, his thin mouth tightened round a stalk of grass showing gold stained teeth, his cold, mean eyes a nearly white blue; and he was sardonically waiting, and his truck, loaded with chairs and bed-iron, stood in the sun where the treeshade had slide beyond it. He was studying Emma coldly and almost without furtiveness, and she was avoiding his eyes. It was impossible to go quite immediately. We all sat around a short while and had lemonade from a pressed-glass pitcher, from which he had already taken at least two propitiatory glasses. It had been made in some hope of helping the leavetaking pass off as a sort of party, from two lemons and spring water, without ice, and it was tepid, heavily sweetened (as if to compensate the lack of lemons), and scarcely tart; there was half a glass for each of us, out of five tumblers, and we all gave most of it to the children. The children of the two families stayed very quiet, shy of each other; the others, save the black-hatted man, tried to talk, without managing much; they tried especially hard when Emma got up, as suddenly as if she had to vomit, and went into the next room and shut the door, and Annie Mae followed her. Gallatin said it was mighty hard on a girl so young as that leaving her kinfolks so far behind. The man in the hat twisted his mouth on the grass and, without opening his teeth, said Yeah-ah, as if he had his own opinions about that. We were trying not to try to hear the voices in the next room, and that same helpless, frozen, creaky weeping I had heard before; and after a little it quieted; and after a little more they came out, Emma flourily powdered straight to the eyes, and the eyes as if she had cried sand instead of tears; and the man said—it was the first kind gesture I had seen in him and one of the few I suspect in his life, and I am sure it was kind by no intention of his: 'Well, we can't hang around here all day. Reckon you'd better come on along, if you're coming.'

With that, Emma and her father kiss, shyly and awkwardly, children doing it   7 before parents; so do she and her brother; she and Annie Mae embrace; she and I shake hands and say goodbye: all this in the sort of broken speed in which a family takes leave beside the black wall of a steaming train when the last crates have been loaded and it seems certain that at any instant the windows, and the leaned un-pitying faces, will begin to slide past on iron. Emma's paper suitcase is lifted into the truck beside the bedsprings which will sustain the years on years of her cold, hopeless nights; she is helped in upon the hard seat beside the driver above the hot and floorless engine, her slippered feet propped askew at the ledges of that pit into the road; the engine snaps and coughs and catches and levels on a hot white mois-tureless and thin metal roar, and with a dreadful rending noise that brings up the mild heads of cattle a quarter of a mile away the truck rips itself loose from the flesh of the planed dirt of the yard and wrings into the road and chucks ahead, we waving, she waving, the black hat straight ahead, she turned away, not bearing it, our hands drooped, and we stand disconsolate and emptied in the sun; and all through these coming many hours while we slow move within the anchored ron-dures of our living, the hot, screaming, rattling, twenty-mile-an-hour traveling elongates steadily crawling, a lost, earnest, and frowning ant, westward on red roads and on white in the febrile sun above no support, suspended, sustained from falling by force alone of its outward growth, like that long and lithe incongruous slender runner a vine spends swiftly out on the vast blank wall of the earth, like snake's head and slim stream feeling its way, to fix, and anchor, so far, so wide of the strong and stationed stalk: and that is Emma.

Rhetorical Focus

1. Identify the places where Agee suggests that he is interweaving the Gudg-ers' language with his own. What is the effect of this technique? Do you find the proportions of each language appropriate? Why or why not?
2. Should Agee have broken down his long sentences into several shorter ones? Why or why not? What about his long paragraphs? Support your reasoning with references to specific passages.
3. Identify where Agee shifts tenses. Note, too, that with the fourth para-graph he leaps forward to the next day. Are these techniques effective? Why or why not?

Thematic Focus

1. Why do you think Agee focuses on Emma here? What does she represent that he apparently thinks important to emphasize? What significance does he appear to find in the scene of her departure?

2. Do you find yourself trusting Agee as an observer of Emma and the rest of the family? Specifically, do you get the impression that he is able to overcome differences of class and gender in writing about these people? Does he reflect sufficiently on his own position as an observer? Support your reasoning with details from the text.
3. Agee engages in various philosophical reflections here. Do you agree with him that "almost any person, no matter how damaged and poisoned and blinded, is infinitely more capable of intelligence and of joy than he can let himself be or than he usually knows" (paragraph 3)? Would you go along with him in defining "the strongest love you can feel" as "pity, and the wish to die for a person, because there isn't anything you can do for them that is at all measurable to your love" (paragraph 6)?

Emma's Story II

Emma McCloud and Bradford Jenkins

In 1976, 40 years after the scene evoked by James Agee at the end of the previous selection, Emma McCloud told her life's story to Bradford Jenkins. Three years later he published it in the journal *Southern Exposure*, along with the section about Emma from Agee's book. More precisely, Jenkins transcribed conversations that he taped with Emma and incorporated excerpts from her diary. We include Jenkins's introduction, along with the text that he fashioned from Emma's reminiscences.

Reflections Before Reading

What does Agee's text lead you to believe Emma's future life will be like? What sorts of experiences would confirm or disconfirm what he seems to predict? What are you especially curious to know as she herself looks back on her life 40 years later?

"Emma's Story: Two Versions," and "So I Sung to Myself," Interview by Bradford Jenkins, SOUTHERN EXPOSURE, Spring, 1979, Vol. VII, No. 1. Copyright © Institute for Southern Studies, Box 531, Durham, N.C. 27702. Reprinted by permission.

Emma McCloud lives today in a rented, four-room frame house at the edge of   1
Cherokee City, Alabama. She dresses neatly in pantsuits from the racks of the
cheaper department stores, but the linoleum on the floors is cracked. At 62, her
only income is the monthly Social Security check. In the winter the oil burner in
the middle of the living room half-heartedly fights the cold air seeping in through
warped window frames and slanted floors.

    On the evening of my first visit, I showed her James Agee and Walker Evans'   2
Let Us Now Praise Famous Men, *the classic portrait of the Depression South.*
Emma's daughter, Patricia, whom she calls Sister, asked "Did they write about
you, Mama, in that book?"

    Emma wasn't sure, so I found the place where Agee spreads forth his   3
description of Emma, "rather a big child, sexual beyond propriety to its years."
She tried to read the words, but her eyes are very weak, and even with the thick
bifocals the small print was too much for her. She handed the book to Sister and
asked her to read it aloud. As she did, first Emma and then the rest of us were
transported back to 1934.

    Emma was 18 then, had been married for two years to a man 20 years her   4
elder, and was about to leave Alabama to join her husband in the red hills of
Mississippi. James Agee, on assignment for Henry Luce's Fortune *magazine, and*
photographer Walker Evans were staying at Emma's sister's home, documenting
the life of a family they believed to be representative of white sharecroppers in
the South. Emma's brief visit, the coming together of her kinfolk and her
departure to another land gave Agee and Evans more than they bargained for.

    As Sister read, Emma kept murmuring, "I remember that," and "Yes, that's   5
just the way it was." When the part came which described the leave-taking,
Emma began crying and her emotion filled the room. When Sister finished, Emma
began talking about leaving her family and going to the red hills of Mississippi.
Then she brightened "You know, I didn't know Jimmy (Agee) felt that way. About
me and all. He was a good-looking man. And I loved to talk to him, but if I had
knowed he felt the way he says he did . . . why, we'd have talked some more."
She chuckled. Her laughter was rich and infectious. We all began to laugh.

    The second version of Emma's story is her own. It was assembled from our   6
taped conversations in November, 1976, and from pages in her diary. Although I
have arranged her story in a chronological sequence and used conventional
spelling, the words and sentences are her own. I have altered the names of the
characters in accordance with Agee's practice and Emma's wish. Needless to say,
Emma's experiences, her life and emotion, though simply expressed, are as
moving as the eloquent ruminations of her accomplished observer, James Agee.

Bradford L. Jenkins

I was born May 27, 1916. Now that seems like a long time ago, but sometimes I get   7
to thinking back and it don't seem long at all. I can remember when I started to
school. We had to walk to school back then three miles and it would be so cold, but
we didn't mind for we didn't know any better.

    Mama would tie a string around my pencil and tie it around my neck so I   8
would not lose so many for they was hard to get. We would take our lunch in a

paper sack. Sometime it would start raining on us before we got to school. The sack would get wet and tear up and we would try to keep our lunch. Sometime we would put it in our pocket.

My brother Clifford, he was smaller than I was and he could not walk as fast as 9 I could for you see I was just a tomboy. But I was real good in school, and I really liked to go for I was going to be a nurse when I finished school—that was always my dream. And I think I would have been if I could have went on to school. But the year I was 13 years old, my mother died. Oh, I can remember that day. You see she was in the hospital—it don't seem like that she was there many days. I know me and Clifford went to see her but once. That is all I remember, but she knew us that day and we were so glad, for we just knew that she was better and would soon be back home with us. But that didn't happen. She died and left us. Clifford 10 and me 13.

Poor old Daddy. There he was left with two children and a big field of cotton 10 to gather, and I know now that his poor old heart was so heavy and he felt so alone and didn't know what to do. I had to start cooking, milking the cow, going to the field too when I had time. I had to wash our clothes and pray for the Lord to come and get me and carry me where Mama was. I didn't know how to do anything and I needed her so bad.

I haven't forgot yet that no one came in to help me and teach me how to do 11 anything. But that poor old daddy of mine done his best and he was always kind. He did not make fun of nothing I tried to do. I don't see how he ate the food I cooked and worked as hard as he did. I can see him now, sitting on his cotton sack, eating the slop I cooked. He didn't stop long enough to come to the house and eat and rest a little while. He ate in the field and went right on picking cotton. I don't guess he could send us to school anymore. I just know we didn't go anymore, and I didn't become that nurse I wanted so bad to be. We just worked hard from year to year—them three years until Daddy married again. We never had any more Christmas. We didn't have anything but one another. We was a pitiful three.

In three years after Mama died, Daddy married again and he married a 12 woman that didn't suit our family. You see I had begun to eye the boys a little when Daddy was not looking. There was one that came along that I thought was it. He was 12 years older than I was. Daddy didn't like him but I did. I think the reason I fell so hard for him was because all the girls around wanted to go with him but he liked me the best. I thought I was something else. I had a lot of life in me when I was growing up. I talked a lot and laughed a lot and I liked to sing. I was just a jolly girl.

This man, Fred Newby, wanted to marry me. Of course, I wanted to marry 13 him too, but I had this friend, Luther Suggs. Me and him was real close. I had more fun with him that I did with anybody and he didn't want me to marry this fellow and he set in to break us up. Me and Luther didn't date but what was so funny we wouldn't let each other date anybody else. If one of us started dating someone, the other wouldn't stop till we broke them up and we could do it every time. We was just good buddies and that was all. He was a doll. I had more fun with that boy than I ever had with any boy and it was clean fun and that is the truth. You know, I bet me and him was really in love and didn't have sense enough to know it. Some nights we would sit in the middle of the road till midnight and after and try to count the stars. And I would think he was the sweetest man on earth, but I never did think of him as a boyfriend and I know he felt the same way about me.

Then I met Fred and we begun to talk about marrying and the only reason we didn't, that buddy of mine found out about it and that was it. He broke us up in one night's time on Christmas Eve night. I didn't really mean to let him do it but he did. It just broke my heart and I cried and cried but it didn't do any good. I was 14 years old at that time.   14

After Daddy married that woman that he had taught me against all my life, I started staying with my sister and her husband. He was a hard-working man, and he believed in everybody working from daylight till dark and that is what we done.   15

I married when I was 17 years old. Right then all I wanted was a home. I was so tired of the way I was living. Work, work, that was all anybody wanted with me.   16

I married in February before I was 17 in May. The first time I saw Lutie he was in bed sick. I remember I saw his eyes that night and I thought they was so pretty. His hair was a light red, not a ugly red and it was pretty and just lay in deep waves. I thought a lots about him the next few weeks.   17

As soon as he could walk, he came over to where we lived. I still thought he looked nice. Well, for some reason his family didn't think too much of him. They always was saying some unpleasant things about him, and I felt sorry for him so I put in a lot of time with him. He was 20 years older than I was. And I was a big mouth—just full of life. But down inside of me I was a lonely girl. I was always searching for something that I couldn't find.   18

Well, he began to talk to me about marrying him. I didn't want to, but I thought that his family and him too was living for God. Now listen, I am not trying to condemn them for God forbids that, but anyway I had been taught you was not supposed to marry anyone that had been married and had a living wife or husband. So I told him that but he went on and showed me where it would be all right in the sight of God for me and him to get married. But I can't remember him just really asking me to marry him and me saying I would.   19

But anyway he got the license and came after me and I ran away when I saw him coming. I went about three miles to Mrs. Suggs' house, that was Luther's mother. I stayed all the rest of the day, and I got a curl of Luther's hair and tied a string around it and put it around my neck. I did not tell him what I was up against though. So it was about dark when I came back home. I thought Lutie would be gone. I knowed I would have. But I had to pass this house on the way home where this old man lived, and I liked that old man and I would listen to what he said. He was a good old thing. Lutie was there at his house so the old man come out in the road and stopped me and stood right there and talked me into going on and marrying Lutie. So we went the very next day and married. I stayed with him three weeks and I ran away and went back to my sister's house. That was the only home I had.   20

Then he came and got me and carried me to his mother's house. I couldn't sing around him or his mother either for I sure love to sing and all kind of stuff and they would say that was what my mind was on. They didn't like for me to sing out loud, so I sung to myself.   21

I just couldn't stay there and Lutie wouldn't get me out so I just got out myself. I went back to Sister and George [Sister's husband]. Boy, you had to work there.   22

Well, Lutie he decided to come to Cherokee City and get him a job so he   23
did and in about two weeks he come and wanted me to come up here with him
and I did. I don't remember just how long we stayed up here, but I do know we
had just one room. We cooked, ate and slept all in the same little room, but it
was fun. We was happy. Then a old man came along—Mr. Jack Jackson. He was
old but he made Lutie think that money growed on trees at Lee, Mississippi. But
you see I had got pregnant with Mildred or I don't believe I would have went.
I thought I would never see Sister again, and looked on her kindly like a mother
I guess, so I went to stay a week with her before I left and that is when I met
them two men—Walker and Jimmy—that has wrote books about us and of the
South.

In them times me and George would go to the woods with a cross-cut saw,   24
course Sister would go with us. I'd get on one end of that saw, he'd get on the other
one. Great old big long tall pine trees and we'd saw them up for stovewood. I'd do
anything he'd do. I didn't know no better. People talked about what was going on.
It was because they was always trying to find something to gossip about. That's
exactly the reason things was said about us. We asked for it.

The only thing that I do regret. I wish Jimmy hadn't wrote just like he did   25
because now all the children's grown and can read and they'll wonder. I tried to
explain to them it wasn't, but I don't know whether they believed it or not.

Well, anyway, on Sunday Lutie and Mrs. Jackson come after me. I was so glad   26
to see Lutie, but I didn't want to go so far away, but I went. Me and Lutie never
had anything much. I won't try to write about how and the way we lived, but we
were happy. I followed him around like a child would their daddy and he treated
me like I was a child.

When Mildred was born, I tried hard to be a grown woman, but I didn't know   27
how. I still wanted Lutie to pet me just as much as he did Mildred and he did. We
had a hard time but we was happy. For that first three years we was married, I only
stayed with him for seven weeks, but after Mildred was born I never left him again.

I guess the only thing I done wrong, I mean about another man, was I day-   28
dreamed for 33 years about Fred for I thought I was really in love with that man.
But in the 33rd year I saw Fred Newby, and I would never have known him anymore. He looked awful. I still can't believe he is the man I thought I loved so
dearly.

Anyway, 17 months after Mildred, May was born. I worked in the field right   29
up till she was borned. I put out soda with Mildred in my arms. May was born the
16th of July and I picked cotton that fall. Oh, it was hard, but I done it. In 13
months, Ruby was borned.

I give up everything when I went to having children. I just wrapped my life   30
around them five kids. Now don't misunderstand me. I growed very close to Lutie
and we had a lot of good times together. With his tongue, he was real good to me,
and I know he loved me and the children with all his heart, but the only thing was if
he couldn't find a job like he wanted, he just wouldn't have one. If he couldn't
make good money, he just wouldn't work. I worked for 50 cents a day and put
bread in their mouths and he wouldn't do it. He would work and play. He would
make a waterwheel down in the ditch somewhere. Now honest to God, I worked
for 50 cents a day and that wasn't by the hour, that was from sun till sun. Fifty cents

to put bread in those kids' mouths. I've worked a lot of days and I'd go home toting a four-pound bucket of lard. That's what I'd be paid for a day's work.

There was a family lived right down below us. It was when Ruby was a baby.   31
And his wife died and he had five boys, and I'd work for him. I'd wash their clothes, I'd iron them, I'd patch them. And they all wore overalls. When they'd put the clothes in a sheet to tie them up, I couldn't pick them up. I'd wash them on a rub-board and boil them in a pot. I'd rinse them and hang them up. I take them up to the spring above the house. I'd carry my washpot up there rather than toting water back and forth. I'd build a fire under the washpot and boil them clothes.

Then Lutie got on the rehabilitation. They called it bull farming, but he got a   32
mule instead of a bull. When he got that mule and cow and some pigs and chickens, I was the happiest woman around. That rehab was a Roosevelt thing. He was the only President I ever knew that done anything. He was the only one that I knowed that I seen what he done.

That year I planted the cotton seed with my hands and Lutie covered them.   33
Sonny was borned the 20th of April and believe it or not I chopped cotton. I could see the house and I would call to Mildred and tell her what to do. When Sonny got to crying hard, I would tell her how to pick him up and bring him on the porch and rock him. Then every once in a while I would run to the house and feed and dry him and then go back to work. It was hard, but I done it and got by. That fall we lost everything.

So the next thing, Lutie went to Mobile and went to work at the shipyard. He   34
was a guard there. I won't never forget—he sent me $30 one time. The rest of the time he always got robbed. He was always getting robbed. So then it was back to stay with his mother, Mrs. McCloud. We went, me and the children.

I worked in the field all I could. Then they transferred Lutie up here to the   35
Northeastern Hospital, still as a guard. We moved to the old C.C.C. [Civilian Conservation Corps] camp at Cookstown. That year, the 23rd day of August, sister [Patricia] came to us. A big 10-pound girl. Lutie was a guard at the gate of the hospital. He dressed like a million dollars, and my children went to school barefooted. He had all his shiny buttons, and when I had to go up town—I didn't unless I had to—I borrowed a dress to wear.

Then he lost his job and we farmed again. And if Lutie took a notion that he   36
would not work, that he was going to the creekbank and fish, he went to the creekbank and fished. And me and the children, as they got big enough, went to the field and we worked and we would sweat.

When Ruby was nine years old she came sick. As it happened they had good   37
health until then. But she taken sick with rheumatic fever, and it was at the bad stage when they found it. The first time she went to the doctor, he put her to bed for six months. After the end of that six months, he told her to stay there for another six months.

What hurt me so bad, and no one really knew but God, was that I would have   38
to go to the field and leave her. Sometime she cried for me just to stay home with her, but believe it or not I couldn't. We all had to eat. I don't mean to be bragging for it is nothing to brag about, but we farmed on the halves and I had to be the one that had to get a place, and I had to give my word, and they looked to me for them

crops to be made, and I had to go. I have just left Ruby a lot of my times with my heart breaking and the tears running down my face with the sweat. I have shed enough tears to do a washing, and God seen me and I bet he felt sorry for me for I prayed as I worked so many, many times. But I can look back now, and I can see that I had a lot of faith.

I'll tell you where I got my first break and the only break I got. I had the asthma, I got down with it so bad I couldn't get up. I had it so bad they would just have to take me to the doctor to get a shot. Somebody from somewhere, I'll never know where, sent to Rehabilitation. They got started to find out what caused the asthma and what could be done. They sent me to Birmingham. They give me all kinds of tests, but they never could figure it out.   39

Then—this man's name was Mr. Johnson—he was with the Rehab. He come down one day and he asked me how would I like a job. I thought to myself: I couldn't lift myself, I didn't have no education, I never could see good. All my life I couldn't see. I didn't have no glasses. But Mr. Johnson—he done me more good than anybody—he wanted to get me a job at a nursing home. He put glasses on my eyes, he got me the job, he put uniforms on my back, and put shoes on my feet. And he set me up. And do you know I went to work there and it wasn't long till I began to feel better. And it wasn't long till I could just go up and down that hall and just do as much as anybody. And I was so happy. I enjoyed it the best in the world. And all the old people loved me, I loved them all. We all got along good—just like a big family. All workers and patients and everything.   40

Well, now my husband, he didn't like this much. He'd grumble about it, and I was making $35 a week. I was taking care of all the expenses. I even paid the rent, and I never got to buy me anything new. Here's where the trouble started. We had two buildings. One of them we called the women's hall, one of them we called the men's hall. There was men over there. You know in wheel chairs and all. The people I worked for was Mr. and Mrs. J. R. Clinton. Well, now they liked me and I could tell they did and they trusted me. They believed in me. And I'd do everything I could. There wasn't nobody working on the men's hall but one colored man. So Mr. Clinton come down one day and got us all in the little old nurses' station. He said, "Now we got so many in here we just run over one another. What about one of you going over to the men's hall and helping John?"   41

Nobody said anything. I didn't say a word, but he kept talking, wanting someone to volunteer to help. Directly he looked over there at me. He said, "Emma, what about you?" and he knowed I'd do anything to help him.   42

I said, "Now Mr. Clinton, I don't know whether I'd like that or not. If I don't like it, what're you going to do about it?"   43

He said, "I'll put you right back there where you were."   44

I said, "All right. That's a deal." So I went over to the men's hall, and we cleaned that men's hall up. Me and this colored man did. And after we got it cleaned up, why, I was the queen over there. Old John wouldn't let me do much of anything, and all them old men just loved me. After lunch I would go in a room and go to bed and one of them old men would sit outside the door and watch to see if anybody was coming over there. If he seen someone, he would call me. I had it so easy all the other aides got jealous as well as Lutie. Then some of them wanted to   45 change places with me, but Mr. Clinton said no, for they all refused to go when he asked them.

Oh, I had a good time. I even planted flowers in our yard, and them old men would help me. That is the ones that was able. We had Sunday School, and I joined the men's class. Even the preacher seemed to like me. I was almost happy. 46

Then my husband he got to throwing all those old men up to me. Wanting me to quit my job. I wouldn't of quit for nothing. He'd say, "With this asthma, you quit and get this disability. Go to the doctor and get on disability." 47

I had sense enough to know that I couldn't get on no disability as long as I was able to work, and I was able then. He ordered me to quit, but I wouldn't quit my job. I came in one day and he was gone. He went to Brockton—that's where his oldest daughter by his first wife was. He got down there and he began to write me bad letters. May and Ruby got to where they would tear them up before I got home, so for a long time I thought he wasn't writing anymore. 48

But one day "Bang!" When I got home, I always went up to May's. So when I went that day she had to tell me that the police had been there with a letter from Lutie saying he was coming to Cherokee City and that he was going to kill me. They wouldn't turn my letter over to me, but several of them got after me to put in for a divorce. I knowed I couldn't pay for it, but I thought if I do that, maybe he'll settle down and stop this mess. So I did. 49

I seen a lawyer, and he put in for the divorce just to stop his mouth. I didn't really want a divorce. I didn't care about one, but one day the lawyer called and told me it was ready for me to pick up, but I didn't have the money to get it. Someways or other some money come in my hands and I went and paid for it. We was divorced. 50

But now all my children was grown and married. After that Lutie came back home. Me and him was friends after that. We didn't live together no more, but we was friends until he died. When he died I was standing by his bed, holding his hand. 51

I worked at the nursing home for about six years. They closed it down. It was just a . . . they called it the poorhouse. It was kept by what people drawed from their social security. They condemned the building and put that one out of commission. Then they put the new ones up over at Northpark, and they have gone up just like hot potatoes. 52

After the nursing home closed down, it wasn't long till a Mr. and Mrs. Frank French got in touch with me, so I went to work there. He was claimed to be one of the richest men in Cherokee City. His wife was down. Well, she wasn't down at that time, but she was senile. I stayed with the Frenches almost six years, and she died in November. I thought when she died my job was over. They had gone up. They was paying me $65 a week. They had two of us. One stayed in the daytime and one stayed at night. When she died, I thought that would be all of it, but they wanted us to stay on just like we was going with him. So we did. 53

Then after he died I knowed my job was done, but do you know I went on backwards and forwards to that house for two or three months after that. And there wasn't a soul over there, but they wouldn't tell me to quit, wouldn't tell me to stay home. I just kept going back. They kept paying me the $65 a week right on. Now 54 they didn't the other ones, but they did me. I stayed there till they got to dividing the things. They put them down in the floor and everywhere and I couldn't walk and get around. I just quit. I quit because I couldn't walk around in the house.

From there I went to a Mrs. Wall's and I worked over there for about two years. While I was working there now the Frenches never did turn me aloose. They kept calling me up. They would call and want to talk to me. I'd talk. One of the boys called me and told me he wanted to see me. When could I get away and come over, away from Mrs. Wall's that was where I worked. I told him anytime after dinnertime. He come over and got me. I didn't know where I was agoing. So he carried me to the courthouse. He carried me up there, and he gave me a $2,000 bond. He had it recorded. So I kept that bond a long time before I cashed it. I finally cashed it. Anyway that's when my break come. When I felt like I was somebody. Could get out. . . .Well, you know how it is when you can get out and make a payday.

I was taking care of an old lady and she fell and got hurt two weeks before Lutie died so they was on the same floor at the hospital so I got to be around him them two weeks. I would go and feed him. The day before he died, he laughed and said "We should go back together. We can't live without each other." So we laughed and I made him sit up in bed and I rubbed his back.

The next day every chance I got I would go and see about him. I remember it was about four o'clock. I went in and they had brought him a milkshake so I told him he had to eat it so I picked it up and fed it to him. He ate it all. Then I had to run back to Mrs. Wall. In a little while, I went back to look in on Lutie. I knew he was going away. I called his name and he looked at me. I ran after a nurse. She said, "Mr. McCloud will pull out."

I said, "Not this time."

So we went back to his room together. She told me to call the kids that was here in town, and she would call the doctor. So we did. I called Sister and she called the rest. I hurried back to him and took his hand in mine. He looked at me. I just prayed that the children would get there. Sister just made it, and I think May was a few minutes late, and the others came as soon as they got the word.

But you see how things can work. I fed him last and I held his hand until he was gone. After all I was with him at the end. We had lots of ups and downs.

Today is Sunday, January 11, 1976. This is the way I talk to myself when I get so lonesome, and it has got to where I stay so lonely. Ruby and [her husband] Will is in bed so I just talk on the phone and write. And I read the Bible a lot too. I've got to where I enjoy it.

It sure is raining this morning. It is so dark, and when you spend as much time as I do just by yourself, it ain't too good. If I don't write or read, I just go crazy with my thoughts.

You remember I just lost the only boy I had September 20, 1975, and it has almost run me crazy. [Sonny worked as an engineer on riverboats pushing barges on the Mississippi and Ohio. He was below deck when a boiler exploded.] We can't understand why these things has to happen so quick. He was so big and healthy we thought, and he went away like a candle blowed out or at least that is what we was told, but as for knowing, we don't. I ask myself, "What did he think about last? What was he thinking about when it happened? Was he hungry for he was just getting off from work?"

Then he lay on the floor of that old boat, burnt up, and me here sleeping in my   64
bed of ease. I won't never get over that. He had to die all by his self, and the way he had to go is killing me. He was so afraid of fire. He never liked for me to even burn trash in the yard. He was a sweet old boy to his mama and he knew that. I miss him so bad sometime I just can't hardly stand it, but I have to keep going a while longer now. No one knows how long.

I hope he is better off than I am tonight. There is one thing I would believe   65
though—he don't have a worried mind and a broken heart tonight. I believe he is sound asleep. He ain't worried about how things are going on here, but I hope to meet him in the morning when we rise up. I want to be right close to him and put my arms around him and say, "Hi, Sonny."

He will pat me on the back and say, "Hi, Emma."   66

Of course, I want all the rest to be there too, and I want us all to set down and   67
have just a happy reunion. Oh, won't it be wonderful there? And there will be Lutie and Bobby [Emma's grandson who was run over by a car] and Mama and Daddy, too. When I get to thinking about it, I can hardly wait. This life has been kindly rugged here. I have never seen too much happiness. My road has been pretty bumpy. The happiest part was when I was trying to bring my children up and I thought I done the best I could. I don't know but Mama tried.

Now I feel kindly alone for a long time. I looked for something real good to   68
happen to me like a little home, a pretty yard of flowers, and a garden, even some chickens. And a good someone to be with, to laugh and talk with. When things was good and when there was trouble and heartaches come about, someone to understand me and help me throw them off and let me be the same way to that someone. But I have give up my dream. That is what I have always done is dream, dream.

So this is just about my life. Not so bad, do you think?   69

Rhetorical Focus

1. How would you characterize the language with which Emma tells her story? What, if any, are the advantages of this language as a means of rendering her life? What, if any, are its disadvantages?
2. Does Emma show pretty much the same emotion as she tells her story, or do her emotions seem to vary? Refer to specific passages in the text.
3. Compare Emma's and Agee's use of details. Does one rely on detail more than the other? Are the details they choose equally evocative, equally rich? Refer to specific passages in each text.

Thematic Focus

1. What are the main themes of Emma's story as she recounts it? What did she find herself having to be mostly concerned about? As she looks back,

what episode(s) in her life does she appear to find the most crucial? Why?

2. Note Emma's assessment of her life in the last sentence. Do you agree with it? Why or why not?

3. How well did Agee predict the woman that Emma became? What, if anything, surprised you about what she became? What does Emma's account suggest about Agee's ability to understand her even as a young woman?

Suggestions for Writing

1. Write an essay identifying the extent to which Emma's own story challenges Agee's account of her. Of course, it's unfair to expect Agee to predict every detail of Emma's life over the next 40 years. Otherwise, though, is his perspective limited in certain ways that her later account exposes? Is there anything in his text that nicely *adds* to Emma's own understanding of herself? Do you consider each text valid? In your analysis, refer to specific passages from each text.

2. Describe a particular occasion when you had difficulty understanding another person's perspective because of your own background. While you can certainly note things about the person that contributed to your difficulty, focus on what about your own background limited your ability to share his or her point of view. To what extent were you ultimately able to understand the other person's perspective? What would you say you learned about yourself from this experience?

3. In a few paragraphs, describe from an observer's point of view a scene involving a real or imaginary person. Then, again in a few paragraphs, assume the identity of this person and describe the scene as he or she would. You may even want to include in this second description the observer from the first, just as Emma later made remarks about Agee. Finally, write a paragraph indicating what you learned from this exercise about the relationship between the observer and the observed.

TIME, PLACE, AND IDENTITY

In reflecting on your personal identity, you may very well find yourself analyzing people and events in your past, trying to understand what they meant for you then and whether the passage of time has led you to put them in a different perspective now. You may also find yourself recalling the places where you have lived, considering whether and how they have influenced your thinking. Because the relationships of time, place, and identity have preoccupied not only writers but also human beings in general, we present essays on these concerns throughout the book. For example, the next unit traces the history of various family relationships, and the third unit focuses on places and communities.

We conclude the present unit, however, with a pair of essays that explicitly introduce such considerations. Both authors attempt to understand their lives by examining continuity and change in a rural setting that has been important to them. E. B. White describes his efforts to recapture his glorious childhood summers at a lake in Maine, while Kathleen Stocking describes her troubled family history and the new politics of ecology on Michigan's Leelanau Peninsula. Both authors ponder whether and how they should identify with their fathers, whom they intimately associate with the place they now contemplate. As you read, consider the extent to which father–son relationships in White's essay resemble the father–daughter relationship in Stocking's. Consider whether these authors' gender differences seem to matter in any other ways. More generally, think about the differences and similarities in the ways these authors depict time, place, and their own concern with self. With what does each author feel obligated to come to terms? How much does each acknowledge other people as he or she grapples with questions of identity? To what extent do they use the same rhetorical strategies in recounting episodes of their personal history and rendering the physical setting bound up with it? For example, do they resort to similar tones, narrative structures, uses of metaphor? Ultimately, do these authors appear equally clear-sighted? Do they seem equally optimistic or pessimistic about their abilities to make peace with the passage of time in the places they write about? You may also find it interesting to consider the different standings of these essays in the curriculum of freshman composition. White's essay has been taught to generations of freshman writers, whereas Stocking's is a much more recent piece and therefore unfamiliar to them. Do you see both as examples of good writing about time, place, and identity? Finally, think about the relationships of these themes in your life, and how you can explore such relationships in your own writing.

Once More to the Lake

E.B. White

You may already know E.B. White (1899–1985) from his children's books *Stuart Little* and *Charlotte's Web*, or from his revision of William Strunk's classic manual *Elements of Style*. He wrote poetry and fiction as well. Yet White was famous mostly for his essays, which he wrote for magazines

---

such as *The New Yorker* and *Harper's* and which were collected in several volumes. "Once More to the Lake" first appeared in *Harper's* in 1941, as part of a series White wrote for this periodical under the title of "One Man's Meat." The essay describes a return visit that White had made with his son to the lakefront camp where his family had spent many summers. This location was actually Bear Spring Camps at Belgrade Lakes, although in the essay White specifies it only as a lake in Maine. The essay went on to become one of his most widely loved works. It has frequently been anthologized in freshman readers such as this one, with its fans often calling attention to its crisp details, adroit repetition of language, and haunting treatment of the relationships among identity, place, and the passage of time.

Reflections Before Beginning

What places and typical experiences in your life would you like to see stay the same? Why do you think you especially value these places and experiences in particular? White describes his return to a lakefront camp that he loved going to each summer while he was growing up. Would such a place appeal to you? Why or why not? White indicates that when he returned to the lake with his own son, he found himself taking on the identity of his father in various ways. Is this kind of experience familiar to you? That is, have you found yourself closely identifying with a parent or parental figure, or have you seen someone else going through such an experience? What do you think are the possible advantages and disadvantages of defining identity in this way?

August 1941

One summer, along about 1904, my father rented a camp on a lake in Maine and took us all there for the month of August. We all got ringworm from some kittens and had to rub Pond's Extract on our arms and legs night and morning, and my father rolled over in a canoe with all his clothes on; but outside of that the vacation was a success and from then on none of us ever thought there was any place in the world like that lake in Maine. We returned summer after summer—always on August 1 for one month. I have since become a salt-water man, but sometimes in summer there are days when the restlessness of the tides and the fearful cold of the sea water and the incessant wind that blows across the afternoon and into the evening make me wish for the placidity of a lake in the woods. A few weeks ago this feeling got so strong I bought myself a couple of bass hooks and a spinner and returned to the lake where we used to go, for a week's fishing and to revisit old haunts.

I took along my son, who had never had any fresh water up his nose and who had seen lily pads only from train windows. On the journey over to the lake I began to wonder what it would be like. I wondered how time would have marred this unique, this holy spot—the coves and streams, the hills that the sun set behind, the camps and the paths behind the camps. I was sure that the tarred road would have found it out, and I wondered in what other ways it would be desolated. It is strange how much you can remember about places like that once you allow your mind to return into the grooves that lead back. You remember one thing, and that suddenly reminds you of another thing. I guess I remembered clearest of all the early mornings, when the lake was cool and motionless, remembered how the bedroom smelled of the lumber it was made of and of the wet woods whose scent entered through the screen. The partitions in the camp were thin and did not extend clear to the top of the rooms, and as I was always the first up I would dress softly so as not to wake the others, and sneak out into the sweet outdoors and start out in the canoe, keeping close along the shore in the long shadows of the pines. I remembered being very careful never to rub my paddle against the gunwale for fear of disturbing the stillness of the cathedral.

The lake had never been what you would call a wild lake. There were cottages sprinkled around the shores, and it was in farming country although the shores of the lake were quite heavily wooded. Some of the cottages were owned by nearby farmers, and you would live at the shore and eat your meals at the farmhouse. That's what our family did. But although it wasn't wild, it was a fairly large and undisturbed lake and there were places in it that, to a child at least, seemed infinitely remote and primeval. 3

I was right about the tar: it led to within half a mile of the shore. But when I got back there, with my boy, and we settled into a camp near a farmhouse and into the kind of summertime I had known, I could tell that it was going to be pretty much the same as it had been before—I knew it, lying in bed the first morning, smelling the bedroom and hearing the boy sneak quietly out and go off along the shore in a boat. I began to sustain the illusion that he was I, and therefore, by simple transposition, that I was my father. This sensation persisted, kept cropping up all the time we were there. It was not an entirely new feeling, but in this setting it grew much stronger. I seemed to be living a dual existence. I would be in the middle of some simple act, I would be picking up a bait box or laying down a table fork, or I would be saying something, and suddenly it would be not I but my father who was saying the words or making the gesture. It gave me a creepy sensation. 4

We went fishing the first morning. I felt the same damp moss covering the worms in the bait can, and saw the dragonfly alight on the tip of my rod as it hovered a few inches from the surface of the water. It was the arrival of this fly that convinced me beyond any doubt that everything was as it always had been, that the years were a mirage and that there had been no years. The small waves were the same, chucking the rowboat under the chin as we fished at anchor, and the boat was the same boat, the same color green and the ribs broken in the same places, and under the floorboards the same fresh-water leavings and débris—the dead helgramite, the wisps of moss, the rusty discarded fishhook, the dried blood from yesterday's catch. We stared silently at the tips of our rods, at the dragonflies that came and went. I lowered the tip of mine into the water, tentatively, pensively dislodging the fly, which darted two feet away, poised, darted two feet back, and came to rest again a little farther up the rod. There had been no years between the ducking of this dragonfly and the other one—the one that was part of memory. I looked at the boy, who was silently watching his fly, and it was my hands that held 5 his rod, my eyes watching. I felt dizzy and didn't know which rod I was at the end of.

We caught two bass, hauling them in briskly as though they were mackerel,   6
pulling them over the side of the boat in a businesslike manner without any landing net, and stunning them with a blow on the back of the head. When we got back for a swim before lunch, the lake was exactly where we had left it, the same number of inches from the dock, and there was only the merest suggestion of a breeze. This seemed an utterly enchanted sea, this lake you could leave to its own devices for a few hours and come back to, and find that it had not stirred, this constant and trustworthy body of water. In the shallows, the dark, water-soaked sticks and twigs, smooth and old, were undulating in clusters on the bottom against the clean ribbed sand, and the track of the mussel was plain. A school of minnows swam by, each minnow with its small individual shadow, doubling the attendance, so clear and sharp in the sunlight. Some of the other campers were in swimming, along the shore, one of them with a cake of soap, and the water felt thin and clear and unsubstantial. Over the years there had been this person with the cake of soap, this cultist, and here he was. There had been no years.

Up to the farmhouse to dinner through the teeming, dusty field, the road   7
under our sneakers was only a two-track road. The middle track was missing, the one with the marks of the hooves and the splotches of dried, flaky manure. There had always been three tracks to choose from in choosing which track to walk in; now the choice was narrowed down to two. For a moment I missed terribly the middle alternative. But the way led past the tennis court, and something about the way it lay there in the sun reassured me; the tape had loosened along the backline, the alleys were green with plantains and other weeds, and the net (installed in June and removed in September) sagged in the dry noon, and the whole place steamed with midday heat and hunger and emptiness. There was a choice of pie for dessert, and one was blueberry and one was apple, and the waitresses were the same country girls, there having been no passage of time, only the illusion of it as in a dropped curtain—the waitresses were still fifteen; their hair had been washed, that was the only difference—they had been to the movies and seen the pretty girls with the clean hair.

Summertime, oh, summertime, pattern of life indelible, the fadeproof lake,   8
the woods unshatterable, the pasture with the sweetfern and the juniper forever and ever, summer without end; this was the background, and the life along the shore was the design, the cottagers with their innocent and tranquil design, their tiny docks with the flagpole and the American flag floating against the white clouds in the blue sky, the little paths over the roots of the trees leading from camp to camp and the paths leading back to the outhouses and the can of lime for sprinkling, and at the souvenir counters at the store the miniature birch-bark canoes and the postcards that showed things looking a little better than they looked. This was the American family at play, escaping the city heat, wondering whether the newcomers in the camp at the head of the cove were "common" or "nice," wondering whether it was true that the people who drove up for Sunday dinner at the farmhouse were turned away because there wasn't enough chicken.

It seemed to me, as I kept remembering all this, that those times and those   9
summers had been infinitely precious and worth saving. There had been jollity and
peace and goodness. The arriving (at the beginning of August) had been so big a
business in itself, at the railway station the farm wagon drawn up, the first smell of
the pine-laden air, the first glimpse of the smiling farmer, and the great importance of the trunks and your father's enormous authority in such matters, and the
feel of the wagon under you for the long ten-mile haul, and at the top of the last
long hill catching the first view of the lake after eleven months of not seeing this
cherished body of water. The shouts and cries of the other campers when they saw
you, and the trunks to be unpacked, to give up their rich burden. (Arriving was less
exciting nowadays, when you sneaked up in your car and parked it under a tree
near the camp and took out the bags and in five minutes it was all over, no fuss, no
loud wonderful fuss about trunks.)

Peace and goodness and jollity. The only thing that was wrong now, really, was   10
the sound of the place, an unfamiliar nervous sound of the outboard motors. This
was the note that jarred, the one thing that would sometimes break the illusion and
set the years moving. In those other summertimes all motors were inboard; and
when they were at a little distance, the noise they made was a sedative, an ingredient of summer sleep. They were one-cylinder and two-cylinder engines, and some
were make-and-break and some were jump-spark, but they all made a sleepy
sound across the lake. The one-lungers throbbed and fluttered, and the twin-cylin-
der ones purred and purred, and that was a quiet sound, too. But now the campers
all had outboards. In the daytime, in the hot mornings, these motors made a petu-
lant, irritable sound; at night, in the still evening when the afterglow lit the water,
they whined about one's ears like mosquitoes. My boy loved our rented outboard,
and his great desire was to achieve single-handed mastery over it, and authority,
and he soon learned the trick of choking it a little (but not too much), and the
adjustment of the needle valve. Watching him I would remember the things you
could do with the old one-cylinder engine with the heavy flywheel, how you could
have it eating out of your hand if you got really close to it spiritually. Motorboats in
those days didn't have clutches, and you would make a landing by shutting off the
motor at the proper time and coasting in with a dead rudder. But there was a way
of reversing them, if you learned the trick, by cutting the switch and putting it on
again exactly on the final dying revolution of the flywheel, so that it would kick
back against compression and begin reversing. Approaching a dock in a strong
following breeze, it was difficult to slow up sufficiently by the ordinary coasting
method, and if a boy felt he had complete mastery over his motor, he was tempted
to keep it running beyond its time and then reverse it a few feet from the dock. It
took a cool nerve, because if you threw the switch a twentieth of a second too soon
you would catch the flywheel when it still had speed enough to go up past center,
and the boat would leap ahead, charging bull-fashion at the dock.

We had a good week at the camp. The bass were biting well and the sun shone   11
endlessly, day after day. We would be tired at night and lie down in the accumulated heat of the little bedrooms after the long hot day and the breeze would stir
almost imperceptibly outside and the smell of the swamp drift in through the rusty
screens. Sleep would come easily and in the morning the red squirrel would be on

the roof, tapping out his gay routine. I kept remembering everything, lying in bed in the mornings—the small steamboat that had a long rounded stern like the lip of a Ubangi, and how quietly she ran on the moonlight sails, when the older boys played their mandolins and the girls sang and we ate doughnuts dipped in sugar, and how sweet the music was on the water in the shining night, and what it had felt like to think about girls then. After breakfast we would go up to the store and the things were in the same place—the minnows in a bottle, the plugs and spinners disarranged and pawed over by the youngsters from the boys' camp, the Fig Newtons and the Beeman's gum. Outside, the road was tarred and cars stood in front of the store. Inside, all was just as it had always been, except there was more Coca-Cola and not so much Moxie and root beer and birch beer and sarsaparilla. We would walk out with the bottle of pop apiece and sometimes the pop would backfire up our noses and hurt. We explored the streams, quietly, where the turtles slid off the sunny logs and dug their way into the soft bottom; and we lay on the town wharf and fed worms to the tame bass. Everywhere we went I had trouble making out which was I, the one walking at my side, the one walking in my pants.

One afternoon while we were there at that lake a thunderstorm came up. It 12 was like the revival of an old melodrama that I had seen long ago with childish awe. The second-act climax of the drama of the electrical disturbance over a lake in America had not changed in any important respect. This was the big scene, still the big scene. The whole thing was so familiar, the first feeling of oppression and heat and a general air around camp of not wanting to go very far away. In midafternoon (it was all the same) a curious darkening of the sky, and a lull in everything that had made life tick; and then the way the boats suddenly swung the other way at their moorings with the coming of a breeze out of the new quarter, and the premonitory rumble. Then the kettle drum, then the snare, then the bass drum and cymbals, then crackling light against the dark, and the gods grinning and licking their chops in the hills. Afterward the calm, the rain steadily rustling in the calm lake, the return of light and hope and spirits, and the campers running out in joy and relief to go swimming in the rain, their bright cries perpetuating the deathless joke about how they were getting simply drenched, and the children screaming with delight at the new sensation of bathing in the rain, and the joke about getting drenched linking the generations in a strong indestructible chain. And the comedian who waded in carrying an umbrella.

When the others went swimming, my son said he was going in, too. He pulled 13 his dripping trunks from the line where they had hung all through the shower and wrung them out. Languidly, and with no thought of going in, I watched him, his hard little body, skinny and bare, saw him wince slightly as he pulled up around his vitals the small, soggy, icy garment. As he buckled the swollen belt, suddenly my groin felt the chill of death.

Rhetorical Focus

1. Where does White repeat language? Identify specific instances. What is the effect of this repetition? Why do you think White engages in it?

2. What sensory details and metaphors here especially strike you? Why do they have such an impact on you? In general, do you find the amount of description in this essay appropriate? Why or why not?

3. To what extent do you think that the writer of this essay shares the perceptions of his subject? To what extent do you think the White who is writing this essay considers the White he is describing to be wrong or naïve? Refer to specific passages.

Thematic Focus

1. Did White's last sentence surprise you? Why or why not? Does it seem an appropriate conclusion to the essay? Why or why not? What earlier statements, if any, does the ending cause you to look at differently?

2. Why does White identify with his father and his son? As he does so, do you find yourself able to identify with White? Why or why not?

3. Do social conditions such as gender and class seem to matter here, or does the essay seem to convey basically a universal human experience? Explain.

The Dunes, My Father
Kathleen Stocking

Kathleen Stocking (b. 1945) grew up on the Leelanau Peninsula, a rural area of northwestern Michigan that juts out into Lake Michigan. After attending the University of Michigan and living in New York City, Stocking returned to her native region in 1974. Over the next several years she turned to writing essays and columns about the area, which she has published in newspapers and journals such as *The Detroit Free Press, Detroit Monthly, Metropolitan Detroit,* and *Travel and Leisure.* In 1990, she collected several of these pieces in a volume entitled *Letters from the Leelanau: Essays of People and Place,* from which the following essay comes. In her introduction to the

---

book, Stocking announces that "What I do . . . is try to meet the need for people to know what rural life is like, without withholding from the writing my awareness of what's going on in the rest of the world." In the various essays that make up the book, Stocking often registers both the recurring aspects of life on the Leelanau as well as the recent social transformations there. She is especially concerned with the area's growing environmental frailty and its transformation into a summer resort. As she notes changes in her time and place, she reflects on her own identity, to varying degrees. What you are about to read comes from the last and most personal of four sections in the book, one that is entitled, aptly enough, "Personals."

Reflections Before Reading

What about White's writing, if anything, would you like to see emulated by later writers on time, place, and identity? What about his writing practice, if anything, would you like them to avoid? The following essay focuses on a relationship between a father and a daughter, rather than on one between a father and a son. Do you expect it to differ in significant ways, then? Why or why not? The essay also refers to the impact of changes in environmental policy and property ownership on a rural region. How might these sorts of changes have affected White's lake since he wrote about it in 1941? Have you experienced such changes in a region you know? Explain. Why, ultimately, might someone care about what happens to the land in the region where she or he lives? Specifically, what might the history of the land have to do with considerations of personal identity?

When you first see the Sleeping Bear Dunes rising massive and golden two hundred feet above a grassy plain, you think you're in the Serengeti or someplace equally strange, not the Midwest. On its eastern slope, this mountain of flesh-colored sand rises like the Taj Mahal to be mirrored in the placid, cattail-bordered Mill Pond below.   1

I never thought too much about it, growing up there. When you're a child your environment is your environment; it could be the far side of the moon and you wouldn't think about it. The Sleeping Bear Dunes were where we always took our end-of-the-school-year picnics, the red, white, and blue school buses of the 1950s lining up at the base of the dunes from all over Michigan. It got so that by third grade we'd complain about going to the dunes *again*—as in vanilla ice cream, *again*. We didn't know that our vanilla ice cream was everyone else's pistachio nut ripple.   2

When the U.S. Army Corps of Engineers first began surveying the land in the dunes in 1957, there were rumblings about a national park some day. This was dismissed as preposterous by most people because everyone knew you didn't put national parks where there were people living. Others thought it was more wishful thinking, grandiose notions, like the one about the mining company that was supposed to come in and mine the sand.   3

Realists believed no one in his right mind would ever want that old pile of   4
sand. My father, a lumberman who already owned large tracts of land in and
around the dunes, began quietly buying up more duneland, even buying some
from the State of Michigan. Most people were only too glad to sell their land in the
dunes to anyone fool enough to buy it.

Did my father know about the park coming in? It's not clear. His secretary   5
with whom he was having an affair, an affair that I was privy to and the unwitting
beard for at the ages of four and five, was active in the statewide Democratic party.
My child's mind was aware only of endless maps, wall-sized blueprints, and the
army cot that mysteriously materialized one day in my father's office and that he
said he needed for "naps." How much my father's secretary may have lobbied for
the park with Democratic senators on the one side, and tipped my father's hand in
his land speculation on the other, is not known. What is known is that in all original
and final plans her land along the base of the dunes on M-109 was excised from the
park. The park boundaries snaked along, encompassing everything in their path,
until coming to her land; then, just as if an invisible snag had been hit, the boundaries blipped up and around her land and then back down to the road again a mile
later.

In 1961, Democratic Senators Philip Hart and Patrick McNamara, both now   6
deceased, first introduced a national park bill to Congress. At this time public
hearings were held around the area. Public sentiment against the park was running
high. I can remember my mingled embarrassment and pride as my father—in
work boots and wool plaid work shirt—walked onto the stage of the Traverse City
High School and demanded, red-faced and using poor grammar, that Senator Hart
and "the big boys" in Washington give him and other landowners fair value for
their land. How smooth and gracious Senator Hart was by comparison, how
schooled in public speaking.

Through all this, local people who hated the idea of, as they phrased it, "the   7
government coming in here and running our lives," saw my father as a champion of
capitalism, synonymous in their minds with democracy. My family was staunchly
Republican and so was the rest of the community. There is nothing like having the
majority on your side to lull you into an unthinking certainty of being right. I mean,
does water run uphill?

Back in the classroom at Glen Lake Community School in Maple City, my   8
English teacher assigned us a "paper" on the dunes controversy. He was what
people in the community called "an odd duck." He wore his hair longer than most,
had students call him "Pete" if they came by his house on weekends, and was the
first English teacher I ever had who assigned anything that wasn't in the textbook.
He was fired the next year. I liked him and never dreamed he would disapprove
when I wrote a paper against the park. He gave me a C+, the lowest grade I ever
got from him, and told me to think about it some more.

I've had three decades to think about it since then. And watch it. Just recently   9
I read in the newspaper, in March of 1989, that a group of Glen Arbor citizens got
together and purchased nonpark land in the village to protect it from development—rampaging development just beyond the boundaries of the park, development that was caused, ironically, by the presence of the national park. This private

purchase of land for public use would have been unthinkable thirty years ago; it simply would not have occurred to anyone.

I've seen the issue change, but mainly I've seen the terminology change. My father, who was viewed in the fifties as "a rugged individualist" and "champion of free enterprise," became by the mid-1970s, "a developer." The tide of public opinion changed through the years so the predominant public mood of wanting to fight the bureaucracy became one of wanting to protect the environment. My father went from hero to villain in the public's eyes in the same time period that he made the reverse journey in mine.

In 1974 I came home from New York City and worked for my father managing his scenic drive in the dunes. I was twenty-nine. I had come home from Manhattan emotionally devastated and thirty thousand dollars in debt following a protracted custody battle and divorce. I did not die of cancer, like Debra Winger in *Terms of Endearment*, but I wanted to. My father told me if I could stop crying long enough to rake the four acres in my front yard at the dunes farmhouse, he'd then talk to me about managing the park. I did both, and for the first time in nearly twenty years we were friends again.

He would come into my orange kitchen at 6:00 A.M. and have a cup of coffee and ask how the trucks were running. Was the backhoe holding up? We would talk with the big dunes behind us, outside the long, high farmhouse windows, somnolent in the early morning light. A goddess. Unnamed. But she made her presence felt.

My father was dark, tense, thick-bodied, quiet, sensual. Ours was a silent communication. This was the man who'd taught me awe and joy as a child, simply by pointing. Birds' nests with tiny blue-speckled eggs. Birds' nests with pink, naked, open-mawed hatchlings. Snake babies under rocks. Ants carrying ant eggs in their mouths. Gordian horse hairs swimming in pools. Dappled newborn fawns motionless in dappled sunlight. Trout guts with caddis flies. Gray milt. Pinkish-yellow roe. The single magenta blossom in the center of the million-blossomed head of the Queen Anne's lace. Pitcher thistle. Bearberry. Arbutus. Bloodroot. The red roots of the sweetgrass in the troughs of the interdunal ponds. The way geese coming north in the spring sound like seagulls, high and mewling, and geese going south in the fall sound like a rocking chair, WONKA, WONKA; all business.

One morning he came in and said, "Your mother was a good woman. But she was awful critical of me. At one point she belonged to twelve different clubs and was president of eleven of them." This was a gloss. My father abandoned my mother, leaving her to raise five daughters alone.

In those days I wore shorts and halters until my father told me to "put some clothes on for Chrissake." My father was a female-dependent male. I know because I keep marrying him. He desperately needed and loved women, desperately needed to escape them, too. His mother kept him alive in a shoe box on the back of the wood stove. Women were his "source," and he feared being absorbed by them as much as he was drawn to them.

Everything is connected. My father's personal life and his treatment of my mother were not a separate thing from his land speculation. When I think of the dunes I think of my mother; I think of my father.

My first day on the job my father showed me how to drive the three-quarter-   17
ton truck, the one with the holes in the floor. He took me and my two children, his
grandchildren, whom he treated as if they were invisible, up into the shady forests
of the back dunes to show us huge red trilliums in bloom.

But we had little contact. "Gran'pa never looks at me," my son said. One   18
morning my daughter said she'd dreamed she'd seen Gran'pa walking up the driveway, bringing a horse on a lead to her. But it never happened.

My children played in the dunes by day, as I had. I knew without asking them   19
how the sand felt like corduroy beneath their feet, how it squeaked. I knew without asking how the dunes were glittery in the daytime heat, heat waves rising like
spirits from the sand, diaphanous. At night when the heat went out of the dunes
they were cold as ice, dry ice.

One day my father showed up earlier than usual, and he didn't come into the   20
kitchen. I felt, rather than saw, him on my porch. When I pulled on a pair of Levis
and a T-shirt and went out onto the still-dark porch, he looked ashen, his skin the
color of creek marl. It was August. I looked past him to the yard, at the trees and
grass, then back. August is an odd time; the light is odd, making everything look
like an overexposed color photo, the grass too yellow, the green trees black-green.

"Cindy died," he said.   21

So taciturn was my father, so closemouthed, that he almost expected to com-   22
municate by ESP, and almost did. It took me several minutes to recall that he had
a black lab named Cindy.

"She was floating in the trout pond this morning," he said. His whole person-   23
ality, or person, had a leaden quality, like weather waiting for rain. He said his wife
had left the day before to go shopping downstate. He said it appeared Cindy had
died of a heart attack.

My father had a second wife. He had not married his secretary after all, a   24
small, dark Southern woman who'd stayed married to her husband. He had miraculously found another big-boned, tall, redheaded woman, almost identical to my
mother in physical type, but unlike her in having an affinity for guns, hunting, and
training dogs. She had been married to a doctor, an anesthesiologist, who'd committed suicide by shooting himself in the head on a deserted road. She had a martial quality.

My father's big black Buick sat shiny on the gravel driveway. I looked from the   25
car shining in the sun to him in the shadow of my porch. He looked odd to me,
oddly weakened. At moments like this I forgave him everything. Forgave him leaving my mother, forgave him for walking away from me and my four sisters. Saw us
all as intimate strangers sucked into the brutality of materialism, how we sold ourselves into marriage, into myriad forms of oppression for the sake of procreating, of
surviving. My redhaired mother, a burning bush. My father, rain. The dog's death.
The shadow of the thing, rather than the thing. It is not this; it is not that. It isn't
the first thing; it isn't the second thing. It is all everything.

It was Cindy's death and the way my father had looked that had me in the   26
blackberries, picking berries for a pie for his birthday September third. But he
died. Suddenly and bizarrely, the day before his sixty-ninth birthday and the day
after the United States government had awarded him three-and-a-half million dol-

lars for his land in the dunes. Heart attack. His wife was in town shopping. A young boy with him had called the ambulance, but by the time it came the thirty miles from Kalkaska, he was dead.

"John Law," my father's wife kept saying and putting her arm around the   27
shoulders of my then companion, a Leelanau County sheriff's deputy, "John Law. We have John Law here to take care of us." She rambled, going on about how her first husband had always cleaned his guns so carefully.

My father was buried in the hot, dry Kalkaska ground. Evergreen Cemetery.   28
The undertaker had a pallor like that of his client, as if he had put powder over his five o'clock shadow. The service was Catholic, although my father was not. My mother attended at a distance, dry-eyed and resolute. My sisters flew in from all over the country and left again. It was not our style to sit around and talk and drink, and so we didn't.

I did not see my father again until November when his apparition accompa-   29
nied me on the way to cut the Christmas tree up in the dunes. He didn't talk, which was normal, but simply walked along beside me, going up and over the furrows of the rows of planted Christmas trees.

I never saw his widow again. She moved to Sun City, Arizona. I never visited   30
his home again. His house burned down six months after he died; burned to the ground before the fire trucks could arrive. I never saw the woman he had an affair with, his secetary, again either. But one day when I was living in Traverse City I called an ad in the classified section of the *Preview*, a shopping weekly. There was an ad for a waffle iron. When I called the woman, she said it was like new and only ten dollars. She asked my name and when I told her she said she was my father's old secretary, that she was disabled and couldn't drive. She said I should come and get the waffle iron, that if she could drive she'd bring it to me. She said she'd give it to me for nothing. That it would be free. If I'd come and get it. She was insistent, sticky, like insect legs caught in wool.

For days the image of this old crone kept coming back to me, this ghost from   31
the past, fluttering her old lady's handkerchief at me across the years, a tiny speck on the horizon behind me, her tiny voice saying, "come and get the waffle iron." I pictured her in her wheelchair, all the raw passion for land and sex gone. My father, too, gone, his life measured more by what his mistresses did him out of than by his daughters, his grandchildren, his wonderful, visionary sense of land. His body, like an outdated piece of machinery, rusting in the ground, the primal urges and the transcendent alike, equally dead.

Only the dunes stay, glittery in the noonday heat and cold under the stars at   32
night. Mythic, monumental, mysterious, the dunes lie like a lovely lady napping, waiting to inspire the next insignificant mortal to take a run at her heights, her steep slopes, her massiveness, her soft yet hard gemlike beauty, her ability to not only outlast, but confound, those who would try to possess her.

Rhetorical Focus

1. What do you take to be Stocking's purpose in this essay? Refer to specific passages in supporting your answer.

2. What tone(s) does Stocking seem to use here? Does she seem to express the same emotion as the essay proceeds? Does her emotion seem appropriate at each moment in the essay? Again, refer to specific passages.

3. Stocking can be said to identify people, places, and historical events more frequently and specifically than White does. He tends to use rather general expressions like "a lake in Maine" and "the boy." Does this difference in style mean that White's essay is universal and Stocking's is not? Explain your reasoning. Do you prefer one author's level of specificity to the other's? Why or why not?

Thematic Focus

1. In what way(s) does Stocking relate the two terms in her title, "my father" and "the dunes"? Does she convince you that they both belong in her title? Why or why not? How does Stocking ultimately perceive her father? In particular, what does she seem to be asserting about their relationship in paragraph 25?

2. To what extent does the father–daughter relationship here resemble the father–son relationships in White's essay? In general, how much do their genders seem to influence the observations that Stocking and White make? Review, for example, the various references that each author makes to people of the same gender and people of the other.

3. Do Stocking and White seem equally self-concerned, self-absorbed? Refer to specific passages in their texts.

Suggestions for Writing

1. Compare the last two paragraphs of White's essay with the last three paragraphs of Stocking's. Both conclusions show the author confronting the passage of time in a particular place, but are they making similar assertions, expressing similar attitudes, wrapping up essays that have essentially resembled each other? Do the climactic references to death and the lake have the same function in White's essay as do the climactic references to death and the dunes in Stocking's?

2. White tries to re-create his childhood summers at the lake, while Stocking tries to understand and reconcile herself to her father's past behavior. Describe your effort to come to terms with a particular situation that pleased or troubled you in the past. What was the situation? How did you react to it back then? Did your attitude toward it change in subsequent years? Why or why not? What is your attitude now?

3. Stocking recalls that her community's increased concern for the environment led it to criticize land developers such as her father. Describe an occasion when you felt pressed to choose sides in a community debate,

perhaps even finding yourself opposing people with whom you had previously identified. *Community* here can range from a closely knit group of people to a school, neighborhood, town, or region. What were the issues and sides involved? What finally happened? What sort of person did you reveal yourself to be on this occasion? In what ways, if any, have you changed from the person you were then?

Chapter
2
Family Relationships

A.s is suggested in the previous unit, we can use writing to explore our personal identity, though we should also acknowledge the role that larger cultural forces play in constructing it. One of the major contexts shaping our sense of self is the family. At its best, it provides us with a nurturing community while enabling us to develop our own powers. At its worst, it can restrict our growth. You may find yourself newly pondering your family's influence on you as you seek the freedom and authority that a college education can bestow, even if you are not leaving home for the first time and already have produced a family yourself.

This unit presents writers who study their own family relationships or who look at other examples of the family as an institution. These writers confront a range of issues that the subject of the family poses. What can the history of a family teach its later generations? How can family members offer mutual support without utterly controlling one another's destinies? What upheavals may a family have to face? What are the various social conditions that different American families endure? What psychological and physical resources does a family need in order to thrive? What do we mean by the term *family* anyway, especially given the fact that the stereotypical image of the nuclear family (mother, father, son, daughter) increasingly fails to describe American society? Obviously, all of these questions call for interpretation. Even when we write about our own families, which we may assume that we know well, we do not simply discover and reproduce the truth about them. Instead, we form a particular vision of them, working with particular details of their history that we think important. To be sure, our family portrait will not convince readers unless we clearly strive to address the complexities of people's lives together.

In the first constellation, N. Scott Momaday and Maxine Hong Kingston suggest the rewards and difficulties that people can face in trying to understand the life of an ancestor. Momaday reflects on his late grandmother, as well as the Native American heritage that she embodied. Kingston speculates about an aunt who died in disgrace back in China and remained a scandalous "no name woman" for her relatives in America. Then, a pair of essays by Scott Russell Sanders highlight the role of interpretation in writing about the family, for they show the same author emphasizing two very different aspects of his father. Next come two contrasting accounts of a mother's influence on her child's restless search for identity. Zora Neale Hurston recalls how her mother's death unfortunately forced her to "wander," while Loren Eiseley describes how he himself became a "wanderer" and "running man" because in part he wanted to avoid his mother.

Finally, we present a pair of texts that deal with single-parent families, an increasingly common phenomenon in American society. Each text focuses on the parent's attempt to affirm family relationships by organizing a festivity. In a nonfiction account, Michael Dorris recalls how he tried to please his adopted son by devising an elaborate cake for his birthday party at a child care center. In a short story, Nicholasa Mohr depicts the struggle of a poor Puerto Rican woman to help her family celebrate Thanksgiving. In effect, both authors raise the issue of what defines and sustains family bonds in an age when the middle class nuclear family has faded as a model. In effect, all of the texts in this unit remind us that we must understand the sheer diversity of families and the various conditions that may surround them. We may be highly conscious of our own family relationships, but we must study as well the relationships of our families to other families and to the larger world.

RELATIONSHIPS WITH ANCESTORS

When we hear the word *family*, many of us first think of parents, children, and siblings. This unit focuses first, though, on what we can learn from family ancestors, including remote generations, grandparents, and other senior relatives. Very often we fail to realize what even the elders we know best can teach us while they are still alive, and so we are left trying to connect with them through memory once they are gone. Very often specific elders of our family are unknown or shadowy figures for us in the first place, their lives either completely lost to us or recounted for us in family stories that may not be accurate.

The two authors here reflect on their efforts to understand and assess particular ancestors whom they also associate with an entire cultural heritage. N. Scott Momaday recalls how his grandmother embodied the vanishing culture of the Kiowas, while Maxine Hong Kingston struggles to imagine exactly what happened to an aunt in China whose adultery, pregnancy, and death not only scandalized her village but also continued to be a taboo subject for her relatives in America. Both essays demonstrate that authors do not just record the past; inevitably, they have to interpret it. Our own family histories are never available to us as a set of indisputable facts and firmly established meanings. Even if we feel that we can genuinely test our recollections against those of other family members, our memory is nevertheless shaped to a significant extent by our present ideas, purposes, and needs.

Our attitudes toward immediate and remote ancestors may even shift over time, especially because we ourselves change. Often we newly appreciate some elders when we ourselves have aged, for they come to represent for us specific values that we now wish to sustain. As you read Momaday's and Kingston's reflections on their ancestors, consider what particular value, if any, they seem to find in the past. Also consider what about these ancestors they seem interested in conveying to you as a reader, as well as the rhetorical strategies they resort to in their efforts to inform and affect you. Which of your ancestors, if any, have been important to you? What about your ancestors would you like to know more about? Examine these essays, too, for ways of getting your own readers to value your speculations about your ancestors and other aspects of your family's past.

The Way to Rainy Mountain

N. Scott Momaday

Of Kiowa and Cherokee descent, N. Scott Momaday (b. 1934) is one of the leading Native American writers of our day. Presently he is Regents Professor of English at the University of Arizona. In 1969 he won the Pulitzer Prize for *House Made of Dawn*, a novel about the plight of a Native American after serving in World War II. More recently he has published another novel, entitled *The Ancient Child*, and a nonfiction account of his family, *The Names*. After first appearing in *The Reporter*, "The Way to Rainy Mountain" served as the introduction to Momaday's 1969 book of the same name. The title is deliberately ambiguous, and in the essay it comes to signify at least four journeys: the centuries-long migration of the Kiowas, ending in despair at Rainy Mountain in Oklahoma; Momaday's own reenactment of their travels; the life and death of Momaday's Kiowa grandmother, now buried at Rainy Mountain; and the spiritual journey necessary to make contact with the values of her tribe.

First published in THE REPORTER, 26 January 1967. Reprinted from THE WAY TO RAINY MOUNTAIN, © 1969, The University of New Mexico Press.

Reflections Before Reading

What scenes, if any, do you associate with your grandparents? Which of their values should the modern world pay more attention to? Which should it ignore? Can you imagine what about a Native American tribe's culture a descendant of it might want to preserve in the modern world? What stereotypes about Native Americans should other people avoid in thinking about this issue?

A single knoll rises out of the plain in Oklahoma, north and west of the Wichita   1
Range. For my people, the Kiowas, it is an old landmark, and they gave it the name Rainy Mountain. The hardest weather in the world is there. Winter brings blizzards, hot tornadic winds arise in the spring, and in summer the prairie is an anvil's edge. The grass turns brittle and brown, and it cracks beneath your feet. There are green belts along the rivers and creeks, linear groves of hickory and pecan, willow and witch hazel. At a distance in July or August the steaming foliage seems almost to writhe in fire. Great green and yellow grasshoppers are everywhere in the tall grass, popping up like corn to sting the flesh, and tortoises crawl about on the red earth, going nowhere in the plenty of time. Loneliness is an aspect of the land. All things in the plain are isolate; there is no confusion of objects in the eye, but *one* hill or *one* tree or *one* man. To look upon that landscape in the early morning, with the sun at your back, is to lose the sense of proportion. Your imagination comes to life, and this, you think, is where Creation was begun.

I returned to Rainy Mountain in July. My grandmother had died in the spring,   2
and I wanted to be at her grave. She had lived to be very old and at last infirm. Her only living daughter was with her when she died, and I was told that in death her face was that of a child.

I like to think of her as a child. When she was born, the Kiowas were living the   3
last great moment of their history. For more than a hundred years they had controlled the open range from the Smoky Hill River to the Red, from the headwaters of the Canadian to the fork of the Arkansas and Cimarron. In alliance with the Comanches, they had ruled the whole of the southern Plains. War was their sacred business, and they were among the finest horsemen the world has ever known. But warfare for the Kiowas was preeminently a matter of disposition rather than of survival, and they never understood the grim, unrelenting advance of the U.S. Cavalry. When at last, divided and ill-provisioned, they were driven onto the Staked Plains in the cold rains of autumn, they fell into panic. In Palo Duro Canyon they abandoned their crucial stores to pillage and had nothing then but their lives. In order to save themselves, they surrendered to the soldiers at Fort Sill and were imprisoned in the old stone corral that now stands as a military museum. My grandmother was spared the humiliation of those high gray walls by eight or ten years, but she must have known from birth the affliction of defeat, the dark brooding of old warriors.

Her name was Aho, and she belonged to the last culture to evolve in North   4
America. Her forebears came down from the high country in western Montana
nearly three centuries ago. They were a mountain people, a mysterious tribe of
hunters whose language has never been positively classified in any major group. In
the late seventeenth century they began a long migration to the south and east. It
was a journey toward the dawn, and it led to a golden age. Along the way the
Kiowas were befriended by the Crows, who gave them the culture and religion of
the Plains. They acquired horses, and their ancient nomadic spirit was suddenly
free of the ground. They acquired Tai-me, the sacred Sun Dance doll, from that
moment the object and symbol of their worship, and so shared in the divinity of the
sun. Not least, they acquired the sense of destiny, therefore courage and pride.
When they entered upon the southern Plains they had been transformed. No
longer were they slaves to the simple necessity of survival; they were a lordly and
dangerous society of fighters and thieves, hunters and priests of the sun. According
to their origin myth, they entered the world through a hollow log. From one point
of view, their migration was the fruit of an old prophecy, for indeed they emerged
from a sunless world.

Although my grandmother lived out her long life in the shadow of Rainy   5
Mountain, the immense landscape of the continental interior lay like memory in
her blood. She could tell of the Crows, whom she had never seen, and of the Black
Hills, where she had never been. I wanted to see in reality what she had seen more
perfectly in the mind's eye, and traveled fifteen hundred miles to begin my pilgrimage.

Yellowstone, it seemed to me, was the top of the world, a region of deep lakes   6
and dark timber, canyons and waterfalls. But, beautiful as it is, one might have the
sense of confinement there. The skyline in all directions is close at hand, the high
wall of the woods and deep cleavages of shade. There is a perfect freedom in the
mountains, but it belongs to the eagle and the elk, the badger and the bear. The
Kiowas reckoned their stature by the distance they could see, and they were bent
and blind in the wilderness.

Descending eastward, the highland meadows are a stairway to the plain. In   7
July the inland slope of the Rockies is luxuriant with flax and buckwheat, stonecrop
and larkspur. The earth unfolds and the limit of the land recedes. Clusters of trees,
and animals grazing far in the distance, cause the vision to reach away and wonder
to build upon the mind. The sun follows a longer course in the day, and the sky is
immense beyond all comparison. The great billowing clouds that sail upon it are
shadows that move upon the grain like water, dividing light. Farther down, in the
land of the Crows and Blackfeet, the plain is yellow. Sweet clover takes hold of the
hills and bends upon itself to cover and seal the soil. There the Kiowas paused on
their way; they had come to the place where they must change their lives. The sun
is at home on the plains. Precisely there does it have the certain character of a god.
When the Kiowas come to the land of the Crows, they could see the dark lees of
the hills at dawn across the Bighorn River, the profusion of light on the grain
shelves, the oldest deity ranging after the solstices. Not yet would they veer south-
ward to the caldron of the land that lay below; they must wean their blood from the

northern winter and hold the mountains a while longer in their view. They bore Tai-me in procession to the east.

A dark mist lay over the Black Hills, and the land was like iron. At the top of a ridge I caught sight of Devil's Tower upthrust against the gray sky as if in the birth of time the core of the earth had broken through its crust and the motion of the world was begun. There are things in nature that engender an awful quiet in the heart of man; Devil's Tower is one of them. Two centuries ago, because they could not do otherwise, the Kiowas made a legend at the base of the rock. My grandmother said:

> Eight children were they at play, seven sisters and their brother. Suddenly the boy was struck dumb; he trembled and began to run upon his hands and feet. His fingers became claws, and his body was covered with fur. Directly there was a bear where the boy had been. The sisters were terrified; they ran, and the bear after them. They came to the stump of a great tree, and the tree spoke to them. It bade them climb upon it, and as they did so it began to rise into the air. The bear came to kill them, but they were just beyond its reach. It reared against the tree and scored the bark all around with its claws. The seven sisters were borne into the sky, and they became the stars of the Big Dipper.

From that moment, and so long as the legend lives, the Kiowas have kinsmen in the night sky. Whatever they were in the mountains, they could be no more. However tenuous their well-being, however much they had suffered and would suffer again, they had found a way out of the wilderness.

My grandmother had a reverence for the sun, a holy regard that now is all but gone out of mankind. There was a wariness in her, and an ancient awe. She was a Christian in her later years, but she had come a long way about, and she never forgot her birthright. As a child she had been to the Sun Dances; she had taken part in those annual rites, and by them she had learned the restoration of her people in the presence of Tai-me. She was about seven when the last Kiowa Sun Dance was held in 1887 on the Washita River above Rainy Mountain Creek. The buffalo were gone. In order to consummate the ancient sacrifice—to impale the head of a buffalo bull upon the medicine tree—a delegation of old men journeyed into Texas, there to beg and barter for an animal from the Goodnight herd. She was ten when the Kiowas came together for the last time as a living Sun Dance culture. They could find no buffalo; they had to hang an old hide from the sacred tree. Before the dance could begin, a company of soldiers rode out from Fort Sill under orders to disperse the tribe. Forbidden without cause the essential act of their faith, having seen the wild herds slaughtered and left to rot upon the ground, the Kiowas backed away forever from the medicine tree. That was July 20, 1890, at the great bend of the Washita. My grandmother was there. Without bitterness, and for as long as she lived, she bore a vision of deicide.

Now that I can have her only in memory, I see my grandmother in the several postures that were peculiar to her: standing at the wood stove on a winter morning and turning meat in a great iron skillet; sitting at the south window, bent above her beadwork, and afterwards, when her vision failed, looking down for a long time into the fold of her hands; going out upon a cane, very slowly as she did when the weight of age came upon her; praying, I remember her most often at prayer. She made long, rambling prayers out of suffering and hope, having seen many things. I was never sure that I had the right to hear, so exclusive were they of all mere custom and company. The last time I saw her she prayed standing by the side of her bed at night, naked to the waist, the light of a kerosene lamp moving upon her dark skin. Her long, black hair, always drawn and braided in the day, lay upon her shoulders and against her breasts like a shawl. I do not speak Kiowa, and I never understood her prayers, but there was something inherently sad in the sound, some merest hesitation upon the syllables of sorrow. She began in a high and descending pitch, exhausting her breath to silence; then again and again—and always the same intensity of effort, of something that is, and is not, like urgency in the human voice. Transported so in the dancing light among the shadows of her room, she seemed beyond the reach of time. But that was illusion; I think I knew then that I should not see her again.

Houses are like sentinels in the plain, old keepers of the weather watch.   11
There, in a very little while, wood takes on the appearance of great age. All colors wear soon away in the wind and rain, and then the wood is burned gray and the grain appears and the nails turn red with rust. The windowpanes are black and opaque; you imagine there is nothing within, and indeed there are many ghosts, bones given up to the land. They stand here and there against the sky, and you approach them for a longer time than you expect. They belong in the distance; it is their domain.

Once there was a lot of sound in my grandmother's house, a lot of coming and   12
going, feasting and talk. The summers there were full of excitement and reunion. The Kiowas are a summer people; they abide the cold and keep to themselves, but when the season turns and the land becomes warm and vital they cannot hold still; an old love of going returns upon them. The aged visitors who came to my grandmother's house when I was a child were made of lean and leather, and they bore themselves upright. They wore great black hats and bright ample shirts that shook in the wind. They rubbed fat upon their hair and wound their braids with strips of colored cloth. Some of them painted their faces and carried the scars of old and cherished enmities. They were an old council of warlords, come to remind and be reminded of who they were. Their wives and daughters served them well. The women might indulge themselves; gossip was at once the mark and compensation of their servitude. They made loud and elaborate talk among themselves, full of jest and gesture, fright and false alarm. They went abroad in fringed and flowered shawls, bright beadwork and German silver. They were at home in the kitchen, and they prepared meals that were banquets.

There were frequent prayer meetings, and great nocturnal feasts. When I was   13
a child I played with my cousins outside, where the lamplight fell upon the ground and the singing of the old people rose up around us and carried away into the darkness. There were a lot of good things to eat, a lot of laughter and surprise. And afterwards, when the quiet returned, I lay down with my grandmother and could hear the frogs away by the river and feel the motion of the air.

Now there is a funeral silence in the rooms, the endless wake of some final   14
word. The walls have closed in upon my grandmother's house. When I returned to
it in mourning, I saw for the first time in my life how small it was. It was late at
night, and there was a white moon, nearly full. I sat for a long time on the stone
steps by the kitchen door. From there I could see out across the land; I could see
the long row of trees by the creek, the low light upon the rolling plains, and the
stars of the Big Dipper. Once I looked at the moon and caught sight of a strange
thing. A cricket had perched upon the handrail, only a few inches away from me.
My line of vision was such that the creature filled the moon like a fossil. It had gone
there, I thought, to live and die, for there, of all places, was its small definition
made whole and eternal. A warm wind rose up and purled like the longing within
me.

The next morning I awoke at dawn and went out on the dirt road to Rainy   15
Mountain. It was already hot, and the grasshoppers began to fill the air. Still, it was
early in the morning, and the birds sang out of the shadows. The long yellow grass
on the mountain shone in the bright light, and a scissortail hied above the land.
There, where it ought to be, at the end of a long and legendary way, was my grandmother's grave. Here and there on the dark stones were ancestral names. Looking
back once, I saw the mountain and came away.

Rhetorical Focus

1. Does it make sense for Momaday to move back and forth between his
   grandmother and larger references to Kiowa history? Should he have
   stayed more with one or the other?
2. The third paragraph deals mostly with the late history of the Kiowas and
   the fourth paragraph mostly with their earlier history. Why do you think
   Momaday chose not to put them in chronological order?
3. Why do you think Momaday feels it is important to describe the landscape
   so much? Refer to specific features of it that he lingers over.

Thematic Focus

1. When he recalls undertaking his pilgrimage from Montana to his grandmother's home at Rainy Mountain, Momaday states that he "wanted to see
   in reality what she had seen more perfectly in her mind's eye" (paragraph
   5). How can this praise of her make sense? What, if anything, do you think
   he gained from his trip?
2. What seems to impress Momaday about the Kiowa value system that his
   grandmother exemplifies? Does he want us to worship Sun Dance dolls?
3. What do you conclude from Momaday's last paragraph? Is it thoroughly
   pessimistic? What do you infer from his use of the words *way* and *away*?

No Name Woman

Maxine Hong Kingston

Maxine Hong Kingston (b. 1940) grew up in Stockton, California, and attended the University of California at Berkeley. For several years now, she has lived in Hawaii. Kingston is primarily known for two books that explore her heritage as a Chinese-American. In *The Woman Warrior: Memoirs of a Girlhood Among Ghosts* (1976), she described the history, experiences, and family values she had to confront growing up as a Chinese-American female. For this book, her first, Kingston won the National Book Critics Circle Award in nonfiction. She then shifted her attention to the history of Chinese and Chinese-American males in her second book, *China Men* (1980), which won the American Book Award. More recently, she has published a novel, *Tripmaster Monkey* (1989), about a Chinese-American man. The following essay is the first of the five sections that compose *The Woman Warrior*. Like much of Kingston's writing, it suggests that we can have trouble distinguishing truth from fiction when we try to fathom the lives of ancestors. Kingston points out the particular complications she faced in imagining what happened back in China to a disgraced aunt, whose very identity was still kept secret by Kingston's parents years later in America.

Reflections Before Reading

Are there aspects of your family history that remain cloudy for you and that you would like to know more about? If so, what are they? Do you think there can be circumstances in which young people are better off not knowing what happened to certain family members? If so, what might those circumstances be? Are there particular relatives who have been held up to you as positive or negative examples for you to keep in mind? If so, what kind of people do you take them to be? In general, when do you think stories about their ancestors can help people, and when do you think such tales can oppress them? In the following essay, Kingston focuses on an aunt who scandalized her village in China when she became pregnant by someone other than her husband. Why might this event disturb a village? Why might the scandal of the aunt continue to haunt relatives of hers, even in America?

"You must not tell anyone," my mother said, "what I am about to tell you. In China   1
your father had a sister who killed herself. She jumped into the family well. We say
that your father has all brothers because it is as if she had never been born.

"In 1924 just a few days after our village celebrated seventeen hurry-up wed-   2
dings—to make sure that every young man who went 'out on the road' would responsibly come home—your father and his brothers and your grandfather and his
brothers and your aunt's new husband sailed for America, the Gold Mountain. It
was your grandfather's last trip. Those lucky enough to get contracts waved goodbye from the decks. They fed and guarded the stowaways and helped them off in
Cuba, New York, Bali, Hawaii. 'We'll meet in California next year,' they said. All of
them sent money home.

"I remember looking at your aunt one day when she and I were dressing; I had   3
not noticed before that she had such a protruding melon of a stomach. But I did
not think, 'She's pregnant,' until she began to look like other pregnant women, her
shirt pulling and the white tops of her black pants showing. She could not have
been pregnant, you see, because her husband had been gone for years. No one said
anything. We did not discuss it. In early summer she was ready to have the child,
long after the time when it could have been possible.

"The village had also been counting. On the night the baby was to be born the   4
villagers raised our house. Some were crying. Like a great saw, teeth strung with
lights, files of people walked zigzag across our land, tearing the rice. Their lanterns
doubled in the disturbed black water, which drained away through the broken
bunds. As the villagers closed in, we could see that some of them, probably men
and women we knew well, wore white masks. The people with long hair hung it
over their faces. Women with short hair made it stand up on end. Some had tied
white bands around their foreheads, arms, and legs.

"At first they threw mud and rocks at the house. Then they threw eggs and   5
began slaughtering our stock. We could hear the animals scream their deaths—the
roosters, the pigs, a last great roar from the ox. Familiar wild heads flared in our
night windows; the villagers encircled us. Some of the faces stopped to peer at us,
their eyes rushing like searchlights. The hands flattened against the panes, framed
heads, and left red prints.

"The villagers broke in the front and the back doors at the same time, even   6
though we had not locked the doors against them. Their knives dripped with the
blood of our animals. They smeared blood on the doors and walls. One woman
swung a chicken, whose throat she had slit, splattering blood in red arcs about her.
We stood together in the middle of our house, in the family hall with the pictures
and tables of the ancestors around us, and looked straight ahead.

"At that time the house had only two wings. When the men came back, we   7
would build two more to enclose our courtyard and a third one to begin a second
courtyard. The villagers pushed through both wings, even your grandparents'
rooms, to find your aunt's, which was also mine until the men returned. From this
room a new wing for one of the younger families would grow. They ripped up her
clothes and shoes and broke her combs, grinding them underfoot. They tore her
work from the loom. They scattered the cooking fire and rolled the new weaving in
it. We could hear them in the kitchen breaking our bowls and banging the pots.

They overturned the great waisthigh earthenware jugs; duck eggs, pickled fruits, vegetables burst out and mixed in acrid torrents. The old woman from the next field swept a broom through the air and loosed the spirits-of-the-broom over our heads. 'Pig.' 'Ghost.' 'Pig,' they sobbed and scolded while they ruined our house.

"When they left, they took sugar and oranges to bless themselves. They cut   8
pieces from the dead animals. Some of them took bowls that were not broken and clothes that were not torn. Afterward we swept up the rice and sewed it back up into sacks. But the smells from the spilled preserves lasted. Your aunt gave birth in the pigsty that night. The next morning when I went for the water, I found her and the baby plugging up the family well.

"Don't let your father know that I told you. He denies her. Now that you have   9
started to menstruate, what happened to her could happen to you. Don't humiliate us. You wouldn't like to be forgotten as if you had never been born. The villagers are watchful."

Whenever she had to warn us about life, my mother told stories that ran like   10
this one, a story to grow up on. She tested our strength to establish realities. Those in the emigrant generations who could not reassert brute survival died young and far from home. Those of us in the first American generations have had to figure out how the invisible world the emigrants built around our childhoods fits in solid America.

The emigrants confused the gods by diverting their curses, misleading them   11
with crooked streets and false names. They must try to confuse their offspring as well, who, I suppose, threaten them in similar ways—always trying to get things straight, always trying to name the unspeakable. The Chinese I know hide their names; sojourners take new names when their lives change and guard their real names with silence.

Chinese-Americans, when you try to understand what things in you are Chi-   12
nese, how do you separate what is peculiar to childhood, to poverty, insanities, one family, your mother who marked your growing with stories, from what is Chinese? What is Chinese tradition and what is the movies?

If I want to learn what clothes my aunt wore, whether flashy or ordinary, I   13
would have to begin, "Remember Father's drowned-in-the-well sister?" I cannot ask that. My mother has told me once and for all the useful parts. She will add nothing unless powered by Necessity, a riverbank that guides her life. She plants vegetable gardens rather than lawns; she carries the odd-shaped tomatoes home from the fields and eats food left for the gods.

Whenever we did frivolous things, we used up energy; we flew high kites. We   14
children came up off the ground over the melting cones our parents brought home from work and the American movie on New Year's Day—*Oh, You Beautiful Doll* with Betty Grable one year, and *She Wore a Yellow Ribbon* with John Wayne another year. After the one carnival ride each, we paid in guilt; our tired father counted his change on the dark walk home.

Adultery is extravagance. Could people who hatch their own chicks and eat   15
the embryos and the heads for delicacies and boil the feet in vinegar for party food, leaving only the gravel, eating even the gizzard lining—could such people engender a prodigal aunt? To be a woman, to have a daughter in starvation time was a

waste enough. My aunt could not have been the lone romantic who gave up every-thing for sex. Women in the old China did not choose. Some man had commanded her to lie with him and be his secret evil. I wonder whether he masked himself when he joined the raid on her family.

Perhaps she had encountered him in the fields or on the mountain where the   16
daughters-in-law collected fuel. Or perhaps he first noticed her in the market-place. He was not a stranger because the village housed no strangers. She had to have dealings with him other than sex. Perhaps he worked an adjoining field, or he sold her the cloth for the dress she sewed and wore. His demand must have sur-prised, then terrified her. She obeyed him; she always did as she was told.

When the family found a young man in the next village to be her husband, she   17
had stood tractably beside the best rooster, his proxy, and promised before they met that she would be his forever. She was lucky that he was her age and she would be the first wife, an advantage secure now. The night she first saw him, he had sex with her. Then he left for America. She had almost forgotten what he looked like. When she tried to envision him, she only saw the black and white face in the group photograph the men had had taken before leaving.

The other man was not, after all, much different from her husband. They both   18
gave orders: she followed. "If you tell your family, I'll beat you. I'll kill you. Be here again next week." No one talked sex, ever. And she might have separated the rapes from the rest of living if only she did not have to buy her oil from him or gather wood in the same forest. I want her fear to have lasted just as long as rape lasted so that the fear could have been contained. No drawn-out fear. But women at sex hazarded birth and hence lifetimes. The fear did not stop but permeated every-where. She told the man, "I think I'm pregnant." He organized the raid against her.

On nights when my mother and father talked about their life back home,   19
sometimes they mentioned an "outcast table" whose business they still seemed to be settling, their voices tight. In a commensal tradition, where food is precious, the powerful older people made wrongdoers eat alone. Instead of letting them start separate new lives like the Japanese, who could become samurais and geishas, the Chinese family, faces averted but eyes glowering sideways, hung on to the offend-ers and fed them leftovers. My aunt must have lived in the same house as my parents and eaten at an outcast table. My mother spoke about the raid as if she had seen it, when she and my aunt, a daughter-in-law to a different household, should not have been living together at all. Daughters-in-law lived with their husbands' parents, not their own; a synonym for marriage in Chinese is "taking a daughter-in-law." Her husband's parents could have sold her, mortgaged her, stoned her. But they had sent her back to her own mother and father, a mysterious act hinting at disgraces not told me. Perhaps they had thrown her out to deflect the avengers.

She was the only daughter; her four brothers went with her father, husband,   20
and uncles "out on the road" and for some years became western men. When the goods were divided among the family, three of the brothers took land, and the youngest, my father, chose an education. After my grandparents gave their daugh-ter away to her husband's family, they had dispensed all the adventure and all the property. They expected her alone to keep the traditional ways, which her broth-

ers, now among the barbarians, could fumble without detection. The heavy, deep-rooted women were to maintain the past against the flood, safe for returning. But the rare urge west had fixed upon our family, and so my aunt crossed boundaries not delineated in space.

The work of preservation demands that the feelings playing about in one's guts   21
not be turned into action. Just watch their passing like cherry blossoms. But perhaps my aunt, my forerunner, caught in a slow life, let dreams grow and fade and after some months or years went toward what persisted. Fear at the enormities of the forbidden kept her desires delicate, wire and bone. She looked at a man because she liked the way the hair was tucked behind his ears, or she liked the question-mark line of a long torso curving at the shoulder and straight at the hip. For warm eyes or a soft voice or a slow walk—that's all—a few hairs, a line, a brightness, a sound, a pace, she gave up family. She offered us up for a charm that vanished with tiredness, a pigtail that didn't toss when the wind died. Why, the wrong lighting could erase the dearest thing about him.

It could very well have been, however, that my aunt did not take subtle enjoy-   22
ment of her friend, but, a wild woman, kept rollicking company. Imagining her free with sex doesn't fit, though. I don't know any women like that, or men either. Unless I see her life branching into mine, she gives me no ancestral help.

To sustain her being in love, she often worked at herself in the mirror, guess-   23
ing at the colors and shapes that would interest him, changing them frequently in order to hit on the right combination. She wanted him to look back.

On a farm near the sea, a woman who tended her appearance reaped a repu-   24
tation for eccentricity. All the married women blunt-cut their hair in flaps about their ears or pulled it back in tight buns. No nonsense. Neither style blew easily into heart-catching tangles. And at their weddings they displayed themselves in their long hair for the last time. "It brushed the backs of my knees," my mother tells me. "It was braided, and even so, it brushed the backs of my knees."

At the mirror my aunt combed individuality into her bob. A bun could have   25
been contrived to escape into black streamers blowing in the wind or in quiet wisps about her face, but only the older woman in our picture album wear buns. She brushed her hair back from her forehead, tucking the flaps behind her ears. She looped a piece of thread, knotted into a circle between her index fingers and thumbs, and ran the double strand across her forehead. When she closed her fingers as if she were making a pair of shadow geese bite, the string twisted together catching the little hairs. Then she pulled the thread away from her skin, ripping the hairs out neatly, her eyes watering from the needles of pain. Opening her fingers, she cleaned the thread, then rolled it along her hairline and the tops of her eyebrows. My mother did the same to me and my sisters and herself. I used to believe that the expression "caught by the short hairs" meant a captive held with a depilatory string. It especially hurt at the temples, but my mother said we were lucky we didn't have to have our feet bound when we were seven. Sisters used to sit on their beds and cry together, she said, as their mothers or their slave removed the bandages for a few minutes each night and let the blood gush back into their veins. I hope that the man my aunt loved appreciated a smooth brow, that he wasn't just a tits-and-ass man.

Once my aunt found a freckle on her chin, at a spot that the almanac said   26
predestined her for unhappiness. She dug it out with a hot needle and washed the
wound with peroxide.

More attention to her looks than these pullings of hairs and pickings at spots   27
would have caused gossip among the villagers. They owned work clothes and good
clothes, and they were good clothes for feasting the new seasons. But since a
woman combing her hair hexes beginnings, my aunt rarely found an occasion to
look her best. Women looked like great sea snails—the corded wood, babies, and
laundry they carried were the whorls on their backs. The Chinese did not admire a
bent back; goddesses and warriors stood straight. Still there must have been a
marvelous freeing of beauty when a worker laid down her burden and stretched
and arched.

Such commonplace loveliness, however, was not enough for my aunt. She   28
dreamed of a lover for the fifteen days of New Year's, the time for families to
exchange visits, money, and food. She plied her secret comb. And sure enough she
cursed the year, the family, the village, and herself.

Even as her hair lured her imminent lover, many other men looked at her.   29
Uncles, cousins, nephews, brothers would have looked, too, had they been home
between journeys. Perhaps they had already been restraining their curiosity, and
they left, fearful that their glances, like a field of nesting birds, might be startled
and caught. Poverty hurt, and that was their first reason for leaving. But another,
final reason for leaving the crowded house was the never-said.

She may have been unusually beloved, the precious only daughter, spoiled   30
and mirror gazing because of the affection the family lavished on her. When her
husband left, they welcomed the chance to take her back from the in-laws; she
could live like the little daughter for just a while longer. There are stories that my
grandfather was different from other people, "crazy ever since the little Jap bayo-
neted him in the head." He used to put his naked penis on the dinner table, laughing. And one day he brought home a baby girl, wrapped up inside his brown west-
ern-style greatcoat. He had traded one of his sons, probably my father, the
youngest, for her. My grandmother made him trade back. When he finally got a
daughter of his own, he doted on her. They must have all loved her, except perhaps
my father, the only brother who never went back to China, having once been
traded for a girl.

Brothers and sisters, newly men and women, had to efface their sexual color   31
and present plain miens. Disturbing hair and eyes, a smile like no other, threatened the ideal of five generations living under one roof. To focus blurs, people
shouted face to face and yelled from room to room. The immigrants I know have
loud voices, unmodulated to American tones even after years away from the village
where they called their friendships out across the fields. I have not been able to
stop my mother's screams in public libraries or over telephones. Walking erect
(knees straight, toes pointed forward, not pigeon-toed, which is Chinese-feminine)
and speaking in an inaudible voice, I have tried to turn myself American-feminine.
Chinese communication was loud, public. Only sick people had to whisper. But at
the dinner table, where the family members came nearest one another, no one
could talk, not the outcasts nor any eaters. Every word that falls from the mouth is

a coin lost. Silently they gave and accepted food with both hands. A preoccupied child who took his bowl with one hand got a sideways glare. A complete moment of total attention is due everyone alike. Children and lovers have no singularity here, but my aunt used a secret voice, a separate attentiveness.

She kept the man's name to herself throughout her labor and dying; she did   32
not accuse him that he be punished with her. To save her inseminator's name she gave silent birth.

He may have been somebody in her own household, but intercourse with a   33
man outside the family would have been no less abhorrent. All the village were kinsmen, and the titles shouted in loud country voices never let kinship be forgotten. Any man within visiting distance would have been neutralized as a lover—"brother," "younger brother," "older brother"—one hundred and fifteen relationship titles. Parents researched birth charts probably not so much to assure good fortune as to circumvent incest in a population that has but one hundred surnames. Everybody has eight million relatives. How useless then sexual mannerisms, how dangerous.

As if it came from an atavism deeper than fear, I used to add "brother" silently   34
to boys' names. It hexed the boys, who would or would not ask me to dance and made them less scary and as familiar and deserving of benevolence as girls.

But, of course, I hexed myself also—no dates. I should have stood up, both   35
arms waving, and shouted out across libraries, "Hey, you! Love me back." I had no idea, though, how to make attraction selective, how to control its direction and magnitude. If I made myself American-pretty so that the five or six Chinese boys in the class fell in love with me, everyone else—the Caucasian, Negro, and Japanese boys—would too. Sisterliness, dignified and honorable, made much more sense.

Attraction eludes control so stubbornly that whole societies designed to orga-   36
nize relationships among people cannot keep order, not even when they bind people to one another from childhood and raise them together. Among the very poor and the wealthy, brothers married their adopted sisters, like doves. Our family allowed some romance, paying adult brides' prices and providing dowries so that their sons and daughters could marry strangers. Marriage promises to turn strangers into friendly relatives—a nation of siblings.

In the village structure, spirits shimmered among the live creatures, balanced   37
and held in equilibrium by time and land. But one human being flaring up into violence could open up a black hole, a maelstrom that pulled in the sky. The frightened villagers, who depended on one another to maintain the real, went to my aunt to show her a personal, physical representation of the break she had made in the "roundness." Misallying couples snapped off the future, which was to be embodied in true offspring. The villagers punished her for acting as if she could have a private life, secret and apart from them.

If my aunt had betrayed the family at a time of large grain yields and peace,   38
when many boys were born, and wings were being built on many houses, perhaps she might have escaped such severe punishment. But the men—hungry, greedy, tired of planting in dry soil—and had been forced to leave the village in order to send food-money home. There were ghost plagues, bandit plagues, wars with the Japanese, floods. My Chinese brother and sister had died of an unknown sickness.

Adultery, perhaps only a mistake during good times, became a crime when the village needed food.

The round moon cakes and round doorways, the round tables of graduated   39
size that fit one roundness inside another, round windows and rice bowls—these talismans had lost their power to warn this family of the law: a family must be whole, faithfully keeping the descent line by having sons to feed the old and the dead, who in turn look after the family. The villagers came to show my aunt and her lover-in-hiding a broken house. The villagers were speeding up the circling of events because she was too shortsighted to see that her infidelity had already harmed the village, that waves of consequences would return unpredictably, sometimes in disguise, as now, to hurt her. This roundness had to be made coin-sized so that she would see its circumference: punish her at the birth of her baby. Awaken her to the inexorable. People who refused fatalism because they could invent small resources insisted on culpability. Deny accidents and wrest fault from the stars.

After the villagers left, their lanterns now scattering in various directions to-   40
ward home, the family broke their silence and cursed her. "Aiaa, we're going to die. Death is coming. Death is coming. Look what you've done. You've killed us. *Ghost! Dead ghost! Ghost!* You've never been born." She ran out into the fields, far enough from the house so that she could no longer hear their voices, and pressed herself against the earth, her own land no more. When she felt the birth coming, she thought that she had been hurt. Her body seized together. "They've hurt me too much," she thought. "This is gall, and it will kill me." With forehead and knees against the earth, her body convulsed and then relaxed. She turned on her back, lay on the ground. The black well of sky and stars went out and out and out forever; her body and her complexity seemed to disappear. She was one of the stars, a bright dot in blackness, without home, without a companion, in eternal cold and silence. An agoraphobia rose in her, speeding higher and higher, bigger and bigger; she would not be able to contain it; there would be no end to fear.

Flayed, unprotected against space, she felt pain return, focusing her body.   41
This pain chilled her—a cold, steady kind of surface pain. Inside, spasmodically, the other pain, the pain of the child, heated her. For hours she lay on the ground, alternately body and space. Sometimes a vision of normal comfort obliterated reality: she saw the family in the evening gambling at the dinner table, the young people massaging their elders' backs. She saw them congratulating one another, high joy on the mornings the rice shoots came up. When these pictures burst, the stars drew yet further apart. Black space opened.

She got to her feet to fight better and remembered that old-fashioned women   42
gave birth in their pigsties to fool the jealous, pain-dealing gods, who do not snatch piglets. Before the next spasms could stop her, she ran to the pigsty, each step a rushing out into emptiness: She climbed over the fence and knelt in the dirt. It was good to have a fence enclosing her, a tribal person alone.

Laboring, this woman who had carried her child as a foreign growth that sick-   43
ened her every day, expelled it at last. She reached down to touch the hot, wet, moving mass, surely smaller than anything human, and could feel that it was human after all—fingers, toes, nails, nose. She pulled it up on to her belly, and it lay curled there, butt in the air, feet precisely tucked one under the other. She opened

her loose shirt and buttoned the child inside. After resting, it squirmed and thrashed and she pushed it up to her breast. It turned its head this way and that until it found her nipple. There, it made little snuffling noises. She clenched her teeth at its preciousness, lovely as a young calf, a piglet, a little dog.

She may have gone to the pigsty as a last act of responsibility: she would pro-   44
tect this child as she had protected its father. It would look after her soul, leaving supplies on her grave. But how would this tiny child without family find her grave when there would be no marker for her anywhere, neither in the earth nor the family hall? No one would give her a family hall name. She had taken the child with her into the wastes. At its birth the two of them had felt the same raw pain of separation, a wound that only the family pressing tight could close. A child with no descent line would not soften her life but only trail after her, ghost-like, begging her to give it purpose. At dawn the villagers on their way to the fields would stand around the fence and look.

Full of milk, the little ghost slept. When it awoke, she hardened her breasts   45
against the milk that crying loosens. Toward morning she picked up the baby and walked to the well.

Carrying the baby to the well shows loving. Otherwise abandon it. Turn its   46
face into the mud. Mothers who love their children take them along. It was prob-ably a girl; there is some hope of forgiveness for boys.

"Don't tell anyone you had an aunt. Your father does not want to hear her   47
name. She has never been born." I have believed that sex was unspeakable and words so strong and fathers so frail that "aunt" would do my father mysterious harm. I have thought that my family, having settled among immigrants who had also been their neighbors in the ancestral land, needed to clean their name, and a wrong word would incite the kinspeople even here. But there is more to this si-lence: they want me to participate in her punishment. And I have.

In the twenty years since I heard this story I have not asked for details nor said   48
my aunt's name; I do not know it. People who can comfort the dead can also chase after them to hurt them further—a reverse ancestor worship. The real punishment was not the raid swiftly inflicted by the villagers, but the family's deliberately for-getting her. Her betrayal so maddened them, they saw to it that she would suffer forever, even after death. Always hungry, always needing, she would have to beg food from other ghosts, snatch and steal it from those whose living descendants give them gifts. She would have to fight the ghosts massed at crossroads for the buns a few thoughtful citizens leave to decoy her away from village and home so that the ancestral spirits could feast unharassed. At peace, they could act like gods, not ghosts, their descent lines providing them with paper suits and dresses, spirit money, paper houses, paper automobiles, chicken, meat, and rice into eternity—essences delivered up in smoke and flames, steam and incense rising from each rice bowl. In an attempt to make the Chinese care for people outside the family, Chairman Mao encourages us now to give our paper replicas to the spirits of out-standing soldiers and workers, no matter whose ancestors they may be. My aunt remains forever hungry. Goods are not distributed evenly among the dead.

My aunt haunts me—her ghost drawn to me because now, after fifty years of   49
neglect, I alone devote pages of paper to her, though not origamied into houses

and clothes. I do not think she always means me well. I am telling on her, and she was a spite suicide, drowning herself in the drinking water. The Chinese are always very frightened of the drowned one, whose weeping ghost, wet hair hanging and skin bloated, waits silently by the water to pull down a substitute.

Rhetorical Focus

1. Kingston begins her essay with a command from her mother: " 'You must not tell anyone . . . what I am about to tell you.' " Yet by immediately telling her readers her mother's story about the aunt, Kingston disobeys this command. Why, then, do you think she begins by quoting it?
2. How would you characterize Kingston's tone in this essay, the feelings she displays? Is her tone consistent? Refer to specific passages.
3. Kingston presents multiple versions of her ancestor's story, while Momaday basically advances one particular account of his grandmother. Is Kingston's credibility as a writer of family history therefore lesser or greater for you than Momaday's is? Explain.

Thematic Focus

1. Why does Kingston's mother tell her the first story about the aunt? List the various stories that Kingston herself then proceeds to tell about her. Do any of these stories come across as more plausible than the others? Why or why not?
2. What, if anything, does Kingston consider to be at least possibly rational about the villagers' treatment of her aunt back in China and her family's treatment of her aunt's memory in America? What, if anything, does Kingston seem to find irrational about the ways that people have treated her aunt in life and in memory? What factors do you yourself think should be considered in analyzing and judging the treatment that the aunt has received?
3. Kingston says of her aunt, "Unless I see her life branching into mine, she gives me no ancestral help" (paragraph 22). By the end of the essay, does Kingston seem to perceive the aunt's life as branching into hers? If so, in what way(s)? Does Kingston seem to find thinking about the aunt ultimately a positive experience, a negative one, or both? Explain. To what extent, finally, does Kingston seem to identify with the no name woman. Do you think she identifies with her aunt to the same degree that Momaday identifies with his grandmother, and with similar effects? Why or why not?

Suggestions for Writing

1. Compare the culture that Momaday depicts with the culture that Kingston does. Do these authors emphasize the same things about their respective

cultures? Do they seem equally committed to the cultures they discuss? Are there aspects of these cultures that you sense Momaday and Kingston have not addressed? If so, what do you think they have chosen to deemphasize?

2. Describe an older member of your family whose values you have come to appreciate. Be sure to describe the particular ways this person demonstrates his or her values. Identify, too, the ways that you would like to demonstrate such values in your own life.

3. Write an essay describing your efforts to learn more about an aspect of your family history that aroused your curiosity—for example, a particular relative, relationship, event, or phase. In your description, identify why you wanted to know more, why your knowledge was limited in the first place, what efforts you made to find out more, what you ultimately were able to learn, and whether you are now satisfied with what you know about this aspect of your family's past.

INTERPRETING A FATHER'S LEGACY

The previous constellation emphasized family ancestors. This one focuses on the role of parents, specifically fathers, in transmitting values to their children and future generations. We may be highly conscious of our genetic inheritance from our parents, the ways we physically resemble them. A more complicated and weightier subject, however, is what we inherit psychologically from them. In what ways do we reproduce their values, attitudes, and dispositions? When should we welcome their influence, and when should we resist it? As was suggested in the previous constellation, questions such as these cannot be resolved simply by pointing to the naked facts of family history. Again, the past has to be interpreted. Depending on their present mood and sense of rhetorical purpose, writers may dwell on some aspect of their parents in one essay and turn to very different aspects of them in another. The two essays here suggest the ways that interpretations of a father's legacy can vary. They were written by the same author, Scott Russell Sanders, but their visions of his father vividly contrast. In effect, they demonstrate that writers can wind up radically altering their treatment of any subject. Indeed, writers often feel that their first presentation of a topic needs to be significantly reworked. In a technical sense, Sanders did not revise his first portrait of his father because it remains in print along with his later one. In a more important sense, however, Sanders clearly undertook a "re-vision" of his father's legacy, choosing to look at a very different aspect of it. As you read his contrasting accounts of "inheritance" and "influence," consider what they imply about the possibilities of "revision" in your own writing.

The Inheritance of Tools

Scott Russell Sanders

Scott Russell Sanders (b. 1945) is a professor of English at Indiana University. In addition to his many essays, he has published fiction (including *Wilderness Plots* and *The Invisible Company*) and literary criticism (*D.H. Lawrence: The World of the Major Novels*). "The Inheritance of Tools" comes from his 1987 collection of essays, *The Paradise of Bombs*, which won the Associated Writing Programs Award for Creative Nonfiction.

Reflections Before Reading

Sanders deals here with the passing down of tools from one generation to another: hammers, saws, chisels, and so forth. Do you own any tools? Do your parents? Do either of you or your parents enjoy working with them? Obviously Sanders also means *inheritance* in a psychological sense, for he indicates that his father transmitted to him a certain ability to use tools properly. What values, habits, and ideas do you think you have inherited from your parents?

At just about the hour when my father died, soon after dawn one February morn-   1
ing when ice coated the windows like cataracts, I banged my thumb with a hammer. Naturally I swore at the hammer, the reckless thing, and in the moment of swearing I thought of what my father would say: "If you'd try hitting the nail it would go in a whole lot faster. Don't you know your thumb's not as hard as that hammer?" We both were doing carpentry that day, but far apart. He was building cupboards at my brother's place in Oklahoma; I was at home in Indiana putting up a wall in the basement to make a bedroom for my daughter. By the time my mother called with news of his death—the long distance wires whittling her voice until it seemed too thin to bear the weight of what she had to say—my thumb was swollen. A week or so later a white scar in the shape of a crescent moon began to show above the cuticle, and month by month it rose across the pink sky of my thumbnail. It took the better part of a year for the scar to disappear, and every time I noticed it I thought of my father.

The hammer had belonged to him, and to his father before him. The three of us have used it to build houses and barns and chicken coops, to upholster chairs and crack walnuts, to make doll furniture and bookshelves and jewelry boxes. The head is scratched and pockmarked, like an old plowshare that has been working rocky fields, and it gives off the sort of dull sheen you see on fast creek water in the shade. It is a finishing hammer, about the weight of a bread loaf, too light really for framing walls, too heavy for cabinetwork, with a curved claw for pulling nails, a rounded head for pounding, a fluted neck for looks, and a hickory handle for strength.   2

The present handle is my third one, bought from a lumberyard in Tennessee down the road from where my brother and I were helping my father build his retirement house. I broke the previous one by trying to pull sixteen-penny nails out of floor joists—a foolish thing to do with a finishing hammer, as my father pointed out. "You ever hear of a crowbar?" he said. No telling how many handles he and my grandfather had gone through before me. My grandfather used to cut down hickory trees on his farm, saw them into slabs, cure the planks in his hayloft, and carve handles with a drawknife. The grain in hickory is crooked and knotty, and therefore tough, hard to split, like the grain in the two men who owned this hammer before me.   3

After proposing marriage to a neighbor girl, my grandfather used this hammer to build a house for his bride on a stretch of river bottom in northern Mississippi. The lumber for the place, like the hickory for the handle, was cut on his own land. By the day of the wedding he had not quite finished the house, and so right after the ceremony he took his wife home and put her to work. My grandmother had worn her Saturday dress for the wedding, with a fringe of lace tacked on around the hem in honor of the occasion. She removed this lace and folded it away before going out to help my grandfather nail siding on the house. "There she was in her good dress," he told me some fifty-odd years after that wedding day, "holding up them long pieces of clapboard while I hammered, and together we got the place covered up before dark." As the family grew to four, six, eight, and eventually thirteen, my grandfather used this hammer to enlarge his house room by room, like a chambered nautilus expanding his shell.   4

By and by the hammer was passed along to my father. One day he was up on the roof of our pony barn nailing shingles with it, when I stepped out the kitchen door to call him for supper. Before I could yell, something about the sight of him straddling the spine of that roof and swinging the hammer caught my eye and made me hold my tongue. I was five or six years old, and the world's commonplaces were still news to me. He would pull a nail from the pouch at his waist, bring the hammer down, and a moment later the *thunk* of the blow would reach my ears. And that is what had stopped me in my tracks and stilled my tongue, that momentary gap between seeing and hearing the blow. Instead of yelling from the kitchen door, I ran to the barn and climbed two rungs up the ladder—as far as I was allowed to go—and spoke quietly to my father. On our walk to the house he explained that sound takes time to make its way through air. Suddenly the world seemed larger, the air more dense, if sound could be held back like any ordinary traveler.   5

By the time I started using this hammer, at about the age when I discovered   6
the speed of sound, it already contained houses and mysteries for me. The smooth
handle was one my grandfather had made. In those days I needed both hands to
swing it. My father would start a nail in a scrap of wood, and I would pound away
until I bent it over.

"Looks like you got ahold of some of those rubber nails," he would tell me.   7
"Here, let me see if I can find you some stiff ones." And he would rummage in a
drawer until he came up with a fistful of more cooperative nails. "Look at the
head," he would tell me. "Don't look at your hands, don't look at the hammer. Just
look at the head of that nail and pretty soon you'll learn to hit it square."

Pretty soon I did learn. While he worked in the garage cutting dovetail joints   8
for a drawer or skinning a deer or tuning an engine, I would hammer nails. I made
innocent blocks of wood look like porcupines. He did not talk much in the midst of
his tools, but he kept up a nearly ceaseless humming, slipping in and out of a dozen
tunes in an afternoon, often running back over the same stretch of melody again
and again, as if searching for a way out. When the humming did cease, I knew he
was faced with a task requiring great delicacy or concentration, and I took care not
to distract him.

He kept scraps of wood in a cardboard box—the ends of two-by-fours, slabs of   9
shelving and plywood, odd pieces of molding—and everything in it was fair game. I
nailed scraps together to fashion what I called boats or houses, but the results
usually bore only faint resemblance to the visions I carried in my head. I would
hold up these constructions to show my father, and he would turn them over in his
hands admiringly, speculating about what they might be. My cobbled-together
guitars might have been alien spaceships, my barns might have been models of
Aztec temples, each wooden contraption might have been anything but what I had
set out to make.

Now and again I would feel the need to have a chunk of wood shaped or   10
shortened before I riddled it with nails, and I would clamp it in a vice and scrape at
it with a handsaw. My father would let me lacerate the board until my arm gave
out, and then he would wrap his hand around mine and help me finish the cut,
showing me how to use my thumb to guide the blade, how to pull back on the saw
to keep it from binding, how to let my shoulder do the work.

"Don't force it," he would say, "just drag it easy and give the teeth a chance to   11
bite."

As the saw teeth bit down the wood released its smell, each kind with its own   12
fragrance, oak or walnut or cherry or pine—usually pine, because it was the softest
and the easiest for a child to work. No matter how weathered and gray the board,
no matter how warped and cracked, inside there was this smell waiting, as of something freshly baked. I gathered every smidgen of sawdust and stored it away in
coffee cans, which I kept in a drawer of the workbench. When I did not feel like
hammering nails I would dump my sawdust on the concrete floor of the garage and
landscape it into highways and farms and towns, running miniature cars and trucks
along miniature roads. Looming as huge as a colossus, my father worked over and
around me, now and again bending down to inspect my work, careful not to tram-
ple my creations. It was a landscape that smelled dizzyingly of wood. Even after a

bath my skin would carry the smell, and so would my father's hair, when he lifted me for a bedtime hug.

I tell these things not only from memory but also from recent observation, 13 because my own son now turns blocks of wood into nailed porcupines, dumps cans full of sawdust at my feet and sculpts highways on the floor. He learns how to swing a hammer from the elbow instead of the wrist, how to lay his thumb beside the blade to guide a saw, how to tap a chisel with a wooden mallet, how to mark a hole with an awl before starting a drill bit. My daughter did the same before him, and even now, on the brink of teenage aloofness, she will occasionally drag out my box of wood scraps and carpenter something. So I have seen my apprenticeship to wood and tools reenacted in each of my children, as my father saw his own apprenticeship renewed in me.

The saw I use belonged to him, as did my level and both of my squares, and all 14 four tools had belonged to his father. The blade of the saw is the bluish color of gun barrels, and the maple handle, dark from the sweat of hands, is inscribed with curving leaf designs. The level is a shaft of walnut two feet long, edged with brass and pierced by three round windows in which air bubbles float in oil-filled tubes of glass. The middle window serves for testing whether a surface is horizontal, the others for testing whether it is plumb or vertical. My grandfather used to carry this level on the gun rack behind the seat in his pickup, and when I rode with him I would turn around to watch the bubbles dance. The larger of the two squares is called a framing square, a flat steel elbow so beat up and tarnished you can barely make out the rows of numbers that show how to figure the cuts on rafters. The smaller one is called a try square, for marking right angles, with a blued steel blade for the shank and a brass-faced block of cherry for the head.

I was taught early on that a saw is not to be used apart from a square: "If you're 15 going to cut a piece of wood," my father insisted, "you owe it to the tree to cut it straight."

Long before studying geometry, I learned there is a mystical virtue in right 16 angles. There is an unspoken morality in seeking the level and the plumb. A house will stand, a table will bear weight, the sides of a box will hold together only if the joints are square and the members upright. When the bubble is lined up between two marks etched in the glass tube of a level, you have aligned yourself with the forces that hold the universe together. When you miter the corners of a picture frame, each angle must be exactly forty-five degrees, as they are in the perfect triangles of Pythagoras, not a degree more or less. Otherwise the frame will hang crookedly, as if ashamed of itself and of its maker. No matter if the joints you are cutting do not show. Even if you are butting two pieces of wood together inside a cabinet, where no one except a wrecking crew will ever see them, you must take pains to insure that the ends are square and the studs are plumb.

I took pains over the wall I was building on the day my father died. Not long 17 after that wall was finished—paneled with tongue-and-groove boards of yellow pine, the nail holes filled with putty and the wood all stained and sealed—I came close to wrecking it one afternoon when my daughter ran howling up the stairs to announce that her gerbils had escaped from their cage and were hiding in my brand-new wall. She could hear them scratching and squeaking behind her bed. Impossible! I said. How on earth could they get inside by drum-tight wall? Through the heating vent, she answered. I went downstairs, pressed by ear to the honey-colored wood, and heard the scritch scratch of tiny feet.

"What can we do?" my daughter wailed. "They'll starve to death, they'll die of thirst, they'll suffocate."   18

"Hold on," I soothed. "I'll think of something."   19

While I thought and she fretted, the radio on her bedside table delivered us the headlines. Several thousand people had died in a city in India from a poisonous cloud that had leaked overnight from a chemical plant. A nuclear-powered submarine had been launched. Rioting continued in South Africa. An airplane had been hijacked in the Mediterranean. Authorities calculated that several thousand homeless people slept on the streets within sight of the Washington Monument. I felt my usual helplessness in face of all these calamities. But here was my daughter weeping because her gerbils were holed up in a wall. This calamity I could handle.   20

"Don't worry," I told her. "We'll set food and water by the heating vent and lure them out. And if that doesn't do the trick, I'll tear the wall apart until we find them."   21

She stopped crying and gazed at me. "You'd really tear it apart? Just for my gerbils? The *wall*? Astonishment slowed her down only for a second, however, before she ran to the workbench and began tugging at drawers, saying, "Let's see, what'll we need? Crowbar. Hammer. Chisels. I hope we don't have to use them— but just in case."   22

We didn't need the wrecking tools. I never had to assault my handsome wall, because the gerbils eventually came out to nibble at a dish of popcorn. But for several hours I studied the tongue-and-groove skin I had nailed up on the day of my father's death, considering where to begin prying. There were no gaps in that wall, no crooked joints.   23

I had botched a great many pieces of wood before I mastered the right angle with a saw, botched even more before I learned to miter a joint. The knowledge of these things resides in my hands and eyes and the webwork of muscles, not in the tools. There are machines for sale—powered miter boxes and radial arm saws, for instance—that will enable any casual soul to cut proper angles in boards. The skill is invested in the gadget instead of the person who uses it, and this is what distinguishes a machine from a tool. If I had to earn my keep by making furniture or building houses, I suppose I would buy powered saws and pneumatic nailers; the need for speed would drive me to it. But since I carpenter only for my own pleasure or to help neighbors or to remake the house around the ears of my family, I stick with hand tools. Most of the ones I own were given to me by my father, who also taught me how to wield them. The tools in my workbench are a double inheritance, for each hammer and level and saw is wrapped in a cloud of knowing.   24

All of these tools are a pleasure to look at and to hold. Merchants would never paste NEW NEW NEW! signs on them in stores. Their designs are old because they work, because they serve their purpose well. Like folksongs and aphorisms and the grainy bits of language, these tools have been pared down to essentials. I   25 look at my claw hammer, the distillation of a hundred generations of carpenters, and consider that it holds up well beside those other classics—Greek vases, Gregorian chants, *Don Quixote*, barbed fishhooks, candles, spoons. Knowledge of hammering stretches back to the earliest humans who squatted beside fires chipping flints. Anthropologists have a lovely name for those unworked rocks that served as the earliest hammers. "Dawn stones" they are called. Their only qualification for the work, aside from hardness, is that they fit the hand. Our ancestors used them for grinding corn, tapping awls, smashing bones. From dawn stones to this claw hammer is a great leap in time, but no great distance in design or imagination.

On that iced-over February morning when I smashed my thumb with the hammer, I was down in the basement framing the wall that my daughter's gerbils would later hide in. I was thinking of my father, as I always did whenever I built anything, thinking how he would have gone about the work, hearing in memory what he would have said about the wisdom of hitting the nail instead of my thumb. I had the studs and plates nailed together all square and trim, and was lifting the wall into place when the phone rang upstairs. My wife answered, and in a moment she came to the basement door and called down softly to me. The stillness in her voice made me drop the framed wall and hurry upstairs. She told me my father was dead. Then I heard the details over the phone from my mother. Building a set of cupboards for my brother in Oklahoma, he had knocked off work early the previous afternoon because of cramps in his stomach. Early this morning, on his way into the kitchen of my brother's trailer, maybe going for a glass of water, so early that no one else was awake, he slumped down on the linoleum and his heart quit.

For several hours I paced around inside my house, upstairs and down, in and out of every room, looking for the right door to open and knowing there was no such door. My wife and children followed me and wrapped me in arms and backed away again, circling and staring as if I were on fire. Where was the door, the door, the door? I kept wondering. My smashed thumb turned purple and throbbed, making me furious. I wanted to cut it off and rush outside and scrape away the snow and hack a hole in the frozen earth and bury the shameful thing.

I went down into the basement, opened a drawer in my workbench, and stared at the ranks of chisels and knives. Oiled and sharp, as my father would have kept them, they gleamed at me like teeth. I took up a clasp knife, pried out the longest blade, and tested the edge on the hair of my forearm. A tuft came away cleanly, and I saw my father testing the sharpness of tools on his own skin, the blades of axes and knives and gouges and hoes, saw the red hair shaved off in patches from his arms and the backs of his hands. "That will cut bear," he would say. He never cut a bear with his blades, now my blades, but he cut deer, dirt, wood. I closed the knife and put it away. Then I took up the hammer and went back to work on my daughter's wall, snugging the bottom plate against a chalkline on the floor, shimming the top plate against the joists overhead, plumbing the studs with my level, making sure before I drove the first nail that every line was square and true.

26

27

28

Rhetorical Focus

1. Sanders begins and ends his essay on the day of his father's death. What occurs in between is mostly scenes from earlier family history. Sanders leaps forward in time, however, with the gerbil episode. It even took place *after* his father's death. Why do you think Sanders inserted it, given that it disrupts the time frame that he otherwise sets up?

2. Is the last paragraph an appropriate conclusion for this essay? Why or why not?

3. Sanders uses various kinds of sentence structure here. Note the following sentences, which all feature a series of parallel expressions:

    It is a finishing hammer, about the weight of a bread loaf, too light really for framing walls, too heavy for cabinetwork, with a curved claw for pulling nails, a rounded head for pounding, a fluted neck for looks, and a hickory handle for strength (paragraph 2).

    My grandfather used to cut down hickory trees on his farm, saw them into slabs, cure the planks in his hayloft, and carve handles with a drawknife (paragraph 3).

    My cobbled-together guitars might have been alien spaceships, my barns might have been models of Aztec temples, each wooden contraption might have been anything but what I had set out to make (paragraph 9).

    My father would let me lacerate the board until my arm gave out, and then he would wrap his hand around mine and help me finish the cut, showing me how to use my thumb to guide the blade, how to pull back on the saw to keep it from binding, how to let my shoulder do the work (paragraph 10).

    Can you find other examples of this sentence structure? Try imitating it yourself. Are there other types of sentences you see the author drawn to?

Thematic Focus

1. What does Sanders mean when he writes, "The tools in my workbench are a double inheritance, for each hammer and level and saw is wrapped in a cloud of knowing" (paragraph 24)?

2. In what ways does Sanders indicate that the inheritance of tools has continued with his children?

3. In this essay, Sanders focuses on a particular aspect of his father. What sorts of things about a father does Sanders leave out?

Under the Influence

Scott Russell Sanders

This second essay about Sanders's father appeared in the November 1989 issue of *Harper's*.

Reflections Before Reading

This essay focuses on the alcoholism of Sanders's father. What sorts of events do you think Sanders may relate as he recalls growing up as the son of an alcoholic? In what ways do you think alcoholics influence their children's lives? What features of Sanders's writing in the first essay do you think you might see in this one?

My father drank. He drank as a gut-punched boxer gasps for breath, as a starving   1
dog gobbles food—compulsively, secretly, in pain and trembling. I use the past
tense not because he ever quit drinking but because he quit living. That is how the
story ends for my father, age sixty-four, heart bursting, body cooling, slumped and
forsaken on the linoleum of my brother's trailer. The story continues for my
brother, my sister, my mother, and me, and will continue as long as memory holds.

In the perennial present of memory, I slip into the garage or barn to see my   2
father tipping back the flat green bottles of wine, the brown cylinders of whiskey,
the cans of beer disguised in paper bags. His Adam's apple bobs, the liquid gurgles,
he wipes the sandy-haired back of a hand over his lips, and then, his bloodshot gaze
bumping into me, he stashes the bottle or can inside his jacket, under the workbench, between two bales of hay, and we both pretend the moment has not occurred.

"What's up, buddy?" he says, thick-tongued and edgy.   3

"Sky's up," I answer, playing along.   4

"And don't forget prices," he grumbles. "Prices are always up. And taxes."   5

In memory, his white 1951 Pontiac with the stripes down the hood and the   6
Indian head on the snout lurches to a stop in the driveway; or it is the 1956 Ford
station wagon, or the 1963 Rambler shaped like a toad, or the sleek 1969 Bonne-

ville that will do 120 miles per hour on straightaways; or it is the robin's-egg-blue pickup, new in 1980, battered in 1981, the year of his death. He climbs out, grinning dangerously, unsteady on his legs, and we children interrupt our game of catch, our building of snow forts, our picking of plums, to watch in silence as he weaves past us into the house, where he drops into his overstuffed chair and falls asleep. Shaking her head, our mother stubs out a cigarette he has left smoldering in the ashtray. All evening, until our bedtimes, we tiptoe past him, as past a snoring dragon. Then we curl fearfully in our sheets, listening. Eventually he wakes with a grunt, Mother slings accusations at him, he snarls back, she yells, he growls, their voices clashing. Before long, she retreats to their bedroom, sobbing—not from the blows of fists, for he never strikes her, but from the force of his words.

Left alone, our father prowls the house, thumping into furniture, rummaging in the kitchen, slamming doors, turning the pages of the newspaper with a savage crackle, muttering back at the late-night drivel from television. The roof might fly off, the walls might buckle from the pressure of his rage. Whatever my brother and sister and mother may be thinking on their own rumpled pillows, I lie there hating him, loving him, fearing him, knowing I have failed him. I tell myself he drinks to ease the ache that gnaws at his belly, an ache I must have caused by disappointing him somehow, a murderous ache I should be able to relieve by doing all my chores, earning A's in school, winning baseball games, fixing the broken washer and the burst pipes, bringing in the money to fill his empty wallet. He would not hide the green bottles in his toolbox, would not sneak off to the barn with a lump under his coat, would not fall asleep in the daylight, would not roar and fume, would not drink himself to death, if only I were perfect. 7

I am forty-four, and I know full well now that my father was an alcoholic, a man consumed by disease rather than by disappointment. What had seemed to me a private grief is in fact, of course, a public scourge. In the United States alone, some ten or fifteen million people share his ailment, and behind the doors they slam in fury or disgrace, countless other children tremble. I comfort myself with such knowledge, holding it against the throb of memory like an ice pack against a bruise. Other people have keener sources of grief: poverty, racism, rape, war. I do not wish to compete to determine who has suffered most. I am only trying to understand the corrosive mixture of helplessness, responsibility, and shame that I learned to feel as the son of an alcoholic. I realize now that I did not cause my father's illness, nor could I have cured it. Yet for all this grown-up knowledge, I am still ten years old, my own son's age, and as that boy I struggle in guilt and confusion to save my father from pain. 8

Consider a few of our synonyms for *drunk*: tipsy, tight, pickled, soused, and plowed; stoned and stewed, lubricated and inebriated, juiced and sluiced; three sheets to the wind, in your cups, out of your mind, under the table; lit up, tanked up, wiped out; besotted, blotto, bombed, and buzzed; plastered, polluted, putrefied; loaded or looped, boozy, woozy, fuddled, or smashed; crocked and shit-faced, corked and pissed, snockered and sloshed. 9

It is a mostly humorous lexicon, as the lore that deals with drunks—in jokes and cartoons, in plays, films, and television skits—is largely comic. Aunt Ma- 10 tilda nips elderberry wine from the sideboard and burps politely during supper. Uncle Fred slouches to the table glassy-eyed, wearing a lampshade for a hat and murmuring, "Candy is dandy, but liquor is quicker." Inspired by cocktails, Mrs. Somebody recounts the events of her day in a fuzzy dialect, while Mr. Somebody nibbles her ear and croons a bawdy song. On the sofa with Boyfriend, Daughter Somebody giggles, licking gin from her lips, and loosens the bows in her hair. Junior knocks back some brews with his chums at the Leopard Lounge and stumbles home to the wrong house, wonders foggily why he cannot locate his pajamas, and crawls naked into bed with the ugliest girl in school. The family dog slurps from a neglected martini and wobbles to the nursery, where he vomits in Baby's shoe.

It is all great fun. But if in the audience you notice a few laughing faces turn   11
grim when the drunk lurches onstage, don't be surprised, for these are the children of alcoholics. Over the grinning mask of Dionysus, the leering face of Bacchus, these children cannot help seeing the bloated features of their own parents. Instead of laughing, they wince, they mourn. Instead of celebrating the drunk as one freed from constraints, they pity him as one enslaved. They refuse to believe *in vino veritas*, having seen their befuddled parents skid away from truth toward folly and oblivion. And so these children bite their lips until the lush staggers into the wings.

My father, when drunk, was neither funny nor honest; he was pathetic, fright-   12
ening, deceitful. There seemed to be a leak in him somewhere, and he poured in booze to keep from draining dry. Like a torture victim who refuses to squeal, he would never admit that he had touched a drop, not even in his last year, when he seemed to be dissolving in alcohol before our very eyes. I never knew him to lie about anything, ever, except about this one ruinous fact. Drowsy, clumsy, unable to fix a bicycle tire, balance a grocery sack, or walk across a room, he was stripped of his true self by drink. In a matter of minutes, the contents of a bottle could transform a brave man into a coward, a buddy into a bully, a gifted athlete and skilled carpenter and shrewd businessman into a bumbler. No dictionary of synonyms for *drunk* would soften the anguish of watching our prince turn into a frog.

Father's drinking became the family secret. While growing up, we children   13
never breathed a word of it beyond the four walls of our house. To this day, my brother and sister rarely mention it, and then only when I press them. I did not confess the ugly, bewildering fact to my wife until his wavering and slurred speech forced me to. Recently, on the seventh anniversary of my father's death, I asked my mother if she ever spoke of his drinking to friends. "No, no, never," she replied hastily. "I couldn't bear for anyone to know."

The secret bores under the skin, gets in the blood, into the bone, and stays   14
there. Long after you have supposedly been cured of malaria, the fever can flare up, the tremors can shake you. So it is with the fevers of shame. You swallow the bitter quinine of knowledge, and you learn to feel pity and compassion toward the drinker. Yet the shame lingers and, because of it, anger.

For a long stretch of my childhood we lived on a military reservation in Ohio,   15
an arsenal where bombs were stored underground in bunkers and vintage airplanes burst into flames and unstable artillery shells boomed nightly at the dump.

We had the feeling, as children, that we played within a minefield, where a heedless footfall could trigger an explosion. When Father was drinking, the house, too, became a minefield. The least bump could set off either parent.

The more he drank, the more obsessed Mother became with stopping him. 16 She hunted for bottles, counted the cash in his wallet, sniffed at his breath. Without meaning to snoop, we children blundered left and right into damning evidence. On afternoons when he came home from work sober, we flung ourselves at him for hugs and felt against our ribs the telltale lump in his coat. In the barn we tumbled on the hay and heard beneath our sneakers the crunch of broken glass. We tugged open a drawer in his workbench, looking for screwdrivers or crescent wrenches, and spied a gleaming six-pack among the tools. Playing tag, we darted around the house just in time to see him sway on the rear stoop and heave a finished bottle into the woods. In his good-night kiss we smelled the cloying sweetness of Clorets, the mints he chewed to camouflage his dragon's breath.

I can summon up that kiss right now by recalling Theodore Roethke's lines 17 about his own father:

> The whiskey on your breath
> Could make a small boy dizzy;
> But I hung on like death:
> Such waltzing was not easy.

Such waltzing was hard, terribly hard, for with a boy's scrawny arms I was trying to hold my tipsy father upright.

For years, the chief source of those incriminating bottles and cans was a grimy 18 store a mile from us, a cinderblock place called Sly's, with two gas pumps outside and a mangy dog asleep in the window. Inside, on rusty metal shelves or in wheezing coolers, you could find pop and Popsicles, cigarettes, potato chips, canned soup, raunchy postcards, fishing gear, Twinkies, wine, and beer. When Father drove anywhere on errands, Mother would send us along as guards, warning us not to let him out of our sight. And so with one or more of us on board, Father would cruise up to Sly's, pump a dollar's worth of gas or plump the tires with air, and then, telling us to wait in the car, he would head for the doorway.

Dutiful and panicky, we cried, "Let us go with you!"   19

"No," he answered. "I'll be back in two shakes."   20

"Please!"   21

"No!" he roared. "Don't you budge or I'll jerk a knot in your tails!"   22

So we stayed put, kicking the seats, while he ducked inside. Often, when he 23 had parked the car at a careless angle, we gazed in through the window and saw Mr. Sly fetching down from the shelf behind the cash register two green pints of Gallo wine. Father swigged one of them right there at the counter, stuffed the other in his pocket, and then out he came, a bulge in his coat, a flustered look on his reddened face.

Because the mom and pop who ran the dump were neighbors of ours, living 24 just down the tar-blistered road, I hated them all the more for poisoning my father. I wanted to sneak in their store and smash the bottles and set fire to the place. I also hated the Gallo brothers, Ernest and Julio, whose jovial faces beamed from the labels of their wine, labels I would find, torn and curled, when I burned the trash. I noted the Gallo brothers' address in California and studied the road atlas to see how far that was from Ohio, because I meant to go out there and tell Ernest and Julio what they were doing to my father, and then, if they showed no mercy, I would kill them.

While growing up on the back roads and in the country schools and cramped   25
Methodist churches of Ohio and Tennessee, I never heard the word *alcoholic*, never happened across it in books or magazines. In the nearby towns, there were no addiction-treatment programs, no community mental-health centers, no Alcoholics Anonymous chapters, no therapists. Left alone with our grievous secret, we had no way of understanding Father's drinking except as an act of will, a deliberate folly or cruelty, a moral weakness, a sin. He drank because he chose to, pure and simple. Why our father, so playful and competent and kind when sober, would choose to ruin himself and punish his family we could not fathom.

Our neighborhood was high on the Bible, and the Bible was hard on drunk-   26
ards. "Woe to those who are heroes at drinking wine and valiant men in mixing strong drink," wrote Isaiah. "The priest and the prophet reel with strong drink, they are confused with wine, they err in vision, they stumble in giving judgment. For all tables are full of vomit, no place is without filthiness." We children had seen those fouled tables at the local truck stop where the notorious boozers hung out, our father occasionally among them. "Wine and new wine take away the understanding," declared the prophet Hosea. We had also seen evidence of that in our father, who could multiply seven-digit numbers in his head when sober but when drunk could not help us with fourth-grade math. Proverbs warned: "Do not look at wine when it is red, when it sparkles in the cup and goes down smoothly. At the last it bites like a serpent and stings like an adder. Your eyes will see strange things, and your mind utter perverse things." Woe, woe.

Dismayingly often, these biblical drunkards stirred up trouble for their own   27
kids. Noah made fresh wine after the flood, drank too much of it, fell asleep without any clothes on, and was glimpsed in the buff by his son Ham, whom Noah promptly cursed. In one passage—it was so shocking we had to read it under our blankets with flashlight—the patriarch Lot fell down drunk and slept with his daughters. The sins of the father set their children's teeth on edge.

Our ministers were fond of quoting St. Paul's pronouncement that drunkards   28
would not inherit the kingdom of God. These grave preachers assured us the wine referred to in the Last Supper was in fact grape juice. Bible and sermons and hymns combined to give us the impression that Moses should have brought down from the mountain another stone tablet, bearing the Eleventh Commandment: Thou shalt not drink.

The scariest and most illuminating Bible story apropos of drunkards was the   29
one about the lunatic and the swine. We knew it by heart: When Jesus climbed out of his boat one day, this lunatic came charging up from the graveyard, stark naked and filthy, frothing at the mouth, so violent that he broke the strongest chains. Nobody would go near him. Night and day for years, this madman had been wailing among the tombs and bruising himself with stones. Jesus took one look at him

and said, "Come out of the man, you unclean spirits!" for he could see that the lunatic was possessed by demons. Meanwhile, some hogs were conveniently rooting nearby. "If we have to come out," begged the demons, "at least let us go into those swine." Jesus agreed, the unclean spirits entered the hogs, and the hogs raced straight off a cliff and plunged into a lake. Hearing the story in Sunday school, my friends thought mainly of the pigs. (How big a splash did they make? Who paid for the lost pork?) But I thought of the redeemed lunatic, who bathed himself and put on clothes and calmly sat at the feet of Jesus, restored—so the Bible said—to "his right mind."

When drunk, our father was clearly in his wrong mind. He became a stranger, as fearful to us as any graveyard lunatic, not quite frothing at the mouth but fierce enough, quick-tempered, explosive; or else he grew maudlin and weepy, which frightened us nearly as much. In my boyhood despair, I reasoned that maybe he wasn't to blame for turning into an ogre: Maybe, like the lunatic, he was possessed by demons.   30

If my father was indeed possessed, who would exorcise him? If he was a sinner, who would save him? If he was ill, who would cure him? If he suffered, who would ease his pain? Not ministers or doctors, for we could not bring ourselves to confide in them; not the neighbors, for we pretended they had never seen him drunk; not Mother, who fussed and pleaded but could not budge him; not my brother and sister, who were only kids. That left me. It did not matter that I, too, was only a child, and a bewildered one at that. I could not excuse myself.   31

On first reading a description of delirium tremens—in a book on alcoholism I smuggled from a university library—I thought immediately of the frothing lunatic and the frenzied swine. When I read stories or watched films about grisly metamorphoses—Dr. Jekyll becoming Mr. Hyde, the mild husband changing into a werewolf, the kindly neighbor inhabited by a brutal alien—I could not help but see my own father's mutation from sober to drunk. Even today, knowing better, I am attracted by the demonic theory of drink, for when I recall my father's transformation, the emergence of his ugly second self, I find it easy to believe in being possessed by unclean spirits. We never knew which version of Father would come home from work, the true or the tainted, nor could we guess how far down the slope toward cruelty he would slide.   32

How far a man *could* slide we gauged by observing our back-road neighbors— the out-of-work miners who had dragged their families to our corner of Ohio from the desolate hollows of Appalachia, the tightfisted farmers, the surly mechanics, the balked and broken men. There was, for example, whiskey-soaked Mr. Jenkins, who beat his wife and kids so hard we could hear their screams from the road. There was Mr. Lavo the wino, who fell asleep smoking time and again, until one night his disgusted wife bundled up the children and went outside and left him in his easy chair to burn; he awoke on his own, staggered out coughing into the yard, and pounded her flat while the children looked on and the shack turned to ash. There was the truck driver, Mr. Simpson, who tripped over his son's tricycle one night while drunk and got mad, jumped into his semi, and drove away, shifting   33 through the dozen gears, and never came back. We saw the bruised children of these fathers clump onto our school bus, we saw the abandoned children huddle in the pews at church, we saw the stunned and battered mothers begging for help at our doors.

Our own father never beat us, and I don't think he beat Mother, but he threat-   34
ened often. The Old Testament Yahweh was not more terrible in His rage. Eyes blazing, voice booming, Father would pull out his belt and swear to give us a whip-ping, but he never followed through, never needed to, because we could imagine it so vividly. He shoved us, pawed us with the back of his hand, not to injure, just to clear a space. I can see him grabbing Mother by the hair as she cowers on a chair during a nightly quarrel. He twists her neck back until she gapes up at him, and then he lifts over her skull a glass quart bottle of milk, the milk spilling down his forearm, and he yells at her, "Say just one more word, one goddamn word, and I'll shut you up!" I fear she will prick him with her sharp tongue, but she is terrified into silence, and so am I, and the leaking bottle quivers in the air, and milk seeps through the red hair of my father's uplifted arm, and the entire scene is there to this moment, the head jerked back, the club raised.

When the drink made him weepy, Father would pack, kiss each of us children   35
on the head, and announce from the front door that he was moving out. "Where to?" we demanded, fearful each time that he would leave for good, as Mr. Simpson had roared away for good in his diesel truck. "Someplace where I won't get hounded every minute," Father would answer, his jaw quivering. He stabbed a look at Mother, who might say "Don't run into the ditch before you get there," or "Good riddance," and then he would slink away. Mother watched him go with arms crossed over her chest, her face closed like the lid on a box of snakes. We children bawled. Where could he go? To the truck stop, that den of iniquity? To one of those dark, ratty flophouses in town? Would he wind up sleeping under a railroad bridge or on a park bench or in a cardboard box, mummied in rags like the bums we had seen on our trips to Cleveland and Chicago? We bawled and bawled, wondering if he would ever come back.

He always did come back, a day or a week later, but each time there was a   36
sliver less of him.

In Kafka's *Metamorphosis*, which opens famously with Gregor Samsa waking   37
up from uneasy dreams to find himself transformed into an insect, Gregor's family keep reassuring themselves that things will be just fine again "when he comes back to us." Each time alcohol transformed our father we held out the same hope, that he would really and truly come back to us, our authentic father, the tender and playful and competent man, and then all things would be fine. We had grounds for such hope. After his tearful departures and chapfallen returns, he would some-times go weeks, even months, without drinking. Those were glad times. Every day without the furtive glint of bottles, every meal without a fight, every bedtime with-out sobs encouraged us to believe that such bliss might go on forever.

Mother was fooled by such a hope all during the forty-odd years she knew   38
Greeley Ray Sanders. Soon after she met him in a Chicago delicatessen on the eve of World War II and fell for his butter-melting Mississippi drawl and his wavy red hair, she learned that he drank heavily. But then so did a lot of men. She would

soon coax or scold him into breaking the nasty habit. She would point out to him how ugly and foolish it was, this bleary drinking, and then he would quit. He refused to quit during their engagement, however, still refused during the first years of marriage, refused until my older sister came along. The shock of fatherhood sobered him, and he remained sober through my birth at the end of the war and right on through until we moved in 1951 to the Ohio arsenal. The arsenal had more than its share of alcoholics, drug addicts, and other varieties of escape artists. There I turned six and started school and woke into a child's flickering awareness, just in time to see my father begin sneaking swigs in the garage.

He sobered up again for most of a year at the height of the Korean War, to   39
celebrate the birth of my brother. But aside from that dry spell, his only breaks from drinking before I graduated from high school were just long enough to raise and then dash our hopes. Then during the fall of my senior year—the time of the Cuban Missile Crisis, when it seemed that the nightly explosions at the munitions dump and the nightly rages in our household might spread to engulf the globe— Father collapsed. His liver, kidneys, and heart all conked out. The doctors saved him, but only by a hair. He stayed in the hospital for weeks, going through a withdrawal so terrible that Mother would not let us visit him. If he wanted to kill himself, the doctors solemnly warned him, all he had to do was hit the bottle again. One binge would finish him.

Father must have believed them, for he stayed dry the next fifteen years. It   40
was an answer to prayer, Mother said, it was a miracle. I believed it was a reflex of fear, which he sustained over the years through courage and pride. He knew a man could die from drink, for his brother Roscoe had. We children never laid eyes on doomed Uncle Roscoe, but in the stories Mother told us he became a fairy-tale figure, like a boy who took the wrong turn in the woods and was gobbled up by the wolf.

The fifteen-year dry spell came to an end with Father's retirement in the   41
spring of 1978. Like many men, he gave up his identity along with his job. One day he was a boss at the factory, with a brass plate on his door and a reputation to uphold; the next day he was a nobody at home. He and Mother were leaving Ontario, the last of the many places to which his job had carried them, and they were moving to a new house in Mississippi, his childhood stomping ground. As a boy in Mississippi, Father sold Coca-Cola during dances while the moonshiners peddled their brew in the parking lot; as a young blade, he fought in bars and in the ring, winning a state Golden Gloves championship; he gambled at poker, hunted pheasant, raced motorcycles and cars, played semiprofessional baseball, and, along with all his buddies—in the Black Cat Saloon, behind the cotton gin, in the woods—he drank hard. It was a perilous youth to dream of recovering.

After his final day of work, Mother drove on ahead with a car full of begonias   42
and violets, while Father stayed behind to oversee the packing. When the van was loaded, the sweaty movers broke open a six-pack and offered him a beer.

"Let's drink to retirement!" they crowed. "Let's drink to freedom! to fishing!   43
hunting! loafing! Let's drink to a guy who's going home!"

At least I imagine some such words, for that is all I can do, imagine, and I see   44
Father's hand trembling in midair as he thinks about the fifteen sober years and about the doctor's warning, and he tells himself, *Goddamnit, I am a free man*, and

Why can't a free man drink one beer after a lifetime of hard work? and I see his arm reaching, his fingers closing, the can tilting to his lips. I even supply a label for the beer, a swaggering brand that promises on television to deliver the essence of life. I watch the amber liquid pour down his throat, the alcohol steal into his blood, the key turn in his brain.

Soon after my parents moved back to Father's treacherous stomping ground, 45 my wife and I visited them in Mississippi with our four-year-old daughter. Mother had been too distraught to warn me about the return of the demons. So when I climbed out of the car that bright July morning and saw my father napping in the hammock, I felt uneasy, and when he lurched upright and blinked his bloodshot eyes and greeted us in a syrupy voice, I was hurled back into childhood.

"What's the matter with Papaw?" our daughter asked.   46

"Nothing," I said. "Nothing!"   47

Like a child again, I pretended not to see him in his stupor, and behind my 48 phony smile I grieved. On that visit and on the few that remained before his death, once again I found bottles in the workbench, bottles in the woods. Again his hands shook too much for him to run a saw, to make his precious miniature furniture, to drive straight down back roads. Again he wound up in the ditch, in the hospital, in jail, in the treatment center. Again he shouted and wept. Again he lied. "I never touched a drop," he swore. "Your mother's making it up."

I no longer fancied I could reason with the men whose names I found on the 49 bottles—Jim Beam, Jack Daniel's—but I was able now to recall the cold statistics about alcoholism: ten million victims, fifteen million, twenty. And yet, in spite of my age, I reacted in the same blind way as I had in childhood, by vainly seeking to erase through my efforts whatever drove him to drink. I worked on their place twelve and sixteen hours a day, in the swelter of Mississippi summers, digging ditches, running electrical wires, planting trees, mowing grass, building sheds, as though what nagged at him was some list of chores, as though by taking his worries upon my shoulders I could redeem him. I was flung back into boyhood, acting as though my father would not drink himself to death if only I were perfect.

I failed of perfection; he succeeded in dying. To the end, he considered him- 50 self not sick but sinful. "Do you want to kill yourself?" I asked him. "Why not?" he answered. "Why the hell not? What's there to save?" To the end, he would not speak about his feelings, would not or could not give a name to the beast that was devouring him.

In silence, he went rushing off the cliff. Unlike the biblical swine, however, he 51 left behind a few of the demons to haunt his children. Life with him and the loss of him twisted us into shapes that will be familiar to other sons and daughters of alcoholics. My brother became a rebel, my sister retreated into shyness, I played the stalwart and dutiful son who would hold the family together. If my father was unstable, I would be a rock. If he squandered money on drink, I would pinch every penny. If he wept when drunk—and only when drunk—I would not let myself weep at all. If he roared at the Little League umpire for calling my pitches balls, I would throw nothing but strikes. Watching him flounder and rage, I came to dread the loss of control. I would go through life without making anyone mad. I vowed never to put in my mouth or veins any chemical that would banish my everyday self. I would never make a scene, never lash out at the ones I loved, never hurt a soul. Through hard work, relentless work, I would achieve something dazzling—in the classroom, on the the basketball court, in the science lab, in the pages of books—and my achievement would distract the world's eyes from his humiliation. I would become a worthy sacrifice, and the smoke of my burning would please God.

It is far easier to recognize these twists in my character than to undo them.   52
Work has become an addiction for me, as drink was an addiction for my father. Knowing this, my daughter gave me a placard for the wall: WORKAHOLIC. The labor is endless and futile, for I can no more redeem myself through work that I could redeem my father. I still panic in the face of other people's anger, because his drunken temper was so terrible. I shrink from causing sadness or disappoint- ment even to strangers, as though I were still concealing the family shame. I still notice every twitch of emotion in those faces around me, having learned as a child to read the weather in faces, and I blame myself for their least pang of unhappiness or anger. In certain moods I blame myself for everything. Guilt burns like acid in my veins.

I am moved to write these pages now because my own son, at the age of ten, is   53
taking on himself the griefs of the world, and in particular the griefs of his father. He tells me that when I am gripped by sadness, he feels responsible; he feels there must be something he can do to spring me from depression, to fix my life. And that crushing sense of responsibility is exactly what I felt at the age of ten in the face of my father's drinking. My son wonders if I, too, am possessed. I write, therefore, to drag into the light what eats at me—the fear, the guilt, the shame—so that my own children may be spared.

I still shy away from nightclubs, from bars, from parties where the solvent is   54
alcohol. My friends puzzle over this, but it is no more peculiar than for a man to shy away from the lions' den after seeing his father torn apart. I took my own first drink at the age of twenty-one, half a glass of burgundy. I knew the odds of my becoming an alcoholic were four times higher than for the children of nonalcoholic fathers. So I sipped warily.

I still do—once a week, perhaps, a glass of wine, a can of beer, nothing stron-   55
ger, nothing more. I listen for the turning of a key in my brain.

Rhetorical Focus

1. Both of Sanders's essays begin with his father's death, but they emphasize different things. If Sanders had written a beginning paragraph combining features of both openings, what would it look like? Both of the essays end by noting the effect that Sanders's father ultimately had on him, but in each, the emphasis is different. If Sanders had written a concluding para- graph combining features of both endings, what would it look like?

2. Early in this essay (paragraph 2), beginning with the words "In the peren- nial present of memory," Sanders writes six paragraphs that recall the past but use the present tense. Is this technique effective? Why do you think Sanders uses it?

3. Are there stylistic similarities between the two essays, despite their differ- ent emphases? For example, do they feature the same amount of concrete detail? Similar kinds of sentence structures?

Thematic Focus

1. In what ways does Sanders elaborate the pun in his title? That is, how does he show not only that his father was physically "under the influence" when drunk, but that Sanders and his own children have been psychologically influenced by his father's alcoholism?

2. More explicitly than in the earlier essay, Sanders here treats his father as an example of a larger social problem. He refers not only to his father's alco- holism, but also to the general problem of excessive drinking in American society. What is a reader justified in concluding about drinking in America from Sanders's descriptions of his father and other alcoholics?

3. Sanders ends his earlier essay with the word *true*, as if he wants to empha- size that he is committed to honesty as a writer. Does the later essay sug- gest that the earlier one is actually false? Should Sanders have mentioned his father's alcoholism in the earlier one and his father's love of tools in the second? What do your answers to these questions imply about the act of "re-vision"?

Suggestions for Writing

1. Do you find Sanders's two essays equally convincing, or is one more con- vincing for you than the other? Write an essay in which you state your answer to this question. Support your answer with specific references to each text.

2. Identify a psychological inheritance or influence you have received from someone. In explaining this quality, tell how the person showed it, as well as how you yourself do. Aim for Sanders's vividness in describing both the person's behavior and yours.

3. Define what *revision* is coming to mean for you. In explaining your defini- tion, tell what you infer from Sanders's act of "revision." Identify, too, what you thought about as you revised drafts of a particular writing assignment.

RELATIONSHIPS WITH MOTHERS

The next selections continue to focus on the theme of parental influence, this time addressing the influence of mothers on their children's development as adults. Historically, our society has been so anxious to maintain particular images of moth- ers that you may find it hard to approach this subject without certain cultural assumptions. Like other societies, Americans have often celebrated the role of the mother, to the extent of viewing it as natural for women and crucial for the maintenance of thriving families. As Loren Eiseley observes here, to a significant extent, ours has been a "mother-worshipping culture." At the same time, both vulgar and sophisticated versions of psychological theory have often blamed mothers for excessively controlling their children. In the mid-1950s, for example, Philip Wylie coined the term *momism* to suggest that Americans were in danger of being overwhelmed by their mothers. Furthermore, maternal activities have usually not been compensated in the same way that work outside the home has been. With these historical facts in mind, recently feminist theory has taken a variety of positions on motherhood. Some feminists emphasize that it has oppressed women; some make proposals for integrating mothering activities with career pursuits; some call for mothers to be paid for their work; some analyze the different conditions of motherhood in different cultures; and some explore the potential virtues of "maternal thinking" (to use a term from the philosopher Sara Ruddick).

The subject of motherhood raises so many questions about women's lives that we deal with it again in our unit on gender. This constellation examines the relationship of mothers and children by presenting two autobiographical texts, both by literary artists who, interestingly enough, were also trained in anthropology. Their memoirs have a similar focus but differ in significant ways. Zora Neale Hurston and Loren Eiseley both examine their mothers' impact on their journeys into adulthood, and both use the term *wandering* as they describe the disorientation of these journeys. Their attitudes toward their mothers sharply contrast, however. Hurston reports that she adored her mother and started "wandering" only after her mother's death. Eiseley reports that in various ways he tried to avoid his mother; he even suggests that he is still "wandering" and "running" from her as he writes.

As with the other constellations on family relationships, this one suggests that they are very much a matter for interpretation. For one thing, the two authors are writing about their childhoods from the vantage point of adults, drawing on their experiences and reflections from the years in between. Both also impart a mystical air to their writing, implying that they have yet to figure out some aspects of their life. Both insistently play with metaphor in describing their life, as if to emphasize that it cannot simply be literally rendered. Moreover, they do not rely on strict chronological order as they recount their personal histories. In particular, Eiseley jumps back and forth between episodes, calling attention to the shifting role of memory as he analyzes his mother's role in his life. As you read these texts, you will undoubtedly think of your personal life: your relationship with your mother and, perhaps, your own experience being a mother. Think also about the rhetorical strategies that various interpretations of motherhood warrant.

Wandering

Zora Neale Hurston

Trained at Columbia University as an anthropologist, Zora Neale Hurston (1891–1960) published African-American folklore she collected in the American South and the Caribbean. During the 1930s and 1940s, she was also widely known for her novels, essays, and autobiography. Yet her career declined thereafter, and she died in poverty. Interest in her revived during the 1970s, partly because she inspired contemporary African-American woman writers such as Alice Walker. Much of her work has now been reprinted, with her 1937 novel *Their Eyes Were Watching God* being taught in many literature courses.

The following is a chapter from Hurston's 1942 autobiography *Dust Tracks on a Road*, which was her most commercially successful book while she was alive. It does not model historical precision. For example, it obscures important relationships in Hurston's adult life, falsifies her age, and barely acknowledges whites' historic mistreatment of African-Americans. Critics have admired, however, sections such as "Wandering," which deal with Hurston's childhood in the all-black town of Eatonville, Florida. The book interestingly reflects, too, its author's lifelong desire to affirm African-American folk culture.

Reflections Before Reading

What sorts of events make children enter the adult world? What might they lose or gain when they do? How might mothers be involved in this process? In the following selection, Hurston is clearly trying to interpret events of her youth. Are there things about your childhood or early adulthood that you have yet to figure out? Hurston uses the term *wandering* to label what happened to her after her mother's death. Have you ever been in a phase of your life where this term applied? If so, what caused your wandering? What did it entail?

I knew that Mama was sick. She kept getting thinner and thinner and her chest   1
cold never got any better. Finally, she took to bed.

She had come home from Alabama that way. She had gone back to her old   2
home to be with her sister during her sister's last illness. Aunt Dinky had lasted on
for two months after Mama got there, and so Mama had stayed on till the last.

It seems that there had been other things there that worried her. Down un-   3
derneath, it appeared that Grandma had never quite forgiven her for the move she
had made twenty-one years before in marrying Papa. So that when Mama suggested that the old Potts place be sold so that she could bring her share back with
her to Florida, her mother, urged on by Uncle Bud, Mama's oldest brother, refused. Not until Grandma's head was cold, was an acre of the place to be sold. She
had long since quit living on it, and it was pretty well run down, but she wouldn't,
that was all. Mama could just go on back to that yaller rascal she had married like
she came. I do not think that the money part worried Mama as much as the injustice and spitefulness of the thing.

Then Cousin Jimmie's death seemed to come back on Mama during her visit.   4
How he came to his death is an unsolved mystery. He went to a party and started
home. The next morning his headless body was found beside the railroad track.
There was no blood, so the train couldn't have killed him. This had happened
before I was born. He was said to have been a very handsome young man, and very
popular with the girls. He was my mother's favorite nephew and she took it hard.
She had probably numbed over her misery, but going back there seemed to
freshen up her grief. Some said that he had been waylaid by three other young
fellows and killed in a jealous rage. But nothing could be proved. It was whispered
that he had been shot in the head by a white man unintentionally, and then beheaded to hide the wound. He had been shot from ambush, because his assailant
mistook him for a certain white man. It was night. The attacker expected the white
man to pass that way, but not Jimmie. When he found out his mistake, he had
forced a certain Negro to help him move the body to the railroad track without the
head, so that it would look as if he had been run over by the train. Anyway, that is
what the Negro wrote back after he had moved to Texas years later. There was
never any move to prove the charge, for obvious reasons. Mama took the whole
thing very hard.

It was not long after Mama came home that she began to be less active. Then   5
she took to bed. I knew she was ailing, but she was always frail, so I did not take it
too much to heart. I was nine years old, and even though she had talked to me very
earnestly one night, I could not conceive of Mama actually dying. She had talked of
it many times.

That day, September 18th, she had called me and given me certain instruc-   6
tions. I was not to let them take the pillow from under her head until she was dead.
The clock was not to be covered, nor the looking-glass. She trusted me to see to it
that these things were not done. I promised her as solemnly as nine years could do,
that I would see to it.

What years of agony that promise gave me! In the first place, I had no idea that   7
it would be soon. But that same day near sundown I was called upon to set my will
against my father, the village dames and village custom. I know now that I could
not have succeeded.

I had left Mama and was playing outside for a little while when I noted a   8 number of women going inside Mama's room and staying. It looked strange. So I went on in. Papa was standing at the foot of the bed looking down on my mother, who was breathing hard. As I crowded in, they lifted up the bed and turned it around so that Mama's eyes would face the east. I thought that she looked to me as the head of the bed was reversed. Her mouth was slightly open, but her breathing took up so much of her strength that she could not talk. But she looked at me, or so I felt, to speak for her. She depended on me for a voice.

The Master-Maker in His making had made Old Death. Made him with big, 9
soft feet and square toes. Made him with a face that reflects the face of all things, but neither changes itself, nor is mirrored anywhere. Made the body of Death out of infinite hunger. Made a weapon for his hand to satisfy his needs. This was the morning of the day of the beginning of things.

But Death had no home and he knew it at once. 10

"And where shall I dwell in my dwelling?" Old Death asked, for he was already 11
old when he was made.

"You shall build you a place close to the living, yet far out of the sight of eyes. 12
Wherever there is a building, there you have your platform that comprehends the four roads of the winds. For your hunger, I give you the first and last taste of all things."

We had been born, so Death had had his first taste of us. We had built things, 13
so he had his platform in our yard.

And now, Death stirred from his platform in his secret place in our yard, and 14
came inside the house.

Somebody reached for the clock, while Mrs. Mattie Clarke put her hand to the 15
pillow to take it away.

"Don't!" I cried out. "Don't take the pillow from under Mama's head! She said 16
she didn't want it moved!"

I made to stop Mrs. Mattie, but Papa pulled me away. Others were trying to 17
silence me. I could see the huge drop of sweat collected in the hollow at Mama's elbow and it hurt me so. They were covering the clock and the mirror.

"Don't cover up that clock! Leave that looking-glass like it is! Lemme put 18
Mama's pillow back where it was!"

But Papa held me tight and the others frowned me down. Mama was still 19
rasping out the last morsel of her life. I think she was trying to say something, and I think she was trying to speak to me. What was she trying to tell me? What wouldn't I give to know! Perhaps she was telling me that it was better for the pillow to be moved so that she could die easy, as they said. Perhaps she was accusing me of weakness and failure in carrying out her last wish. I do no know. I shall never know.

Just then, Death finished his prowling through the house on his padded feet 20
and entered the room. He bowed to Mama in his way, and she made her manners and left us to act out our ceremonies over unimportant things.

I was to agonize over that moment for years to come. In the midst of play, in 21
wakeful moments after midnight, on the way home from parties, and even in the classroom during lectures. My thoughts would escape occasionally from their confines and stare me down.

Now, I know that I could not have had my way against the world. The world 22
we lived in required those acts. Anything else would have been sacrilege, and no

nine-year-old voice was going to thwart them. My father was with the mores. He had restrained me physically from outraging the ceremonies established for the dying. If there is any consciousness after death, I hope that Mama knows that I did my best. She must know how I have suffered for my failure.

But life picked me up from the foot of Mama's bed, grief, self-despisement and all, and set my feet in strange ways. That moment was the end of a phase in my life I was old before my time with grief of loss, of failure, and of remorse. No matter what the others did, my mother had put her trust in me. She had felt that I could and would carry out her wishes, and I had not. And then in that sunset time, I failed her. It seemed as she died that the sun went down on purpose to flee away from me.   23

That hour began my wanderings. Not so much in geography, but in time. Then not so much in time as in spirit.   24

Mama died at sundown and changed a world. That is, the world which had been built out of her body and her heart. Even the physical aspects fell apart with a suddenness that was startling.   25

My oldest brother was up in Jacksonville in school, and he arrived home after Mama had passed. By then, she had been washed and dressed and laid out on the ironing-board in the parlor.   26

Practically all of the village was in the front yard and on the porch, talking in low tones and waiting. They were not especially waiting for my brother Bob. They were doing that kind of waiting that people do around death. It is a kind of sipping up the drama of the thing. However, if they were asked, they would say it was the sadness of the occasion which drew them. In reality it is a kind of feast of the Passover.   27

Bob's grief was awful when he realized that he was too late. He could not conceive at first that nothing could be done to straighten things out. There was no ear for his excuse nor explanation—no way to ease what was in him. Finally it must have come to him that what he had inside, he must take with him wherever he went. Mama was there on the cooling board with the sheet draped over her blowing gently in the wind. Nothing there seemed to hear him at all.   28

There was my sister Sarah in the kitchen crying and trying to quiet Everett, who was just past two years old. She was crying and trying to make him hush at the same time. He was crying because he sensed the grief around him. And then, Sarah, who was fifteen, had been his nurse and he would respond to her mood, whatever it was. We were all grubby bales of misery, huddled about lamps.   29

I have often wished I had been old enough at the time to look into Papa's heart that night. If I could know what that moment meant to him, I could have set my compass towards him and been sure. I know that I did love him in a way, and that I admired many things about him. He had a poetry about him that I loved. That had made him a successful preacher. He could hit ninety-seven out of a hundred with a gun. He could swim Lake Maitland from Maitland to Winter Park, and no man in the village could put my father's shoulders to the ground. We were so certain of Papa's invincibility in combat that when a village woman scolded Everett for some misdemeanor, and told him that God would punish him, Everett, just two years old, reared back and told her, "He better not bother me. Papa will shoot Him down." He found out better later on, but that goes to show you how big our Papa   30 looked to us. We had seen him bring down bears and panthers with his gun, and chin the bar more times than any man in competing distance. He had to our knowledge licked two men who Mama told him had to be licked. All that part was just fine with me. But I was Mama's child. I knew that she had not always been happy, and I wanted to know just how sad he was that night.

I have repeatedly called up that picture and questioned it. Papa cried some too, as he moved in his awkward way about the place. From the kitchen to the front porch and back again. He kept saying, "Poor thing! She suffered so much." I do not know what he meant by that. It could have been love and pity for her suffering ending at last. It could have been remorse mixed with relief. The hard-driving force was no longer opposed to his easy-going pace. He could put his potentialities to sleep and be happy in the laugh of the day. He could do next year or never, what Mama would have insisted must be done today. Rome, the eternal city, meant two different things to my parents. To Mama, it meant, you must build it today so it could last through eternity. To Papa, it meant that you could plan to lay some bricks today and you have the rest of eternity to finish it. With all time, why hurry? God had made more time than anything else, anyway. Why act so stingy about it?   31

Then too, I used to notice how Mama used to snatch Papa. That is, he would start to put up an argument that would have been terrific on the store porch, but Mama would pitch in with a single word or a sentence and mess it all up. You could tell he was mad as fire with no words to blow it out with. He would sit over in the corner and cut his eyes at her real hard. He was used to being a hero on the store porch and in church affairs, and I can see how he must have felt to be always outdone around home. I know now that that is a griping thing to a man—not to be able to whip his woman mentally. Some women know how to give their man that conquesting feeling. My mother took her over-the-creek man and bare-knuckled him from brogans to broadcloth, and I am certain that he was proud of the change, in public. But in the house, he might have always felt over-the-creek, and because that was not the statue he had made for himself to look at he resented it. But then, you cannot blame my mother too much if she did not see him as his entranced congregations did. The one who makes the idols never worships them, however tenderly he might have molded the clay. You cannot have knowledge and worship at the same time. Mystery is the essence of divinity. Gods must keep their distances from men.   32

Anyway, the next day, Sam Moseley's span of fine horses, hitched to our wagon, carried my mother to Macedonia Baptist Church for the last time. The finality of the thing came to me fully when the earth began to thud on the coffin.   33

That night, all of Mama's children were assembled together for the last time on earth. The next day, Bob and Sarah went back to Jacksonville to school. Papa was away from home a great deal, so two weeks later I was on my way to Jacksonville, too. I was under age, but the school had agreed to take me in under the circumstances. My sister was to look after me, in a way.   34

The midnight train had to be waved down at Maitland for me. That would put me into Jacksonville in the daytime.   35

As my brother Dick drove the mile with me that night, we approached the 36
curve in the road that skirts Lake Catherine, and suddenly I saw the first picture of
my visions. I had seen myself upon that curve at night leaving the village home,
bowed down with grief that was more than common. As it all flashed back to me, I
started violently for a minute, then I moved closer beside Dick as if he could shield
me from those others that were to come. He asked me what was the matter, and I
said I thought I heard something moving down by the lake. He laughed at that, and
we rode on, the lantern showing the roadway, and me keeping as close to Dick as I
could. A little, humped-up, shabby-backed trunk was behind us in the buckboard.
I was on my way from the village, never to return to it as a real part of the town.

Jacksonville made me know that I was a little colored girl. Things were all 37
about the town to point this out to me. Streetcars and stores and then talk I heard
around the school. I was no longer among the white people whose homes I could
barge into with a sure sense of welcome. These white people had funny ways. I
could tell that even from a distance. I didn't get a piece of candy or a bag of crackers just for going into a store in Jacksonville as I did when I went into Galloway's or
Hill's at Maitland, or Joe Clarke's in Eatonville.

Around the school I was an awful bother. The girls complained that they 38
couldn't get a chance to talk without me turning up somewhere to be in the way. I
broke up many good "He said" conferences just by showing up. It was not my
intention to do so. What I wanted was for it to go full steam ahead and let me listen.
But that didn't seem to please. I was not in the "he said" class, and they wished I
would kindly please stay out of the way. My underskirt was hanging, for instance.
Why didn't I go some place and fix it? My head looked like a hoo-raw's nest. Why
didn't I go comb it? If I took time enough to match my stockings, I wouldn't have
time to be trying to listen in on grown folk's business. These venerable old ladies
were anywhere from fifteen to eighteen.

In the classroom I got along splendidly. The only difficulty was that I was rated 39
as sassy. I just had to talk back at established authority and that established authority hated backtalk worse than barbed-wire pie. My brother was asked to speak to
me in addition to a licking or two. But on the whole, things went along all right. My
immediate teachers were enthusiastic about me. It was the guardians of study-
hour and prayer meetings who felt that their burden was extra hard to bear.

School in Jacksonville was one of those twilight things. It was not dark, but it 40
lacked the bold sunlight that I craved. I worshipped two of my teachers and loved
gingersnaps with cheese, and sour pickles. But I was deprived of the loving pine,
the lakes, the wild violets in the woods and the animals I used to know. No more
holding down first base on the team with my brothers and their friends. Just a
jagged hole where my home used to be.

At times, the girls of the school were lined up two and two and taken for a 41
walk. On one of these occasions, I had an experience that set my heart to fluttering.
I saw a woman sitting on a porch who looked at a distance like Mama. Maybe it *was*
Mama! Maybe she was not dead at all. They had made some mistake. Mama had
gone off to Jacksonville and they thought that she was dead. The woman was sitting
in a rocking-chair just like Mama always did. It must be Mama! But before I came

abreast of the porch in my rigid place in line, the woman got up and went inside. I wanted to stop and go in. But I didn't even breathe my hope to anyone. I made up my mind to run away someday and find the house and let Mama know where I was. But before I did, the hope that the woman really was my mother passed. I accepted my bereavement.

Rhetorical Focus

1. Hurston extensively uses figurative language. Identify a few of her metaphors or turns of phrase that especially appeal to you. Explain why you like them.
2. Into what main parts can this chapter from Hurston's autobiography be divided? Does its focus shift, or does it tend to deal with the same theme?
3. Hurston seems interested in conveying the dramatic immediacy of her mother's death. In the middle of the chapter, however, she goes at some length back into the past, describing her parents' marriage. Is this leap back in time justified? Why or why not?

Thematic Focus

1. In what ways does the term *wandering* apply to this chapter?
2. In what ways does Hurston suggest that she is writing from the perspective of an adult, even though she is describing her youth?
3. Hurston refers at times to folklore and the supernatural. Note in particular the way she personifies death. Is this moment in her text effective for you as a modern reader, or is it simply too fantastic?

The Running Man

Loren Eiseley

Like Zora Neale Hurston, Loren Eiseley (1907–1977) was trained in
anthropology but also gained praise for his literary artistry. Unlike Hurston's,
his fame was sustained. Working mostly with the essay form, Eiseley made
topics in archaeology and natural history both haunting and accessible to a
general public. Collections of his essays include *The Immense Journey, The
Unexpected Universe*, and *Night Country*.

"The Running Man" is a chapter from Eiseley's 1975 autobiography *All
The Strange Hours: The Excavation of a Life*. Although by the time he wrote
it he had been acclaimed as a writer, archaeologist, and university professor,
the book is marked by personal despair. Often, it anticipates its author's
death, and in fact Eiseley did die two years later. The Colorado cabin
referred to at the start of this chapter is where the young Eiseley went to
recover from tuberculosis. You may find the selection difficult to follow, as it
abruptly flashes back and forth in time. Instead of methodically developing a
single idea, Eiseley stresses how turbulent his mind still is as he looks back
over the drama of his life. Instead of trying to figure out right away the
meanings and relationships of the events he recalls, consider what Eiseley's
method of writing reveals about his present state of mind. In particular, note
how this writer still struggles to confront distressing truths about his
relationship with his mother.

Reflections Before Reading

If someone described himself as a "running man," what might he be saying
about himself? Think of the term's possible meanings. In the following
selection, Eiseley expresses negative feelings toward his mother. Do you
think you can appreciate such a text, or are you prepared to dismiss it?

While I endured the months in the Colorado cabin, my mother, who had been   1
offered a safe refuge in the home of her sister, quarreled and fought with everyone. Finally, in her own inelegant way of putting things, she had "skipped town" to
work as a seamstress, domestic, or housekeeper upon farms. She was stone deaf. I
admired her courage, but I also knew by then that she was paranoid, neurotic and

Reprinted with permission of Charles Scribner's Sons, an imprint of Macmillan Publishing Company
from ALL THE STRANGE HOURS by Loren Eiseley. Copyright © 1975 Loren Eiseley.

unstable. What ensued on these various short-lived adventures I neither know to this day, nor wish to know.

It comes to me now in retrospect that I never saw my mother weep; it was her   2
gift to make others suffer instead. She was an untutored, talented artist and she left me, if anything, a capacity for tremendous visual impressions just as my father, a one-time itinerant actor, had in that silenced household of the stone age—a house of gestures, of daylong facial contortion—produced for me the miracle of words when he came home. My mother had once been very beautiful. It is only thus that I can explain the fatal attraction that produced me. I have never known how my parents chanced to meet.

There will be those to say, in this mother-worshipping culture, that I am harsh,   3
embittered. They will be quite wrong. Why should I be embittered? It is far too late. A month ago, after a passage of many years, I stood above her grave in a place called Wyuka. We, she and I, were close to being one now, lying like the skeletons of last year's leaves in a fence corner. And it was all nothing. Nothing, do you understand? All the pain, all the anguish. Nothing. We were, both of us, merely the debris life always leaves in its passing, like the maimed, discarded chicks in the hatchery trays—no more than that. For a little longer I would see and hear, but it was nothing, and to the world it would mean nothing.

I murmured to myself and tried to tell her this belatedly: Nothing, mama,   4
nothing. Rest. You could never rest. That was your burden. But now, sleep. Soon I will join you, although, forgive me, not here. Neither of us then would rest. I will go far to lie down; the time draws on; it is unlikely that I will return. Now you will understand, I said, touching the October warmth of the gravestone. It was for nothing. It has taken me all my life to grasp this one fact.

I am, it is true, wandering out of time and place. This narrative is faltering. To   5
tell the story of a life one is bound to linger above gravestones where memory blurs and doors can be pushed ajar, but never opened. Listen, or do not listen, it is all the same.

I am every man and no man, and will be so to the end. This is why I must tell   6
the story as I may. Not for the nameless name upon the page, not for the trails behind me that faded or led nowhere, not for the rooms at nightfall where I slept from exhaustion or did not sleep at all, not for the confusion of where I was to go, or if I had a destiny recognizable by any star. No, in retrospect it was the loneliness of not knowing, not knowing at all.

I was a child of the early century, American man, if the term may still be   7
tolerated. A creature molded of plains' dust and the seed of those who came west with the wagons. The names Corey, Hollister, Appleton, McKee lie strewn in graveyards from New England to the broken sticks that rotted quickly on the Oregon trail. That ancient contingent, with a lost memory and a gene or two from the Indian, is underscored by the final German of my own name.

How, among all these wanderers, should I have absorbed a code by which to   8
live? How should I have answered in turn to the restrained Puritan, and the long hatred of the beaten hunters? How should I have curbed the flaring rages of my maternal grandfather? How should—

But this I remember out of deepest childhood—I remember the mad Shep-   9
ards as I heard the name whispered among my mother's people. I remember the
pacing, the endless pacing of my parents after midnight, while I lay shivering in the
cold bed and tried to understand the words that passed between my mother and
my father.

Once, a small toddler, I climbed from bed and seized their hands, pleading   10
wordlessly for sleep, for peace, peace. And surprisingly they relented, even my
unfortunate mother. Terror, anxiety, ostracism, shame; I did not understand the
words, I learned only the feelings they represent. I repeat, I am an American
whose profession, even his life, is no more than a gambler's throw by the firelight
of a western wagon.

What have I to do with the city in which I live? Why, far to the west, does my   11
mind still leap to great windswept vistas of grass or the eternal snows of the Cas-
cades? Why does the sight of wolves in cages cause me to avert my eyes?

I will tell you only because something like this was at war in the heart of every   12
American at the final closing of the westward trails. One of the most vivid memories I retain from my young manhood is of the wagon ruts of the Oregon trail still
visible on the unplowed short-grass prairie. They stretched half a mile in width and
that was only yesterday. In his young years, my own father had carried a gun and
remembered the gamblers at the green tables in the cow towns. I dream inexplica-
bly at times of a gathering of wagons, of women in sunbonnets and black-garbed,
bewhiskered men. Then I wake and the scene dissolves.

I have strayed from the Shepards. It was a name to fear but this I did not learn   13
for a long time. I thought they were the people pictured in the family Bible, men
with white beards and long crooks with which they guided sheep.

In the house, when my father was away and my mother's people came to visit,   14
the Shepards were spoken of in whispers. They were the mad Shepards, I slowly
gathered, and they lay somewhere in my line of descent. When I was recalcitrant
the Shepards were spoken of and linked with my name.

In that house there was no peace, yet we loved each other fiercely. Perhaps   15
the adults were so far on into the midcountry that mistakes were never rectifiable,
flight disreputable. We were Americans of the middle border where the East was
forgotten and the one great western road no longer crawled with wagons.

A silence had fallen. I was one of those born into that silence. The bison had   16
perished; the Sioux no longer rode. Only the yellow dust of the cyclonic twisters
still marched across the landscape. I know the taste of that dust in my youth. I
knew it in the days of the dust bowl. No matter how far I travel it will be a fading
memory upon my tongue in the hour of my death. It is the taste of one dust only,
the dust of a receding ice age.

So much for my mother, the mad Shepards, and the land, but this is not all,   17
certainly not. Some say a child's basic character is formed by the time he is five. I
can believe it, I who begged for peace at four and was never blessed for long by its
presence.

The late W.H. Auden once said to me over a lonely little dinner in New York   18
before he left America, "What public event do you remember first from child-

hood?" I suppose the massive old lion was in his way encouraging a shy man to speak. Being of the same age we concentrated heavily upon the subject.

"I think for me, the Titanic disaster," he ventured thoughtfully.   19

"Of course," I said. "That would be 1912. She was a British ship and you British have always been a sea people."   20

"And you?" he questioned, holding me with his seamed features that always gave him the aspect of a seer.   21

I dropped my gaze. Was it 1914? Was it Pancho Villa's raid into New Mexico in 1916? All westerners remembered that. We wandered momentarily among dead men and long-vanished events. Auden waited patiently.   22

"Well," I ventured, for it was a long-held personal secret, "It was an escape, just an escape from prison."   23

"Your own?" Auden asked with a trace of humor.   24

"No," I began, "it was the same year as the Titanic sinking. He blew the gates with nitroglycerin. I was five years old, like you." Then I paused, considering the time. "You are right," I admitted hesitantly. "I was already old enough to know one should flee from the universe but I did not know where to run." I identified with the man as I always had across the years. "We never made it," I added glumly, and shrugged. "You see, there was a warden, a prison, and a blizzard. Also there was an armed posse and a death." I could feel the same snow driving beside the window in New York. "We never made it," I repeated unconsciously.   25

Auden sighed and looked curiously at me. I knew he was examining the pronoun. "There are other things that constitute a child," I added hastily. "Sandpiles, for example. There was a lot of building being done then on our street. I used to spend hours turning over the gravel. Why, I wouldn't know. Finally I had a box of pretty stones and some fossils. I prospected for hours alone. It was like today in book stores, old book stores," I protested defensively.   26

Auden nodded in sympathy.   27

"I still can't tell what started it," I went on. "I was groping, I think, childishly into time, into the universe. It was to be my profession but I never understood in the least, not till much later. No other child on the block wasted his time like that. I have never understood my precise motivation, never. For actually I was retarded in the reading of clock time. Was it because, in the things found in the sand, I was already lost and wandering instinctively—amidst the debris of vanished eras?"   28

"Ah," Auden said kindly, "who know these things?"   29

"Then there was the period of the gold crosses," I added. "Later, in another house, I had found a little bottle of liquid gilt my mother used on picture frames. I made some crosses, carefully whittled out of wood, and gilded them till they were gold. Then I placed them over an occasional dead bird I buried. Or, if I read of a tragic, heroic death like those of the war aces, I would put the clipping—I could read by then—into a little box and bury it with a gold cross to mark the spot. One day a mower in the empty lot beyond our backyard found the little cemetery and carried away all of my carefully carved crosses. I cried but I never told anyone. How could I? I had sought in my own small way to preserve the memory of what always in the end perishes: life and great deeds. I wonder what the man with the scythe did with my crosses. I wonder if they still exist."   30

"Yes, it was a child's effort against time," commented Auden. "And perhaps   31
the archaeologist is just that child grown up."

It was time for Auden to go. We stood and exchanged polite amenities while   32
he breathed in that heavy, sad way he had. "Write me at Oxford," he had said at the
door. But then there was Austria and soon he was gone. Besides one does not
annoy the great. Their burdens are too heavy. They listen kindly with their eyes far
away.

After that dinner I was glumly despondent for days. Finally a rage possessed   33
me, started unwittingly by that gentle, gifted man who was to die happily after a
recitation of his magnificent verse. For nights I lay sleepless in a New York hotel
room and all my memories in one gigantic catharsis were bad, spewed out of hell's
mouth, invoked by that one dinner, that one question, *what do you remember
first*? My God, they were all firsts. My brain was so scarred it was a miracle it had
survived in any fashion.

For example, I remembered for the first time a ruined farmhouse that I had   34
stumbled upon in my solitary ramblings after school. The road was one I had never
taken before. Rain was falling. Leaves lay thick on the abandoned road. Hesitantly
I approached and stood in the doorway. Plaster had collapsed from the ceiling;
wind mourned through the empty windows. I crunched tentatively over shattered
glass upon the floor. Papers lay scattered about in wild disorder. Some looked like
school examination papers. I picked one up in curiosity, but this, my own mature
judgment tells me, no one will believe. The name Eiseley was scrawled across the
cover. I was too shocked even to read the paper. No such family had ever been
mentioned by my parents. We had come from elsewhere. But here, in poverty like
our own, at the edge of town, had subsisted in this ruined house a boy with my own
name. Gingerly I picked up another paper. There was the scrawled name again,
not too unlike my own rough signature. The date was what might have been expected in that tottering clapboard house. It read from the last decade of the century before. They were gone, whoever they were, and another Eiseley was tiptoing
through the ruined house.

All that remained in a room that might in those days have been called the   35
parlor were two dice lying forlornly amidst the plaster, forgotten at the owners' last
exit. I picked up the pretty cubes uncertainly in the growing sunset through the
window, and on impulse cast them. I did not know how adults played, I merely cast
and cast again, making up my own game as I played. Sometimes I thought I won
and murmured to myself as children will. Sometimes I thought I lost, but I liked
the clicking sound before I rolled the dice. For what stakes did I play, with my
childish mind gravely considering? I think I was too naïve for such wishes as money
and fortune. I played, and here memory almost fails me. I think I played against
the universe as the universe was represented by the wind, stirring papers on the
plaster-strewn floor. I played against time, remembering my stolen crosses, I
played for adventure and escape. Then, clutching the dice, but not the paper with
my name, I fled frantically down the leaf-sodden unused road, never to return.
One of the dice survives still in my desk drawer. The time is sixty years away.

I have said that, though almost ostracized, we loved each other fiercely there   36
in the silent midcountry because there was nothing else to love, but was it true?

Was the hour of departure nearing? My mother lavished affection upon me in her tigerish silent way, giving me cakes when I should have had bread, attempting protection when I was already learning without brothers the grimness and realities of the street.

There had been the time I had just encountered the neighborhood bully. His   37
father's shoulder had been long distorted and rheumatic from the carrying of ice, and the elder son had just encountered the law and gone to prison. My antagonist had inherited his brother's status in the black Irish gang that I had heretofore succeeded in avoiding by journeying homeward from school through alleys and occasional thickets best known to me. But now brother replaced brother. We confronted each other on someone's lawn.

"Get down on your knees," he said contemptuously, knowing very well what   38
was coming. He had left me no way out. At that moment I hit him most inexpertly in the face, whereupon he began very scientifically, as things go in childish circles, to cut me to ribbons. My nose went first.

But then came the rage, the utter fury, summoned up from a thousand home   39
repressions, adrenalin pumped into me from my Viking grandfather, the throwback from the long ships, the berserk men who cared nothing for living when the mood came on them and they stormed the English towns. It comes to me now that the Irishman must have seen it in my eyes. By nature I was a quiet reclusive boy, but then I went utterly mad.

The smashed nose meant nothing, the scientific lefts and rights slicing up my   40
features meant nothing. I went through them with body punches and my eyes. When I halted we were clear across the street and the boy was gone, running for home. Typically I, too, turned homeward but not for succor. All I wanted was access to the outside watertap to wash off the blood cascading down my face. This I proceeded to do with the stoical indifference of one who expected no help.

As I went about finishing my task, my mother, peering through the curtains,   41
saw my face and promptly had hysterics. I turned away then. I always turned away. In the end, not too far distant, there would be an unbridgeable silence between us. Slowly I was leaving the world she knew and desperation marked her face.

I was old enough that I obeyed my father's injunction, reluctantly given out of   42
his own pain. "Your mother is not responsible, son. Do not cross her. Do you understand?" He held me with his eyes, a man I loved, who could have taken the poor man's divorce, desertion, at any moment. The easy way out. He stayed for me. That was the simple reason. He stayed when his own closest relatives urged him to depart.

I cast down my eyes. "Yes, father," I promised, but I could not say for always. I   43
think he knew it, but work and growing age were crushing him. We looked at each other in a blind despair.

I was like a rag doll upon whose frame skins were tightening in a distorted   44
crippling sequence; the toddler begging for peace between his parents at midnight; the lad suppressing fury till he shook with it; the solitary with his books; the projected fugitive running desperately through the snows of 1912; the dice player in the ruined house of his own name. Who was he, really? The man, so the psychologists would say, who had to be shaped or found in five years' time. I was inarticulate but somewhere, far forward, I would meet the running man; the peace I

begged for between my parents would, too often, leave me sleepless. There was another thing I could not name to Auden. The fact that I remember it at all reveals the beginning of adulthood and a sense of sin beyond my years.

To grow is a gain, an enlargement of life; is not this what they tell us? Yet it is also a departure. There is something lost that will not return. We moved one fall to Aurora, Nebraska, a sleepy country town near the Platte. A few boys gathered to watch the van unload. "Want to play?" ventured one. "Sure," I said. I followed them off over a rise to a creek bed. "We're making a cave in the bank," they explained. It was a great raw gaping hole obviously worked on by more than one generation of troglodytes. They giggled. "But first you've got to swear awful words. We'll all swear." 45

I was a silent boy, who went by reading. My father did not use these words. I was, in retrospect, a very funny little boy. I was so alone I did not know how to swear, but clamoring they taught me. I wanted to belong, to enter the troglodytes' existence. I shouted and mouthed the uncouth, unfamiliar words with the rest. 46

Mother was restless in the new environment, though again my father had wisely chosen a house at the edge of town. The population was primarily Scandinavian. She exercised arbitrary judgment. She drove good-natured, friendly boys away if they seemed big, and on the other hand encouraged slighter youngsters whom I had every reason to despise. 47

Finally, because it was farmland over which children roamed at will, mother's ability to keep track of my wide-ranging absences faltered. On one memorable occasion her driving, possessive restlessness passed out of bounds. She pursued us to a nearby pasture and in the rasping voice of deafness ordered me home. 48

My comrades of the fields stood watching. I was ten years old by then. I sensed my status in this gang was at stake. I refused to come. I had refused a parental order that was arbitrary and uncalled for and, in addition, I was humiliated. My mother was behaving in the manner of a witch. She could not hear, she was violently gesticulating without dignity, and her dress was somehow appropriate to the occasion. 49

Slowly I turned and looked at my companions. Their faces could not be read. They simply waited, doubtless waited for me to break the apron strings that rested lightly and tolerably upon themselves. And so in the end I broke my father's injunction; I ran, and with me ran my childish companions, over fences, tumbling down haystacks, chuckling, with the witch, her hair flying, her clothing disarrayed, stumbling after. Escape, escape, the first stirrings of the running man. Miles of escape. 50

Of course she gave up. Of course she never caught us. Walking home alone in the twilight I was bitterly ashamed. Ashamed for the violation of my promise to my father. Ashamed at what I had done to my savage and stone-deaf mother who could not grasp the fact that I had to make my way in a world unknown to her. Ashamed for the story that would penetrate the neighborhood. Ashamed for my own weakness. Ashamed, ashamed. 51

I do not remember a single teacher from that school, a single thing I learned there. Men were then drilling in a lot close to our house. I watched them every day. Finally they marched off. It was 1917. I was ten years old. I wanted to go. Either that or back to sleeping the troglodyte existence we had created in the cave bank. 52

But never home, not ever. Even today, as though in a far-off crystal, I can see my running, gesticulating mother and her distorted features cursing us. And they laughed, you see, my companions. Perhaps I, in anxiety to belong, did also. That is what I could not tell Auden. Only an unutterable savagery, my savagery at myself, scrawls it once and once only on this page.

Rhetorical Focus

1. In what ways does the organization of this chapter from Eiseley's autobiography relate to the chapter's title? For example, why does Eiseley defer the crucial last scene (in which he literally runs from his mother) until the very end?
2. Eiseley presents other episodes in this chapter, such as the destruction of his gold crosses, his discovery of the farmhouse, and his dinner with the poet W. H. Auden. Choose one of these scenes and explain its function in the chapter. What would have been lost if Eiseley had cut it?
3. What do you think is Eiseley's ultimate motive for writing this chapter? Do you believe that his motive differs from Hurston's in writing hers? Both of their last sentences have an air of finality. Do you think it justified in each case?

Thematic Focus

1. When Eiseley identifies himself with a larger regional heritage, on what aspects of it does he focus? Does this context for his behavior make sense to you? Why or why not?
2. Is Eiseley's "running" in any way like Hurston's "wandering"? Note that he refers to "wandering" himself (paragraphs 5, 8).
3. Obviously Eiseley is not as warm toward his mother as Hurston is toward hers. Is the difference to Eiseley's discredit? Can you appreciate his perspective? What do your answers say about his contention that ours is a "mother-worshipping culture" (paragraph 3)?

Suggestion for Writing

1. Now that you have read Hurston's and Eiseley's accounts of their relationships with their mothers, explain the extent to which you ultimately sympathize with both authors. How much do you sympathize with each? In the end, do you find yourself able to sympathize equally with them? Support your reasoning with evidence from both texts.
2. Describe a time in your life when you very much sensed yourself "wandering" in search of your identity. This time may be the present. As part of your description, explain what issues this "wandering" involved, whom you were "wandering" from, and whether your "wandering" has ended.
3. Auden asked Eiseley, "What public event do you remember first from childhood?" (paragraph 18). Auden's own answer was the Titanic disaster.

Eiseley's answer was the prison break. Many of us from a later generation would answer the John Kennedy assassination. Write an essay in which you give your own answer to Auden's question, speculating at the same time about why you remember the particular event you do.

SINGLE-PARENT FAMILIES

We conclude this unit with a constellation focused on single-parent families, for they have become much more common in America than they previously were. Indeed, the traditional nuclear family with two parents has faded as an institution of our society, despite the central position it has long enjoyed in America's cultural mythology. Even when this model fit many American families, it did not fit all. Today, however, policy planners and other analysts are compelled to acknowledge the existence of single-parent families. As you read the following texts about particular ones, consider the causes and effects of our society's long investment in the two-parent model, as well as the social developments that have now made single-parent families more evident in American life.

One important aspect of this trend is that women head single-parent families much more often than men do. It should also be noted that many of these women struggle to help their families overcome poverty. Various analysts have even invoked the term *feminization of poverty* to indicate that the American poor increasingly consists of single mothers and other women. To help you ponder these specific realities, we include here a short story by Nicholasa Mohr, which depicts how a single mother draws on her willpower and Puerto Rican heritage to sustain her family amidst harsh urban living conditions. Because men also head single-parent families, we begin with Michael Dorris's nonfiction account of an occasion when, as a single father, he labored to please his adopted son. Besides similarly focusing on a single-parent family, the two texts both describe how a particular celebration affirmed its members' relationship. Dorris recalls trying to compete with other parents by making an elaborate cake for his son's birthday party at a child care center. Mohr describes her heroine's effort to make Thanksgiving joyous for her family despite their poverty. Think about the cultural forces and the personal character traits that these texts reveal through their respective celebrations. Think, too, about the similarities and differences in the ways that gender, ethnicity, and socioeconomic class figure in these stories. Like other texts in this unit, the ones here suggest that even if we prefer to think of our family relationships as self-contained, all of us should ponder the ways they reflect and interact with a larger social context.

The Train Cake

Michael Dorris

Michael Dorris (b. 1945) is a professor of anthropology and Native American studies at Dartmouth College. A member of the Modoc tribe, he has published *Native Americans: Five Hundred Years After*, as well as many articles on Native American life. He has also published a novel, *A Yellow Raft in Blue Water*, besides collaborating with his wife, Louise Erdrich, on the 1991 novel *The Crown of Columbus*. The following selection comes from Dorris's 1989 autobiographical work *The Broken Cord*, which won the National Book Critics Circle Award for nonfiction. The book focuses on Dorris's relationship with Adam, a Native American youth whom he adopted before his marriage, when he was 26 years old. From early childhood, Adam suffered seizures and various learning disabilities. Ultimately, Dorris realized that Adam's condition resulted from his mother's having drunk a great deal of alcohol, even while pregnant. As he reports this discovery in the book, Dorris also discusses the general problem of fetal alcohol syndrome on Indian reservations. Our excerpt here, however, which we call "The Train Cake," focuses on a single episode in Adam's youth, when Dorris did his best as a single parent to celebrate his son's birthday in style.

Reflections Before Reading

Why do you think there are many more families headed by a single woman than ones headed by a single man? Why might a single man choose to adopt a child? If you were a staff member at the adoption agency, would you be more cautious about letting a single man adopt a child than you would if the prospective parent were a single woman? Why or why not? Do you assume that a single man would face greater or other challenges as a parent than a single woman would? Why or why not?

. . . Adam was enrolled in what I assumed to be an enlightened day care cen-   1
ter, and I had thrown myself into the role of professional single parent. Still in my twenties, I was young enough to believe that all it took to juggle family and career was organization and good intent. I was aggressively confident, well versed in the

literature and jargon of child rearing, and prepared to quote statistics to prove that nurturing was a *human*, and not exclusively female, potential.

I was ready for the doubtful look or the arched eyebrow, I was ready to ex- 2
change recipes and remedies while folding clothes in laundromats or waiting in line at Sears to have family portraits taken. I was not, however, expecting to vie with a population of high-achieving working parents—single or married—every bit as defensive as I about being employed outside the home.

The competition, I soon realized, would not be easy. The other moms and 3
dads had read and taken notes on every how-to-be-perfect manual on the market. Their progeny arrived in the morning dressed in color-coordinated outfits with matching watches and down-filled winter gear. Each boy and girl sported hair-styles that had to have taken an hour of dextrous adult early-morning labor to create. These kids all had famous idiosyncratic habits—aversions to synthetic cloth or allergies to dust—that required special instructions.

Birthdays were the one occasion for each child to be center stage. And so 4
lavish had the festivities apparently become the year before we arrived that the day care center had made a rule limiting the gala spread to foods explicitly made *by* the actual parents *in* their actual homes. This seemed reasonable enough, but as fall turned into winter and I witnessed, at the end of occasional days, the excessive remains of one extravaganza after another, I began to suspect that some people were cheating. How else to explain the ice-cream cupcakes, the individual hot-dog-and-baked-bean quiches, the fluted papaya cups filled with *crème fraiche?*

Adam and I still lived in the small wooden house by Mascoma Lake—the price 5
was right for an instructor's salary. It was there that I retreated to think and plan as Adam's January birthday neared. Under no circumstances was I about to send him off with a concoction sneakily purchased at the bakery. I had something to prove.

I considered briefly the phyla of cream puffs and éclairs but rejected them as 6
too risky. I was not an experienced cook, and my oven, while dutifully heating, was not up to wild extremes or precise temperature calibrations. I contemplated the possibilities of puddings but rejected them as too unorthodox, too bizarre. From every unconventional excursion, I came back to cake.

"What would be the best cake you could imagine?" I asked Adam one night as 7
he played on the carpet with our Husky, Skahota. His reply was immediate and unsurprising, the declaration of his enduring passion.

"A choo choo train!" he announced, and went back to his game. 8

It was his birthday, so I didn't argue, didn't try to widen his horizon. This once 9
I took his fierce attachment seriously and called Nina,* who knew more about baking than I. Culling through her recipe collection, she uncovered directions for specialized pans made from cardboard wrapped in aluminum foil. Boxcars and caboose were a cinch, the coal car was a problem, and the locomotive was a chal-lenge. But it was possible, it was Adam's enduring, maddening fantasy, and done

---

*Friend of Dorris.

right, it could be the most spectacular dessert ever to grace the two-foot-high day care table. I gave the project a week of my life.

Mounted on a piece of plywood, each of the six cars was at base an eight-by- 10 four-inch-long rectangle of trimmed sponge cake, to which I attached paper wheels and connected toggles made of taffy. No food colors at the local grocery seemed bright or impressive enough, so I traveled one Sunday afternoon to a specialty outlet where, for two dollars each, I purchased small vials of blues and reds and yellows and greens so vivid, so ceramic in their luster, that a mere drop was sufficient to tint a bowl of white icing. But I was looking for more than a tint; I was after *bold*, so for good measure I mixed more and more edible dye into my palette until the hues that confronted me were dazzling. No caboose was ever so barn-red, no passenger car so grass-green, no plucky little locomotive, decorated with gumdrops, a hand mirror and a cheerful expression, so sky-blue. This was a little engine that *could*, and knew it. Black, for the coal car, was tricker, but I solved that dilemma with melted licorice that, when spread warm and allowed to harden, cemented the fragile sides into indestructible steel. I got behind in my lecture preparations, but finished the train at midnight the day before Adam's party. All around it I had constructed toy houses, cutout happy families (more than one shepherded by a lone adult male), grazing cartoon animals. Before going to bed, exhausted but smug, I asked Bea° to come over and take photographs of Adam, Nina, and me standing before my creation. My son would have nothing to apologize for.

And it all came to pass just as I had imagined. When I carefully carried the 11 plywood base from the car, and negotiated the door of the center, the train cake was greeted with exclamations of delight and disbelief by the staff and children alike. Other parents, disrobing their sons and daughters from layers of mittens and boots and snowsuits, looked from the cake to me with expressions of betrayal and chagrin.

I had become the act to beat, the standard against which to measure. With a 12 spin of the mixer I had achieved the status of Ideal Parent, the adult for whom no task was too great, no child's dream too onerous to grant. Yes, I was employed full time, but did I let that get in the way of my fatherly duties? The train cake told the story in capital letters.

The party, to which I returned to preside over later in the day, was memora- 13 ble. In the flickering light of six candles (one to grow on), the children's eyes were sugar-glazed. The volume of their voices was loud with greed, and once the clapping ceased, they made fast work of all my labors. Within twenty minutes my ordered platter had become a surrealistic swatch of colors, with only the indestructible coal car, chipped at but undismantled, remaining as solitary witness.

Adam, who had eaten almost none of the cake in his excitement, was every- 14 one's best friend, the hero of the day, and when we got into our blue VW station wagon to go home, he leaned across the seat with a smile so wide and happy it startled me.

°Friends of Dorris.

"Thank you, Daddy," he said.   15

I looked at him, this little boy who really was, after all, what this was for and   16
about. In his dark eyes there was one message only, one idea: his wish had come
true. And I looked back in turn with a single realization of my own: in him, my wish
had come true, too.

"Happy Birthday," I said.   17

The story should have ended there, with the cake eaten and Adam content and   18
me reacquainted with the real meaning of things, but there was one final chapter.
About ten o'clock that night, I was at the kitchen table trying hard to organize the
next day's class notes when the phone rang. It was the director of the day care
center, and her voice was frantic.

"What did you put in that thing?" she demanded.   19

"Why, nothing," I answered, worried that I had somehow violated some inter-   20
diction about natural ingredients. "Just flour and sugar and a few pieces of candy.
What's wrong?"

"The parents have been calling me all night," she said. "They're hysterical.   21
They're ready to take their children to the emergency room at the hospital."

"Why?" Now I was scared.   22

"It's when they put the kids to bed," she said. "When they took them to the   23
potty. They noticed before they flushed! The water in the toilet bowl was green! Or
bright blue! Electric yellow! *Orange!*"

I closed my eyes and saw again the jaunty cars, lined up and ready to roll. The   24
train cake had made more of an impression than I had planned.

Days later, when every expensive hue had passed safely but remarkably   25
through the digestive system of each child, the day care center's governing council
inaugurated an amendment to the party rule: henceforth, all birthday fixings must
be normal. The like of the train cake would never be seen again.

Rhetorical Focus

1. Where, if anywhere, is Dorris's tone ironic as he describes his own behavior and that of others? Where, if anywhere, does he manage to get you to
   sympathize with his younger self? Refer to specific passages.
2. What does Dorris do to foster a sense of mounting tension or excitement as
   his story proceeds?
3. Dorris carries this story through to its chronological conclusion, the unfortunate effects of the train cake. Do you think this conclusion also expresses
   the main point that Dorris wishes to make about the whole experience?
   Why or why not?

Thematic Focus

1. Dorris writes, "With a spin of the mixer I had achieved the status of an
   Ideal Parent, the adult for whom no task was too great, no child's dream
   too onerous to grant" (paragraph 12). Do you think Dorris's ambition was

sound? Why or why not? If you object to it, what alternative ambition do you think Dorris should have had as a single parent? Ultimately, do you think the train cake was worth making? Why or why not?

2. To what extent, do you think, was Dorris responding to outside pressure? To what extent do you think the pressure he felt was self-imposed? Support your reasoning by referring to specific passages in the text.

3. Note the child care center's policies. Do you think it should have had other policies for the children's birthday celebrations? Explain.

A Thanksgiving Celebration (Amy)

Nicholasa Mohr

Nicholasa Mohr (b. 1935) was originally trained as a visual artist, and she has worked as a painter, printmaker, and art instructor. She also has written several works of fiction reflecting her Puerto Rican heritage, including *Nilda, Felita, Going Home, El Bronx Remembered: A Novella and Stories, In Nueva York*, and *Rituals of Survival: A Woman's Portfolio*, a 1985 volume from which the following story comes. The book is divided into six sections, each focusing on a particular Puerto Rican woman who is fighting to survive admist urban poverty. Amy's story is the fourth.

Reflections Before Reading

In recent years, analysts have increasingly used the term *feminization of poverty* to indicate that more and more of the poor in America are women trying to raise families alone. Why do you suppose that the feminization of poverty has occurred? What sorts of details do you associate with single women's struggles to raise a family without much money? How might such

a family celebrate Thanksgiving? Under what circumstances would you call
for government to assist such a family? What sorts of personal qualities do
you think a single mother would need in order to help her family survive
amidst poverty?

Amy sat on her bed thinking. Gary napped soundly in his crib, which was placed   1
right next to her bed. The sucking sound he made as he chewed on his thumb
interrupted her thoughts from time to time. Amy glanced at Gary and smiled. He
was her constant companion now; he shared her bedroom and was with her during
those frightening moments when, late into the night and early morning, she wondered if she could face another day just like the one she had safely survived. Amy
looked at the small alarm clock on the bedside table. In another hour or so it would
be time to wake Gary and give him his milk, then she had just enough time to shop
and pick up the others, after school.

She heard the plopping sound of water dropping into a full pail. Amy hurried   2
into the bathroom, emptied the pail into the toilet, then replaced it so that the floor
remained dry. Last week she had forgotten, and the water had overflowed out of
the pail and onto the floor, leaking down into Mrs. Wynn's bathroom. Now, Mrs.
Wynn was threatening to take her to small claims court, if the landlord refused to
fix the damage done to her bathroom ceiling and wallpaper. All right, Amy
shrugged, she would try calling the landlord once more. She was tired of the countless phone calls to plead with them to come and fix the leak in the roof.

"Yes, Mrs. Guzman, we got your message and we'll send somebody over. Yes,   3
just as soon as we can . . . we got other tenants with bigger problems, you know.
We are doing our best, we'll get somebody over; you gotta be patient . . ."

Time and again they had promised, but no one had ever showed up. And it was   4
now more than four months that she had been forced to live like this. Damn, Amy
walked into her kitchen, they never refuse the rent for that, there's somebody
ready any time! Right now, this was the best she could do. The building was still
under rent control and she had enough room. Where else could she go? No one in
a better neighborhood would rent to her, not the way things were.

She stood by the window, leaning her side against the molding, and looked   5
out. It was a crisp sunny autumn day, mild for the end of November. She remembered it was the eve of Thanksgiving and felt a tightness in her chest. Amy took a
deep breath, deciding not to worry about that right now.

Rows and rows of endless streets scattered with abandoned buildings and   6
small houses stretched out for miles. Some of the blocks were almost entirely leveled, except for clumps of partial structures charred and blackened by fire. From a
distance they looked like organic masses pushing their way out of the earth. Garbage, debris, shattered glass, bricks and broken, discarded furniture covered the
ground. Rusting carcasses of cars that had been stripped down to the shell shone
and glistened a bright orange under the afternoon sun.

There were no people to be seen nor traffic, save for a group of children   7
jumping on an old filthy mattress that had been ripped open. They were busy

pulling the stuffing out of the mattress and tossing it about playfully. Nearby, several stray dogs searched the garbage for food. One of the boys picked up a brick, then threw it at the dogs, barely missing them. Reluctantly, the dogs moved on.

Amy sighed and swallowed, it was all getting closer and closer. It seemed as if only last month, when she had looked out of this very window, all of that was much further away; in fact, she recalled feeling somewhat removed and safe. Now the decay was creeping up to this area. The fire engine sirens screeching and screaming in the night reminded her that the devastation was constant, never stopping even for a night's rest. Amy was fearful of living on the top floor. Going down four flights to safety with the kids in case of a fire was another source of worry for her. She remembered how she had argued with Charlie when they had first moved in. 8

"All them steps to climb with Michele and Carlito, plus carrying the carriage for Carlito, is too much." 9

"Come on baby," Charlie had insisted "it's only temporary. The rent's cheaper and we can save something towards buying our own place. Come on . . ." 10

That was seven years ago. There were two more children now, Lisabeth and Gary; and she was still here, without Charlie. 11

"Soon it'll come right to this street and to my doorstep. God Almighty!" Amy whispered. It was like a plague: a disease for which there seemed to be no cure, no prevention. Gangs of youngsters occupied empty store fronts and basements; derelicts, drunk or wasted on drugs, positioned themselves on street corners and in empty doorways. Every day she saw more abandoned and burned-out sections. 12

As Amy continued to look out, a feeling that she had been in this same situation before, a long time ago, startled her. The feeling of deja vu so real to her, reminded Amy quite vividly of the dream she had had last night. In that dream, she had been standing in the center of a circle of little girls. She herself was very young and they were all singing a rhyme. In a soft whisper, Amy sang the rhyme: "London Bridge is falling down, falling down, falling down, London Bridge is falling down, my fair lady . . . ." She stopped and saw herself once again in her dream, picking up her arms and chanting, "wave your arms and fly away, fly away, fly away . . ." 13

She stood in the middle of the circle waving her arms, first gently, then more forcefully, until she was flapping them. The other girls stared silently at her. Slowly, Amy had felt herself elevated above the circle, higher and higher until she could barely make out the human figures below. Waving her arms like the wings of a bird, she began to fly. A pleasant breeze pushed her gently, and she glided along, passing through soft white clouds into an intense silence. Then she saw it. Beneath her, huge areas were filled with crumbling buildings and large caverns; miles of destruction spread out in every direction. Amy had felt herself suspended in this silence for a moment and then she began to fall. She flapped her arms and legs furiously, trying to clutch at the air, hoping for a breeze, something to get her going again, but there was nothing. Quickly she fell, faster and faster, as the ground below her swirled and turned, coming closer and closer, revealing destroyed, burned buildings, rubble and a huge dark cavern. In a state of hysteria, Amy had fought against the loss of control and helplessness, as her body descended into the large black hole and had woken up with a start just before she hit bottom. 14

Amy stepped away from the window for a moment, almost out of breath as she   15
recollected the fear she had felt in her dream. She walked over to the sink and
poured herself a glass of water.

"That's it, Europe and the war," she said aloud. "In the movies, just like my   16
dream.

Amy clearly remembered how she had sat as a very little girl in a local movie   17
theatre with her mother and watched horrified at the scenes on the screen. News-
reels showed entire cities almost totally devastated. Exactly as it had been in her
dream, she recalled seeing all the destruction caused by warfare. Names like "Mu-
nich, Nuremburg, Berlin" and "the German people" identified the areas. Most of
the streets were empty, except for the occasional small groups of people who rum-
maged about, searching among the ruins and huge piles of debris, sharing the
spoils with packs of rats who scavenged at a safe distance. Some people pulled
wagons and baby carriages loaded with bundles and household goods. Others carried what they owned on their backs.

Amy remembered turning to her mother, asking "What was going on? Mami,   18
who did this? Why did they do it? Who are those people living there?"

"The enemy, that's who," her mother had whispered emphatically. "Bad peo-   19
ple who started the war against our country and did terrible things to other people
and to us. That's where your papa was for so long, fighting in the army. Don't you
remember, Amy?"

"What kinds of things, Mami?" Who were the other people they did bad things   20
to?"

"Don't worry about them things. These people got what they deserved. Be-   21
sides, they are getting help from us, now that we won the war. There's a plan to
help them, even though they don't deserve no help from us."

Amy had persisted. "Are there any little kids there? Do they go to school? Do   22
they live in them holes?"

"Shh . . . let me hear the rest of the news . . ." her mother had responded,   23
annoyed. Amy had sat during the remainder of the double feature, wondering
where those people lived and all about the kids there. And she continued to wonder and worry for several days, until one day she forgot all about it.

Amy sipped from the glass she held, then emptied most of the water back into   24
the sink. She sat and looked around at her small kitchen. The ceiling was peeling
and flakes of paint had fallen on the kitchen table. The entire apartment was in
urgent need of a thorough plastering and paint job. She blinked and shook her
head, and now? Who are we now? What have I done? Who is the enemy? Is there
a war? Are we at war? Amy suppressed a loud chuckle.

"Nobody answered my questions then, and nobody's gonna answer them   25
now," she spoke out loud.

Amy still wondered and groped for answers about Charlie. No one could tell   26
her what had really happened . . . how he had felt and what he was thinking before
he died. Almost two years had gone by, but she was still filled with an overwhelming sense of loneliness. That day was just like so many other days; they were together, planning about the kids, living from one crisis to the next, fighting, barely

finding the time to make love without being exhausted; then late that night, it was all over. Charlie's late again, Amy had thought, and didn't even call me. She was angry when she heard the doorbell. He forgot the key again. Dammit, Charlie! You would forget your head if it weren't attached to you!

They had stood there before her; both had shown her their badges, but only one had spoken.   27

"Come in . . . sit down, won't you."   28

"You better sit down, miss." The stranger told her very calmly and soberly that Charlie was dead.   29

"On the Bruckner Boulevard Expressway . . . head on collision . . . dead on arrival . . . didn't suffer too long . . . nobody was with him, but we found his wallet."   30

Amy had protested and argued—No way! They were lying to her. But after a while she knew they brought the truth to her, and Charlie wasn't coming back.   31

Tomorrow would be the second Thanksgiving without him and one she could not celebrate. Celebrate with what? Amy stood and walked over and opened the refrigerator door. She had enough bread, a large pitcher of powdered milk which she had flavored with Hershey's cocoa and powdered sugar. There was plenty of peanut butter and some graham crackers she had kept fresh by sealing them in a plastic bag. For tonight she had enough chopped meat and macaroni. But tomorrow? What could she buy for tomorrow?   32

Amy shut the refrigerator door and reached over to the money tin set way back on one of the shelves. Carefully she took out the money and counted every cent. There was no way she could buy a turkey, even a small one. She still had to manage until the first; she needed every penny just to make it to the next check. Things were bad, worse than they had ever been. In the past, when things were rough, she had turned to Charlie and sharing had made it all easier. Now there was no one. She resealed the money tin and put it away.   33

Amy had thought of calling the lawyers once more. What good would that do? What can they do for me? Right now . . . today!   34

"These cases take time before we get to trial. We don't want to take the first settlement they offer. That wouldn't do you or the children any good. You have a good case, the other driver was at fault. He didn't have his license or the registration, and we have proof he was drinking. His father is a prominent judge who doesn't want that kind of publicity. I know . . . yes, things are rough, but just hold on a little longer. We don't want to accept a poor settlement and risk your future and the future of your children, do we?" Mr. Silverman of Silverman, Knapp and Ullman was handling the case personally. "By early Spring we should be making a date for trial . . . just hang in there a bit longer . . ." And so it went every time she called: the promise that in just a few more months she could hope for relief, some money, enough to live like people.   35

Survivor benefits had not been sufficient, and since they had not kept up premium payments on Charlie's G.I. insurance policy, she had no other income. Amy was given a little more assistance from the Aid to Dependent Children agency. Somehow she had managed so far.   36

The two food stores that extended her credit were still waiting for Amy to   37
settle overdue accounts. In an emergency she could count on a few friends; they
would lend her something, but not for this, not for Thanksgiving dinner.

She didn't want to go to Papo and Mary's again. She knew her brother meant   38
well, and that she always had an open invitation. They're good people, but we are
five more mouths to feed, plus they've been taking care of Papa all these years,
ever since Mami died. Enough is enough. Amy shut her eyes. I want my own
dinner this year, just for my family, for me and the kids.

If I had the money, I'd make a dinner tomorrow and invite Papa and Lou   39
Ann from downstairs and her kids. She's been such a good friend to us. I'd get a
gallon of cider and a bottle of wine . . . a large cake at the bakery by Alexander's,
some dried fruits and nuts . . . even a holiday centerpiece for the table. Yes, it
would be my dinner for us and my friends. I might even invite Jimmy. She
hadn't seen Jimmy for a long time. Must be over six months . . . almost a year? He
worked with Charlie at the plant. After Charlie's death, Jimmy had come by often,
but Amy was not ready to see another man, not just then, so she discouraged him.
From time to time, she thought of Jimmy and hoped he would visit her again.

Amy opened her eyes and a sinking feeling flowed through her, as she looked   40
down at the chips of paint spread out on the kitchen table. Slowly, Amy brushed
them with her hand, making a neat pile.

These past few months, she had seriously thought of going out to work. Be-   41
fore she had Michele, she had worked as a clerk–typist for a large insurance
company, but that was almost ten years ago. She would have to brush up on her
typing and math. Besides, she didn't know if she could earn enough to pay for a
sitter. She couldn't leave the kids alone; Gary wasn't even three and Michele had
just turned nine. Amy had applied for part-time work as a teacher's aide, but when
she learned that her check from Aid to Dependent Children could be discontin-
ued, she withdrew her application. Better to go on like this until the case comes to
trial.

Amy choked back the tears. I can't let myself get like this. I just can't! Lately,   42
she had begun to find comfort at the thought of never waking up again. What about
my kids, then? I must do something. I have to. Tomorrow is going to be for us, just
us, our day.

Her thoughts went back to her own childhood and the holiday dinners with   43
her family. They had been poor, but there was always food. We used to have such
good times, Amy remembered the many stories her grandmother used to tell
them. She spoke about her own childhood on a farm in a rural area of Puerto Rico.
Her grandmother's stories were about the animals, whom she claimed to know
personally and very well. Amy laughed, recalling that most of the stories her grandmother related were too impossible to be true, such as a talking goat who saved the
town from a flood, and the handsome mouse and beautiful lady beetle who fell in
love, got married and had the biggest and fanciest wedding her grandmother had
ever attended. Her grandmother was very old and had died before Amy was ten.
Amy had loved her best, more than her own parents, and she still remembered the
old woman quite clearly.

"Abuelita, did them things really happen? How come them animals talked?   44
Animals don't talk. Everybody knows that."

"Oh, but they do talk! And yes, everything I tell you is absolutely the truth. I   45
believe it and you must believe it too." The old woman had been completely convincing. And for many years Amy had secretly believed that when her grandmother
was a little girl, somewhere in a special place, animals talked, got married and were
heroes.

"Abuelita," Amy whispered, "I wish you were here and could help me now."   46
And then she thought of it. Something special for tomorrow. Quickly, Amy took
out the money tin, counting out just the right amount of money she needed. She
hesitated for a moment. What if it won't work and I can't convince them? Amy took
a deep breath. Never mind, I have to try, I must. She counted out a few more
dollars. I'll work it all out somehow. Then she warmed up Gary's milk and got
ready to leave.

Amy heard the voices of her children with delight. Shouts and squeals of   47
laughter bounced into the kitchen as they played in the living room. Today they
were all happy, anticipating their mother's promise of a celebration. Recently, her
frequent moods of depression and short temper had frightened them. Privately,
the children had blamed themselves for their mother's unhappiness, fighting with
each other in helpless confusion. The children welcomed their mother's energy
and good mood with relief.

Lately Amy had begun to realize that Michele and Carlito were constantly   48
fighting. Carlito was always angry and would pick on Lisabeth. Poor Lisabeth, she's
always so sad. I never have time for her and she's not really much older than Gary.
This way of life has been affecting us all . . . but not today. Amy worked quickly.
The apartment was filled with an air of festivity. She had set the kitchen table with
a paper tablecloth, napkins and paper cups to match. These were decorated with
turkeys, pilgrims, Indian corn and all the symbols of the Thanksgiving holiday.
Amy had also bought a roll of orange paper streamers and decorated the kitchen
chairs. Each setting had a name-card printed with bright magic markers. She had
even managed to purchase a small holiday cake for dessert.

As she worked, Amy fought moments of anxiety and fear that threatened to   49
weaken her sense of self-confidence. What if they laugh at me? Dear God in
heaven, will my children think I'm a fool? But she had already spent the money,
cooked and arranged everything; she had to go ahead. If I make it through this day,
Amy nodded, I'll be all right.

She set the food platter in the center of the table and stepped back. A mound   50
of bright yellow rice, flavored with a few spices and bits of fatback, was surrounded
by a dozen hardboiled eggs that had been colored a bright orange. Smiling, Amy
felt it was all truly beautiful; she was ready for the party.

"All right," Amy walked into the living room. "We're ready!" The children   51
quickly followed her into the kitchen.

"Oooh, Mommy," Lisabeth shouted, "everything looks so pretty."   52

"Each place has got a card with your own name, so find the right seat." Amy   53
took Gary and sat him down on his special chair next to her.

"Mommy," Michele spoke, "is this the whole surprise?"   54

"Yes," Amy answered, "just a minute, we also have some cider." Amy brought   55
a small bottle of cider to the table.

"Easter eggs for Thanksgiving?" Carlito asked.   56

"Is that what you think they are, Carlito?" Amy asked. "Because they are not   57
Easter eggs."

The children silently turned to one another, exchanging bewildered looks.   58

"What are they?" Lisabeth asked.   59

"Well," Amy said, "these are . . . turkey eggs, that's what. What's better than a   60
turkey on Thanksgiving day? Her eggs, right?" Amy continued as all of them
watched her. "You see, it's not easy to get these eggs. They're what you call a
delicacy. But I found a special store that sells them, and they agreed to sell me a
whole dozen for today."

"What store is that, Mommy?" Michele asked. "Is it around here?"   61

"No. They don't have stores like that here. It's special, way downtown."   62

"Did the turkey lay them eggs like that? That color?" Carlito asked.   63

"I want an egg," Gary said pointing to the platter.   64

"No, no . . . I just colored them that way for today, so everything goes together   65
nicely, you know . . ." Amy began to serve the food. "All right, you can start eating."

"Well then, what's so special about these eggs? What's the difference between   66
a turkey egg and an egg from a chicken?" Carlito asked.

"Ah, the taste, Carlito, just wait until you have some." Amy quickly finished   67
serving everyone. "You see, these eggs are hard to find because they taste so fantastic." She chewed a mouthful of egg. "Ummm . . . fantastic, isn't it?" She nodded
at them.

"Wonderful, Mommy," said Lisabeth. "It tastes real different."   68

"Oh yeah," Carlito said, "you can taste it right away. Really good."   69

Everyone was busy eating and commenting on how special the eggs tasted. As   70
Amy watched her children, a sense of joy filled her, and she knew it had been a
very long time since they had been together like this, close and loving.

"Mommy, did you ever eat these kinds of eggs before?" asked Michele.   71

"Yes, when I was little," she answered. "My grandmother got them for me.   72
You know, I talked about my abuelita before. When I first ate them, I couldn't get
over how good they tasted, just like you." Amy spoke with assurance, as they listened to every word she said. "Abuelita lived on a farm when she was very little.
That's how come she knew all about turkey eggs. She used to tell me the most
wonderful stories about her life there."

"Tell us!"   73

"Yeah, please Mommy, please tell us."   74

All right, I'll tell you one about a hero who saved her whole village from a big   75
flood. He was . . . a billy goat."

"Mommy," Michele interrupted, "a billy goat?"   76

"That's right, and you have to believe what I'm going to tell you. All of you   77
have to believe me. Because everything I'm going to say is absolutely the truth.

Promise? All right, then, in the olden days, when my grandmother was very little, far away in a small town in Puerto Rico . . ."

Amy continued, remembering stories that she had long since forgotten. The children listened, intrigued by what their mother had to say. She felt a calmness within. Yes, Amy told herself, today's for us, for me and the kids.   78

Rhetorical Focus

1. Do you consider Mohr's style of writing to be realistic? What features of it do you have in mind when you respond to this question?
2. Through what techniques does Mohr gradually impart the information about Amy's life we need in order to grasp and sympathize with her present situation?
3. This story can be divided into two parts: Amy's reflections on Thanksgiving Eve and the dinner the next day. The story leaps from one to the other. Does this jump forward in time work, or should Mohr have made the transition more gradual, describing Amy's concrete planning of the celebration as Dorris describes at length his creation of the train cake? Explain.

Thematic Focus

1. What resources does Amy draw on as she and her family struggle to survive? What does she achieve by the end of the story? Does the story leave you thinking that society should do more for the Amys of this world? Why or why not?
2. Drawing on her childhood memories of World War II, Amy wonders whether the term *war* can apply to her present condition. Does the analogy seem plausible to you? Can we say there is a war going on in this story? Support your answers with specific references to the text.
3. Does social class seem to matter equally in Mohr's story and Dorris's as an influence on family life? Explain.

Suggestions for Writing

1. Compare Amy's Thanksgiving dinner and Dorris's birthday celebration as revelations of character. To what extent do they reveal similar values in these two people? To what extent do they point to different outlooks? Bear in mind that when Dorris writes about the train cake, he may do so with a perspective different from the one he had at the time.
2. Describe an occasion when a family you know revealed something significant about its nature. You may want to focus on a birthday celebration or holiday festivity, as Dorris and Mohr do. Be sure not only to state a thesis about the family, but also to re-create vividly for your readers the family episode that supports your thesis.

3. Write an essay recommending some ways that a particular kind of institution can show that it is sensitive to the situation of single-parent families. Possible institutions include child care centers, schools, charitable organizations, religious institutions, places where the parent may work, and city, state, or federal governments. You may find it useful to refer to Dorris's and/or Mohr's accounts as you state and explain your recommendations.

Chapter
3

Places and
Communities

Most human beings don't just glide unaffected through their physical surroundings. Although we may entertain the notion that we are self-enclosed egoes, walled off from the influences of environment, almost all of us are shaped by and respond to the scenes we directly experience as well as larger social forces. Indeed, the spaces that people inhabit or pass through are often charged with meaning for them, whether the impressions they take away from these spaces are conscious or not. Consider how, at various times, you have been influenced by a social setting, even if you ultimately rejected it by going somewhere else. Perhaps you have just left home and are wondering not only what values of it you will retain but also how much the campus community will affect you. Even if you are commuting to campus from home, entering college may very well lead you to examine what these two settings in your life represent and how you will balance your attachments to them. Whatever your present situation, you can learn a great deal by writing about places and communities you have lived in, visited, or encountered through texts. Such a project encourages you to summon up concrete detail, to identify social forces that shape personal identity, to analyze what holds groups together, and to examine how different groups relate to one another and among themselves.

The following sections reflect these activities. They also show how writers interpret a place or community, emphasizing particular aspects of it for a particular purpose and audience, rather than simply recreating it. Two writers may choose the very same place or community on which to focus, but their personal histories and predispositions may cause them to take different angles on it—in other words, to "locate" themselves differently when they set out to write about it. As we do throughout *Constellations*, we have paired texts here to suggest the range of experiences, ideas, viewpoints, and techniques that writers draw upon even if they address similar topics. For example, even though Alfred Kazin and Paule Marshall recall the same kind of room—both referring to a kitchen from their youth in Brooklyn—their accounts vary in form and content, partly because Kazin grew up among Eastern European Jews and Marshall among immigrants from Barbados. Moving outward to encompass whole communities, both Gretel Ehrlich and Margaret Laurence depict "open spaces" that have been important to them; however, Ehrlich focuses on a community she fell in love with, the ranch culture of Wyoming, while Laurence reflects on a community she left, a small, isolated village on the Canadian prairie. Next, even though both Marianna De Marco Torgovnick and Barbara Grizzuti Harrison examine concepts of "insiders" and "outsiders" held by their native community of Bensonhurst, New York, they resort to different rhetorical strategies that perhaps reflect different ideas they want to convey. Finally, John Didion and Michael Ventura each use Las Vegas as a target for cultural critique, but they show different ways of relating the same place or community to a thesis about American society. As you read these texts, we hope that you will consider them invitations to discuss the perspectives on community life they offer. We encourage you, too, to mine them for strategies as you write about the places and communities that you would like to investigate.

MEMORIES OF ROOMS

We begin our unit on places and communities with a pair of essays on rooms—specifically, kitchens. This way of starting may strike you as curious. The kitchens and other rooms you have encountered over the years may not seem significant enough for you to write about. When you contemplate the rooms in your life, however, you can indeed start to understand how to write on a larger scale about various settings. After all, rooms are not always just backgrounds for human beings occupied with more important things. If you look back seriously on the rooms you have passed through, you are likely to find several charged with meaning for you—either because momentous events occurred in them, or because you simply spent enough time in them that you can see how they encapsulate a whole way of life. Recalling and analyzing particular rooms can in effect lead you metaphorically to knock down their walls, exposing the personal history and social context in which they are embedded. At the same time, describing a room can give you practice in focused writing that will help you when you set out to analyze larger, more complex settings.

Here, Alfred Kazin and Paule Marshall both recall kitchens from their childhood in Brooklyn, New York. They even refer to roughly the same time period (Kazin was born in 1915, Marshall in 1928). Their recollections of kitchen life differ, however. For one thing, they use their kitchens to evoke different ethnic backgrounds: for Kazin, the culture of Jewish immigrants from Eastern Europe; for Marshall, the African-American culture of immigrants from Barbados. Also, they emphasize different kinds of details when they describe their kitchens, evidently because they want to convey different overall impressions to their readers. Taken together, these essays indicate the choices that writers make in detail, theme, and rhetorical purpose, even when they focus on a place as apparently simple as a room. What rooms do you recall when you review your own life? How and why do they resonate with meaning for you? What about them would you convey to a present audience, such as your classmates? Think about questions such as these as Kazin and Marshall take you several decades back to the kitchens of their Brooklyn youths.

The Kitchen

Alfred Kazin

Alfred Kazin (b. 1915) grew up in a neighborhood of poor, Yiddish-speaking Eastern European Jews in Brooklyn, New York. Especially interested in American literature, he launched a reputation as a critic and scholar of it with his 1942 book *On Native Grounds*. His later books of literary analysis have included *Contemporaries, Bright Book of Life*, and *An American Procession*. Kazin has also taught at several universities, most recently the City University of New York. In addition to his academic work, however, Kazin has won acclaim for his series of memoirs. Based on the private journal that he has maintained throughout his life—and that has itself grown to more than 30 volumes—the series includes *A Walker in the City* (1951), *Starting Out in the Thirties* (1965), and *New York Jew* (1978). The following is an excerpt from the first of these books. As its title suggests, the book depicts Kazin walking through his old neighborhood recalling the physical details and psychological experiences of his childhood there. The book is divided into four sections, and what you are about to read comes from the second of these, entitled "The Kitchen." In the introduction that precedes this excerpt, Kazin, in London after World War II, is stimulated to recall the kitchen of his youth by a broadcast of the first Sabbath service at the recently liberated Belsen Concentration Camp.

Reflections Before Reading

Why might people recall the kitchens of their youth? What might kitchens reveal about the people who use them? List details of a kitchen you know well. What chief impression of it would you convey to people asking you about the life lived there? The following text specifically refers to the kitchen of poor Eastern European Jews who immigrated to America. What, if anything, do you associate with this cultural group or with other European immigrants to America during the late nineteenth and early twentieth centuries?

In Brownsville tenements the kitchen is always the largest room and the center of the household. As a child I felt that we lived in a kitchen to which four other rooms were annexed. My mother, a "home" dressmaker, had her workshop in the kitchen. She told me once that she had begun dressmaking in Poland at thirteen; as far back as I can remember, she was always making dresses for the local women. She had an innate sense of design, a quick eye for all subtleties in the latest fashions, even when she despised them, and great boldness. For three or four dollars she would study the fashion magazines with a customer, go with the customer to the remnants store on Belmont Avenue to pick out the material, argue the owner down—all remnants stores, for some reason, were supposed to be shady, as if the owners dealt in stolen goods—and then for days would patiently fit and baste and sew and fit again. Our apartment was always full of women in their housedresses sitting around the kitchen table waiting for a fitting. My little bedroom next to the kitchen was the fitting room. The sewing machine, an old nut-brown Singer with golden scrolls painted along the black arm and engraved along the two tiers of little drawers massed with needles and thread on each side of the treadle, stood next to the window and the great coal-black stove which up to my last year in college was our main source of heat. By December the two outer bedrooms were closed off, and used to chill bottles of milk and cream, cold borscht and jellied calves' feet.

The kitchen held our lives together. My mother worked in it all day long, we ate in it almost all meals except the Passover *seder*, I did my homework and first writing at the kitchen table, and in winter I often had a bed made up for me on three kitchen chairs near the stove. On the wall just over the table hung a long horizontal mirror that sloped to a ship's prow at each end and was lined in cherry wood. It took up the whole wall, and drew every object in the kitchen to itself. The walls were a fiercely stippled whitewash, so often rewhitened by my father in slack seasons that the paint looked as if it had been squeezed and cracked into the walls. A large electric bulb hung down the center of the kitchen at the end of a chain that had been hooked into the ceiling; the old gas ring and key still jutted out of the wall like antlers. In the corner next to the toilet was the sink at which we washed, and the square tub in which my mother did our clothes. Above it, tacked to the shelf on which were pleasantly ranged square, blue-bordered white sugar and spice jars, hung calendars from the Public National Bank on Pitkin Avenue and the Minsker Progressive Branch of the Workman's Circle; receipts for the payment of insurance premiums, and household bills on a spindle; two little boxes engraved with Hebrew letters. One of these was for the poor, the other to buy back the Land of Israel. Each spring a bearded little man would suddenly appear in our kitchen to salute us with a hurried Hebrew blessing, empty the boxes (sometimes with a side-long look of disdain if they were not full), hurriedly bless us again for remembering our less fortunate Jewish brothers and sisters, and so take his departure until the next spring, after vainly trying to persuade my mother to take still another box. We did occasionally remember to drop coins in the boxes, but this was usually only on the dreaded morning of "mid-terms" and final examinations, because my mother thought it would bring me luck. She was extremely superstitious, but embarrassed about it, and always laughed at herself whenever, on the morning of an examination, she counseled me to leave the house on my right foot. "I know it's silly," her smile seemed to say, "but what harm can it do? It may calm God down."

3   The kitchen gave a special character to our lives; my mother's character. All my memories of that kitchen are dominated by the nearness of my mother sitting all day long at her sewing machine, by the clacking of the treadle against the lino-leum floor, by the patient twist of her right shoulder as she automatically pushed at the wheel with one hand or lifted the foot to free the needle where it had got stuck in a thick piece of material. The kitchen was her life. Year by year, as I began to take in her fantastic capacity for labor and her anxious zeal, I realized it was our-selves she kept stitched together. I can never remember a time when she was not working. She worked because the law of her life was work, work and anxiety; she worked because she would have found life meaningless without work. She read almost no English; she could read the Yiddish paper, but never felt she had time to. We were always talking of a time when I would teach her how to read, but somehow there was never time. When I awoke in the morning she was already at her machine, or in the great morning crowd of housewives at the grocery getting fresh rolls for breakfast. When I returned from school she was at her machine, or conferring over *McCall's* with some neighborhood woman who had come in point-ing hopefully to an illustration—"Mrs. Kazin! Mrs. Kazin! Make me a dress like it shows here in the picture!" When my father came home from work she had some-how mysteriously interrupted herself to make supper for us, and the dishes cleared and washed, was back at her machine. When I went to bed at night, often she was still there, pounding away at the treadle, hunched over the wheel, her hands steer-ing a piece of gauze under the needle with a finesse that always contrasted sharply with her swollen hands and broken nails. Her left hand had been pierced through when as a girl she had worked in the infamous Triangle Shirtwaist Factory on the East Side. A needle had gone straight through the palm, severing a large vein. They had sewn it up for her so clumsily that a tuft of flesh always lay folded over the palm.

4   The kitchen was the great machine that set our lives running; it whirred down a little only on Saturdays and holy days. From my mother's kitchen I gained my first picture of life as a white, overheated, starkly lit workshop redolent with Jewish cooking, crowded with women in housedresses, strewn with fashion magazines, patterns, dress material, spools of thread—and at whose center, so lashed to her machine that bolts of energy seemed to dance out of her hands and feet as she worked, my mother stamped the treadle hard against the floor, hard, hard, and silently, grimly at war, beat out the first rhythm of the world to me.

Every sound from the street roared and trembled at our windows—a mother   5
feeding her child on the doorstep, the screech of the trolley cars on Rockaway
Avenue, the eternal smash of a handball against the wall of our house, the clatter of
"der Italyéner" 's cart packed with watermelons, the sing-song of the old-clothes
men walking Chester Street, the cries *"Arbes! Arbes! Kinder! Kinder! Heyse gute
árbes!"* All day long people streamed into our apartment as a matter of course—
"customers," upstairs neighbors, downstairs neighbors, women who would stop in
for a half-hour's talk, salesmen, relatives, insurance agents. Usually they came in
without ringing the bell—everyone knew my mother was always at home. I would
hear the front door opening, the wind whistling through our front hall, and then
some familiar face would appear in our kitchen with the same bland, matter-of-fact
inquiring look: no need to stand on ceremony: my mother and her kitchen were
available to everyone all day long.

At night the kitchen contracted around the blaze of the light on the cloth, the   6
patterns, the ironing board where the iron had burned a black border around the
tear in the muslin cover; the finished dresses looked so frilly as they jostled on their
wire hangers after all the work my mother had put into them. And then I would get
that strangely ominous smell of tension from the dress fabrics and the burn in the
cover of the ironing board—as if each piece of cloth and paper crushed with light
under the naked bulb might suddenly go up in flames. Whenever I pass some small
tailoring shop still lit up at night and see the owner hunched over his steam press;
whenever in some poorer neighborhood of the city I see through a window some
small crowded kitchen naked under the harsh light glittering in the ceiling, I still
smell that fiery breath, that warning of imminent fire. I was always holding my
breath. What I must have felt most about ourselves, I see now, was that we ourselves were like kindling—that all the hard-pressed pieces of ourselves and all the
hard-used objects in that kitchen were like so many slivers of wood that might go
up in flames if we came too near the white-blazing filaments in that naked bulb.
Our tension itself was fire, we ourselves were forever burning—to live, to get down
the foreboding in our souls, to make good.

Twice a year, on the anniversaries of her parents' deaths, my mother placed on   7
top of the ice-box an ordinary kitchen glass packed with wax, the *yortsayt*, and lit
the candle in it. Sitting at the kitchen table over my homework, I would look across
the threshold to that mourning-glass and sense that for my mother the distance
from our kitchen to *der heym*, from life to death, was only a flame's length away.
Poor as we were, it was not poverty that drove my mother so hard; it was loneliness—some endless bitter brooding over all those left behind, dead or dying or
soon to die; a loneliness locked up in her kitchen that dwelt every day on the
hazardousness of life and the nearness of death, but still kept struggling in the lock,
trying to get us through by endless labor.

With us, life started up again only on the last shore. There seemed to be no   8
middle ground between despair and the fury of our ambition. Whenever my
mother spoke of her hopes for us, it was with such unbelievingness that the likes of
us would ever come to anything, such abashed hope and readiness for pain, that I
finally came to see in the flame burning on top of the ice-box death itself burning

away the bones of poor Jews, burning out in us everything but courage, the blind resolution to live. In the light of that mourning-candle, there were ranged around me how many dead and dying—how many eras of pain, of exile, of dispersion, of cringing before the powers of this world!

It was always at dusk that my mother's loneliness came home most to me. 9 Painfully alert to every shift in the light at her window, she would suddenly confess her fatigue by removing her pince-nez, and then wearily pushing aside the great mound of fabrics on her machine, would stare at the street as if to warm herself in the last of the sun. "How sad it is!" I once heard her say. "It grips me! It grips me!" Twilight was the bottommost part of the day, the chilliest and loneliest time for her. Always so near to her moods, I knew she was fighting some deep inner dread, struggling against the returning tide of darkness along the streets that invariably assailed her heart with the same foreboding—Where? Where now? Where is the day taking us now?

Yet one good look at the street would revive her. I see her now, perched 10 against the windowsill, with her face against the glass, her eyes almost asleep in enjoyment, just as she starts up with the guilty cry—"What foolishness is this in me!"—and goes to the stove to prepare supper for us: a moment, only a moment, watching the evening crowd of women gathering at the grocery for fresh bread and milk. But between my mother's pent-up face at the window and the winter sun dying in the fabrics—"Alfred, see how beautiful!"—she has drawn for me one single line of sentience.

Rhetorical Focus

1. Kazin makes a general statement about life in his family's kitchen at the start of almost every paragraph. Are these statements equally general, or are some more specific than others? Which would you choose as the best guide to what his description of the kitchen emphasizes?
2. What is the central image that Kazin uses to organize the material in his sixth, seventh, and eighth paragraphs? Why do you think he chooses this particular image? What do you yourself associate with it?
3. Consider how and for what rhetorical purpose Kazin uses various sentence structures and lengths in this essay. For example, note the kind of structure he uses in these three long sentences about his mother.

> All my memories of that kitchen are dominated by the nearness of my mother sitting all day long at her sewing machine, by the clacking of the treadle against the linoleum floor, by the patient twist of her right shoulder as she automatically pushed at the wheel with one hand or lifted the foot to free the needle where it had got stuck in a thick piece of material. (paragraph 3)

> When I went to bed at night, often she was still there, pounding away at the treadle, hunched over the wheel, her hands steering a piece of gauze under the needle with a finesse that always contrasted sharply with her swollen hands and broken nails. (paragraph 3)

From my mother's kitchen I gained my first picture of life as a white, overheated, starkly lit workshop redolent with Jewish cooking, crowded with women in house-dresses, strewn with fashion magazines, patterns, dress material, spools of thread—and at whose center, so lashed to her machine that bolts of energy seemed to dance out of her hands and feet as she worked, my mother stamped the treadle hard against the floor, hard, hard, and silently, grimly at war, beat out the first rhythm of the world to me. (paragraph 4)

How would you describe this kind of sentence? What effect(s) do you think Kazin is aiming for with it? Is it effective for you? What would be the effect if each of the preceding sentences were broken into several shorter ones?

Thematic Focus

1. Think again of the kitchen you recalled in "Reflections Before Reading." How does it compare with the one Kazin describes?
2. List three adjectives you would use to describe Kazin's mother as he depicts her. What is your overall impression of her?
3. Autobiographies often reflect both the past and the present perspectives of the author. As Kazin describes life in his family's kitchen, how much does he seem to reproduce what he thought about that life as a boy? How much does he seem to express an adult's perspective? Support your judgment by referring to specific statements he makes.

From the Poets in the Kitchen

Paule Marshall

Paule Marshall is primarily known as a fiction writer. She has also taught or lectured on creative writing and on African-American literature at several universities, including Yale, Columbia, Cornell, Oxford, Michigan State, and Virginia Commonwealth. Born in 1929 to recent immigrants from Barbados in the Caribbean, Marshall grew up in a neighborhood of Brooklyn, New York oriented toward her parents' culture. In much of her work, she examines the relationship of later generations to this culture. Her first novel, *Brown Girl, Brownstones* (1959) essentially describes how she, as a youth, resisted her parents while still sensing her kinship with them. Her subsequent novels *The Chosen Place, The Timeless People* (1969), and *Praisesong for the Widow* (1983) are actually set in the Caribbean and emphasize the spiritual import of its marginalized native societies. Marshall has also produced two collections of short stories, *Soul Clap Hands and Sing* (1961) and *Reena and Other Stories*, a 1983 volume in which the following essay serves as a preface. It also appeared that same year as part of a *New York Times Book Review* series entitled "The Making of a Writer."

Reflections Before Reading

Marshall describes the kitchen of her Barbadian immigrant family. Do you expect that her culture led her to have experiences different from Kazin's? Why or why not? Do you think their differences in gender will matter in their descriptions of kitchens? If so, how? Note Marshall's title. In what sense may her mother and her mother's friends have been "poets?"

Some years ago, when I was teaching a graduate seminar in fiction at Columbia University, a well known male novelist visited my class to speak on his development as a writer. In discussing his formative years, he didn't realize it but he seri-

1

ously endangered his life by remarking that women writers are luckier than those of his sex because they usually spend so much time as children around their mothers and their mothers' friends in the kitchen.

What did he say that for? The women students immediately forgot about being in awe of him and began readying their attack for the question and answer period later on. Even I bristled. There again was the awful image of women locked away from the world in the kitchen with only each other to talk to, and their daughters locked in with them. 2

But my guest wasn't really being sexist or trying to be provocative or even spoiling for a fight. What he meant—when he got around to explaining himself more fully—was that, given the way children are (or were) raised in our society, with little girls kept closer to home and their mothers, the woman writer stands a better chance of being exposed, while growing up, to the kind of talk that goes on among women, more often than not in the kitchen; and that this experience gives her an edge over her male counterpart by instilling in her an appreciation for ordinary speech. 3

It was clear that my guest lecturer attached great importance to this, which is understandable. Common speech and the plain, workaday words that make it up are, after all, the stock in trade of some of the best fiction writers. They are the principal means by which characters in a novel or story reveal themselves and give voice sometimes to profound feelings and complex ideas about themselves and the world. Perhaps the proper measure of a writer's talent is skill in rendering everyday speech—when it is appropriate to the story—as well as the ability to tap, to exploit, the beauty, poetry and wisdom it often contains. 4

"If you say what's on your mind in the language that comes to you from your parents and your street and friends you'll probably say something beautiful." Grace Paley tells this, she says, to her students at the beginning of every writing course. 5

It's all a matter of exposure and training of the ear for the would-be writer in those early years of apprenticeship. And, according to my guest lecturer, this training, the best of it, often takes place in as unglamorous a setting as the kitchen. 6

He didn't know it, but he was essentially describing my experience as a little girl. I grew up among poets. Now they didn't look like poets—whatever that breed is supposed to look like. Nothing about them suggested that poetry was their calling. They were just a group of ordinary housewives and mothers, my mother included, who dressed in a way (shapeless housedresses, dowdy felt hats and long, dark, solemn coats) that made it impossible for me to imagine they had ever been young. 7

Nor did they do what poets were supposed to do—spend their days in an attic room writing verses. They never put pen to paper except to write occasionally to their relatives in Barbados. "I take my pen in hand hoping these few lines will find you in health as they leave me fair for the time being," was the way their letters invariably began. Rather, their day was spent "scrubbing floor," as they described the work they did. 8

Several mornings a week these unknown bards would put an apron and a pair of old house shoes in a shopping bag and take the train or streetcar from our 9 section of Brooklyn out to Flatbush. There, those who didn't have steady jobs would wait on certain designated corners for the white housewives in the neighborhood to come along and bargain with them over pay for a day's work cleaning their houses. This was the ritual even in the winter.

Later, armed with the few dollars they had earned, which in their vocabulary became "a few raw-mouth pennies," they made their way back to our neighborhood, where they would sometimes stop off to have a cup of tea or cocoa together before going home to cook dinner for their husbands and children.   10

The basement kitchen of the brownstone house where my family lived was the usual gathering place. Once inside the warm safety of its walls the women threw off the drab coats and hats, seated themselves at the large center table, drank their cups of tea or cocoa, and talked. While my sister and I sat at a smaller table over in a corner doing our homework, they talked—endlessly, passionately, poetically, and with impressive range. No subject was beyond them. True, they would indulge in the usual gossip: whose husband was running with whom, whose daughter looked slightly "in a way" (pregnant) under her bridal gown as she walked down the aisle. That sort of thing. But they also tackled the great issues of the time. They were always, for example, discussing the state of the economy. It was the mid and late 30's then, and the aftershock of the Depression, with its soup lines and suicides on Wall Street, was still being felt.   11

Some people, they declared, didn't know how to deal with adversity. They didn't know that you had to "tie up your belly" (hold in the pain, that is) when things got rough and go on with life. They took their image from the bellyband that is tied around the stomach of a newborn baby to keep the navel pressed in.   12

They talked politics. Roosevelt was their hero. He had come along and rescued the country with relief and jobs, and in gratitude they christened their sons Franklin and Delano and hoped they would live up to the names.   13

If F.D.R. was their hero, Marcus Garvey was their God. The name of the fiery, Jamaican-born black nationalist of the 20's was constantly invoked around the table. For he had been their leader when they first came to the United States from the West Indies shortly after World War I. They had contributed to his organization, the United Negro Improvement Association (UNIA), out of their meager salaries, bought shares in his ill-fated Black Star Shipping Line, and at the height of the movement they had marched as members of his "nurses' brigade" in their white uniforms up Seventh Avenue in Harlem during the great Garvey Day parades. Garvey: He lived on through the power of their memories.   14

And their talk was of war and rumors of wars. They raged against World War II when it broke out in Europe, blaming it on the politicians. "It's these politicians. They're the ones always starting up all this lot of war. But what they care? It's the poor people go to suffer and mothers with their sons." If it was *their* sons, they swore they would keep them out of the Army by giving them soap to eat each day to make their hearts sound defective. Hitler? He was for them "the devil incarnate."   15

Then there was home. They reminisced often and at length about home. The old country. Barbados—or Bimshire, as they affectionately called it. The little Caribbean island in the sun they loved but had to leave. "Poor—poor but sweet" was the way they remembered it.   16

And naturally they discussed their adopted home. America came in for   17
both good and bad marks. They lashed out at it for the racism they encountered.
They took to task some of the people they worked for, especially those who gave
them only a hardboiled egg and a few spoonfuls of cottage cheese for lunch.
"As if anybody can scrub floor on an egg and some cheese that don't have no taste
to it!"

Yet although they caught H in "this man country," as they called America, it   18
was nonetheless a place where "you could at least see your way to make a dollar."
That much they acknowledged. They might even one day accumulate enough dollars, with both them and their husbands working, to buy the brownstone houses
which, like my family, they were only leasing at that period. This was their consuming ambition: to "buy house" and to see the children through.

There was no way for me to understand it at the time, but the talk that filled   19
the kitchen those afternoons was highly functional. It served as therapy, the cheapest kind available to my mother and her friends. Not only did it help them recover
from the long wait on the corner that morning and the bargaining over their labor,
it restored them to a sense of themselves and reaffirmed their self-worth. Through
language they were able to overcome the humiliations of the work-day.

But more than therapy, that freewheeling, wide-ranging, exuberant talk func-   20
tioned as an outlet for the tremendous creative energy they possessed. They were
women in whom the need for self-expression was strong, and since language was
the only vehicle readily available to them they made of it an art form that—in
keeping with the African tradition in which art and life are one—was an integral
part of their lives.

And their talk was a refuge. They never really ceased being baffled and over-   21
whelmed by America—its vastness, complexity and power. Its strange customs and
laws. At a level beyond words they remained fearful and in awe. Their uneasiness
and fear were even reflected in their attitude toward the children they had given
birth to in this country. They referred to those like myself, the little Brooklyn-born
Bajans (Barbadians), as "these New York children" and complained that they
couldn't discipline us properly because of the laws here. "You can't beat these
children as you would like, you know, because the authorities in this place will dash
you in jail for them. After all, these is New York children." Not only were we
different, American, we had, as they saw it, escaped their ultimate authority.

Confronted therefore by a world they could not encompass, which even lim-   22
ited their rights as parents, and at the same time finding themselves permanently
separated from the world they had known, they took refuge in language. "Language is the only homeland," Czeslaw Milosz, the emigré Polish writer and Nobel
Laureate, has said. This is what it became for the women at the kitchen table.

It served another purpose also, I suspect. My mother and her friends were   23
after all the female counterpart of Ralph Ellison's invisible man. Indeed, you might
say they suffered a triple invisibility, being black, female and foreigners. They really didn't count in American society except as a source of cheap labor. But given
the kind of women they were, they couldn't tolerate the fact of their invisibility,
their powerlessness. And they fought back, using the only weapon at their command: the spoken word.

Those late afternoon conversations on a wide range of topics were a way for   24
them to feel they exercised some measure of control over their lives and the events
that shaped them. "Soully-gal, talk yuh talk!" they were always exhorting each
other. "In this man world you got to take yuh mouth and make a gun!" They were
in control, if only verbally and if only for the two hours or so that they remained in
our house.

For me, sitting over in the corner, being seen but not heard, which was the   25
rule for children in those days, it wasn't only what the women talked about—the
content—but the way they put things—their style. The insight, irony, wit and humor they brought to their stories and discussions and their poet's inventiveness and
daring with language—which of course I could only sense but not define back
then.

They had taken the standard English taught them in the primary schools of   26
Barbados and transformed it into an idiom, an instrument that more adequately
described them—changing around the syntax and imposing their own rhythm and
accent so that the sentences were more pleasing to their ears. They added the few
African sounds and words that had survived, such as the derisive suck-teeth sound
and the word "yam," meaning to eat. And to make it more vivid, more in keeping
with their expressive quality, they brought to bear a raft of metaphors, parables,
Biblical quotations, sayings and the like:

"The sea ain' got no back door," they would say, meaning that it wasn't like a   27
house where if there was a fire you could run out the back. Meaning that it was not
to be trifled with. And meaning perhaps in a larger sense that man should treat all
of nature with caution and respect.

"I has read hell by heart and called every generation blessed!" They sometimes   28
went in for hyperbole.

A woman expecting a baby was never said to be pregnant. They never used   29
that word. Rather, she was "in the way" or, better yet, "tumbling big." "Guess who
I butt up on in the market the other day tumbling big again!"

And a woman with a reputation of being too free with her sexual favors was   30
known in their book as a "thoroughfare"—the sense of men like a steady stream of
cars moving up and down the road of her life. Or she might be dubbed "a free-
bee," which was my favorite of the two. I liked the image it conjured up of a woman
scandalous perhaps but independent, who flitted from one flower to another in a
garden of male beauties, sampling their nectar, taking her pleasure at will, the
roles reversed.

And nothing, no matter how beautiful, was ever described as simply beautiful.   31
It was always "beautiful-ugly": the beautiful-ugly dress, the beautiful-ugly house,
the beautiful-ugly car. Why the word "ugly," I used to wonder, when the thing they
were referring to was beautiful, and they knew it. Why the antonym, the contradiction, the linking of opposites? It used to puzzle me greatly as a child.

There is the theory in linguistics which states that the idiom of a people, the   32
way they use language, reflects not only the most fundamental views they hold of
themselves and the world but their very conception of reality. Perhaps in using the
term "beautiful-ugly" to describe nearly everything, my mother and her friends
were expressing what they believed to be a fundamental dualism in life: the idea

that a thing is at the same time its opposite, and that these opposites, these contradictions make up the whole. But theirs was not a Manichaean brand of dualism
that sees matter, flesh, the body, as inherently evil, because they constantly addressed each other as "soully-gal"—soul: spirit; gal: the body, flesh, the visible self.
And it was clear from their tone that they gave one as much weight and importance
as the other. They had never heard of the mind/body split.

As for God, they summed up His essential attitude in a phrase. "God," they   33
would say, "don't love ugly and He ain't stuck on pretty."

Using everyday speech, the simple commonplace words—but always with   34
imagination and skill—they gave voice to the most complex ideas. Flannery
O'Connor would have approved of how they made ordinary language work, as she
put it, "doubletime," stretching, shading, deepening its meaning. Like Joseph Con-
rad they were always trying to infuse new life in the "old old words worn thin
. . . by . . . careless usage." And the goals of their oral art were the same as his: "to
make you hear, to make you feel . . . to make you *see*." This was their guiding
esthetic.

By the time I was 8 or 9, I graduated from the corner of the kitchen to the   35
neighborhood library, and thus from the spoken to the written word. The Macon
Street Branch of the Brooklyn Public Library was an imposing half block long
edifice of heavy gray masonry, with glass-paneled doors at the front and two tall
metal torches symbolizing the light that comes of learning flanking the wide steps
outside.

The inside was just as impressive. More steps—of pale marble with gleam-   36
ing brass railings at the center and sides—led up to the circulation desk, and a
great pendulum clock gazed down from the balcony stacks that faced the entrance.
Usually stationed at the top of the steps like the guards outside Buckingham
Palace was the custodian, a stern-faced West Indian type who for years, until I was
old enough to obtain an adult card, would immediately shoo me with one hand into
the Children's Room and with the other threaten me into silence, a finger to his
lips. You would have thought he was the chief librarian and not just someone
whose job it was to keep the brass polished and the clock wound. I put him in a
story called "Barbados" years later and had terrible things happen to him at the
end.

I sheltered from the storm of adolescence in the Macon Street library, reading   37
voraciously, indiscriminately, everything from Jane Austen to Zane Grey, but with
a special passion for the long, full-blown, richly detailed 18th- and 19th-century
picaresque tales: "Tom Jones," "Great Expectations," "Vanity Fair."

But although I loved nearly everything I read and would enter fully into the   38
lives of the characters—indeed, would cease being myself and become them—I
sensed a lack after a time. Something I couldn't quite define was missing. And then
one day, browsing in the poetry section, I came across a book by someone called
Paul Laurence Dunbar, and opening it I found the photograph of a wistful, sad-
eyed poet who to my surprise was black. I turned to a poem at random. "Little
brown-baby wif spa'klin / eyes / Come to yo' pappy an' set on his knee." Although I
had a little difficulty at first with the words in dialect, the poem spoke to me as

nothing I had read before of the closeness, the special relationship I had had with my father, who by then had become an ardent believer in Father Divine and gone to live in Father's "kingdom" in Harlem. Reading it helped to ease somewhat the tight knot of sorrow and longing I carried around in my chest that refused to go away. I read another poem. " 'Lias! 'Lias! Bless de Lawd! / Don' you know de day's / erbroad? / Ef you don' get up, you scamp / Dey'll be trouble in dis camp." I laughed. It reminded me of the way my mother sometimes yelled at my sister and me to get out of bed in the mornings.

And another: "Seen my lady home las' night / Jump back, honey, jump back. / Hel' huh han' an' sque'z it tight . . ." About love between a black man and a black woman. I had never seen that written about before and it roused in me all kinds of delicious feelings and hopes. 39

And I began to search then for books and stories and poems about "The Race" (as it was put back then), about my people. While not abandoning Thackeray, Fielding, Dickens and the others, I started asking the reference librarian, who was white, for books by Negro writers, although I must admit I did so at first with a feeling of shame—the shame I and many others used to experience in those days whenever the word "Negro" or "colored" came up. 40

No grade school literature teacher of mine had ever mentioned Dunbar or James Weldon Johnson or Langston Hughes. I didn't know that Zora Neale Hurston existed and was busy writing and being published during those years. Nor was I made aware of people like Frederick Douglass and Harriet Tubman—their spirit and example—or the great 19th-century abolitionist and feminist Sojourner Truth. There wasn't even Negro History Week when I attended P.S. 35 on Decatur Street! 41

What I needed, what all the kids—West Indian and native black American alike—with whom I grew up needed, was an equivalent of the Jewish shul, someplace where we could go after school—the schools that were shortchanging us— and read works by those like ourselves and learn about our history. 42

It was around that time also that I began harboring the dangerous thought of someday trying to write myself. Perhaps a poem about an apple tree, although I had never seen one. Or the story of a girl who could magically transplant herself to wherever she wanted to be in the world—such as Father Divine's kingdom in Harlem. Dunbar—his dark, eloquent face, his large volume of poems—permitted me to dream that I might someday write, and with something of the power with words my mother and her friends possessed. 43

When people at readings and writers' conferences ask me who my major influences were, they are sometimes a little disappointed when I don't immediately name the usual literary giants. True, I am indebted to those writers, white and black, whom I read during my formative years and still read for instruction and pleasure. But they were preceded in my life by another set of giants whom I always acknowledge before all others: the group of women around the table long ago. They taught me my first lessons in the narrative art. They trained my ear. They set a standard of excellence. This is why the best of my work must be attributed to them; it stands as testimony to the rich legacy of language and culture they so freely passed on to me in the wordshop of the kitchen. 44

Rhetorical Focus

1. Marshall does not actually start describing life in her family's kitchen until her eleventh paragraph. How do her first ten paragraphs establish the purpose and focus of her description?
2. How does bringing in the library help Marshall make points about the kitchen?
3. Do Marshall and Kazin use the same tone in describing their families' kitchens? If not, how do their tones differ? Do they each give concrete evidence for feeling the way they do?

Thematic Focus

1. How was the "talk" of Marshall's mother and her friends "highly functional" (paragraph 19)? Does she succeed in getting you to consider these women to be "poets"? Support your answers by referring to Marshall's quotations from the women.
2. Marshall suggests that "the proper measure of a writer's talent is skill in rendering everyday speech—when it is appropriate to the story—as well as the ability to tap, to exploit, the beauty, poetry and wisdom it often contains" (paragraph 4). Do you expect to use everyday speech in your academic writing? Why or why not?
3. Marshall suggests that "being black, female, and foreigners" (paragraph 23) affected these women's lives. Do you find yourself agreeing with her? Do gender and ethnic background matter much in Kazin's account?

Suggestions for Writing

1. Marshall thinks of her family's kitchen as a "wordshop." Kazin thinks of his family's kitchen as a "workshop." Write an essay explaining how these different conceptions lead them to emphasize different things. Use details from each text to support your answer.
2. Describe a kitchen or another room you know well, choosing and organizing details so that your readers get one dominant impression of the life lived in this room. Note the possible approaches that Kazin and Marshall demonstrate. As you use various details to convey one main impression of your room, you may find that you also wish to compare it with the kitchens these two authors describe.
3. Not atypically, Kazin and Marshall associate the kitchens of their youth with women. A mother presides over the kitchen in each text, and in Marshall's, the kitchen becomes a refuge for a whole community of women. Choose a place in your home or community that you associate with one sex much more than another. Then, write an essay explaining the ways that this is or was a "gendered" space. As part of your explanation, indicate whether you are content that the space is "gendered" and whether the people there would agree with your perspective on it.

DEPICTING LIFE IN A COMMUNITY

This constellation moves beyond rooms to suggest ways of depicting life in a wider community. When writers set out to describe communities they know, they face a number of rhetorical decisions. Above all, they need to determine their audience's prior knowledge about the community, the main impression they want to convey about it, and the details that will best achieve their aim. For example, think what you need to focus on if you want to help people unfamiliar with your community begin to understand and appreciate it. How important are the community's population size, landscape, climate, history, majority and minority groups, leaders, eccentrics, language, ethnic background, forms of work, forms of entertainment, meeting places, political affiliations, and ethical codes, among other things? What assumptions about your community, if any, do you need to counter?

Here, Gretel Ehrlich and Margaret Laurence set out to depict communities that they know many of their readers would normally disregard. Ehrlich describes the "open spaces" of Wyoming, where she moved after living elsewhere for 30 years. Laurence describes a kind of "open space" where she once lived, the small, isolated prairie town of her youth in the Canadian province of Manitoba. You will probably find yourself wondering if and how it matters that Ehrlich discusses a community she embraced and Laurence a community she left. What do you think is the relationship between your present sense of your life's design and the ways you might describe places where you lived? Whatever their ultimate differences in perspective, though, Ehrlich and Laurence both show ways of helping readers to see a community that otherwise might have been neglected. For example, note how each uses the changing seasons to evoke setting. In effect, both also raise the question of just what community feeling is because the people they describe have to build relationships away from mass society. Both suggest, too, that their communities represent specific principles that the larger culture should esteem. As you read Ehrlich's and Laurence's essays, think what values you associate with the communities you have known, and how your depictions of these communities might emphasize their ideals.

The Solace of Open Spaces

Gretel Ehrlich

A native of California, Gretel Ehrlich (b. 1946) attended Bennington College, the film school of the University of California at Los Angeles, and the New School for Social Research in New York City. When she visited Wyoming in 1976 to film a documentary on sheepherders, she found herself increasingly attracted to the state. Eventually she settled there, and today she and her husband own a ranch in the Big Horn Basin. Much of Ehrlich's writing lyrically describes and celebrates the region she now calls home. Her essays about Wyoming have appeared in such publications as *Harper's, The Atlantic, The New York Times*, and *Time*. Ehrlich has also published short stories and, in 1988, a novel entitled *Heart Mountain*, which concerns the internment of Japanese-Americans in Wyoming during World War II. "The Solace of Open Spaces" comes from her first collection of essays, published in 1985 under the same title.

Reflections Before Reading

What would you want to know about a geographical area before deciding whether to live there? Are there particular areas of North America where you would never want to live? If so, explain your reasoning. What do you associate with Wyoming, the state that Ehrlich describes in the following essay? What do you think are the characteristics of someone who enjoys living there?

It's May and I've just awakened from a nap, curled against sagebrush the way my 1
dog taught me to sleep—sheltered from wind. A front is pulling the huge sky over me, and from the dark a hailstone has hit me on the head. I'm trailing a band of two thousand sheep across a stretch of Wyoming badlands, a fifty-mile trip that takes five days because sheep shade up in hot sun and won't budge until it's cool. Bunched together now, and excited into a run by the storm, they drift across dry

land, tumbling into draws like water and surge out again onto the rugged, choppy plateaus that are the building blocks of this state.

The name Wyoming comes from an Indian word meaning "at the great plains," but the plains are really valleys, great arid valleys, sixteen hundred square miles, with the horizon bending up on all sides into mountain ranges. This gives the vastness a sheltering look. 2

Winter lasts six months here. Prevailing winds spill snowdrifts to the east, and new storms from the northwest replenish them. This white bulk is sometimes dizzying, even nauseating, to look at. At twenty, thirty, and forty degrees below zero, not only does your car not work, but neither do your mind and body. The landscape hardens into a dungeon of space. During the winter, while I was riding to find a new calf, my jeans froze to the saddle, and in the silence that such cold creates I felt like the first person on earth, or the last. 3

Today the sun is out—only a few clouds billowing. In the east, where the sheep have started off without me, the benchland tilts up in a series of eroded red-earthed mesas, planed flat on top by a million years of water; behind them, a bold line of muscular scarps rears up ten thousand feet to become the Big Horn Mountains. A tidal pattern is engraved into the ground, as if left by the sea that once covered this state. Canyons curve down like galaxies to meet the oncoming rush of flat land. 4

To live and work in this kind of open country, with its hundred-mile views, is to lose the distinction between background and foreground. When I asked an older ranch hand to describe Wyoming's openness, he said, "It's all a bunch of nothing—wind and rattlesnakes—and so much of it you can't tell where you're going or where you've been and it don't make much difference." John, a sheepman I know, is tall and handsome and has an explosive temperament. He has a perfect intuition about people and sheep. They call him "Highpockets," because he's so long-legged; his graceful stride matches the distances he has to cover. He says, "Open space hasn't affected me at all. It's all the people moving in on it." The huge ranch he was born on takes up much of one county and spreads into another state; to put 100,000 miles on his pickup in three years and never leave home is not unusual. A friend of mine has an aunt who ranched on Powder River and didn't go off her place for eleven years. When her husband died, she quickly moved to town, bought a car, and drove around the States to see what she'd been missing. 5

Most people tell me they've simply driven through Wyoming, as if there were nothing to stop for. Or else they've skied in Jackson Hole, a place Wyomingites acknowledge uncomfortably because its green beauty and chic affluence are mismatched with the rest of the state. Most of Wyoming has a "lean-to" look. Instead of big, roomy barns and Victorian houses, there are dugouts, low sheds, log cabins, sheep camps, and fence lines that look like driftwood blown haphazardly into place. People here still feel pride because they live in such a harsh place, part of the glamorous cowboy past, and they are determined not to be the victims of a mining-dominated future. 6

Most characteristic of the state's landscape is what a developer euphemistically describes as "indigenous growth right up to your front door"—a reference to waterless stands of salt sage, snakes, jack rabbits, deerflies, red dust, a brief respite 7 of wildflowers, dry washes, and no trees. In the Great Plains the vistas look like music, like Kyries of grass, but Wyoming seems to be the doing of a mad architect—tumbled and twisted, ribboned with faded, deathbed colors, thrust up and pulled down as if the place had been startled out of a deep sleep and thrown into a pure light.

I came here four years ago. I had not planned to stay, but I couldn't make   8 myself leave. John, the sheepman, put me to work immediately. It was spring, and shearing time. For fourteen days of fourteen hours each, we moved thousands of sheep through sorting corrals to be sheared, branded, and deloused. I suspect that my original motive for coming here was to "lose myself" in new and unpopulated territory. Instead of producing the numbness I thought I wanted, life on the sheep ranch woke me up. The vitality of the people I was working with flushed out what had become a hallucinatory rawness inside me. I threw away my clothes and bought new ones; I cut my hair. The arid country was a clean slate. Its absolute indifference steadied me.

Sagebrush covers 58,000 square miles of Wyoming. The biggest city has a   9 population of fifty thousand, and there are only five settlements that could be called cities in the whole state. The rest are towns, scattered across the expanse with as much as sixty miles between them, their populations two thousand, fifty, or ten. They are fugitive-looking, perched on a barren, windblown bench, or tagged onto a river or a railroad, or laid out straight in a farming valley with implement stores and a block-long Mormon church. In the eastern part of the state, which slides down into the Great Plains, the new mining settlements are boomtowns, trailer cities, metal knots on flat land.

Despite the desolate look, there's a coziness to living in this state. There are so   10 few people (only 470,000) that ranchers who buy and sell cattle know one another statewide; the kids who choose to go to college usually go to the state's one university, in Laramie; hired hands work their way around Wyoming in a lifetime of hirings and firings. And despite the physical separation, people stay in touch, often driving two or three hours to another ranch for dinner.

Seventy-five years ago, when travel was by buckboard or horseback, cowboys   11 who were temporarily out of work rode the grub line—drifting from ranch to ranch, mending fences or milking cows, and receiving in exchange a bed and meals. Gossip and messages traveled this slow circuit with them, creating an intimacy between ranchers who were three and four weeks' ride apart. One old-time couple I know, whose turn-of-the-century homestead was used by an outlaw gang as a relay station for stolen horses, recall that if you were traveling, desperado or not, any lighted ranch house was a welcome sign. Even now, for someone who lives in a remote spot, arriving at a ranch or coming to town for supplies is cause for celebration. To emerge from isolation can be disorienting. Everything looks bright, new, vivid. After I had been herding sheep for only three days, the sound of the camp tender's pickup flustered me. Longing for human company, I felt a foolish grin take over my face; yet I had to resist an urgent temptation to run and hide.

Things happen suddenly in Wyoming, the change of seasons and weather; for   12 people, the violent swings in and out of isolation. But good-naturedness is concomitant with severity. Friendliness is a tradition. Strangers passing on the road wave hello. A common sight is two pickups stopped side by side far out on a range, on a dirt track winding through the sage. The drivers will share a cigarette, uncap their thermos bottles, and pass a battered cup, steaming with coffee, between windows. These meetings summon up the details of several generations, because, in Wyoming, private histories are largely public knowledge.

Because ranch work is a physical and, these days, economic strain, being "at   13
home on the range" is a matter of vigor, self-reliance, and common sense. A person's life is not a series of dramatic events for which he or she is applauded or exiled but a slow accumulation of days, seasons, years, fleshed out by the generational weight of one's family and anchored by a land-bound sense of place.

In most parts of Wyoming, the human population is visibly outnumbered by   14
the animal. Not far from my town of fifty, I rode into a narrow valley and startled a herd of two hundred elk. Eagles look like small people as they eat car-killed deer by the road. Antelope, moving in small, graceful bands, travel at sixty miles an hour, their mouths open as if drinking in the space.

The solitude in which westerners live makes them quiet. They telegraph   15
thoughts and feelings by the way they tilt their heads and listen; pulling their Stetsons into a steep dive over their eyes, or pigeon-toeing one boot over the other, they lean against a fence with a fat wedge of Copenhagen beneath their lower lips and take in the whole scene. These detached looks of quiet amusement are sometimes cynical, but they can also come from a dry-eyed humility as lucid as the air is clear.

Conversation goes on in what sounds like a private code; a few phrases imply a   16
complex of meanings. Asking directions, you get a curious list of details. While trailing sheep I was told to "ride up to that kinda upturned rock, follow the pink wash, turn left at the dump, and then you'll see the water hole." One friend told his wife on roundup to "turn at the salt lick and the dead cow," which turned out to be a scattering of bones and no salt lick at all.

Sentence structure is shortened to the skin and bones of a thought. Descrip-   17
tive words are dropped, even verbs; a cowboy looking over a corral full of horses will say to a wrangler, "Which one needs rode?" People hold back their thoughts in what seems to be a dumbfounded silence, then erupt with an excoriating perceptive remark. Language, so compressed, becomes metaphorical. A rancher ended a relationship with one remark: "You're a bad check," meaning bouncing in and out was intolerable, and even coming back would be no good.

What's behind this laconic style is shyness. There is no vocabulary for the   18
subject of feelings. It's not a hangdog shyness, or anything coy—always there's a robust spirit in evidence behind the restraint, as if the earth-dredging wind that pulls across Wyoming had carried its people's voices away but everything else in them had shouldered confidently into the breeze.

I've spent hours riding to sheep camp at dawn in a pickup when nothing was   19
said; eaten meals in the cookhouse when the only words spoken were a mumbled "Thank you, ma'am" at the end of dinner. The silence is profound. Instead of

talking, we seem to share one eye. Keenly observed, the world is transformed. The landscape is engorged with detail, every movement on it chillingly sharp. The air between people is charged. Days unfold, bathed in their own music. Nights become hallucinatory; dreams, prescient.

Spring weather is capricious and mean. It snows, then blisters with heat. 20 There have been tornadoes. They lay their elephant trunks out in the sage until they find houses, then slurp everything up and leave. I've noticed that melting snowbanks hiss and rot, viperous, then drip into calm pools where ducklings hatch and livestock, being trailed to summer range, drink. With the ice cover gone, rivers churn a milkshake brown, taking culverts and small bridges with them. Water in such an arid place (the average annual rainfall where I live is less than eight inches) is like blood. It festoons drab land with green veins; a line of cottonwoods following a stream; a strip of alfalfa; and, on ditch banks, wild asparagus growing.

I've moved to a small cattle ranch owned by friends. It's at the foot of the Big 21 Horn Mountains. A few weeks ago, I helped them deliver a calf who was stuck halfway out of his mother's body. By the time he was freed, we could see a heartbeat, but he was straining against a swollen tongue for air. Mary and I held him upside down by his back feet, while Stan, on his hands and knees in the blood, gave the calf mouth-to-mouth resuscitation. I have a vague memory of being pneumonia-choked as a child, my mother giving me her air, which may account for my romance with this windswept state.

If anything is endemic to Wyoming, it is wind. This big room of space is swept 22 out daily, leaving a bone yard of fossils, agates, and carcasses in every stage of decay. Though it was water that initially shaped the state, wind is the meticulous gardener, raising dust and pruning the sage.

I try to imagine a world in which I could ride my horse across uncharted land. 23 There is no wilderness left; wildness, yes, but true wilderness has been gone on this continent since the time of Lewis and Clark's overland journey.

Two hundred years ago, the Crow, Shoshone, Arapaho, Cheyenne, and Sioux 24 roamed the intermountain West, orchestrating their movements according to hunger, season, and warfare. Once they acquired horses, they traversed the spines of all the big Wyoming ranges—the Absarokas, the Wind Rivers, the Tetons, the Big Horns—and wintered on the unprotected plains that fan out from them. Space was life. The world was their home.

What was life-giving to Native Americans was often nightmarish to sodbusters 25 who had arrived encumbered with families and ethnic pasts to be transplanted in nearly uninhabitable land. The great distances, the shortage of water and trees, and the loneliness created unexpected hardships for them. In her book *O Pioneers!*, Willa Cather gives a settler's version of the bleak landscape:

> The little town behind them had vanished as if it had never been, had fallen behind the swell of the prairie, and the stern frozen country received them into its bosom. The homesteads were few and far apart; here and there a windmill gaunt against the sky, a sod house crouching in a hollow.

The emptiness of the West was for others a geography of possibility. Men and 26 women who amassed great chunks of land and struggled to preserve unfenced empires were, despite their self-serving motives, unwitting geographers. They understood the lay of the land. But by the 1850s the Oregon and Mormon trails sported bumper-to-bumper traffic. Wealthy landowners, many of them aristocratic absentee landlords, known as remittance men because they were paid to come West and get out of their families' hair, overstocked the range with more than a million herd of cattle. By 1885 the feed and water were desperately short, and the winter of 1886 laid out the gaunt bodies of dead animals so closely together that when the thaw came, one rancher from Kaycee claimed to have walked on cowhide all the way to Crazy Woman Creek, twenty miles away.

Territorial Wyoming was a boy's world. The land was generous with every- 27 thing but water. At first there was room enough, food enough, for everyone. And, as with all beginnings, an expansive mood set in. The young cowboys, drifters, shopkeepers, schoolteachers, were heroic, lawless, generous, rowdy, and tenacious. The individualism and optimism generated during those times have endured.

John Tisdale rode north with the trail herds from Texas. He was a college- 28 educated man with enough money to buy a small outfit near the Powder River. While driving home from the town of Buffalo with a buckboard full of Christmas toys for his family and a winter's supply of food, he was shot in the back by an agent of the cattle barons who resented the encroachment of small-time stockmen like him. The wealthy cattlemen tried to control all the public grazing land by restricting membership in the Wyoming Stock Growers Association, as if it were a country club. They ostracized from roundups and brandings cowboys and ranchers who were not members, then denounced them as rustlers. Tisdale's death, the second such cold-blooded murder, kicked off the Johnson County cattle war, which was no simple good-guy–bad-guy shoot-out but a complicated class struggle between landed gentry and less affluent settlers—a shocking reminder that the West was not an egalitarian sanctuary after all.

Fencing ultimately enforced boundaries, but barbed wire abrogated space. It 29 was stretched across the beautiful valleys, into the mountains, over desert badlands, through buffalo grass. The "anything is possible" fever—the lure of any new place—was constricted. The integrity of the land as a geographical body, and the freedom to ride anywhere on it, were lost.

I punched cows with a young man named Martin, who is the great-grandson of 30 John Tisdale. His inheritance is not the open land that Tisdale knew and prematurely lost but a rage against restraint.

Wyoming tips down as you head northeast; the highest ground—the Laramie 31 Plains—is on the Colorado border. Up where I live, the Big Horn River leaks into difficult, arid terrain. In the basin where it's dammed, sandhill cranes gather and, with delicate legwork, slice through the stilled water. I was driving by with a rancher one morning when he commented that cranes are "old-fashioned." When I asked why, he said, "Because they mate for life." Then he looked at me with a twinkle in his eyes, as if to say he really did believe in such things but also understood why we break our own rules.

In all this open space, values crystallize quickly. People are strong on scruples   32
but tenderhearted about quirky behavior. A friend and I found one ranch hand,
who's "not quite right in the head," sitting in front of the badly decayed carcass of a
cow, shaking his finger and saying, "Now, I don't want you to do this ever again!"
When I asked what was wrong with him, I was told, "He's goofier than hell, just
like the rest of us." Perhaps because the West is historically new, conventional
morality is still felt to be less important than rock-bottom truths. Though there's
always a lot of teasing and sparring, people are blunt with one another, sometimes
even cruel, believing honesty is stronger medicine than sympathy, which may console but often conceals.

The formality that goes hand in hand with the rowdiness is known as the West-   33
ern Code. It's a list of practical do's and don'ts, faithfully observed. A friend, Cliff,
who runs a trapline in the winter, cut off half his foot while chopping a hole in the
ice. Alone, he dragged himself to his pickup and headed for town, stopping to open
the ranch gate as he left, and getting out to close it again, thus losing, in his obser-
vance of rules, precious time and blood. Later, he commented, "How would it
look, them having to come to the hospital to tell me their cows had gotten out?"

Accustomed to emergencies, my friends doctor each other from the vet's bag   34
with relish. When one old-timer suffered a heart attack in hunting camp, his partner quickly stirred up a brew of red horse liniment and hot water and made the
half-conscious victim drink it, then tied him onto a horse and led him twenty miles
to town. He regained consciousness and lived.

The roominess of the state has affected political attitudes as well. Ranchers   35
keep up with world politics and the convulsions of the economy but are basically
isolationists. Being used to running their own small empires of land and livestock,
they're suspicious of big government. It's a "don't fence me in" holdover from a
century ago. They still want the elbow room their grandfathers had, so they're
strongly conservative, but with a populist twist.

Summer is the season when we get our "cowboy tans"—on the lower parts of   36
our faces and on three fourths of our arms. Excessive heat, in the nineties and
higher, sends us outside with the mosquitoes. In winter we're tucked inside our
houses, and the white wasteland outside appears to be expanding, but in summer
all the greenery abridges space. Summer is a go-ahead season. Every living thing is
off the block and in the race: battalions of bugs in flight and biting; bats swinging
around my log cabin as if the bases were loaded and someone had hit a home run.
Some of summer's high-speed growth is ominous: larkspur, death camas, and
green greasewood can kill sheep—an ironic idea, dying in this desert from eating
what is too verdant. With sixteen hours of daylight, farmers and ranchers irrigate
feverishly. There are first, second, and third cuttings of hay, some crews averaging
only four hours of sleep a night for weeks. And, like the cowboys who in summer
ride the night rodeo circuit, nighthawks make daredevil dives at dusk with an eerie
whirring sound like a plane going down on the shimmering horizon.

In the town where I live, they've had to board up the dance-hall windows   37
because there have been so many fights. There's so little to do except work that
people wind up in a state of idle agitation that becomes fatalistic, as if there were

nothing to be done about all this untapped energy. So the dark side to the grandeur of these spaces is the small-mindedness that seals people in. Men become hermits; women go mad. Cabin fever explodes into suicides, or into grudges and lifelong family feuds. Two sisters in my area inherited a ranch but found they couldn't get along. They fenced the place in half. When one's cows got out and mixed with the other's, the women went at each other with shovels. They ended up in the same hospital room but never spoke a word to each other for the rest of their lives.

After the brief lushness of summer, the sun moves south. The range grass is   38
brown. Livestock is trailed back down from the mountains. Water holes begin to frost over at night. Last fall Martin asked me to accompany him on a pack trip. With five horses, we followed a river into the mountains behind the tiny Wyoming town of Meeteetse. Groves of aspen, red and orange, gave off a light that made us look toasted. Our hunting camp was so high that clouds skidded across our foreheads, then slowed to sail out across the warm valleys. Except for a bull moose who wandered into our camp and mistook our black gelding for a rival, we shot at nothing.

One of our evening entertainments was to watch the night sky. My dog, a   39
dingo bred to herd sheep, also came on the trip. He is so used to the silence and empty skies that when an airplane flies over he always looks up and eyes the distant intruder quizzically. The sky, lately, seems to be much more crowded than it used to be. Satellites make their silent passes in the dark with great regularity. We counted eighteen in one hour's viewing. How odd to think that while they circumnavigated the planet, Martin and I had moved only six miles into our local wilderness and had seen no other human for the two weeks we stayed there.

At night, by moonlight, the land is whittled to slivers—a ridge, a river, a strip   40
of grassland stretching to the mountains, then the huge sky. One morning a full moon was setting in the west just as the sun was rising. I felt precariously balanced between the two as I loped across a meadow. For a moment, I could believe that the stars, which were still visible, work like cooper's bands, holding together everything above Wyoming.

Space has a spiritual equivalent and can heal what is divided and burdensome   41
in us. My grandchildren will probably use space shuttles for a honeymoon trip or to recover from heart attacks, but closer to home we might also learn how to carry space inside ourselves in the effortless way we carry our skins. Space represents sanity, not a life purified, dull, or "spaced out" but one that might accommodate intelligently any idea or situation.

From the clayey soil of northern Wyoming is mined bentonite, which is used   42
as a filler in candy, gum, and lipstick. We Americans are great on fillers, as if what we have, what we are, is not enough. We have a cultural tendency toward denial, but, being affluent, we strangle ourselves with what we can buy. We have only to look at the houses we build to see how we build *against* space, the way we drink against pain and loneliness. We fill up space as if it were a pie shell, with things whose opacity further obstructs our ability to see what is already there.

Rhetorical Focus

1. Ehrlich begins with a particular day, describing it in the present tense. After the fourth paragraph, however, she stops referring to it. What may be her rhetorical purpose, then, in starting with this day? Should she have returned to it at some point?
2. In what ways does Ehrlich organize her essay? Do you as her reader have any difficulty following it? Why or why not?
3. What knowledge of Wyoming does Ehrlich seem to assume that her audience already has? What knowledge does she seem to assume that her readers need? What, ultimately, do you think she wants her readers to do? Is she suggesting that we all move to Wyoming, for example?

Thematic Focus

1. Ehrlich relates several anecdotes in this essay. Choose the one that strikes you the most, and explain why it is effective. Consider not only the language of the anecdote, but also how it helps Ehrlich make an important point about the community she is depicting.
2. What are the basic elements of the "Western Code," as Ehrlich describes it? Would you be comfortable living under this code? Why or why not?
3. Would you respond to this essay differently if the author were a male rancher instead of a female one? Explain.

Where the World Began

Margaret Laurence

A native of the small town of Neepawa in the Canadian province of
Manitoba, Margaret Laurence (1926–1987) became one of her country's
leading novelists and short-story writers. Many of her writings explore the
struggle of various characters to establish a personal identity and sustaining
values within the changing culture of her homeland. Even her works of
fiction often deal with her native village in disguised form. Laurence's fiction
includes *The Tomorrow Tamer and Other Stories*, *The Stone Angel*, *The Fire
Dwellers*, *The Diviners*, and *A Jest of God*, a 1966 novel on which the film
Rachel, Rachel was based. Laurence also translated and edited a volume of
prose and poetry from Somaliland, an African country where she lived for a
time. She lived in England as well before finally settling in a small town in
Ontario, Canada. The following autobiographical essay first appeared in the
December 1972 issue of *Maclean's*, a Canadian magazine. Laurence then
included it with others of her personal essays in her 1977 book *Heart of a
Stranger*.

Reflections Before Reading

What do you associate with Canada? Have you thought of it as having a
distinct culture, or have you thought that it pretty much resembles the
United States? Try to identify the source of your assumptions about this
country. The following essay describes a small, isolated prairie town about
40 years ago. What do you anticipate that life would be like in such a town?

A strange place it was, that place where the world began. A place of incredible   1
happenings, splendors and revelations, despairs like multitudinous pits of isolated
hells. A place of shadow-spookiness, inhabited by the unknowable dead. A place of
jubilation and of mourning, horrible and beautiful.

It was, in fact, a small prairie town.   2

Because that settlement and that land were my first and for many years my   3
only real knowledge of this planet, in some profound way they remain my world,
my way of viewing. My eyes were formed there. Towns like ours, set in a sea of

France. My own young mother lay in that graveyard, beside other dead of our kin, and when I was 10, my father too, only 40, left the living town for the dead dwelling on the hill.

When I was 18, I couldn't wait to get out of that town, away from the prairies. I did not know then that I would carry the land and town all my life within my skull, that they would form the mainspring and source of the writing I was to do, wherever and however far away I might live. [12]

This was my territory in the time of my youth, and in a sense my life since then has been an attempt to look at it, to come to terms with it. Stultifying to the mind it could certainly be, and sometimes was, but not to the imagination. It was many things, but it was never dull. [13]

The same, I now see, could be said for Canada in general. Why on earth did generations of Canadians pretend to believe this country dull? We knew perfectly well it wasn't. Yet for so long we did not proclaim what we knew. If our upsurge of so-called nationalism seems odd or irrelevant now to outsiders, and even to some of our own people (*what's all the fuss about?*), they might try to understand that for many years we valued ourselves insufficiently, living as we did under the huge shadows of those two dominating figures, Uncle Sam and Britannia. We have only just begun to value ourselves, our land, our abilities. We have only just begun to recognize our legends and to give shape to our myths. [14]

There are, God knows, enough aspects to deplore about this country. When I see the killing of our lakes and rivers with industrial wastes, I feel rage and despair. When I see our industries and natural resources increasingly taken over by America, I feel an overwhelming discouragement, especially as I cannot simply say, "damn Yankees." It should never be forgotten that it is we ourselves who have sold such a large amount of our birthright for a mess of plastic Progress. When I saw the War Measures Act being invoked, I lost forever the vestigial remains of the naïve wish-belief that repression could not happen here, or would not. And yet of course I had known all along in the deepest and often hidden cave of the heart that anything can happen anywhere, for the seeds both of man's freedom and of his captivity are found everywhere, even in the microcosm of a prairie town. But in raging against our injustices, our stupidities, I do so *as family*, as I did, and still do in writing, about those aspects of my town which I hated and which are always in some ways aspects of myself. [15]

The land still draws me more than other lands. I have lived in Africa and in England, but splendid as both can be they do not have the power to move me in the same way as, for example, that part of southern Ontario where I spent four months last summer in a cedar cabin beside a river. "Scratch a Canadian and you find a phony pioneer," I used to say to myself, in warning. But all the same it is true, I think, that we are not yet totally alienated from physical earth, and let us only pray we do not become so. I once thought that my lifelong fear and mistrust of cities made me a kind of old-fashioned freak; now I see it differently. [16]

The cabin has a long window across its front western wall, and sitting at the oak table there, in the mornings, I used to look out at the river and at the tall trees beyond, green-gold in the early light. The river was bronze; the sun caught it [17] strangely, reflecting upon its surface the near-shore sand ripples underneath, making it seem momentarily as though a whole flotilla of gold flickerings sailed there. Suddenly, the silver crescenting of a fish, gone before the eye could clearly give image to it. The old man next door said these leaping fish were carp. Himself, he preferred muskie, for he was a real fisherman and the muskie gave him a fight. The wind most often blew from the south, and the river flowed toward the south, so when the water was wind-riffled and the current was strong, the river seemed to be flowing both ways. I liked this, and interpreted it as an omen, a natural symbol.

A few years ago, when I was back in Winnipeg, I gave a talk at my old college. It was open to the public, and afterward a very old man came up to me and asked me if my maiden name had been Wemyss. I said yes, thinking that he might have known my father or my grandfather. But no. "When I was a young lad," he said, "I once worked for your great-grandfather, Robert Wemyss, when he had the sheep ranch." I think that was the moment when I realized something of great importance to me. My long-ago families came from Scotland and Ireland, but in a sense that no longer mattered so much. My true roots were here and would remain so, whatever happened.   18

I am not very patriotic, in the usual meaning of that word. I cannot say, "My country right or wrong" in any political, social or literary context. But one thing is inalterable, for better or worse.   19

This is not only where my world began. It is also the land of my ancestors.   20

Rhetorical Focus

1. Laurence originally wrote her essay for a Canadian audience. Does this fact seem related to the essay's content and purpose? Do you think the essay might have been different if Laurence had written it for a magazine in the United States? Explain.

2. Laurence begins several paragraphs with a topic sentence that the rest of the paragraph develops. Identify a few examples. Then explain why you think she begins some of her other paragraphs the way she does.

3. Early in her essay Margaret Laurence reports, "I have had it said to me that the railway trip across Canada is spectacular, except for the prairies, when it would be desirable to go to sleep for several days, until the ordeal is over" (paragraph 2). Early in her essay Gretel Ehrlich reports, "Most people tell me they've simply driven through Wyoming, as if there were nothing to stop for" (paragraph 6). What does including these statements then obligate Laurence and Ehrlich to do in their essays? Do you find them equally successful in meeting the obligation? Cite details from their texts.

Thematic Focus

1. Summarize in your own words what you take to be Laurence's attitude toward her home town as she looks back on it. What has shaped her attitude over the years? How much does her attitude seem to have changed? Support your answers with details from the text.

2. Do Ehrlich and Laurence consider the same kinds of things important when they discuss their respective communities? For example, do they attach the same importance to landscape, work activities, individual people, language, codes of living, and ancestors? Do they use their depictions of their communities to make the same cultural criticisms?

3. Ehrlich moved to Wyoming; Laurence got out of her home town. Do their actions reflect different values or needs? As you read their essays, do you find that it matters in other ways that one author depicts a community she embraced and the other a community she left?

Suggestions for Writing

1. Explain how much isolation and community there is in Ehrlich's Wyoming and in the small prairie town that Laurence depicts. Is there a balance of isolation and community in each case? Be sure to make clear how you are defining these terms. Also, make sure to support your claims with details from the essays.

2. Explain how your attitude toward a particular geographical area has changed over the years. As part of your explanation, identify what about the area sticks in your mind and what has led you to change your attitude toward it.

3. Describe a community you know that many people have looked at superficially or even misperceived. Focus on one or two aspects of the community that you would like these people to recognize. If you like, you can even address them as your audience. *Community* in this context can range from a group of friends, to a residential living complex, to a large geographical area.

INSIDERS AND OUTSIDERS

Many communities, especially in the United States, like to think of themselves as being open to all kinds of people. Consciously or unconsciously, though, communities often distinguish between "insiders" and "outsiders." In fact, a good way of studying communities is to see whom they consciously or unconsciously assign to these categories. Outsiders can, of course, be people new to the community and seeking to enter it in some way. This term can also apply, however, to people who have lived within the community yet have not felt accepted by it or part of its mainstream. Similarly, even though insiders can be people who have remained within the community, they can also be people who have left it but still feel attached to it somehow. Here Marianna De Marco Torgovnick and Barbara Grizzuti Harrison bring all of these meanings into play as they focus on the community in which they both grew up, the Bensonhurst section of Brooklyn, New York. Both authors deal with an August 23, 1989, incident in which an African-American youth was killed when he entered this largely white neighborhood. Torgovnick and Harrison analyze what this murder of an outsider reveals about the community's values. As part of their analysis, both also discuss ways in which they themselves were outsiders to the community even while living there. Yet although they have now left the neighborhood, they indicate that to some degree they are still Benson-hurst insiders, for their experience growing up there continues to haunt them. This pair of essays offers you, therefore, a rare opportunity to see how writers from the same community use the same incident there to explore various things implied by its notion of insiders and outsiders. You will also find it worthwhile to compare the rhetorical strategies that Torgovnick and Harrison use to convey their perspectives. For example, do they focus on the same kinds of details? Display the same tone? Use similar methods of organization? Seem to write with a common purpose? Consider, finally, how you yourself can analyze communities you have known or researched by examining the concepts of insider and outsider that they seem to hold.

On Being White, Female, and Born in Bensonhurst

Marianna De Marco Torgovnick

Marianna De Marco Torgovnick (b. 1949) grew up in the Bensonhurst section of Brooklyn, New York. She received a bachelor's degree in English from New York University, as well as a master's degree and a doctorate in English from Columbia University. Presently, she is Professor and Associate Chair of English at Duke University in Durham, North Carolina. Torgovnick has published two books of literary criticism, *Closure in the Novel* and *Visual Arts, Pictorialism, and the Novel: James, Lawrence, and Woolf.* Recently, however, she has turned to the wider realm of cultural analysis. Her 1990 book *Gone Primitive: Savage Intellects, Modern Lives* examines images of the so-called primitive Other in various works of Western culture, ranging

"On Being White, Female, and Born in Bensonhurst," by Marianna Torgovnick, PARTISAN RE-VIEW, Volume LVII, Number 3. Reprinted by permission of the author.

from post-Impressionist paintings to the Tarzan novels to contemporary museum exhibitions. The book also shows Torgovnick's effort to bring her personal experience and feelings more into her academic writing. As she explained in a paper she gave at the 1989 meeting of the Modern Language Association, "I could not think of myself as a writer until I risked exposing myself as a writer. . . . writerly writing is personal writing, whether or not it is autobiographical. Even if it offers no facts from the writer's life, or offers just a hint of them here and there, it makes the reader know some things about the writer—a fundamental condition, it seems to me, of any real act of communication." The essay that follows, which *is* autobiographical, appeared in the Summer 1990 issue of *Partisan Review*, a journal of cultural and political analysis geared mostly to academics and other intellectuals. Note that Torgovnick does not usually incorporate her maiden name into her byline, as she does here.

Reflections Before Reading

What kinds of people does your community seem to consider outsiders? Think not only of people who actually live outside the community, but also people living within it whom it has not truly accepted. Can you see yourself becoming an outsider to the community you grew up in or the one you know best? Why or why not? This essay and the next describe the particular community of Bensonhurst, suggesting that it opposes people from various ethnic groups and social change in general. Do you know any communities like this? If so, what forms does their attitude toward outsiders take? Why do you think such communities act the way they do?

The Mafia protects the neighborhood, our fathers say, with that peculiar satisfied   1
pride with which law-abiding Italian-Americans refer to the Mafia: the Mafia protects the neighborhood from "the coloreds." In the fifties and sixties, I heard that
information repeated, in whispers, in neighborhood parks and in the yard at school
in Bensonhurst. The same information probably passes today in the parks (the
word now "blacks," not "coloreds") but perhaps no longer in the schoolyards. From
buses each morning, from neighborhoods outside Bensonhurst, spill children of all
colors and backgrounds—American black, West-Indian black, Hispanic, and
Asian. But the blacks are the only ones especially marked for notice. Bensonhurst
is no longer entirely protected from "the coloreds." But in a deeper sense, at least
for Italian-Americans, Bensonhurst never changes.

Italian-American life continues pretty much as I remember it. Families with   2
young children live side by side with older couples whose children are long gone to
the suburbs. Many of those families live "down the block" from the last generation
or, sometimes still, live together with parents or grandparents. When a young family leaves, as sometimes happens, for Long Island or New Jersey or (very common
now) for Staten Island, another arrives, without any special effort being required,
from Italy or a poorer neighborhood in New York. They fill the neat but anony-

mous houses that make up the mostly tree-lined streets: two-, three-, or four-family houses for the most part (this is a working, lower to middle-middle class area, and people need rents to pay mortgages), with a few single family or small apartment houses tossed in at random. Tomato plants, fig trees, and plaster madonnas often decorate small but well-tended yards which face out onto the street; the grassy front lawn, like the grassy backyard, is relatively uncommon.

Crisscrossing the neighborhood and marking out ethnic zones—Italian, Irish, and Jewish, for the most part, though there are some Asian-Americans and some people (usually Protestants) called simply Americans—are the great shopping streets: 86th Street, Kings Highway, Bay Parkway, 18th Avenue, each with its own distinctive character. On 86th Street, crowds bustle along sidewalks lined with ample, packed fruit stands. Women wheeling shopping carts or baby strollers check the fruit carefully, piece by piece, and often bargain with the dealer, cajoling for a better price or letting him know that the vegetables, this time, aren't up to snuff. A few blocks down the fruit stands are gone and the streets are lined by clothing and record shops, mobbed by teenagers. Occasionally, the El rumbles overhead, a few stops out of Coney Island on its way to the city, a trip of around one hour.   3

On summer nights, neighbors congregate on stoops which during the day serve as play yards for children. Air conditioning exists everywhere in Bensonhurst, but people still sit outside in the summer—to supervise children, to gossip, to stare at strangers. "Buona sera," I say, or "Buona notte," as I am ritually presented to Sal and Lily and Louie, the neighbors sitting on the stoop. "Grazie," I say when they praise my children or my appearance. It's the only time I use Italian, which I learned at high school, although my parents (both second generation Italian-Americans, my father Sicilian, my mother Calabrian) speak it at home to each other but never to me or my brother. My accent is the Tuscan accent taught at school, not the southern Italian accents of my parents and the neighbors.   4

It's important to greet and please the neighbors; any break in this decorum would seriously offend and aggrieve my parents. For the neighbors are the stern arbiters of conduct in Bensonhurst. Does Mary keep a clean house? Did Gina wear black long enough after her mother's death? Was the food good at Tony's wedding? The neighbors know and pass judgement. Any news of family scandal (my brother's divorce, for example) provokes from my mother the agonized words: "But what will I *tell* people?" I sometimes collaborate in devising a plausible script.   5

A large sign on the church I attended as a child sums up for me the ethos of Bensonhurst. The sign urges contributions to the church building fund with the message, in huge letters: "EACH YEAR ST. SIMON AND JUDE SAVES THIS NEIGHBORHOOD ONE MILLION DOLLARS IN TAXES." Passing the church on the way from largely Jewish and middle-class Sheepshead Bay (where my in-laws live) to Bensonhurst, year after year, my husband and I look for the sign and laugh at the crass level of its pitch, its utter lack of attention to things spiritual. But we also understand *exactly* the values it represents.   6

In the summer of 1989, my parents were visiting me at my house in Durham, North Carolina from the apartment in Bensonhurst where they have lived since 1942: three small rooms, rent-controlled, floor clean enough to eat off, every cor-   7 ner and crevice known and organized. My parents' longevity in a single apartment is unusual even for Bensonhurst, but not that unusual; many people live for decades in the same place or move within a ten-block radius. When I lived in this apartment, there were four rooms; one has since been ceded to a demanding landlord, one of the various landlords who have haunted my parents' life and must always be appeased lest the ultimate threat—removal from the rent-controlled apartment—be brought into play. That summer, during their visit, on August 23rd (my younger daughter's birthday) a shocking, disturbing, news report issued from the neighborhood: it had become another Howard Beach.

Three black men, walking casually through the streets at night, were attacked   8 by a group of whites. One was shot dead, mistaken, as it turned out, for another black youth who was dating a white, although part-Hispanic, girl in the neighborhood. It all made sense: the crudely protective men, expecting to see a black arriving at the girl's house and overreacting; the rebellious girl dating the outsider boy; the black dead as a sacrifice to the feelings of the neighborhood.

I might have felt outrage, I might have felt guilt or shame, I might have de-   9 spised the people among whom I grew up. In a way I felt all four emotions when I heard the news. I expect that there were many people in Bensonhurst who felt the same rush of emotions. But mostly I felt that, given the set-up, this was the only way things could have happened. I detested the racial killing; but I also understood it. Those streets, which should be public property available to all, belong to the neighborhood. All the people sitting on the stoops on August 23rd knew that as well as they knew their own names. The black men walking through probably knew it too—though their casual walk sought to deny the fact that, for the neighbors, even the simple act of blacks walking through the neighborhood would be seen as invasion.

Italian-Americans in Bensonhurst are notable for their cohesiveness and pro-   10 vinciality; the slightest pressure turns those qualities into prejudice and racism. Their cohesiveness is based on the stable economic and ethical level that links generation to generation, keeping Italian-Americans in Bensonhurst and the Italian-American community alive as the Jewish-American community of my youth is no longer alive. (Its young people routinely moved to the suburbs or beyond, and were never replaced, so that Jews in Bensonhurst today are almost all very old people.) Their provinciality results from the Italian-Americans' devotion to jealous distinctions and discriminations. Jews are suspect, but (the old Italian women admit) "they make good husbands." The Irish are okay, fellow Catholics, but not really "like us"; they make bad husbands because they drink and gamble. Even Italians come in varieties by region (Sicilian, Calabrian, Neapolitan, very rarely any region further north), and by history in this country (the newly arrived and ridiculed "gaffoon" versus the second or third generation.)

Bensonhurst is a neighborhood dedicated to believing that its values are the   11 only values; it tends toward certain forms of inertia. When my parents visit me in Durham, they routinely take chairs from the kitchen and sit out on the lawn in front of the house, not on the chairs on the back deck; then they complain that the streets are too quiet. When they walk around my neighborhood (these De Marcos who have friends named Travaglianti and Occhipinti), look at the mailboxes and report that my neighbors have strange names. Prices at my local supermarket are compared, in unbelievable detail, with prices on 86th Street. Any rearrangement of my kitchen since their last visit is registered and criticized. Difference is not only unwelcome, it is unacceptable. One of the most characteristic things my mother ever said was in response to my plans for renovating my house in Durham. When she heard my plans, she looked around, crossed her arms, and said, "If it was me, I wouldn't change nothing." My father once asked me to level with him about a Jewish boyfriend who lived in a different part of the neighborhood, reacting to his Jewishness, but even more to the fact that he often wore Bermuda shorts: "Tell me something, Marianna. Is he a Communist?" Such are the standards of normality and political thinking in Bensonhurst.

I often think that one important difference between Italian-Americans in New   12
York neighborhoods like Bensonhurst and Italian-Americans elsewhere is that the others moved on—to upstate New York, to Pennsylvania, to the Midwest. Though they frequently settled in communities of fellow Italians, they did move on. Bensonhurst Italian-Americans seem to have felt that one large move, over the ocean, was enough. Future moves could be only local: from the Lower East Side, for example, to Brooklyn, or from one part of Brooklyn to another. Bensonhurst was for many of these people the summa of expectations. If their America were to be drawn as a *New Yorker* cover, Manhattan itself would be tiny in proportion to Bensonhurst, and to its satellites, Staten Island, New Jersey, and Long Island.

"Oh, no," my father says when he hears the news about the shooting. Though   13
he still refers to blacks as "coloreds," he's not really a racist and is upset that this innocent youth was shot in his neighborhood. He has no trouble acknowledging the wrongness of the death. But then, like all the news accounts, he turns to the fact, repeated over and over, that the blacks had been on their way to look at a used car when they encountered the hostile mob of whites. The explanation is right before him but, "Yeah," he says, still shaking his head, "yeah, but what were they *doing* there? They didn't belong."

Over the next few days, the television news is even more disturbing. Rows of   14
screaming Italians, lining the streets, most of them looking like my relatives. I focus especially on one woman who resembles almost completely my mother: stocky but not fat, mid-seventies but well-preserved, full face showing only minimal wrinkles, ample steel-gray hair neatly if rigidly coiffed in a modified beehive hairdo left over from the sixties. She shakes her fist at the camera, protesting the arrest of the Italian-American youths in the neighborhood and the incursion of more blacks into the neighborhood, protesting the shooting. I look a little nervously at my mother (the parent I resemble), but she had not even noticed the woman and stares impassively at the television.

What has Bensonhurst to do with what I teach today and write? Why did I   15
need to write about this killing in Bensonhurst, but not in the manner of a news account or a statistical sociological analysis? Within days of hearing the news, I began to plan this essay, to tell the world what I knew, even though I was aware that I could publish the piece only some place my parents or their neighbors would never see or hear about it. I sometimes think that I looked around from my baby carriage and decided that someday, the sooner the better, I would get out of Ben-

sonhurst. Now, much to my surprise, Bensonhurst—the antipodes of the intellectual life I sought, the least interesting of places—had become a respectable intellectual topic. People would be willing to hear about Bensonhurst—and all by the dubious virtue of a racial killing in the streets.

The story as I would have to tell it would be to some extent a class narrative: 16 about the difference between working class and upper middle class, dependence and a profession, Bensonhurst and a posh suburb. But I need to make it clear that I do not imagine myself as writing from a position of enormous self-satisfaction, or even enormous distance. You can take the girl out of Bensonhurst (that much is clear); but you may not be able to take Bensonhurst out of the girl. And upward mobility is not the essence of the story, though it is an important marker and symbol.

In Durham today, I live in a twelve-room house, surrounded by an acre of 17 trees. When I sit on my back deck, on summer evenings, no houses are visible through the trees. I have a guaranteed income, teaching English at an excellent university, removed by my years of education from the fundamental economic and social conditions of Bensonhurst. The one time my mother ever expressed pleasure at my work was when I got tenure, what my father still calls, with no irony intended, "ten years." "What does that mean?" my mother asked when she heard the news. Then she reached back into her experience as a garment worker, subject to periodic lay-offs. "Does it mean they can't fire you just for nothing and can't lay you off?" When I said that was exactly what it means, she said, "Very good. Congratulations. That's *wonderful*." I was free from the *padrones*, from the network of petty anxieties that had formed, in large part, her very existence. Of course, I wasn't really free of petty anxieties: would my salary increase keep pace with my colleagues', how would my office compare, would this essay be accepted for publication, am I happy? The line between these worries and my mother's is the line between the working class and the upper middle class.

But getting out of Bensonhurst never meant to me a big house, or nice clothes, 18 or a large income. And it never meant feeling good about looking down on what I left behind or hiding my background. Getting out of Bensonhurst meant freedom—to experiment, to grow, to change. It also meant knowledge in some grand, abstract way. All the material possessions I have acquired, I acquired simply along the way—and for the first twelve years after I left Bensonhurst, I chose to acquire almc t nothing at all. Now, as I write about the neighborhood, I recognize that although I've come far in physical and material distance, the emotional distance is harder to gauge. Bensonhurst has everything to do with who I am and even with what I write. Occasionally I get reminded of my roots, of their simultaneously choking and nutritive power.

Scene one: It's after a lecture at Duke, given by a visiting professor from Prin- 19 cetc.. The lecture was long and a little dull and—bad luck—I had agreed to be one of the people having dinner with the lecturer afterwards. We settle into our table at the restaurant: this man, me, the head of the Comparative Literature program (also a professor of German) and a couple I like who teach French—the husband at my university, the wife at one nearby. The conversation is sluggish, as it often is when a stranger, like the visiting professor, has to be assimilated into a group, so I ask the visitor from Princeton a question to personalize things a bit. "How did you get interested in what you do? What made you become a professor of German?" The man gets going and begins talking about how it was really unlikely that he, a nice Jewish boy from Bensonhurst, would have chosen, in the midfifties, to study German. Unlikely indeed.

I remember seeing *Judgment at Nuremberg* in a local movie theater and hav- 20 ing a woman in the row in back of me get hysterical when some clips of a concentration camp were shown; "My God," she screamed in a European accent, "Look at what they did. Murderers, MURDERERS!"—and she had to be supported out by her family. I couldn't see, in the dark, whether her arm bore the neatly tattooed numbers that the arms of some of my classmates' parents did—and that always affected me with a thrill of horror. Ten years older than me, this man had lived more directly through those feelings, lived with and *among* those feelings. The first chance he got he raced to study in Germany. I myself have twice chosen not to visit Germany—but I understand his impulse to identify with the Other as a way of getting out of the neighborhood.

At the dinner, the memory of the movie pops into my mind but I pick up 21 instead on the Bensonhurst—I'm also from there, but Italian-American. Like a flash, he asks something I haven't been asked in years: Where did I go to high school and (a more common question) What was my maiden name? I went to Lafayette High School, I say, and my name was De Marco. Everything changes: his facial expression, his posture, his accent, his voice. "Soo Dee Maw-ko," he says, "Dun anything wrong at school today—got enny pink slips? Wanna meet me later at the parrk or maybe bye the Baye?" When I laugh, recognizing the stereotype that Italians get pink slips for misconduct at school and the notorious chemistry between Italian women and Jewish men, he says, back in his Princetonian voice: "My God, for a minute I felt like I was turning into a werewolf."

It's odd that although I can remember almost nothing else about this man— 22 his face, his body type, even his name—I remember this lapse into his "real self" with enormous vividness. I am especially struck by how easily he was able to slip into the old, generic Brooklyn accent. I myself have no memory of ever speaking in that accent, though I also have no memory of trying not to speak it, except for teaching myself, carefully, to say "oil" rather than "earl."

But the surprises aren't over. The female French professor, whom I have 23 known for at least five years, reveals for the first time that she is also from the neighborhood, though she lived across the other side of Kings Highway, went to a different, more elite high school, and was Irish-American. Three of six professors, sitting at an eclectic vegetarian restaurant in Durham, all from Bensonhurst—a neigborhood where (I swear) you couldn't get *The New York Times* at any of the local stores.

Scene Two: I still live in Bensonhurst. I'm waiting for my parents to return 24 from a conference at my school, where they've been summoned to discuss my transition from elementary to junior high school. I am already a full year younger than any of my classmates, having skipped a grade, a not uncommon occurrence for "gifted" youngsters. Now the school is worried about putting me in an accelerated track through junior high, since that would make me two years younger. A compromise was reached: I would be put in a special program for gifted children, but one that took three, not two years. It sounds okay.

Three years later, another wait. My parents have gone to school this time to   25 make another decision. Lafayette High School has three tracks: academic, for potentially college-bound kids; secretarial, mostly for Italian-American girls or girls with low aptitude scores (the high school is segregated *de facto* so none of the tracks is as yet racially coded, though they are coded by ethnic group and gender), and vocational, mostly for boys with the same attributes, ethnic or intellectual. Although my scores are superb, the guidance counselor has recommended the secretarial track: when I protested, the conference with my parents was arranged. My mother's preference is clear: the secretarial track—college is for boys; I will need to make a "good living" until I marry and have children. My father also prefers the secreterial track, but he wavers, half proud of my aberrantly high scores, half worried. I press the attack, saying that if I were Jewish I would have been placed, without question, in the academic track. I tell him I have sneaked a peek at my files and know that my I.Q. is genius level. I am allowed to insist on the change into the academic track.

What I did, and I was ashamed of it even then, was to play upon my father's   26 competitive feeling with Jews: his daughter could and should be as good as theirs. In the bank where he was a messenger and the insurance company where he worked in the mail room, my father worked with Jews, who were almost always his immediate supervisors. Several times, my father was offered the supervisory job but turned it down, after long conversations with my mother about the dangers of making a change, the difficulty of giving orders to friends. After her work in a local garment shop, after cooking dinner and washing the floor each night, my mother often did piece work making bows; sometimes I would help her for fun, but it *wasn't* fun, and I was free to stop while she continued for long, tedious hours to increase the family income. Once a week, her part-time boss, Dave, would come by to pick up the boxes of bows. Short, round, with his shirt-tails sloppily tucked into his pants and a cigar almost always dangling from his lips, Dave was a stereotyped Jew but also, my parents always said, a nice guy, a decent man.

Years later, similar choices came up, and I show the same assertiveness I   27 showed with my father, the same ability to deal for survival, but tinged with Bensonhurst caution. Where will I go to college? Not to Brooklyn College, the flagship of the city system—I know that, but don't press the invitations I have received to apply to prestigious schools outside of New York. The choice comes down to two: Barnard, which gives me a full scholarship, minus five hundred dollars a year that all scholarship students are expected to contribute from summer earnings, or New York University, which offers me one thousand dollars above tuition as a bribe. I waver. My parents stand firm: they are already losing money by letting me go to college. I owe it to the family to contribute the extra thousand dollars plus my summer earnings. Besides, my mother adds, harping on a favorite theme, there are no boys at Barnard; at N.Y.U. I'm more likely to meet someone to marry. I go to N.Y.U. and do marry in my senior year, but he is someone I didn't meet at college. I was secretly relieved, I now think (though at the time I thought I was just placating my parents' conventionality), to be out of the marriage sweepstakes.

The first boy who ever asked me for a date was Robert Lubitz, in eighth grade;   28
tall and skinny to my average height and teenage chubbiness. I turned him down,
thinking we would make a ridiculous couple. Day after day, I cast my eyes at stylish
Juliano, the class cut-up; day after day, I captivated Robert Lubitz. Occasionally,
one of my brother's Italian-American friends would ask me out, and I would go,
often to R.O.T.C. dances. My specialty was making political remarks so shocking
that the guys rarely asked me again. After awhile, I recognized destiny: the Jewish
man was a passport out of Bensonhurst. I of course did marry a Jewish man, who
gave me my freedom and, very important, helped remove me from the expectations of Bensonhurst. Though raised in a largely Jewish section of Brooklyn, he had
gone to college in Ohio and knew how important it was (as he put it) "to get past
the Brooklyn Bridge"; we met on neutral ground, in Central Park, at a performance of Shakespeare. The Jewish-Italian marriage is a common enough catastrophe in Bensonhurst for my parents to have accepted, even welcomed mine—
though my parents continued to treat my husband as an outsider for the first
twenty years ("Now Marianna. Here's what's going on with you' brother. But don't
tell a' you' husband.")

Along the way, I make other choices, more fully marked by Bensonhurst cau-   29
tiousness. I am attracted to journalism or the arts as careers, but the prospects for
income seem iffy. I choose instead to imagine myself as a teacher. Only the availability of NDEA Fellowships when I graduate, with their generous terms, propels
me from high school teaching (a thought I never much relished) to college teaching (which seems like a brave new world). Within the college teaching profession, I
choose off-beat specializations: the novel, interdisciplinary approaches (not something clear and clubby, like Milton or the eighteenth century). Eventually I write
the book I like best about primitive others as they figure within Western obsessions: my identification with "the Other," my sense of being "Other," surfaces at
last. I avoid all mentoring structures for a long time but accept aid when it comes to
me on the basis of what I perceive to be merit. I'm still, deep down, Italian-American Bensonhurst, though by this time I'm a lot of other things as well.

Scene Three: In the summer of 1988, a little more than a year before the   30
shooting in Bensonhurst, my father woke up trembling in what appeared to be a fit.
Hospitalization revealed that he had a pocket of blood on his brain, a frequent
consequence of falls for older people. About a year earlier, I had stayed home,
using my children as an excuse, when my aunt, my father's much loved sister died,
missing her funeral; only now does my mother tell me how much my father resented my taking his suggestion that I stay home. Now, confronted with what is
described as brain surgery but turns out to be less dramatic than it sounds, I fly
home immediately.

My brother drives three hours back and forth from New Jersey every day to   31
chauffeur me and my mother to the hospital: he is being a fine Italian-American
son. For the first time in years, we have long conversations alone. He is two years
older than I am, a chemical engineer who has also left the neighborhood but has
remained closer to its values, with a suburban, Republican inflection. He talks a lot

about New York, saying that (except for neighborhoods like Bensonhurst) it's a "third world city now." It's the summer of the Tawana Brawley incident, when Brawley accused white men of abducting her and smearing racial slurs on her body with her own excrement. My brother is filled with dislike for Al Sharpton and Brawley's other vocal supporters in the black community—not because they're black, he says, but because they're troublemakers, stirring things up. The city is drenched in racial hatred that makes itself felt in the halls of the hospital: Italians and Jews in the beds and as doctors; blacks as nurses and orderlies.

This is the first time since I left New York in 1975 that I have visited Brooklyn   32 without once getting into Manhattan. It's the first time I have spent several days alone with my mother, living in her apartment in Bensonhurst. My every move is scrutinized and commented on. I feel like I am going to go crazy.

Finally, it's clear that my father is going to be fine, and I can go home. She   33 insists on accompanying me to the travel agent to get my ticket for home, even though I really want to be alone. The agency (a Mafia front?) has no one who knows how to ticket me for the exotic destination of North Carolina and no computer for doing so. The one person who can perform this feat by hand is out. I have to kill time for an hour and suggest to my mother that she go home, to be there for my brother when he arrives from Jersey. We stop in a Pork Store, where I buy a stash of cheeses, sausages, and other delicacies unavailable in Durham. My mother walks home with the shopping bags, and I'm on my own.

More than anything I want a kind of *sorbetto* or ice I remember from my   34 childhood, a *cremolata*, almond-vanilla flavored with large chunks of nuts. I pop into the local bakery (at the unlikely hour of eleven a.m.) and ask for a *cremolata*, usually eaten after dinner. The woman—a younger version of my mother—refuses: they haven't made a fresh ice yet and what's left from the day before is too icy, no good. I explain that I'm about to get on a plane for North Carolina and want that ice, good or not. But she has her standards and holds her ground, even though North Carolina has about the same status in her mind as Timbuktoo and she knows I will be banished, perhaps forever, from the land of *cremolata*.

Then, while I'm taking a walk, enjoying my solitude, I have another idea. On   35 the block behind my parents' house, there's a club for men, for men from a particular town or region in Italy: six or seven tables, some on the sidewalk beneath a garish red, green, and white sign; no women allowed or welcome unless they're with men; and no women at all during the day when the real business of the club—a game of cards for old men—is in progress. Still, I know that inside the club would be coffee and a *cremolata* ice. I'm thirty-eight, well-dressed, very respectable looking. I know what I want, I also know I'm not supposed to enter that club. I enter anyway, asking the teenage boy behind the counter firmly, in my most professional tones, for a *cremolata* ice. Dazzled, he complies immediately. The old men at the card table have been staring at this scene, unable to place me exactly, though my facial type is similar. Finally, a few old men's hisses pierce the air. "Strega," I hear as I leave, "mala strega," "witch," or "brazen whore." I have been in Bensonhurst less than a week, but I have managed to reproduce, on my final day there for this visit, the conditions of my youth. Knowing the rules, I have broken them. I shake hands with my discreetly rebellious past, still an outsider walking through the neighborhood, marked and insulted—though unlikely to be shot.

Rhetorical Focus

1. What seems to be Torgovnick's purpose in writing this essay? What does she seem to assume about her audience? Support your answers with references to her text.
2. How consistent is the tone that Torgovnick uses in this essay? Does she always show the same emotion? Refer to specific passages in her text.
3. In the second half of her essay, Torgovnick presents three scenes from her life. How does she organize the first half, before she gets to these scenes?

Thematic Focus

1. How would you describe Torgovnick's attitude toward her parents, her native community, and her present life? What, if anything, does she seem still undecided about? Refer to specific places in the text.
2. What is Torgovnick's main point in each of the three scenes she re-creates? Are the points similar, or different?
3. How do race, gender, and social class matter in this essay? Again, refer to specific places in the text.

Women and Blacks and Bensonhurst

Barbara Grizzuti Harrison

Like Marianna De Marco Torgovnick, Barbara Grizzuti Harrison (b. 1934) grew up in the Bensonhurst section of Brooklyn, New York. Although she has published a novel entitled *Foreign Bodies*, Harrison is primarily known as a free-lance journalist. For example, she has contributed book reviews, celebrity profiles, and reportage to such journals as *The Village Voice, The Nation, The New Republic, The New York Times Book Review*, and *Vanity Fair*. Several of her early pieces are collected in her book *Off Center*. Often, Harrison uses writing to explore social or historical issues related to her personal experience. Her first book, *Unlearning the Lie*, grew out of her effort to introduce nonsexist materials into her daughter's school curriculum. Her later book *Visions of Glory: A History and a Memory of Jehovah's Witnesses* reflects her childhood religious life. *Italian Days* (1989), Harrison's most recent book, reports her travels through the land of her ancestors. Interestingly, Harrison now lives again in Brooklyn. Explaining why in a 1984 *Contemporary Authors* interview why she returned to the area, she identified a key element of her whole writing career: "I really believe that the seeds of all good writing come from childhood. That doesn't mean that one writes about one's childhood endlessly, which obviously I don't. But I think that's where it starts, and somehow that geographical proximity to where those enormous events took place is important." The following essay about her native community first appeared in the March 1990 issue of *Harper's*.

Reflections Before Reading

Which of Torgovnick's observations about Bensonhurst are you curious to see whether Harrison will verify? What does comparing their titles lead you to think Harrison might do?

On August 23, 1989, a sixteen-year-old black kid, Yusuf K. Hawkins, was shot to death in Bensonhurst, an almost entirely white section of Brooklyn, allegedly by

Joseph Fama, a brain-damaged, neurologically impaired high-school dropout with a "low normal" IQ of 72 and the academic achievement of a second- to fifth-grade child. According to reports, Hawkins was confronted by about thirty white kids, some of them carrying baseball bats. Fama, eighteen, and Keith Mondello, nineteen, have been charged with intentional murder. Four other whites are charged with "depraved indifference to human life" and "acting in concert with other persons" to kill Yusuf Hawkins. On September 18, pleas of not guilty were entered for all defendants; separate trials are expected to begin this spring.

Keith Mondello was once the boyfriend of eighteen-year-old Gina Feliciano, whose father, no longer alive, was Puerto Rican. Feliciano, who is under police protection and is expected to be a key witness for the prosecution, favored black and Hispanic boyfriends; interviewed on CBS's *60 Minutes*, she was not at all reluctant to talk about her preferences. 2

One of the defense attorneys, Benjamin Brafman, questioned why the district attorney's office had not sought to indict Feliciano, whom he called an "instigating force" in the attack. 3

"Was she down there and did she fire a shot? Was she armed with a baseball bat?" Justice Thaddeus Owens asked. She wasn't. But it is more than defense strategy to implicate Feliciano: It is the prevailing feeling in Bensonhurst that she was responsible for the killing of a man . . . *the woman made me do it.* 4

My friend Biagio, who was brought up in Bensonhurst, as was I, says the thing he misses most is the honeysuckle. "And pig's rind," he says. Pig's skin, pink-white and waxy, is stuffed with pine nuts and raisins and garlic and parsley, and rolled and tied with string and put—along with sweet and hot sausages, fresh pork shoulder, gravy-beef, and chicken—into the "gravy," the tomato sauce for pasta. Of course we never used the food-trendy word *pasta* in Bensonhurst; *macaronies* was our generic term, macaronies and gravy our Sunday ritual . . . The pork rind gets gelatinous in the gravy, chewy, fragrant . . . 5

Sometimes Biagio and I go back to Bensonhurst to buy the ingredients for gravy (nostalgia takes strange forms). Biagio patronizes a pork store on Avenue P. I like to shop on Eighteenth Avenue. I grew up in "the Numbers"; Biagio grew up in "the Letters"; each of us has trouble believing the other grew up in the heart of the heart of Italian Brooklyn. Bensonhurst, a series of villages within a village, is about territory, territory strictly defined and fiercely defended. Besides the Numbers and the Letters, there are "the Bays," those streets that stretch toward the body of water called the Narrows. The girl who was to become my brother's wife lived on a pie-shaped block where the Letters and the Numbers converged; he met her at a dance in the Bays. And these facts of geography seemed to him liberating; he drove his Edsel to get to Carol's house and regarded their courtship as an event not unlike the Yalta Conference. 6

It isn't possible to overestimate the importance of the Sunday gravy; the amount of meat one ate was the most significant measure of affluence in Bensonhurst in the Forties and Fifties: You could live on top of a store, but if you ate meat six days a week, you counted yourself prosperous. And hospitality and generosity— character—were measured by the amount of meat you served your guests: "The 7

kind of woman your mother was," my Uncle Pat once said, summarily and suc-
cinctly defining my mother's nature, "was if four people came to dinner, there
would be four pork chops." My mother was not prodigal; she was unnaturally fru-
gal. Luigi Barzini had it that Italians in postwar Italy ate poorly, preferring to wear
their money on their backs, where it showed, in the form of clothes, so as to make a
bel' figura. But Barzini was a northern Italian. Bensonhurst's Italian immigrants
came from the poverty-stricken south—from Naples and Calabria and Abruzzo—
and food was both comfort and tangible proof of success, as well as justification and
revenge, a way to show off to one's friends and neighbors and a perceived way of
assimilating, just as the Host (the "Communion cookie") was the way to God. We
processed the world through our digestive systems. My mother served organ meat
a lot, and appendages—heart stew and chicken-feet soup; many things rubbery
and many things slippery; and she went comparison-shopping for broccoli and
fought with my maternal grandmother over whether to use the dandelions that
grew in an empty lot next to us for salad or (as my grandmother wished) for wine.
From such evidence I tried to assess our relative position in the world.

When there are internecine fights in Bensonhurst—when, for example, the   8
new immigrants, not as impoverished as my grandparents, who came to America at
the turn of the century, at the time of the *grande immigrazione*, are made objects
of scorn or become the source of bewilderment—Italians of my generation use the
understood language of food to express uneasiness. In 1974, there was a race riot at
my high school, New Utrecht, blacks having been brought in from other neighborhoods to attend; and when my brother and I went back to the old neighborhood to
talk to some of his friends about it, one of them said: "We got this big influx of
Italians from the Old Country—geeps. They're not like us. They got a chip on their
shoulder. Mouth-y. They say, Blacks have been here for a hundred years and they
couldn't make it; now it's our turn. It was a geep who beat up on a black kid at
Utrecht. The geeps are here three years, and they got money to buy a four-family
house. That's all they think of is money. They never heard of going to the movies.
They never heard of anisette. They never even heard of *coffee*. What kind of Italian
is that? They work two jobs, and they eat macaroni every night—*pasta lenticci*,
pasta fazool, that's it. We're here eating steaks and drinking highballs, and we hear
them every night cracking macaroni into the pot—unbelievable." And food is used
to signify opprobrium: a dope is called a *zhadrool*, slang from the word for a cu-
cumber or a squash. *Zhadrool* has quasi-affectionate overtones. Blacks are called
mulanyam, a corruption of *melanzane*, eggplants . . . and in that there is no affection at all—only blackness so opaque as to defy comprehension.

I remember skipping rope, Double Dutch, in the magic dusk. "Come in, the   9
chicken's ready," my brother yells out the window. "Don't let the Jews down the
street know what we're having for dinner," my aunt calls out.

So embattled. The Indians were always circling around the wagons. It was that   10
way in the Old Country, where only silence brought a measure of peace—*don't
interfere*—if not of economic freedom; and it was that way in America, too. Italian
immigrants of my grandparents' and my parents' generations lived with the conviction that *they*—the "Americans," the Jews, the *others*—were out to get them, cheat
them, kill them. *Don't let them know anything. What they don't know can't hurt*

you. In the days of his senile dementia, my grandfather believed he'd flown with Lindbergh across the Atlantic—but that *they*, the Americans, wouldn't give an Italian credit for it. When Grandpa got cancer, it was "a sin" (not "what a shame," but "what a sin"), the greater sin being to tell anybody about it. The world was malevolent; it existed to be held off and thus controlled.

As for the honeysuckle: Perhaps honeysuckle grows somewhere else in New   11
York; if it does, I don't know about it. Or maybe—this heretical thought has occurred to me—what Biagio and I both think of as honeysuckle is the flower of the
privet hedges that decorously contain Bensonhurst's tidy one- and two- and four-
family houses. But I am prepared to swear that it was the sweetness of honeysuckle
that threaded its way through my waking and sleeping dreams when I was young
and tempestuously in love—years and years of invalidated love—in Bensonhurst.

The first man I loved was a Jew.   12

My first lover was a black man.   13

It'll kill Mommy and Daddy, I thought (not without a delicate thrill of plea-   14
sure); Mommy and Daddy will kill me, I thought (feeling what I had never felt
before: a sense of latent power absurdly coupled with ennui and a sense of hope-
lessness).

There was a honeysuckle bush on the corner of Sixty-sixth Street and Nine-   15
teenth Avenue; its perfume restored me to a love of an enlarged world when I was
desperately unhappy—and simultaneously fed the unlicensed ardors that were a
source of my unhappiness. Now I dream not of those lost loves but of the honeysuckle bush, which has itself become an object of intense love, flowering in my
reveries . . .

Yusuf Hawkins was shot dead on Sixty-eighth Street and Twentieth Avenue,   16
two blocks away from the building my parents lived in till they died. Hawkins,
together with three black friends, came to Bensonhurst to look at a used car. It was
an act of singular naïveté, and the timing was deadly: Eighteen-year-old Gina Feliciano's birthday fell on August 23. The young woman had invited black and Hispanic friends to celebrate with her and told her ex-boyfriend, Keith Mondello;
perhaps she taunted him. According to Feliciano, Mondello and his friends called
her a "spic lover," told her her "friends don't belong in the neighborhood." Feliciano called the celebration off. On the night of her birthday, she and her mother
and a girlfriend ate potato chips in her apartment, while, according to her, white
kids milled around her apartment house; by a horrible accident of fate, Hawkins
and his friends, who knew nothing of Feliciano, walked by. The white kids chased
them with bats; Hawkins was killed with a shot from a .32-caliber automatic pistol.

Some white residents of Bensonhurst claimed later that Feliciano tried to   17
frighten the white kids—that she said black guys were coming into the neighborhood to beat them up. She denies this. She says she knows she's being called "a
prostitute, crackhead, a liar," and she says she was "with black guys in Coney Island . . . a couple of them" (the implication is that she was "with" them sexually),
but that it's nobody's business, especially not the business of the "Guidos" who
have "sixty chains and hair spray in one hand and a mirror in the other" and use
"jumper cables" to style their hair. "They ain't paying my rent, they ain't putting

clothes on my back, and they ain't feeding me," and she's not sleeping with *them*, she says.

Bensonhurst's response to the tragedy in their community is not monolithic. 18 But when I hear Gina Feliciano say that her neighbors tell her she "brought Bensonhurst down," I hear a chorus of voices from the past—the immediate past and the mythological past: *The woman made me do it.*

According to Gina Feliciano, who is under round-the-clock police protection, 19 there is a $100,000 contract out on her life.

I ran away from Bensonhurst—as fast and as hard and as far as I could (across 20 the bridge, to Manhattan, the emancipating city of calculated dreams). I fled from insularity and provincialism and suspicion of all that was not *us* and from familial love that was both careless and claustrophobic. I fled, and now I grieve. One cannot separate oneself from the landscape of earliest desire, the crucible, the wellspring, the source. I still want what I owned and what owned me—the honeysuckle bush on the corner. In memory I walk those streets; I look for clues, for the stuff that binds me to Yusuf Hawkins, and to his killers.

It is an established fact in my family that I am crazy; my Aunt Mary, who loves 21 me, dissents, but since she is Sicilian, her word does not count for much among my Calabrian and Abruzzesi aunts and uncles. Italians are tribal. Bensonhurst is tribal. My family called Aunt Mary "the Arab," Sicilians not being regarded as properly Italian.

My mother had a friend called "Rosie the Spic." One day I answered the door- 22 bell when Rosie the Spic came to visit (I can remember when doors in Bensonhurst were never locked, and so can generations of Italians—that was before, they say, "the element" moved among them). "Rosie the Spic is here," I shouted, having no idea whatsoever that "the Spic" was not her proper name. I didn't know about racial enmities then; I was four. Naturally Rosie the Spic never came back, and naturally I got a beating.

Sometimes we went to Prospect Park. I used—this is how, very early, I estab- 23 lished my craziness—to run up to black people and touch their skin and tell them they were beautiful. This was an aesthetic, not an ideology; I was five years old, and I don't know how or why I came to it. One of my aunts gave me a black doll and told me I could play with it if I never ever again touched a black person. It was a Little Black Sambo doll; I hated it. So then we never went to Prospect Park again, only to the Botanic Garden, because the park was "full of *them.*"

It did not surprise me when black protest marchers in Bensonhurst were 24 greeted with cries of "nigger go home" and with watermelons. Of course the kids we used to call "geeps," the kids Gina Feliciano calls "Guidos," would use the language of food.

When I went to New Utrecht High School in Bensonhurst, there was only one 25 black student, Joan Smith. She never spoke to anyone and no one ever spoke to her. At the end of her senior year, she was nominated for most popular. (I have told this story so often I believe it to be wholly true. But if it is not true, it will, as they say in Italy, "serve"; it is to the point.) It is not true that Joan Smith never spoke to anyone and no one ever spoke to her. I spoke to her. I spoke to her because I was raised a Jehovah's Witness, and it was my (hated and hateful) duty to proselytize. So I tried to convert Joan Smith. It didn't take. (I did convert Fatima Ouida, though, an Egyptian girl who kept snakes in the apartment underneath the elevated train line where she lived. Fatima used to invite people over to watch her father pray toward Mecca; he became known as "the guy who prays to the West End train.") In the lunchroom at New Utrecht High School, I sat with a girl who had one eye, her father having knocked the other out of her head with a broomstick; and I sat with a girl whose makeup was puddled all over her face—she was mad; and I sat with the class slut, who was stupid. I tried to convert them all. In any case, no one else would have much to do with me, my religion having made me an outsider and a freak.

There are, of course, voyeuristic advantages to being an outsider and a freak.   26

I was an outsider and a freak, but I was smart. (I was pretty, too, but I didn't   27
know that; I didn't know what my father meant when he said, "The world eats up pretty, smart girls like you." Eats them up and spits them out, he meant; he meant, Beware.) One day a teacher approached me in the hallway of New Utrecht and said—genuinely bewildered, I think—"Why do you have an Italian last name?" "Because I'm Italian," I said. He did not know what to do with this. Jews were smart—they took academic college-preparatory courses; Italians were dumb, or going to be married immediately. (Jewish girls wore charm bracelets; Italian girls wore engagement rings.)

I took hold of this view of my world early; we all did. I can remember when   28
Miss Silver, my third-grade teacher, a chunky woman who wore chunky Mexican silver jewelry (which jewelry I associate with lesbians, perhaps because of Miss Silver's interest in me, which my father considered untoward), came to my house rustling with sibilant *s*'s when I had viral pneumonia to tell my mother I was going to skip a grade; my mother took a dim view of what she regarded as interference. Actually Miss Silver came really, I think, to say, Look at your daughter, pay attention to her (she held my fevered hand); and this is what my mother, who introduced herself as "Barbara's relative" and dwelt in the clouds with Jehovah, having heavenly fish to fry, took a dim view of.

In junior high school there also was one black kid; and my brother, at the time   29
of the race riots at New Utrecht, said, "That kid was lucky. He was bright and good-looking. If he was just a regular black kid, he'd have had bad trouble. Every time teachers talked about black history or slavery, my word of honor I felt sorry for the kid. If they'd talked about Italian history, there'd have been thirty of us Italians, we wouldn't be embarrassed . . . not that they ever talked about Italian history." In high school Italian was offered as a second language. Nobody took it. Everybody took French.

My brother got beat up badly when some kids in the Bays mouthed him and   30
Carol, and he, gallant, answered them back. He got in his Edsel and drove to the station house all bloody, his nose and several ribs broken. "Were the kids white or

colored?" the desk sergeant asked. "White." "Go home and forget about it," the
sergeant said.

The first day of freshman English, New Utrecht: David Zeiger is our teacher;   31
he says, "Everyone with blue eyes has to do homework." Our world is divided into
three parts: Italian, Jewish, and "American." The Americans have blue eyes. They
protest: "It isn't fair," making his point for him. David Zeiger spent a forty-minute
English period, in 1948, telling freshman English students in Bensonhurst—many
of whom had never seen a Negro—why it was wrong to judge people by the color
of their eyes or their skin.

According to the dogma by which I lived, beginning at the age of nine, when   32
my mother became a Jehovah's Witness, Jehovah was a god of justice and mercy,
and whatever happened—including the drowning of infants in their own blood at
an imminent Armageddon—was by definition fair. But I knew—I viscerally knew,
I was laceratingly divided—that my world was governed by caprice, that punish-
ments and rewards were arbitrary. I lived, after all, with my mother.

My mother, who was beautiful, had blue eyes, like an American; she was very   33
nearly blind. She went to a doctor, a quack, who gave her eye exercises to do; one
of them involved resting her head on the windowsill while she rolled her eyes in
her head. A passing motorist saw her and thought she was convulsing; I came
home to a fire-engine rescue team. Why didn't you tell them I was doing eye
exercises? she asked me, her need to place the blame a rigorous passion. I must
assume that given her voracious and discordant needs she was mad, and that her
religion accommodated her madness. Mad. Sad. Of course the eye exercises didn't
work. Thereafter, rain or shine, she carried a red umbrella so that cars could see
her when she crossed the street. A beautiful woman with blue eyes carrying a red
umbrella.

My mother was incapable of dual allegiances. After she fell in love with Jeho-   34
vah, she no longer wanted to sleep with my father. She made me tell him so. I was
ten. He cried. But he slept in the mahogany double bed with my brother, and my
mother slept in the pickled-oak twin bed next to mine. She cried. One Christmas
Eve my mother went out, against my father's protests, to proselytize from door to
door. My father got drunk. I washed the dishes. The doors of all the kitchen cupboards flew open and everything in them—cups, saucers, pots—came flying out.
For years I remembered that poltergeist phenomenon without remembering what
had directly preceded it: My father put a dish towel around my neck and, yanking
it, started to strangle me; then he fell in a wet heap on the floor; and then the
cupboards flew open and everything in them flew out. I was twelve. The downstairs neighbors heard the noise. Weeks later they said to me, "We mind our business." All of our neighbors minded their business. They wouldn't have heard the
sound of a shot, and if they had, they wouldn't have done anything about it.

In particular, my father hated an uncle of mine who, after coming home from   35
the war with a Purple Heart, had been converted by my mother. This uncle
worked in a doll factory. At dinner my father would say, "Did you stuff dolls today?" This is how it was: The house was hot with sex, but nobody talked about sex.
"What's Tampax?" I asked my mother. She left the room.

My aunts, my godmother among them, knew that my mother and my father   36
did not sleep together. They blamed this on "the Jehovahs." But they maintained a
stony silence; it was important for them to believe that they were "nice," and "nice"
people—like the "Americans"—didn't talk about sex. When I was an adult, my
godmother told me that Daddy had wanted to leave my mother to marry a woman
who worked in the bargain-hats department of Gimbels department store. She
talked her brother out of it, my godmother said, there never having been a divorce
in the family. Italians didn't get divorced and Italians didn't talk about sex.

Which was what made it possible for my mother to have a romantic affair   37
without a guilty conscience. After the war, the Witnesses who had been imprisoned for not serving in the Armed Forces came home. One of them, Louis, fell in
love with my beautiful mother. They went from door to door together, holding
hands. They considered, having consulted various Bible concordances, that they
were married in the eyes of God, the pledge being as good as the deed; they would
celebrate their marriage in Jehovah's "New World," after Armageddon had disposed of my father. Future-sex. Louis painted her toenails; I'm sure they never
talked about sex. They talked about the New World, when the lion and the lamb
would lie down together. I was told to regard Louis, whom I loathed, as my proper
father-in-the-Lord. At dinner one night my father said, "You were seen walking
mano a mano with that Louis, the one who stuffs dolls with your brother." My
mother cried all night long in the twin bed next to mine. "What did you tell him.
Oh, what did you tell him," she cried. I hadn't told him anything. Everybody in the
Numbers knew. Word gets around. What you don't want known in Bensonhurst
you don't do. "You've ruined my life," my mother said.

So all in all it wasn't race relations I learned from David Zeiger (or "tolerance,"   38
which was the word we used back then) as much as the idea, new to me and radical, that lives could and should exemplify fairness, that justice wasn't exercised only
by God but by human beings.

David Zeiger is still my friend, though it is hard for me to change his place in   39
the story of my life. In reveries, he belongs to the past—the runic past I spend the
present reading, the past that contains Arnold Horowitz, who is dead.

Arnold Horowitz was David Zeiger's best friend, and he was my English   40
teacher when I was fifteen. A lot of the girls—the smart girls, the point of him not
being obvious to the dumb girls—had a crush on Arnold Horowitz; I myself didn't
see the point of him until he wrote this sentence on the blackboard: *The beautiful
girl with hair the color of ripe wheat* . . . That's as far as I got in the sentence, and
then I fell in love and could not believe there was a time I hadn't been in love with
Arnold Horowitz.

Almost all of my Italian neighbors were casually anti-Semitic; it wasn't a mat-   41
ter of creed. Some of my neighbors and some of my family members were viru-
lently anti-Semitic—when my brother brought home a loaf of Arnold's bread from
the market one day, my mother threw it out the kitchen window. But that was not
so much because Arnold was Jewish but because Arnold, like Miss Silver, paid
attention to me. He was more dangerous than Miss Silver. Miss Silver only taught
me I was smart. Arnold told me I was good. (I have loved him all my life.)

He sent pepperoni to the hoods, the hard guys in jail. In 1945, ahead of his   42
time, he co-edited a book for young adults called *This Way to Unity: For the Pro-*

motion of Goodwill and Teamwork Among Racial, Religious, and National Groups.
(He published it under a pseudonym, Arnold Herrick, bland and WASP. The
Board of Education banned it; it contained the word *womb*.) Jehovah's Witnesses
are forbidden to salute the flag; Arnold came into the school auditorium at assembly time during the flag salute and held my hand. How could I not have loved him?

I met a black teacher in his house in the Bays one hot summer night. It was   43
awkward in the big living room with the window seat and the blond Danish furniture and the Picasso prints. The others—David Zeiger and his wife, Lila, and some
people whose faces I cannot recall—made very little conversation. We blamed it
on the heat. One treated a black person as one treated an invalid—with courtesy
and caution.

Anti-Semitism seemed a most peculiar thing to me. The halls of all our build-   44
ings smelled ecumenically of chicken fat and gravy. The girls I had talked dirty
with before talking dirty became a sin were Italian and Jewish and equally inven-
tive and equally ignorant of sex. The girls I'd played the Ouija board with under the
stairs of apartment buildings were Jewish and Italian and equally titillated (the
Ouija board said I was going to marry DICK, which was my father's name) and
equally scared. The girls I most admired were Jewish. They were named Barbara
and Violet, and they were twins. (I thought it would be lovely to be a twin; one
would never be lonely, and one could look for proof of one's existence in the mirror
of another face.) I'd jumped across roofs with Jewish and with Italian girls, and
ridden up and down dumbwaiters with Jewish and Italian girls, and what was the
difference?

When my world became full of catalogued sin, both Jewish and Italian girls   45
became equally remote to me, to be envied because they had, it seemed to me, two
gifts that I had not: the freedom to play and, within limits, to choose.

On Friday evenings my Jewish neighbors gave me two cents—they gave boys   46
three—to turn on the stove and the lights for Sabbath.

Sometimes my family and my neighbors counted the number of Jews on the   47
subway train; they were afraid of being overwhelmed.

On Bay Parkway a self-possessed, smiling young woman walked to the ele-   48
vated subway every morning in a silk dress underneath which there was no bra.
(This was in the days before Doris Day became a virgin; the single most potent
image of freedom I cherished was that of a girl with long blond hair sitting at a
lunch counter in a raincoat, her unstockinged feet out of her shoes.) "She must be
Jewish," the Italians said.

They were afraid of sexual perdition and contagion. They wanted their daugh-   49
ters pink and white and girdled and pure. Angela, one of Arnold's students, got a
scholarship to Radcliffe. *The New Yorker* published Harold Brodkey's short story
about the love affair of a Harvard boy and a Radcliffe girl. Angela bought every
copy of *The New Yorker* to be had in Bensonhurst. That was what Angela's family
feared: that they *did it* there. Angela was the only Italian girl from Bensonhurst I
knew who went to college. Italians didn't believe in college; it threatened family
authority. (And this has not changed.)

When I was twenty-two, and Arnold had not married me or asked me to marry   50
him or for that matter declared his love for me, I fell in love, at Minton's, on 128th

Street in Harlem, with a jazz drummer. It was a clever thing for me to have done; I had left my childhood religion but not the bed in the room where my mother cried at night. I wanted a baptism of fire into the world, and I got it.

I had never once seen a black man walk the streets of Bensonhurst. I loved the 51 nights. In those days it was safe to take the subway late at night; and full of love, replete, I'd walk at dawn to the apartment house, where, in the lobby, my father, longing for proof of what he most feared, my sexual indiscretion, lurked. (I always harbored a suspicion that the lady in the bargain-hats department was black.) Even in Manhattan, it was hard for me and G., my musician, to walk in safety; even in Birdland it was dicey to hold hands.

Once at Minton's an angry black man asked me who the Mau Mau were. 52 "Kenyan terrorists," I said promptly; I was ignorant and innocent and did not suspect black people of laying traps. (G. laughed and laughed because I couldn't say the word *nigger*, a word he and his friends used all the time. He made me say it; and, taking a leaf from my mother's book, I cried.) The angry black man scolded me up and down and all around. (G. was busy playing a set.) "Don't you call her no names," a whiskey voice said. "She's a woman, she's a nigger—she can be raped." The voice belonged to Billie Holiday, whom as a consequence I loved.

It would not have occurred to me to walk the streets of Bensonhurst with G. 53 Sometimes, to test me and, I suppose, himself, he'd stop me on a busy Manhattan street and kiss me on the lips. But it would not have occurred to him to walk the streets of Bensonhurst with me; he was very much dedicated to his own survival. Once or twice he came to my door in a car or in a cab, laughing his husky laugh (Camel cigarettes), amused, defiant, proud to think of my father waiting there. My father took to following us around Harlem. He'd crouch beneath the areaways of brownstones that housed after-hours clubs; surely there was an illicit thrill in his determined vigilance.

Arnold said, "Are you happy?" 54

G. was married. Three years after I fell in love with him I married a white 55 man, a man I could take home to Bensonhurst but never took to my heart.

The thing about taking G. to Bensonhurst was, he would have been killed. 56 That was what we understood.

Arnold taught us, echoing Camus, that people were not so much good or bad 57 as ignorant. I don't know. I believe in good and evil; and I believe in forgiveness. What I have written here, torn from a bloody past, is not the whole truth. In the whole truth belongs the safety of the stoops in the friendly dark; trips to Ebbets Field; my growing love for my sister-in-law Carol; the steadfast love of my grandmother Concetta, who prayed for me even when I despised her Catholic prayers; *Jack Armstrong* and *Inner Sanctum* and a linen closet full of sugar cubes that smelled of lavender; the smell of glue and new paper and old books in the library on Eighteenth Avenue; Mrs. Scalia, the junior high school teacher who wanted more than anything else to see my Italian name inscribed on the marble honor roll; my meanness to my brother and his to me and the restoration of our love for each other (and the time when he hit a kid on the head with a shovel—he was four—and I packed the bleeding wound with mud); the time Mike Collura drove me to my job in the Secretariat Building of the UN in his ice truck—right to the door; the bakeries and the lemon ices and the fish carts and the kosher butchers; the bike rides to Coney Island and the parachute ride; my maternal grandfather's grape-vine, the yeasty smell of his wine pervading the house; the sun room my paternal grandfather built and Aunt Louise's tailor's dummy and the big radio that were in it; trips to the rodeo (I cried) and the circus and to the World's Fair (I shook hands with Johnny Weissmuller); Miss Isaacs, who would not let Shirley Gottlieb play with me in eighth grade because I might convert her; Aunt Louise's death when she was twenty-three and Dr. Greenberg, who could not bring himself to present the family with a bill; the kindness I received from strangers, all those people, Italians and Jews, whose doorbells I rang in Bensonhurst with my message of su-periority and doom; the goodness of teachers and nuns and priests who listened to a wild, unhappy girl preach; the high school girls I thought despised me and who now, when I meet them, say, We remember you, you were nice. I think it is a sin to have left out all the good things and not to have told all the truth . . . But I am thinking of Yusuf Hawkins, and Gina Feliciano.

"It was the woman's fault." The first lie, the lie the serpent told.   58

Bensonhurst is full of coffee bars now, social clubs for men, they really are,   59
and I've tried to sit in them; and I've been—even with my brother and my son and my nephews—scared. Because they don't belong to us. Bensonhurst was territorial when I grew up. It is more territorial now. It is more defended, and more fright-ened.

If I had told the whole truth—if I had given equal time to what is good and   60
what I loved—I would still not feel welcome there. If I had spoken of their broken dreams, of their hard working-class lives, their economic nightmares, their fear of dope and crime and invasion and change—and their guts and their love—I would still not be welcome there. Because the first survival lesson, the first thing you have to understand to live in Bensonhurst, is to honor "the blood." And when family warmth and tribal feeling have been perverted by fear and alienation, corrupted to form an incubator for hatred, the duty of "the blood" to "the blood" is silence: It is held true that even a single reproach pollutes the stream of love: "We mind our business."

I am afraid of black men now, and I am afraid of being afraid but cannot   61
reason my way out of fear. I am different from the murderers of Yusuf Hawkins; but perhaps not so different from the people who have spun a net of protection, a net of silence, around them. All the time I have been writing this, I have fought the inclination to do the same.

When I was a child, I loved the way the girls receiving First Communion   62
looked; I envied them. I did not understand how I would ever be married if I didn't first become a child-bride in this ceremony that prefigures marriage and looks so much like it. I loved the way their missals smelled and looked, white leather and onionskin paper; I wanted flowers in my hair. It seemed to me a kind of doom that I could not join them, a prefiguration of loneliness . . .

A special Mass was said for Yusuf Hawkins in Bensonhurst. Priests led their   63
parishioners, who looked solemn, grave, frightened, in a march to protest the kill-ing, a march to express solidarity with the people of a child shot dead. They looked

as if they were in shock; count-me-among-the-just/I-am-not-worthy, their looks said. They were brave.

You'd have to have lived there to know how brave. You'd have to have lived   64
there, an outsider and a freak like I was, to know how good their goodness feels.

My brother says: "Thirty years ago, honest to God, I would have been with the   65
guys with the bats. In August, I swear to God, I would have been with the protest-
ors." I can't tell you how hopeful that makes me feel.

On an Alitalia flight from Rome a few weeks after the killing, I sat next to an   66
immigrant from Calabria who lives in the Bays. I asked him if he'd heard about the
trouble in Bensonhurst. "You mean the Chinese?" he said. "It hasn't been the same
since Chinks came to live in the Bays, making trouble."

What can you do with a man like that?   67

I called a friend who lives on West Fifth Street and Avenue S—the Letters.   68
"Bensonhurst," I began . . . "I don't live in Bensonhurst," she said. "I live in Grave-
send." "You've said you live in Bensonhurst all your life!" I said. "No more," she
said . . . and, with what I have come to think of as characteristic Italian logic, she
added, "I never lived in Bensonhurst."

Then we talked about food.   69

Update as This Book Goes to Press in Spring 1991

Eight men were indicted in the killing of Yusuf Hawkins, seven of them charged
with second-degree murder as well as lesser offenses. The prosecution had trouble
proving all the charges, however, partly because of uncooperative witnesses. Joseph Fama was convicted of murder and sentenced to 32 years to life in prison.
Keith Mondello was acquitted of murder but convicted of related charges; he received a sentence of 5½ to 16 years in prison. Another man, convicted of riot and
related charges, was sentenced to 2⅔ to 8 years. For lesser convictions, two were
sentenced to community service; one of these men was also put on probation and
had to pay a $500 fine. Three were acquitted of all charges.

Rhetorical Focus

1. Rather than follow a more linear structure, Harrison chooses to jump back
   and forth between her own life and the Hawkins case. Note, for example,
   the sudden transitions between certain paragraphs. Do you think these
   transitions ultimately make sense? Why or why not?
2. Harrison refers to the Hawkins case right away. Torgovnick mentions it
   only after several paragraphs. What do you infer from this difference in
   rhetorical strategy? For example, do you think that Harrison is more interested in jolting us than Torgovnick is? That she takes the killing of Yusuf
   Hawkins more seriously than Torgovnick does? That she has a different
   overall purpose for her essay?

3. Compare and contrast Harrison's and Torgovnick's writing styles. For example, does one write more concretely than the other, or one more straightforwardly, or one more intensely? When comparing their styles, do you consider their styles basically the same? Refer to passages from both texts.

Thematic Focus

1. Think of Harrison's essay as at least in part a cause-and-effect analysis. Why, according to Harrison, was Yusuf Hawkins killed? What leads her to this conclusion? What explanation(s) does she reject?
2. What do Harrison and Torgovnick both identify as significant features of Bensonhurst? Does Harrison emphasize any significantly different aspects of it? If so, what are they?
3. Recall Torgovnick's statement, "You can take the girl out of Bensonhurst (that much is clear); but you may not be able to take Bensonhurst out of the girl" (paragraph 16). In what ways have Harrison and Torgovnick been outsiders to Bensonhurst themselves? In what ways are they still part of it and is Bensonhurst still part of them? How does each use her brother's present thinking about Bensonhurst to emphasize her own?

Suggestions for Writing

1. Compare a town or neighborhood you know with Bensonhurst as Torgovnick and Harrison describe it. Focus on just a few of the most important similarities and/or differences. Be sure to support your generalizations with details.
2. Write an essay in which you identify the values of a community you belonged to by describing an instance where the community treated an outsider in a particular way. *Community* can mean a close group of friends, a club or organization, a living unit, a neighborhood, or a town. You may find it interesting to focus on an incident where you learned something about the community's values that you had not realized before.
3. Write an essay in which you identify the values of a community that you struggled to join. *Community* can have the range of meanings identified in Assignment 2. You may want to describe your effort to enter your present community or some group within it.

THE ROLE OF PLACES AND COMMUNITIES IN CULTURAL ANALYSIS

When describing various places and communities, the previous authors in this unit have by no means simply jotted down every detail they can remember. They selected particular aspects of the locales they described and worked with a certain overall purpose as they did so. Furthermore, the authors described their place or community in ways that evoke a whole set of cultural values. Our final constellation in this unit emphasizes the cultural context of places and communities, showing how a writer can use them to make points about their larger society. More specifically, Joan Didion and Michael Ventura both see aspects of Las Vegas, Nevada, as indicating problems with the whole American social fabric. Of course, this particular community has long been a favorite object of study for various cultural critics. Other contemporary essayists who have examined it include Tom Wolfe, Hunter Thompson, Jan Morris, and Nancy Mairs. Writing in the mid-1960s, Didion uses the Las Vegas ritual of fast wedding ceremonies to point out deep confusion in American youth. Writing almost 20 years later, Ventura takes Las Vegas as a microcosm of America's obsession with media imagery. Both authors are visitors to Las Vegas rather than inhabitants of it, so you should consider whether their perspectives as outsiders are necessarily more or less objective than the insiders' perspectives conveyed earlier in the unit. Because these authors are not the same person and, in fact, write almost 20 years apart, you should also compare their main points. Do their basic conclusions about Las Vegas wind up being the same, despite their different backgrounds and time periods? Think, too, about the rhetorical strategies of these authors as they use the same city to comment on American culture. For example, do they focus on similar details of Las Vegas or radically different aspects of it? What about the ways they state and develop their theses about it? What about their tones as they elaborate what they observed there? Finally, think of ways that the places and communities you have visited or studied can exemplify cultural trends.

Marrying Absurd

Joan Didion

One of America's most distinguished contemporary writers, Joan Didion
was born in Sacramento, California in 1934 and graduated from the
University of California at Berkeley. After moving to New York, she began
her career as a writer for *Vogue* in 1956. Subsequently, she returned to
California. Although today she is well-known for novels such as *Play It As It
Lays, A Book of Common Prayer*, and *Democracy*, she is perhaps even
more highly regarded for her ironic nonfiction commentaries on people,
places, and trends in America. "Marrying Absurd" first appeared in *The
Saturday Evening Post* in 1967. It was one of Didion's contributions to a
column entitled "Points West" that she alternated writing with her husband
John Gregory Dunne. It was then included in her first collection of essays,
Slouching Towards Bethlehem (1968). Throughout that volume and a
subsequent one entitled *The White Album* (1979), Didion chronicles what
she takes to be America's increasing moral and psychological disorientation
since the 1960s. She has also written two other books of reportage on
places of social turmoil, *Salvador* (1983) and *Miami* (1987). In recent years,
Didion has lived in both Los Angeles and New York and has written
magazine profiles of both cities that reflect the same probing skepticism
with which she here discusses Las Vegas.

Reflections Before Reading

What do you associate with Las Vegas? List images and typical scenes that
come to mind for you. What point(s) about American society do you think a
writer can use Las Vegas to make? Note Didion's title. What can it mean? In
what ways, that is, can the act of marrying be "absurd"? Do you think that
"marrying absurd" is a common practice in America? Why or why not?

To be married in Las Vegas, Clark County, Nevada, a bride must swear that she is   1
eighteen or has parental permission and a bridegroom that he is twenty-one or has
parental permission. Someone must put up five dollars for the license. (On Sundays and holidays, fifteen dollars. The Clark County Courthouse issues mar-

riage licenses at any time of the day or night except between noon and one in the afternoon, between eight and nine in the evening, and between four and five in the morning.) Nothing else is required. The State of Nevada, alone among these United States, demands neither a premarital blood test nor a waiting period before or after the issuance of a marriage license. Driving in across the Mojave from Los Angeles, one sees the signs way out on the desert, looming up from that moon-scape of rattlesnakes and mesquite, even before the Las Vegas lights appear like a mirage on the horizon: "GETTING MARRIED? Free License Information First Strip Exit." Perhaps the Las Vegas wedding industry achieved its peak operational efficiency between 9:00 p.m. and midnight of August 26, 1965, an otherwise unremarkable Thursday which happened to be, by Presidential order, the last day on which anyone could improve his draft status merely by getting married. One hundred and seventy-one couples were pronounced man and wife in the name of Clark County and the State of Nevada that night, sixty-seven of them by a single justice of the peace, Mr. James A. Brennan. Mr. Brennan did one wedding at the Dunes and the other sixty-six in his office, and charged each couple eight dollars. One bride lent her veil to six others. "I got it down from five to three minutes," Mr. Brennan said later of his feat. "I could've married them *en masse*, but they're people, not cattle. People expect more when they get married."

What people who get married in Las Vegas actually do expect—what, in the largest sense, their "expectations" are—strikes one as a curious and self-contradictory business. Las Vegas is the most extreme and allegorical of American settlements, bizarre and beautiful in its venality and in its devotion to immediate gratification, a place the tone of which is set by mobsters and call girls and ladies' room attendants with amyl nitrite poppers in their uniform pockets. Almost everyone notes that there is no "time" in Las Vegas, no night and no day and no past and no future (no Las Vegas casino, however, has taken the obliteration of the ordinary time sense quite so far as Harold's Club in Reno, which for a while issued, at odd intervals in the day and night, mimeographed "bulletins" carrying news from the world outside); neither is there any logical sense of where one is. One is standing on a highway in the middle of a vast hostile desert looking at an eighty-foot sign which blinks "STARDUST" or "CAESAR'S PALACE." Yes, but what does that explain? This geographical implausibility reinforces the sense that what happens there has no connection with "real" life; Nevada cities like Reno and Carson are ranch towns, Western towns, places behind which there is some historical imperative. But Las Vegas seems to exist only in the eye of the beholder. All of which makes it an extraordinarily stimulating and interesting place, but an odd one in which to want to wear a candlelight satin Priscilla of Boston wedding dress with Chantilly lace insets, tapered sleeves and a detachable modified train.

And yet the Las Vegas wedding business seems to appeal to precisely that impulse. "Sincere and Dignified Since 1954," one wedding chapel advertises. There are nineteen such wedding chapels in Las Vegas, intensely competitive, each offering better, faster, and, by implication, more sincere services than the next: Our Photos Best Anywhere, Your Wedding on A Phonograph Record, Candlelight with Your Ceremony, Honeymoon Accommodations, Free Transportation from Your Motel to Courthouse to Chapel and Return to Motel, Religious or Civil

Ceremonies, Dressing Rooms, Flowers, Rings, Announcements, Witnesses Available, and Ample Parking. All of these services, like most others in Las Vegas (sauna baths, payroll-check cashing, chinchilla coats for sale or rent) are offered twenty-four hours a day, seven days a week, presumably on the premise that marriage, like craps, is a game to be played when the table seems hot.

But what strikes one most about the Strip chapels, with their wishing wells and   4
stained-glass paper windows and their artificial bouvardia, is that so much of their business is by no means a matter of simple convenience, of late-night liaisons between show girls and baby Crosbys. Of course there is some of that. (One night about eleven o'clock in Las Vegas I watched a bride in an orange minidress and masses of flame-colored hair stumble from a Strip chapel on the arm of her bridegroom, who looked the part of the expendable nephew in movies like *Miami Syndicate*. "I gotta get the kids," the bride whimpered. "I gotta pick up the sitter, I gotta get to the midnight show." "What you gotta get," the bridegroom said, opening the door of a Cadillac Coupe de Ville and watching her crumple on the seat, "is sober.") But Las Vegas seems to offer something other than "convenience"; it is merchandising "niceness," the facsimile of proper ritual, to children who do not know how else to find it, how to make the arrangements, how to do it "right." All day and evening long on the Strip, one sees actual wedding parties, waiting under the harsh lights at a crosswalk, standing uneasily in the parking lot of the Frontier while the photographer hired by The Little Church of the West ("Wedding Place of the Stars") certifies the occasion, takes the picture: the bride in a veil and white satin pumps, the bridegroom usually in a white dinner jacket, and even an attendant or two, a sister or a best friend in hot-pink *peau de soie*, a flirtation veil, a carnation nosegay. "When I Fall in Love It Will Be Forever," the organist plays, and then a few bars of Lohengrin. The mother cries; the stepfather, awkward in his role, invites the chapel hostess to join them for a drink at the Sands. The hostess declines with a professional smile; she has already transferred her interest to the group waiting outside. One bride out, another in, and again the sign goes up on the chapel door: "One moment please—Wedding."

I sat next to one such wedding party in a Strip restaurant the last time I was in   5
Las Vegas. The marriage had just taken place; the bride still wore her dress, the mother her corsage. A bored waiter poured out a few swallows of pink champagne ("on the house") for everyone but the bride, who was too young to be served. "You'll need something with more kick than that," the bride's father said with heavy jocularity to his new son-in-law; the ritual jokes about the wedding night had a certain Panglossian character, since the bride was clearly several months pregnant. Another round of pink champagne, this time not on the house, and the bride began to cry. "It was just as nice," she sobbed, "as I hoped and dreamed it would be."

Rhetorical Focus

1. Four of the five paragraphs in this essay focus on wedding services in Las Vegas. What do you take to be Didion's purpose in writing paragraph 2, the one that does not?

2. Didion can be said to state her thesis when she writes, "But Las Vegas seems to offer something other than 'convenience'; it is merchandising 'niceness,' the facsimile of proper ritual, to children who do not know how else to find it, how to make the arrangements, how to do it 'right' " (paragraph 4). Why do you think she decided not to place this statement at the beginning? How does she connect with it at the end?

3. Much of this essay lists concrete details, tells anecdotes, and quotes other people. Didion explicitly refers to herself only in the last paragraph. To what extent, then, is she indicating her own attitude toward what she records? Obviously she expresses a judgment in her title, but how much does she express one in the body of her essay? Support your answer by referring to specific statements she makes.

Thematic Focus

1. Do you think Didion's title is fair? Would you agree that the marrying she describes is "absurd"?

2. Does Las Vegas, as Didion describes it, strike you as unusual? Can you think of other places or communities that in some sense "merchandise 'niceness' "?

3. The people Didion met in Las Vegas probably would not like what she writes about them. Does she, as a writer, have any responsibility toward her subjects?

Report from El Dorado

Michael Ventura

Prior to starting a career in journalism with the *Austin [Texas] Sun* in 1974, Michael Ventura (b. 1945) held several jobs. In his own words, he "did everything—sold vacuum cleaners, flipped hamburgers, typed, hammered nails, poured concrete." Presently he is a columnist for the *L.A. Weekly* in California. In addition, he has done work in films: writing *Echo Park*, co-authoring *Roadie*, and directing—as well as writing—a documentary on the actor–filmmaker John Cassavetes. The following is part of an essay in Ventura's 1985 collection *Shadow Dancing in the U.S.A.* This selection is representative of the spirited cultural criticism pervading the volume. Here, almost 20 years after Joan Didion used Las Vegas to identify what she felt were distorted American values, Ventura turns to it as an emblem of his society's continuing illusions.

Reflections Before Reading

Didion wrote her essay on Las Vegas in the 1960s. Ventura uses his essay on Las Vegas to emphasize what he sees as disturbing trends in the America of the 1980s. What, if any, are American trends that currently disturb you? When you have looked around cities, your campus, or other communities, what recent evidence of these trends have you seen? Note Ventura's title. What, if anything, do you associate with El Dorado?

To go from a job you don't like to watching a screen on which others live more 1
intensely than you . . . is American life, by and large.

This is our political ground. This is our artistic ground. This is what we've done 2
with our immense resources. We have to stop calling it "entertainment" or "news"
or "sports" and start calling it what it is: our most immediate environment.

This is a very, very different America from the America that built the indus- 3
trial capacity to win the Second World War and to surge forward on the multiple
momentums of that victory for thirty years. That was an America that worked at
mostly menial tasks during the day (now we work at mostly clerical tasks) and had
to look at each other at night.

"Report from El Dorado," from DANCING IN THE USA, by Michael Ventura. Reprinted with special permission from Jeremy P. Tarcher, Inc., Los Angeles.

I'm not suggesting a nostalgia for that time. It was repressive and bigoted to an 4
extent that is largely forgotten today, to cite only two of its uglier aspects. But in
that environment America meant *America:* the people and the land. The land was
far bigger than what we'd done with the land.

This is no longer true. Now the environment of America is media. Not the 5
land itself, but the image of the land. The focus is not on the people so much as it is
on the interplay between people and screens. What we've done with the land is far
more important now than the land—we're not dealing with the land anymore,
we're dealing with our manipulation and pollution of it.

And what we've done with the very concept of "image" is taking on far more 6
importance for many of us than the actual sights and sounds of our lives.

For instance: Ronald Reagan stands on a cliff in Normandy to commemorate 7
the day U.S. Army Rangers scaled those cliffs in the World War II invasion. Today's Rangers reenact the event while some of the original Rangers, in their sixties
now, look on. Except that it is the wrong cliff. The cliff that was actually scaled is a
bit further down the beach, but it's not as photogenic as this cliff, so this cliff has
been chosen for everybody to emote over. Some of the old Rangers tell reporters
that the historical cliff is over yonder, but the old Rangers are swept up (as well
they might be) in the ceremonies, and nobody objects enough. This dislocation,
this choice, this stance that the real cliff is not important, today's photograph is
more important, is a media event. It insults the real event, and overpowers it.
Multiplied thousands of times over thousands of outlets of every form and size,
ensconced in textbooks as well as screenplays, in sales presentations as well as
legislative packages, in religious revivals as well as performance-art pieces, this is
the process that has displaced what used to be called "culture."

"I'm not even sure it's a culture anymore. It's like this careening hunger splat- 8
tering out in all directions."

Jeff Nightbyrd was trying to define "culture" in the wee hours at the Four 9
Queens in Las Vegas. It was a conversation that had been going on since we'd
become friends working on the *Austin Sun* in 1974, trying to get our bearing now
that the sixties were *really* over. He'd spent that triple-time decade as an SDS
organizer and editor of *Rat*, and I'd hit Austin after a few years of road-roving,
commune-hopping, and intensive (often depressive) self-exploration—getting by,
as the song said, with a little help from my friends, as a lot of us did then. This
particular weekend Nightbyrd had come to Vegas from Austin for a computer convention, and I had taken off from my duties at the *L.A. Weekly* for some lessons in
craps (at which Jeff is quite good) and to further our rap. The slot machines clat-
tered around us in unison, almost comfortingly, the way the sound of a large shaky
air-conditioner can be comforting in a cheap hotel room when you're trying to
remember to forget. We were, after all, trying to fathom an old love: America.

There are worse places to indulge in this obsession than Las Vegas. It is the 10
most American, the most audacious, of cities. Consuming unthinkable amounts of
energy in the midst of an unlivable desert (Death Valley is not far away), its decor is
based on various cheap-to-luxurious versions of a 1930s Busby Berkeley musical.
Indeed, no studio backlot could ever be more of a set, teeming with extras, people

who come from all over America, and all over the world, to see the topless, taste-
less shows, the Johnny Carson guests on parade doing their utterly predictable
routines, the dealers and crap-table croupiers who combine total boredom with
ruthless efficiency and milk us dry—yet at least these tourists are risking something they genuinely value: money. It's a quiz show turned into a way of life, where
you can get a good Italian dinner at dawn. Even the half-lit hour of the wolf doesn't
faze Las Vegas. How could it, when the town has survived the flash of atom bombs
tested just over the horizon?

The history books will tell you that, ironically enough, the town was founded   11
by Mormons in 1855. Even their purity of vision couldn't bear the intensity of this
desert, and they abandoned the place after just two years. But they had left a
human imprint, and a decade later the U.S. Army built a fort here. The settlement
hung on, and the railroad came through in 1905. During the Second World War
the Mafia started to build the city as we know it now. Religious zealots, the Army,
and the Mafia—quite a triad of founding fathers.

Yet one could go back even further, some 400 years, when the first Europeans   12
discovered the deserts of the American West—Spaniards who, as they slowly began to believe that there might be no end to these expansive wilds, became more
and more certain that somewhere, somewhere to the north, lay El Dorado—a city
of gold. Immeasurable wealth would be theirs, they believed, and eternal youth.
What would they have thought if they had suddenly come upon modern Las Vegas,
lying as it does in the midst of this bleached nowhere, glowing at night with a
brilliance that would have frightened them? We have built our desert city to their
measure—for they were gaudy and greedy, devout and vicious, jovial and frenzied,
like this town. They had just wasted the entire Aztec civilization because their
fantasies were so strong they couldn't see the ancient cultural marvels before their
eyes. The Aztecs, awed and terrified, believed they were being murdered by gods;
and in the midst of such strangeness, the Spaniards took on godlike powers even in
their own eyes. As many Europeans would in America, they took liberties here
they would never have taken within sight of their home cathedrals. Their hungers
dominated them, and in their own eyes the New World seemed as inexhaustible as
their appetites. So when Nightbyrd described our present culture as "a careening
hunger splattering out in all directions," he was also, if unintentionally, speaking
about our past. Fittingly, we were sitting in the midst of a city that had been fantasized by those seekers of El Dorado 400 years ago. In that sense, America had Las
Vegas a century before it had Plymouth Rock. And our sensibility has been caught
between the fantasies of the conquistadors and the obsessions of the Puritans ever
since.

Yes, a fitting place to try to think about American culture.   13

"There are memories of culture," Nightbyrd was saying, "but the things that   14
have given people strength have dissolved. And because they've dissolved, people
are into distractions. And distractions aren't culture."

Are there even memories? The media have taken over our memories. That   15
day Nightbyrd had been driving through the small towns that dot this desert, towns
for which Vegas is only a dull glow to the southwest. In a bar in one of those towns,
"like that little bar in *The Right Stuff*," he'd seen pictures of cowboys on the wall.

"Except that they weren't cowboys. They were movie stars. Guys who grew up in Glendale [John Wayne] and Santa Monica [Robert Redford]." Surely this desert had its own heroes once, in the old gold-mining towns where a few people still hang on, towns like Goldfield and Tonopah. Remembering those actual heroes would be "culture." Needing pictures of movie stars for want of the real thing is only a nostalgia for culture.

Nostalgia is not memory. Memory is specific. One has a relationship to a memory, and it may be a difficult relationship, because a memory always makes a demand upon the present. But nostalgia is vague, a sentimental wash that obscures memory and acts as a narcotic to dull the importance of the present.   16

Media as we know it now thrives on nostalgia and is hostile to memory. In a television bio-pic, Helen Keller is impersonated by Mare Winningham. But the face of Helen Keller was marked by her enormous powers of concentration, while the face of Mare Winningham is merely cameo-pretty. A memory has been stolen. It takes a beauty in you to see the beauty in Helen Keller's face, while to cast the face of a Mare Winningham in the role is to suggest, powerfully, that one can come back from the depths unscathed. No small delusion is being sold here. Yet this is a minor instance in a worldwide, twenty-four-hour-a-day onslaught.   17

An onslaught that gathers momentum every twenty-four hours. Remember that what drew us to Las Vegas was a computer fair. One of these new computers does interesting things with photographs. You can put a photograph into the computer digitally. This means the photograph is in there without a negative or print, each element of the image stored separately. In the computer, you can change any element of the photograph you wish, replacing it or combining it with elements from other photographs. In other words, you can take composites of different photographs and put them into a new photograph of your own composition. Combine this with computer drawing, and you can touch up shadows that don't match. When it comes out of the computer the finished product bears no evidence of tampering with any negative. The possibilities for history books and news stories are infinite. Whole new histories can now be written. Events which never happened can be fully documented.   18

The neo-Nazis who are trying to convince people that the Holocaust never happened will be able to show the readers of their newsletter an Auschwitz of well-fed, happy people being watched over by kindly S.S. men while tending gardens. And they will be able to make the accusation that photographs of the *real* Auschwitz were created in a computer by manipulative Jews. The Soviet Union can rewrite Czechoslovakia and Afghanistan, the United States can rewrite Vietnam, and atomic weapons proponents can prove that the average resident of Hiroshima was unharmed by the blast. On a less sinister, but equally disruptive, level, the writers of business prospectuses and real-estate brochures can have a field day.   19

Needless to say, when any photograph can be processed this way then all photographs become suspect. It not only becomes easier to lie, it becomes far harder to tell the truth.   20

But why should this seem shocking when under the names of "entertainment" and "advertising" we've been filming history, and every facet of daily life, in just   21 this way for nearly a century now? It shouldn't surprise us that the ethics of our entertainment have taken over, and that we are viewing reality itself as a form of entertainment. And, as entertainment, reality can be rewritten, transformed, played with, in any fashion.

These considerations place us squarely at the center of our world—and we have no choice, it's the only world there is anymore. *Electronic media has done for everyday reality what Einstein did for physics:* everything is shifting. Even the shifts are shifting. And a fact is not so crucial anymore, not so crucial as the process that turns a fact into an image. For we live now with images as much as facts, and the images seem to impart more life than facts *precisely because they are so capable of transmutation, of transcendence, able to transcend their sources and their uses.* And all the while the images goad us on, so that we become partly images ourselves, imitating the properties of images as we surround ourselves with images.   22

This is most blatant in our idea of "a vacation"—an idea only about 100 years old. To "vacation" is to enter an image. Las Vegas is only the most shrill embodiment of this phenomenon. People come here not so much to gamble (individual losses are comparatively light), nor for the glittery entertainment, but to step into an image, a daydream, a filmlike world where "everything" is promised. No matter that the Vegas definition of "everything" is severely limited, what thrills tourists is the sense of being surrounded in "real life" by the same images that they see on TV. But the same is true of the Grand Canyon, or Yellowstone National Park, or Yosemite, or Death Valley, or virtually any of our "natural" attractions. What with all their roads, telephones, bars, cable-TV motels, the visitors are carefully protected from having to *experience* the place. They view its image, they camp out on its image, ski down or climb up its image, take deep breaths of its image, let its image give them a tan. Or, when they tour the cities, they ride the quaint trolley cars of the city's image, they visit the Latin Quarter of its image, they walk across the Brooklyn Bridge of its image—our recreation is a *re*-creation of America into one big Disneyland.   23

And this is only one way we have stripped the very face of America of any content, any reality, concentrating only on its power as image. We also elect images, groom ourselves as images, make an image of our home, our car, and now, with aerobics, of our very bodies. For in the aerobics craze the flesh becomes a garment, susceptible to fashion. So it becomes less *our* flesh, though the exercise may make it more serviceable. It becomes "my" body, like "my" car, "my" house. What, within us, is saying "my"? What is transforming body into image? We shy away from asking. In this sense it can be said that after the age of about twenty-five we no longer *have* bodies anymore—we have possessions that are either more or less young, which we are constantly trying to transform and through which we try to breathe.   24

It's not that all this transmutation of realities into un- or non- or supra-realities is "bad," but that it's unconscious, compulsive, reductive. We rarely make things more than they were; we simplify them into less. Though surely the process *could*—at least theoretically—go both ways. Or so India's mediators and Zen's   25 monks say. But that would be to *increase* meaning, and we seem bent on the elimination of meaning. We're Reagan's Rangers, climbing a cliff that *is* a real cliff, except it's not the cliff we say it is, so that the meaning of both cliffs—not to mention of our act of climbing—is reduced.

As I look out onto a glowing city that is more than 400 years old but was built   26
only during the last forty years, as I watch it shine in blinking neon in a desert that has seen the flash of atom bombs, it becomes more and more plain to me that America is at war with meaning. America is form opposed to content. Not just form *instead* of content. Form opposed. Often violently. There are few things resented so much among us as the suggestion that what we do *means*. It *means* something to watch so much TV. It *means* something to be obsessed with sports. It *means* something to vacation by indulging in images. It means something, and therefore it has consequences. Other cultures have argued over their meanings. We tend to deny that there is any such thing, insisting instead that what you see is what you get and that's *it*. All we're doing is having a *good time*, all we're doing is making a buck, all we're doing is enjoying the spectacle, we insist. So that when we export American culture what we are really exporting is an attitude toward content. Media is the American war on content with all the stops out, with meaning in utter rout, frightened nuances dropping their weapons as they run.

Rhetorical Focus

1. Unlike Didion, Ventura does not mention Las Vegas until his ninth paragraph. How does he use it to develop a thesis he has previously established?
2. Ventura is more dramatically present in his essay than Didion is in hers. Do you think it was wise of him to inject himself so explicitly into it? Why or why not?
3. These two authors seem to work with at least somewhat different visions of their audience. Ventura implicates himself and his readers in what he is criticizing. He even calls Las Vegas *"our* desert city" (paragraph 12). By contrast, Didion seems to consider herself and her readers detached from the people she describes. Do these authors' stances toward their audiences make equal sense?

Thematic Focus

1. Ventura's essay pivots around certain terms and distinctions between them. How does he oppose "culture" to "media"? How does he distinguish "nostalgia" from "memory"?
2. Why do you think Ventura gives a history of Las Vegas and even goes back 400 years to the search for El Dorado?
3. Are Ventura and Didion equally plausible in what they argue about their culture, or is one more convincing than the other? Explain.

Suggestions for Writing

1. Explain the ways that Didion and Ventura both use Las Vegas to make larger criticisms of American society. When they discuss Las Vegas, are they pointing to essentially the same problem in American life, or do their concerns significantly differ?
2. Explain how a particular aspect of a community you know indicated to you something important about American life in general. As part of your explanation, indicate whether the inhabitants of the community would share your perspective on it.
3. At the conclusion of "Marrying Absurd," Didion presents a concrete anecdote without stating its moral. Write a real-life anecdote, trying to express a central idea simply through your details. On a separate piece of paper, state the moral you wish to convey. Exchange anecdotes (but not morals) with a classmate, and see whether the two of you are able to guess each other's moral.

Chapter
4
Education

*A*lthough Americans have always prided themselves on their democratic educational system, there have been some grumblings lately from those who feel slighted by America's schools. Industrial nations try to educate their population to read and write at a rather high level. Some are, however, more successful than others. Japan, for example, has a high rate of literacy among the general population even though only a small percentage go to college. Although almost half of American secondary students continue their schooling beyond graduation, many minority students and a growing number of women now feel that their education has been faulty, that they have been either poorly educated or educated in a biased fashion. Such dissent is no longer unusual.

Although we have long had universal education, many critics still think that the content of education reflects the cultural values and ideas of an elite, specifically the upper middle-class white men in power. Others find this position extreme, suggesting instead that teachers emphasize the "western" classics as a way to unify our diverse society.

In the first constellation, Adrienne Rich, Malcolm X, and Maya Angelou find their own values and experiences missing from their educational setting. In the second constellation of readings, Norman Podhoretz and Toni Cade Bambara also describe education from the "wrong" end of the social ladder, but they are transformed through interactions with a significant teacher. In the third constellation, Richard Rodriguez and George Orwell provide outsiders' perspectives, as working-class children confused by the resolutely middle-class world of school. In the last section, "Canons," the actual content of the curriculum is debated by E. D. Hirsch and Mike Rose, who, in turn, take conservative and liberal stances about what should be read in high school and college. These and other debates revolve around some basic questions of schooling: Is education a way to socialize students into society or to transform society? Should we pass on the Western tradition or critique it? As you read through these sections, compare your own experiences in school to those of the writers in this unit.

LEARNING TO LEARN

Most students accept the education they are given without wondering whether there is something better, something more connected to their lives and their futures. However, some do resist, refusing to accept what they see as the school's lower expectation for them as women or as African-Americans, for example. Adrienne Rich and Maya Angelou want something more than the traditional fare, and they have the resources to get it. Malcolm X, who was not even taught how to read in school, also refuses to accept illiteracy, thereby forging a powerful statement about a person's ability to overcome the indifference of an educational system that could not or would not learn how to teach difficult students. Admittedly, that task in many inner city schools is awesome, but when we look at the vast number of poorly educated and hostile students in America, we must ask ourselves whether our society has really committed itself financially and philosophically to educating all its citizens or only those who are prepared enough or cooperative enough to accept what is offered, regardless of its relevance.

Claiming an Education

Adrienne Rich

Adrienne Rich (b. 1929), one of the most respected of contemporary American poets, was the product of a traditional education. She attended a private all-girls high school in Baltimore and went on to Radcliffe, where—by her own account—she was taught the white male poets by white male teachers. Profoundly influenced by the feminist movement of the 1960s and 1970s, Rich became known as an outspoken and radical feminist with a particular interest in women's anger and its creative uses. In the following lecture given to undergraduate women at Douglass College, Rutgers University, in 1977, Rich urges women to take responsibility for their own education, to actively pursue a "life of meaningful work," to recognize and claim their potential as contributors to society.

Reflections Before Reading

Do you think you were given a preordained education, or did you make a decision to claim an education you wanted? Do you think it is possible to decide to be in charge of your own education? Do you think the education you have received so far primarily supports the values of white middle-class males? Be specific.

For this convocation, I planned to separate my remarks into two parts: some thoughts about you, the women students here, and some thoughts about us who teach in a women's college. But ultimately, those two parts are indivisible. If university education means anything beyond the processing of human beings into expected roles, through credit hours, tests, and grades (and I believe that in a women's college especially it *might* mean much more), it implies an ethical and intellectual contract between teacher and student. This contract must remain intuitive, dynamic, unwritten; but we must turn to it again and again if learning is to be reclaimed from the depersonalizing and cheapening pressures of the present-day academic scene.

1

The first thing I want to say to you who are students, is that you cannot afford to think of being here to *receive* an education; you will do much better to think of yourselves as being here to *claim* one. One of the dictionary definitions of the verb "to claim" is: *to take as the rightful owner; to assert in the face of possible contradiction.* "To receive" is *to come into possession of; to act as receptacle or container for; to accept as authoritative or true.* The difference is that between acting and being acted-upon, and for women it can literally mean the difference between life and death.

2

One of the devastating weaknesses of university learning, of the store of knowledge and opinion that has been handed down through academic training, has been its almost total erasure of women's experience and thought from the curriculum, and its exclusion of women as members of the academic community. Today, with increasing numbers of women students in nearly every branch of higher learning, we still see very few women in the upper levels of faculty and administration in most institutions. Douglass College itself is a women's college in a university administered overwhelmingly by men, who in turn are answerable to the state legislature, again composed predominantly of men. But the most significant fact for you is that what you learn here, the very texts you read, the lectures you hear, the way your studies are divided into categories and fragmented one from the other—all this reflects, to a very large degree, neither objective reality, nor an accurate picture of the past, nor a group of rigorously tested observations about human behavior. What you can learn here (and I mean not only at Douglass but

3

any college in any university) is how *men* have perceived and organized their experience, their history, their ideas of social relationships, good and evil, sickness and health, etc. When you read or hear about "great issues," "major texts," "the mainstream of Western thought," you are hearing about what men, above all white men, in their male subjectivity, have decided is important.

Black and other minority peoples have for some time recognized that their   4
racial and ethnic experience was not accounted for in the studies broadly labeled human; and that even the sciences can be racist. For many reasons, it has been more difficult for women to comprehend our exclusion, and to realize that even the sciences can be sexist. For one thing, it is only within the last hundred years that higher education has grudgingly been opened up to women at all, even to white, middle-class women. And many of us have found ourselves poring eagerly over books with titles like: *The Descent of Man; Man and His Symbols; Irrational Man; The Phenomenon of Man; The Future of Man; Man and the Machine; From Man to Man; May Man Prevail?; Man, Science and Society;* or *One-Dimensional Man*—books pretending to describe a "human" reality that does not include over one-half the human species.

Less than a decade ago, with the rebirth of a feminist movement in this coun-   5
try, women students and teachers in a number of universities began to demand and set up women's studies courses—to *claim* a woman-directed education. And, despite the inevitable accusations of "unscholarly," "group therapy," "faddism," etc., despite backlash and budget cuts, women's studies are still growing, offering to more and more women a new intellectual grasp on their lives, new understanding of our history, a fresh vision of the human experience, and also a critical basis for evaluating what they hear and read in other courses, and in the society at large.

But my talk is not really about women's studies, much as I believe in their   6
scholarly, scientific, and human necessity. While I think that any Douglass student has everything to gain by investigating and enrolling in women's studies courses, I want to suggest that there is a more essential experience that you owe yourselves, one which courses in women's studies can greatly enrich, but which finally depends on you, in all your interactions with yourself and your world. This is the experience of *taking responsibility toward yourselves*. Our upbringing as women has so often told us that this should come second to our relationships and responsibilities to other people. We have been offered ethical models of the self-denying wife and mother; intellectual models of the brilliant but slapdash dilettante who never commits herself to anything the whole way, or the intelligent woman who denies her intelligence in order to seem more "feminine," or who sits in passive silence even when she disagrees inwardly with everything that is being said around her.

Responsibility to yourself means refusing to let others do your thinking, talk-   7
ing, and naming for you; it means learning to respect and use your own brains and instincts; hence, grappling with hard work. It means that you do not treat your body as a commodity with which to purchase superficial intimacy or economic security; for our bodies and minds are inseparable in this life, and when we allow our bodies to be treated as objects, our minds are in mortal danger. It means insisting that those to whom you give your friendship and love are able to respect your mind. It means being able to say, with Charlotte Brontë's *Jane Eyre:* "I have

an inward treasure born with me, which can keep me alive if all the extraneous delights should be withheld or offered only at a price I cannot afford to give."

Responsibility to yourself means that you don't fall for shallow and easy solu-   8
tions—predigested books and ideas, weekend encounters guaranteed to change your life, taking "gut" courses instead of ones you know will challenge you, bluffing at school and life instead of doing solid work, marrying early as an escape from real decisions, getting pregnant as an evasion of already existing problems. It means that you refuse to sell your talents and aspirations short, simply to avoid conflict and confrontation. And this, in turn, means resisting the forces in society which say that women should be nice, play safe, have low professional expectations, drown in love and forget about work, live through others, and stay in the places assigned to us. It means that we insist on a life of meaningful work, insist that work be as meaningful as love and friendship in our lives. It means, therefore, the courage to be "different"; not to be continuously available to others when we need time for ourselves and our work; to be able to demand of others—parents, friends, room-mates, teachers, lovers, husbands, children—that they respect our sense of pur-pose and our integrity as persons. Women everywhere are finding the courage to do this, more and more, and we are finding that courage both in our study of women in the past who possessed it, and in each other as we look to other women for comradeship, community, and challenge. The difference between a life lived actively, and a life of passive drifting and dispersal of energies, is an immense difference. Once we begin to feel committed to our lives, responsible to ourselves, we can never again be satisfied with the old, passive way.

Now comes the second part of the contract. I believe that in a women's college   9
you have the right to expect your faculty to take you seriously. The education of women has been a matter of debate for centuries, and old, negative attitudes about women's role, women's ability to think and take leadership, are still rife both in and outside the university. Many male professors (and I don't mean only at Douglass) still feel that teaching in a women's college is a second-rate career. Many tend to eroticize their women students—to treat them as sexual objects—instead of de-manding the best of their minds. (At Yale a legal suit [*Alexander* v. *Yale*] has been brought against the university by a group of women students demanding a stated policy against sexual advances toward female students by male professors.) Many teachers, both men and women, trained in the male-centered tradition, are still handing the ideas and texts of that tradition on to students without teaching them to criticize its antiwoman attitudes, its omission of women as part of the species. Too often, all of us fail to teach the most important thing, which is that clear think-ing, active discussion, and excellent writing are all necessary for intellectual free-dom, and that these require *hard work*. Sometimes, perhaps in discouragement with a culture which is both anti-intellectual and antiwoman, we may resign our-selves to low expectations for our students before we have given them half a chance to become more thoughtful, expressive human beings. We need to take to heart the words of Elizabeth Barrett Browning, a poet, a thinking woman, and a femi-nist, who wrote in 1845 of her impatience with studies which cultivate a "passive recipiency" in the mind, and asserted that "women want to be made to *think ac-tively*: their apprehension is quicker than that of men, but their defect lies for the

most part in the logical faculty and in the higher mental activities." Note that she implies a defect which can be remedied by intellectual training; *not* an inborn lack of ability.

I have said that the contract on the student's part involves that you demand to   10
be taken seriously so that you can also go on taking yourself seriously. This means seeking out criticism, recognizing that the most affirming thing anyone can do for you is demand that you push yourself further, show you the range of what you *can* do. It means rejecting attitudes of "take-it-easy," "why-be-so-serious," "why-worry-you'll-probably-get-married-anyway." It means assuming your share of responsibility for what happens in the classroom, because that affects the quality of your daily life here. It means that the student sees herself engaged *with* her teachers in an active, ongoing struggle for a real education. But for her to do this, her teachers must be committed to the belief that women's minds and experience are intrinsically valuable and indispensable to any civilization worthy of the name; that there is no more exhilarating and intellectually fertile place in the academic world today than a women's college—*if* both students and teachers in large enough numbers are trying to fulfill this contract. The contract is really a pledge of mutual seriousness about women, about language, ideas, methods, and values. It is our shared commitment toward a world in which the inborn potentialities of so many women's minds will no longer be wasted, raveled-away, paralyzed, or denied.

Rhetorical Focus

1. Rich's thesis does not seem to appear until the middle of the sixth paragraph. Is this effective? What is she doing in the previous five?
2. After her announced thesis, Rich gives two paragraphs of examples. Why is she so concrete here?
3. Notice how many times in the last paragraph Rich uses "it means." What is she trying to do? Is this an effective way to achieve her goal?

Thematic Focus

1. Can you remember studying, either in English, history, or elsewhere, about the contributions of women and their experiences? Be specific.
2. Rich writes about various traditional roles women have been offered. Do they ring true from your experience? What comparable role models are men encouraged to emulate?
3. Should there be courses enabling all minorities to gain insight into their experiences? Would this hold true for Hispanics, American Indians, Quakers, gay men and lesbians, atheists, Marxists?

Learning to Read

Malcolm X

Malcolm X (born Malcolm Little) began his career as a street hustler in pre–civil rights America. He was convicted of robbery in 1946 and spent the next seven years in prison, where he taught himself to read history, religion, and philosophy. He also became a member of the Black Muslims, a radical religious sect. During the 1960s, Malcolm X was a prominent leader of the African-American community. He was assassinated in 1965. In the following excerpt from *The Autobiography of Malcolm X*, he describes the process by which he educated himself in prison, and the devastating conclusions to which he came about the relationship between whites and nonwhites throughout history.

Reflections Before Reading

Can you remember when you first started reading? Were your early experiences positive? Are you surprised that someone who was once an illiterate criminal would later be represented in a college anthology in a writing course? Explain. Of course, even with Alex Haley's help, Malcolm X was quite literate when he wrote this. Does that say anything about the connection between illiteracy and intelligence? If you were in prison, what would you do with your time? If you were a prison warden, what would you do about the education of the inmates?

Many who today hear me somewhere in person, or on television, or those who read something I've said, will think I went to school far beyond the eighth grade. This impression is due entirely to my prison studies. 1

It had really begun back in the Charlestown Prison, when Bimbi first made me feel envy of his stock of knowledge. Bimbi had always taken charge of any conversation he was in, and I had tried to emulate him. But every book I picked up had few sentences which didn't contain anywhere from one to nearly all of the words that might as well have been in Chinese. When I just skipped those words, of course, I really ended up with little idea of what the book said. So I had come to the Norfolk Prison Colony still going through only book-reading motions. Pretty 2 soon, I would have quit even these motions, unless I had received the motivation that I did.

I saw that the best thing I could do was get hold of a dictionary—to study, to learn some words. I was lucky enough to reason also that I should try to improve my penmanship. It was sad. I couldn't even write in a straight line. It was both ideas together that moved me to request a dictionary along with some tablets and pencils from the Norfolk Prison Colony school.   3

I spent two days just riffling uncertainly through the dictionary's pages. I'd never realized so many words existed! I didn't know *which* words I needed to learn. Finally, just to start some kind of action, I began copying.   4

In my slow, painstaking, ragged handwriting, I copied into my tablet everything printed on that first page, down to the punctuation marks.   5

I believe it took me a day. Then, aloud, I read back, to myself, everything I'd written on the tablet. Over and over, aloud, to myself, I read my own handwriting.   6

I woke up the next morning, thinking about those words—immensely proud to realize that not only had I written so much at one time, but I'd written words that I never knew were in the world. Moreover, with a little effort, I also could remember what many of these words meant. I reviewed the words whose meanings I didn't remember. Funny thing, from the dictionary first page right now, that "aardvark" springs to my mind. The dictionary had a picture of it, a long-tailed, long-eared, burrowing African mammal, which lives off termites caught by sticking out its tongue as an anteater does for ants.   7

I was so fascinated that I went on—I copied the dictionary's next page. And the same experience came when I studied that. With every succeeding page, I also learned of people and places and events from history. Actually the dictionary is like a miniature encyclopedia. Finally the dictionary's A section had filled a whole tablet—and I went on into the B's. That was the way I started copying what eventually became the entire dictionary. It went a lot faster after so much practice helped me to pick up handwriting speed. Between what I wrote in my tablet, and writing letters, during the rest of my time in prison I would guess I wrote a million words.   8

I suppose it was inevitable that as my word-base broadened, I could for the first time pick up a book and read and now begin to understand what the book was saying. Anyone who has read a great deal can imagine the new world that opened. Let me tell you something: from then until I left that prison in every free moment I had, if I was not reading in the library, I was reading on my bunk. You couldn't have gotten me out of books with a wedge. Between Mr. Muhammad's teachings, my correspondence, my visitors—usually Ella and Reginald—and my reading of books, months passed without my even thinking about being imprisoned. In fact, up to then, I never had been so truly free in my life.   9

The Norfolk Prison Colony's library was in the school building. A variety of classes was taught there by instructors who came from such places as Harvard and Boston universities. The weekly debates between inmate teams were also held in the school building. You would be astonished to know how worked up convict debaters and audiences would get over subjects like "Should Babies Be Fed Milk?"   10

Available on the prison library's shelves were books on just about every general subject. Much of the big private collection that Parkhurst had willed to the   11 prison was still in crates and boxes in the back of the library—thousands of old books. Some of them looked ancient: covers faded, old-time parchment-looking binding. Parkhurst, I've mentioned, seemed to have been principally interested in history and religion. He had the money and the special interest to have a lot of books that you wouldn't have in general circulation. Any college library would have been lucky to get that collection.

As you can imagine, especially in a prison where there was heavy emphasis on   12
rehabilitation, an inmate was smiled upon if he demonstrated an unusually intense interest in books. There was a sizable number of well-read inmates, especially the popular debaters. Some were said by many to be practically walking encyclopedias. They were almost celebrities. No university would ask any student to devour literature as I did when this new world opened to me, of being able to read and *understand*.

I read more in my room than in the library itself. An inmate who was known to   13
read a lot could check out more than the permitted maximum number of books. I preferred reading in the total isolation of my own room.

When I had progressed to really serious reading, every night at about ten P.M. I   14
would be outraged with the "lights out." It always seemed to catch me right in the middle of something engrossing.

Fortunately, right outside my door was a corridor light that cast a glow into my   15
room. The glow was enough to read by, once my eyes adjusted to it. So when "lights out" came, I would sit on the floor where I could continue reading in that glow.

At one-hour intervals the night guards paced past every room. Each time I   16
heard the approaching footsteps, I jumped into bed and feigned sleep. And as soon as the guard passed, I got back out of bed onto the floor area of that light-glow, where I would read for another fifty-eight minutes—until the guard approached again. That went on until three or four every morning. Three or four hours of sleep a night was enough for me. Often in the years in the streets I had slept less than that.

Mr. Muhammad, to whom I was writing daily, had no idea of what a new world   17
had opened up to me through my efforts to document his teachings in books.

When I discovered philosophy, I tried to touch all the landmarks of philosoph-   18
ical development. Gradually, I read most of the old philosophers, Occidental and Oriental. The Oriental philosophers were the ones I came to prefer; finally, my impression was that most Occidental philosophy had largely been borrowed from the Oriental thinkers. Socrates, for instance, traveled in Egypt. Some sources even say that Socrates was initiated into some of the Egyptian mysteries. Obviously Socrates got some of his wisdom among the East's wise men.

I have often reflected upon the new vistas that reading opened to me. I knew   19
right there in prison that reading had changed forever the course of my life. As I see it today, the ability to read awoke inside me some long dormant craving to be mentally alive. I certainly wasn't seeking any degree, the way a college confers a status symbol upon its students. My homemade education gave me, with every additional book that I read, a little bit more sensitivity to the deafness, dumbness,

and blindness that was afflicting the black race in America. Not long ago, an English writer telephoned me from London, asking questions. One was, "What's your alma mater?" I told him, "Books." You will never catch me with a free fifteen minutes in which I'm not studying something I feel might be able to help the black man.

Yesterday I spoke in London, and both ways on the plane across the Atlantic I   20
was studying a document about how the United Nations proposes to insure the human rights of the oppressed minorities of the world. The American black man is the world's most shameful case of minority oppression. What makes the black man think of himself as only an internal United States issue is just a catch-phrase, two words, "civil rights." How is the black man going to get "civil rights" before first he wins his *human* rights? If the American black man will start thinking about his *human* rights, and then start thinking of himself as part of one of the world's great peoples, he will see he has a case for the United Nations.

I can't think of a better case! Four hundred years of black blood and sweat   21
invested here in America, and the white man still has the black man begging for what every immigrant fresh off the ship can take for granted the minute he walks down the gangplank.

But I'm digressing. I told the Englishman that my alma mater was books, a   22
good library. Every time I catch a plane, I have with me a book that I want to read—and that's a lot of books these days. If I weren't out here every day battling the white man, I could spend the rest of my life reading, just satisfying my curiosity—because you can hardly mention anything I'm not curious about. I don't think anybody ever got more out of going to prison than I did. In fact, prison enabled me to study far more intensively than I would have if my life had gone differently and I had attended some college. I imagine that one of the biggest troubles with colleges is there are too many distractions, too much panty-raiding, fraternities, and boola-boola and all of that. Where else but in a prison could I have attacked my ignorance by being able to study intensely sometimes as much as fifteen hours a day?

Schopenhauer, Kant, Nietzsche, naturally, I read all of those. I don't respect   23
them; I am just trying to remember some of those whose theories I soaked up in those years. These three, it's said, laid the groundwork on which the Fascist and Nazi philosophy was built. I don't respect them because it seems to me that most of their time was spent arguing about things that are not really important. They remind me of so many of the Negro "intellectuals," so-called, with whom I have come in contact—they are always arguing about something useless.

Spinoza impressed me for a while when I found out that he was black. A black   24
Spanish Jew. The Jews excommunicated him because he advocated a pantheistic doctrine, something like the "allness of God," or "God in everything." The Jews read their burial services for Spinoza, meaning that he was dead as far as they were concerned; his family was run out of Spain, they ended up in Holland, I think.

I'll tell you something. The whole stream of Western philosophy has now   25
wound up in a cul-de-sac. The white man has perpetrated upon himself, as well as upon the black man, so gigantic a fraud that he has put himself into a crack. He did it through his elaborate, neurotic necessity to hide the black man's true role in history.

And today the white man is faced head on with what is happening on the Black 26
Continent, Africa. Look at the artifacts being discovered there, that are proving
over and over again, how the black man had great, fine, sensitive civilizations before the white man was out of the caves. Below the Sahara, in the places where
most of America's Negroes' foreparents were kidnapped, there is being unearthed
some of the finest craftsmanship, sculpture and other objects, that has ever been
seen by modern man. Some of these things now are on view in such places as New
York City's Museum of Modern Art. Gold work of such fine tolerance and workmanship that it has no rival. Ancient objects produced by black hands . . . refined
by those black hands with results that no human hand today can equal.

History has been so "whitened" by the white man that even the black profes- 27
sors have known little more than the most ignorant black man about the talents and
rich civilizations and cultures of the black man of millenniums ago. I have lectured
in Negro colleges and some of these brainwashed black Ph.D.'s, with their sus-
penders dragging the ground with degrees, have run to the white man's newspapers calling me a "black fanatic." Why, a lot of them are fifty years behind the
times. If I were president of one of these black colleges, I'd hock the campus if I
had to, to send a bunch of black students off digging in Africa for more, more and
more proof of the black race's historical greatness. The white man now is in Africa
digging and searching. An African elephant can't stumble without falling on some
white man with a shovel. Practically every week, we read about some great new
find from Africa's lost civilizations. All that's new is white science's attitude. The
ancient civilizations of the black man have been buried on the Black Continent all
the time.

Here is an example: a British anthropologist named Dr. Louis S. B. Leakey is 28
displaying some fossil bones—a foot, part of a hand, some jaws, and skull fragments. On the basis of these, Dr. Leakey has said it's time to rewrite completely
the history of man's origin.

This species of man lived 1,818,036 years before Christ. And these bones were 29
found in Tanganyika. In the Black Continent.

It's a crime, the lie that has been told to generations of black men and white 30
men both. Little innocent black children, born of parents who believed that their
race had no history. Little black children seeing, before they could talk, that their
parents considered themselves inferior. Innocent black children growing up, living
out their lives, dying of old age—and all of their lives ashamed of being black. But
the truth is pouring out of the bag now.

Rhetorical Focus

1. From the second paragraph on, Malcolm X uses "I" a great deal. Is this a
   good idea? Are his sentences simple or complex? Read some of these sentences aloud. How do they sound: confident? tentative?
2. Do you find it odd that the content here is so provocative and the tone so
   calm? Would you say this about Rich?
3. Has Malcolm X provided appropriate proof for his assertions? Explain.

Thematic Focus

1. What do you know about black history in America? How about women's history or the history of the Irish immigrants or Hispanic writers or African artists? Whose history do we study? Whose literature do we read? Why do we study English literature?
2. What is your response to Malcolm X's claim that the "collective white man had been actually nothing but a piratical opportunist"?
3. Would you object if Malcolm X were commissioned to write a history of slavery to be used in all high schools? Why?

Graduation

Maya Angelou

Maya Angelou was born in St. Louis in 1928. She has been a singer, actress, poet, and playwright, but she is best known for her autobiographical writings, particularly *I Know Why the Caged Bird Sings* (1970). In her writing, Angelou explores the pain she experienced growing up as an African-American woman in the pre–civil rights South. In the essay that follows, she relates a moving incident in which an eighth-grade black boy helps a school community to transcend the crippling and demeaning view of blacks shown by a white "educator."

Reflections Before Reading

Do you remember your high school graduation? What were the speakers like? What were your reactions? Do you think there were varied responses to your graduation ceremony? Were ethnic minorities in your class? Were they going on to college? Did this affect their response? Can you speculate as to what your thoughts might be when you attend your college graduation? What might the response of others be?

The children in Stamps trembled visibly with anticipation. Some adults were ex-   1
cited too, but to be certain, the whole young population had come down with
graduation epidemic. Large classes were graduating from both the grammar
school and the high school. Even those who were years removed from their own
day of glorious release were anxious to help with preparations as a kind of dry run.
The junior students who were moving into the vacating classes' chairs were tradi-
tion-bound to show their talents for leadership and management. They strutted
through the school and around the campus exerting pressure on the lower grades.
Their authority was so new that occasionally if they pressed a little too hard it had
to be overlooked. After all, next term was coming, and it never hurt a sixth grader
to have a play sister in the eighth grade, or a tenth-year student to be able to call a
twelfth grader Bubba. So all was endured in a spirit of shared understanding. But
the graduating classes themselves were the nobility. Like travelers with exotic destinations on their minds, the graduates were remarkably forgetful. They came to
school without their books, or tablets or even pencils. Volunteers fell over themselves to secure replacements for the missing equipment. When accepted, the willing workers might or might not be thanked, and it was of no importance to the
pregraduation rites. Even teachers were respectful of the now quiet and aging
seniors, and tended to speak to them, if not as equals, as beings only slightly lower
than themselves. After tests were returned and grades given, the student body,
which acted like an extended family, knew who did well, who excelled, and what
piteous ones had failed.

Unlike the white high school, Lafayette County Training School distinguished   2
itself by having neither lawn, nor hedges, nor tennis court, nor climbing ivy. Its two
buildings (main classrooms, the grade school and home economics) were set on a
dirt hill with no fence to limit either its boundaries or those of bordering farms.
There was a large expanse to the left of the school which was used alternately as a
baseball diamond or a basketball court. Rusty hoops on the swaying poles represented the permanent recreational equipment, although bats and balls could be
borrowed from the P. E. teacher if the borrower was qualified and if the diamond
wasn't occupied.

Over this rocky area relieved by a few shady tall persimmon trees the graduat-   3
ing class walked. The girls often held hands and no longer bothered to speak to the
lower students. There was a sadness about them, as if this old world was not their
home and they were bound for higher ground. The boys, on the other hand, had
become more friendly, more outgoing. A decided change from the closed attitude
they projected while studying for finals. Now they seemed not ready to give up the
old school, the familiar paths and classrooms. Only a small percentage would be
continuing on to college—one of the South's A & M (agricultural and mechanical)
schools, which trained Negro youths to be carpenters, farmers, handymen, ma-
sons, maids, cooks and baby nurses. Their future rode heavily on their shoulders,
and blinded them to the collective joy that had pervaded the lives of the boys and
girls in the grammar school graduating class.

Parents who could afford it had ordered new shoes and ready-made clothes   4
for themselves from Sears and Roebuck or Montgomery Ward. They also engaged

the best seamstresses to make the floating graduating dresses and to cut down secondhand pants which would be pressed to a military slickness for the important event.

Oh, it was important, all right. Whitefolks would attend the ceremony, and two or three would speak of God and home, and the Southern way of life, and Mrs. Parsons, the principal's wife, would play the graduation march while the lower-grade graduates paraded down the aisles and took their seats below the platform. The high school seniors would wait in empty classrooms to make their dramatic entrance.

In the Store I was the person of the moment. The birthday girl. The center. Bailey had graduated the year before, although to do so he had had to forfeit all pleasures to make up for his time lost in Baton Rouge.

My class was wearing butter-yellow piqué dresses, and Momma launched out on mine. She smocked the yoke into tiny crisscrossing puckers, then shirred the rest of the bodice. Her dark fingers ducked in and out of the lemony cloth as she embroidered raised daisies around the hem. Before she considered herself finished she had added a crocheted cuff on the puff sleeves, and a pointy crocheted collar.

I was going to be lovely. A walking model of all the various styles of fine hand sewing and it didn't worry me that I was only twelve years old and merely graduating from the eighth grade. Besides, many teachers in Arkansas Negro schools had only that diploma and were licensed to impart wisdom.

The days had become longer and more noticeable. The faded beige of former times had been replaced with strong and sure colors. I began to see my classmates' clothes, their skin tones, and the dust that waved off pussy willows. Clouds that lazed across the sky were objects of great concern to me. Their shiftier shapes might have held a message that in my new happiness and with a little bit of time I'd soon decipher. During that period I looked at the arch of heaven so religiously my neck kept a steady ache. I had taken to smiling more often, and my jaws hurt from the unaccustomed activity. Between the two physical sore spots, I suppose I could have been uncomfortable, but that was not the case. As a member of the winning team (the graduating class of 1940) I had outdistanced unpleasant sensations by miles. I was headed for the freedom of open fields.

Youth and social approval allied themselves with me and we trammeled memories of slights and insults. The wind of our swift passage remodeled my features. Lost tears were pounded to mud and then to dust. Years of withdrawal were brushed aside and left behind, as hanging ropes of parasitic moss.

My work alone had awarded me a top place and I was going to be one of the first called in the graduating ceremonies. On the classroom blackboard, as well as on the bulletin board in the auditorium, there were blue stars and white stars and red stars. No absences, no tardinesses, and my academic work was among the best of the year. I could say the preamble to the Constitution even faster than Bailey. We timed ourselves often: "WethepeopleoftheUnitedStatesinordertoformamoreperfectunion . . ." I had memorized the Presidents of the United States from Washington to Roosevelt in chronological as well as alphabetical order.

My hair pleased me too. Gradually the black mass had lengthened and thick-   12
ened, so that it kept at last to its braided pattern, and I didn't have to yank my scalp off when I tried to comb it.

Louise and I had rehearsed the exercises until we tired out ourselves. Henry   13
Reed was class valedictorian. He was a small, very black boy with hooded eyes, a long, broad nose and an oddly shaped head. I had admired him for years because each term he and I vied for the best grades in our class. Most often he bested me, but instead of being disappointed I was pleased that we shared top places between us. Like many Southern Black children, he lived with his grandmother, who was as strict as Momma and as kind as she knew how to be. He was courteous, respectful and soft-spoken to elders, but on the playground he chose to play the roughest games. I admired him. Anyone, I reckoned, sufficiently afraid or sufficiently dull could be polite. But to be able to operate at a top level with both adults and children was admirable.

His valedictory speech was entitled "To Be or Not to Be." The rigid tenth-   14
grade teacher had helped him write it. He'd been working on the dramatic stresses for months.

The weeks until graduation were filled with heady activities. A group of small   15
children were to be presented in a play about buttercups and daisies and bunny rabbits. They could be heard throughout the building practicing their hops and their little songs that sounded like silver bells. The older girls (nongraduates, of course) were assigned the task of making refreshments for the night's festivities. A tangy scent of ginger, cinnamon, nutmeg and chocolate wafted around the home economics building as the budding cooks made samples for themselves and their teachers.

In every corner of the workshop, axes and saws split fresh timber as the wood-   16
shop boys made sets and stage scenery. Only the graduates were left out of the general bustle. We were free to sit in the library at the back of the building or look in quite detachedly, naturally, on the measures being taken for our event.

Even the minister preached on graduation the Sunday before. His subject   17
was, "Let your light so shine that men will see your good works and praise your Father, Who is in Heaven." Although the sermon was purported to be addressed to us, he used the occasion to speak to backsliders, gamblers and general ne'er-do-wells. But since he had called our names at the beginning of the service we were mollified.

Among Negroes the tradition was to give presents to children going only from   18
one grade to another. How much more important this was when the person was graduating at the top of the class. Uncle Willie and Momma had sent away for a Mickey Mouse watch like Bailey's. Louise gave me four embroidered handker-chiefs. (I gave her three crocheted doilies.) Mrs. Sneed, the minister's wife, made me an underskirt to wear for graduation, and nearly every customer gave me a nickel or maybe even a dime with the instruction "Keep on moving to higher ground," or some such encouragement.

Amazingly the great day finally dawned and I was out of bed before I knew it.   19
I threw open the back door to see it more clearly, but Momma said, "Sister, come
away from that door and put your robe on."

I hoped the memory of that morning would never leave me. Sunlight was itself   20
still young, and the day had none of the insistence maturity would bring it in a few
hours. In my robe and barefoot in the backyard, under cover of going to see about
my new beans, I gave myself up to the gentle warmth and thanked God that no
matter what evil I had done in my life He had allowed me to live to see this day.
Somewhere in my fatalism I had expected to die, accidentally, and never have the
chance to walk up the stairs in the auditorium and gracefully receive my hard-
earned diploma. Out of God's merciful bosom I had won reprieve.

Bailey came out in his robe and gave me a box wrapped in Christmas paper.   21
He said he had saved his money for months to pay for it. It felt like a box of
chocolates, but I knew Bailey wouldn't save money to buy candy when we had all
we could want under our noses.

He was as proud of the gift as I. It was a soft-leather-bound copy of a collection   22
of poems by Edgar Allan Poe, or, as Bailey and I called him, "Eap." I turned to
"Annabel Lee" and we walked up and down the garden rows, the cool dirt between
our toes, reciting the beautifully sad lines.

Momma made a Sunday breakfast although it was only Friday. After we fin-   23
ished the blessing, I opened my eyes to find the watch on my plate. It was a dream
of a day. Everything went smoothly and to my credit. I didn't have to be reminded
or scolded for anything. Near evening I was too jittery to attend to chores, so Bailey
volunteered to do all before his bath.

Days before, we had made a sign for the Store, and as we turned out the lights   24
Momma hung the cardboard over the doorknob. It read clearly: CLOSED. GRADUA-
TION.

My dress fitted perfectly and everyone said that I looked like a sunbeam in it.   25
On the hill, going toward the school, Bailey walked behind with Uncle Willie, who
muttered, "Go on, Ju." He wanted him to walk ahead with us because it embarrassed him to have to walk so slowly. Bailey said he'd let the ladies walk together,
and the men would bring up the rear. We all laughed, nicely.

Little children dashed by out of the dark like fireflies. Their crepe-paper   26
dresses and butterfly wings were not made for running and we heard more than
one rip, dryly, and the regretful "uh uh" that followed.

The school blazed without gaiety. The windows seemed cold and unfriendly   27
from the lower hill. A sense of ill-fated timing crept over me, and if Momma hadn't
reached for my hand I would have drifted back to Bailey and Uncle Willie, and
possibly beyond. She made a few slow jokes about my feet getting cold, and tugged
me along to the now-strange building.

Around the front steps, assurance came back. There were my fellow "greats,"   28
the graduating class. Hair brushed back, legs oiled, new dresses and pressed
pleats, fresh pocket handkerchiefs and little handbags, all homesewn. Oh, we were
up to snuff, all right. I joined my comrades and didn't even see my family go in to
find seats in the crowded auditorium.

The school band struck up a march and all classes filed in as had been re-   29
hearsed. We stood in front of our seats, as assigned, and on a signal from the choir
director, we sat. No sooner had this been accomplished than the band started to
play the national anthem. We rose again and sang the song, after which we recited
the pledge of allegiance. We remained standing for a brief minute before the choir
director and the principal signaled to us, rather desperately I thought, to take our
seats. The command was so unusual that our carefully rehearsed and smooth-run-
ning machine was thrown off. For a full minute we fumbled for our chairs and
bumped into each other awkwardly. Habits change or solidify under pressure, so in
our state of nervous tension we had been ready to follow our usual assembly pattern: the American national anthem, then the pledge of allegiance, then the song
every Black person I knew called the Negro National Anthem. All done in the
same key, with the same passion and most often standing on the same foot.

Finding my seat at last, I was overcome with a presentiment of worse things to   30
come. Something unrehearsed, unplanned, was going to happen, and we were
going to be made to look bad. I distinctly remember being explicit in the choice of
pronoun. It was "we," the graduating class, the unit, that concerned me then.

The principal welcomed "parents and friends" and asked the Baptist minister   31
to lead us in prayer. His invocation was brief and punchy, and for a second I
thought we were getting back on the high road to right action. When the principal
came back to the dais, however, his voice had changed. Sounds always affected me
profoundly and the principal's voice was one of my favorites. During assembly it
melted and lowed weakly into the audience. It had not been in my plan to listen to
him, but my curiosity was piqued and I straightened up to give him my attention.

He was talking about Booker T. Washington, our "late great leader," who said   32
we can be as close as the fingers on the hand, etc. . . . Then he said a few vague
things about friendship and the friendship of kindly people to those less fortunate
than themselves. With that his voice nearly faded, thin, away. Like a river dimin-
ishing to a stream and then to a trickle. But he cleared his throat and said, "Our
speaker tonight, who is also our friend, came from Texarkana to deliver the commencement address, but due to the irregularity of the train schedule, he's going to,
as they say, 'speak and run.' " He said that we understood and wanted the man to
know that we were most grateful for the time he was able to give us and then
something about how we were willing always to adjust to another's program, and
without more ado—"I give you Mr. Edward Donleavy."

Not one but two white men came through the door off-stage. The shorter one   33
walked to the speaker's platform, and the tall one moved over to the center seat
and sat down. But that was our principal's seat, and already occupied. The dis-
lodged gentleman bounced around for a long breath or two before the Baptist
minister gave him his chair, then with more dignity than the situation deserved,
the minister walked off the stage.

Donleavy looked at the audience once (on reflection, I'm sure that he wanted   34
only to reassure himself that we were really there), adjusted his glasses and began
to read from a sheaf of papers.

He was glad "to be here and to see the work going on just as it was in the other   35
schools."

At the first "Amen" from the audience I willed the offender to immediate   36
death by choking on the word. But Amens and Yes, sir's began to fall around the
room like rain through a ragged umbrella.

He told us of the wonderful changes we children in Stamps had in store. The   37
Central School (naturally, the white school was Central) had already been granted
improvements that would be in use in the fall. A well-known artist was coming
from Little Rock to teach art to them. They were going to have the newest micro-
scopes and chemistry equipment for their laboratory. Mr. Donleavy didn't leave us
long in the dark over who made these improvements available to Central High.
Nor were we to be ignored in the general betterment scheme he had in mind.

He said that he had pointed out to people at a very high level that one of the   38
first-line football tacklers at Arkansas Agricultural and Mechanical College had
graduated from good old Lafayette County Training School. Here fewer Amen's
were heard. Those few that did break through lay dully in the air with the heaviness of habit.

He went on to praise us. He went on to say how he had bragged that "one of   39
the best basketball players at Fisk sank his first ball right here at Lafayette County
Training School."

The white kids were going to have a chance to become Galileos and Madame   40
Curies and Edisons and Gauguins, and our boys (the girls weren't even in on it)
would try to be Jesse Owenses and Joe Louises.

Owens and the Brown Bomber were great heroes in our world, but what   41
school official in the white-goddom of Little Rock had the right to decide that
those two men must be our only heroes? Who decided that for Henry Reed to
become a scientist he had to work like George Washington Carver, as a bootblack,
to buy a lousy microscope? Bailey was obviously always going to be too small to be
an athlete, so which concrete angel glued to what country seat had decided that if
my brother wanted to become a lawyer he had to first pay penance for his skin by
picking cotton and hoeing corn and studying correspondence books at night for
twenty years?

The man's dead words fell like bricks around the auditorium and too many   42
settled in my belly. Constrained by hard-learned manners I couldn't look behind
me, but to my left and right the proud graduating class of 1940 had dropped their
heads. Every girl in my row had found something new to do with her handkerchief.
Some folded the tiny squares into love knots, some into triangles, but most were
wadding them, then pressing them flat on their yellow laps.

On the dais, the ancient tragedy was being replayed. Professor Parsons sat, a   43
sculptor's reject, rigid. His large, heavy body seemed devoid of will or willingness,
and his eyes said he was no longer with us. The other teachers examined the flag
(which was draped stage right) or their notes, or the windows which opened on our
now-famous playing diamond.

Graduation, the hush-hush magic time of frills and gifts and congratulations   44
and diplomas, was finished for me before my name was called. The accomplishment was nothing. The meticulous maps, drawn in three colors of ink, learning and
spelling decasyllabic words, memorizing the whole of *The Rape of Lucrece*—it was
for nothing. Donleavy had exposed us.

We were maids and farmers, handymen and washerwomen, and anything   45
higher that we aspired to was farcical and presumptuous.

Then I wished that Gabriel Prosser and Nat Turner had killed all whitefolks in   46
their beds and that Abraham Lincoln had been assassinated before the signing of
the Emancipation Proclamation, and that Harriet Tubman had been killed by that
blow on her head and Christopher Columbus had drowned in the *Santa María*.

It was awful to be Negro and have no control over my life. It was brutal to be   47
young and already trained to sit quietly and listen to charges brought against my
color with no chance of defense. We should all be dead. I thought I should like to
see us all dead, one on top of the other. A pyramid of flesh with the whitefolks on
the bottom, as the broad base, then the Indians with their silly tomahawks and
teepees and wigwams and treaties, the Negroes with their mops and recipes and
cotton sacks and spirituals sticking out of their mouths. The Dutch children should
all stumble in their wooden shoes and break their necks. The French should choke
to death on the Louisiana Purchase (1803) while silkworms ate all the Chinese with
their stupid pigtails. As a species, we were an abomination. All of us.

Donleavy was running for election, and assured our parents that if he won we   48
could count on having the only colored paved playing field in that part of Arkansas.
Also—he never looked up to acknowledge the grunts of acceptance—also, we
were bound to get some new equipment for the home economics building and the
workshop.

He finished, and since there was no need to give any more than the most   49
perfunctory thank-you's, he nodded to the men on the stage, and the tall white
man who was never introduced joined him at the door. They left with the attitude
that now they were off to something really important. (The graduation ceremonies
at Lafayette County Training School had been a mere preliminary.)

The ugliness they left was palpable. An uninvited guest who wouldn't leave.   50
The choir was summoned and sang a modern arrangement of "Onward, Christian
Soldiers," with new words pertaining to graduates seeking their place in the world.
But it didn't work. Elouise, the daughter of the Baptist minister, recited "Invictus,"
and I could have cried at the impertinence of "I am the master of my fate, I am the
captain of my soul."

My name had lost its ring of familiarity and I had to be nudged to go and   51
receive my diploma. All my preparations had fled. I neither marched up to the
stage like a conquering Amazon, nor did I look in the audience for Bailey's nod of
approval. Marguerite Johnson, I heard the name again, my honors were read,
there were noises in the audience of appreciation, and I took my place on the stage
as rehearsed.

I thought about colors I hated: ecrù, puce, lavender, beige and black.   52

There was shuffling and rustling around me, then Henry Reed was giving his   53
valedictory address, "To Be or Not to Be." Hadn't he heard the whitefolks? We
couldn't *be*, so the question was a waste of time. Henry's voice came out clear and
strong. I feared to look at him. Hadn't he got the message? There was no "nobler in
the mind" for Negroes because the world didn't think we had minds, and they let
us know it. "Outrageous fortune"? Now, that was a joke. When the ceremony was

over I had to tell Henry Reed some things. That is, if I still cared. Not "rub," Henry, "erase." "Ah, there's the erase." Us.

Henry had been a good student in elocution. His voice rose on tides of prom-   54
ise and fell on waves of warnings. The English teacher had helped him to create a sermon winging through Hamlet's soliloquy. To be a man, a doer, a builder, a leader, or to be a tool, an unfunny joke, a crusher of funky toadstools. I marveled that Henry could go through with the speech as if we had a choice.

I had been listening and silently rebutting each sentence with my eyes closed;   55
then there was a hush, which in an audience warns that something unplanned is happening. I looked up and saw Henry Reed, the conservative, the proper, the A student, turn his back to the audience and turn to us (the proud graduating class of 1940) and sing, nearly speaking,

> "Lift ev'ry voice and sing
> Till earth and heaven ring
> Ring with the harmonies of Liberty . . ."

It was the poem written by James Weldon Johnson. It was the music composed by J. Rosamond Johnson. It was the Negro national anthem. Out of habit we were singing it.

Our mothers and fathers stood in the dark hall and joined the hymn of encour-   56
agement. A kindergarten teacher led the small children onto the stage and the buttercups and daisies and bunny rabbits marked time and tried to follow:

> "Stony the road we trod
> Bitter the chastening rod
> Felt in the days when hope, unborn, had died.
> Yet with a steady beat
> Have not our weary feet
> Come to the place for which our fathers sighed?"

Every child I knew had learned that song with his ABC's and along with "Jesus   57
Loves Me This I Know." But I personally had never heard it before. Never heard the words, despite the thousands of times I had sung them. Never thought they had anything to do with me.

On the other hand, the words of Patrick Henry had made such an impression   58
on me that I had been able to stretch myself tall and trembling and say, "I know not what course others may take, but as for me, give me liberty or give me death."

And now I heard, really for the first time: 59

> "We have come over a way that with tears
> has been watered,
> We have come, treading our path through
> the blood of the slaughtered."

"Lift Ev'ry Voice and Sing"—words by James Weldon Johnson and music by J. Rosamond Johnson. Copyright by Edward B. Marks Music Corporation. Used by permission.

While echoes of the song shivered in the air, Henry Reed bowed his head, said   60
"Thank you," and returned to his place in the line. The tears that slipped down
many faces were not wiped away in shame.

We were on top again. As always, again. We survived. The depths had been icy   61
and dark, but now a bright sun spoke to our souls. I was no longer simply a member
of the proud graduating class of 1940; I was a proud member of the wonderful,
beautiful Negro race.

Oh, Black known and unknown poets, how often have your auctioned pains   62
sustained us? Who will compute the lonely nights made less lonely by your songs,
or the empty pots made less tragic by your tales?

If we were a people much given to revealing secrets, we might raise monu-   63
ments and sacrifice to the memories of our poets, but slavery cured us of that
weakness. It may be enough, however, to have it said that we survive in exact
relationship to the dedication of our poets (include preachers, musicians and blues
singers).

Rhetorical Focus

1. In her narrative, Angelou creates whole paragraphs of concrete detail (see
   paragraph 7). What is the purpose of such concreteness?
2. In her central episode, the graduation speech, Angelou both describes and
   interprets the talk given by Mr. Donleavy. Point to examples.
3. Examine the sentences of the last three paragraphs. Are rules being broken? Do these sentences sound more like poetry than prose?

Thematic Focus

1. Did you sense a feeling of community, of shared values and expectations as
   Angelou described the pregraduation preparations? Is that part of your
   experience? Would it have been Rich's?
2. At one point, during Donleavy's speech, Angelou writes, "On the dais, the
   ancient tragedy was being replayed." (see paragraph 43.) Be specific about
   what you think she means. Would it make a difference if she were a man? A
   member of a different minority?
3. Was the speaker a racist or just culturally uninformed? What do you think
   he intended? Why did it fail?

Suggestions for Writing

1. Suppose that you had been asked to give a commencement address for a
   junior high school at an American Indian reservation. Describe what you
   would say in a ten-minute talk. How about a Hispanic ghetto in Los Angeles, or an exclusive prep school for girls (or boys) in Boston?
2. Write a narrative about the specifics of your early reading experiences.
   What generalization or themes do you find? Are there strong feelings? Patterns of any kind?

3. Based on Rich's notion of claiming an education, write a letter to your high school principal describing the kind of education you would have preferred. Try to be clear about the relationship between that education and the one you actually received. Try to include your sense of the purpose of an education and its connection to democracy.

TEACHERS THAT MATTERED

Sometimes, it seems as if every think tank, parents' group, and educational association in America has a new, improved solution for the complex social and intellectual problems of contemporary education. Most often, curriculum is their focus. Less art and more math urges one group; more classic literature and less trendy relevance shouts another. Somehow, almost all of these critics forget that when they think back to their own schooling, what they remember most is a teacher that mattered, someone who changed them, motivated them, and opened their eyes to the realities of the world, someone who taught them a lesson that endured. Also, that lesson is usually not some interesting historical event, some scientific insight or some impressive literary character; it is usually a lesson about life.

Norman Podhoretz, like Richard Rodriquez and George Orwell in the following section, has mixed feelings about his education. For him, leaving the values of his working-class family is a kind of treason. Like many bright students, the move from the neighborhood to college is simultaneously exciting and sad. Many are reluctant to make such a bargain, but Podhoretz had a teacher who wanted him to succeed, wanted him to move up the social ladder. Although his essay is a kind of success story, the character of Mrs. K is problematic. She is a snob; she has little respect for local cultures. She represents a teacher who matters, but not necessarily one we endorse. Toni Cade Bambara's teacher is easier to admire—She has a simple mission: to teach a lesson about the inequality of our society. The narrator learns that lesson with a vengeance. These readings remind us that however important we think content is in our education, it is more often the human contact that affects us most deeply, and often in ways we cannot anticipate.

A Question of Class

Norman Podhoretz

Norman Podhoretz (b. 1930) grew up in a working-class neighborhood in
Brooklyn. He won a scholarship to Columbia and later studied at Cambridge.
During the 1960s, as the editor of *Commentary,* he was considered one of
the most promising of the young literary intellectuals living in Manhattan. "A
Question of Class" is taken from his autobiography *Making It,* which caused
a stir for his claim that "ambition . . . seems to be replacing erotic lust as the
dirty little secret of the well-educated American soul." The following essay
describes a teacher who had a lot to do with motivating that ambition.

Reflections Before Reading

Can you remember a teacher who took a special interest in you? What do
you remember? Why? Can you remember teachers who ignored you or who
paid special attention to others? Do you think race or class or gender played
any part in how teachers treated students?

One of the longest journeys in the world is the journey from Brooklyn to Manhat- 1
tan—or at least from certain neighborhoods in Brooklyn to certain parts of Manhattan. I have made that journey, but it is not from the experience of having made
it that I know how very great the distance is, for I started on the road many years
before I realized what I was doing, and by the time I did realize it I was for all
practical purposes already there. At so imperceptible a pace did I travel, and with
so little awareness, that I never felt footsore or out of breath or weary at the
thought of how far I still had to go. Yet whenever anyone who has remained back
there where I started—remained not physically but socially and culturally, for the
neighborhood is now a Negro ghetto and the Jews who have "remained" in it
mostly reside in the less affluent areas of Long Island—whenever anyone like that
happens into the world in which I now live with such perfect ease, I can see that in
his eyes I have become a fully acculturated citizen of a country as foreign to him as
China and infinitely more frightening.

That country is sometimes called the upper middle class; and indeed I am a 2
member of that class, less by virtue of my income than by virtue of the way my
speech is accented, the way I dress, the way I furnish my home, the way I entertain

and am entertained, the way I educate my children—the way, quite simply, I look and I live. It appalls me to think what an immense transformation I had to work on myself in order to become what I have become: if I had known what I was doing I would surely not have been able to do it, I would surely not have wanted to. No wonder the choice had to be blind; there was a kind of treason in it: treason toward my family, treason toward my friends. In choosing the road I chose, I was pronouncing a judgment upon them, and the fact that they themselves concurred in the judgment makes the whole thing sadder but no less cruel.

When I say that the choice was blind, I mean that I was never aware—obviously not as a small child, certainly not as an adolescent, and not even as a young man already writing for publication and working on the staff of an important intellectual magazine in New York—how inextricably my "noblest" ambitions were tied to the vulgar desire to rise above the class into which I was born; nor did I understand to what an astonishing extent these ambitions were shaped and defined by the standards and values and tastes of the class into which I did not know I wanted to move. It is not that I was or am a social climber as that term is commonly used. High society interests me, if at all, only as a curiosity; I do not wish to be a member of it; and in any case, it is not, as I have learned from a small experience of contact with the very rich and fashionable, my "scene." Yet precisely because social climbing is not one of my vices (unless what might be called celebrity climbing, which very definitely *is* one of my vices, can be considered the contemporary variant of social climbing), I think there may be more than a merely personal significance in the fact that class has played so large a part both in my life and in my career. 3

But whether or not the significance is there, I feel certain that my longtime blindness to the part class was playing in my life was not altogether idiosyncratic. "Privilege," Robert L. Heilbroner has shrewdly observed in *The Limits of American Capitalism,* "is not an attribute we are accustomed to stress when we consider the construction of *our* social order." For a variety of reasons, says Heilbroner, "privilege under capitalism is much less 'visible,' especially to the favored groups, than privilege under other systems" like feudalism. This "invisibility" extends in America to class as well. 4

No one, of course, is so naïve as to believe that America is a classless society or that the force of egalitarianism, powerful as it has been in some respects, has ever been powerful enough to wipe out class distinctions altogether. There was a moment during the 1950's, to be sure, when social thought hovered on the brink of saying that the country had to all intents and purposes become a wholly middle-class society. But the emergence of the civil-rights movements in the 1960's and the concomitant discovery of the poor—to whom, in helping to discover them, Michael Harrington interestingly enough applied, in *The Other America,* the very word ("invisible") that Heilbroner later used with reference to the rich—has put at least a temporary end to that kind of talk. And yet if class has become visible again, it is only in its grossest outlines—mainly, that is, in terms of income levels—and to the degree that manners and style of life are perceived as relevant at all, it is generally in the crudest of terms. There is something in us, it would seem, which resists the idea of class. Even our novelists, working in a genre for which class has 5 traditionally been a supreme reality, are largely indifferent to it—which is to say, blind to its importance as a factor in the life of the individual.

In my own case, the blindness to class always expressed itself in an outright   6 and very often belligerent refusal to believe that it had anything to do with me at all. I no longer remember when or in what form I first discovered that there was such a thing as class, but whenever it was and whatever form the discovery took, it could only have coincided with the recognition that criteria existed by which I and everyone I knew were stamped as inferior: we were in the *lower* class. This was not a proposition I was willing to accept, and my way of not accepting it was to dismiss the whole idea of class as a prissy triviality.

Given the fact that I had literary ambitions even as a small boy, it was inevita-   7 ble that the issue of class would sooner or later arise for me with a sharpness it would never acquire for most of my friends. But given the fact also that I was on the whole very happy to be growing up where I was, that I was fiercely patriotic about Brownsville (the spawning-ground of so many famous athletes and gang-sters), and that I felt genuinely patronizing toward other neighborhoods, especially the "better" ones like Crown Heights and East Flatbush which seemed by compar-ison colorless and unexciting—given the fact, in other words, that I was not, for all that I wrote poetry and read books, an "alienated" boy dreaming of escape—my confrontation with the issue of class would probably have come later rather than sooner if not for an English teacher in high school who decided that I was a gem in the rough and who took it upon herself to polish me to as high a sheen as she could manage and I would permit.

I resisted—far less effectively, I can see now, than I then thought, though   8 even then I knew that she was wearing me down far more than I would ever give her the satisfaction of admitting. Famous throughout the school for her altogether outspoken snobbery, which stopped short by only a hair, and sometimes did not stop short at all, of an old-fashioned kind of patrician anti-Semitism, Mrs. K. was also famous for being an extremely good teacher; indeed, I am sure that she saw no distinction between the hopeless task of teaching the proper use of English to the young Jewish barbarians whom fate had so unkindly deposited into her charge and the equally hopeless task of teaching them the proper "manners." (There were as many young Negro barbarians in her charge as Jewish ones, but I doubt that she could ever bring herself to pay very much attention to them. As she never hesitated to make clear, it was punishment enough for a woman of her background—her family was old-Brooklyn and, she would have us understand, extremely distin-guished—to have fallen among the sons of East European immigrant Jews.)

For three years, from the age of thirteen to the age of sixteen, I was her special   9 pet, though that word is scarcely adequate to suggest the intensity of the relation-ship which developed between us. It was a relationship right out of *The Corn Is Green*, which may, for all I know, have served as her model; at any rate, her objec-tive was much the same as the Welsh teacher's in that play: she was determined that I should win a scholarship to Harvard. But whereas (an irony much to the point here) the problem the teacher had in *The Corn Is Green* with her coal-miner pupil in the traditional class society of Edwardian England was strictly academic, Mrs. K.'s problem with me in the putatively egalitarian society of New Deal America was strictly social. My grades were very high and would obviously remain so, but what would they avail me if I continued to go about looking and sounding like a "filthy little slum child" (the epithet she would invariably hurl at me whenever we had an argument about "manners")?

Childless herself, she worked on me like a dementedly ambitious mother with   10 a somewhat recalcitrant son; married to a solemn and elderly man (she was then in her early forties or thereabouts), she treated me like a callous, ungrateful adolescent lover on whom she had humiliatingly bestowed her favors. She flirted with me and flattered me, she scolded me and insulted me. Slum child, filthy little slum child, so beautiful a mind and so vulgar a personality, so exquisite in sensibility and so coarse in manner. What would she do with me, what would become of me if I persisted out of stubbornness and perversity in the disgusting ways they had taught me at home and on the streets?

To her the most offensive of these ways was the style in which I dressed: a tee   11 shirt, tightly pegged pants, and a red satin jacket with the legend "Cherokees, S.A.C." (social–athletic club) stitched in large white letters across the back. This was bad enough, but when on certain days I would appear in school wearing, as a particular ceremonial occasion required, a suit and tie, the sight of those immense padded shoulders and my white-on-white shirt would drive her to even greater heights of contempt and even lower depths of loving despair than usual. *Slum child, filthy little slum child.* I was beyond saving; I deserved no better than to wind up with all the other horrible little Jewboys in the gutter (by which she meant Brooklyn College). If only I would listen to her, the whole world could be mine: I could win a scholarship to Harvard, I could get to know the best people, I could grow up into a life of elegance and refinement and taste. Why was I so stupid as not to understand?

In those days it was very unusual, and possibly even against the rules, for   12 teachers in public high schools to associate with their students after hours. Nevertheless, Mrs. K. sometimes invited me to her home, a beautiful old brownstone located in what was perhaps the only section in the whole of Brooklyn fashionable enough to be intimidating. I would read her my poems and she would tell me about her family, about the schools she had gone to, about Vassar, about writers she had met, while her husband, of whom I was frightened to death and who to my utter astonishment turned out to be Jewish (but not, as Mrs. K. quite unnecessarily hastened to inform me, *my* kind of Jewish), sat stiffly and silently in an armchair across the room, squinting at his newspaper through the first *pince-nez* I had ever seen outside the movies. He spoke to me but once, and that was after I had read Mrs. K. my tearful editorial for the school newspaper on the death of Roosevelt—an effusion which provoked him into a full five-minute harangue whose blasphemous contents would certainly have shocked me into insensibility if I had not been even more shocked to discover that he actually had a voice.

But Mrs. K. not only had me to her house; she also—what was even more   13 unusual—took me out a few times, to the Frick Gallery and the Metropolitan Museum, and once to the theater, where we saw a dramatization of *The Late George Apley,* a play I imagine she deliberately chose with the not wholly mistaken idea that it would impress upon me the glories of aristocratic Boston.

One of our excursions into Manhattan I remember with particular vividness   14
because she used it to bring the struggle between us to rather a dramatic head. The
familiar argument began this time on the subway. Why, knowing that we would be
spending the afternoon together "in public," had I come to school that morning
improperly dressed? (I was, as usual, wearing my red satin club jacket over a white
tee shirt.) She realized, of course, that I owned only one suit (this said not in
compassion but in derision) and that my poor parents had, God only knew where,
picked up the idea that it was too precious to be worn except at one of those bar
mitzvahs I was always going to. Though why, if my parents were so worried about
clothes, they had permitted me to buy a suit which made me look like a young
hoodlum she found it very difficult to imagine. Still, much as she would have been
embarrassed to be seen in public with a boy whose parents allowed him to wear a
zoot suit, she would have been somewhat less embarrassed than she was now by
the ridiculous costume I had on. Had I no consideration for her? Had I no consideration for myself? Did I want everyone who laid eyes on me to think that I was
nothing but an ill-bred little slum child?

My standard ploy in these arguments was to take the position that such things   15
were of no concern to me: I was a poet and I had more important matters to think
about than clothes. Besides, I would feel silly coming to school on an ordinary day
dressed in a suit. Did Mrs. K. want me to look like one of those "creeps" from
Crown Heights who were all going to become doctors? This was usually an effective counter, since Mrs. K. despised her middle-class Jewish students even more
than she did the "slum children," but probably because she was growing desperate
at the thought of how I would strike a Harvard interviewer (it was my senior year),
she did not respond according to form on that particular occasion. "At least," she
snapped, "they reflect well on their parents."

I was accustomed to her bantering gibes at my parents, and sensing, probably,   16
that they arose out of jealousy, I was rarely troubled by them. But this one bothered me; it went beyond banter and I did not know how to deal with it. I remember
flushing, but I cannot remember what if anything I said in protest. It was the
beginning of a very bad afternoon for both of us.

We had been heading for the Museum of Modern Art, but as we got off the   17
subway, Mrs. K. announced that she had changed her mind about the museum.
She was going to show me something else instead, just down the street on Fifth
Avenue. This mysterious "something else" to which we proceeded in silence
turned out to be the college department of an expensive clothing store, de Pinna. I
do not exaggerate when I say that an actual physical dread seized me as I followed
her into the store. I had never been inside such a store; it was not a store, it was
enemy territory, every inch of it mined with humiliations. "I am," Mrs. K. declared
in the coldest human voice I hope I shall ever hear, "going to buy you a suit that
you will be able to wear at your Harvard interview." I had guessed, of course, that
this was what she had in mind, and even at fifteen I understood what a fantastic act
of aggression she was planning to commit against my parents and asking me to
participate in. Oh no, I said in a panic (suddenly realizing that I *wanted* her to buy
me that suit), I can't, my mother wouldn't like it. "You can tell her it's a birthday
present. Or else I will tell her. If I tell her, I'm sure she won't object." The idea of

Mrs. K. meeting my mother was more than I could bear: my mother, who spoke with a Yiddish accent and of whom, until that sickening moment, I had never known I was ashamed and so ready to betray.

To my immense relief and my equally immense disappointment, we left the store, finally, without buying a suit, but it was not to be the end of clothing or "manners" for me that day—not yet. There was still the ordeal of a restaurant to go through. Where I came from, people rarely ate in restaurants, not so much because most of them were too poor to afford such a luxury—although most of them certainly were—as because eating in restaurants was not regarded as a luxury at all; it was, rather, a necessity to which bachelors were pitiably condemned. A home-cooked meal was assumed to be better than anything one could possibly get in a restaurant, and considering the class of restaurants in question (they were really diners or luncheonettes), the assumption was probably correct. In the case of my own family, myself included until my late teens, the business of going to restaurants was complicated by the fact that we observed the Jewish-dietary laws, and except in certain neighborhoods, few places could be found which served kosher food; in midtown Manhattan in the 1940's, I believe there were only two and both were relatively expensive. All this is by way of explaining why I had had so little experience of restaurants up to the age of fifteen and why I grew apprehensive once more when Mrs. K. decided after we left de Pinna that we should have something to eat.   18

The restaurant she chose was not at all an elegant one—I have, like a criminal, revisited it since—but it seemed very elegant indeed to me: enemy territory again, and this time a mine exploded in my face the minute I set foot through the door. The hostess was very sorry, but she could not seat the young gentleman without a coat and tie. If the lady wished, however, something could be arranged. The lady (visibly pleased by this unexpected—or was it expected?—object lesson) did wish, and the so recently defiant but by now utterly docile young gentleman was forthwith divested of his so recently beloved but by now thoroughly loathsome red satin jacket and provided with a much oversized white waiter's coat and a tie—which, there being no collar to a tee shirt, had to be worn around his bare neck. Thus attired, and with his face supplying the touch of red which had moments earlier been supplied by his jacket, he was led into the dining room, there to be taught the importance of proper table manners through the same pedagogic instrumentality that had worked so well in impressing him with the importance of proper dress.   19

Like any other pedagogic technique, however, humiliation has its limits, and Mrs. K. was to make no further progress with it that day. For I had had enough, and I was not about to risk stepping on another mine. Knowing she would subject me to still more ridicule if I made a point of my revulsion at the prospect of eating nonkosher food, I resolved to let her order for me and then to feign lack of appetite or possibly even illness when the meal was served. She did order—duck for both of us, undoubtedly because it would be a hard dish for me to manage without using my fingers.   20

The two portions came in deep oval-shaped dishes, swimming in a brown sauce and each with a sprig of parsley sitting on top. I had not the faintest idea of   21 what to do—should the food be eaten directly from the oval dish or not?—nor which of the many implements on the table to do it with. But remembering that Mrs. K. herself had once advised me to watch my hostess in such a situation and then to do exactly as she did, I sat perfectly still and waited for her to make the first move. Unfortunately, Mrs. K. also remembered having taught me that trick, and determined as she was that I should be given a lesson that would force me to mend my ways, she waited too. And so we both waited, chatting amiably, pretending not to notice the food while it sat there getting colder and colder by the minute. Thanks partly to the fact that I would probably have gagged on the duck if I had tried to eat it—dietary taboos are very powerful if one has been conditioned to them—I was prepared to wait forever. And in fact it was Mrs. K. who broke first.

"Why aren't you eating?" she suddenly said after something like fifteen min- 22 utes had passed. "Aren't you hungry?" Not very, I answered. "Well," she said, "I think we'd better eat. The food is getting cold." Whereupon, as I watched with great fascination, she deftly captured the sprig of parsley between the prongs of her serving fork, set it aside, took up her serving spoon and delicately used those two esoteric implements to transfer a piece of duck from the oval dish to her plate. I imitated the whole operation as best I could, but not well enough to avoid splat- tering some partly congealed sauce onto my borrowed coat in the process. Still, things could have been worse, and having more or less successfully negotiated my way around that particular mine, I now had to cope with the problem of how to get out of eating the duck. But I need not have worried. Mrs. K. took one bite, pro- nounced it inedible (it must have been frozen by then), and called in quiet fury for the check.

Several months later, wearing an altered but respectably conservative suit 23 which had been handed down to me in good condition by a bachelor uncle, I presented myself on two different occasions before interviewers from Harvard and from the Pulitzer Scholarship Committee. Some months after that, Mrs. K. had her triumph: I won the Harvard scholarship on which her heart had been so pas- sionately set. It was not, however, large enough to cover all expenses, and since my parents could not afford to make up the difference, I was unable to accept it. My parents felt wretched but not, I think, quite as wretched as Mrs. K. For a while it looked as though I would wind up in the "gutter" of Brooklyn College after all, but then the news arrived that I had also won a Pulitzer Scholarship which paid full tuition if used at Columbia and a small stipend besides. Everyone was consoled, even Mrs. K.: Columbia was at least in the Ivy League.

The last time I saw her was shortly before my graduation from Columbia and just after a story had appeared in the *Times* announcing that I had been awarded a fellowship which was to send me to Cambridge University. Mrs. K. had passion- ately wanted to see me in Cambridge, Massachusetts, but Cambridge, England was even better. We met somewhere near Columbia for a drink, and her happiness over my fellowship, it seemed to me, was if anything exceeded by her delight at discovering that I now knew enough to know that the right thing to order in a cocktail lounge was a very dry martini with lemon peel, please.

Rhetorical Focus

1. Podhoretz divided this essay into three parts: an introduction of ideas, a narrative with a couple of concrete episodes, and a brief, one-paragraph coda. Is the sequence he chooses invariant; that is, could he have effectively arranged his essay otherwise?
2. Compare two paragraphs, one expository the other narrative (for example, paragraphs 5 and 21). After reading both aloud, do you hear any difference in syntax or tone?
3. Podhoretz's last sentence is rather concrete. To what specific idea in the opening seven paragraphs might this be thematically connected?

Thematic Focus

1. Does Podhoretz say what specific values he betrayed by joining the upper middle class? What values would he have betrayed if he ignored Mrs. K?
2. From reading this piece, how would you say class is determined in America? Is this a matter of interpretation or a fact?
3. Are we to assume that Podhoretz changed his class dramatically in college, or did he just mature?

The Lesson
Toni Cade Bambara

Toni Cade Bambara (b. 1939) was born and educated in New York City, where she received her B.A. (Queens College 1959) and M.A. (City College 1964). She has been a dancer, editor, activist, film critic, free-lance writer, as well as a professor at various universities. "The Lesson" is taken from her short story collection, *Gorilla, My Love* (1972), a book praised for its inspirational themes, its poetic Black dialect, and the affection and warmth with which her characters are developed. A recent collection, *If Blessing Comes* (1987), has also been highly praised.

Reflections Before Reading

When you were growing up, did you feel that your life-style was typical of the rest of America? Describe when you knew there were people richer and poorer than you. Can you remember having contact with adults in your neighborhood other than your parents? Try to remember how you felt about them.

Back in the days when everyone was old and stupid or young and foolish and me   1
and Sugar were the only ones just right, this lady moved on our block with nappy hair and proper speech and no makeup. And quite naturally we laughed at her, laughed the way we did at the junk man who went about his business like he was some big-time president and his sorry-ass horse his secretary. And we kinda hated her too, hated the way we did the winos who cluttered up our parks and pissed on our handball walls and stank up our hallways and stairs so you couldn't halfway play hide-and-seek without a goddamn gas mask. Miss Moore was her name. The only woman on the block with no first name. And she was black as hell, cept for her feet, which were fish-white and spooky. And she was always planning these boring-ass things for us to do, us being my cousin, mostly, who lived on the block cause we all moved North the same time and to the same apartment then spread out gradual to breathe. And our parents would yank our heads into some kinda shape and crisp up our clothes so we'd be presentable for travel with Miss Moore, who always looked like she was going to church, though she never did. Which is just one of the things the grown-ups talked about when they talked behind her back like a dog. But when she came calling with some sachet she'd sewed up or some gingerbread she'd made or some book, why then they'd all be too embarrassed to turn her down and we'd get handed over all spruced up. She'd been to college and said it was only right that she should take responsibility for the young ones' education, and she not even related by marriage or blood. So they'd go for it. Specially Aunt Gretchen. She was the main gofer in the family. You got some ole dumb shit foolishness you want somebody to go for, you send for Aunt Gretchen. She been screwed into the go-along for so long, it's a blood-deep natural thing with her. Which is how she got saddled with me and Sugar and Junior in the first place while our mothers were in a la-de-da apartment up the block having a good ole time.

So this one day Miss Moore rounds us all up at the mailbox and it's puredee   2
hot and she's knockin herself out about arithmetic. And school suppose to let up in summer I heard, but she don't never let up. And the starch in my pinafore scratching the shit outta me and I'm really hating this nappy-head bitch and her goddamn college degree. I'd much rather go to the pool or to the show where it's cool. So me and Sugar leaning on the mailbox being surly, which is a Miss Moore word. And Flyboy checking out what everybody brought for lunch. And Fat Butt already wasting his peanut-butter-and-jelly sandwich like the pig he is. And Junebug punchin on Q.T.'s arm for potato chips. And Rosie Giraffe shifting from one hip to the other waiting for somebody to step on her foot or ask her if she from Georgia so she can

kick ass, perferable Mercedes'. And Miss Moore asking us do we know what money is, like we a bunch of retards. I mean real money, she say, like it's only poker chips or monopoly papers we lay on the grocer. So right away I'm tired of this and say so. And would much rather snatch Sugar and go to the Sunset and terrorize the West Indian kids and take their hair ribbons and their money too. And Miss Moore files that remark away for next week's lesson on brotherhood, I can tell. And finally I say we oughta get to the subway cause it's cooler and besides we might meet some cute boys. Sugar done swiped her mama's lipstick, so we ready.

So we heading down the street and she's boring us silly about what things cost 3 and what our parents make and how much goes for rent and how money ain't divided up right in this country. And then she gets to the part about we all poor and live in the slums, which I don't feature. And I'm ready to speak on that, but she steps out in the street and hails two cabs just like that. Then she hustles half the crew in with her and hands me a five-dollar bill and tells me to calculate 10 percent tip for the driver. And we're off. Me and Sugar and Junebug and Flyboy hangin out the window and hollering to everybody, putting lipstick on each other cause Flyboy a faggot anyway, and making farts with our sweaty armpits. But I'm mostly trying to figure how to spend this money. But they all fascinated with the meter ticking and Junebug starts laying bets as to how much it'll read when Flyboy can't hold his breath no more. Then Sugar lays bets as to how much it'll be when we get there. So I'm stuck. Don't nobody want to go for my plan, which is to jump out at the next light and run off to the first bar-b-que we can find. Then the driver tells us to get the hell out cause we there already. And the meter reads eighty-five cents. And I'm stalling to figure out the tip and Sugar say give him a dime. And I decide he don't need it bad as I do, so later for him. But then he tries to take off with Junebug foot still in the door so we talk about his mama something ferocious. Then we check out that we on Fifth Avenue and everybody dressed up in stockings. One lady in a fur coat, hot as it is. White folks crazy.

"This is the place," Miss Moore say, presenting it to us in the voice she uses at 4 the museum. "Let's look in the windows before we go in."

"Can we steal?" Sugar asks very serious like she's getting the ground rules 5 squared away before she plays. "I beg your pardon," say Miss Moore, and we fall out. So she leads us around the windows of the toy store and me and Sugar screamin, "This is mine, that's mine, I gotta have that, that was made for me, I was born for that," till Big Butt drowns us out.

"Hey, I'm goin to buy that there." 6

"That there? You don't even know what it is, stupid." 7

"I do so," he say punchin on Rosie Giraffe. "It's a microscope." 8

"Whatcha gonna do with a microscope, fool?" 9

"Look at things." 10

"Like what, Ronald?" ask Miss Moore. And Big Butt ain't got the first notion. 11 So here go Miss Moore gabbing about the thousands of bacteria in a drop of water and the somethinorother in a speck of blood and the million and one living things in the air around us is invisible to the naked eye. And what she say that for? Junebug go to town on that "naked" and we rolling. Then Miss Moore ask what it cost.

So we all jam into the window smudgin it up and the price tag say $300. So then she ask how long'd take for Big Butt and Junebug to save up their allowances. "Too long," I say. "Yeh," adds Sugar, "outgrown it by that time." And Miss Moore say no, you never outgrow learning instruments. "Why, even medical students and interns and," blah, blah, blah. And we ready to choke Big Butt for bringing it up in the first damn place.

"This here costs four hundred eighty dollars," say Rosie Giraffe. So we pile up   12
all over her to see what she pointin out. My eyes tell me it's a chunk of glass cracked with something heavy, and different-color inks dripped into the splits, then the whole thing put into a oven or something. But the $480 it don't make sense.

"That's a paperweight made of semi-precious stones fused together under tre-   13
mendous pressure," she explains slowly, with her hands doing the mining and all the factory work.

"So what's a paperweight?" asks Rosie Giraffe.   14

"To weigh paper with, dumbbell," say Flyboy, the wise man from the East.   15

"Not exactly," say Miss Moore, which is what she say when you warm or way   16
off too. "It's to weigh paper down so it won't scatter and make your desk untidy." So right away me and Sugar curtsy to each other and then to Mercedes who is more the tidy type.

"We don't keep paper on top of the desk in my class," say Junebug, figuring   17
Miss Moore crazy or lyin one.

"At home, then," she say. "Don't you have a calendar and a pencil case and a   18
blotter and a letter-opener on your desk at home where you do your homework?" And she know damn well what our homes look like cause she nosys around in them every chance she gets.

"I don't even have a desk," say Junebug. "Do we?"   19

"No. And I don't get no homework neither," say Big Butt.   20

"And I don't even have a home," say Flyboy like he do at school to keep the   21
white folks off his back and sorry for him. Send this poor kid to camp posters is his specialty.

"I do," says Mercedes. "I have a box of stationery on my desk and a picture of   22
my cat. My godmother bought the stationery and the desk. There's a big rose on each sheet and the envelopes smell like roses."

"Who wants to know about your smelly-ass stationery," say Rosie Giraffe fore I   23
can get my two cents in.

"It's important to have a work area all your own so that . . ."   24

"Will you look at this sailboat, please," say Flyboy, cuttin her off and pointin to   25
the thing like it was his. So once again we tumble all over each other to gaze at this magnificent thing in the toy store which is just big enough to maybe sail two kittens across the pond if you strap them to the posts tight. We all start reciting the price tag like we in assembly. "Handcrafted sailboat of fiberglass at one thousand one hundred ninety-five dollars."

"Unbelievable," I hear myself say and am really stunned. I read it again for   26
myself just in case the group recitation put me in a trance. Same thing. For some

reason this pisses me off. We look at Miss Moore and she lookin at us, waiting for I dunno what.

Who'd pay all that when you can buy a sailboat set for a quarter at Pop's, a tube   27
of blue for a dime, and a ball of string for eight cents? "It must have a motor and a whole lot else besides," I say. "My sailboat cost me about fifty cents."

"But will it take water?" say Mercedes with her smart ass.   28

"Took mine to Alley Pond Park once," say Flyboy. "String broke. Lost it. Pity."   29

"Sailed mine in Central Park and it keeled over and sank. Had to ask my father   30
for another dollar."

"And you got the strap," laugh Big Butt. "The jerk didn't even have a string on   31
it. My old man wailed on his behind."

Little Q.T. was staring hard at the sailboat and you could see he wanted it bad.   32
But he too little and somebody'd just take it from him. So what the hell. "This boat for kids, Miss Moore?"

"Parents silly to buy something like that just to get all broke up," say Rosie   33
Giraffe.

"That much money it should last forever," I figure.   34

"My father'd buy it for me if I wanted it."   35

"Your father, my ass," say Rosie Giraffe getting a chance to finally push Mer-   36
cedes.

"Must be rich people shop here," say Q.T.   37

"You are a very bright boy," say Flyboy. "What was your first clue?" And he rap   38
him on the head with the back of his knuckles, since Q.T. the only one he could get away with. Though Q.T. liable to come up behind you years later and get his licks in when you half expect it.

"What I want to know," I says to Miss Moore though I never talk to her, I   39
wouldn't give the bitch that satisfaction, "is how much a real boat costs? I figure a thousand'd get you a yacht any day."

"Why don't you check that out," she says, "and report back to the group?"   40
Which really pains my ass. If you gonna mess up a perfectly good swim day least you could do is have some answers. "Let's go in," she say like she got something up her sleeve. Only she don't lead the way. So me and Sugar turn the corner to where the entrance is, but when we get there I kinda hang back. Not that I'm scared, what's there to be afraid of, just a toy store. But I feel funny, shame. But what I got to be shamed about? Got as much right to go in as anybody. But somehow I can't seem to get hold of the door, so I step away for Sugar to lead. But she hangs back too. And I look at her and she looks at me and this is ridiculous. I mean, damn, I have never ever been shy about doing nothing or going nowhere. But then Mer- cedes steps up and then Rosie Giraffe and Big Butt crowd in behind and shove, and next thing we all stuffed into the doorway with only Mercedes squeezing past us, smoothing out her jumper and walking right down the aisle. Then the rest of us tumble in like a glued-together jigsaw done all wrong. And people lookin at us. And it's like the time me and Sugar crashed into the Catholic church on a dare. But once we got in there and everything so hushed and holy and the candles and the bowin and the handkerchiefs on all the drooping heads, I just couldn't go through

with the plan. Which was for me to run up to the altar and do a tap dance while Sugar played the nose flute and messed around in the holy water. And Sugar kept givin me the elbow. Then later teased me so bad I tied her up in the shower and turned it on and locked her in. And she'd be there till this day if Aunt Gretchen hadn't finally figured I was lyin about the boarder takin a shower.

Same thing in the store. We all walkin on tiptoe and hardly touchin the games and puzzles and things. And I watched Miss Moore who is steady watchin us like she waitin for a sign. Like Mama Drewery watches the sky and sniffs the air and takes note of just how much slant is in the bird formation. Then me and Sugar bump smack into each other, so busy gazing at the toys, 'specially the sailboat. But we don't laugh and go into our fat-lady bump-stomach routine. We just stare at that price tag. Then Sugar run a finger over the whole boat. And I'm jealous and want to hit her. Maybe not her, but I sure want to punch somebody in the mouth. 41

"Watcha bring us here for, Miss Moore?" 42

"You sound angry, Sylvia. Are you mad about something?" Givin me one of them grins like she tellin a grown-up joke that never turns out to be funny. And she's lookin very closely at me like maybe she plannin to do my portrait from memory. I'm mad, but I won't give her that satisfaction. So I slouch around the store bein very bored and say, "Let's go." 43

Me and Sugar at the back of the train watchin the tracks whizzin by large then small then gettin gobbled up in the dark. I'm thinkin about this tricky toy I saw in the store. A clown that somersaults on a bar then does chin-ups just cause you yank lightly at his leg. Cost $35. I could see me askin my mother for a $35 birthday clown. "You wanna who that costs what?" she'd say, cocking her head to the side to get a better view of the hole in my head. Thirty-five dollars could buy new bunk beds for Junior and Gretchen's boy. Thirty-five dollars and the whole household could visit Grandaddy Nelson in the country. Thirty-five dollars would pay for the rent and the piano bill too. Who are these people that spend that much for performing clowns and $1,000 for toy sailboats? What kinda work they do and how they live and how come we ain't in on it? Where we are is who we are, Miss Moore always pointin out. But it don't necessarily have to be that way, she always adds then waits for somebody to say that poor people have to wake up and demand their share of the pie and don't none of us know what kind of pie she talkin about in the first damn place. But she ain't so smart cause I still got her four dollars from the taxi and she sure ain't gettin it. Messin up my day with this shit. Sugar nudges me in my pocket and winks. 44

Miss Moore lines us up in front of the mailbox where we started from, seem like years ago, and I got a headache for thinkin so hard. And we lean all over each other so we can hold up under the draggy-ass lecture she always finishes us off with at the end before we thank her for borin us to tears. But she just looks at us like she readin tea leaves. Finally she say, "Well, what did you think of F.A.O. Schwarz?" 45

Rosie Giraffe mumbles, "White folks crazy." 46

"I'd like to go there again when I get my birthday money," says Mercedes, and we shove her out the pack so she has to lean on the mailbox by herself. 47

"I'd like a shower. Tiring day," say Flyboy. 48

Then Sugar surprises me by sayin, "You know, Miss Moore, I don't think all of   49
us here put together eat in a year what that sailboat costs." And Miss Moore lights
up like somebody goosed her. "And?" she say, urging Sugar on. Only I'm standin
on her foot so she don't continue.

"Imagine for a minute what kind of society it is in which some people can   50
spend on a toy what it would cost to feed a family of six or seven. What do you
think?"

"I think," say Sugar pushing me off her feet like she never done before, cause I   51
whip her ass in a minute, "that this is not much of a democracy if you ask me. Equal
chance to pursue happiness means an equal crack at the dough, don't it?" Miss
Moore is besides herself and I am disgusted with Sugar's treachery. So I stand on
her foot one more time to see if she'll shove me. She shuts up, and Miss Moore
looks at me, sorrowfully I'm thinkin. And somethin weird is goin on, I can feel it in
my chest.

"Anybody else learn anything today?" lookin dead at me. I walk away and   52
Sugar has to run to catch up and don't even seem to notice when I shrug her arm
off my shoulder.

"Well, we got four dollars anyway," she says.   53
"Uh hunh."   54
"We could go to Hascombs and get half a chocolate layer and then go to the   55
Sunset and still have plenty money for potato chips and ice-cream sodas."
"Uh hunh."   56
"Race you to Hascombs," she say.   57
We start down the block and she gets ahead which is O.K. by me cause I'm   58
going to the West End and then over to the Drive to think this day through. She
can run if she want to and even run faster. But ain't nobody gonna beat me at
nuthin.

Rhetorical Focus

1. Was it an effective decision to use the first person here instead of the third?
   Explain.
2. Much of this narrative is dialogue or monologue. What is gained and lost by
   using this technique? Suggest alternatives.
3. If this is a traditional narrative with a beginning, middle, and end, where
   would the climax or turning point be?

Thematic Focus

1. What is the lesson that the narrator learns? How would you compare it to
   Podhoretz's?
2. Is a society that has expensive toys as well as an underclass unjust? Explain.
3. What would Mrs. K think of Sylvia and her group, and vice versa?

Suggestions for Writing

1. "Translate" the first paragraph of "The Lesson" into standard English. Try to do the reverse for "A Question of Class," using black dialect.
2. Narrate a personal experience in which a teacher played an important part either positively or negatively. You might want to use the expository approach of Podhoretz or Bambara's more fictional style.
3. In Eiseley's "The Running Man," the narrator claims that "To grow is a gain, an enlargement of life; is not this what they tell us? Yet it is also a departure." Using this as an opening premise, write an essay about your own education and the teachers who mattered.

TROUBLED EDUCATIONS

Although many persons think of schools as a site of learning, as a place to teach students about the Western tradition of art and science, schools also have as a goal the socialization of students into mainstream culture, encouraging, even demanding, that the values of the middle-class—its speech, its hopes and dreams—be seen as the standard, as appropriate and normal for all. Minority cultures are rarely given much attention. In a culture as ethnically diverse as ours, a student's neighborhood culture is rarely valued. In fact, to succeed in school culture, with its emphasis on achievement and cooperation, students often have to abandon many aspects of their parents' way of life. They have to learn a new culture, as it were. The emotional consequences are often severe for the student and for the family left behind. Richard Rodriguez is quite explicit about the pride and the guilt he feels in adopting the ways of a different culture at school. George Orwell's account of his experience as a "scholarship boy" in an elite British school had such a harrowing effect on him that even as a world-famous author, he could not forgive his schoolmasters for being so filled with class bias and cruelty.

Often, middle-class students are surprised when others complain about the psychological damage done by an education that is too narrowly conceived. They are usually surprised because most of us are so used to the content and method of our schooling that it seems natural, commonsensical. However, the form education takes is not natural; it is developed by people with certain values and experiences. There can be alternatives to the ways things have been done. Tradition is not sacred.

Achievement of Desire

Richard Rodriguez

Richard Rodriguez, born (1944) in San Francisco to Mexican immigrant parents, spoke only Spanish when he entered a Catholic school at the age of six years. However, Rodriguez proved to be a precocious student, distinguishing himself academically, doing undergraduate work at Stanford, winning a Fulbright fellowship, and ultimately earning a Ph.D. in English Renaissance literature. This essay, an excerpt from his book *Hunger of Memory* (1982), describes the tremendous sadness and conflict Rodriguez experienced as a "scholarship boy" who was doubly alienated—set apart from the academic world by his ethnic background and separated from his uneducated family by the very education he had labored so hard to obtain.

Reflections Before Reading

Were you conscious of going to a school where your social class mattered? When were you aware of class distinctions in school? What was your response? Are you planning to carry on your parents' values? Your neighborhood's?

The boy who first entered a classroom barely able to speak English, twenty years later concluded his studies in the stately quiet of the reading room in the British Museum. Thus with one sentence I can summarize my academic career. It will be harder to summarize what sort of life connects the boy to the man.

With every award, each graduation from one level of education to the next, people I'd meet would congratulate me. Their refrain always the same: 'Your parents must be very proud.' Sometimes then they'd ask me how I managed it—my 'success.' (How?) After a while, I had several quick answers to give in reply. I'd admit, for one thing, that I went to an excellent grammar school. (My earliest teachers, the nuns, made my success their ambition.) And my brother and both my sisters were very good students. (They often brought home the shiny school trophies I came to want.) And my mother and father always encouraged me. (At every graduation they were behind the stunning flash of the camera when I turned to look at the crowd.)

As important as these factors were, however, they account inadequately for my academic advance. Nor do they suggest what an odd success I managed. For although I was a very good student, I was also a very bad student. I was a 'scholarship boy,' a certain kind of scholarship boy. Always successful, I was always unconfident. Exhilarated by my progress. Sad. I became the prized student—anxious and eager to learn. Too eager, too anxious—an imitative and unoriginal pupil. My brother and two sisters enjoyed the advantages I did, and they grew to be as successful as I, but none of them ever seemed so anxious about their schooling. A second-grade student, I was the one who came home and corrected the 'simple' grammatical mistakes of our parents. ('Two negatives make a positive.') Proudly I announced—to my family's startled silence—that a teacher had said I was losing all trace of a Spanish accent. I was oddly annoyed when I was unable to get parental help with a homework assignment. The night my father tried to help me with an arithmetic exercise, he kept reading the instructions, each time more deliberately, until I pried the textbook out of his hands, saying, 'I'll try to figure it out some more by myself.'

When I reached the third grade, I outgrew such behavior. I became more tactful, careful to keep separate the two very different worlds of my day. But then, with ever-increasing intensity, I devoted myself to my studies. I became bookish, puzzling to all my family. Ambition set me apart. When my brother saw me struggling home with stacks of library books, he would laugh, shouting: 'Hey, Four Eyes!' My father opened a closet one day and was startled to find me inside, reading a novel. My mother would find me reading when I was supposed to be asleep or helping around the house or playing outside. In a voice angry or worried or just curious, she'd ask: 'What do you see in your books?' It became the family's joke. When I was called and wouldn't reply, someone would say I must be hiding under my bed with a book.

(How did I manage my success?)

What I am about to say to you has taken me more than twenty years to admit: *A primary reason for my success in the classroom was that I couldn't forget that schooling was changing me and separating me from the life I enjoyed before becoming a student.* That simple realization! For years I never spoke to anyone about it. Never mentioned a thing to my family or my teachers or classmates. From a very early age, I understood enough, just enough about my classroom experiences to keep what I knew repressed, hidden beneath layers of embarrassment. Not until my last months as a graduate student, nearly thirty years old, was it possible for me to think much about the reasons for my academic success. Only then. At the end of my schooling, I needed to determine how far I had moved from my past. The adult finally confronted, and now must publicly say, what the child shuddered from knowing and could never admit to himself or to those many faces that smiled at his every success. ('Your parents must be very proud. . . .')

I

At the end, in the British Museum (too distracted to finish my dissertation) for weeks I read, speed-read, books by modern educational theorists, only to find infrequent and slight mention of students like me. (Much more is written about the more typical case, the lower-class student who barely is helped by his schooling.) Then one day, leafing through Richard Hoggart's *The Uses of Literacy*, I found, in his description of the scholarship boy, myself. For the first time I realized that there were other students like me, and so I was able to frame the meaning of my academic success, its consequent price—the loss.

Hoggart's description is distinguished, at least initially, by deep understand- 8 ing. What he grasps very well is that the scholarship boy must move between environments, his home and the classroom, which are at cultural extremes, opposed. With his family, the boy has the intense pleasure of intimacy, the family's consolation in feeling public alienation. Lavish emotions texture home life. *Then,* at school, the instruction bids him to trust lonely reason primarily. Immediate needs set the pace of his parents' lives. From his mother and father the boy learns to trust spontaneity and nonrational ways of knowing. *Then,* at school, there is mental calm. Teachers emphasize the value of a reflectiveness that opens a space between thinking and immediate action.

Years of schooling must pass before the boy will be able to sketch the cultural 9 differences in his day as abstractly as this. But he senses those differences early. Perhaps as early as the night he brings home an assignment from school and finds the house too noisy for study.

> He has to be more and more alone, if he is going to 'get on'. He will have, probably unconsciously, to oppose the ethos of the hearth, the intense gregariousness of the working-class family group. Since everything centres upon the living-room, there is unlikely to be a room of his own; the bedrooms are cold and inhospitable, and to warm them or the front room, if there is one, would not only be expensive, but would require an imaginative leap—out of the tradition—which most families are not capable of making. There is a corner of the living-room table. On the other side Mother is ironing, the wireless is on, someone is singing a snatch of song or Father says intermittently whatever comes into his head. The boy has to cut himself off mentally, so as to do his homework, as well as he can.°

The next day, the lesson is as apparent at school. There are even rows of desks. Discussion is ordered. The boy must rehearse his thoughts and raise his hand before speaking out in a loud voice to an audience of classmates. And there is time enough, and silence, to think about ideas (big ideas) never considered at home by his parents.

Not for the working-class child alone is adjustment to the classroom difficult. 10 Good schooling requires that any student alter early childhood habits. But the working-class child is usually least prepared for the change. And, unlike many middle-class children, he goes home and sees in his parents a way of life not only different but starkly opposed to that of the classroom. (He enters the house and hears his parents talking in ways his teachers discourage.)

°All quotations in this reading are from Richard Hoggart, *The Uses of Literacy* (London: Chatto and Windus, 1957), chapter 10.

Without extraordinary determination and the great assistance of others—at 11
home and at school—there is little chance for success. Typically most working-class children are barely changed by the classroom. The exception succeeds. The relative few become scholarship students. Of these, Richard Hoggart estimates, most manage a fairly graceful transition. Somehow they learn to live in the two very different worlds of their day. There are some others, however, those Hoggart pejoratively terms 'scholarship boys,' for whom success comes with special anxiety. Scholarship boy: good student, troubled son. The child is 'moderately endowed,' intellectually mediocre, Hoggart supposes—though it may be more pertinent to note the special qualities of temperament in the child. High-strung child. Brooding. Sensitive. Haunted by the knowledge that one *chooses* to become a student. (Education is not an inevitable or natural step in growing up.) Here is a child who cannot forget that his academic success distances him from a life he loved, even from his own memory of himself.

Initially, he wavers, balances allegiance. ('The boy is himself [until he reaches, 12
say, the upper forms] very much of *both* the worlds of home and school. He is enormously obedient to the dictates of the world of school, but emotionally still strongly wants to continue as part of the family circle.') Gradually, necessarily, the balance is lost. The boy needs to spend more and more time studying, each night enclosing himself in the silence permitted and required by intense concentration. He takes his first step toward academic success, away from his family.

From the very first days, through the years following, it will be with his par- 13
ents—the figures of lost authority, the persons toward whom he feels deepest love—that the change will be most powerfully measured. A separation will unravel between them. Advancing in his studies, the boy notices that his mother and father have not changed as much as he. Rather, when he sees them, they often remind him of the person he once was and the life he earlier shared with them. He realizes what some Romantics also know when they praise the working class for the capacity for human closeness, qualities of passion and spontaneity, that the rest of us experience in like measure only in the earliest part of our youth. For the Romantic, this doesn't make working-class life childish. Working-class life challenges precisely because it is an *adult* way of life.

The scholarship boy reaches a different conclusion. He cannot afford to ad- 14
mire his parents. (How could he and still pursue such a contrary life?) He permits himself embarrassment at their lack of education. And to evade nostalgia for the life he has lost, he concentrates on the benefits education will bestow upon him. He becomes especially ambitious. Without the support of old certainties and consolations, almost mechanically, he assumes the procedures and doctrines of the classroom. The kind of allegiance the young student might have given his mother and father only days earlier, he transfers to the teacher, the new figure of authority. '[The scholarship boy] tends to make a father-figure of his form-master,' Hoggart observes.

But Hoggart's calm prose only makes me recall the urgency with which I came 15
to idolize my grammar school teachers. I began by imitating their accents, using their diction, trusting their every direction. The very first facts they dispensed, I grasped with awe. Any book they told me to read, I read—then waited for them to

tell me which books I enjoyed. Their every casual opinion I came to adopt and to trumpet when I returned home. I stayed after school 'to help'—to get my teacher's undivided attention. It was the nun's encouragement that mattered most to me. (She understood exactly what—my parents never seemed to appraise so well—all my achievements entailed.) Memory gently caressed each word of praise bestowed in the classroom so that compliments teachers paid me years ago come quickly to mind even today.

The enthusiasm I felt in second-grade classes I flaunted before both my par- 16 ents. The docile, obedient student came home a shrill and precocious son who insisted on correcting and teaching his parents with the remark: 'My teacher told us. . . .'

I intended to hurt my mother and father. I was still angry at them for having 17 encouraged me toward classroom English. But gradually this anger was exhausted, replaced by guilt as school grew more and more attractive to me. I grew increasingly successful, a talkative student. My hand was raised in the classroom; I yearned to answer any question. At home, life was less noisy than it had been. (I spoke to classmates and teachers more often each day than to family members.) Quiet at home, I sat with my papers for hours each night. I never forgot that schooling had irretrievably changed my family's life. That knowledge, however, did not weaken ambition. Instead, it strengthened resolve. Those times I remembered the loss of my past with regret, I quickly reminded myself of all the things my teachers could give me. (They could make me an educated man.) I tightened my grip on pencil and books. I evaded nostalgia. Tried hard to forget. But one does not forget by trying to forget. One only remembers. I remembered too well that education had changed my family's life. I would not have become a scholarship boy had I not so often remembered.

Once she was sure that her children knew English, my mother would tell us, 18 'You should keep up your Spanish.' Voices playfully groaned in response. '¡Pochos!' my mother would tease. I listened silently.

After a while, I grew more calm at home. I developed tact. A fourth-grade 19 student, I was no longer the show-off in front of my parents. I became a conventionally dutiful son, politely affectionate, cheerful enough, even—for reasons beyond choosing—my father's favorite. And much about my family life was easy then, comfortable, happy in the rhythm of our living together: hearing my father getting ready for work; eating the breakfast my mother had made me; looking up from a novel to hear my brother or one of my sisters playing with friends in the backyard; in winter, coming upon the house all lighted up after dark.

But withheld from my mother and father was any mention of what most mat- 20 tered to me: the extraordinary experience of first-learning. Late afternoon: In the midst of preparing dinner, my mother would come up behind me while I was trying to read. Her head just over mine, her breath warmly scented with food. 'What are you reading?' Or, 'Tell me all about your new courses.' I would barely respond, 'Just the usual things, nothing special.' (A half smile, then silence. Her head moving back in the silence. Silence! Instead of the flood of intimate sounds that had once flowed smoothly between us, there was this silence.) After dinner, I would rush to a bedroom with papers and books. As often as possible, I resisted parental pleas to 'save lights' by coming to the kitchen to work. I kept so much, so often, to myself. Sad. Enthusiastic. Troubled by the excitement of coming upon new ideas. Eager. Fascinated by the promising texture of a brand-new book. I hoarded the pleasures of learning. Alone for hours. Enthralled. Nervous. I rarely looked away from my books—or back on my memories. Nights when relatives visited and the front rooms were warmed by Spanish sounds, I slipped quietly out of the house.

It mattered that education was changing me. It never ceased to matter. My   21
brother and sisters would giggle at our mother's mispronounced words. They'd correct her gently. My mother laughed girlishly one night, trying not to pronounce *sheep* as *ship*. From a distance I listened sullenly. From that distance, pretending not to notice on another occasion, I saw my father looking at the title pages of my library books. That was the scene on my mind when I walked home with a fourth-grade companion and heard him say that his parents read to him every night. (A strange-sounding book—*Winnie the Pooh*.) Immediately, I wanted to know, 'What is it like?' My companion, however, thought I wanted to know about the plot of the book. Another day, my mother surprised me by asking for a 'nice' book to read. 'Something not too hard you think I might like.' Carefully I chose one, Willa Cather's *My Ántonia*. But when, several weeks later, I happened to see it next to her bed unread except for the first few pages, I was furious and suddenly wanted to cry. I grabbed up the book and took it back to my room and placed it in its place, alphabetically on my shelf.

Rhetorical Focus

1. Throughout the essay, Rodriguez uses parentheses. Try to generalize about the purpose for the unusual frequency (see paragraph 2) of this device.
2. Rodriguez uses both "I" and "the scholarship boy" as a way to narrate his experiences. What do you think about his use of the first and third person? What is he trying to do? Does he succeed?
3. Check the last sentence in a paragraph and then the first one in the next. Does the author use transitions? Explain.

Thematic Focus

1. Is the situation Rodriguez describes inevitable in our culture? Could school be structured to prevent such alienation?
2. Are all good students good imitators of their instructor's ideas and verbal behavior?
3. At the end, Rodriguez seems rather bitter. Is this natural?

All the Rich Boys

George Orwell

George Orwell, an English novelist and essayist best known for his novels
Animal Farm (1945) and *1984* (1949), was born in India, the son of an
English civil servant. He was educated as a scholarship boy in the English
boarding-school system, where he encountered considerable discrimination,
both from his schoolmasters and from his upper-class peers, due to his
so-called inferior social status. Orwell recounts his schooldays in the essay
"Such, Such Were the Joys," from which the following selection is taken.
The essay is concerned with the relationship between social class and
education and the ways in which both are intertwined with political ideology.

Reflections Before Reading

How would you describe your high school in terms of class; were there
poor students, rich students, mostly middle-class students? Were they
treated differently? How do you feel now about some injustice either you or
a peer suffered in elementary or junior high school?

Crossgates was an expensive and snobbish school which was in process of becom- 1
ing more snobbish, and, I imagine, more expensive. The public school with which
it had special connections was Harrow, but during my time an increasing proportion of the boys went on to Eton. Most of them were the children of rich parents,
but on the whole they were the unaristocratic rich, the sort of people who live in
huge shrubberied houses in Bournemouth or Richmond, and who have cars and
butlers but not country estates. There were a few exotics among them—some
South American boys, sons of Argentine beef barons, one or two Russians, and
even a Siamese prince, or someone who was described as a prince.

Sim had two great ambitions. One was to attract titled boys to the school, and 2
the other was to train up pupils to win scholarships at public schools, above all
Eton. He did, towards the end of my time, succeed in getting hold of two boys with
real English titles. One of them, I remember, was a wretched little creature, almost an albino, peering upward out of weak eyes, with a long nose at the end of
which a dewdrop always seemed to be trembling. Sim always gave these boys their

titles when mentioning them to a third person, and for their first few days he actually addressed them to their faces as "Lord So-and-so." Needless to say he found ways of drawing attention to them when any visitor was being shown round the school. Once, I remember, the little fair-haired boy had a choking fit at dinner, and a stream of snot ran out of his nose onto his plate in a way horrible to see. Any lesser person would have been called a dirty little beast and ordered out of the room instantly: but Sim and Bingo laughed it off in a "boys will be boys" spirit.

All the very rich boys were more or less undisguisedly favored. The school still had a faint suggestion of the Victorian "private academy" with its "parlor boarders," and when I later read about that kind of school in Thackeray I immediately saw the resemblance. The rich boys had milk and biscuits in the middle of the morning, they were given riding lessons once or twice a week, Bingo mothered them and called them by their Christian names, and above all they were never caned. Apart from the South Americans, whose parents were safely distant, I doubt whether Sim ever caned any boy whose father's income was much above £2,000 a year. But he was sometimes willing to sacrifice financial profit to scholastic prestige. Occasionally, by special arrangement, he would take at greatly reduced fees some boy who seemed likely to win scholarships and thus bring credit on the school. It was on these terms that I was at Crossgates myself: otherwise my parents could not have afforded to send me to so expensive a school.

I did not at first understand that I was being taken at reduced fees; it was only when I was about eleven that Bingo and Sim began throwing the fact in my teeth. For my first two or three years I went through the ordinary educational mill: then soon after I had started Greek (one started Latin at eight, Greek at ten), I moved into the scholarship class, which was taught, so far as classics went, largely by Sim himself. Over a period of two or three years the scholarship boys were crammed with learning as cynically as a goose is crammed for Christmas. And with what learning! This business of making a gifted boy's career depend on a competitive examination, taken when he is only twelve or thirteen, is an evil thing at best, but there do appear to be preparatory schools which send scholars to Eton, Winchester, etc., without teaching them to see everything in terms of marks. At Crossgates the whole process was frankly a preparation for a sort of confidence trick. Your job was to learn exactly those things that would give an examiner the impression that you knew more than you did know, and as far as possible to avoid burdening your brain with anything else. Subjects which lacked examination value, such as geography, were almost completely neglected, mathematics was also neglected if you were a "classical," science was not taught in any form—indeed it was so despised that even an interest in natural history was discouraged—and the books you were encouraged to read in your spare time were chosen with one eye on the "English Paper." Latin and Greek, the main scholarship subjects, were what counted, but even these were deliberately taught in a flashy, unsound way. We never, for example, read right through even a single book of a Greek or Latin author: we merely read short passages which were picked out because they were the kind of thing likely to be set as an "unseen translation." During the last year or so before we went up for our scholarships, most of our time was spent in simply working our way through the scholarship papers of previous years. Sim had sheaves of these in his possession, from every one of the major public schools. But the greatest outrage of all was the teaching of history.

There was in those days a piece of nonsense called the Harrow History   5
Prize, an annual competition for which many preparatory schools entered. At Crossgates we mugged up every paper that had been set since the competition started. They were the kind of stupid question that is answered by rapping out a name or a quotation. Who plundered the Begams? Who was beheaded in an open boat? Who caught the Whigs bathing and ran away with their clothes? Almost all our historical teaching was on this level. History was a series of unrelated, unintelligible but—in some way that was never explained to us—important facts with resounding phrases tied to them. Disraeli brought peace with honor. Clive was astonished at his moderation. Pitt called in the New World to redress the balance of the Old. And the dates, and the mnemonic devices! (Did you know, for example, that the initial letters of "A black Negress was my aunt: there's her house behind the barn" are also the initial letters of the battles in the Wars of the Roses?) Bingo, who "took" the higher forms in history, revelled in this kind of thing. I recall positive orgies of dates, with the keener boys leaping up and down in their places in their eagerness to shout out the right answers, and at the same time not feeling the faintest interest in the meaning of the mysterious events they were naming.

"1587?"   6
"Massacre of St. Bartholomew!"   7
"1707?"   8
"Death of Aurangzeeb!"   9
"1713?"   10
"Treaty of Utrecht!"   11
"1773?"   12
"The Boston Tea Party!"   13
"1520?"   14
"Oh, Mum, please, Mum—"   15
"Please, Mum, please, Mum! Let me tell him, Mum!"   16
"Well; 1520?"   17
"Field of the Cloth of Gold!"   18
And so on.   19

But history and such secondary subjects were not bad fun. It was in "classics"   20
that the real strain came. Looking back, I realize that I then worked harder than I have ever done since, and yet at the time it never seemed possible to make quite the effort that was demanded of one. We would sit round the long shiny table, made of some very pale-colored, hard wood, with Sim goading, threatening, exhorting, sometimes joking, very occasionally praising, but always prodding, prodding away at one's mind to keep it up to the right pitch of concentration, as one might keep a sleepy person awake by sticking pins into him.

"Go on, you little slacker! Go on, you idle, worthless little boy! The whole   21
trouble with you is that you're bone and horn idle. You eat too much, that's why.

You wolf down enormous meals, and then when you come here you're half asleep. Go on, now, put your back into it. You're not *thinking.* Your brain doesn't sweat."

He would tap away at one's skull with his silver pencil, which, in my memory,   22
seems to have been about the size of a banana, and which certainly was heavy enough to raise a bump: or he would pull the short hairs round one's ears, or, occasionally, reach out under the table and kick one's shin. On some days nothing seemed to go right, and then it would be: "All right, then, I know what you want. You've been asking for it the whole morning. Come along, you useless little slacker. Come into the study." And then whack, whack, whack, whack, and back one would come, red-wealed and smarting—in later years Sim had abandoned his riding crop in favor of a thin rattan cane which hurt very much more—to settle down to work again. This did not happen very often, but I do remember more than once being led out of the room in the middle of a Latin sentence, receiving a beating and then going straight ahead with the same sentence, just like that. It is a mistake to think such methods do not work. They work very well for their special purpose. Indeed, I doubt whether classical education ever has been or can be successfully carried on without corporal punishment. The boys themselves believed in its efficacy. There was a boy named Beacham, with no brains to speak of, but evidently in acute need of a scholarship. Sim was flogging him towards the goal as one might do with a foundered horse. He went up for a scholarship at Uppingham, came back with a consciousness of having done badly, and a day or two later received a severe beating for idleness. "I wish I'd had that caning before I went up for the exam," he said sadly—a remark which I felt to be contemptible, but which I perfectly well understood.

The boys of the scholarship class were not all treated alike. If a boy were the   23
son of rich parents to whom the saving of fees was not all-important, Sim would goad him along in a comparatively fatherly way, with jokes and digs in the ribs and perhaps an occasional tap with the pencil, but no hair-pulling and no caning. It was the poor but "clever" boys who suffered. Our brains were a gold mine in which he had sunk money, and the dividends must be squeezed out of us. Long before I had grasped the nature of my financial relationship with Sim, I had been made to understand that I was not on the same footing as most of the other boys. In effect there were three castes in the school. There was the minority with an aristocratic or millionaire background, there were the children of the ordinary suburban rich, who made up the bulk of the school, and there were a few underlings like myself, the sons of clergymen, Indian civil servants, struggling widows and the like. These poorer ones were discouraged from going in for "extras" such as shooting and carpentry, and were humiliated over clothes and petty possessions. I never, for instance, succeeded in getting a cricket bat of my own, because "your parents wouldn't be able to afford it." This phrase pursued me throughout my schooldays. At Crossgates we were not allowed to keep the money we brought back with us, but had to "give it in" on the first day of term, and then from time to time were allowed to spend it under supervision. I and similarly placed boys were always choked off from buying expensive toys like model aeroplanes, even if the necessary money stood to our credit. Bingo, in particular, seemed to aim consciously at inculcating a humble outlook in the poorer boys. "Do you think that's the sort of thing a

boy like you should buy?" I remember her saying to somebody—and she said this in front of the whole school; "You know you're not going to grow up with money, don't you? Your people aren't rich. You must learn to be sensible. Don't get above yourself!" There was also the weekly pocket-money, which we took out in sweets, dispensed by Bingo from a large table. The millionaires had sixpence a week, but the normal sum was threepence. I and one or two others were only allowed twopence. My parents had not given instructions to this effect, and the saving of a penny a week could not conceivably have made any difference to them: it was a mark of status. Worse yet was the detail of the birthday cakes. It was usual for each boy, on his birthday, to have a large iced cake with candles, which was shared out at tea between the whole school. It was provided as a matter of routine and went on his parents' bill. I never had such a cake, though my parents would have paid for it readily enough. Year after year, never daring to ask, I would miserably hope that this year a cake would appear. Once or twice I even rashly pretended to my companions that this time I *was* going to have a cake. Then came teatime, and no cake, which did not make me more popular.

Very early it was impressed upon me that I had no chance of a decent future 24
unless I won a scholarship at a public school. Either I won my scholarship, or I must leave school at fourteen and become, in Sim's favorite phrase, "a little office boy at forty pounds a year." In my circumstances it was natural that I should believe this. Indeed, it was universally taken for granted at Crossgates that unless you went to a "good" public school (and only about fifteen schools came under this heading) you were ruined for life. It is not easy to convey to a grown-up person the sense of strain, of nerving oneself for some terrible, all-deciding combat, as the date of the examination crept nearer—eleven years old, twelve years old, then thirteen, the fatal year itself! Over a period of about two years, I do not think there was ever a day when "the exam," as I called it, was quite out of my waking thoughts. In my prayers it figured invariably: and whenever I got the bigger portion of a wishbone, or picked up a horseshoe, or bowed seven times to the new moon, or succeeded in passing through a wishing-gate without touching the sides, then the wish I earned by doing so went on "the exam" as a matter of course. And yet curiously enough I was also tormented by an almost irresistible impulse *not* to work. There were days when my heart sickened at the labors ahead of me, and I stood stupid as an animal before the most elementary difficulties. In the holidays, also, I could not work. Some of the scholarship boys received extra tuition from a certain Mr. Batchelor, a likeable, very hairy man who wore shaggy suits and lived in a typical bachelor's "den"—booklined walls, overwhelming stench of tobacco— somewhere in the town. During the holidays Mr. Batchelor used to send us extracts from Latin authors to translate, and we were supposed to send back a wad of work once a week. Somehow I could not do it. The empty paper and the black Latin dictionary lying on the table, the consciousness of a plain duty shirked, poisoned my leisure, but somehow I could not start, and by the end of the holidays I would only have sent Mr. Batchelor fifty or a hundred lines. Undoubtedly part of the reason was that Sim and his cane were far away. But in term time, also, I would go through periods of idleness and stupidity when I would sink deeper and deeper into disgrace and even achieve a sort of feeble defiance, fully

conscious of my guilt and yet unable or unwilling—I could not be sure which—to do any better. Then Bingo or Sim would send for me, and this time it would not even be a caning.

Bingo would search me with her baleful eyes. (What color were those eyes, I wonder? I remember them as green, but actually no human being has green eyes. Perhaps they were hazel.) She would start off in her peculiar, wheedling, bullying style, which never failed to get right through one's guard and score a hit on one's better nature.   25

"I don't think it's awfully decent of you to behave like this, is it? Do you think it's quite playing the game by your mother and father to go on idling your time away, week after week, month after month? Do you *want* to throw all your chances away? You know your people aren't rich, don't you? You know they can't afford the same things as other boys' parents. How are they to send you to a public school if you don't win a scholarship? I know how proud your mother is of you. Do you *want* to let her down?"   26

"I don't think he wants to go to a public school any longer," Sim would say, addressing himself to Bingo with a pretense that I was not there. "I think he's given up that idea. He wants to be a little office boy at forty pounds a year."   27

The horrible sensation of tears—a swelling in the breasts, a tickling behind the nose—would already have assailed me. Bingo would bring out her ace of trumps: 28

"And do you think it's quite fair to *us*, the way you're behaving? After all we've done for you? You *do* know what we've done for you, don't you?" Her eyes would pierce deep into me, and though she never said it straight out, I did know. "We've had you here all these years—we even had you here for a week in the holidays so that Mr. Batchelor could coach you. We don't *want* to have to send you away, you know, but we can't keep a boy here just to eat up our food, term after term. *I* don't think it's very straight, the way you're behaving. Do you?"   29

I never had any answer except a miserable "No, Mum," or "Yes, Mum" as the case might be. Evidently it was *not* straight, the way I was behaving. And at some point or other the unwanted tear would always force its way out of the corner of my eye, roll down my nose, and splash.   30

Bingo never said in plain words that I was a non-paying pupil, no doubt because vague phrases like "all we've done for you" had a deeper emotional appeal. Sim, who did not aspire to be loved by his pupils, put it more brutally, though, as was usual with him, in pompous language. "You are living on my bounty" was his favorite phrase in this context. At least once I listened to these words between blows of the cane. I must say that these scenes were not frequent, and except on one occasion they did not take place in the presence of other boys. In public I was reminded that I was poor and that my parents "wouldn't be able to afford" this or that, but I was not actually reminded of my dependent position. It was a final unanswerable argument, to be brought forth like an instrument of torture when my work became exceptionally bad.   31

To grasp the effect of this kind of thing on a child of ten or twelve, one has to remember that the child has little sense of proportion or probability. A child may be a mass of egoism and rebelliousness, but it has not accumulated experience to give it confidence in its own judgments. On the whole it will accept what it is told,   32 and it will believe in the most fantastic way in the knowledge and power of the adults surrounding it. Here is an example.

I have said that at Crossgates we were not allowed to keep our own money. 33 However, it was possible to hold back a shilling or two, and sometimes I used furtively to buy sweets which I kept hidden in the loose ivy on the playing-field wall. One day when I had been sent on an errand I went into a sweetshop a mile or more from the school and bought some chocolates. As I came out of the shop I saw on the opposite pavement a small sharp-faced man who seemed to be staring very hard at my school cap. Instantly a horrible fear went through me. There could be no doubt as to who the man was. He was a spy placed there by Sim! I turned away unconcernedly, and then, as though my legs were doing it of their own accord, broke into a clumsy run. But when I got round the next corner I forced myself to walk again, for to run was a sign of guilt, and obviously there would be other spies posted here and there about the town. All that day and the next I waited for the summons to the study, and was surprised when it did not come. It did not seem to me strange that the headmaster of a private school should dispose of an army of informers, and I did not even imagine that he would have to pay them. I assumed that any adult, inside the school or outside, would collaborate voluntarily in preventing us from breaking the rules. Sim was all-powerful, and it was natural that his agents should be everywhere. When this episode happened I do not think I can have been less than twelve years old.

I hated Bingo and Sim, with a sort of shamefaced, remorseful hatred, but it 34 did not occur to me to doubt their judgment. When they told me that I must either win a public school scholarship or become an office boy at fourteen, I believed that those were the unavoidable alternatives before me. And above all, I believed Bingo and Sim when they told me they were my benefactors. I see now, of course, that from Sim's point of view I was a good speculation. He sank money in me, and he looked to get it back in the form of prestige. If I had "gone off," as promising boys sometimes do, I imagine that he would have got rid of me swiftly. As it was I won him two scholarships when the time came, and no doubt he made full use of them in his prospectuses. But it is difficult for a child to realize that a school is primarily a commercial venture. A child believes that the school exists to educate and that the schoolmaster disciplines him either for his own good, or from a love of bullying. Sim and Bingo had chosen to befriend me, and their friendship included canings, reproaches, and humiliations, which were good for me and saved me from an office stool. That was their version, and I believed in it. It was therefore clear that I owed them a vast debt of gratitude. But I was *not* grateful, as I very well knew. On the contrary, I hated both of them. I could not control my subjective feelings, and I could not conceal them from myself. But it is wicked, is it not, to hate your benefactors? So I was taught, and so I believed. A child accepts the codes of behavior that are presented to it, even when it breaks them. From the age of eight, or even earlier, the consciousness of sin was never far away from me. If I contrived to seem callous and defiant, it was only a thin cover over a mass of shame and dismay. All through my boyhood I had a profound conviction that I was no good, that I was wasting my time, wrecking my talents, behaving with monstrous folly and wickedness and ingratitude—and all this, it seemed, was inescapable, because I lived among laws which were absolute, like the law of gravity, but which it was not possible for me to keep.

Rhetorical Focus

1. Do any of the words Orwell uses seem specifically British or out-of-date? Give examples.
2. How would you compare Orwell's voice and tone here to that of Rodriguez? Give examples.
3. In this narrative, Orwell gives concrete details, sometimes episodes, to support his interpretations of Sim and Bingo and Crossgates in general. Would you have drawn the same conclusion as Orwell about, say, the Harrow History Prizes?

Thematic Focus

1. What do you think of Orwell's description of his history instruction? Was yours different? How should history be taught?
2. Both Rodriguez and Orwell describe scenes where guilt played a significant role. Why is this so? What is guilt? Is it related to class?
3. Can you tell something about a culture from the way students are treated in school? Would girls be treated differently in such a boarding school?

Suggestions for Writing

1. Try to recount several significant events from your own elementary school education, then in the manner of Orwell's last paragraph, write a generalization about these experiences.
2. Has your education made your values and expectations different from those of your parents? Your grandparents? Write an essay that explains these changes.
3. Write a letter to a teacher from your past that you still have negative or mixed feelings about. Try to explain what went wrong, what could have happened and what the teacher might do to prevent future misunderstandings.

CANONS

To many educated people, classic works such as *Macbeth*, *The Iliad*, and *The Scarlet Letter* have endured because they are indisputably great. They speak to all ages and to all people of universal truths about society and the human heart. They assume that freedom and equality, self-esteem and loneliness are constants regardless of place and time. Shakespeare's Hamlet and Twain's Huck Finn are both part of American culture, and, they argue, all citizens should know who they are. Although that might seem obvious to some, many other teachers and students think education is more complicated than exposing everyone to the same reading list. These critics want to know how certain works get to be classics, why everyone should read them, and what is the purpose of elite culture.

Critics of E. D. Hirsch's notion of cultural literacy—most popularly understood as a list of information any culturally literate person should know in order to function in society—dispute the validity of the traditional canon on the grounds that who gets included and who does not is completely subjective. Mike Rose and Barbara Herrnstein Smith, for example, think women and persons belonging to ethnic minorities have been excluded not because they lack interest or merit but because the standards of judgment were created by middle- and upper-class white males. The canon, so goes this argument, reflects the world view of those with the most power. The classics are about their aspirations, their fears, and their desires. The values and experiences of others are dismissed as trivial or sentimental or simply too alien. For a democracy to survive, they suggest that a cultural pluralism be created where the values and lives of women, African-Americans, and others can enrich the experiences of all readers, not just a privileged few.

Cultural Literacy

E. D. Hirsch, Jr.

E. D. Hirsch, Jr., a Professor of English at the University of Virginia, is a widely respected critic and scholar who has recently turned his attention to the question of American cultural literacy. In the following excerpt from his book *Cultural Literacy: What Every American Needs to Know,* Hirsch explains his belief that America's current educational system is causing a cultural fragmentation that can only be remedied by having all students learn a standardized body of knowledge that all Americans could use to communicate with one another. Hirsch believes that culturally disadvantaged students would benefit because they would acquire the tools of literacy necessary to participate in the discourses of power, which have traditionally belonged only to the socially privileged.

Reflections Before Reading

Is there an American culture? Are TV and the movies an important part of it? Is it natural to feel uncomfortable with those who have different cultural values? Be specific about the kind of cultural information you share with your friends, your family, and your classmates.

During the period 1970–1985, the amount of shared knowledge that we have been   1
able to take for granted in communicating with our fellow citizens has also been declining. More and more of our young people don't know things we used to assume they knew.

A side effect of the diminution in shared information has been a noticeable   2
increase in the number of articles in such publications as *Newsweek* and the *Wall Street Journal* about the surprising ignorance of the young. My son John, who recently taught Latin in high school and eighth grade, often told me of experiences which indicate that these articles are not exaggerated. In one of his classes he mentioned to his students that Latin, the language they were studying, is a dead language that is no longer spoken. After his pupils had struggled for several weeks with Latin grammar and vocabulary, this news was hard for some of them to accept. One girl raised her hand to challenge my son's claim. "What do they speak in Latin America?" she demanded.

At least she had heard of Latin America. Another day my son asked his Latin   3
class if they knew the name of an epic poem by Homer. One pupil shot up his hand and eagerly said, "The Alamo!" Was it just a slip for *The Iliad?* No, he didn't know what the Alamo was, either. To judge from other stories about information gaps in the young, many American schoolchildren are less well informed than this pupil. The following, by Benjamin J. Stein, is an excerpt from one of the most evocative recent accounts of youthful ignorance.

I spend a lot of time with teenagers. Besides employing three of them part-time, I frequently conduct focus groups at Los Angeles area high schools to learn about teenagers' attitudes towards movies or television shows or nuclear arms or politicians. . . .

I have not yet found one single student in Los Angeles, in either college or high school, who could tell me the years when World War II was fought. Nor have I found one who could tell me the years when World War I was fought. Nor have I found one who knew when the American Civil War was fought. . . .

A few have known how many U.S. senators California has, but none has known how many Nevada or Oregon has. ("Really? Even though they're so small?") . . . Only two could tell me where Chicago is, even in the vaguest terms. (My particular favorite geography lesson was the junior at the University of California at Los Angeles who thought that Toronto must be in Italy. My second-favorite geography lesson is the junior at USC, a pre-law student, who thought that Washington, D.C. was in Washington State.) . . .

Only two could even approximately identify Thomas Jefferson. Only one could place the date of the Declaration of Independence. None could name even one of the first ten amendments to the Constitution or connect them with the Bill of Rights. . . .

On and on it went. On and on it goes. I have mixed up episodes of ignorance of facts with ignorance of concepts because it seems to me that there is a connection. . . . The kids I saw (and there may be lots of others who are different) are not mentally prepared to continue the society because they basically do not understand the society well enough to value it.

My son assures me that his pupils are not ignorant. They know a great deal. 4 Like every other human group they share a tremendous amount of knowledge among themselves, much of it learned in school. The trouble is that, from the standpoint of their literacy and their ability to communicate with others in our culture, what they know is ephemeral and narrowly confined to their own generation. Many young people strikingly lack the information that writers of American books and newspapers have traditionally taken for granted among their readers from all generations. For reasons explained in this book, our children's lack of intergenerational information is a serious problem for the nation. The decline of literacy and the decline of shared knowledge are closely related, interdependent facts.

The evidence for the decline of shared knowledge is not just anecdotal. In 5 1978 NAEP [National Assessment of Educational Progress] issued a report which analyzed a large quantity of data showing that our children's knowledge of American civics had dropped significantly between 1969 and 1976. The performance of thirteen-year-olds had dropped an alarming 11 percentage points. That the drop has continued since 1976 was confirmed by preliminary results from a NAEP study conducted in late 1985. It was undertaken both because of concern about declining knowledge and because of the growing evidence of a causal connection between the drop in shared information and in literacy. The Foundations of Literacy project is measuring some of the specific information about history and literature that American seventeen-year-olds possess.

Although the full report will not be published until 1987, the preliminary field 6 tests are disturbing. If these samplings hold up, and there is no reason to think they will not, then the results we will be reading in 1987 will show that two thirds of our seventeen-year-olds do not know that the Civil War occurred between 1850 and 1900. Three quarters do not know what *reconstruction* means. Half do not know the meaning of the *Brown decision* and cannot identify either Stalin or Churchill. Three quarters are unfamiliar with the names of standard American and British authors. Moreover, our seventeen-year-olds have little sense of geography or the relative chronology of major events. Reports of youthful ignorance can no longer be considered merely impressionistic.

My encounter in the seventies with this widening knowledge gap first caused 7 me to recognize the connection between specific background knowledge and mature literacy. The research I was doing on the reading and writing abilities of college students made me realize two things. First, we cannot assume that young people today know things that were known in the past by almost every literate person in the culture. For instance, in one experiment conducted in Richmond, Virginia, our seventeen- and eighteen-year-old subjects did not know who Grant and Lee were. Second, our results caused me to realize that we cannot treat reading and writing as empty skills, independent of specific knowledge. The reading skill of a person may vary greatly from task to task. The level of literacy exhibited in each task depends on the relevant background information that the person possesses.

◦   ◦   ◦

The Decline of Teaching Cultural Literacy

Why have our schools failed to fulfill their fundamental acculturative responsibil-   8
ity? In view of the immense importance of cultural literacy for speaking, listening, reading, and writing, why has the need for a definite, shared body of information been so rarely mentioned in discussions of education? In the educational writings of the past decade, I find almost nothing on this topic, which is not arcane. People who are introduced to the subject quickly understand why oral or written communication requires a lot of shared background knowledge. It's not the difficulty or novelty of the idea that has caused it to receive so little attention.

Let me hazard a guess about one reason for our neglect of the subject. We   9
have ignored cultural literacy in thinking about education—certainly I as a researcher also ignored it until recently—precisely because it was something we have been able to take for granted. We ignore the air we breathe until it is thin or foul. Cultural literacy is the oxygen of social intercourse. Only when we run into cultural illiteracy are we shocked into recognizing the importance of the information that we had unconsciously assumed.

To be sure, a minimal level of information is possessed by any normal person   10
who lives in the United States and speaks elementary English. Almost everybody knows what is meant by *dollar* and that cars must travel on the right-hand side of the road. But this elementary level of information is not sufficient for a modern democracy. It isn't sufficient to read newspapers (a sin against Jeffersonian democracy), and it isn't sufficient to achieve economic fairness and high productivity. Cultural literacy lies *above* the everyday levels of knowledge that everyone possesses and *below* the expert level known only to specialists. It is that middle ground of cultural knowledge possessed by the "common reader." It includes information that we have traditionally expected our children to receive in school, but which they no longer do.

During recent decades Americans have hesitated to make a decision about the   11
specific knowledge that children need to learn in school. Our elementary schools are not only dominated by the content-neutral ideas of Rousseau and Dewey, they are also governed by approximately sixteen thousand independent school districts. We have viewed this dispersion of educational authority as an insurmountable obstacle to altering the fragmentation of the school curriculum even when we have questioned that fragmentation. We have permitted school policies that have shrunk the body of information that Americans share, and these policies have caused our national literacy to decline.

At the same time we have searched with some eagerness for causes such as   12
television that lie outside the schools. But we should direct our attention undeviat-

ingly toward what the schools teach rather than toward family structure, social class, or TV programming. No doubt, reforms outside the schools are important, but they are harder to accomplish. Moreover, we have accumulated a great deal of evidence that faulty policy in the schools is the chief cause of deficient literacy. Researchers who have studied the factors influencing educational outcomes have found that the school curriculum is the most important controllable influence on what our children know and don't know about our literate culture.

It will not do to blame television for the state of our literacy. Television watch-   13
ing does reduce reading and often encroaches on homework. Much of it is admittedly the intellectual equivalent of junk food. But in some respects, such as its use of standard written English, television watching is acculturative. Moreover, as Herbert Walberg points out, the schools themselves must be held partly responsible for excessive television watching, because they have not firmly insisted that students complete significant amounts of homework, an obvious way to increase time spent on reading and writing. Nor should our schools be excused by an appeal to the effects of the decline of the family or the vicious circle of poverty, important as these factors are. Schools have, or should have, children for six or seven hours a day, five days a week, nine months a year, for thirteen years or more. To assert that they are powerless to make a significant impact on what their students learn would be to make a claim about American education that few parents, teachers, or students would find it easy to accept.

Just how fragmented the American public school curriculum has become is   14
described in *The Shopping Mall High School*, a report on five years of firsthand study inside public and private secondary schools. The authors report that our high schools offer courses of so many kinds that "the word 'curriculum' does not do justice to this astonishing variety." The offerings include not only academic courses of great diversity, but also courses in sports and hobbies and a "services curriculum" addressing emotional or social problems. All these courses are deemed "educationally valid" and carry course credit. Moreover, among academic offerings are numerous versions of each subject, corresponding to different levels of student interest and ability. Needless to say, the material covered in these "content area" courses is highly varied.

Cafeteria-style education, combined with the unwillingness of our schools to   15
place demands on students, has resulted in a steady diminishment of commonly shared information between generations and between young people themselves. Those who graduate from the same school have often studied different subjects, and those who graduate from different schools have often studied different material even when their courses have carried the same titles. The inevitable consequence of the shopping mall high school is a lack of shared knowledge across and within schools. It would be hard to invent a more effective recipe for cultural fragmentation.

The formalistic educational theory behind the shopping mall school (the the-   16
ory that any suitable content will inculcate reading, writing, and thinking skills) has had certain political advantages for school administrators. It has allowed them to stay scrupulously neutral with regard to content. Educational formalism enables them to regard the indiscriminate variety of school offerings as a positive virtue, on

the grounds that such variety can accommodate the different interests and abilities of different students. Educational formalism has also conveniently allowed school administrators to meet objections to the traditional literate materials that used to be taught in the schools. Objectors have said that traditional materials are class-bound, white, Anglo-Saxon, and Protestant, not to mention racist, sexist, and excessively Western. Our schools have tried to offer enough diversity to meet these objections from liberals and enough Shakespeare to satisfy conservatives. Caught between ideological parties, the schools have been attracted irresistibly to a quantitative and formal approach to curriculum making rather than one based on sound judgments about what should be taught.

Some have objected that teaching the traditional literate culture means teaching conservative material. Orlando Patterson answered that objection when he pointed out that mainstream culture is not the province of any single social group and is constantly changing by assimilating new elements and expelling old ones. Although mainstream culture is tied to the written word and may therefore seem more formal and elitist than other elements of culture, that is an illusion. Literate culture is the most democratic culture in our land: it excludes nobody; it cuts across generations and social groups and classes; it is not usually one's first culture, but it should be everyone's second, existing as it does beyond the narrow spheres of family, neighborhood, and region.   17

Rhetorical Focus

1. Hirsch's thesis is clear enough. Do you think his evidence supports his point, is it conclusive enough? If you disagree, what other kinds of evidence would he have to present to convince you?
2. Hirsch begins his second section with a simple question which he then answers. Briefly describe his train of thought in dealing with the failure of schools.
3. Describe the last sentence in this essay. How has Hirsch put it together? Try to imitate the pattern with an original sentence of your own.

Thematic Focus

1. Does Hirsch equate knowing how to read with information about culture? Do you agree that your friends and classmates are culturally uninformed?
2. Do you agree with Hirsch that traditional culture is neutral, without a specific political point of view?
3. If everyone in your class read a particular novel, would that increase understanding in the class? Expand on what some possible results might be.

The following excerpted lists from *Cultural Literacy* is entitled, "What Literate Americans Know: A Preliminary List." Do you know everything on this list? Are there omissions that seem serious? What about the very idea of such a list? What could be said for and against it?

lemmings to the sea
lend lease
Lenin
Leningrad
lens
Lent
Leonardo da Vinci
leopard doesn't change its spots, A
leprechaun
leprosy
lesbian
Let bygones be bygones.
Let sleeping dogs lie.
Letter from the Birmingham Jail (title)
let the cat out of the bag
Levant, the
Lewis, Sinclair
Lewis and Clark expedition
Lexington, Battle of
Leyden jar
liaison
libel
liberal
liberal arts
liberalism
Liberty, Statue of
Liberty Bell
libido
Library of Congress
Libya
lien
lightning (electricity)
lightning rod
light year
Lilliputian
Lima
Limbo
limerick
limestone
Lincoln, Abraham
Lincoln–Douglas debates
Lincoln Memorial
Lincoln's Second Inaugural Address
    (title)
Lindbergh, Charles A.
linear momentum
Linnaeus
Lippmann, Walter
lip service
liquid asset

liquidation
liquidity
Lisbon
list price
Liszt, Franz
litany
literati
litmus test
Little Big Horn
Little Bo-Peep (text)
Little Boy Blue (text)
Little Jack Horner (text)
little learning is a dangerous thing, A
Little Miss Muffet (text)
Little pitchers have big ears.
Little Red Hen, The (title)
Little Red Riding Hood (title)
Little Rock, Arkansas
Little strokes fell great oaks.
Little Women (title)
Live and learn.
Live and let live.
liver (detoxification)
tariff
tar with the same brush
Tarzan
Tasmania
taste bud
tax-deductible
tax loophole
taxonomic classification
tax shelter
Tchaikovsky
Teapot Dome
technological unemployment
technology
Tecumseh
teenybopper
Teflon-coated
Teheran
Tel Aviv
telemetry
telepathy
telephoto
telescope
Tell, William
Teller, Edward
tell tales out of school
Tempest, The (title)
tempest in a teapot

temple	Thames River
tempo	Thatcher, Margaret
tenant farming	theme
Ten Commandments	therapy
tenderfoot	There are lots of fish in the sea.
Tennessee	There is a tide in the affairs of men (text)
Tennessee River	There is a time to be born and a time to die.
Tennessee Valley Authority (TVA)	
Tennyson, Alfred Lord	There is no joy in Mudville.
tenor (music)	There is no new thing under the sun.
tense (grammar)	There's more than one way to skin a cat.
tenure	There's no fool like an old fool.
terra firma	There's no place like home.
testes	There was an old woman who lived in a shoe (text)
testosterone	
tetanus	thermal equilibrium
tête-a-tête	thermal pollution
Tet offensive	thermodynamics
Texas	thermonuclear
Thailand	thermostat
thalidomide	These are the times that try men's souls.

Cult-Lit

Barbara Herrnstein Smith

Barbara Herrnstein Smith is a professor of English at Duke University, where she teaches literary theory and aesthetics. She was born in New York City in 1932 and received her Ph.D. at Brandeis. She taught for a number of years at the University of Pennsylvania. The following excerpt appeared in the *South Atlantic Quarterly.* Smith is concerned that the "vague and muddled" models of educational reform promoted by conservatives such as Hirsch and Bloom will do more harm than good. She does not want a national culture and thinks Hirsch is naïve to hope that a common vocabulary will solve our social problems, breaking the "cycle of illiteracy for deprived children" and

"Cut-Lit" by Barbara Herrnstein Smith, *The South Atlantic Quarterly,* Winter 1990, Vol. 89, Number 1. Published by Duke University Press. Reprinted by permission.

"enabling all citizens to participate in the political process." The solution is much more complex, involving substantial political, financial, and educational resources.

Reflections Before Reading

Smith strongly objects to Hirsch's ideas. Based on the brief notes about her, can you anticipate some of her objections? If you were to create a list of information students should have, how would you proceed? What would happen if all students knew everything on Hirsch's list?

It should be a matter of some concern, I think, that the current movement for 1 educational reform duplicates so many of the perennial (indeed classic) themes of apocalyptic cultural criticism: most obviously, of course, the recurrent images of a civilization in decline (the young corrupted, the masses stupefied, barbarians at the gates of the *polis*), but also the nostalgic invocations of an allegedly once "whole" but now "fragmented" community (lost shared values, lost shared knowledge, lost shared attitudes, and so forth), where historical as well as contemporary diversities are, in one stroke, both forgotten and wishfully obliterated.

The force of this general concern will be apparent in my remarks, but I mean 2 to focus specifically on E. D. Hirsch's book, *Cultural Literacy*, and I don't mean to mince words. I believe that the immediate objective it proposes—that is, the ac- quisition, by every American child, of the alleged "common," "traditional," infor- mation, attitudes, and values shared by all literate Americans or, as Hirsch also refers to it, *"the* national culture"—is meaningless as stated and if not meaningless then, given what it evidently means to Hirsch, undesirable; that such an objective, if it were desirable, could not be achieved by the pedagogic methods it proposes; and that, if it were actually adopted on a national scale (as is clearly Hirsch's serious and now institutionalized intention), the pursuit of that objective by those meth- ods—that is, the attempt to equip every child in the country with a putatively finite, determinate, measurable store of basic "American knowledge" in the form of standard definitions or "sets of associations" attached to disarticulated terms and phrases—would not only *not* alleviate the conditions it is supposedly designed to cure (among them, widespread illiteracy and a cycle of economic deprivation, so- cial marginalization, and political ineffectuality), but would postpone even longer adequate analyses of, and appropriate responses to, those and other problems of the nation's schools.

I will amplify these points by examining several key passages in *Cultural Lit-* 3 *eracy,* beginning with the one, early in the book, in which Hirsch introduces the notion of a "national culture" and sets up his argument for a uniform national school curriculum based on his now-famous List.

The failure of our schools, Hirsch tells us, can be attributed to the educational 4 theories of Rousseau, Dewey, and "their present-day disciples." In contrast to these, he writes, his own "anthropological" theory of education deems it neither wrong nor unnatural to teach young children adult information before they fully understand it. The anthropological view stresses the universal fact that a human group must have effective communications to function effectively, that effective communications require shared culture, and that shared culture requires transmission of specific information to children.

Each link in this argument bears scrutiny, as does also the nature of the logical/ rhetorical syntax by which they are joined.

To begin with, the term "human group" is vague and, as Hirsch uses it here,   5
slippery. The statement containing the phrase—that is, "a human group must have effective communications to function effectively"—makes sense when we think of a relatively small group of mutually interacting people, such as a family, a company of co-workers, or, given the quasi-anthropological auspices, a tribal community. A *nation,* however, and particularly what Hirsch refers to repeatedly as "a modern industrial nation," is not a "human group" in that sense; and, although his subsequent allusions to "our national community" manage to evoke, under the sign of scientific precision, a questionable (and, as will be seen, otherwise disturbing) nationalist communitarianism, the phrase is clearly question-begging here and the concept has no anthropological or other scientific credentials whatsoever.

The existence of an American "national culture" is by no means self-evident.   6
Every citizen of this nation belongs to numerous communities (regional, ethnic, religious, occupational, etc.) and shares different sets of beliefs, interests, assumptions, attitudes, and practices—and, in that sense, cultures—with the other members of each of those communities. There is, however, no single, comprehensive macroculture in which all or even most of the citizens of this nation actually participate, no numerically preponderant majority culture in relation to which any or all of the others are "minority" cultures, and no culture that, in Hirsch's term, "transcends" any or all other cultures. Nor do these multiplicities describe a condition of cultural "fragmentation" except by implicit contrast to some presumed prior condition of cultural unity and uniformity—a condition that could obtain only among the members of a relatively isolated, demographically homogeneous and stable community, and has never obtained in this nation at any time in its history.

The invocation of *transcendence* noted above is justified in the book by an   7
illegitimate analogy between language and culture: indeed, doubly illegitimate, for not only are cultures not like languages in the way Hirsch implies (that is, sets of discrete items of "information" analogous to "vocabulary" lists), but languages themselves are not the way he describes them and requires them to be for the analogies in question. Just as every national language, Hirsch writes, "*transcends* any particular dialect, region, or social class," so also does the "national culture." There is, however, no "national language," either in the United States or anywhere else, that all or most of the inhabitants of a nation speak *over and above* various regional and other (ethnic, class, etc.) dialects. There are only *particular* regional and other dialects, some—or one—of which may be privileged over and above all others in the state educational system and/or by various cultural agencies. An analogy from language to culture, then, would support a view of the latter quite different from that urged by Hirsch. Indeed, as his critics observe, what he refers to as

"*the* national culture," and exemplifies by his List, is nothing but a *particular* (egregiously classbound and otherwise parochial) set of items of "knowledge" that Hirsch himself privileges and that he *wants* the state educational system to make "standard." (His recurrent reply to this observation is to dismiss it as "ideological," in presumed contrast to his own beliefs and proposals.)

Hirsch puts the culture/language analogy to other, remarkable uses. "[F]ixing   8 the vocabulary of a national culture," he writes, "is analogous to fixing a standard grammar, spelling, and pronunciation"; and, he claims, Americans "need to learn not just the associations of such words as *to run* but also the associations of such terms as *Teddy Roosevelt, DNA,* and *Hamlet.*" Indeed, he assures us, if children can all learn the associations of common words such as *to run,* there is no reason why they cannot all learn the associations of *Teddy Roosevelt, DNA,* and *Hamlet.* To speak of the "vocabulary" of a culture, however, is to presuppose the altogether Hirsch-generated culture/language analogy and thus, as usual, to beg the question. (It is because Hirsch characteristically presupposes the key points of his arguments—either as self-evident or as already proved by his mere statement of them—that question-begging formulations are so recurrent in *Cultural Literacy.*) Moreover, the dubiousness—and, in fact, absurdity—of the analogy becomes increasingly apparent from the very use he makes of it. Can we really speak of "*the* associations" of *Teddy Roosevelt, DNA,* and *Hamlet* or, to choose some other items from Hirsch's List, of *Woodie Guthrie* or *Harlem?* Are there "standard associations" and, as he also claims, "traditional values" already in existence for such items, and are they really shared by all literate Americans? Or, if they are not already in existence (Hirsch is equivocal on the point), could associations and values for such items be "fixed" or "standardized" so that they really would be *independent,* as he implies, of the specific personal histories of whoever was doing the sharing and associating and valuing? And, if we really managed to teach children from Houston, Boston, Alaska, and Nebraska to memorize and recite standard associations and values for *Teddy Roosevelt, Woodie Guthrie, Hamlet, Harlem, DNA,* and five thousand other terms, do we really suppose that the "human group" constituted by the citizens of this country would have acquired a "shared culture," and would only then "have effective communications," and would only thereby and thereupon "function effectively"? What *are* we talking about?

Hirsch's claim that "effective communications require shared culture" is, in   9 fact, false. For, given any sense of the term "culture" relevant to the passage under discussion—that is, either (a) as anthropologists would define it, the system of beliefs, skills, routine practices, and communal institutions shared by the members of some society as such, or (b) as Hirsch implies, familiarity with a list of academic set-phrases and vintage items of middle-class cultural lore—then it is a "universal fact" that people can communicate *without* a "shared culture" and that they do it all the time. Japanese suppliers, for example (a group whose presence hovers over the pages of *Cultural Literacy*), communicate with European and African buyers without sharing the latter's cultures in the anthropological sense; and, just to speak of other Americans, I communicate quite effectively with my eighty-five-year-old ex-mother-in-law from Altoona, Pennsylvania, my twenty-five-year-old hairdresser from Hillsborough, North Carolina, my five-year-old grandson from Brooklyn,

New York, and my *cat*, without sharing much, if anything, of what Hirsch calls "the shared national culture" with any of them. The reason I can do so is that all the activities that Hirsch classifies as "communication" and sees as *duplicative transmissions* that presuppose *sameness*—"common" knowledge, "shared" culture, "standardized" associations—are, in fact, always *ad hoc*, context-specific, pragmatically adjusted negotiations of (and through) *difference*. We never have sameness; we cannot produce sameness; we do not need sameness.

°   °   °

What literate Americans know. What every American needs to know. So Hirsch   10
claims for his List, and so Americans in the hundreds of thousands may now be inclined to believe. The force of the claim is equivocal, however, and hedged throughout the book. Hirsch states, for example, that the appendix to *Cultural Literacy* is not meant to be "prescriptive" but is only "a *descriptive* list of the information actually possessed by literate Americans," forgetting the book's subtitle and his recurrent imperatives concerning the centrality of the List to the educational reforms he is proposing. The continuous eliding of the prescriptive/descriptive distinction is significant because it permits Hirsch to evade the responsibilities of each kind of claim by moving to the other when criticisms are pressed. Thus, if the List's claims to descriptive adequacy and accuracy are questioned (is it really what literate Americans—*all* of them?—"actually" know?), Hirsch can claim to be offering only provisional recommendations and "guideposts"; conversely, when objections are raised to the manifestly patrician, self-privileging norms promoted by the List, Hirsch can claim that it has nothing to do with what *he* knows or thinks should be known, but simply describes the way things are among "literate Americans."

The method by which the List was generated is, in any case, exceedingly mys-   11
terious. According to Hirsch, it is not "a complete catalogue of American knowledge," but "is intended to illustrate the character and range of the knowledge literate Americans tend to share" and to "establish guideposts that can be of practical use to teachers, students, and all others who need to know our literate culture" (which is, of course, according to Hirsch, "every American"). But, one might ask (granting the double absurdity of a specifically "*American* knowledge" and a possible catalog of *any* actual human knowledge), what sorts of persons *are* the "literate Americans" whose knowledge is illustrated or represented by the List? How, for example, could one distinguish them from Americans who merely know how to read? And how does Hirsch himself know what "the literate reader" knows?

The answers to these questions cannot be determined from any explicit state-   12
ments of procedure in the book. Indeed, the accounts of the List given by way of introduction and explanation could hardly be briefer or vaguer. Hirsch notes that "different literate Americans have slightly *[sic]* different conceptions of our shared knowledge," but assures his readers that "more than one hundred consultants reported agreement on over 90 percent of the items listed." Wonderful: more than one hundred, over 90 percent. But agreement on *what?* Was each "consultant" asked to compile an individual list and then all the lists compared for overlap? Or, quite differently, were the consultants asked, for each item on an already compiled list, to say whether they were themselves familiar with it? Or, again, and again

quite differently, were the consultants asked, for each item, whether they agreed that every "literate American" (however defined for them—if at all) *knew* it—or, and also quite differently, whether they thought every literate American *should* know it? Nor does Hirsch indicate how the consultants themselves were chosen. At random from the Charlottesville telephone directory? From among his classiest friends, best students, and most congenial colleagues at the University of Virginia? Were they, by any chance, selected to be representative of various regions of the nation, and a range of ages, occupations, and degrees of formal education? Were they chosen, in fact, by any consistent and appropriate sampling principle?

The questions raised here are important because, depending on the specific   13 procedures and selection criteria used, very different lists would have been produced. Moreover, without consistent and appropriate procedures and criteria, the claims of representativeness (not to mention implications of unbiased, statistical authority) made for Hirsch's List—copies of which are now being delivered by the truckful to teachers and children across the nation—might seem, relative to the standards of responsible social science research, dubious. But never mind all that: like the old Ivory Soap ads, *99 and 44/100 percent pure—it floats!*

Rhetorical Focus

1. In the second paragraph, Herrnstein Smith wants to be clear and direct in stating her opposition to Hirsch. Is she? Paraphrase her point as simply as you can.
2. Herrnstein Smith does not present the usual factual evidence to refute Hirsch. Instead she uses logic and what she calls "close" analytical reading. Briefly explain some of her objections to Hirsch's words in paragraph 3.
3. Herrnstein Smith chooses to conclude this phase of her argument with a rather indirect analogy. Do you like it? What is the point she is trying to make?

Thematic Focus

1. Herrnstein Smith does not seem surprised by the enthusiasm generated by Hirsch's lists. Why?
2. Herrnstein Smith objects to Hirsch's project on several grounds. Which of her arguments seemed the most cogent?
3. Herrnstein Smith says we do not need sameness. What does she mean, and do you agree?

The Context of Literacy

Mike Rose

Mike Rose was born to Italian immigrant parents and grew up in a poor Los Angeles neighborhood. Due to his own experiences as a disadvantaged so-called problem student, Rose has made the education of such students his specific mission. He is now associate director of UCLA Writing Programs, where he works with educationally underprivileged children and adults. In this excerpt from his book *Lives on the Boundary,* Rose considers the issue of canonicity. He acknowledges the value of classic texts, but he objects to the arguments of theorists such as Hirsch and Bloom, claiming that by focusing on the hypothetical social unity to be found in a shared body of knowledge, these canonists deflect attention from the serious problems—economic, social, and political—that lie at the root of what is, it appears, wide disparities among the classes in America today.

Reflections Before Reading

Were there different tracks at your high school, such as one for the college bound and another called "vocational?" What do you remember about that arrangement? Rose writes mostly about working-class neighborhoods. Do you think different neighborhoods have differing values about education? Explain.

There is a strong impulse in American education—curious in a country with such an ornery streak of antitraditionalism—to define achievement and excellence in terms of the acquisition of a historically validated body of knowledge, an authoritative list of books and allusions, a canon. We seek a certification of our national intelligence, indeed, our national virtue, in how diligently our children can display this central corpus of information. This need for certification tends to emerge most dramatically in our educational policy debates during times of real or imagined threat: economic hard times, political crises, sudden increases in immigration. Now is such a time, and it is reflected in a number of influential books and commission reports. E. D. Hirsch argues that a core national vocabulary, one oriented toward the English literate tradition—Alice in Wonderland to zeitgeist—will build a knowledge base that will foster the literacy of all Americans. Diane Ravitch and Chester Finn call for a return to a traditional historical and literary curriculum: the valorous historical figures and the classical literature of the once-elite course of study. Allan Bloom, Secretary of Education William Bennett, Mortimer Adler and the Paideia Group, and a number of others have affirmed, each in their very different ways, the necessity of the Great Books: Plato and Aristotle and Sophocles; Dante and Shakespeare and Locke, Dickens and Mann and Faulkner. We can call this orientation to educational achievement the canonical orientation.

At times in our past, the call for a shoring up of or return to a canonical curric-   2
ulum was explicitly elitist, was driven by a fear that the education of the select was being compromised. Today, though, the majority of the calls are provocatively framed in the language of democracy. They assail the mediocre and grinding curriculum frequently found in remedial and vocational education. They are disdainful of the patronizing perceptions of student ability that further restrict the already restricted academic life of disadvantaged youngsters. They point out that the canon—its language, conventions, and allusions—is central to the discourse of power, and to keep it from poor kids is to assure their disenfranchisement all the more. The books of the canon, claim the proposals, the Great Books, are a window onto a common core of experience and civic ideals. There is, then, a spiritual, civic, and cognitive heritage here, and *all* our children should receive it. If we are sincere in our desire to bring Mario, Chin, the younger versions of Caroline, current incarnations of Frank Marell, and so many others who populate this book—if we truly want to bring them into our society—then we should provide them with this stable and common core. This is a forceful call. It promises a still center in a turning world.

I see great value in being challenged to think of the curriculum of the many in   3
the terms we have traditionally reserved for the few; it is refreshing to have common assumptions about the capacities of underprepared students so boldly challenged. Many of the people we have encountered in these pages have displayed the ability to engage books and ideas thought to be beyond their grasp. There were the veterans: Willie Oates writing, in prison, ornate sentences drawn from *The Mill on the Floss.* Sergeant Gonzalez coming to understand poetic ambiguity in "Butch Weldy." There was the parole aide Olga who no longer felt walled off from *Macbeth.* There were the EOP students at UCLA, like Lucia who unpackaged *The Myth of Mental Illness* once she had an orientation and overview. And there was Frank Marell who, later in his life, would be talking excitedly to his nephew about this guy Edgar Allan Poe. Too many people are kept from the books of the canon, the Great Books, because of misjudgments about their potential. Those books eventually proved important to me, and, as best I know how, I invite my students to engage them. But once we grant the desirability of equal curricular treatment and begin to consider what this equally distributed curriculum would contain, problems arise: If the canon itself is the answer to our educational inequities, why has it historically invited few and denied many? Would the canonical orientation provide adequate guidance as to how a democratic curriculum should be constructed and how it should be taught? Would it guide us in opening up to Olga that "fancy talk" that so alienated her?

Those who study the way literature becomes canonized, how linguistic creations are included or excluded from a tradition, claim that the canonical curriculum students would most likely receive would not, as is claimed, offer a common core of American experience. Caroline would not find her life represented in it, nor would Mario. The canon has tended to push to the margin much of the literature of our nation: from American Indian songs and chants to immigrant fiction to working-class narratives. The institutional messages that students receive in the books they're issued and the classes they take are powerful and, as I've witnessed since my Voc. Ed. days, quickly internalized. And to revise these messages and redress past wrongs would involve more than adding some new books to the existing canon—the very reasons for linguistic and cultural exclusion would have to become a focus of study in order to make the canon act as a democratizing force. Unless this happens, the democratic intent of the reformers will be undercut by the content of the curriculum they propose.

And if we move beyond content to consider basic assumptions about teaching and learning, a further problem arises, one that involves the very nature of the canonical orientation itself. The canonical orientation encourages a narrowing of focus from learning to that which must be learned: It simplifies the dynamic tension between student and text and reduces the psychological and social dimensions of instruction. The student's personal history recedes as the what of the classroom is valorized over the how. Thus it is that the encounter of student and text is often portrayed by canonists as a transmission. Information, wisdom, virtue will pass from the book to the student if the student gives the book the time it merits, carefully traces its argument or narrative or lyrical progression. Intellectual, even spiritual, growth will *necessarily* result from an encounter with Roman mythology, *Othello,* and "I heard a Fly buzz—when I died—," with biographies and historical sagas and patriotic lore. Learning is stripped of confusion and discord. It is stripped, as well, of strong human connection. My own initiators to the canon— Jack MacFarland, Dr. Carothers, and the rest—knew there was more to their work than their mastery of a tradition. What mattered most, I see now, were the relationships they established with me, the guidance they provided when I felt inadequate or threatened. This mentoring was part of my entry into that solemn library of Western thought—and even with such support, there were still times of confusion, anger, and fear. It is telling, I think, that once that rich social network slid away, once I was in graduate school in intense, solitary encounter with that tradition, I abandoned it for other sources of nurturance and knowledge.

The model of learning implicit in the canonical orientation seems, at times, more religious than cognitive or social: Truth resides in the printed texts, and if they are presented by someone who knows them well and respects them, that truth will be revealed. Of all the advocates of the canon, Mortimer Adler has given most attention to pedagogy—and his Paideia books contain valuable discussions of instruction, coaching, and questioning. But even here, and this is doubly true in the other manifestos, there is little acknowledgment that the material in the canon can be not only difficult but foreign, alienating, overwhelming.

We need an orientation to instruction that provides guidance on how to determine and honor the beliefs and stories, enthusiasms, and apprehensions that students reveal. How to build on them, and when they clash with our curriculum—as I saw so often in the Tutorial Center at UCLA—when they clash, how to encourage a discussion that will lead to reflection on what students bring and what they're currently confronting. Canonical lists imply canonical answers, but the manifestos offer little discussion of what to do when students fail. If students have been exposed to at least some elements of the canon before—as many have—why didn't it take? If they're encountering it for the first time and they're lost, how can we determine where they're located—and what do we do then?

Each member of a teacher's class, poor *or* advantaged, gives rise to endless decisions, day-to-day determinations about a child's reading and writing: decisions on how to tap strength, plumb confusion, foster growth. The richer your conception of learning and your understanding of its social and psychological dimensions, the more insightful and effective your judgments will be. Consider the sources of literacy we saw among the children in El Monte: shopkeepers' signs, song lyrics, auto manuals, the conventions of the Western, family stories and tales, and more. Consider Chin's sources—television and *People* magazine—and Caroline's oddly generative mix of the Bible and an American media illusion. Then there's the jarring confluence of personal horror and pop cultural flotsam that surfaces in Mario's drawings, drawings that would be a rich, if volatile, point of departure for language instruction. How would these myriad sources and manifestations be perceived and evaluated if viewed within the framework of a canonical tradition, and what guidance would the tradition provide on how to understand and develop them? The great books and central texts of the canon could quickly become a benchmark against which the expressions of student literacy would be negatively measured, a limiting band of excellence that, ironically, could have a dispiriting effect on the very thing the current proposals intend: the fostering of mass literacy. 8

To understand the nature and development of literacy we need to consider the social context in which it occurs—the political, economic, and cultural forces that encourage or inhibit it. The canonical orientation discourages deep analysis of the way these forces may be affecting performance. The canonists ask that schools transmit a coherent traditional knowledge to an ever-changing, frequently uprooted community. This discordance between message and audience is seldom examined. Although a ghetto child can rise on the lilt of a Homeric line—books *can* spark dreams—appeals to elevated texts can also divert attention from the conditions that keep a population from realizing its dreams. The literacy curriculum is being asked to do what our politics and our economics have failed to do: diminish differences in achievement, narrow our gaps, bring us together. Instead of analysis of the complex web of causes of poor performance, we are offered a faith in the unifying power of a body of knowledge, whose infusion will bring the rich and the poor, the longtime disaffected and the uprooted newcomers into cultural unanimity. If this vision is democratic, it is simplistically so, reductive, not an invitation for people truly to engage each other at the point where cultures and classes intersect. 9

I worry about the effects a canonical approach to education could have on cultural dialogue and transaction—on the involvement of an abandoned underclass and on the movement of immigrants like Mario and Chin into our nation. A 10 canonical uniformity promotes rigor and quality control; it can also squelch new thinking, diffuse the generative tension between the old and the new. It is significant that the canonical orientation is voiced with most force during times of challenge and uncertainty, for it promises the authority of tradition, the seeming stability of the past. But the authority is fictive, gained from a misreading of American cultural history. No period of that history was harmoniously stable; the invocation of a golden age is a mythologizing act. Democratic culture is, by definition, vibrant and dynamic, discomforting and unpredictable. It gives rise to apprehension; freedom is not always calming. And, yes, it can yield fragmentation, though often as not the source of fragmentation is intolerant misunderstanding of diverse traditions rather than the desire of members of those traditions to remain hermetically separate. A truly democratic vision of knowledge and social structure would honor this complexity. The vision might not be soothing, but it would provide guidance as to how to live and teach in a country made up of many cultural traditions.

We are in the middle of an extraordinary social experiment: the attempt to provide education for all members of a vast pluralistic democracy. To have any prayer of success, we'll need many conceptual blessings: A philosophy of language and literacy that affirms the diverse sources of linguistic competence and deepens our understanding of the ways class and culture blind us to the richness of those sources. A perspective on failure that lays open the logic of error. An orientation toward the interaction of poverty and ability that undercuts simple polarities, that enables us to see simultaneously the constraints poverty places on the play of mind and the actual mind at play within those constraints. We'll need a pedagogy that encourages us to step back and consider the threat of the standard classroom and that shows us, having stepped back, how to step forward to invite a student across the boundaries of that powerful room. Finally, we'll need a revised store of images of educational excellence, ones closer to egalitarian ideals—ones that embody the reward and turmoil of education in a democracy, that celebrate the plural, messy human reality of it. At heart, we'll need a guiding set of principles that do not encourage us to retreat from, but move us closer to, an understanding of the rich mix of speech and ritual and story that is America.

Rhetorical Focus

1. In developing his argument, Rose begins by describing the position of his opposition. Do you think he does this fairly in the first two paragraphs?
2. What specific points does Rose use to refute those who want students to study the canon at the expense of all else?
3. A good argument is supposed to end with positive solutions, with an agenda, a call to action, with alternatives. Does Rose do this effectively?

Thematic Focus

1. Has it been your experience that canonical lists imply canonical answers?
2. Although Rose sees value in the canon, he worries that it alone will not "diminish differences in achievement." Do you agree?

3. Is Rose, in his last two paragraphs, suggesting that education in America should be unpredictable, plural, and discomforting? Is this your vision of education? What would the business community think? The arts community? How about Hirsch? Herrnstein Smith?

Suggestions for Writing

1. Write a letter to E. D. Hirsch in which you first objectively summarize his position and then raise one important reservation you have about his project.
2. Write an essay in which you either agree or disagree with the cultural literacy program of E. D. Hirsch. Be sure to include the ideas of Mike Rose and Barbara Herrnstein Smith. You might also want to refer to earlier writers in this chapter.
3. You have been asked to speak before an audience of concerned parents and teachers from your former high school on the topic, "The Debate over the Canon: Where I Stand." Write a five-minute talk appropriate for this group.

Chapter
5
Gender

Gender conditioning affects every aspect of our lives; unfortunately we do not yet know enough about how men and women differ or how gender conditioning is influenced by biological or social factors. Every interaction is gendered in some way. Discussions with teachers, with classmates, with parents are directly affected by the gender of the participants. The women's movement of the past three decades has stimulated considerable research on the topic, though no clear consensus has emerged. Some researchers argue that men and women are basically alike but that obstacles have arisen that have kept women from participating fully in the range of activities available to men. Others argue that men and women are basically different but that women's different strengths and contributions have been suppressed, thus creating an imbalance in the social order. Do you think you are similar to or different from individuals of the opposite gender?

The essays included in this chapter explore the effects of gender conditioning on personality, taking into consideration the effects of social and political phenomena. The institution of the family is explored. What difference does it make, do you think, that both boys and girls, traditionally at least, have been parented by the mother? What happens to gender role identity formation when both parents share child care? What effect has male domination of institutions beyond the family had on the socialization of males and females?

Alice Walker and Patricia Hampl explore the feminine cultural imperative of beauty from different perspectives, demonstrating that age, race, and class influence gender socialization. Susan Brownmiller focuses on the ways in which such socialization has been detrimental to women's development. Noel Perrin and Nicholas Bromell explore changing definitions of masculinity as a result of the women's movement. Nancy Chodorow, Deborah Tannen, and Francine du Plessix Gray focus on gender differences within different contexts, Chodorow focusing on

282

psychological development, Tannen on speech, and du Plessix Gray on socialization patterns in the Soviet Union. In the final constellation of essays, David Osborne and Barbara Neely make evident the difficulties of parenting under adverse circumstances—for a man whose wife has professional commitments that limit the amount of time she can spend with her infant and for a mother whose son is a convicted rapist. Adrienne Rich's powerful essay on motherhood concludes the chapter, giving voice not only to what has been but to what might be.

FEMININITY

Our introduction from our earliest years into gendered patterns of behavior and attitudes may be even more powerful than the influence of racial or class background. Above all, a girl, regardless of background, learns that she must be feminine, that she must be beautiful. The message encourages girls to see themselves as secondary to boys and focuses her attention on her appearance rather than on the development of her intellectual or other abilities. The concept of femininity prevails because it arises out of and contributes to the domination of males over females.

The essays in this constellation explore the theme of femininity, suggesting that the gendered expectations placed on young girls are destructive. No one is able to fully live up to the feminine ideal, and so everyone is made to feel inadequate in some way. If the gap between the ideal and the reality is great, a girl's feelings of inferiority may be extreme. Alice Walker speaks of having been crippled psychologically for a time by a physical deformity that resulted when her brother shot her in the eye with a BB gun, an act that no doubt resulted from his socialization into violent behavior patterns. Patricia Hampl speaks of beauty as a "disease." Susan Brownmiller speaks of femininity as a "romantic sentiment, a nostalgic tradition of imposed limitations." To achieve fulfillment and maturity, according to these authors, young girls must learn to resist these societal expectations. Walker, Hampl, and Brownmiller suggest that doing so is possible but extremely difficult.

Beauty: When the Other Dancer Is the Self

Alice Walker

Alice Walker was born February 9, 1944, the eighth and last child of Willie Lee and Minnie Lou Grant Walker, in Eatonton, Georgia. She attended Spelman College in Atlanta and Sarah Lawrence in New York. She has published poetry, short stories, and novels, including *In Love and Trouble: Stories of Black Women, Revolutionary Petunias and Other Poems, Meridian, You Can't Keep a Good Woman Down: Stories,* and *The Color Purple. The Color Purple* (1983) was awarded the Pulitzer Prize and the American Book Award and has been made into a popular film. She received the Lillian Smith Award (1979), a Rosenthal Award (1973), and a Guggenheim Foundation Award (1979). Her most recent novel is *The Temple of My Familiar* (1989). Walker has taught at numerous universities including Wellesley, Yale, Brandeis, and the University of California at Berkeley. Currently she runs a publishing company, Wild Trees Press. "Beauty: When the Other Dancer Is the Self" was first published in *In Search of Our Mothers' Gardens: Womanist Prose.*

Reflections Before Reading

How do you define the word *beauty?* Does the word suggest a physical or a spiritual state? In what sense is the concept a gendered one? What are some connections between beauty and femininity? Are these cultural concepts imprisoning or liberating or both? Walker subtitles her essay, "When the Other Dancer Is the Self." What do you suppose she means by this phrase? What is your own conception of beauty? of femininity?

It is a bright summer day in 1947. My father, a fat, funny man with beautiful eyes   1
and a subversive wit, is trying to decide which of his eight children he will take with him to the county fair. My mother, of course, will not go. She is knocked out from getting most of us ready: I hold my neck stiff against the pressure of her knuckles as she hastily completes the braiding and then beribboning of my hair.

My father is the driver for the rich old white lady up the road. Her name is   2
Miss Mey. She owns all the land for miles around, as well as the house in which we
live. All I remember about her is that she once offered to pay my mother thirty-five
cents for cleaning her house, raking up piles of her magnolia leaves, and washing
her family's clothes, and that my mother—she of no money, eight children, and a
chronic earache—refused it. But I do not think of this in 1947. I am two and a half
years old. I want to go everywhere my daddy goes. I am excited at the prospect of
riding in a car. Someone has told me fairs are fun. That there is room in the car for
only three of us doesn't faze me at all. Whirling happily in my starchy frock, showing off my biscuit-polished patent-leather shoes and lavender socks, tossing my
head in a way that makes my ribbons bounce, I stand, hands on hips, before my
father. "Take me, Daddy," I say with assurance; "I'm the prettiest!"

Later, it does not surprise me to find myself in Miss Mey's shiny black car,   3
sharing the back seat with the other lucky ones. Does not surprise me that I thoroughly enjoy the fair. At home that night I tell the unlucky ones all I can remember
about the merry-go-round, the man who eats live chickens, and the teddy bears,
until they say: that's enough, baby Alice. Shut up now, and go to sleep.

It is Easter Sunday, 1950. I am dressed in a green, flocked, scalloped-hem   4
dress (handmade by my adoring sister, Ruth) that has its own smooth satin petti-
coat and tiny hot-pink roses tucked into each scallop. My shoes, new T-strap patent
leather, again highly biscuit-polished. I am six years old and have learned one of
the longest Easter speeches to be heard that day, totally unlike the speech I said
when I was two: "Easter lilies / pure and white / blossom in / the morning light."
When I rise to give my speech I do so on a great wave of love and pride and
expectation. People in the church stop rustling their new crinolines. They seem to
hold their breath. I can tell they admire my dress, but it is my spirit, bordering on
sassiness (womanishness), they secretly applaud.

"That girl's a little *mess*," they whisper to each other, pleased.   5

Naturally I say my speech without stammer or pause, unlike those who stutter,   6
stammer, or, worst of all, forget. This is before the word "beautiful" exists in people's vocabulary, but "Oh, isn't she the *cutest* thing!" frequently floats my way.
"And got so much sense!" they gratefully add . . . for which thoughtful addition I
thank them to this day.

It was great fun being cute. But then, one day, it ended.   7

I am eight years old and a tomboy. I have a cowboy hat, cowboy boots, check-   8
ered shirt and pants, all red. My playmates are my brothers, two and four years
older than I. Their colors are black and green, the only difference in the way we are
dressed. On Saturday nights we all go to the picture show, even my mother; Westerns are her favorite kind of movie. Back home, "on the ranch," we pretend we are
Tom Mix, Hopalong Cassidy, Lash LaRue (we've even named one of our dogs
Lash LaRue); we chase each other for hours rustling cattle, being outlaws, deliver-
ing damsels from distress. Then my parents decide to buy my brothers guns. These
are not "real" guns. They shoot "BBs," copper pellets my brothers say will kill

birds. Because I am a girl, I do not get a gun. Instantly I am relegated to the position of Indian. Now there appears a great distance between us. They shoot and shoot at everything with their new guns. I try to keep up with my bow and arrows.

One day while I am standing on top of our makeshift "garage"—pieces of tin nailed across some poles—holding my bow and arrow and looking out toward the fields, I feel an incredible blow in my right eye. I look down just in time to see my brother lower his gun.   9

Both brothers rush to my side. My eye stings, and I cover it with my hand. "If you tell," they say, "we will get a whipping. You don't want that to happen, do you?" I do not. "Here is a piece of wire," says the older brother, picking it up from the roof; "say you stepped on one end of it and the other flew up and hit you." The pain is beginning to start. "Yes," I say. "Yes, I will say that is what happened." If I do not say this is what happened, I know my brothers will find ways to make me wish I had. But now I will say anything that gets me to my mother.   10

Confronted by our parents we stick to the lie agreed upon. They place me on a bench on the porch and I close my left eye while they examine the right. There is a tree growing from underneath the porch that climbs past the railing to the roof. It is the last thing my right eye sees. I watch as its trunk, its branches, and then its leaves are blotted out by the rising blood.   11

I am in shock. First there is intense fever, which my father tries to break using lily leaves bound around my head. Then there are chills: my mother tries to get me to eat soup. Eventually, I do not know how, my parents learn what has happened. A week after the "accident" they take me to see a doctor. "Why did you wait so long to come?" he asks, looking into my eye and shaking his head. "Eyes are sympathetic," he says. "If one is blind, the other will likely become blind too."   12

This comment of the doctor's terrifies me. But it is really how I look that bothers me most. Where the BB pellet struck there is a glob of whitish scar tissue, a hideous cataract, on my eye. Now when I stare at people—a favorite pastime, up to now—they will stare back. Not at the "cute" little girl, but at her scar. For six years I do not stare at anyone, because I do not raise my head.   13

Years later, in the throes of a mid-life crisis, I ask my mother and sister whether I changed after the "accident." "No," they say, puzzled. "What do you mean?"   14

What do I mean?   15

I am eight, and, for the first time, doing poorly in school, where I have been something of a whiz since I was four. We have just moved to the place where the "accident" occurred. We do not know any of the people around us because this is a different county. The only time I see the friends I knew is when we go back to our old church. The new school is the former state penitentiary. It is a large stone building, cold and drafty, crammed to overflowing with boisterous, ill-disciplined children. On the third floor there is a huge circular imprint of some partition that has been torn out.   16

"What used to be here?" I ask a sullen girl next to me on our way past it to lunch.   17

"The electric chair," says she.   18

At night I have nightmares about the electric chair, and about all the people   19
reputedly "fried" in it. I am afraid of the school, where all the students seem to be
budding criminals.

"What's the matter with your eye?" they ask, critically.   20

When I don't answer (I cannot decide whether it was an "accident" or not),   21
they shove me, insist on a fight.

My brother, the one who created the story about the wire, comes to my res-   22
cue. But then brags so much about "protecting" me, I become sick.

After months of torture at the school, my parents decide to send me back to   23
our old community, to my old school. I live with my grandparents and the teacher
they board. But there is no room for Phoebe, my cat. By the time my grandparents
decide there *is* room, and I ask for my cat, she cannot be found. Miss Yarborough,
the boarding teacher, takes me under her wing, and begins to teach me to play the
piano. But soon she marries an African—a "prince," she says—and is whisked away
to his continent.

At my old school there is at least one teacher who loves me. She is the teacher   24
who "knew me before I was born" and bought my first baby clothes. It is she who
makes life bearable. It is her presence that finally helps me turn on the one child at
the school who continually calls me "one-eyed bitch." One day I simply grab him
by his coat and beat him until I am satisfied. It is my teacher who tells me my
mother is ill.

My mother is lying in bed in the middle of the day, something I have never   25
seen. She is in too much pain to speak. She has an abscess in her ear. I stand
looking down on her, knowing that if she dies, I cannot live. She is being treated
with warm oils and hot bricks held against her cheek. Finally a doctor comes. But I
must go back to my grandparents' house. The weeks pass but I am hardly aware of
it. All I know is that my mother might die, my father is not so jolly, my brothers still
have their guns, and I am the one sent away from home.

"You did not change," they say.   26

Did I imagine the anguish of never looking up?   27

I am twelve. When relatives come to visit I hide in my room. My cousin   28
Brenda, just my age, whose father works in the post office and whose mother is a
nurse, comes to find me. "Hello," she says. And then she asks, looking at my recent
school picture, which I did not want taken, and on which the "glob," as I think of it,
is clearly visible, "You still can't see out of that eye?"

"No," I say, and flop back on the bed over my book.   29

That night, as I do almost every night, I abuse my eye. I rant and rave at it, in   30
front of the mirror. I plead with it to clear up before morning. I tell it I hate and
despise it. I do not pray for sight. I pray for beauty.

"You did not change," they say.   31

I am fourteen and baby-sitting for my brother Bill, who lives in Boston. He is   32
my favorite brother and there is a strong bond between us. Understanding my
feelings of shame and ugliness he and his wife take me to a local hospital, where

the "glob" is removed by a doctor named O. Henry. There is still a small bluish crater where the scar tissue was, but the ugly white stuff is gone. Almost immediately I become a different person from the girl who does not raise her head. Or so I think. Now that I've raised my head I win the boyfriend of my dreams. Now that I've raised my head I have plenty of friends. Now that I've raised my head classwork comes from my lips as faultlessly as Easter speeches did, and I leave high school as valedictorian, most popular student, and *queen,* hardly believing my luck. Ironically, the girl who was voted most beautiful in our class (and was) was later shot twice through the chest by a male companion, using a "real" gun, while she was pregnant. But that's another story in itself. Or is it?

"You did not change," they say.   33

It is now thirty years since the "accident." A beautiful journalist comes to visit   34
and to interview me. She is going to write a cover story for her magazine that focuses on my latest book. "Decide how you want to look on the cover," she says. "Glamorous, or whatever."

Never mind "glamorous," it is the "whatever" that I hear. Suddenly all I can   35
think of is whether I will get enough sleep the night before the photography session: if I don't, my eye will be tired and wander, as blind eyes will.

At night in bed with my lover I think up reasons why I should not appear on   36
the cover of a magazine. "My meanest critics will say I've sold out," I say. "My family will now realize I write scandalous books."

"But what's the real reason you don't want to do this?" he asks.   37

"Because in all probability," I say in a rush, "my eye won't be straight."   38

"It will be straight enough," he says. Then, "Besides, I thought you'd made   39
your peace with that."

And I suddenly remember that I have.   40

I remember: 41

I am talking to my brother Jimmy, asking if he remembers anything unusual   42
about the day I was shot. He does not know I consider that day the last time my father, with his sweet home remedy of cool lily leaves, chose me, and that I suffered and raged inside because of this. "Well," he says, "all I remember is standing by the side of the highway with Daddy, trying to flag down a car. A white man stopped, but when Daddy said he needed somebody to take his little girl to the doctor, he drove off."

I remember.   43

I am in the desert for the first time. I fall totally in love with it. I am so over-   44
whelmed by its beauty, I confront for the first time, consciously, the meaning of the doctor's words years ago: "Eyes are sympathetic. If one is blind, the other will likely become blind too." I realize I have dashed about the world madly, looking at this, looking at that, storing up images against the fading of the light. *But I might have missed seeing the desert!* The shock of that possibility—and gratitude for over twenty-five years of sight—sends me literally to my knees. Poem after poem comes—which is perhaps how poets pray.

On Sight

I am so thankful I have seen
The Desert
And the creatures in the desert
And the desert Itself.

The desert has its own moon
Which I have seen
With my own eye.
There is no flag on it.

Trees of the desert have arms
All of which are always up
That is because the moon is up
The sun is up
Also the sky
The stars
Clouds
None with flags.

If there *were* flags, I doubt
the trees would point.
Would you?

But mostly, I remember this: 45
I am twenty-seven, and my baby daughter is almost three. Since her birth I   46
have worried about her discovery that her mother's eyes are different from other
people's. Will she be embarrassed? I think. What will she say? Every day she
watches a television program called "Big Blue Marble." It begins with a picture of
the earth as it appears from the moon. It is bluish, a little battered-looking, but full
of light, with whitish clouds swirling around it. Every time I see it I weep with love,
as if it is a picture of Grandma's house. One day when I am putting Rebecca down
for her nap, she suddenly focuses on my eye. Something inside me cringes, gets
ready to try to protect myself. All children are cruel about physical differences, I
know from experience, and that they don't always mean to be is another matter. I
assume Rebecca will be the same.

But no-o-o-o. She studies my face intently as we stand, her inside and me   47
outside her crib. She even holds my face maternally between her dimpled little
hands. Then, looking every bit as serious and lawyerlike as her father, she says, as if
it may just possibly have slipped my attention: "Mommy, there's a *world* in your
eye." (As in, "Don't be alarmed, or do anything crazy.") And then, gently, but with
great interest: "Mommy, where did you *get* that world in your eye?"

For the most part, the pain left then. (So what, if my brothers grew up to buy   48
even more powerful pellet guns for their sons and to carry real guns themselves. So
what, if a young "Morehouse man" once nearly fell off the steps of Trevor Arnett
Library because he thought my eyes were blue.) Crying and laughing I ran to the
bathroom, while Rebecca mumbled and sang herself off to sleep. Yes indeed, I
realized, looking into the mirror. There *was* a world in my eye. And I saw that it

was possible to love it: that in fact, for all it had taught me of shame and anger and inner vision, I *did* love it. Even to see it drifting out of orbit in boredom, or rolling up out of fatigue, not to mention floating back at attention in excitement (bearing witness, a friend has called it), deeply suitable to my personality, and even characteristic of me.

That night I dream I am dancing to Stevie Wonder's song "Always" (the name of the song is really "As," but I hear it as "Always"). As I dance, whirling and joyous, happier than I've ever been in my life, another bright-faced dancer joins me. We dance and kiss each other and hold each other through the night. The other dancer has obviously come through all right, as I have done. She is beautiful, whole and free. And she is also me.

49

Rhetorical Focus

1. Walker's subtitle suggests that the essay deals with multiple selves. How does the structure of the piece reinforce this idea?
2. Why do you think Walker uses the present tense throughout much of the essay? What effect would a shift to past tense have? Why do you think Walker disrupts chronological sequence in the essay?
3. Repetition can serve a number of different purposes in essays. What are some of the ways in which Walker uses repetition and what do you think her purpose in using it is?

Thematic Focus

1. Identify the ways in which the words *beauty* or *beautiful* are used throughout the essay. What thematic purpose does this variety serve?
2. Draw parallels between the story of the girl who was voted the most beautiful in Walker's high school class and Walker's own story. Are these stories gendered ones? If so, how?
3. What does Walker seem to be saying about the connection between self-esteem and creativity?

Beauty

Patricia Hampl

Patricia Hampl was born in St. Paul, Minnesota, in 1946. She received her education at the University of Minnesota and the University of Iowa. Her prose memoir, *A Romantic Education*, from which the essay included here is excerpted, was awarded the Houghton Mifflin Literary Fellowship in 1981. She has also published *Spillville*, a re-creation of one summer in the life of Czech composer Antonín Dvořák, and two collections of poetry. She teaches creative writing and literary studies at the University of Minnesota and is a contributor to various literary journals, including *Paris Review*, *The New Yorker*, *The New York Times Book Review*, and *American Poetry Review*. The essay included here is from "Beauty," the second section of *A Romantic Education*. The first part of the book is entitled "St Paul: The Garden," and the third "Prague: The Castle."

Reflections Before Reading

Hampl's background is quite different from Walker's. How do you think her Czechoslovakian heritage and her middle class, white upbringing will affect her attitudes toward beauty and toward femininity? How do you think her definition of beauty will differ from Walker's? Hampl begins the passage by indicating that she will be describing figures of the "romantic quest" in her life. What do you think she means by this phrase? What do you think the figures she will introduce will be like? Are there individuals in your life who are figures of a "romantic quest"?

There are other figures of the romantic quest in my life. Orna Tews was one. She was an artist (I never saw any of her paintings—maybe she was a sculptor). She was invited by the nuns every year to give one of the weekly "assembly speeches" at our school. To most of the girls she was a plain woman wearing aggressively homely clothes, shod in sensible shoes like our own uniform Girl Scout oxfords. How lucky we were to be wearing them, too, we were always told. How happy we would be years later when our metatarsal bones were straight and true, unlike the deformed and painful feet of foolish public school girls who wore penny loafers or—worse—moccasins.

Here in this holding-pool for ugly ducklings who, one fine day, would give   2
geeselike cackles when they turned into the swans that were Catholic wives-and-
mothers, Orna Tews, spinster artist, was invited by the Sisters to address us. To me
Orna Tews with her odd and faintly elderly name and her aggressive disregard for
fashion (a far cry from Aunt Lillian), was the epitome of a spinsterishness that was
positively glamorous. I hung on her every assembly hall word (I believe she had an
accent) as if she were a missionary only briefly returned to the tepid homeland
before rejoining, drab herself, the world of macaws and jaguars and savage religion
to which she belonged. An artist, speaking of art.

She said to observe everything. Actually, she said *Observe perpetually.* I went   3
around for a week with my head on a swivel, eyes popping, looking so diligently for
"the significant detail" that I was in a state of chronic peevishness. I could hardly
fall asleep at night because of my earnest attention. I was an exhausted, querulous
wreck. But I was observing—perpetually.

Fifteen years later when I found that Orna Tews's dictum was the final entry   4
in Virginia Woolf's *Writer's Diary,* a line itself quoted from Henry James, I didn't
feel deceived. In fact, I was often drawn to people who lived only the shell of life in
our measly present, in St. Paul where God had absent-mindedly dropped them,
speaking in their own inauthentic, timorous voices. They lived, actually, in literature. The first boy who kissed me, a French horn player who soon after explained
that he had to be careful of his lip, held me in a long embrace and said, "My God,
you're fun to kiss!" Scott Fitzgerald, *Tender Is the Night,* book II, chapter 9, spoken by Dick Diver to Nicole: *their* first kiss. My French horn player didn't care if I
found out his magic line was not his own; it was he, soon after, who loaned me the
novel and said I ought to read it. The language of the art crazed is rarely our own,
almost never in youth. Orna Tews quoting from Virginia Woolf's diary, the boy of
my first kiss copping an exclamation from Fitzgerald—we spoke the same language though it wasn't ours. It was the alluringly aged, dusty voice of an author. It
was prose. We bowed our heads and spoke in quotation, excising the citations for
the sake of the moment.

Miss Tews talked about art in life, the beauty of dailiness. I was all agog. She   5
was a sort of arty Aunt Lillian, the next step; an intellectual providing theory where
my aunt had been all wonderful praxis. Her message seemed to be that art was
made of nothing. Or perhaps that nothing—that is, everything—was art. She dwelt
at length on the art that went into baking a *truly beautiful* cake, the care in sifting,
the delicate folding of egg whites into batter, the attention to preheated ovens and
well-creamed butter and sugar mixtures. Details, details, the art of the tiny could
fill a lifetime. Our mothers were artists! Our fathers, oiling a creaking hinge on a
door, were artists! Our grandmothers were artists ("the fine old American art of
darning—how many of you girls have ever thought of darning as an art?"). The
well-driven bus, the carefully plowed street in winter, the beautifully set dinner
table, the diligently written history theme: art, art, all art!

I wanted to sign up for the whole package: the lifetime of oxfords, the doughy   6
resilience of a belief in the beauty that resided in all things, the fanatic's ecstasy as
she toiled her way through the art of cakes and pastries, the itty-bitty harmless-
nesses that, translated into what Miss Tews called at the end of her speech "formal

art," were the business of perpetual observation. And perpetual observation was the first tool of any questor. Which is what, though she stayed at home to practice her formal and informal arts in her manic way, Orna Tews was.

Though deeply unbeautiful, she had further involved me in this pursuit of   7
beauty. I didn't know it, I only knew what attracted me. But now I see her, and Aunt Lillian (who was beautiful) and my grandmother (who also was) as the trium- virate they were: my figures for the pursuit of what I felt I did not possess myself but which, I sensed, the world might provide: beauty, the loveliness I was willing to seek, to make, if I could not *be* it, as I understood was woman's way.

There were kindred spirits my own age too. A girl in our parish fascinated me,   8
and although I didn't know her well—she was two or three years older—I was always aware of her. Her name was Helen. I can remember with unusual clarity our few conversations, Helen looking directly at me as we talked, curious, so curi- ous to hear what I would say next. She was genuinely interested in other people. She was the ugliest girl I had ever seen, ugly beyond her years, with an elderly witchlike angularity that thrilled me and made me shy as if it was love I was feeling. It was pity, though, and it made my heart move toward her. She loved to read and was very intelligent; this somehow consolidated her homeliness. She was a hero- ine, I thought, in the best mode: brilliant, original mind, hopelessly unbeautiful, like Jane Eyre, my great favorite.

The last time I saw Helen, the summer before she began the university, she   9
told me, "I tested out of freshman English. I can go straight ahead and take litera- ture courses." We had met by chance on the St. Clair bus, she coming home from the University of Minnesota, I from the St. Paul library downtown. I was deeply impressed. I resolved, when the time came, to test out of freshman English myself, a thing I hadn't known was possible.

We sat in the darkened St. Clair bus, the forest-green upholstery worn smooth   10
and almost gray, the two narrow bands of yellowish light running along both sides of the interior above the windows. Romantic, gauzy light, even then. The light of our town with its buttery streetlights, the softened light of memory and dream. Helen's face that night is one of the clearest pictures I have of any human being. She sat in the shadowy glow, all the angularity of her strange face and attenuated body throwing their own shadows. "Hey, that's great," I said. It was somehow only fair that such homeliness should at least test out of freshman English. The thing about her that took my breath away was the poise of her ugliness. She was smiling, a perfectly natural and yet somehow alarming smile. It dawned on me: she doesn't know she's ugly.

How this had occurred—the vast deception of a brilliant mind, a mind that   11
could test out of freshman English at the university—I couldn't begin to under- stand. She was not troubled, she was not downcast, she was not even self-con- scious. She didn't care that she wasn't pretty. Apparently, she didn't think about it. Beyond the ugliness, which she hadn't registered, she was simply a very eager girl. Eager to live. Testing out of freshman English was just another stroke that cleared away the intervening dross, a little leap that brought her nearer to experience. Like me, she was literary and she "wanted to experience life." I wanted to ask her . . . so many things. But mainly, how had she received this inoculation against beauty?

Like the women of my grandmother and aunts' coffee conversations on the subject, she was plain: she was free. She had tested out of freshman English, she had tested out of the rougher course, the college of good looks from which the rest of us sensed we would never graduate.

But who asks questions, who even knows, staring fascinated at another person   12
and absorbing her mystery, that these things are *questions* that beat their wings on just the other side of consciousness? I asked nothing. Yet I felt our kinship was complete. I'd always felt the sisterhood of gawky homeliness was ours and that, just as she was smarter than I, she was homelier. Not essentially different, just *more* ugly, *more* undesirable. But twins, all the same. Two homely girls who liked to read long novels about English governesses.

She left the bus before I did, getting off at Victoria Street, queenly and unaf-   13
fected herself, stunning me again with her mystery which I finally understood was grace. She waved gaily from the curb as I, a lit face in a darkened rectangle, passed down St. Clair Avenue toward home.

A couple of years later, when I was at the university (where I had not tested   14
out of freshman English and had gotten an F on my first theme: "didn't follow directions," the notation said), I heard Helen had gone to Paris to study. She got married there. She's settled down in Paris, my mother said, who liked Helen's mother and liked Helen and likes life, I sometimes think, because she likes fiction. She is always trailing after somebody's dénouement, keeping track of her old friends, my old friends, the deaths of other people's relatives, reading to the end of everybody's book to see how things turn out. It's because of my mother that I know what happened to Helen.

I was living in a different state when my mother sent me a clipping from the   15
Pioneer Press, which she reads every morning with her X-acto knife in hand. It was an article from the Women's Page, as it used to be called and as my mother still calls it, though the title now is Trends.

The article was about Helen who had come home to visit her family. Home   16
from Paris. The picture was huge, a three-column portrait of a beautiful woman, her elegant head looking from atop the languid frame, looking not at the camera, not at anything in particular, absorbed apparently in her thought: selfless, *thinking*. The expressive hands were held out slightly in some gesture of thought, grasping her idea.

What was she explaining, this enigma of my girlhood, this proof of the mystery   17
and transformative power of time? It didn't matter. She had become gorgeous, utterly, utterly beautiful.

Helen had become a fashion model in Paris after she married. You're just right   18
for my clothes, Coco Chanel had told her. She was on the cover of *Elle*, *Vogue*, whatever the rest of them are called. She only worked part-time, here and there. It wasn't a career so much as a lark. "Clothes are toys," she said in the article. She explained it wasn't a matter of beauty. She said she saw girls all the time, everywhere, to whom she wanted to say, "You could be a model if you want to." It wasn't beauty, she said. All you needed was to have high cheekbones and be skinny.

The reporter wrote that Helen seemed *unable* to gain weight, that she ate   19
what she wanted—according to the reporter, a whole bag of Tom Thumb donuts

just that morning—yet kept her bony beauty, throwing her stylish shadows from the planes of her high cheekbones.

    She had taken a professional name. She had chosen the name of our bus line: 20 to Coco Chanel, to the editors of *Vogue* and *Elle,* she was Helen St. Clair. Helen of St. Clair, of the shabby and romantic St. Clair bus, poised on the hills of our town, as Helen, that night, had been poised on the curb, waving, our emissary to the light, to the City of Light.

Rhetorical Focus

1. In the section immediately preceding the Hampl piece excerpted here, she says, "To be a woman of taste and sensibility is the accepted way (for those in the middle class) to bind the self together, to make the fragmented, frustrated parts a working whole." In what ways is the excerpt itself a "working whole"? How is it organized? What images and structural devices bind it together?
2. How would you characterize Hampl's style? What devices does she employ to achieve emphasis in the essay? How are these devices related to the content Hampl is discussing?
3. How does light and darkness imagery function in the essay?

Thematic Focus

1. Hampl says elsewhere in *A Romantic Education* that beauty is our problem, our lack, and our obsession. Does the piece illustrate this idea? If so, how? If not, why not?
2. Hampl says she is drawn to people who live "in literature." Find evidence in the essay that Hampl is such a person.
3. As in the Walker essay, the words *beauty* and *beautiful* are used in a number of different ways. Identify two ways that would seem to be contradictory. Does Hampl resolve these contradictions? If so, how. If not, why not?

Femininity

Susan Brownmiller

Susan Brownmiller, born in 1935, is a journalist who has been a network
newswriter for the American Broadcasting Company and a staff reporter for
The Village Voice. She published *Against Our Will,* a study of rape, in 1975.
Femininity, published in 1984, is her second book. Her novel *Waverly Place,*
published in 1989, has been translated into eight languages. She resides in
New York City and is working on a book on friendship, tentatively entitled
The Limits of Friendship.

Reflections Before Reading

Brownmiller begins her essay with a description of a childhood ritual that
was decidedly gendered. Can you think of rituals in your past that were
gendered? She also describes being dressed in a very feminine way, in
organdy pinafores and Mary Jane shoes. Were you or the girls in your
childhood dressed in such a way, or was your clothing more androgynous?
Brownmiller also speaks of the strong messages she received as an
adolescent to hold onto her femininity. Were such messages strong for you
or the young women you grew up with in high school? Brownmiller also
feels that strongly delineated distinctions between masculinity and
femininity result in female competition for scarce resources—men and jobs.
Do the women in your life compete fiercely for scarce resources?

We had a game in our house called "setting the table" and I was Mother's   1
helper. Forks to the left of the plate, knives and spoons to the right. Placing the
cutlery neatly, as I recall, was one of my first duties, and the event was alive with
meaning. When a knife or a fork dropped to the floor, that meant a man was unex-
pectedly coming to dinner. A falling spoon announced the surprise arrival of a
female guest. No matter that these visitors never arrived on cue, I had learned a
rule of gender identification. Men were straight-edged, sharply pronged and formidable, women were softly curved and held the food in a rounded well. It made
perfect sense, like the division of pink and blue that I saw in babies, an orderly way
of viewing the world. Daddy, who was gone all day at work and who loved to putter
at home with his pipe, tobacco and tool chest, was knife and fork. Mommy and

Grandma, with their ample proportions and pots and pans, were grownup soup spoons, large and capacious. And I was a teaspoon, small and slender, easy to hold and just right for pudding, my favorite dessert.

Being good at what was expected of me was one of my earliest projects, for not only was I rewarded, as most children are, for doing things right, but excellence gave pride and stability to my childhood existence. Girls were different from boys, and the expression of that difference seemed mine to make clear. Did my loving, anxious mother, who dressed me in white organdy pinafores and Mary Janes and who cried hot tears when I got them dirty, give me my first instruction? Of course. Did my doting aunts and uncles with their gifts of pretty dolls and miniature tea sets add to my education? Of course. But even without the appropriate toys and clothes, lessons in the art of being feminine lay all around me and I absorbed them all: the fairy tales that were read to me at night, the brightly colored advertisements I pored over in magazines before I learned to decipher the words, the movies I saw, the comic books I hoarded, the radio soap operas I happily followed whenever I had to stay in bed with a cold. I loved being a little girl, or rather I loved being a fairy princess, for that was who I thought I was.

As I passed through a stormy adolescence to a stormy maturity, femininity increasingly became an exasperation, a brilliant, subtle esthetic that was bafflingly inconsistent at the same time that it was minutely, demandingly concrete, a rigid code of appearance and behavior defined by do's and don't-do's that went against my rebellious grain. Femininity was a challenge thrown down to the female sex, a challenge no proud, self-respecting young woman could afford to ignore, particularly one with enormous ambition that she nursed in secret, alternately feeding or starving its inchoate life in tremendous confusion.

"Don't lose your femininity" and "Isn't it remarkable how she manages to retain her femininity?" had terrifying implications. They spoke of a bottom-line failure so irreversible that nothing else mattered. The pinball machine had registered "tilt," the game had been called. Disqualification was marked on the forehead of a woman whose femininity was lost. No records would be entered in her name, for she had destroyed her birthright in her wretched, ungainly effort to imitate a man. She walked in limbo, this hapless creature, and it occurred to me that one day I might see her when I looked in the mirror. If the danger was so palpable that warning notices were freely posted, wasn't it possible that the small bundle of resentments I carried around in secret might spill out and place the mark on my own forehead? Whatever quarrels with femininity I had I kept to myself; whatever handicaps femininity imposed, they were mine to deal with alone, for there was no women's movement to ask the tough questions, or to brazenly disregard the rules.

Femininity, in essence, is a romantic sentiment, a nostalgic tradition of imposed limitations. Even as it hurries forward in the 1980s, putting on lipstick and high heels to appear well dressed, it trips on the ruffled petticoats and hoopskirts of an era gone by. Invariably and necessarily, femininity is something that women had more of in the past, not only in the historic past of prior generations, but in each woman's personal past as well—in the virginal innocence that is replaced by knowledge, in the dewy cheek that is coarsened by age, in the "inherent nature" that a woman seems to misplace so forgetfully whenever she steps out of bounds.

Why should this be so? The XX chromosomal message has not been scrambled, the estrogen-dominated hormonal balance is generally as biology intended, the reproductive organs, whatever use one has made of them, are usually in place, the breasts of whatever size are most often where they should be. But clearly, biological femaleness is not enough.

Femininity always demands more. It must constantly reassure its audience by a willing demonstration of difference, even when one does not exist in nature, or it must seize and embrace a natural variation and compose a rhapsodic symphony upon the notes. Suppose one doesn't care to, has other things on her mind, is clumsy or tone-deaf despite the best instruction and training? To fail at the feminine difference is to appear not to care about men, and to risk the loss of their attention and approval. To be insufficiently feminine is viewed as a failure in core sexual identity, or as a failure to care sufficiently about oneself, for a woman found wanting will be appraised (and will appraise herself) as mannish or neutered or simply unattractive, as men have defined these terms.

We are talking, admittedly, about an exquisite esthetic. Enormous pleasure can be extracted from feminine pursuits as a creative outlet or purely as relaxation; indeed, indulgence for the sake of fun, or art, or attention, is among femininity's great joys. But the chief attraction (and the central paradox, as well) is the competitive edge that femininity seems to promise in the unending struggle to survive, and perhaps to triumph. The world smiles favorably on the feminine woman: it extends little courtesies and minor privilege. Yet the nature of this competitive edge is ironic, at best, for one works at femininity by accepting restrictions, by limiting one's sights, by choosing an indirect route, by scattering concentration and not giving one's all as a man would to his own, certifiably masculine, interests. It does not require a great leap of imagination for a woman to understand the feminine principle as a grand collection of compromises, large and small, that she simply must make in order to render herself a successful woman. If she has difficulty in satisfying femininity's demands, if its illusions go against her grain, or if she is criticized for her shortcomings and imperfections, the more she will see femininity as a desperate strategy of appeasement, a strategy she may not have the wish or the courage to abandon, for failure looms in either direction.

It is fashionable in some quarters to describe the feminine and masculine principles as polar ends of the human continuum, and to sagely profess that both polarities exist in all people. Sun and moon, yin and yang, soft and hard, active and passive, et cetera, may indeed be opposites, but a linear continuum does not illuminate the problem. (Femininity, in all its contrivances, is a very active endeavor.) What, then, is the basic distinction? The masculine principle is better understood as a driving ethos of superiority designed to inspire straightforward, confident success, while the feminine principle is composed of vulnerability, the need for protection, the formalities of compliance and the avoidance of conflict—in short, an appeal of dependence and good will that gives the masculine principle its romantic validity and its admiring applause.

Femininity pleases men because it makes them appear more masculine by contrast; and, in truth, conferring an extra portion of unearned gender distinction on men, an unchallenged space in which to breathe freely and feel stronger, wiser,

6

7

8

9

more competent, is femininity's special gift. One could say that masculinity is often an effort to please women, but masculinity is known to please by displays of mastery and competence while femininity pleases by suggesting that these concerns, except in small matters, are beyond its intent. Whimsy, unpredictability and patterns of thinking and behavior that are dominated by emotion, such as tearful expressions of sentiment and fear, are thought to be feminine precisely because they lie outside the established route to success.

If in the beginnings of history the feminine woman was defined by her physi- 10
cal dependency, her inability for reasons of reproductive biology to triumph over the forces of nature that were the tests of masculine strength and power, today she reflects both an economic and emotional dependency that is still considered "natural," romantic and attractive. After an unsettling fifteen years in which many basic assumptions about the sexes were challenged, the economic disparity did not disappear. Large numbers of women—those with small children, those left high and dry after a mid-life divorce—need financial support. But even those who earn their own living share a universal need for connectedness (call it love, if you wish). As unprecedented numbers of men abandon their sexual interest in women, others, sensing opportunity, choose to demonstrate their interest through variety and a change in partners. A sociological fact of the 1980s is that female competition for two scarce resources—men and jobs—is especially fierce.

So it is not surprising that we are currently witnessing a renewed interest in 11
femininity and an unabashed indulgence in feminine pursuits. Femininity serves to reassure men that women need them and care about them enormously. By incorporating the decorative and the frivolous into its definition of style, femininity functions as an effective antidote to the unrelieved seriousness, the pressure of making one's way in a harsh, difficult world. In its mandate to avoid direct confrontation and to smooth over the fissures of conflict, femininity operates as a value system of niceness, a code of thoughtfulness and sensitivity that in modern society is sadly in short supply.

There is no reason to deny that indulgence in the art of feminine illusion can 12
be reassuring to a woman, if she happens to be good at it. As sexuality undergoes some dizzying revisions, evidence that one is a woman "at heart" (the inquisitor's question) is not without worth. Since an answer of sorts may be furnished by piling on additional documentation, affirmation can arise from such identifiable but trivial feminine activities as buying a new eyeliner, experimenting with the latest shade of nail color, or bursting into tears at the outcome of a popular romance novel. Is there anything destructive in this? Time and cost factors, a deflection of energy and an absorption in fakery spring quickly to mind, and they need to be balanced, as in a ledger book, against the affirming advantage.

Throughout this book I have attempted to trace significant feminine principles 13
to basic biology, for feminine expression is conventionally praised as an enhancement of femaleness, or the raw materials of femaleness shaped and colored to perfection. Sometimes I found that a biological connection did exist, and sometimes not, and sometimes I had to admit that many scientific assumptions about the nature of femaleness were unresolved and hotly debated, and that no sound conclusion was possible before all the evidence was in. It was more enlightening to

explore the origins of femininity in borrowed affectations of upper-class status, and in the historic subjugation of women through sexual violence, religion and law, where certain myths about the nature of women were put forward as biological fact. It was also instructive to approach femininity from the angle of seductive glamour, which usually does not fit smoothly with aristocratic refinement, accounting for some contradictory feminine messages that often appear as an unfathomable puzzle.

The competitive aspect of femininity, the female-against-female competition   14 produced by the effort to attract and secure men, is one of the major themes I have tried to explore. Male-against-male competition for high rank and access to females is a popular subject in anthropology, in the study of animals as well as humans, but few scholars have thought to examine the pitched battle of females for ranking and access to males. Yet the struggle to approach the feminine ideal, to match the femininity of other women, and especially to outdo them, is the chief competitive arena (surely it is the only sanctioned arena) in which the American woman is wholeheartedly encouraged to contend. Whether or not this absorbing form of competition is a healthy or useful survival strategy is a critical question.

Hymns to femininity, combined with instruction, have never been lacking.   15 Several generations of us are acquainted with sugar and spice, can recite the job description for "The Girl That I Marry" (doll-size, soft and pink, wears lace and nail polish, gardenia in the hair), or wail the payoff to "Just Like a Woman" ("She breaks like a little girl"). My contribution may be decidedly unmusical, but it is not a manual of how-not-to, nor a wholesale damnation. Femininity deserves some hard reckoning, and this is what I have tried to do.

A powerful esthetic that is built upon a recognition of powerlessness is a slip-   16 pery subject to grapple with, for its contradictions are elusive, ephemeral and ultimately impressive. A manner that combines a deferential attitude with ornaments of the upper class and an etiquette composed in equal parts of modesty and exhibition are paradoxes that require thoughtful interpretation. A strategy of survival that is based on overt concession and imposed restrictions deserves close study, for what is lost and what is gained is not always apparent. By organizing my chapters along pragmatic lines—body, hair, clothes, voice, et cetera—I have attempted a rational analysis that is free of mystification. Coming down hard on certain familiar aspects while admitting a fond tolerance for some others has been unavoidable in my attempt to give an honest appraisal of the feminine strategies as I have myself practiced or discarded them. I do not mean to project my particular compromises and choices as the better way, or the final word, nor do I mean to condemn those women who practice the craft in ways that are different from mine. I offer this book as a step toward awareness, in the hope that one day the feminine ideal will no longer be used to perpetuate inequality between the sexes, and that exaggeration will not be required to rest secure in biological gender.

Rhetorical Focus

1. Brownmiller's essay serves as a prologue to her book, *Femininity*. Why do you think Brownmiller decided to introduce her essay (and her book) in

2. Brownmiller sometimes uses repetition to emphasize an idea. Identify places in which she does so and explain what she is trying to emphasize and why.

3. Who is Brownmiller's audience? What stylistic devices does she employ to reach that audience?

Thematic Focus

1. Brownmiller's essay was published in 1983. In what ways are her arguments dated? In what ways are they still relevant?

2. Brownmiller makes clear distinctions between masculinity and femininity. Do you think her categories are rigid? Why might she want to emphasize differences rather than similarities?

3. Does Brownmiller define femininity as a positive term with its own characteristics, or does she define it largely as a negative term, a reaction against masculinity?

Suggestions for Writing

1. Walker and Hampl speak of teachers or other role models who were important to them as they attempted to free themselves from the constraints of stereotypical conceptions of femininity. Describe a teacher or other role model who was important to you as you developed a gendered identity.

2. Try out Hampl's technique of "observing perpetually" for a day or two, focusing especially on the ways in which women conform to or react against traditional definitions of womanhood. Then write an essay in which you analyze your observations.

3. Brownmiller says her adolescence was stormy because the rigid code of femininity went against her rebellious nature. Describe your own adolescence in terms of the ease or difficulty with which you dealt with socially prescribed gender roles.

MASCULINITY

The women's movement has encouraged men to reflect on their masculinity and on the topic of gender differences. This reflection has, in turn, resulted in an emerging men's movement aimed at exploring and perhaps recovering masculine character traits. Individuals such as the poet Robert Bly conduct workshops designed to facilitate such soul searching.

The essays by Noel Perrin and Nicholas Bromell included here represent essentially different responses to the challenge of the women's movement. Perrin celebrates freedom from restricting gender stereotypes. Bromell, in contrast, is disturbed by a blurring of distinctions between masculinity and femininity and thinks certain traits traditionally associated with masculinity need to be defended. With whom do you agree? How do you think Walker, Hampl, and Brownmiller would respond to these essays?

The Androgynous Man
Noel Perrin

Noel Perrin was born September 18, 1927, in New York. He attended Williams College, Duke University, and Cambridge University and teaches American literature at Dartmouth College. A collection of essays, *A Passport Secretly Green,* was published by St. Martin's Press in 1961. Other books he has had published are *Vermont in All Weathers* (1973), *First Person Rural* (1978), and *Second Person Rural* (1980). He is also a contributor to the *New Yorker* magazine. "The Androgynous Male" first appeared in the "On Men" column in the *New York Times Magazine* in February 1984.

Reflections Before Reading

How would you distinguish between masculine and feminine traits? Perrin claims that androgynous individuals have the greatest freedom. Do you have androgynous characteristics? Do you agree that people with androgynous characteristics are the most free?

The summer I was 16, I took a train from New York to Steamboat Springs, Colo., where I was going to be assistant horse wrangler at a camp. The trip took three days, and since I was much too shy to talk to strangers, I had quite a lot of time for reading. I read all of "Gone With the Wind." I read all the interesting articles in a couple of magazines I had, and then I went back and read all the dull stuff. I also took all the quizzes, a thing of which magazines were even fuller then than now.

The one that held my undivided attention was called "How Masculine/   2
Feminine Are You?" It consisted of a large number of inkblots. The reader was
supposed to decide which of four objects each blot most resembled. The choices
might be a cloud, a steam engine, a caterpillar and a sofa.

When I finished the test, I was shocked to find that I was barely masculine at   3
all. On a scale of 1 to 10, I was about 1.2. Me, the horse wrangler? (And not just
wrangler, either. That summer, I had to skin a couple of horses that died—the
camp owner wanted the hides.)

The results of that test were so terrifying to me that for the first time in my life   4
I did a piece of original analysis. Having unlimited time on the train, I looked at the
"masculine" answers over and over, trying to find what it was that distinguished
real men from people like me—and eventually I discovered two very simple patterns. It was "masculine" to think the blots looked like man-made objects, and
"feminine" to think they looked like natural objects. It was masculine to think they
looked like things capable of causing harm, and feminine to think of innocent
things.

Even at 16, I had the sense to see that the compilers of the test were using   5
rather limited criteria—maleness and femaleness are both more complicated than
that—and I breathed a huge sigh of relief. I wasn't necessarily a wimp, after all.

That the test did reveal something other than the superficiality of its makers I   6
realized only many years later. What it revealed was that there is a large class of
men and women both, to which I belong, who are essentially androgynous. That
doesn't mean we're gay, or low in the appropriate hormones, or uncomfortable
performing the jobs traditionally assigned our sexes. (A few years after that summer, I was leading troops in combat and, unfashionable as it now is to admit this,
having a very good time. War is exciting. What a pity the 20th century went and
spoiled it with high-tech weapons.)

What it does mean to be spiritually androgynous is a kind of freedom. Men   7
who are all-male, or he-man, or 100 percent red-blooded Americans, have a little
biological set that causes them to be attracted to physical power, and probably also
to dominance. Maybe even to watching football. I don't say this to criticize them.
Completely masculine men are quite often wonderful people: good husbands,
good (though sometimes overwhelming) fathers, good members of society. Furthermore, they are often so unself-consciously at ease in the world that other men
seek to imitate them. They just aren't as free as us androgynes. They pretty nearly
have to be what they are; we have a range of choices open.

The sad part is that many of us never discover that. Men who are not 100   8
percent red-blooded Americans—say, those who are only 75 percent red-
blooded—often fail to notice their freedom. They are too busy trying to copy the
he-men ever to realize that men, like women, come in a wide variety of acceptable
types. Why this frantic imitation? My answer is mere speculation, but not casual. I
have speculated on this for a long time.

Partly they're just envious of the he-man's unconscious ease. Mostly they're   9
terrified of finding that there may be something wrong with them deep down,
some weakness at the heart. To avoid discovering that, they spend their lives acting
out the role that the he-man naturally lives. Sad.

One thing that men owe to the women's movement is that this kind of failure is   10
less common than it used to be. In releasing themselves from the single ideal of the
dependent woman, women have more or less incidentally released a lot of men
from the single ideal of the dominant male. The one mistake the feminists have
made, I think, is in supposing that *all* men need this release, or that the world
would be a better place if all men achieved it. It wouldn't. It would just be duller.

So far I have been pretty vague about just what the freedom of the androgy-   11
nous man is. Obviously it varies with the case. In the case I know best, my own, I
can be quite specific. It has freed me most as a parent. I am, among other things, a
fairly good natural mother. I like the nurturing role. It makes me feel good to see a
child eat—and it turns me to mush to see a 4-year-old holding a glass with both
small hands, in order to drink. I even enjoyed sewing patches on the knees of my
daughter Amy's Dr. Dentons when she was at the crawling stage. All that pleasure
I would have lost if I had made myself stick to the notion of the paternal role that I
started with.

Or take a smaller and rather ridiculous example. I feel free to kiss cats. Until   12
recently it never occurred to me that I would want to, though my daughters have
been doing it all their lives. But my elder daughter is now 22, and in London. Of
course, I get to look after her cat while she is gone. He's a big, handsome farm cat
named Petrushka, very unsentimental, though used from kittenhood to being
kissed on the top of the head by Elizabeth. I've gotten very fond of him (he's the
adventurous kind of cat who likes to climb hills with you), and one night I simply
felt like kissing him on the top of the head, and did. Why did no one tell me sooner
how silky cat fur is?

Then there's my relation to cars. I am completely unembarrassed by my in-   13
ability to diagnose even minor problems in whatever object I happen to be driving,
and don't have to make some insider's remark to mechanics to try to establish that
I, too, am a "Man With His Machine."

The same ease extends to household maintenance. I do it, of course. Service   14
people are expensive. But for the last decade my house has functioned better than
it used to because I've had the aid of a volume called "Home Repairs Any Woman
Can Do," which is pitched just right for people at my technical level. As a youth, I'd
as soon have touched such a book as I would have become a transvestite. Even
though common sense says there is really nothing sexual whatsoever about fixing
sinks.

Or take public emotion. All my life I have easily been moved by certain kinds   15
of voices. The actress Siobhan McKenna's, to take a notable case. Give her an
emotional scene in a play, and within 10 words my eyes are full of tears. In boyhood, my great dread was that someone might notice. I struggled manfully, you
might say, to suppress this weakness. Now, of course, I don't see it as a weakness at
all, but as a kind of fulfillment. I even suspect that the true he-men feel the same
way, or one kind of them does, at least, and it's only the poor imitators who have to
struggle to repress themselves.

Let me come back to the inkblots, with their assumption that masculine   16
equates with machinery and science, and feminine with art and nature. I have no
idea whether the right pronoun for God is He, She or It. But this I'm pretty sure

of. If God could somehow be induced to take that test, God would not come out macho, and not feminismo, either, but right in the middle. Fellow androgynes, it's a nice thought.

Rhetorical Focus

1. Perrin claims he is an androgynous male. Do you think he employs an androgynous writing style? What might such a style look like?
2. Would a woman have written the essay differently? If so, how? If not, why not?
3. Is Perrin writing for other men or for men and women alike? What rhetorical features of the essay led you to your decision?

Thematic Focus

1. Can you think of additional ways in which androgyny might be liberating for men?
2. Perrin says that the one mistake feminists have made is in supposing that all men need to be released from traditional gender roles. Do you agree with him? Why or why not?
3. Is there any evidence in the essay that Perrin is still influenced to an extent by traditional gender roles? If so, explain.

Man Hunt

Nicholas Bromell

Nicholas Bromell was born in 1950 in New York and received his B.A. from
Amherst in 1972 and his Ph.D. from Stanford in 1987. He teaches English
and American studies at the University of Massachusetts, Amherst, and is a
visiting assistant professor in the English department at Harvard University.
He is a contributing editor of the *Boston Review* and has published essays
in the *Georgia Review*, the *New York Times Magazine*, *Harper's Magazine*,
and the *Boston Globe*. He is working on a book about nineteenth-century
American cultural construction of the meaning of work in contemporary
America.

Reflections Before Reading

Bromell thinks that certain traits that have traditionally been associated with
males should be preserved. What might such traits be? Do you agree that
they are valuable and should be encouraged? Like Perrin, Bromell also
suggests that gender differences may be biologically determined. Do you
agree?

Is there anything worth saving from the wreck of masculinity? In my world, at   1
least, barnacles encrust the old virtues of manhood: courage and physical strength
have become the marks of bullies and macho-men; independence and initiative, of
selfish capitalists; pride in family honor, of mafiosi and petty dictators. When we
probe the blackness below decks, we find that the hold is empty. The seas have
carried everything away.

Yet the wreck itself is evidence that something of manhood remains. Expedi-   2
tion leaders like Robert Bly take men back to explore, and perhaps recover, the
best of what they once were. Anthropologists have also joined the search, circling
the globe to find vestiges of real manhood in cultures that have escaped, or with-
stood, the levelling influences of the West. David Gilmore's recent overview of
their work reports that anthropologists have found an essentially similar cluster of
traits and behaviors being ascribed to and performed by men among such diverse
peoples as Andalusians, Truk Islanders in the South Pacific, Mehinaku Indians in

"Manhunt" by Nicholas Bromell, *The Boston Review*, December 1990. Reprinted by permission of the
author.

the Amazon rain forest, the Gurumba of New Guinea, and the Samburu of East Africa. All of these cultures demand that men be brave in the face of danger, willing to take risks, quick to defend their honor, ready to pit physical strength against physical hardship. They must also be sexually aggressive and manifestly potent.

Moreover, in all these and many other cultures manhood is something a male   3
can never take for granted. Again and again, both through elaborate rituals and the trials of everyday life, cultures test men, demanding that they continually show evidence of their masculinity.

A man who tries to decide whether to preserve and perform these features of   4
manhood is likely to find himself wondering about their origins. Setting aside the possibility of a biological source for masculinity (which, if he has small children to observe, may be hard to do), he is left with two ways of explaining its cultural sources. The first focuses on the individual psyche. Certain Freudian anthropologists, for example, argue that men everywhere use masculinity as a psychic defense against the castration fears which inevitably accompany Oedipal trauma. Certain post-Freudians, to take another example, focus on the ways a boy's biological maleness seems to require that he, much more than his sister, develop a gender identity separate and different from that of his mother. In both cases, the notion of masculinity has its deepest source in the individual male psyche and is "projected" onto the "screen" of culture.

The second explanation focuses on masculinity as performing a social func-   5
tion. According to this view, which takes some of its assumptions from the post-Freudians, a boy's separation from a sense of primal unity with his mother is an enormously difficult, and tenuous, achievement. The temptation to regress to a state of passive dependence and blissful union is strong indeed. On the other hand, every society needs its men. Many societies have needed them to hunt for high-protein food sources (i.e., animals and fish). More generally, men provide an energetic labor source that is always free from the demands of childbirth and childrearing. Society conscripts men into performing these roles, but since at a deep psychic level all men resist (wanting to stay home with Mommy), society develops the concept of performative masculinity to reward men who obey and punish those who don't.

This thesis has a number of problems (why, for example, is a state of unity with   6
the mother necessarily "passive"?), but what seems most important is that it shares with the other explanations the assumption that asymmetrical parenting is at the root of gender (as distinct from sexual) differentiation. There would be no Oedipal complex or castration anxiety if boys were loved and nurtured as much by their fathers as their mothers. There would be no special need for boys, relative to girls, to develop a separate gender identity from their mother if they were cared for equally by their father. There would be no primary and exclusive "enclitic" unity with the mother if boys and girls also knew their fathers as persons with whom the deepest of bonds could be formed. Take away the traditional division of the labor of childrearing, and, these theories imply, you take away all need for masculinity as it traditionally has been defined.

But in the tiny culture of my home, where my wife and I share equally the   7
work of raising two small boys, some aspects of masculinity flourish. At times, I

even find myself being a hesitant advocate of it. More publicly, an emergent men's movement seeks to recover whatever might be valuable in traditional masculinity and to invent, if necessary, a new brand. Why does masculinity continue to exercise such resistance and appeal?

It makes sense to assume that we cannot explain masculinity or femininity   8
unless we deal with the two sexes and their relations with each other. Certainly I, as a man, think of my manhood far more in relation to women and to what they find attractive, than in relation to men. Even as a kid, I performed feats of der- ring-do much more enthusiastically when a girl was present to witness them than when I was alone with my gang of guys. It is true that we boys constantly tested each other. "I dare you" was our daily refrain. But we posed and passed these tests grimly; they were work. Only when a girl was around to admire us did we feel ourselves infused with a divine energy, uplifted by an urge to excel that carried us beyond our known capabilities.

A grown-up now, I still feel the same way. My public performance as a man,   9
not as a person, is directed to the female gaze. If I force myself to jog regularly and bridle my appetite for Dove Bars, it's because I want to appear to be "in shape." And if I ask myself, in shape for what, or whom, I can only reply, for women. Why would a man care? Similarly, if I cultivate a mien with certain manly attributes— slow to anger or panic, deliberate in my approach to problems, scrupulously objec- tive and fairminded, ready to face danger—it is because I imagine that most women want, and sometimes even need, such qualities in a man.

Surely a woman wants the feel of strong arms and admires the lines of defined   10
muscles. Surely she wants a man who can negotiate with contractors, fix broken machines, get out of bed and patrol the house when she hears a noise at night, and help her adjudicate, by recourse to certain abstract principles, the bewildering and conflicting claims of love, life, work, and children. To whatever degree I have de- veloped these traits, I've done so for women, not for men.

If I don't perform my manhood for men, maybe it's because I don't know any   11
real men. I know some other guys—but they're sort of like me. When we get together, our wives or lovers are usually with us (in fact, they've usually brought us together). We talk about some manly things—the Red Sox, life insurance, what we would have done if we had caught the crooks who stole our car—and sometimes we do manly things—basketball is the only one that comes to mind. But these are not the men I'd pick to go with me if for some reason I had to lead an expedition to the North Pole or rescue hostages from a besieged American embassy. I'd pick— well, real men. And presumably such men would pick other real men, not me.

So I'm never entirely confident that my performance of manhood is genuine,   12
since I'm performing it for women not for men. To make matters worse, most women I've talked to about masculinity say they couldn't care less. What distinc- tively manly things do you find attractive in a man? I ask. My women friends' eyes widen at the question itself. Distinctively manly traits? They can't think of one. They start to go on about a certain gentle look in the eyes, an ability to talk about feelings. I interrupt: no, I mean traditionally manly things. You know, like a strong

body, like courage, independence, resourcefulness. But they just look blank. Those things aren't that important, they insist.

I'm not convinced. Not long ago my wife and a female friend of hers were   13
talking about their high school days and my wife said she always wondered what
had become of—we'll call him Dave. "He was the sexiest guy I've ever met," she
sighed, and the friend responded with a knowing laugh. "That's what I mean," I
pounced. "What exactly was so attractive about this guy?" His eyes, my wife replied, there was an extraordinary depth to his eyes. Because my wife had already
told me a little about Dave, I kept asking until she finally went further.

"There was something dangerous about him."   14

Dangerous?   15

"Going out with him was crossing a line. Sleeping with him would have been   16
crossing a further line."

In the tempting "danger" of "crossing a line" I read at first a desire for differ-   17
ence. Dave was not a musclebound boy scout who could find his way out of the
woods unaided, but he was different from my wife in other ways: to a girl who had
been taught to be "innocent," he projected undisguised sexual desire and experience: to a girl who had learned to accept social regulations, he projected indifference toward a code that sought to tame desire by linking it to romantic love and,
ultimately, to matrimony.

But like all Byronic heroes, Dave was a contradiction. He was desirable as long   18
as he was "dangerous"—that is, as long as he posed a direct threat to the safe,
domestic world to which middle-class women have been consigned and through
which they have also managed to protect themselves from irresponsible male desire. At the same time, he was also desirable insofar as he represented an opportunity to the girls' reformist impulses; he was a boy who would have to be won over
and subtly subdued, and thus he offered them the chance to exercise their powers
in a culture that for the most part renders them relatively powerless.

If this understanding of Dave's appeal is correct, however, the precise location   19
of his "difference" is hard to pin down. When he appeals to a woman's fascination
with unregulated desire, he may be appealing to the true woman, the real woman
in her, that is, to the woman who has not been entirely subjugated by patriarchy's
regulations. Thus the point of apparently greatest difference might be more accurately seen as the appeal of sameness. Conversely, when Dave appeals to a woman's reformist impulse, he offers her another kind of empowerment; she is "like" a
man insofar as she exercises her powers, and she makes him "like" her insofar as
she domesticates him. Here, too, an apparent difference can also be read as simi-
larity.

When a teenaged girl felt she could plunge into Dave's eyes and keep going   20
"forever," did she think she would lose herself or find herself? The answer seems
to be, "both."

If sameness, not just difference, is a crucial instigator of female heterosexual   21
desire, what about heterosexual men? When I try to identify what I find appealing
in the womanliness of a woman, I keep coming back to individual women I have

known, to their particular qualities rather than to a generalized essence of desirability. Do I know any women like Dave, women with whom I was never intimate but who exercised a mesmeric appeal? Yes. I have always been starstruck by the kind of woman, let us call her Lois, who is upfront with her sexuality, who has got it and shows it without worrying that she is being undignified or, worse, the tool of a sexploitative patriarchal culture. Lois wears low-cut dresses, tight clothes, and her eyes have that look—bold, a little hard, and at the same time inviting. They seem to say, "Here I am. Come and get me if you dare."

But I don't dare. I'm held back, I think, mainly by a fear of inadequacy. I   22
assume that women like Lois are attracted only to their male counterparts—to real men?—and I'm just too restrained and regulated to have a chance with them. I have learned to be a safe man, the kind of man who appeals to women who want a relationship, a marriage, a husband. What could I possibly have to offer to a woman whose whole bearing expresses nothing but enjoyment and desire?

My fear of inadequacy is also an intuition that with such women I would lack   23
sexual leverage. By this I mean that the role I play when I have sex with my counterparts, safe women, would not work with Lois. With safe women, I think, I remain myself but pretend, for a while, to be Dave. Or perhaps I discover the Dave within me and become Dave for a while. But Lois doesn't want that. She already has Dave, and she wants Dave to play a role, to become something else, to leverage himself and her into a different performance. But what Dave becomes, and what that performance is, I'll never know.

Am I drawn to Lois because she is "different" from or the "same" as me? Here,   24
too, the distinctions blur. Lois is different from me in that she is, relatively speaking, defiant toward social regulations concerning sexual attitudes and behavior. But the expression her defiance takes—that is, more explicitly announcing her sexual desire—makes her more like a conventional male, and thus more like me. She is like me also in that she does not think that a male conception of female sexiness—a conception that includes provocativeness, display—is wrong, dirty, or demeaning. She is different from me in that she is not afraid to appear sexy, but she is like me in that we share a notion of what is sexy.

Does the sexual desirability of difference, then, explain why we hold on to   25
gender distinctions and certain traditional notions of masculinity and femininity? I don't think so. After all, I seem not to know whether I desire sameness or difference because (patriarchal) culture has inextricably connected these, not just semantically, in that one has no meaning without the other, but actually, in that each keeps turning into the other. Difference seems to be less the sole incitement to desire than part of a metaphor for desire—the other part of which is sameness.

If it's not required by sexual desire, does masculinity serve any requirements   26
at all? Are there any qualities I associate with masculinity that I would not give up and that would be jeopardized in a world of gender uniformity? I take them one by one:

Courage: No reason at all why this should be a masculine virtue and no reason   27
to think that a culture without gender differences would cease to value it.

Willingness to take risks: David Gilmore theorizes that men are deputed to take risks because they are biologically more expendable than females. A culture can survive with many women and only a few males, but not under the reverse circumstances. For this reason, among others, men are trained to become hunters and warriors, to do whatever dangerous work is required in order to acquire and defend land and food. As a male, I would welcome a new order of things in which the burden of such risk-taking was more evenly distributed among both males and females.   28

Physical strength: Cultures will value strength as long as there is a need for it. Although biology has apparently designed men to be stronger than women, I see no reason at all why strength should be accorded a special value.   29

Pride in family honor: Definitely expendable, along with other tribal loyalties.   30

Independence: Here we get to the sticking point. I see no reason why this quality, and the closely related one of objectivity, should be associated with males. But it is a quality I value and it is one that might be jeopardized—as I hope to show—in a world of perfectly symmetrical parenting and no gender differences.   31

Many feminists are quick to ridicule the male obsession with independence. The rugged hero's desire for solitude is shown to be nothing but a boyish fantasy of escape from the responsibilities of adult life. When Huck Finn lights out for the wilderness ahead of Widow Douglass and her civilizing ways, he is really trying to avoid the inevitable fate of growing up—of marrying, having children, loving and being loved, and so on.   32

I have difficulty justifying male independence to women, not only because I have a personal stake in it, but because it has long served as a smokescreen for pernicious and irresponsible behavior. The moment the individual claims an identity apart from that of the community, and rights distinct from the needs of the society, problems are bound to occur. Nevertheless, as a male from a middle-class culture I feel that so much of my humanness is contingent on the right to be alone that I cannot imagine going without it—existing always in a web of interconnectedness. Solitude and loneliness, the existential situation of radical solipsism—these are the flip side of independence, and I am ready to accept (though I do not embrace) them. Selfishness, egoism, greed—these are the flip side of self-reliance, and I am ready to accept them also if they are the price we have to pay for the sense (and I know it might be an illusion) that we can guide our own actions toward our own ends. That we can (or are fated to) stand isolate over and against the whole rest of existence, imprisoned or enthroned in our own spark of existence. "Our own": so much is bound up in this notion of individualism, not least the right to ownership and the concept of property. These, too, I am willing to accept, if they are the inevitable corollaries of ontological individualism.   33

My argument, obviously, is not just with a certain strain of feminism, but with Marxism and with many of the world's great religions. To base the meaning of life on the value of community is not essentially different, from my perspective, than to base it on the value of a larger social collectivity, or on the value of a featureless soul whose primal desire is reunification with the divine. Clearly, then, there is nothing essentially male or masculine about an emphasis on individual selfhood. In   34 a gender-free culture, as many women as men might come to its defense. But the fact that it has for so long been associated with masculinity would, I imagine, jeopardize its survival in such a culture.

Similarly, a number of feminists have criticized the traditional masculine emphasis on the value of objectivity in intellectual life and judicial process—the notion that truth and fairness are best arrived at by distancing one's self from the subject under consideration—as an escape into abstraction from the more confusing, but also more rich and rewarding, realities of everyday life. Moreover, as postmodernists in general are apt to point out, objectivity is impossible anyway, so idealizing it serves mainly to obscure the fact that self-interest, often male self-interest, is at work everywhere. That "objective" scientific inquiry has led to global pollution and threat of nuclear war while enriching corporate research sponsors is a case in point. By contrast, women, according to some researchers, have developed an alternative sense of values, one that recognizes the impossibility of objectivity and roots intellectual life and ethical decisions in a complex web of loyalties. They think and make decisions not on the basis of abstractions like love of God and country, but in terms of specific situations, personal experience, and personal affiliations.   35

I understand the critiques of objectivity that have been advanced by feminists, Foucauldians, Marxists, and others, but I am not convinced that our manifest inability to be objective should stop us from trying to make the effort. Objectivity is enshrined not just in the Western tradition of scientific inquiry, but in our judicial procedures and in some of our deepest assumptions about intellectuality. Although it has been challenged on many different fronts, objectivity still holds the field against rival modes of ascertaining what is true and what is just.   36

It dominates, I suspect, as much because the culture recognizes the need to have one mode prevail over others as because it is intrinsically better. It's hard to imagine, for example, how a culture could survive if it allowed epistemological and judicial pluralism to flourish in its courts of law. How could a Supreme Court function if each justice had a fundamentally different mode of determining what was true and just? What would happen if one were to ignore the Constitution with its abstract principles, such as "All men are created equal," and rely on personal experience of what is good and right, and on a personal understanding of a particular situation? Chaos is the only conceivable outcome of such a sanctioned pluralism.   37

If a striving for objectivity is constructive and desirable, we must next ask what makes objectivity possible. This is where we run into trouble, since we find that the most compelling psychosocial explanation of objectivity has linked it to gender differentiation and asymmetrical parenting. The writings of Nancy Chodorow, Carol Gilligan, and Evelyn Fox Keller, among others, view objectivity not as a universal, but a gender-specific trait; boys acquire it as a by-product of the maturation process in which they feel compelled to distance themselves from their mother (because they are sexually different from her) in order to achieve an adequate sense of self.   38

Girls, according to this account, make epistemological and ethical decisions on a different basis. Because they share their mother's gender, they can remain like   39 her even as they grow apart from her. Their sense of self is thus less isolate, more connected with others, than that of their male siblings and counterparts. When they have to decide what is true, or just, they are more apt to consider a wide range of personal and particular factors than to keep themselves out of it and depend upon an abstract principle for guidance.

We can't know whether this account is accurate. But assuming for the moment   40
that it is, I find myself asking what would happen to the masculine desire/need for objectivity in a culture where parenting was equally shared by mother and father. Presumably the boy who has bonded deeply with both parents would feel far less need to distinguish himself from his mother in order to achieve a sense of self. Of course, the girl's maturational process and needs would change also. She would have to come to terms with the fact that she was sexually different from one of her (equally primary) parents and she might acquire more of the separational needs that formerly troubled only her brother. But I don't think that this adjustment would suffice to make up what has been "lost" through the change in her brother's process. The nicely balanced arrangement of symmetrical parenting defuses that rage for difference that is required in order to achieve the highly unnatural and unpleasant separation that splits the boy apart from his mother. Symmetrical parenting, it seems to me, is more likely to infuse boys with a sense of interconnectedness than to burden girls with a need for difference sufficient to create an ethic of objectivity.

Exploring these possibilities underscores how artificial and achieved is the   41
male craving for independence that creates, among other things, the conception (or sensation) of an isolate self and the notion (or apperceptive mode) of objectivity. It suggests that these hard-won cultural achievements have come into being by way of asymmetrical parenting (which in effect tells the father that he should not love, as a mother loves, his children) and a developmental process that causes one gender (currently boys) enormous psychic pain but then rewards them with, in certain realms, cultural dominance.

Thus we are left facing the conclusion that if objectivity is a necessity, then   42
cultures must employ drastic methods—traditionally asymmetrical parenting—to bring it into being. It is clear to me that in a culture where male strength and freedom from the labor of pregnancy and childbirth are no longer required, the male sex has no claim to a privileged, masculine role. It is less clear to me that a culture in which symmetrical parenting becomes the norm could devise another method of bringing into being, nurturing, and making dominant in some realms certain hitherto masculine traits. Certainly I haven't heard any proponents of symmetrical parenting recognize the need for, much less propose, some such method.

The choice my wife and I face now is whether to encourage any traditionally   43
masculine behavior in our boys, whether to applaud or discourage their rough play, their fascination with tools and weapons, their eagerness to put their bodies at risk, their experiments with violence and destruction, and so on.

Take, for example, what seems to be the most egregious issue, weapons. My   44
wife feels strongly that we should actively discourage all weapon-play. We should

not only refrain from giving them weapons as toys, but we should intercede whenever we see them pretending that a stick, or a stone, or a finger is a weapon.

The case she makes is a compelling one. We both acknowledge a parent's   45
right, and responsibility, to intrude upon and guide a child's fantasy play. Certainly
we would intercede if we saw our sons playing games in which they fantasized acts
of cruelty or racism. If Sam and Leon pretended that some of their toy figures were
slaves and enjoyed chaining them together to march them to the fields, we would
step in and talk to the boys, wouldn't we? It seems reasonable, then, that we should
exercise this same sense of parental obligation with regard to weapons.

But what if weapon-play were an expression of a wider phenomenon, call it   46
fighting-play, and if fighting-play were an essential developmental method of experimenting with and actually achieving a sense of independence? When a boy
swipes at the air with a stick, he might be carving a space for himself in the world.
When he mows down legions of toy soldiers, he might be rehearsing the fantasy
that he can survive even when all others die. What if, by taking away their weapons
repeatedly, we are in effect saying to our children: do not fight the world even
when it appears to be wrong? What if a prohibition on weapon-play were interpreted by them as a prohibition of individualism: do not seek to distance yourself
from a network of interconnectedness, from a complex pattern of loyalties, but
remain forever embedded in, responsible to, and nurtured by, your world?

I think my wife and I part ways here. I think she would say that such implica-   47
tions pose no problem for her, that they might be desirable even. I disagree. I am
not about to buy the boys toy assault rifles and grenade launchers (toys that, by the
way, I had when I was a kid), but I don't want to embark on a course that imperils
their acquisition of a sense of self that is essentially isolate. One could rejoin that
many people develop such a sense of self without weapon-play or fighting-play. In
our culture, for example, many girls do. But this begs the question of whether any
girls would do so if the culture at large had not already promoted such a sense of
self by (among many other ways) allowing, or encouraging, boys to engage in such
play. My hunch is that they would not.

When all is said and done, however, masculinity may not need me to defend it.   48
In spite of all my wife and I have done to be equal partners and to gentle our sons
within the new order of symmetrical parenting, they retain a roughness at the core.
When their fingers curl around a new object, they assume that it must be a weapon
or a tool. In their little hands, Legos become swords, blocks become forts, sticks
become spears. They love nothing so much as the heft of a hammer or wrench
swiped from my toolbox. Sometimes a flower is beauty to behold and smell, sometimes it is fragility to pluck apart and destroy. They fling their bodies against the
world's resistance, testing the strength of their muscles against everything they
encounter—stairs, chairs, fence palings, newel posts, and of course bodies: their
own, each other's, and ours.

Where did the little Rambo in each of them come from? Because they are so   49
young, and because we have sheltered them from so many of society's images of
manhood, my wife and I uneasily confront the possibility that their masculine behavior might have genetic, not social origins. Like all good liberals, we are appalled. Surely nurture, not nature, is responsible for most of what we are. Surely
that aggressive hunch in our older son's shoulder as he runs full tilt toward his baby

brother is something that time, patience, and the model of a gentle father can eradicate? Surely we can weed out, not just come to terms with, the fury with which he beats a tree with a fallen branch? But when our younger son grins from his stroller and growlingly says "carrrr"—his first word—we wonder. I, perhaps, with a shade less misgiving than she.

Rhetorical Focus

1. Explore the ramifications of the image Bromell uses to introduce his essay, that of the wreck.
2. What audience has Bromell defined for himself? What rhetorical devices does he use to attempt to persuade that audience?
3. How would you describe the tone of Bromell's essay? Does it shift within the piece? If so, where and why? How does it compare to the tone employed by Perrin?

Thematic Focus

1. Bromell says that his argument challenges the major tenets of feminism, Marxism, and the world's great religions. Do you agree that it does? If so, in what ways. If not, why not?
2. Bromell is also clearly arguing against specific feminist researchers, namely Nancy Chodorow, Carol Gilligan, and Evelyn Fox Keller. What does Bromell find disturbing about their positions? Do you find his counterarguments convincing? Why or why not?
3. Bromell and his wife disagree about whether to encourage any traditionally masculine behavior in their two boys. Who do you sympathize with in this disagreement? Why?

Suggestions for Writing

1. Describe people you know who have masculine, feminine, or androgynous characteristics, focusing especially on their conformity to or freedom from gender stereotypes.
2. Both Perrin and Bromell suggest that gender identity may be biologically determined, to an extent. Construct an argument in which you support or refute this position.
3. Compare Bromell's conceptions of masculinity and femininity with Perrin's.

GENDER DIFFERENCES

Books and articles on gender differences have proliferated in the past few years. Inquiry into the behavior and attitudes of men and women is multidisciplinary, arising out of fields such as psychology, sociology, anthropology, literary studies, linguistics, the study of reading, composition studies, and others. This inquiry is also multicultural, reflecting both indigenous American and European influences. Findings to date are often contradictory. Some researchers emphasize difference, insisting that inattention to the ways in which men and women differ can lead to the oppression of women. Others celebrate women's distinctive attributes, seeing them as providing refreshing alternatives to our present structures and attitudes. Still others criticize this emphasis on difference, arguing that rigid gender-role stereotypes have been oppressive to women and calling for greater emphasis on commonalities between women and men.

Nancy Chodorow, Deborah Tannen, and Francine du Plessix Gray discuss differences in different modalities. Chodorow finds that asymmetrical parenting, in which the mother is the primary caregiver in the early years, leads to different developmental patterns for girls and boys. She calls for the institutionalization of symmetrical parenting and hence for the elimination of difference. Tannen seems to feel that differences between men and women are essential to their natures and that an understanding of these differences can eliminate conflict and bring about understanding between men and women. Gray sees gender difference as a cultural construct and finds that historical circumstances have brought about a situation within the Soviet Union in which women are in many ways more powerful than men.

Where do you situate yourself in this conversation? Should gender differences be celebrated or eliminated? Are our present modes of socialization injurious to girls or to boys or to both? Can we only speak of the problem within the context of a particular culture at a particular historical moment, or do these issues transcend the particularities of culture, class, and race?

The Sexual Sociology of Adult Life

Nancy Chodorow

Nancy Chodorow was born January 20, 1944, and is professor of sociology
at the University of California, Berkeley. She is the author of *The
Reproduction of Mothering*, 1978, from which this essay is taken, and of
Feminism and Psychoanalytic Theory, published in 1989. She received her
A.B. degree from Radcliffe and her M.A. and her Ph.D. from Brandeis.

Reflections Before Reading

The excerpt included in this chapter is from Chodorow's book, *The
Reproduction of Mothering*. What might such a title mean? What do you
think the title of the essay itself means? Chodorow explores the differing
developmental processes of girls and boys as a result of the asymmetrical
parenting that Bromell speaks about. Do you feel that your psychological
development is different from that of individuals of the opposite gender?

*Hence, there is a typically asymmetrical relation of the marriage pair to
the occupational structure.*
*This asymmetrical relation apparently both has exceedingly important
positive functional significance and is at the same time an important
source of strain in relation to the patterning of sex roles.*

Talcott Parsons,
"The Kinship System of the Contemporary United States"

Girls and boys develop different relational capacities and senses of self as a result   1
of growing up in a family in which women mother. These gender personalities are
reinforced by differences in the identification processes of boys and girls that also
result from women's mothering. Differing relational capacities and forms of identification prepare women and men to assume the adult gender roles which situate
women primarily within the sphere of reproduction in a sexually unequal society.

Gender Identification and Gender Role Learning

All social scientists who have examined processes of gender role learning and the development of a sense of identification in boys and girls have argued that the asymmetrical organization of parenting in which women mother is the basic cause of significant contrasts between feminine and masculine identification processes. Their discussions range from concern with the learning of appropriate gender role behavior—through imitation, explicit training and admonitions, and cognitive learning processes—to concern with the development of basic gender identity. The processes these people discuss seem to be universal, to the extent that all societies are constituted around a structural split, growing out of women's mothering, between the private, domestic world of women and the public, social world of men. Because the first identification for children of both genders has always been with their mother, they argue, and because children are first around women, women's family roles and being feminine are more available and often more intelligible to growing children than masculine roles and being masculine. Hence, male development is more complicated than female because of the difficult shifts of identification which a boy must make to attain his expected gender identification and gender role assumption. Their view contrasts sharply to the psychoanalytic stress on the difficulties inherent in feminine development as girls make their convoluted way to heterosexual object choice.°

Because all children identify first with their mother, a girl's gender and gender role identification processes are continuous with her earliest identifications and a boy's are not. A girl's oedipal identification with her mother, for instance, is continuous with her earliest primary identification (and also in the context of her early dependence and attachment). The boy's oedipal crisis, however, is supposed to enable him to shift in favor of an identification with his father. He gives up, in addition to his oedipal and preoedipal attachment to his mother, his primary identification with her.

What is true specifically for oedipal identification is equally true for more general gender identification and gender role learning. A boy, in order to feel himself adequately masculine, must distinguish and differentiate himself from others in a way that a girl need not—must categorize himself as someone apart. Moreover, he defines masculinity negatively as that which is not feminine and/or connected to women, rather than positively. This is another way boys come to deny and repress relation and connection in the process of growing up.

These distinctions remain even where much of a girl's and boy's socialization is the same, and where both go to school and can participate in adulthood in the labor force and other nonfamilial institutions. Because girls at the same time grow up in a family where mothers are the salient parent and caretaker, they also can

2

3

4

5

°The extent of masculine difficulty varies, as does the extent to which identification processes for boys and girls differ. This variance depends on the extent of the public–domestic split in a subculture or society—the extent to which men, men's work, and masculine activities are removed from the home, and therefore masculinity and personal relations with adult men are hard to come by for a child.

begin to identify more directly and immediately with their mothers and their mothers' familial roles than can boys with their fathers and men. Insofar as a woman's identity remains primarily as a wife/mother, moreover, there is greater generational continuity in role and life-activity from mother to daughter than there can be from father to son. This identity may be less than totally appropriate, as girls must realistically expect to spend much of their life in the labor force, whereas their mothers were less likely to do so. Nevertheless, family organization and ideology still produce these gender differences, and generate expectations that women much more than men will find a primary identity in the family.

Permanent father-absence, and the "father absence" that is normal in our so-   6
ciety, do not mean that boys do not learn masculine roles or proper masculine behavior, just as there is no evidence that homosexuality in women correlates with father absence. What matters is the extent to which a child of either gender can form a personal relationship with their object of identification, and the differences in modes of identification that result from this. Mitscherlich, Slater, Winch, and Lynn all speak to these differences. They suggest that girls in contemporary society develop a personal identification with their mother, and that a tie between affective processes and role learning—between libidinal and ego development—characterizes feminine development. By contrast, boys develop a positional identification with aspects of the masculine role. For them, the tie between affective processes and role learning is broken.

Personal identification, according to Slater and Winch, consists in diffuse   7
identification with someone else's general personality, behavioral traits, values, and attitudes. Positional identification consists, by contrast, in identification with specific aspects of another's role and does not necessarily lead to the internalization of the values or attitudes of the person identified with. According to Slater, children preferentially choose personal identification because this grows out of a positive affective relationship to a person who is there. They resort to positional identification residually and reactively, and identify with the perceived role or situation of another when possibilities for personal identification are not available.

In our society, a girl's mother is present in a way that a boy's father, and other   8
adult men, are not. A girl, then, can develop a personal identification with her mother, because she has a real relationship with her that grows out of their early primary tie. She learns what it is to be womanlike in the context of this personal identification with her mother and often with other female models (kin, teachers, mother's friends, mothers of friends). Feminine identification, then, can be based on the gradual learning of a way of being familiar in everyday life, exemplified by the relationship with the person with whom a girl has been most involved.

A boy must attempt to develop a masculine gender identification and learn the   9
masculine role in the absence of a continuous and ongoing personal relationship to his father (and in the absence of a continuously available masculine role model). This positional identification occurs both psychologically and sociologically. Psychologically, as is clear from descriptions of the masculine oedipus complex, boys appropriate those specific components of the masculinity of their father that they fear will be otherwise used against them, but do not as much identify diffusely with him as a person. Sociologically, boys in father-absent and normally father-remote

families develop a sense of what it is to be masculine through identification with cultural images of masculinity and men chosen as masculine models.

Boys are taught to be masculine more consciously than girls are taught to be feminine. When fathers or men are not present much, girls are taught the heterosexual components of their role, whereas boys are assumed to learn their heterosexual role without teaching, through interaction with their mother. By contrast, other components of masculinity must be more consciously imposed. Masculine identification, then, is predominantly a gender role identification. By contrast, feminine identification is predominantly *parental:* "Males tend to identify with a cultural stereotype of the masculine role; whereas females tend to identify with aspects of their own mother's role specifically."

Girls' identification processes, then, are more continuously embedded in and mediated by their ongoing relationship with their mother. They develop through and stress particularistic and affective relationships to others. A boy's identification processes are not likely to be so embedded in or mediated by a real affective relation to his father. At the same time, he tends to deny identification with and relationship to his mother and reject what he takes to be the feminine world; masculinity is defined as much negatively as positively. Masculine identification processes stress differentiation from others, the denial of affective relation, and categorical universalistic components of the masculine role. Feminine identification processes are relational, whereas masculine identification processes tend to deny relationship.

These distinctions do not mean that the development of femininity is all sugar and spice for a girl, but that it poses different *kinds* of problems for her than the development of masculinity does for a boy. The feminine identification that a girl attains and the masculine identification about which a boy remains uncertain are valued differently. In their unattainability, masculinity and the masculine role are fantasized and idealized by boys (and often by girls), whereas femininity and the feminine role remain for a girl all too real and concrete. The demands on women are often contradictory—for instance, to be passive and dependent in relation to men, and active and independently initiating toward children. In the context of the ego and object-relational issues I described in the preceding chapters, moreover, it is clear that mother-identification presents difficulties. A girl identifies with and is expected to identify with her mother in order to attain her adult feminine identification and learn her adult gender role. At the same time she must be sufficiently differentiated to grow up and experience herself as a separate individual—must overcome primary identification while maintaining and building a secondary identification.

Studies suggest that daughters in American society have problems with differentiation from and identification with their mothers. Slater reports that all forms of personal parental identification (cross-gender and same-gender) correlate with freedom from psychosis or neurosis except personal identification of a daughter with her mother. Johnson reports that a boy's identification with his father relates to psychological adjustment, whereas a girl's with her mother does not. The implication in both accounts is that for a girl, just as for a boy, there can be too much of

10

11

12

13

mother. It may be easy, but possibly too easy, for a girl to attain a feminine gender identification.°

Gender and gender-role identification processes accord with my earlier account of the development of psychic structure. They reinforce and replicate the object-relational and ego outcomes which I have described. Externally, as internally, women grow up and remain more connected to others. Not only are the roles which girls learn more interpersonal, particularistic, and affective than those which boys learn. Processes of identification and role learning for girls also tend to be particularistic and affective—embedded in an interpersonal relationship with their mothers. For boys, identification processes and masculine role learning are not likely to be embedded in relationship with their fathers or men but rather to involve the denial of affective relationship to their mothers. These processes tend to be more role-defined and cultural, to consist in abstract or categorical role learning rather than in personal identification.   14

Rhetorical Focus

1. Unlike the other writers in this chapter, Chodorow is a social scientist. How does her writing differ from the reflective essays we have encountered in this chapter so far?
2. Compare Chodorow's style to that of a humanistic essay employing considerably more narrative. Which do you prefer? Why?
3. Identify terms that Chodorow uses that are unfamiliar to you. Define them either by drawing on contextual cues within the passage or by referring to a dictionary or psychology textbook.

Thematic Focus

1. In paragraph 11, Chodorow says, "Feminine identification processes are relational, whereas masculine identification processes tend to deny relationship." Do you agree with this statement? Does it describe your experience?
2. Femininity is sometimes defined as the negation of masculinity. Chodorow, however, reverses this idea, suggesting in paragraph 11 that "masculinity is defined as much negatively as positively." How do you respond to this idea?
3. Chodorow says masculinity and femininity are idealized by boys, whereas femininity and feminine roles remain for a girl too real and concrete. Does this assertion coincide with your own experience? Why or why not?

°Recall also Deutsch's description of the prepubertal girl's random attempts to break her identification with her mother.

Different Words, Different Worlds

Deborah Tannen

Deborah Tannen, born in 1945 in Brooklyn, New York, is a professor of
linguistics at Georgetown University, where she has taught since 1979. Her
Ph.D. is from the University of California, Berkeley. She has received grants
from the National Endowment for the Humanities, the Rockefeller
Foundation, and the National Science Foundation and has made her research
available to the general public through articles in *The New York Times
Magazine*, *New York* magazine, and *The Washington Post*. She is the author
of *That's Not What I Meant!* The essay reprinted here is from her
bestselling book, *You Just Don't Understand: Women and Men in
Conversation*.

Reflections Before Reading

Tannen sees that men and women interpret reality in different ways. Do you
think that you interpret your experiences and the behavior and conversations
of others differently from individuals of the opposite gender? If so, what are
some of those differences? How do you account for them? If not, how do
you account for positions such as Tannen's? Tannen's essay is from her
book entitled *You Just Don't Understand*. What do you think her title
means?

Many years ago I was married to a man who shouted at me, "I do not give you the 1
right to raise your voice to me, because you are a woman and I am a man." This was
frustrating, because I knew it was unfair. But I also knew just what was going on. I
ascribed his unfairness to his having grown up in a country where few people
thought women and men might have equal rights.

Now I am married to a man who is a partner and friend. We come from similar 2
backgrounds and share values and interests. It is a continual source of pleasure to
talk to him. It is wonderful to have someone I can tell everything to, someone who
understands. But he doesn't always see things as I do, doesn't always react to things
as I expect him to. And I often don't understand why he says what he does.

Abridgement of "Different Words, Different Worlds", *You Just Don't Understand* by Deborah Tannen, Ph.D. Copyright © 1990 by Deborah Tannen, Ph.D. Published by William Morrow & Company,
Inc. Reprinted by permission.

At the time I began working on this book, we had jobs in different cities.   3
People frequently expressed sympathy by making comments like "That must be
rough," and "How do you stand it?" I was inclined to accept their sympathy and say
things like "We fly a lot." Sometimes I would reinforce their concern: "The worst
part is having to pack and unpack all the time." But my husband reacted differently, often with irritation. He might respond by de-emphasizing the inconve-
nience: As academics, we had four-day weekends together, as well as long vacations throughout the year and four months in the summer. We even benefited
from the intervening days of uninterrupted time for work. I once overheard him
telling a dubious man that we were lucky, since studies have shown that married
couples who live together spend less than half an hour a week talking to each other;
he was implying that our situation had advantages.

I didn't object to the way my husband responded—everything he said was   4
true—but I was surprised by it. I didn't understand why he reacted as he did. He
explained that he sensed condescension in some expressions of concern, as if the
questioner were implying, "Yours is not a real marriage; your ill-chosen profession
has resulted in an unfortunate arrangement. I pity you, and look down at you from
the height of complacence, since my wife and I have avoided your misfortune." It
had not occurred to me that there might be an element of one-upmanship in these
expressions of concern, though I could recognize it when it was pointed out. Even
after I saw the point, though, I was inclined to regard my husband's response as
slightly odd, a personal quirk. He frequently seemed to see others as adversaries
when I didn't.

Having done the research that led to this book, I now see that my husband was   5
simply engaging the world in a way that many men do: as an individual in a hierarchical social order in which he was either one-up or one-down. In this world, conversations are negotiations in which people try to achieve and maintain the upper
hand if they can, and protect themselves from others' attempts to put them down
and push them around. Life, then, is a contest, a struggle to preserve independence and avoid failure.

I, on the other hand, was approaching the world as many women do: as an   6
individual in a network of connections. In this world, conversations are negotiations for closeness in which people try to seek and give confirmation and support,
and to reach consensus. They try to protect themselves from others' attempts to
push them away. Life, then, is a community, a struggle to preserve intimacy and
avoid isolation. Though there are hierarchies in this world too, they are hierarchies
more of friendship than of power and accomplishment.

Women are also concerned with achieving status and avoiding failure, but   7
these are not the goals they are *focused* on all the time, and they tend to pursue
them in the guise of connection. And men are also concerned with achieving involvement and avoiding isolation, but they are not *focused* on these goals, and they
tend to pursue them in the guise of opposition.

Discussing our differences from this point of view, my husband pointed out to   8
me a distinction I had missed: He reacted the way I just described only if expressions of concern came from men in whom he sensed an awareness of hierarchy.
And there were times when I too disliked people's expressing sympathy about our

commuting marriage. I recall being offended by one man who seemed to have a leering look in his eye when he asked, "How do you manage this long-distance romance?" Another time I was annoyed when a woman who knew me only by reputation approached us during the intermission of a play, discovered our situation by asking my husband where he worked, and kept the conversation going by asking us all about it. In these cases, I didn't feel put down; I felt intruded upon. If my husband was offended by what he perceived as claims to superior status, I felt these sympathizers were claiming inappropriate intimacy.

Intimacy and Independence

Intimacy is key in a world of connection where individuals negotiate complex networks of friendship, minimize differences, try to reach consensus, and avoid the appearance of superiority, which would highlight differences. In a world of status, *independence* is key, because a primary means of establishing status is to tell others what to do, and taking orders is a marker of low status. Though all humans need both intimacy and independence, women tend to focus on the first and men on the second. It is as if their lifeblood ran in different directions.   9

These differences can give women and men differing views of the same situation, as they did in the case of a couple I will call Linda and Josh. When Josh's old high-school chum called him at work and announced he'd be in town on business the following month, Josh invited him to stay for the weekend. That evening he informed Linda that they were going to have a houseguest, and that he and his chum would go out together the first night to shoot the breeze like old times. Linda was upset. She was going to be away on business the week before, and the Friday night when Josh would be out with his chum would be her first night home. But what upset her the most was that Josh had made these plans on his own and informed her of them, rather than discussing them with her before extending the invitation.   10

Linda would never make plans, for a weekend or an evening, without first checking with Josh. She can't understand why he doesn't show her the same courtesy and consideration that she shows him. But when she protests, Josh says, "I can't say to my friend, 'I have to ask my wife for permission'!"   11

To Josh, checking with his wife means seeking permission, which implies that he is not independent, not free to act on his own. It would make him feel like a child or an underling. To Linda, checking with her husband has nothing to do with permission. She assumes that spouses discuss their plans with each other because their lives are intertwined, so the actions of one have consequences for the other. Not only does Linda not mind telling someone, "I have to check with Josh"; quite the contrary—she likes it. It makes her feel good to know and show that she is involved with someone, that her life is bound up with someone else's.   12

Linda and Josh both felt more upset by this incident, and others like it, than seemed warranted, because it cut to the core of their primary concerns. Linda was hurt because she sensed a failure of closeness in their relationship: He didn't care about her as much as she cared about him. And he was hurt because he felt she was trying to control him and limit his freedom.   13

A similar conflict exists between Louise and Howie, another couple, about   14
spending money. Louise would never buy anything costing more than a hundred
dollars without discussing it with Howie, but he goes out and buys whatever he
wants and feels they can afford, like a table saw or a new power mower. Louise is
disturbed, not because she disapproves of the purchases, but because she feels he
is acting as if she were not in the picture.

Many women feel it is natural to consult with their partners at every turn,   15
while many men automatically make more decisions without consulting their partners. This may reflect a broad difference in conceptions of decision making.
Women expect decisions to be discussed first and made by consensus. They appreciate the discussion itself as evidence of involvement and communication. But
many men feel oppressed by lengthy discussions about what they see as minor
decisions, and they feel hemmed in if they can't just act without talking first. When
women try to initiate a freewheeling discussion by asking, "What do you think?"
men often think they are being asked to decide.

Communication is a continual balancing act, juggling the conflicting needs for   16
intimacy and independence. To survive in the world, we have to act in concert with
others, but to survive as ourselves, rather than simply as cogs in a wheel, we have to
act alone. In some ways, all people are the same: We all eat and sleep and drink
and laugh and cough, and often we eat, and laugh at, the same things. But in some
ways, each person is different, and individuals' differing wants and preferences
may conflict with each other. Offered the same menu, people make different
choices. And if there is cake for dessert, there is a chance one person may get a
larger piece than another—and an even greater chance that one will *think* the
other's piece is larger, whether it is or not.

Asymmetries

If intimacy says, "We're close and the same," and independence says, "We're sep-   17
arate and different," it is easy to see that intimacy and independence dovetail with
connection and status. The essential element of connection is symmetry: People
are the same, feeling equally close to each other. The essential element of status is
asymmetry: People are not the same; they are differently placed in a hierarchy.

This duality is particularly clear in expressions of sympathy or concern, which   18
are all potentially ambiguous. They can be interpreted either symmetrically, as
evidence of fellow feeling among equals, or asymmetrically, offered by someone
one-up to someone one-down. Asking if an unemployed person has found a job, if
a couple have succeeded in conceiving the child they crave, or whether an unten-
ured professor expects to get tenure can be meant—and interpreted, regardless of
how it is meant—as an expression of human connection by a person who understands and cares, or as a reminder of weakness from someone who is better off and
knows it, and hence as condescending. The latter view of sympathy seems self-
evident to many men. For example, a handicapped mountain climber named Tom
Whittaker, who leads groups of disabled people on outdoor expeditions, remarked,
"You can't feel sympathetic for someone you admire"—a statement that struck me
as not true at all.

The symmetry of connection is what creates community: If two people are   19
struggling for closeness, they are both struggling for the same thing. And the asymmetry of status is what creates contest: Two people can't both have the upper
hand, so negotiation for status is inherently adversarial. In my earlier work, I explored in detail the dynamics of intimacy (which I referred to as involvement) and
independence, but I tended to ignore the force of status and its adversarial nature.
Once I identified these dynamics, however, I saw them all around me. The puzzling behavior of friends and co-workers finally became comprehensible.

Differences in how my husband and I approached the same situation, which   20
previously would have been mystifying, suddenly made sense. For example, in a
jazz club the waitress recommended the crab cakes to me, and they turned out to
be terrible. I was uncertain about whether or not to send them back. When the
waitress came by and asked how the food was, I said that I didn't really like the
crab cakes. She asked, "What's wrong with them?" While staring at the table, my
husband answered, "They don't taste fresh." The waitress snapped, "They're frozen! What do you expect?" I looked directly up at her and said, "We just don't like
them." She said, "Well, if you don't like them, I could take them back and bring
you something else."

After she left with the crab cakes, my husband and I laughed because we   21
realized we had just automatically played out the scripts I had been writing about.
He had heard her question "What's wrong with them?" as a challenge that he had
to match. He doesn't like to fight, so he looked away, to soften what he felt was an
obligatory counterchallenge: He felt instinctively that he had to come up with
something wrong with the crab cakes to justify my complaint. (He was fighting for
me.) I had taken the question "What's wrong with them?" as a request for information. I instinctively sought a way to be right without making her wrong. Perhaps it
was because she was a woman that she responded more favorably to my approach.

When I have spoken to friends and to groups about these differences, they too   22
say that now they can make sense of previously perplexing behavior. For example,
a woman said she finally understood why her husband refused to talk to his boss
about whether or not he stood a chance of getting promoted. He wanted to know
because if the answer was no, he would start looking for another job. But instead of
just asking, he stewed and fretted, lost sleep, and worried. Having no others at her
disposal, this wife had fallen back on psychological explanations: Her husband
must be insecure, afraid of rejection. But then, everyone is insecure, to an extent.
Her husband was actually quite a confident person. And she, who believed herself
to be at least as insecure as he, had not hesitated to go to her boss to ask whether he
intended to make her temporary job permanent.

Understanding the key role played by status in men's relations made it all   23
come clear. Asking a boss about chances for promotion highlights the hierarchy in
the relationship, reminding them both that the employee's future is in the boss's
hands. Taking the low-status position made this man intensely uncomfortable. Although his wife didn't especially relish taking the role of supplicant with respect to
her boss, it didn't set off alarms in her head, as it did in his.

In a similar flash of insight, a woman who works in sales exclaimed that now   24
she understood the puzzling transformation that the leader of her sales team had

undergone when he was promoted to district manager. She had been sure he would make a perfect boss because he had a healthy disregard for authority. As team leader, he had rarely bothered to go to meetings called by management and had encouraged team members to exercise their own judgment, eagerly using his power to waive regulations on their behalf. But after he became district manager, this man was unrecognizable. He instituted more regulations than anyone had dreamed of, and insisted that exceptions could be made only on the basis of written requests to him.

This man behaved differently because he was now differently placed in the hierarchy. When he had been subject to the authority of management, he'd done all he could to limit it. But when the authority of management was vested in him, he did all he could to enlarge it. By avoiding meetings and flouting regulations, he had evidenced not disregard for hierarchy but rather discomfort at being in the subordinate position within it. 25

Yet another woman said she finally understood why her fiancé, who very much believes in equality, once whispered to her that she should keep her voice down. "My friends are downstairs," he said. "I don't want them to get the impression that you order me around." 26

That women have been labeled "nags" may result from the interplay of men's and women's styles, whereby many women are inclined to do what is asked of them and many men are inclined to resist even the slightest hint that anyone, especially a woman, is telling them what to do. A woman will be inclined to repeat a request that doesn't get a response because she is convinced that her husband would do what she asks, if he only understood that she *really* wants him to do it. But a man who wants to avoid feeling that he is following orders may instinctively wait before doing what she asked, in order to imagine that he is doing it of his own free will. Nagging is the result, because each time she repeats the request, he again puts off fulfilling it. 27

◦   ◦   ◦

Mixed Judgments and Misjudgments

Because men and women are regarding the landscape from contrasting vantage points, the same scene can appear very different to them, and they often have opposite interpretations of the same action. 28

A colleague mentioned that he got a letter from a production editor working on his new book, instructing him to let her know if he planned to be away from his permanent address at any time in the next six months, when his book would be in production. He commented that he hadn't realized how like a parole officer a production editor could be. His response to this letter surprised me, because I have received similar letters from publishers, and my response is totally different: I like them, because it makes me feel important to know that my whereabouts matter. When I mentioned this difference to my colleague, he was puzzled and amused, as I was by his reaction. Though he could understand my point of view intellectually, emotionally he could not imagine how one could not feel framed as 29 both controlled and inferior in rank by being told to report one's movements to someone. And though I could understand his perspective intellectually, it simply held no emotional resonance for me.

In a similar spirit, my colleague remarked that he had read a journal article 30 written by a woman who thanked her husband in the acknowledgments section of her paper for helpful discussion of the topic. When my colleague first read this acknowledgment, he thought the author must be incompetent, or at least insecure: Why did she have to consult her husband about her own work? Why couldn't she stand on her own two feet? After hearing my explanation that women value evidence of connection, he reframed the acknowledgment and concluded that the author probably valued her husband's involvement in her work and made reference to it with the pride that comes of believing one has evidence of a balanced relationship.

If my colleague's reaction is typical, imagine how often women who think they 31 are displaying a positive quality—connection—are misjudged by men who perceive them as revealing a lack of independence, which the men regard as synonymous with incompetence and insecurity.

In Pursuit of Freedom

A woman was telling me why a long-term relationship had ended. She recounted a 32 recurrent and pivotal conversation. She and the man she lived with had agreed that they would both be free, but they would not do anything to hurt each other. When the man began to sleep with other women, she protested, and he was incensed at her protest. Their conversation went like this:

SHE: How can you do this when you know it's hurting me?
HE: How can you try to limit my freedom?
SHE: But it makes me feel awful.
HE: You are trying to manipulate me.

On one level, this is simply an example of a clash of wills: What he wanted conflicted with what she wanted. But in a fundamental way, it reflects the difference in focus I have been describing. In arguing for his point of view, the key issue for this man was his independence, his freedom of action. The key issue for the woman was their interdependence—how what he did made her feel. He interpreted her insistence on their interdependence as "manipulation": She was using her feelings to control his behavior.

The point is not that women do not value freedom or that men do not value 33 their connection to others. It is rather that the desire for freedom and independence becomes more of an issue for many men in relationships, whereas interdependence and connection become more of an issue for many women. The difference is one of focus and degree.

In a study of how women and men talk about their divorces, Catherine Kohler 34 Riessman found that both men and women mentioned increased freedom as a benefit of divorce. But the word *freedom* meant different things to them. When women told her they had gained freedom by divorce, they meant that they had gained "independence and autonomy." It was a relief for them not to have to worry about how their husbands would react to what they did, and not have to be "responsive to a disgruntled spouse." When men mentioned freedom as a benefit of divorce, they meant freedom from obligation—the relief of feeling "less confined," less "claustrophobic," and having "fewer responsibilities."

Riessman's findings illuminate the differing burdens that are placed on women and men by their characteristic approaches to relationships. The burden from which divorce delivered the women was perceived as internally motivated: the continual preoccupation with how their husbands would respond to them and how they should respond to their husbands. The burden from which it delivered the men was perceived as externally imposed: the obligations of the provider role and a feeling of confinement from having their behavior constrained by others. Independence was not a gift of divorce for the men Riessman interviewed, because, as one man put it, "I always felt independent and I guess it's just more so now." 35

The Chronicle of Higher Education conducted a small survey, asking six university professors why they had chosen the teaching profession. Among the six were four men and two women. In answering the question, the two women referred to teaching. One said, "I've always wanted to teach." The other said, "I knew as an undergraduate that I wanted to join a faculty. . . . I realized that teaching was the thing I wanted to do." The four men's answers had much in common with each other and little in common with the women's. All four men referred to independence as their main motive. Here are excerpts from each of their responses: 36

> I decided it was academe over industry because I would have my choice of research. There's more independence.

> I wanted to teach, and I like the freedom to set your own research goals.

> I chose an academic job because the freedoms of academia outweighed the money disadvantages—and to pursue the research interest I'd like to, as opposed to having it dictated.

> I have a problem that interests me. . . . I'd rather make $30,000 for the rest of my life and be allowed to do basic research than to make $100,000 and work in computer graphics.

Though one man also mentioned teaching, neither of the women mentioned freedom to pursue their own research interests as a main consideration. I do not believe this means that women are not interested in research, but rather that independence, freedom from being told what to do, is not as significant a preoccupation for them.

In describing what appealed to them about teaching, these two women focused on the ability to influence students in a positive way. Of course, influencing students reflects a kind of power over them, and teaching entails an asymmetrical relationship, with the teacher in the higher-status position. But in talking about their profession, the women focused on connection to students, whereas the men focused on their freedom from others' control. 37

Male–Female Conversation Is
Cross-cultural Communication

If women speak and hear a language of connection and intimacy, while men speak   38
and hear a language of status and independence, then communication between
men and women can be like cross-cultural communication, prey to a clash of conversational styles. Instead of different dialects, it has been said they speak different
genderlects.

The claim that men and women grow up in different worlds may at first seem   39
patently absurd. Brothers and sisters grow up in the same families, children to
parents of both genders. Where, then, do women and men learn different ways of
speaking and hearing?

It Begins at the Beginning

Even if they grow up in the same neighborhood, on the same block, or in the same   40
house, girls and boys grow up in different worlds of words. Others talk to them
differently and expect and accept different ways of talking from them. Most important, children learn how to talk, how to have conversations, not only from their
parents but from their peers. After all, if their parents have a foreign or regional
accent, children do not emulate it; they learn to speak with the pronunciation of
the region where they grow up. Anthropologists Daniel Maltz and Ruth Borker
summarize research showing that boys and girls have very different ways of talking
to their friends. Although they often play together, boys and girls spend most of
their time playing in same-sex groups. And, although some of the activities they
play at are similar, their favorite games are different, and their ways of using language in their games are separated by a world of difference.

Boys tend to play outside, in large groups that are hierarchically structured.   41
Their groups have a leader who tells others what to do and how to do it, and resists
doing what other boys propose. It is by giving orders and making them stick that
high status is negotiated. Another way boys achieve status is to take center stage by
telling stories and jokes, and by sidetracking or challenging the stories and jokes of
others. Boys' games have winners and losers and elaborate systems of rules that are
frequently the subjects of arguments. Finally, boys are frequently heard to boast of
their skill and argue about who is best at what.

Girls, on the other hand, play in small groups or in pairs; the center of a girl's   42
social life is a best friend. Within the group, intimacy is key: Differentiation is
measured by relative closeness. In their most frequent games, such as jump rope
and hopscotch, everyone gets a turn. Many of their activities (such as playing
house) do not have winners or losers. Though some girls are certainly more skilled
than others, girls are expected not to boast about it, or show that they think they
are better than the others. Girls don't give orders; they express their preferences as
suggestions, and suggestions are likely to be accepted. Whereas boys say, "Gimme
that!" and "Get outta here!" girls say, "Let's do this," and "How about doing that?"
Anything else is put down as "bossy." They don't grab center stage—they don't
want it—so they don't challenge each other directly. And much of the time, they

simply sit together and talk. Girls are not accustomed to jockeying for status in an obvious way; they are more concerned that they be liked.

Gender differences in ways of talking have been described by researchers observing children as young as three. Amy Sheldon videotaped three- to four-year-old boys and girls playing in threesomes at a day-care center. She compared two groups of three—one of boys, one of girls—that got into fights about the same play item: a plastic pickle. Though both groups fought over the same thing, the dynamics by which they negotiated their conflicts were different. In addition to illustrating some of the patterns I have just described, Sheldon's study also demonstrates the complexity of these dynamics. 43

While playing in the kitchen area of the day-care center, a little girl named Sue wanted the pickle that Mary had, so she argued that Mary should give it up because Lisa, the third girl, wanted it. This led to a conflict about how to satisfy Lisa's (invented) need. Mary proposed a compromise, but Sue protested: 44

MARY: I cut it in half. One for Lisa, one for me, one for me.
SUE: But, Lisa wants a *whole* pickle!

Mary comes up with another creative compromise, which Sue also rejects:

MARY: Well, it's a whole *half* pickle.
SUE: No, it isn't.
MARY: Yes, it is, a whole *half* pickle.
SUE: *I'll* give her a whole half. I'll give her a *whole whole*. I gave her a whole one.

At this point, Lisa withdraws from the alliance with Sue, who satisfies herself by saying, "I'm pretending I gave you one."

On another occasion, Sheldon videotaped three boys playing in the same kitchen play area, and they too got into a fight about the plastic pickle. When Nick saw that Kevin had the pickle, he demanded it for himself: 45

NICK: [Screams] Kevin, but the, oh, I *have* to cut! I want to cut it! It's mine!

Like Sue, Nick involved the third child in his effort to get the pickle:

NICK: [Whining to Joe] Kevin is not letting me cut the pickle.
JOE: Oh, I know! I can pull it away from him and give it back to you. That's an idea!

The boys' conflict, which lasted two and a half times longer than the girls', then proceeded as a struggle between Nick and Joe on the one hand and Kevin on the other.

In comparing the boys' and girls' pickle fights, Sheldon points out that, for the most part, the girls mitigated the conflict and preserved harmony by compromise and evasion. Conflict was more prolonged among the boys, who used more insis- 46 tence, appeals to rules, and threats of physical violence. However, to say that these little girls and boys used *more* of one strategy or another is not to say that they didn't use the other strategies at all. For example, the boys did attempt compromise, and the girls did attempt physical force. The girls, like the boys, were struggling for control of their play. When Sue says by mistake, "*I'll* give her a whole half," then quickly corrects herself to say, "I'll give her a *whole whole*," she reveals that it is not really the size of the portion that is important to her, but who gets to serve it.

While reading Sheldon's study, I noticed that whereas both Nick and Sue tried   47
to get what they wanted by involving a third child, the alignments they created with the third child, and the dynamics they set in motion, were fundamentally different. Sue appealed to Mary to fulfill someone else's desire; rather than saying that *she* wanted the pickle, she claimed that Lisa wanted it. Nick asserted his own desire for the pickle, and when he couldn't get it on his own, he appealed to Joe to get it for him. Joe then tried to get the pickle by force. In both these scenarios, the children were enacting complex lines of affiliation.

Joe's strong-arm tactics were undertaken not on his own behalf but, chival-   48
rously, on behalf of Nick. By making an appeal in a whining voice, Nick positioned himself as one-down in a hierarchical structure, framing himself as someone in need of protection. When Sue appealed to Mary to relinquish her pickle, she wanted to take the one-up position of serving food. She was fighting not for the right to *have* the pickle, but for the right to *serve* it. (This reminded me of the women who said they'd become professors in order to teach.) But to accomplish her goal, Sue was depending on Mary's desire to fulfill others' needs.

This study suggests that boys and girls both want to get their way, but they   49
tend to do so differently. Though social norms encourage boys to be openly competitive and girls to be openly cooperative, different situations and activities can result in different ways of behaving. Marjorie Harness Goodwin compared boys and girls engaged in two task-oriented activities: The boys were making slingshots in preparation for a fight, and the girls were making rings. She found that the boys' group was hierarchical: The leader told the others what to do and how to do it. The girls' group was egalitarian: Everyone made suggestions and tended to accept the suggestions of others. But observing the girls in a different activity—playing house—Goodwin found that they too adopted hierarchical structures: The girls who played mothers issued orders to the girls playing children, who in turn sought permission from their play-mothers. Moreover, a girl who was a play-mother was also a kind of manager of the game. This study shows that girls know how to issue orders and operate in a hierarchical structure, but they don't find that mode of behavior appropriate when they engage in task activities with their peers. They do find it appropriate in parent–child relationships, which they enjoy practicing in the form of play.

These worlds of play shed light on the world views of women and men in   50
relationships. The boys' play illuminates why men would be on the lookout for signs they are being put down or told what to do. The chief commodity that is bartered in the boys' hierarchical world is status, and the way to achieve and maintain status is to give orders and get others to follow them. A boy in a low-status

position finds himself being pushed around. So boys monitor their relations for subtle shifts in status by keeping track of who's giving orders and who's taking them.

These dynamics are not the ones that drive girls' play. The chief commodity that is bartered in the girls' community is intimacy. Girls monitor their friendships for subtle shifts in alliance, and they seek to be friends with popular girls. Popularity is a kind of status, but it is founded on connection. It also places popular girls in a bind. By doing field work in a junior high school, Donna Eder found that popular girls were paradoxically—and inevitably—disliked. Many girls want to befriend popular girls, but girls' friendships must necessarily be limited, since they entail intimacy rather than large group activities. So a popular girl must reject the overtures of most of the girls who seek her out—with the result that she is branded "stuck up."   51

The Key Is Understanding

If adults learn their ways of speaking as children growing up in separate social worlds of peers, then conversation between women and men is cross-cultural communication. Although each style is valid on its own terms, misunderstandings arise because the styles are different. Taking a cross-cultural approach to male–female conversations makes it possible to explain why dissatisfactions are justified without accusing anyone of being wrong or crazy.   52

Learning about style differences won't make them go away, but it can banish mutual mystification and blame. Being able to understand why our partners, friends, and even strangers behave the way they do is a comfort, even if we still don't see things the same way. It makes the world into more familiar territory. And having others understand why we talk and act as we do protects us from the pain of their puzzlement and criticism.   53

In discussing her novel *The Temple of My Familiar*, Alice Walker explained that a woman in the novel falls in love with a man because she sees in him "a giant ear." Walker went on to remark that although people may think they are falling in love because of sexual attraction or some other force, "really what we're looking for is someone to be able to hear us."   54

We all want, above all, to be heard—but not merely to be heard. We want to be understood—heard for what we think we are saying, for what we know we meant. With increased understanding of the ways women and men use language should come a decrease in frequency of the complaint "You just don't understand."   55

Rhetorical Focus

1. How would you describe the audience Tannen is writing for? What stylistic features of the essay provide evidence in support of your choice?
2. Contrast Tannen's style with Chodorow's. In what ways do their differing audiences determine their differing styles?

3. Analyze Tannen's organizational structure. Does she employ a tight, linear approach or a loose, associative approach? Why do you think she organized her material in the way she did?

Thematic Focus

1. Tannen has a number of paired oppositions in the essay. How many of these can you identify? Do you agree with the ways in which Tannen has associated them with a particular gender?
2. Do you think Tannen overstates her case? Explain your answer.
3. Compare Tannen's explanation for why gender differences occur with Chodorow's. Are they fundamentally in agreement or in disagreement?

Soviet Women
Francine du Plessix Gray

Born in 1930 in France, Francine du Plessix Gray came to the United States when she was 11 years old. She has been a free-lance writer for many years, contributing to *Vogue,* the *New Yorker,* the *New Republic, Saturday Review,* and the *New York Review of Books.* She has taught at Yale University and Columbia University, and won the National Catholic Book Award for *Divine Disobedience: Profiles in Catholic Radicalism* (1970) and the Front Page Award for *Hawaii: The Sugar-Coated Fortress* (1972). Gray has written the novels *Lovers and Tyrants* (1976), *World Without End* (1981), and *October Blood* (1985). In 1987, she published a collection of essays called *Adam and Eve in the City.* Her book *Soviet Women* was published in 1990.

Reflections Before Reading

Gray's essay suggests that attitudes toward gender may differ somewhat from culture to culture. To what extent are your own attitudes a result of the culture in which you were raised? Gray is describing attitudes of and toward women in the Soviet Union today. What do you suppose those attitudes are? How do you think they might differ from attitudes of and toward women in the United States?

Throughout my stays in the Soviet Union, I kept remembering these early glimpses of male passivity and disillusionment, of female power and self-esteem, while talking to the few scholars who are beginning to research patterns of sex differences in Soviet society. Because of the distaste for such analysis that prevails in any Marxist state, it is an area of psychology that has been virtually untouched in the Soviet Union until recently.   1

Olga Voronina, my philosopher friend in Moscow who is one of the even smaller group of scholars who consider themselves "feminists" (she estimates that no more than twenty women in Moscow would accept that label), views the situation this way: Soviet girls are favored by teachers from the earliest preschool days, because, having stronger role models, they are more obedient than boys and do far better in school. "Even in such patriarchal organizations as Pioneer groups, until the age of fourteen or so the girls were always far more active—I say 'were' because the popularity of such Party organizations has much decreased lately," she said. "Look at their role models: mother often alone at home ruling the roost, an all-female cast of teachers, and, all around them, women handling the double shift of career and home. The girls absorb this female energy and are more active on every level throughout their school years. But as they reach adolescence they tend consciously to slow down, and curb themselves; they think an overactive woman is less appealing. Well, God only knows how aggressive we'd be if we *didn't* curb ourselves a little bit!"   2

"I know that a majority of public-school teachers in the U.S.A. are also women," my friend Elvira Novikova, another feminist scholar, said. "But it's a Soviet phenomenon for teachers to favor girls as much as we do. That creates a pattern of anti-social behavior among boys. It leads them to feel that it's not 'cool' to get good grades, and it reinforces their resentment of women. A boy's ego is further undermined because he spends most of his time at home with his mother; his father—if he has one—is often too passive or too macho or not sensitive enough to deal with a child's problems and become a proper role model."   3

"Our young men have gone out into the world with the attitude that they're little boys, still under the wings of their mommies," said Monika Zile, the magazine editor. "When they've had to take a responsibility or make a decision, a woman has always stepped in to take over."   4

Mariya Osorina, a Leningrad psychologist, offered more complex historical reasons for what one could call "the Powerful Woman Syndrome" in Russian society. She sees a breaking point in nineteenth-century history, in the Decembrist rebellion of 1825: when that first wave of political dissent was brutally crushed by the czar, Russia's male intelligentsia lost much of its self-esteem, began to feel marginal and helpless before an immutable authoritarian regime. She also believes that the deepest traditions of Russian culture—the high value on inner emotional   5 life, the life of the spirit—are far more feminine than those of most other nations. "Compare our traditional values, for instance, with the very masculine, pragmatic, utilitarian German ethos," she said. "For some eight centuries, we praised and upheld all that was connected with *dukhovnye tsennosty*—'spiritual values'—and we were taught to disdain most practical aspects of existence. This reverence for values associated with the female principle gave women an immense psychic power, even through the feudalism and repression that lasted until the late nineteenth century, even before they were allowed to have schooling and careers. Ironically, the union of feminine and national values has continued right into postrevolutionary times. Teachers have favored girls because their behavior is more closely modelled on the Soviet system of social values—on communitarian obedience, orderliness, altruism, dutifulness."

On all levels of Soviet society, one is constantly impressed by women's keen   6
sense of their greater patience, diligence, optimism, endurance, shrewdness, and self-esteem—a self-esteem apparently heightened by the very arduousness of their everyday duties, their incessant foraging for basic necessities of food and clothing. This sense of female superiority is summed up with eerie precision by a Russian proverb: "Women can do everything; men can do the rest."

What are some other reasons that make it easier for women than for men to   7
grow into powerful, responsible citizens with superior work habits? When answering that question today, in the *glasnost* era, most Soviet citizens feel free to put the blame on their nation's history: through centuries of serfdom and seven decades of dictatorship, men have never had a chance to develop their initiative.

In a culture in which men have never felt themselves to be masters of their   8
fates, never felt any real worth in their work, "how could they ever become responsible?" Monika Zile asks. "Women, on the other hand, kept right on ruling over their little domestic kingdoms, and never suffered an equal sense of helplessness. And at the time of the revolution, when only some ten per cent of our women were literate, they had to take such huge leaps that somehow they just kept leaping on and on, bypassing the men in many ways—in levels of education, of steadfastness, and, particularly, of diligence."

Soviet women's remarkable self-assurance (not to say their superiority complex) leads to an often derisive view of men that might make the most committed   9
American feminist uncomfortable. I felt it painfully during a discussion with a group of women who were television producers in Riga. They had expressed the recurring complaint of *peregruzhennost*, "overburdening," and one member of the group had cited some striking figures that are often mentioned in women's conversations: Soviet husbands have some thirty hours more free time a week than their wives, enjoying a total of nearly two "stolen days"; women, because of their chores, enjoy one hour less sleep at night than men; and women have an average of only twelve minutes a day to spend on their children's education.

I asked my Riga acquaintances what the average man might be doing with that   10
free time.

The group burst into raucous laughter.   11

"He takes out the dog," one said. (Much giggling.)   12

"He looks at television and occasionally remembers to play with the children,"   13
a second one said. ("Yes, yes!" and hoots of derision.)

"He mostly takes out the dog," a third one repeated. (More laughter.)   14

"He tinkers with the car." (Further hilarity.)   15

"He tinkers with the car to *pretend* he's doing something." (More approving   16
laughter.)

Analyzing the mysterious force of Russian females and the relative passivity of   17
Russian men, some of the more thoughtful women I talked to put the blame on
their own sex. "Russian women have a need to control that verges on the tyranni-
cal, the sadistic," said Elvira Osipova, a professor of British and American literature at Leningrad State University, and a wise observer of national habits. "If our
men can't manage to curb the aggressive, sadistic element in their spouses' characters, women will always end up tyrannizing over them, like no other women I can
think of in history."

After dozens of evenings spent with distraught, henpecked men and with a   18
dismaying abundance of superwomen, I reached the conclusion that the Soviet
Union might be as much in need of a men's movement as of a women's movement.
I tried out the idea on some of my female acquaintances, and found it very well
received.

"The principal function of a women's movement in this country would be to   19
quiet our women down, make them more capable of reassuring their men," Mariya
Osorina said. "A good feminist movement would make our women more gentle,
restore the sexes to that fine balance they had in Pushkin's time. . . . Look at the
Decembrist men—powerful, positive heroes, with heroic, strong, but gentle
wives."

"With emancipation, we not only freed ourselves but created a generation in   20
which too many women tried to be the heads of families," I was told by a Riga
marriage counsellor named Anna Livmane. "Excuse the rudeness, but I shall put it
this way: Man should always be the Minister of Exterior Affairs, the woman should
be the Minister of Interior Affairs. Now women try too often to be both kinds of
minister, and men, who are lazier by nature, withdraw."

Thus one of the important benefits of *perestroika*, many Soviet citizens would   21
agree, is that by freeing women from some part of their historic double burden it
may allow them to step back and relax. "*Perestroika* is about waking up the
lichnost—'individualism'—in our men, so that they cease feeling superfluous,"
Monika Zile said. "It is about creating a society of less aggressive females, who can
at last regain their womanliness."

One day in Leningrad, a few hours after arriving from Riga, Nonna Volenko   22
and I found ourselves in the apartment of an attractive and affable woman, a program editor at the local television station, who lived alone with a twenty-year-old
daughter. "My husband couldn't stand my having a career equal to his, my earning
a salary larger than his," she said as she served us tea from an old-fashioned samo-
var that stood on a table in her living room. "My success threatened him terribly.
He began forcing me to make a choice between marriage and career, and, of

course, I chose my career." She added casually, "That wasn't a difficult choice at all."

On my hostess's living-room couch sat her daughter, a determined-looking   23
university student in faded bluejeans. "Mama was right on target," she said. "She's just like my generation. Here's the way our order of priorities goes: first, career; second, a child. As for a man, that's irrelevant. He can go on his way as soon as the child is conceived."

On my left sat a smart, handsome, cool-mannered young man, a graduate stu-   24
dent named Vadim who had been assigned by the local Goskomizdat to guide us through his city. A few hours earlier, Nonna and I had been asking Vadim, who is in his late twenties, which domestic responsibilities he felt ready to take on when he married. He had previously been aloof, but his aloofness had melted as he described his love of children and vaunted his gift for cooking. "I'm a good chef," he said, with pride. "I've watched my mother make borscht, shchi, kisel, and pirozhki, and I can make them almost as well as she can."

I asked him whether his father also had domestic talents.   25

His reserved manner immediately returned. "I've never met my father," he   26
said curtly.

Now, at the television editor's home in Leningrad, as I sampled my hostess's   27
delicious homemade cake, I thought about some impressive Latvian women I'd met earlier that week.

There was Dasya, our Riga guide. She was an athletic young woman who lived   28
alone with her mother, an engineer. As we toured the city's superbly restored medieval landmarks, whose Westernness manifests Latvia's centuries-old links with Germany and Scandinavia, I'd asked Dasya if her father also lived in Riga. "Yes, he does," she had replied, as curtly as Vadim would later. "But I've seen him only a few times in my life."

On our first morning in Riga, Dasya had taken us to visit Monika Zile, who   29
lives with her teen-age daughter and her mother. "My family is a mirror image of our national matriarchate," Monika had said. "My husband's father was killed in the war, and he and his four siblings grew up with only a mother. My husband and I were divorced after seventeen years of marriage. At some point, a jealousy sprang up between us—but he still helps to bring up my daughter. My mother lives with me, and also helps to bring up my daughter." She sighed, and then said, "You see, thirty, forty years after the war we seem to continue this all-woman tradition through sheer force of habit. I fear that my daughter will follow my example, take me as a model. Our matriarchal ways have become chronic, infectious."

Another Rigan I had been much impressed by was Dr. Anita Tsaune, the head   30
gynecologist at a maternity clinic in Riga which is regarded as the finest in the Soviet Union. Dr. Tsaune, an attractive divorcée in her early fifties with a beehive of teased blond hair, is also the director of the Maternal and Child Health Protection Agency for the entire republic of Latvia. She had given me an account of her daily morning schedule.

"I live alone with Mama, who is a wonderful eighty-nine years old," Dr.   31
Tsaune had said. "And the first thing I do when I get up, at six, is prepare breakfast for Mama, and rearrange the flowers and change their water so that everything will

be ready and pretty and cheerful for her when she gets up. All her life, she got breakfast for me and my children, so I do that for her. Then I get to work by seven-thirty, and since I live across the street from the maternity clinic I go home for lunch, and give Mama a chance to show her love for me."

Dr. Tsaune and her assistant director, Dr. Sarmite Khartmane, an equally   32
attractive divorcée, who was once a slalom ski champion, are pioneers in "family birthing," the psychological preparation of both husband and wife for their baby's delivery. Sitting in the flower-filled office of these archetypal Soviet superwomen—ebullient, brilliant, and intensely feminine—I had teased them about the prevalence of women on their staff, for during an hour's visit at their clinic I had not seen one male doctor.

"Oh, yes, we have a few men doctors," Dr. Tsaune said, laughing. "A few tall,   33
thin, very handsome men. We keep them around as a tonic. Without any men, women don't dress as well, don't behave as nicely."

"So the men are here for decoration?" I asked.   34

"The men are a tonic," she repeated.   35

"Like a Finnish sauna?"   36

"Yes, that's it. They're like a Finnish sauna!" Hearty laughter from all the women.   37

A few moments later, I asked the two divorcées whether they envied women with   38
husbands.

"A husband, that's, how can I say . . ." Dr. Tsaune hesitated.   39

"It's an elective obligation," Dr. Khartmane suggested.   40

Approving laughter again greeted these views of man-as-disposable-commodity.   41
"Absolutely correct, an elective obligation," Dr. Tsaune repeated.

Later, at the Leningrad tea party, I recalled a description given by my friend   42
Elvira Novikova of the only unhappy days in her life: "They're the summer days when Mama is at our little dacha out of town, and I worry about her so much I can barely work. She's alone there, seventy-nine years old, and I call her several times a day to check that she's all right." I also recalled the many women I knew in Moscow who had divorced because their mothers did not get on with their husbands and, in choosing between the two, "Mother always comes first."

So on that afternoon in Leningrad I looked around the homey living room in   43
which my hostess and her very independent daughter were graciously pouring tea, at walls hung with travel souvenirs from Poland, Hungary, and India, at its mantelpiece and tables filled with photographs of what seemed to be exclusively female progenitors—mothers, grandmothers, great-aunts. There was not a male in sight. Observing these tokens of indissoluble mother–daughter ties, I thought of the gaily painted wooden *matryoshka* dolls that are a staple of Russian folk art: breaking apart at the stomach, they spill out many identical dolls, generations of parthenogenetic females fitting snugly into each other. No artifact, I mused that day in Leningrad, is more symbolic of this country's sovereign matriarchies.

In the notebooks in which I recorded my months of Soviet research, I listed sev-   44
eral dozen basic categories of human experience with which to organize my themes: friendship, family, childhood, heroism, education, sex, marriage, religion. I realized upon finishing my list that one fundamental category was missing from it: love.

It was not an oversight. Throughout my time in the Soviet Union, I barely, if   45
ever, heard one mention of the word *lyubov*—"love" in its romantic sense. It confirmed my suspicion that love in the Soviet Union is a luxury, an accessory, but
hardly the prerequisite for marriage or happiness that it is in Western Europe or
the United States.

Conversations with Soviet women made it clear to me that heterosexual love   46
tends to recede in importance before the far deeper bonds of blood kinship, filial
responsibility, and matriarchal ties, and that they tend to look on marriage as a
coolly pragmatic commodity resorted to for a variety of utilitarian reasons: a
chance to move to a larger, more attractive city; an improvement in housing conditions; a way of escaping the appalling lack of sexual privacy which results from
living with parents; an enhancement in job opportunity and social status. In sum,
some form of marriage, past or present, loving or loveless, is a cornerstone of social
and professional respectability.

For in the Soviet Union it is just splendid, and utterly normal, to be a single,   47
divorced mother. Outside the circles of the progressive intelligentsia, a considerable stigma is attached to being a spinster, and to never having experienced marriage and procreation. When Soviet women are asked why the great majority of
them get married when they could be economically independent, and when marriage is so often nightmarish, most answer that it is essential to their career ad-
vancement: the Soviet system penalizes unmarried women by considering them
"morally unstable"; the word *starukha*—"old maid"—seems to be a greater pejorative in the Soviet Union than in any other developed nation.

The rigid paternalism that has guided Soviet attitudes on sexual equality has   48
no roots in the central, libertarian principle of Western feminism—women's right
to self-determination. It has been shaped solely by instrumental concerns that the
state can mold and alter according to its needs. And since the nineteen-sixties the
Soviet government's approach to women's social roles has been far narrower and
more conservative than it was in the first decades of its history. The notion that sex
differences are biologically rather than socially created, and are thus immutable,
and that woman's "natural" role is wifehood and child rearing—a concept that
would have been looked on as subversively bourgeois by the first Bolshevik generation—has become a staple of government propaganda.

This stereotyping of sex differences is one of the many aspects of current So-   49
viet culture that contradict original Marxist theory. In its efforts to create "the new
Soviet person," and to combat Western Freudianism, early Marxist psychology
fiercely attacked the notion of biologically innate traits; it singled out the social
environment as the central force in the shaping of human behavior, and saw personality as created only through "the process of activity." Accordingly, women in
the new Soviet state could easily acquire "masculine" characteristics of "rationality"
and "self-control," and men could naturally develop those traits of "gentleness"
and "nurturing" that current Soviet propaganda assigns exclusively to females (and
whose cultivation by husbands would so ease wives' difficult schedules). But in the
past two decades, because of demographers' panic about a dwindling work force,
the Soviet regime's former egalitarianism has been replaced by a fixation on sex
roles that verges on the neurotic. Parents have been advised to reprimand boys for

displaying emotion ("You're crying just like a girl!") and to encourage in their daughters an obsessive concern for personal appearance and conventional domestic skills.

When a contemporary Soviet mother is asked what trait of character she most   50
wishes her daughters to possess, for instance, nine times out of ten she will answer *"Zhenstvennost"*—"femininity." The word is made almost nauseating by its repetition. And a foreign traveller in the Soviet Union is immediately struck by the passionate interest evidenced by Soviet women under forty-five in traditional domestic rituals—cooking, sewing, embroidery—which their grandmothers never had the time (or perhaps even the license) to indulge in.

Except among a small but growing sector of university students, this new cult   51
of femininity has led to an increasing trend toward early marriage. In Soviet hospitals, a woman of twenty-five or over giving birth to her first child is often referred to as an "aging first-time mother." And however tragic the statistics showing that over a third of Soviet marriages are ending in divorce, the government-bred anxiety to rush into wedlock is shown in a striking feature of the Soviet press which was unheard of before the *glasnost* era: "Getting Acquainted" columns ("25-year-old girl of middle height, attractive, sociable . . . would like to meet serious young man of 24–30 years of age, clean-living, kind—of Tartar or European origins" or "I would like to start a family with a man 34–40, not shorter than 1 metre 76 cent. in height"). I would wager that the ratio of women to men placing such ads is approximately four to one.

These observations, however, apply primarily to middle-class women of me-   52
dian age, income, status. Attitudes based on class differences differ quite as much in the Soviet Union as in any capitalist country. And among the young intellectual élite a very different picture emerges.

On a crystal-cold winter morning, Professor Elvira Novikova, the feminist his-   53
torian and writer who has become a good friend, took me to visit a branch of her alma mater, the Moscow Lenin State Pedagogical Institute. Founded in 1877, it was one of the first centers of higher learning in Moscow to open its doors to women. The institute now graduates many of the young people, mostly women, who will become the next generation of high-school teachers and university professors.

The interior walls of the institute—a handsome neoclassical building with   54
Doric colonnades—are blue and green and are still hung with 1942-vintage posters that remind all onlookers of the Great Patriotic War: mother and child clutching each other before a bloodied Nazi bayonet, with the slogan "WARRIORS OF THE RED ARMY, SAVE US!," and, the most famous war image of all, a powerful woman, her head wrapped in a peasant kerchief, pointing at the timeless slogan "THE MOTHERLAND CALLS YOU!"

For several hours, Elvira and I met with the rector of the institute, a genial   55
woman of starkly old-fashioned style, with gray hair escaping from a bun, and flat, masculine shoes. She had asked eight students to talk to us over tea. These young women were enrolled in different "faculties" of the university, which has a student body of eleven thousand, and were scarcely acquainted with one another. Our first topic of conversation was what seems to be an obsession of college-age Soviet

women: the rapidly growing divorce rate, which they link to their mothers' tendency to pressure them into early marriage.

"My mother and I are absolutely at odds on the issue," said Tatyana, a thoughtful twenty-year-old with long brown hair, whose parents are both factory workers. "All she can think of for me is marriage and kids, whereas my principal goal is to be wise and learned. So we argue a lot. The only support I get is from my grandmother, because, of course, in the nineteen-thirties women never questioned the central role of work and career." 56

"My grandmother, my parents, my brother, his wife, their child, and I all share a two-room apartment," said Natasha, a young woman with alert blue eyes, who is also the child of factory workers. "Seven people in two rooms. It's kind of wonderful to all dine together every night. We get a lot of discussion time together. I have the same problem as Tatyana: Mother believes that women must start a family early. My babushka's the one who says it's essential to have both a career and a family." 57

"My babushka's also the only one who understands why young people want to live together before marriage," Tatyana chimed in. "Morals were much freer in her time, in the twenties." 58

All the young women nodded in agreement. 59

"Our mothers' postwar generation passed on this dangerous attitude—that it's a stigma to stay unmarried, that if you wait too long you'll never get a man," said Olga, an aspiring zoologist. "It's a horrible side of our society—when a girl isn't married at nineteen or twenty-one, she says, 'I'm a left-behind, useless woman, useless to all.'" 60

"I'm a very unusual case," said Ira, who, at twenty-three, was the oldest of the group. A trim blonde, she was a linguist who had recently married a career Army officer. "My mother is Estonian, so my parents are perhaps more geared to the Western tradition; they simply put me out of the house when I finished high school, and I had to get a room of my own." 61

Ira's fellow-students all turned their heads to stare at her. A room of her own! It was clear that they'd never before set eyes on a peer who had become independent so early. 62

"And I'll be grateful to them to the end of my days," Ira went on proudly. "I worked for two years before entering the institute, and that gave me time to prepare for marriage. My husband and I were twenty-three and twenty-eight when we married, and I think our union is perfect." 63

"I was married at age eighteen and had two children in the following four years," said Masha, a smart-looking young matron with the round pink face of a *matryoshka* doll. "But I couldn't have started my studies here without my husband's help. He's twelve years older than I, a very serious man, and he helps out with everything in the house—diapers, cooking." 64

This, too, seemed extremely unusual. There were gasps of "Oh, you lucky thing!" 65

"Thirty per cent of our divorces are caused by too many people living in one crowded apartment," said Ira. "My husband and I were careful to wait two years. We married only when we were settled in a decent apartment and each of us was 66 earning a good salary." *"Molodets"*—"Smart girl"—the rector observed, from her desk.

"For my part, I wish to bring up a child by myself, without a man," Tatyana   67
said. "A man! Who needs a *second* child?"

The young women laughed and clapped in approval, and the rector rocked   68
approvingly in her chair. I asked for a show of hands on the issue. Six out of the eight young women asserted that if they hadn't found "an adequate husband" by the age of twenty-six or so they'd have a child without one.

"And I'm going to wait until I've finished my dissertation to have my first   69
child," said provident Ira. "My field is the British contemporary novel. I'm writing my thesis on Graham Greene, and as soon as that's behind me I'll feel ready for pregnancy."

"Tovarishch!" Elvira exclaimed. "Tell us how you go about planning a family   70
that carefully."

"It's very simple," Ira answered forthrightly. "The IUD."   71

The young women shook their heads with envy. The group compared notes on   72
the immense difficulty of obtaining IUDs, or any effective contraceptive, outside the country's main urban centers—Leningrad, Moscow. And even there, they agreed, you had to find a particularly privileged doctor, for only one out of ten gynecologists has access to IUDs.

Throughout the discussion, at the back of the room there had sat a pretty,   73
silent young woman with heavy eye makeup, who was wearing a gold-embroidered scarf and a large amount of gold jewelry. Her style differed strikingly from her peers', which was carefully groomed but simple, and I asked her for her view of the issues we had been discussing.

"My father is a military man and my mother hasn't worked for twenty years,"   74
she said with a touch of self-consciousness. "She has brought us up and happily busied herself with her sewing and knitting, and I want to be just like her and have a husband and three children."

Heads turned toward this anomaly with looks of annoyance and dismissal. The   75
young woman pouted and appeared sorry to have spoken at all.

"Look at her, decked out like a strumpet and selling herself like a slave in the   76
marriage market," Elvira whispered to me.

"To think that our government spends its precious money educating her, and   77
all she wants to do is stay home with the kids and do needlework," the rector grumbled to Elvira.

I then asked the young women to describe what they saw as their ideal life   78
fifteen years from now.

"My first priority is to love my work—to become an outstanding specialist in   79
the field of teaching English," Tatyana announced. "Once that's established, I can support a child."

"I also want a beloved work, above all else," Nadia agreed. "I wish to go to   80
work every day as if it were a festival."

"In fifteen years, I want to have finished my *doctoral* dissertation in contem-   81
porary British fiction," the energetic Ira announced. "I want to continue with my community work and Komsomol activities. I want my husband, who's now a major,

to have become a colonel. I also want him to have finished his advanced degree in political science. And we've agreed that we want two children, so we'll need a slightly larger apartment."

"I want a beloved work above all," said Natasha, the girl who lived with six   82
members of her family in a two-room apartment. "I perhaps want a husband and children, but, even more important, I want to remain very close to my parents, and continue living with them."

"Bravo!" the rector applauded.   83

"What if your husband doesn't like it that way?" I asked.   84

"The marriage will end," Natasha announced.   85

After the young women had left—we had talked for almost three hours—   86
Elvira and I stayed on and chatted with the rector.

The two educators continued to deplore the societal pressures that forced   87
women into early marriage. And then the rector—who has been married for thirty-five years to a man she describes as "a marvellous person, charmingly infantile"—made a statement that might well sum up Soviet women's attitudes toward life.

"I'll tell you," she said. "I have only a son. But if I had a daughter I'd suggest   88
she go and have a child without a man. Because the most important duty of a woman, along with her work, is to have children, far beyond the duty of being a wife."

"And the *next* most important thing is to keep a sense of duty toward your   89
parents," Elvira said.

"Bravo!" said the rector of the institute.   90

The following day, I got together with Tatyana, the serious young woman with   91
aspirations to teach English and to bring up a child by herself. We talked for several hours over dinner.

She was formidable. She had just read eight novels of Iris Murdoch's in a row.   92
As a teen-ager, she had read Bulgakov's "Master and Margarita" half a dozen times, shortly after the government allowed publication of the long-suppressed novel. She knew her Stalinist history to perfection. "Among other things, he surrounded himself—excuse me—with ass-kissers," she commented, obviously relishing her command of American slang.

Most of the young men of her generation whom she'd met were "immature   93
and terribly lacking in respect for women," she said. Apart from books, her favorite distraction was ballroom dancing—waltz, tango—but her male friends disdained such music and liked only heavy-metal rock, which she detested. So she went to ballroom-dancing clubs with groups of women friends, and they danced together, "as our grandmothers did in wartime."

I asked Tatyana how she proposed to support her child.   94

"I'll wait until a few years after I've finished my dissertation, because after that   95
I'll be receiving three hundred and fifty or four hundred rubles a month, and I can save up from my salary," she said. "So after the child is born I'll stay home with him or her for two or three years, giving English lessons and making homemade sweaters—a child needs to be with its mother for at least that length of time. I can get forty-five rubles for a good homemade sweater, and my babushka taught me to knit so well I can easily turn out three or four sweaters a month."

Her three closest women friends, Tatyana said, all planned to raise a child in   96
approximately the same circumstances. And when one of them went out to attend
classes or to shop, the others would take turns minding her babies.

I asked Tatyana what role, in her view and that of her friends, a child played in   97
a woman's life.

"A child is . . ." She thought a little. "A child is a woman's best friend."   98

Mother and a cherished vocation as the first loves of a woman's life, the child   99
as the indispensable friend—that seemed to be the prevailing view among these
future educators of the nation's youth.

Rhetorical Focus

1. Why do you think Gray includes so many quotations in the essay? What
   rhetorical effect do they have?
2. Like Tannen, Gray uses examples to support her main ideas. Are her examples similar to or different from Tannen's? Do they serve a similar function
   in each essay?
3. "Soviet Women" was first published in a section of the *New Yorker* called
   "Reflections." What stylistic features indicate that Gray is reflecting on her
   experience? How does her style differ from Chodorow's?

Thematic Focus

1. Gray speaks of male passivity and disillusionment and female power and
   self-esteem in the Soviet Union. How does this characterization differ
   from Tannen's? Are you convinced by Gray's account, or do you think she
   overstates her case?
2. Gray seems to celebrate the asymmetrical parenting she observed in the
   Soviet Union. In what ways does her view differ from Chodorow's? In what
   ways is it similar?
3. Gray observes that the Soviet Union needs a men's movement to bolster
   the spirits of its passive males. Would Chodorow and Tannen agree? Why
   or why not?

Suggestions for Writing

1. Write an essay in which you describe your gender role socialization, focusing especially on your relationship with your parents in the early years.
2. Listen carefully to a conversation between a male and a female. Then analyze the conversational patterns you identify, and make connections between what you find and what Tannen has found.
3. Write an essay in which you compare and contrast the Soviet women described by Gray and the American women described by Tannen.

PARENTING

The institution of parenthood would seem to be the site where transformation of gender-role stereotypes could be enacted. Children, after all, first learn masculine or feminine behavior patterns from their parents. As we have seen, theorists such as Nancy Chodorow call for an end to asymmetrical parenting and for the institutionalization of symmetrical parenting.

As the pieces in this section demonstrate, though, parenting is deeply affected by institutions beyond the family, so changes in this one institution are not sufficient to bring about changes in gender-role identity formation. The Osborne essay, for instance, describes the experience of a new father as he attempts to deal with parental responsibilities he has taken on as a result of his wife's 100-hour per week commitment to her residency in obstetrics and gynecology. A woman who is training to become an obstetrician has very little time to care for her own child. The Neely story suggests that misogyny is such a powerful cultural phenomenon that a mother is unable to prevent her son from becoming a rapist or to mother him after he has served his prison sentence. The Rich essay deals explicitly with connections between parenting and larger social phenomena, especially gynephobia.

Beyond the Cult of Fatherhood

David Osborne

David Osborne is a free-lance writer who has published essays in *Harper's, The New York Times Magazine, The Washington Post,* the *Atlantic, Mother Jones,* and elsewhere. His book, *Laboratories of Democracy,* was published by the Harvard Business School Press in 1988, and he is working on a book entitled *Reinventing Government.* He and his wife, a practicing physician with a specialty in obstetrics and gynecology, are expecting their fourth child. The essay reprinted here was originally published in *Ms.* in 1985.

Reflections Before Reading

Theorists such as Nancy Chodorow suggest that developmental differences between boys and girls will be minimized if men have an equal share in the parenting of children. Do you agree that shared parenting is desirable? What kinds of changes in our institutional structures beyond the family would be needed to make shared parenting possible? Are men as capable as women in the area of child rearing?

If I ever finish this article, it will be a miracle. Nicholas woke up this morning with   1
an earache and a temperature, and I spent half the day at the doctor's office and pharmacy. Another ear infection.

Nicholas is my son. Twenty months old, a stout little bundle of energy and   2
affection.

I will never forget the moment when I realized how completely Nick would   3
change my life. My wife is a resident in obstetrics and gynecology, which means, among other things, that she works 100 hours a week, leaves the house every day by six and works all night several times a week, and often all weekend too. I'm not a househusband; I take Nick to day care five days a week. But I come about as close to house-husbandry as I care to. I am what you might call a "nontraditional" father.

Nick was three weeks old when I learned what that actually meant. Rose had   4
just gone back to work, and Nick and I were learning about bottles. I don't remember if it was Rose's first night back or her second, but she wasn't home.

I stayed up too late; I had not yet learned that, with a baby in the house, you   5
grab sleep whenever you can—even if it means going to bed at nine. Just as I drifted off, about 11:30, Nick woke up. I fed him and rocked him and put him back to sleep. About 2 A.M. he woke again, crying, and I rocked him for 45 minutes before he quieted down.

When he started screaming at four, I was in the kitchen by the time I woke up.   6
As every parent knows, the sound of an infant—your infant—screaming sends lightning bolts up the spine. Bells ring in the head; nerves jangle. Racing against my son's hunger, I boiled water, poured it into the little plastic sack, slipped the sack into the plastic bottle, put on the top, and plunged the bottle into a bowl of cold water to cool it. I had not yet learned that in Connecticut, where I live, the water need not be sterilized. (Fathers are the last to know.)

It takes a long time to boil water and cool it back to body temperature, and I   7
was dead on my feet even before the screams rearranged my vertebrae. By the time the water had cooled, I was half-crazed, my motions rapid and jerky. I mixed in the powdered formula and slipped the nipple back on. I ran toward Nick's room, shaking the bottle as hard as I could to make sure it was thoroughly mixed. As I reached his crib, the top flew off—and the contents sprayed all over the room.

At that point, I lost it. I swore at the top of my lungs, I stomped around the   8
room, I slammed the changing table, and I swore some more. That was when I realized what I had gotten myself into—and how much I had to learn.

With baby boomers well ensconced in the nation's newsrooms, fatherhood is   9
sweeping American journalism. You can pick up the *New York Times Magazine,* or
Esquire, or Bob Greene's best-seller, *Good Morning, Merry Sunshine: A Father's
Journal of His Child's First Year* (Penguin), and read all about the wonders of
being a father.

By all accounts, today's fathers are more involved and more sensitive than   10
their own fathers were. But as warm and tender as their writing may be, it rings
false. Rosalie Ziomek, a mother in Evanston, Illinois, said it perfectly in a letter to
the *New Republic,* after it printed a scathing review of Bob Greene's book. "I was
enraged by Greene's book," Ziomek wrote. "Anyone taking care of a newborn infant doesn't have time to write about it. Greene was cashing in on the experiences
that most women have quietly and painfully lived without the glorification of fame
and money. Meanwhile, because of the structure of his work/social life, which he is
unwilling to alter, he avoids the thing that is the hardest part of new motherhood:
the moment-to-moment dependency of a tiny, helpless, and demanding human
being. I have more to say on the subject, but I have three children to take care of
and writing is a luxury I can't afford right now."

Ziomek is right. I've been trying to keep a journal, as Greene did, and it's   11
impossible. There's no time. And how do you capture the essence of an exhausting,
never-ending 24-hour day in a few paragraphs? Snapshots work if you spend an
hour or two with a child, but if you spend days, everything dissolves in a blur.

My experience is different from that of the fathers I read about. Certainly I am   12
not fulfilling the role of a traditional mother, and certainly no child could ask for a
more loving mother than Nick has. But I do fix most of the meals and do most of
the laundry and change a lot of the diapers and get Nick up and dressed in the
morning and shuttle him back and forth to day care and cart him to the grocery
store and sing him to sleep and clean up his toys and wipe his nose and deal with
his tantrums and cuddle with him and tickle him and all the other wonderful and
exhausting things mothers do. If you ask me what it all means, I can't say. After 20
months, I'm still dizzy, still desperate for a free hour or two, and still hopelessly in
love with my little boy. All I have to offer are fragments; profound thoughts are for
people who have more time. But if you want to go beyond the cult of fatherhood, I
think I've been there.

My day starts about 6:30 or 7 A.M., when Nick stands up in his crib and calls out   13
for me. I stumble into his room, pick him up, give him a kiss and a "Good morning,
Pumpkin," and carry him back to bed. I lay him down on his mother's empty pillow, lie down beside him, and sometimes I drowse again before it's really time to
get up. But most mornings Nick is ready to start his day, and he gradually drags me
up toward consciousness. He smiles at me, climbs up on me, and rests his head
against my cheek—even kisses me if I'm really lucky, or sits on my bladder and
bounces, if I'm not. I tickle him, and he laughs and squirms and shrieks for more.

Sometimes he lies there for a few minutes, thinking his little boy thoughts,   14
before sliding himself backward off the bed and going in search of something to
do. Often he arrives back with a toy or two and asks to be picked "Up! Up!" Then
he plays for a few minutes, making sure to keep an eye on my progress toward

wakefulness. When he has waited long enough, he hands me my glasses, takes my hand, and pulls me out of bed.

While I shower, Nick plays in the bathroom, sitting on the floor with his toys. By the time I'm dressed, the kettle is whistling, and he's ready for breakfast. We always eat together; he has hot cereal, I have cold cereal, and often we share a bagel. I wish you could hear him say "cream cheese."   15

The rough times come on weekends. After 24 hours, I'm ready to be hung out on the line to dry. After 48 hours, I'm ready to pin medals on women who stay home every day with their kids. For single mothers, I'm ready to build monuments.   16

Don't let anyone tell you otherwise: traditional mothers work harder than anyone else can even imagine. They are on duty 24 hours a day, 365 days a year. I remember wondering, as a youth, why my own mother always rushed around with such urgency when she was cooking or cleaning. To me, she was like a woman possessed. Now I do the same thing. When you have a young child (or two, or three), you have very little time to get the dishes done, or cook dinner, or vacuum, or do the laundry. So when you get a moment, you proceed with all possible haste. If your children are asleep, they might wake up. If they're playing, they might get bored and demand your attention.   17

Friends who visit me nowadays probably think I'm crazy, the way I rush compulsively to get dinner ready or mow the lawn or finish the laundry. I do feel somewhat self-conscious about it. But the fact is, if I'm cooking, Nick is going to start demanding his meal soon, and if it's not ready, he's going to get very cranky. And with all the chores that pile up on a weekend—the lawn, the laundry, the groceries, and so on—I have to seize every possible instant. If he naps, that may give me an hour and a half. If he wakes up before I'm done, whatever I'm doing will never get finished.   18

In any case, it is on weekends alone with Nick that I feel the full brunt of child-rearing. Consider a typical weekend: Nick wakes at 7:00, and we lie in bed and play for half an hour before getting up. But this morning he feels feverish, so I take his temperature. It is 101.6—not high for a young child, but a fever nonetheless.   19

The first thing I do is call Maureen, who takes care of him during the week. Both of her kids have a bug, and I want to find out what the symptoms are, to see if Nick has the same thing. From what we can tell, he does. On that basis, I decide to give him Tylenol for the fever, rather than taking him in to the pediatrician to see if he's got an ear infection. Besides, he wants to lie down for a nap at 10:00, before I have decided, and doesn't wake until 1:00. By then the office is closed.   20

After lunch he feels much better—cool, happy, and bubbling. We play with his lock-blocks for a while, then watch a basketball game. He's very cuddly, because he's not feeling well. After the game it's off to the bank and grocery store. He falls asleep on the way home, at 5:45. It's an awkward time for a nap, but he only sleeps until 6:30. He wakes up crying, with a high fever, feeling miserable.   21

To get him to swallow more Tylenol, which he hates, I promise him ice cream. I give him half an ice-cream sandwich while I rush around the kitchen cooking   22 dinner, and when he finishes it, he cries for the other half. I tell him he can have it after he eats his dinner. But when dinner is ready, he won't eat; he just sits there pointing at the freezer, where the ice cream is, and wailing. This is a major tantrum—hot tears, red face. I can't help but sympathize, though, because it's born of feeling absolutely wretched. How should I respond? I don't want to give in and teach him he can get his way by screaming. I try to comfort him by holding him in my lap, but he just sobs. Finally I take him into his room and rock him, holding him close. Gradually the sobs subside, and after 10 minutes I take him back into the kitchen, hold him on my lap, and feed him myself. He doesn't eat much, but enough to deserve his ice cream.

Though Nick gets over the incident in no time, I am traumatized. The fever is frightening—it has hit 102 by dinnertime, and it only drops to 101.4 by 8 P.M. Should I have taken him to the doctor? Will he spike a really high fever tonight? Am I being too relaxed? And what will Rose say? I cannot stop worrying; I feel heartsick as I read him his bedtime stories, though he cools down as he drifts off to sleep in my arms. Would a mother feel so uncertain, I wonder? Do mothers feel adequate at moments like this? Or am I in a father's territory here?   23

Sunday morning Nick wakes at 6:30 and devours his breakfast, but pretty soon his temperature begins to rise. I call our pediatrician, who reassures me that it doesn't sound like an ear infection, and that I'm doing the right thing. Still, Nick isn't feeling well, and it makes him more demanding. He wants to be held; he wants me with him constantly; he insists that I do what he wants me to do and cries if I balk. It is a wearing day. He naps late, and when I wake him at seven, he is again miserable—temperature at 102.4, crying, refusing to let me change his diaper. But after more Tylenol and a good dinner he feels better.   24

I haven't heard from Rose all weekend, so I decide to call her at the hospital. She is furious that I haven't taken Nick to the doctor. A child who gets ear infections as often as he does has to be checked, she yells at me. He could blow out an eardrum! And why haven't I called her—she's his mother, for God's sake! I'm exhausted, I've been busting my hump all weekend, alone, doing the best I can, and now I'm being abused. I don't like it. My first impulse is to hang up on her, but instead I hand the phone to Nicholas, who has a long talk with her. He says "Mommy!" she says "Nicholas!" and he laughs and laughs.   25

Rose may be right, I know, but that doesn't help my anger. We part tersely, and I promise to take him to the pediatrician the next morning before I leave for California on an article assignment. After that's out of the way, Nick and I have a good evening. We read books, and several times he leads me into his room to get another handful. A short bath, more books, then off to bed. He wants to take two of his trucks to bed with him—a new wrinkle—but I finally convince him to say "night-night" to his trucks and turn out the lights.   26

I have several hours of work to do before I leave, so I don't get to bed until after midnight. I'm absolutely shot. When the alarm rings at 6:00, I haul myself out of bed, shower, get dressed, and get Nick up and fed and dressed. We speed down to the library to return several books, then to the doctor's office. No ear infection; it's just a bug, says the doc, and he should be over it by nightfall. I drop Nick off at Maureen's by 9:30, race home, and spend the next hour packing, vacuuming,   27 cleaning up the dishes and defrosting something for Rose and Nick's dinner. When I get to the airport, I realize I've misread my ticket and I'm half an hour early. I'm exhausted, and the trip has yet to begin.

Two nights later I call Rose. When I ask how she is, she bursts into tears. Nicholas has fallen at Maureen's and cut his forehead on a metal toy. Rose was caught in an ice storm between the hospital and home, so Maureen had to take her own kids to a neighbor's and rush Nick to the pediatrician's office for stitches. They gave him a local anesthetic, but he screamed the whole time.   28

"I feel so awful," Rose sobs, over and over. "I should have been there. I just feel awful." Guilt floods in, but it is nothing to match Rose's guilt. This is one of the differences I have discovered between mothers and fathers.   29

Rose has felt guilty since the day she went back to work—the hardest single thing I've ever watched her do. Deep inside her psyche lies a powerful message that she belongs at home, that if she is not with her child she is terribly irresponsible.   30

I feel guilty only occasionally. When I dropped Nick off at day care the first day after returning from California, and he sobbed because he thought I was leaving him again, the guilt just about killed me. I turned into a classic mother: as soon as I got home, I called to see if he was still crying. (He was.) Two guilt-ridden hours later I called again, desperate to hear that everything was fine. (It was.)   31

Deep within my psyche, however, the most powerful message is that I belong at work, that if I am not out making my mark on the world I am worth nothing.   32

The contradiction between family and career is nothing new; it is perhaps the central unresolved conflict in the lives of American women today. What I did not expect was the force with which that conflict would erupt in my life.   33

Like an addict, I now find myself squeezing in every last minute of work that I can. I wait until the last possible instant before rushing out the door to pick Nick up in the afternoon. I dart out to my studio while he naps on weekends, using a portable intercom to listen for his cries. At night I compulsively page through old newspapers that pile up because I can no longer read them over breakfast, afraid I've missed something important. As I hit deadline time, I pray that Nicholas doesn't get sick. I have even tried writing on a Saturday afternoon, with Nick playing in my studio. That experiment lasted half an hour, at which point he hit the reset button on the back of my computer and my prose was lost to the ages.   34

This frantic effort to keep up is clearly not good for me, but I cannot seem to abandon it. I constantly feel as if I live in a pressure cooker. I long for a free day, even a free hour. But my career has taken off just as my responsibilities as a father have hit their peak, and I cannot seem to scale down my commitment to either.   35

When Nick was four months old, I took him to a Christmas party, one Saturday when Rose was working. After an hour or so he got cranky, so I took him upstairs with a bottle. A little girl followed, and soon her brother and sister—equally bored by the goings-on downstairs—had joined us. It wasn't long before Dad came looking for them.   36

We introduced ourselves and talked for a bit. His wife, it turned out, was also a   37
doctor. The curious part came when I asked what he did. First he told me all the
things he had done in the past: carpentry, business, you name it. Then he said he'd
done enough—he was about 40—and felt no need to prove himself any more.
Finally he told me he stayed at home with the kids. And frankly, he pulled it off
with far more dignity and less stammering than I would have, had our places been
reversed.

I don't think I could do what he does. If I were to stay home full-time with   38
Nick, I would quickly lose my self-esteem, and within months I would be deep into
an identity crisis. Part of the reason I love my role as a father is that I am secure in
my role as a writer. Without that, I would not feel good enough about myself to be
the kind of father I am.

This is not simply a problem inside male heads. How many women would be   39
content with men who stayed home with the kids? Not many, I'll wager. And not
my wife, I know. From my experience, modern women want a man who will share
the responsibilities at home but still be John Wayne in the outside world. They
don't want any wimps wearing aprons. And men know it.

We are in a Burger King, in Fall River, Massachusetts. We are not having a   40
good day. We drove two hours to shop in the factory outlets here, and all but a
handful are closed because it's Sunday.

Nick likes Burger King, but he's not having a great day either. He has recently   41
learned about tantrums, and as we get ready to leave, he decides to throw one. He
doesn't want to leave; he doesn't want to put on his coat; he just doesn't want to be
hauled around any more. So he stands up and wails.

Rose is mortified; she takes any misbehavior in public as an advertisement of   42
her failings as a mother. It triggers all her guilt about working. This time, the
timing couldn't be worse, because she is already on edge.

Our tantrum strategy is generally to let him yell, to ignore him, and thus to   43
teach him that it does no good. But in a public restaurant, I don't have the stamina
to ignore him, so I cross the room to pick him up.

Rose orders me away from him, in no uncertain terms. There are no negotia-   44
tions, no consultations. We are going to do this her way or no way.

That lights my fuse, of course, and after simmering for 10 minutes, I bring it   45
up. "Let it go," she tells me, almost in tears over Nicholas. "It's not important."

It's not important.   46

Ah, the double bind. You're in charge one day, playing mother and father all   47
wrapped into one, depended upon to feed him and clothe him and change him and
bathe him and rock him and meet his every need. And the next day you're a third
wheel, because Mom is around. You are expected to put in the long hours, but to
pretend in public that you don't, for fear of undercutting your wife's sense of self-
worth as a mother. How could she be doing her job, her psyche seems to whisper,
if she's letting someone else make half the decisions and give half the care? There
are many double binds in modern relationships, and this is the one I like the least.

I didn't let it drop that day, of course. At home, when Rose asserts the tradi-   48
tional mother's prerogative to make decisions and handle problems alone, on her

terms, I often let it go. But when it happens in public, or in front of family, it is too much. It is as if my entire contribution to raising Nicholas is being denied, as if the world is being told that I am nothing more than a spectator. Luckily, as Nick grows older, and it becomes clear to Rose that she will always be number one in his heart, she has begun to relax her public vigilance, and this problem seems to have abated.

This is the first time I've ever been part of a woman's world. I'm not really a part of it, of course; the chasm between the sexes is too wide to step across so lightly. But when it comes to children, I have instant rapport with most mothers. We talk about the same things, think about the same things, joke about the same things. With men, it is almost never that way, even when the men are fathers and the subject is kids. We can share enthusiasms, but the sense of being there, on the inside—the unspoken understanding that comes out of shared experience—that is missing.   49

In fact, most men don't have the slightest idea what my life with Nick is like. When I tell colleagues—even those with children—that I have no time to read, or to watch television, I get blank stares. (I never tell mothers that; they already know. Who has time to read?) One friend, also a writer, stopped in the middle of a recent conversation and said, "You have Nick at home while you're working, don't you? What do you do with him?" No such thought could pass a mother's lips.   50

None of this would have been possible had I not been forced into taking care of Nick on my own much of the time. In fact, my entire relationship with Nick would have been different had I not been forced off the sidelines. I am convinced that in our society, when Mom is home with the kids, it is almost impossible for Dad to be an equal partner in their upbringing, even if he wants to be.   51

I believe this because for three weeks, while Rose was home after Nick's birth, it felt impossible to me. Rose had carried Nick for nine months; Rose had been through labor; and Rose was nursing him. For nine months he had listened to her heartbeat, felt her pulse, been a part of her being. Now he hunted her scent and drank from her body, and the bond between them was awesome. I was like some voyeur, peeking through the window at an ancient and sacred rite.   52

Then Rose went back to work, and I had no choice but to get off the sidelines. I *had* to get Nick dressed in the morning. I *had* to feed him. I *had* to burp him and rock him and change him and get up with him in the night. He may have wanted his mother, but she wasn't there.   53

Gradually, it all began to come naturally. I learned to carry him on my (nonexistent) hip and do anything—or any combination of things—with one hand. I learned to whip up a bottle in no time, to change a diaper and treat diaper rash and calm his tears.   54

Even on vacation, it is remarkably easy to slip back into a traditional role—for both Rose and me. But the day Rose goes back to work, I am always yanked back to reality. I complain a lot, but in truth, this is my great good fortune.   55

Last night Nick asked to go to the beach—"Go? Beach? Go? Beach?" I walked him the two blocks down, one of his hands firmly in mine, the other proudly holding the leash for Sam, our dog. We played on the swings for a long time, then   56 strolled along the beach while Sam went swimming. It was that very still hour before dark, when the world slows to a hush, and little boys and girls slowly wind down. It was almost dark when we returned. Nick asked his daddy to give him his bath, then his mommy to put him to bed.

This morning when I woke he was lying beside me, on his mother's empty pillow. I looked over and he gave me a big smile, his eyes shining with that special, undiluted joy one sees only in children. Then he propped himself up on his elbows, leaned over and kissed me. If there are any better moments in life, I've never found them. 57

Rhetorical Focus

1. Like several of the other authors in this chapter, Osborne disrupts chrono-logical sequence in the essay. Why do you think he does this? What is its rhetorical effect?
2. Why do you think Osborne shifts tenses in the essay? What connections can you make between these tense shifts and the disruption of chronologi-cal sequence just mentioned?
3. What is the thesis of Osborne's essay? Do you find it convincing?

Thematic Focus

1. Osborne's essay suggests that shared parenting has benefits. What are some of them? What does Osborne suggest are some of the disadvantages?
2. What are some of the "powerful messages" Osborne and his wife are coun-tering in their nontraditional family structure? What conflicts result from disruptions of traditional patterns? How successful are they in dealing with these conflicts?
3. Osborne claims that modern women want a man who will share with the responsibilities at home but still be John Wayne in the outside world. Do you agree?

Spilled Salt

Barbara Neely

Barbara Neely was born in Lebanon, Pennsylvania and grew up in Philadelphia. She has a master's degree in urban and regional planning from the University of Pittsburgh. She has published short stories in *Essence* and in anthologies such as *Things that Divide Us: Stories of Racism, Sexism, and Classism* edited by Faith Conlon and published by Seal Press. St. Martin's Press will publish her mystery novel in 1992. She is involved in social change work and is an African-American feminist socialist.

Reflections Before Reading

Theorist Sara Ruddick suggests that there is such a thing as "maternal thinking," a kind of nurturing that involves the development of intellectual capacities, judgments, metaphysical attitudes, and the affirmation of values. Maternal thinking, according to Ruddick, involves meeting a child's demands for preservation, growth, and social acceptance. Do you agree that mothering is a complex activity necessitating highly developed skills?

Nel Noddings, another theorist, speaks of the caring relationship between mother and child as one in which the caregiver develops a "reactive," "responsive," and "receptive" posture toward the one being cared for. The one being cared for has an obligation to reciprocate by being responsive to the care received, thus sustaining and invigorating the person who is doing the caring. Do you agree that there should be an element of reciprocity in the relationship between a parent and a child? If so, what forms might this reciprocity take?

"I'm home, Ma."   1

Myrna pressed down hard on the doorknob and stared blankly up into Kenny's large brown eyes and freckled face so much like her own he was nearly her twin. But he was taller than she remembered. Denser.   2

He'd written to say he was getting out. She hadn't answered his letter, hoping her lack of response would keep him away.   3

"You're here." She stepped back from the door, pretending not to see him reach out and try to touch her.   4

But a part of her had leaped to life at the sight of him. No matter what, she was   5
glad he hadn't been maimed or murdered in prison. He at least looked whole and
healthy of body. She hoped it was a sign that he was all right inside, too.

She tried to think of something to say as they stood staring at each other in the   6
middle of the living room. A fly buzzed against the window screen in a desperate
attempt to get out.

"Well, Ma, how've you—"   7

"I'll fix you something to eat," Myrna interrupted. "I know you must be starved   8
for decent cooking." She rushed from the room as though a meal were already in
the process of burning.

For a moment she was lost in her own kitchen. The table, with its dented   9
metal legs, the green-and-white cotton curtains, and the badly battered coffeepot
were all familiar-looking strangers. She took a deep breath and leaned against the
back of a chair.

In the beginning she'd flinched from the very word. She couldn't even think it,   10
let alone say it. Assault, attack, molest, anything but rape. Anyone but her son, her
bright and funny boy, her high school graduate.

At the time, she'd been sure it was a frame-up on the part of the police. They   11
did things like that. It was in the newspapers every day. Or the girl was trying to get
revenge because he hadn't shown any interest in her. Kenny's confession put paid
to all those speculations.

She'd have liked to believe that remorse had made him confess. But she knew   12
better. He'd simply told the wrong lie. If he'd said he'd been with the girl but it
hadn't been rape, he might have built a case that someone would have believed—
although she didn't know how he could have explained away the wound on her
neck where he'd held his knife against her throat to keep her docile. Instead, he'd
claimed not to have offered her a ride home from the bar where she worked, never
to have had her in his car. He'd convinced Myrna. So thoroughly convinced her
that she'd fainted dead away when confronted with the semen, fiber, and hair
evidence the police quickly collected from his car, and the word of the woman who
reluctantly came forth to say she'd seen Kenny ushering Crystal Roberts into his
car on the night Crystal was raped.

Only then had Kenny confessed. He'd said he'd been doing the girl a favor by   13
offering her a ride home. In return, she'd teased and then refused him, he'd said.
"I lost my head," he'd said.

"I can't sleep. I'm afraid to sleep." The girl had spoken in barely a whisper.   14
The whole courtroom had seemed to tilt as everyone leaned toward her. "Every
night he's there in my mind, making me go through it all over again, and again, and
again."

Was she free now that Kenny had done his time? Or was she flinching from   15
hands with short, square fingers, and crying when the first of September came
near? Myrna moved around the kitchen like an old, old woman with bad feet.

After Kenny had confessed, Myrna spent days that ran into weeks rifling   16
through memories of the past she shared with him, searching for some incident,
some trait or series of events that would explain why he'd done such a thing. She'd
tried to rationalize his actions with circumstances: Kenny had seen his father beat
her. They'd been poorer than dirt. And when Kenny had just turned six, she'd

finally found the courage to leave Buddy to raise their son alone. What had she really known about raising a child? What harm might she have done out of ignorance, out of impatience and concentration on warding off the pains of her own life?

Still, she kept stumbling over the knowledge of other boys, from far worse   17
circumstances, with mothers too tired and worried to do more than strike out at them. Yet those boys had managed to grow up and not do the kind of harm Kenny had done. The phrases "I lost my head," and "doing the girl a favor," reverberated through her brain, mocking her, making her groan out loud and startle people around her.

Myrna dragged herself around the room, turning eggs, bacon, milk, and mar-   18
garine into a meal. In the beginning the why of Kenny's crime was like a tapeworm in her belly, consuming all her strength and sustenance, all her attention. In the first few months of his imprisonment she'd religiously paid a neighbor to drive her the long distance to the prison each visiting day. The visits were as much for her benefit as for his.

"But why?" she'd kept asking him, just as she'd asked him practically every day   19
since he'd confessed.

He would only say that he knew he'd done wrong. As the weeks passed, silence   20
became his only response—a silence that had remained intact despite questions like: "Would you have left that girl alone if I'd bought a shotgun and blown your daddy's brains out after the first time he hit me in front of you?" and, "Is there a special thrill you feel when you make a woman ashamed of her sex?" and, "Was this the first time? The second? The last?"

Perhaps silence was best, now, after so long. Anything could happen if she   21
let those five-year-old questions come rolling out of her mouth. Kenny might begin to question her, might ask her what there was about her mothering that made him want to treat a woman like a piece of toilet paper. And what would she say to that?

It was illness that had finally put an end to her visits with him. She'd written   22
the first letter—a note really—to say she was laid up with the flu. A hacking cough had lingered. She hadn't gotten her strength back for nearly two months. By that time their correspondence was established. Letters full of: How are you? I'm fine. . . . The weather is . . . The print shop is . . . The dress I made for Mrs. Rothstein was . . . were so much more manageable than those silence-laden visits. And she didn't have to worry about making eye contact with Kenny in a letter.

Now Myrna stood staring out the kitchen window while Kenny ate his bacon   23
and eggs. The crisp everydayness of clothes flapping on the line surprised her. A leaf floated into her small cemented yard and landed on a potted pansy. Outside, nothing had changed; the world was still in spring.

"I can't go through this again," she mouthed soundlessly to the breeze.   24

"Come talk to me, Ma," her son called softly around a mouthful of food.   25

Myrna turned to look at him. He smiled an egg-flecked smile she couldn't   26
return. She wanted to ask him what he would do now, whether he had a job lined up, whether he planned to stay long. But she was afraid of his answers, afraid of how she might respond if he said he had no job, no plans, no place to stay except with her and that he hadn't changed in any important way.

"I'm always gonna live with you, Mommy," he'd told her when he was a child, 27
"Always." At the time, she'd wished it was true, that they could always be together, she and her sweet, chubby boy. Now the thought frightened her.

"Be right back," she mumbled, and scurried down the hall to the bathroom. 28
She eased the lock over so that it made barely a sound.

"He's my son!" she hissed at the drawn woman in the mirror. Perspiration 29
dotted her upper lip and glistened around her hair line.

"My son!" she repeated pleadingly. But the words were not as powerful as the 30
memory of Crystal Roberts sitting in the courtroom, her shoulders hunched and her head hung down, as though she were the one who ought to be ashamed. Myrna wished him never born, before she flushed the toilet and unlocked the door.

In the kitchen Kenny had moved to take her place by the window. His dishes 31
littered the table. He'd spilled the salt, and there were crumbs on the floor.

"It sure is good to look out the window and see something besides guard tow- 32
ers and cons." Kenny stretched, rubbed his belly, and turned to face her.

"It's good to see you, Ma." His eyes were soft and shiny. 33

Oh, Lord! Myrna moaned to herself. She turned her back to him and began 34
carrying his dirty dishes to the sink: first the plate, then the cup, the knife, fork, and spoon, drawing out the chore.

"This place ain't got as much room as the old place," she told him while she 35
made dishwater in the sink.

"It's fine, Ma, just fine." 36

Oh, Lord, Myrna prayed. 37

Kenny came to lean against the stove to her right. She dropped a knife and 38
made the dishwater too cold.

"Seen Dad?" 39

"Where and why would I see *him*?" She tried to put ice in her voice. It trem- 40
bled.

"Just thought you might know where he is." Kenny moved back to the window. 41

Myrna remembered the crippling shock of Buddy's fist in her groin and 42
scoured Kenny's plate and cup with a piece of steel wool before rinsing them in scalding water.

"Maybe I'll hop a bus over to the old neighborhood. See some of the guys, how 43
things have changed."

He paced the floor behind her. Myrna sensed his uneasiness and was startled 44
by a wave of pleasure at his discomfort.

After he'd gone, she fixed herself a large gin and orange juice and carried it 45
into the living room. She flicked on the TV and sat down to stare at it. After two minutes of frenetic, over-bright commercials, she got up and turned it off again. Outside, children screamed each other to the finish line of a footrace. She remembered that Kenny had always liked to run. So had she. But he'd had more childhood than she'd had. She'd been hired out as a mother's helper by the time she was twelve, and pregnant and married at sixteen. She didn't begrudge him his childhood fun. It just seemed so wasted now.

Tears slid down her face and salted her drink. Tears for the young Myrna who 46
hadn't understood that she was raising a boy who needed special handling to keep

him from becoming a man she didn't care to know. Tears for Kenny who was so twisted around inside that he could rape a woman. Myrna drained her gin, left Kenny a note reminding him to leave her door key on the kitchen table, and went to bed.

Of course, she was still awake when he came in. He bumped into the coffee table, ran water in the bathroom sink for a long time, then quiet. Myrna lay awake in the dark blue-gray night listening to the groan of the refrigerator, the hiss of the hot-water heater, and the rumble of large trucks on a distant street. *He* made no sound where he lay on the opened-out sofa, surrounded by her sewing machine, dress dummy, marking tape, and pins.

When sleep finally came, it brought dreams of walking down brilliantly lit streets, hand in hand with a boy about twelve who looked, acted, and talked like Kenny but who she knew with certainty was not her son, at the same time she also knew he could be no one else.

She woke to a cacophony of church bells. It was late. Too late to make it to church service. She turned her head to look at the crucifix hanging by her bed and tried to pray, to summon up that feeling of near weightlessness that came over her in those moments when she was able to free her mind of all else and give herself over to prayer. Now nothing came but a dull ache in the back of her throat.

She had begun attending church regularly after she stopped visiting Kenny. His refusal to respond to her questions made it clear she'd have to seek answers elsewhere. She'd decided to talk to Father Giles. He'd been at St. Mark's, in their old neighborhood, before she and Kenny had moved there. He'd seen Kenny growing up. Perhaps he'd noticed something, understood something about the boy, about her, that would explain what she could not understand.

"It's God's will, my child—put it in His hands," he'd urged, awkwardly patting her arm and averting his eyes.

Myrna took his advice wholeheartedly. She became quite adept at quieting the questions boiling in her belly with, "His will," or "My cross to bear." Many nights she'd "Our Fathered" herself to sleep. Acceptance of Kenny's inexplicable act became a test God had given her. One she passed by visiting the sick, along with other women from the church; working on the neighborhood cleanup committee; avoiding all social contact with men. With sex. She put "widowed" on job applications and never mentioned a son to new people she met. Once she'd moved away from the silent accusation of their old apartment, prayer and good works became a protective shield separating her from the past.

Kenny's tap on her door startled her back to the present. She cleared her throat and straightened the covers before calling to him to come in.

A rich, aromatic steam rose from the coffee he'd brought her. The toast was just the right shade of brown, and she was sure that when she cracked the poached egg it would be cooked exactly to her liking. Not only was everything perfectly prepared, it was the first time she'd had breakfast in bed since he'd been arrested. Myrna couldn't hold back the tears or the flood of memories of many mornings, just so: him bending over her with a breakfast tray.

"You wait on people in the restaurant all day and sit up all night making other people's clothes. You need some waiting on, too."

Had he actually said that, this man as a boy? Could this man have been such a   56
boy? Myrna nearly tilted the tray in her confusion.

"I need to brush my teeth." She averted her face and reached for her bath-   57
robe.

But she couldn't avoid her eyes in the medicine cabinet mirror, eyes that re-   58
minded her that despite what Kenny had done, she hadn't stopped loving him. But
her love didn't need his company. It thrived only on memories of him that were
more than four years old. It was as much a love remembered as a living thing. But
it was love, nonetheless. Myrna pressed her clenched fist against her lips and wondered if love was enough. She stayed in the bathroom until she heard him leave her
bedroom and turn on the TV in the living room.

When he came back for the tray, she told him she had a sick headache and had   59
decided to stay in bed. He was immediately sympathetic, fetching aspirin and a
cool compress for her forehead, offering to massage her neck and temples, to
lower the blinds and block out the bright morning sun. Myrna told him she wanted
only to rest.

All afternoon she lay on her unmade bed, her eyes on the ceiling or idly roam-   60
ing the room, her mind moving across the surface of her life, poking at old wounds,
so amazingly raw after all these years. First there'd been Buddy. He'd laughed at
her country ways and punched her around until he'd driven her and their child into
the streets. But at least she was rid of him. Then there was his son. Her baby. He'd
tricked a young woman into getting into his car where he proceeded to ruin a great
portion of her life. Now he'd come back to spill salt in her kitchen.

I'm home, Ma, homema, homema. His words echoed in her inner ear and   61
made her heart flutter. Her neighbors would want to know where he'd been all this
time and why. Fear and disgust would creep into their faces and voices. Her nights
would be full of listening. Waiting.

And she would have to live with the unblanketed reality that whatever anger   62
and meanness her son held toward the world, he had chosen a woman to take it
out on.

A woman.   63

Someone like me, she thought, like Great Aunt Faye, or Valerie, her eight-   64
year-old niece; like Lucille, her oldest friend, or Dr. Ramsey, her dentist. A woman
like all the women who'd helped feed, clothe, and care for Kenny; who'd tried their
damnedest to protect him from as much of the ugly and awful in life as they could;
who'd taught him to ride a bike and cross the street. All women. From the day
she'd left Buddy, not one man had done a damned thing for Kenny. Not one.

And he might do it again, she thought. The idea sent Myrna rolling back and   65
forth across the bed as though she could actually escape her thoughts. She'd allowed herself to believe she was done with such thoughts. Once she accepted Kenny's crime as the will of God, she immediately saw that it wouldn't have made any
difference how she'd raised him if this was God's unfathomable plan for him. It
was a comforting idea, one that answered her question of why and how her much-
loved son could be a rapist. One that answered the question of the degree of her
responsibility for Kenny's crime by clearing her of all possible blame. One that
allowed her to forgive him. Or so she'd thought.

Now she realized all her prayers, all her studied efforts to accept and forgive   66
were like blankets thrown on a forest fire. All it took was the small breeze created
by her opening the door to her only child to burn those blankets to cinders and
release her rage—as wild and fierce as the day he'd confessed.

She closed her eyes and saw her outraged self dash wildly into the living room   67
to scream imprecations in his face until her voice failed. Specks of froth gathered at
the corners of her mouth. Her flying spit peppered his face. He cringed before
her, his eyes full of shame as he tore at his own face and chest in self-loathing.

Yet, even as she fantasized, she knew Kenny could no more be screamed into   68
contrition than Crystal or any woman could be bullied into willing sex. And what,
in fact, was there for him to say or do that would satisfy her? The response she
really wanted from him was not available: there was no way he could become the
boy he'd been before that night four years ago.

No more than I can treat him as if he were that boy, she thought.   69

And the thought stilled her. She lay motionless, considering.   70

When she rose from her bed, she dragged her old green Samsonite suitcase   71
out from the back of the closet. She moved with the easy, effortless grace of someone who knows what she is doing and feels good about it. Without even wiping off
the dust, she plopped the suitcase on the bed. When she lifted the lid, the smell of
leaving and good-bye flooded the room and quickened her pulse. For the first time
in two days, her mouth moved in the direction of a smile.

She hurried from dresser drawer to closet, choosing her favorites: the black   72
two-piece silk knit dress she'd bought on sale, her comfortable gray shoes, the
lavender sweater she'd knitted as a birthday present to herself but had never worn,
both her blue and her black slacks, the red crepe blouse she'd made to go with
them, and the best of her underwear. She packed in a rush, as though her bus or
train were even now pulling out of the station.

When she'd packed her clothes, Myrna looked around the room for other   73
necessary items. She gathered up her comb and brush and the picture of her
mother from the top of her bureau, then walked to the wall on the left side of her
bed and lifted down the shiny metal and wooden crucifix that hung there. She ran
her finger down the slim, muscular body. The Aryan plaster-of-Paris Christ
seemed to writhe in bittersweet agony. Myrna stared at the crucifix for a few moments, then gently hung it back on the wall.

When she'd finished dressing, she sat down in the hard, straight-backed chair   74
near the window to think through her plan. Kenny tapped at her door a number of
times until she was able to convince him that she was best left alone and would be
fine in the morning. When dark came, she waited for the silence of sleep, then
quietly left her room. She set her suitcase by the front door, tiptoed by Kenny,
where he slept on the sofa, and went into the kitchen. By the glow from the back
alley streetlight, she wrote him a note and propped it against the sugar bowl:

> Dear Kenny,
>   I'm sorry. I just can't be your mother right now. I will be back in one week. Please be
> gone. Much love, Myrna.

Kenny flinched and frowned in his sleep as the front door clicked shut.   75

Rhetorical Focus

1. How does the image of silence function in the story? Is the word always used in the same way?
2. The story begins and ends with the opening and shutting of the front door. Why do you think Neely chose to focus on the door in this way? Are there other doors in the story? Do they function in the same way as the door that frames the story?
3. Provide explanations for the recurring images in the story, such as eyes, salt, and the crucifix.

Thematic Focus

1. Is Myrna a good mother? Why or why not? Is she more or less secure in her parenting than is Osborne? Does Kenny reciprocate in any way for the care she has given him?
2. Neely describes in detail the nature of Myrna's love for Kenny. How does she love him? What is the relationship between her love and her rage?
3. Compare the theme of parental guilt in the Osborne essay and the Neely story. If you see differences, are they differences in degree or in kind?

Motherhood: The Contemporary Emergency and the Quantum Leap

Adrienne Rich

Adrienne Rich was born in Baltimore, Maryland, on May 16, 1929. She was educated at Radcliffe College, graduating in 1951. That same year she won the Yale Series of Younger Poets prize for *A Change of World*. Since then, she has published numerous volumes of poetry, including *Snapshots of a Daughter-in-Law: Poems, Diving into the Wreck: Poems, 1971–1972, The Dream of a Common Language: Poems, 1974–1977,* and *The Fact of a Doorframe: Poems Selected and New, 1950–1984.* She is also the author of *Of Woman Born: Motherhood as Experience and Institution* and has published several volumes of selected essays. "Motherhood" is collected in *On Lies, Secrets, and Silence: Selected Prose, 1966–1978*. She is the mother of three sons and is now teaching at Stanford University.

Reflections Before Reading

Rich insists that motherhood is not "private and personal." What do you suppose she means by this? In what ways is motherhood a public institution? What do you think she means by the "contemporary emergency" and the "quantum leap" of her title? Do you think the Osborne essay and the Neely story demonstrate that motherhood is very much a public institution? If so, how? If not, why not? Rich's essay was originally delivered at a conference on the future of mothering held in Columbus, Ohio in 1978. What do you think mothering will be like in the future?

I want to begin by saying something that has been on my mind ever since I was   1
asked to participate in this conference. I hope, and believe, that every woman in
this room knows that on the subject of motherhood there are no experts. What we
need, in any case, as women, is not experts on our lives, but the opportunity and

"Motherhood: The Contemporary Emergency and the Quantum Leap" is reprinted from *On Lies, Secrets, and Silence, Selected Prose 1966–1978*, by Adrienne Rich, by permission of W.W. Norton & Company, Inc. Copyright © 1979 by W.W. Norton & Company, Inc.

the validation to name and describe the truths of our lives, as we have known them. Whatever you hear from me, from Jessie Bernard, from Dorothy Dinnerstein, from Tillie Olsen [the three other invited speakers at the conference], remember that it is your own sense of urgency, your own memories, needs, questions, and hopes, your own painfully gathered knowledge of daughterhood and motherhood, which you must above all trust. Listen to us, then, as to four women who through certain kinds of luck, privilege, struggle, exceptional status, and at certain kinds of cost, have been able not only to live the experience of daughterhood and motherhood, but also to reflect and write about it. But listen even more closely to yourselves.

One of the most powerful social and political catalysts of the past decade has been the speaking of women with other women, the telling of our secrets, the comparing of wounds and the sharing of words. This hearing and saying of women has been able to break many a silence and taboo; literally to transform forever the way we see. Let this be a time, then, for hearing and speaking together, for breaking silences, not only within yourselves but among all our selves: the daughter and the mother; the black woman and the white; the lesbian mother and the married housewife; the woman who has chosen single or communal motherhood and the woman who has chosen to use her life in ways which do not include the raising of children; the woman who has given up custody of her children and the woman who is fighting to keep hers; the step-daughter, the foster-mother, the pregnant woman; the daughter who has never known her mother, the mother who has no daughters. What we all, collectively, have lived, as the daughters of women, as the mothers of children, is a tale far greater than any three or four of us can encompass: a tale only beginning to be told. I hope that here, speaking to and hearing one another, we can begin to fling cables of recognition and attention across the conditions that have divided us. And so I begin tonight by urging each of you to take responsibility for the voicing of her experience, to take seriously the work of listening to each other and the work of speaking, whether in private dialogue or in larger groups. In order to change what is, we need to give speech to what *has been,* to imagine together what *might be.*

I have seen massive sculpturelike weavings, of jute, hemp, and wool, in which many varicolored strands are quickly visible like vines or striations; but when you come closer and try to touch this or that strand, your hand enters a dense, bristling mesh, thick with knotted and twisted filaments, some harsh and rough to the fingers, others surprisingly silky and strong. In writing *Of Woman Born,* and in thinking about motherhood ever since, I have felt a similar sensation, of elemental exploration and of complex discovery. Let us try then to do justice to the complexity of this immense weaving, even as we single out particular strands or finger particular knots that seem to account for the whole. For motherhood is the great mesh in which all human relations are entangled, in which lurk our most elemental assumptions about love and power.

If we speak of motherhood at all, we are inevitably speaking of something far more than the relationship of a woman with her children. And even this relationship has been shaped long before the first child's birth. All women are daughters of women—is this an obvious, a simple-minded statement? or does it reach through the layers of the weaving to inner chambers only now beginning to be explored by women? It has been suggested by Margaret Mead that possibly a deep chemical affinity exists, of which we as yet know nothing, between the body of the mother and her still unborn female child. It has been affirmed by Nancy Chodorow, that through the intense mother–daughter relationship women come into a deep and richer inner life than men, and, even when heterosexual, tend to be more deeply attached to women than to men, and more capable than men of relationship.[1] Both Chodorow and Dorothy Dinnerstein feel strongly that the solution to sexual inequality would be a radical change in the system of parenting, that is, that parenting must be shared equally between women and men. I wish here to suggest other forces which sit in wait in the birth-chamber as a woman completes her first nine months of mothering.

Historically, cross-culturally, a woman's status as childbearer has been the test 5 of her womanhood. Through motherhood, every woman has been defined from outside herself: mother, matriarch, matron, spinster, barren, old maid—listen to the history of emotional timbre that hangs about each of these words. Even by default motherhood has been an enforced identity for women, while the phrases "childless man" and "nonfather" sound absurd and irrelevant to us.

And so this woman in labor is on the one hand, even perhaps in terror and 6 pain, doing what history has told her it was her duty and destiny to do; while at the same time doing what her mother did, reenacting a scene, which both separates her from her own mother (for now she is, supposedly, herself a woman and no longer a child) and creates her more intensely in her mother's image.

Motherhood is also, of course, at the crux of the self-determination of women 7 over our bodies. Many of you need no reminding that here in Ohio we meet on soil already shaken by the fire-bombing and burning of four women's health clinics within the past four months, part of a nationwide pattern of terrorism against the hard-won and fragile right of women to make the invariably difficult choice to end an unwanted pregnancy. But these attacks on the grassroots, spreading movement of women to repossess our bodies are only one small piece of the larger picture to which I allude, in the title of this talk, as "the contemporary emergency." Sometimes referred to as "the backlash," this emergency is many-pronged, and I believe it is important to grasp it as clearly and as realistically as we can.

Motherhood, the family, are still too often relegated to the realm of the "pri- 8 vate and personal." "For love," women are assumed to provide unflagging emotional care, not only to children but to men; while in terms of the physical work we do, our enormous, unpaid contribution to every economy is everywhere dismissed as only the natural service of women to men and children. We would rightly be skeptical of a feminism which denied the value and dignity of traditional women's work in the home. But in fact it is not feminists who have belittled and devalued the work of the housewife and mother: It is the statisticians, the political scientists, the economists, the image-makers of television and other advertising, the profes-

---

[1] *The Reproduction of Mothering* (Berkeley: University fo California, 1978), p. 198.

sionals, who depict the woman at home as "not working," as invisible, as an empty-headed consumer. Listen to the idiotic baby-voices allotted to women in canned radio commercials, look at the grimacing smiles of housewives and mothers as depicted on television, observe the obscene patronizing of women on game shows, read the childraising and sex manuals, equally patronizing, written by the male doctor experts.[2] The feminist movement has from the first demanded choice as each woman's right, respect for each woman's being; feminist artists, historians, anthropologists have been the first to show concern and respect for the crafts of the midwives and grandmothers, the anonymous work of women's hands, the oral culture of women sitting in kitchens, the traditional arts and remedies passed on from mother to daughter, the female culture never granted the reverence accorded to "high art." A recognition of women's unquenchable creativity—contained so often within domestic limits, yet astounding in its diversity—has been one of the deep perceptions of a feminism which looks with fresh eyes on all that has been trivialized, devalued, forbidden, or silenced in female history. And so we can both take pride in all that women have done for "love"—including the resourceful, heroic coping of ordinary women everywhere—and also ask: "Why should women, and women only, work for love only? And what kind of love is this, which means always to be for others, never for ourselves?"

But the dismissal of the traditional work of women as nonwork, of our art as mere "decoration" or "craft" or "scribbling," the condescension to the housewife and mother, the long and violent campaign against voluntary motherhood, the suspect status of women who are neither wives nor mothers—these are merely symptoms of the much larger phenomenon of *gynephobia*—fear and hatred of women—which in its less virulent and savage forms we have called "sexism." Much is being written these days about gender-identity—and about how we can change the restricting images of self that both girls and boys learn so early, as the chief lessons of culture. I believe that the issue of gender-identity may well mask a reality much deeper and more terrifying to contemplate than the superstitions which impose one set of qualities upon one sex and another set on the other.   9

Beneath sexism, beneath socially enforced gender-identity and stereotype, lies *gynephobia*. It is an ancient and well-documented phenomenon,[3] and it is not a simple one, neither in its origins nor in the many faces it wears in the present day. Certainly male contempt and loathing for women and for women's bodies is embedded in language, art, folklore, and legend; the need to contain and restrict women's creativity and power within the mothering role is an insistent theme in all   10

---

[2]For a detailed documentation and analysis of the creation of "the woman problem" by postindustrial science, especially medicine, see B. Ehrenreich and D. English, *For Her Own Good; 150 Years of the Experts' Advice to Women* (New York: Doubleday/Anchor, 1978), a brilliant study marred only by its failure to deal with heterosexuality itself as a primary mandate to women.

[3]See H. R. Hays, *The Dangerous Sex: The Myth of Feminine Evil* (New York: Pocket Books, 1972), first published 1964; Katherine M. Rogers, *The Troublesome Helpmate: A History of Misogyny in Literature* (Seattle: University of Washington, 1966); Andrea Dworkin, *Woman Hating* (New York: Dutton, 1974); Mary Daly, *Gyn/Ecology: The Metaethics of Radical Feminism* (Boston: Beacon, 1979).

social institutions; what has been called "the backlash" is, I think, only an intensification of the long assault upon every effort by women to repossess ourselves, to lay hold on our integrity, to refuse to hate ourselves as we have been hated.

There has been a basic contradiction throughout patriarchy: between the laws   11
and sanctions designed to keep women essentially powerless, and the attribution to mothers of almost superhuman power (of control, of influence, of life-support). The other side of the contradiction, of course, is the negation of women who are not mothers, or who are woman-identified. The unmarried or childless woman may be more acceptable today than when she was perceived as so threatening that she was burned as a witch. But the socialization of every girl toward heterosexual romance and childbearing is still probably the most intense socialization practiced by society as a whole. At the same time, once a woman has borne a child she is viewed as the primary and uttermost source of that child's good and evil, its survival, health, sanity, and selfhood. A society which penalizes some children because they are not white, others because they are not male, indoctrinating in them a sense of worthlessness, can still lay the blame for the waste of its young on the "bad" mothers who have somehow failed to be superhuman, who have somehow failed to rear, in a callous and ruthless social order, well-adjusted, obedient, achieving, nonalienated children.

Gynephobia supposes the eternal, universal guilt of women, and most women   12
carry in us a learned, internalized version of that guilt. Maternal guilt is perhaps the most familiar to many of us; but many also know the guilt leveled at the woman who affirms herself, who is centered-in-herself, and who, in a woman-hating environment, dares to love herself and other women. It is ironic, to say the least, that the first verbal attack slung at the woman who demonstrates a primary loyalty to herself and other women is *man-hater*. The fear of appearing or being named as a man-hater still causes many women to deny the reality of gynephobia, the concrete evidences of woman-hating embedded in our culture, in language, image, and act.

Gynephobia is an old historical reality; what creates an emergency today is the   13
fusion of gynephobia with technology. To deal fully with the implications of this— the acceleration of technological change over the past century, the rapidly increasing complexity of systems and the training of elite males who will decide how and for what technology is to be used—this would take several volumes, and some of these are already written. In response to this crisis, a strong feminist ecology movement is beginning to take shape, as exemplified by the Women's Conference on the Environment in Albany, June 17–18, 1978, and by the publication of two major books on women, manmade technology, and nature: Susan Griffin's *Woman and Nature* and Mary Daly's *Gyn/Ecology*.[4] What I want to do here is look at some things that are happening with respect to the control of motherhood, the exploitation of women's reproductive power by male-dominated institutions and systems.

---

[4]Susan Griffin, *Woman and Nature: The Roaring Inside Her* (New York: Harper & Row, 1978); Mary Daly, op. cit. For an analysis of a specific application of technology, see Janice Raymond, *The Transsexual Empire: The Making of the She-Male* (Boston: Beacon, 1979).

The Supreme Court decision leading to state withdrawal of Medicaid funds   14
for abortion is a legal attack upon a hard-won freedom for women. It is also directly
linked with the growing use of sterilization as a population-control device—first in
Latin America and other Third World areas, but soon to be attempted in the States
as a major form of "family planning." If poor women cannot afford abortion, and
cannot afford to raise their children, they are more likely to give what is often
cynically termed "informed consent" to sterilization.[5] Already by 1968, 35.3 per
cent of Puerto Rican women of childbearing age, two-thirds of them under thirty,
had been sterilized—under funding by the department cynically termed Health,
Education, and Welfare. Experimental contraceptives are tested by AID [Agency
for International Development] in Puerto Rico for dissemination in the Third
World although they fail to meet the admittedly low standards of the United States
drug industry. Sterilization is being used on poor women and women of color in
the continental United States, even where abortion is legal and has been requested.

Here are some examples quoted from an article on sterilization of Native   15
American women from the Denver, Colorado, feminist newspaper, *Big Mama
Rag:*

> Sterilization of women in this country has increased 300% since 1970. . . . An esti-
> mated 32% of all black women under thirty have been sterilized. . . . Over 25% of all
> American Indian women of childbearing age have been sterilized since 1973, leaving
> only about 100,000 women of childbearing age who can have children. Among those
> sterilized, 10% were under the age of 21. . . . Many Indian women are coerced into
> signing forms agreeing to sterilization. It is frequently insinuated that they will lose
> welfare payments and benefits if they refuse. A large number of women agree to ster-
> ilization operations because they are afraid that their children will be taken away from
> them if they don't. To avoid this type of misunderstanding government agencies are
> now required to inform women that there are other forms of birth control available to
> them and that other benefits may not be withheld if they refuse. However, there is no
> indication that these laws are being followed or enforced.[6]

The agencies implementing sterilization policies here and abroad are among those
which present a "humanitarian" image to the public: HEW, VISTA, the Peace

---

[5]The importance of "guidelines" in the performance of elective sterilization is unquestionable. But, as
we examine the social and economic conditions under which women give consent, and the absence of
alternatives, it becomes clear that "the question of poverty is inseparable from reproductive freedom
for women" and the meaning of "voluntary" becomes inseparable from a woman's entire life-situation,
the actual range of her choices, her view of sterilization as "an escape from abject poverty." For an
excellent overview of the issue, with emphasis on Puerto Rico, see *Workbook on Sterilization and
Sterilization Abuse* (Ad Hoc Women's Studies Committee Against Sterilization Abuse, Women's Studies, Sarah Lawrence College, Bronxville, N.Y. 10708). See also "Who Controls Reproduction: Birth
Control, Population Control, Sterilization Abuse" in *Isis* International Bulletin no. 7, spring 1978 (Case
Postale 301, 1227 Carouge/Geneva, Switzerland).
[6]Judy Barlow, "Sterilization of Native American Women," *Big Mama Rag*, vol. 6, no. 5, May 1978.

Corps, AID.[7] But women must be deeply skeptical of apparent solutions to human distress which may deprive any woman or group of women of the decision as to how their bodies are to be used. The assumptions justifying coercive sterilization are part of the objectification and exploitation of women's bodies that we see in pornography and in cultural imagery everywhere that degrades women. And no woman, or group of women, is finally exempt from these attitudes.

Meanwhile, in underdeveloped countries, the multinational corporations manufacturing commercial infant formula have been aggressively marketing their products as a better, Western replacement for breast milk. In Africa, the Caribbean, Latin America, the Philippines, areas where protein–calorie malnutrition can be an acute problem, and where mothers have successfully breastfed their children for centuries, samples of formula are given away at prenatal clinics, pushed by company employees costumed as "milk nurses," while clinic walls are plastered with posters alleging the superiority of powdered formula. Hospitals are bribed to permit advertising and sales with free gifts of medical equipment and other largesse. Very large numbers of children are dying from malnutrition—the mothers want to do the best, the most modern thing, for their infants, cannot afford to feed them the full formula, have in any case no refrigeration or sterile water supply, and often dilute or reduce the formula to save money.[8] When we hear of "population control" as a solution to famine, we must not forget starvation caused by the ruthlessness of "free" enterprise, and by a profound indifference to the lives of women and children. 16

I believe—as my poem "Hunger" attempts to delineate in a different kind of language—that the problem of world hunger is a central issue for women, that it is inextricably bound up with motherhood, and with the control of women's bodies by male-dominated interests. We hear a great deal about the "population explosion," but little about the withholding of resources, the waste and misuse of protein, the use of food as a tool of international pressure. "Population control" is targeted at women from groups considered expendable or "unfit" on the basis of income, class, and race. Instead of finding ways of supporting human life humanely on the planet, instead of controlling the expansion of corporate power and profiteering in agriculture, such male-dominated, and utterly nonfeminist, groups as Zero Population Growth and International Planned Parenthood seek to remove all choice from women as to the use of their potential for motherhood; sterilization is to replace contraception or abortion. Obviously, sterilization itself is no evil, so 17

---

[7]"Humanitarian" at least in name. " 'The United States plans to sterilize one-quarter of the world's women,' said Dr. R. T. Ravenholt, director of AID's office on population control. According to Ravenholt, population control is necessary to maintain 'the normal operation of commercial interests around the world.' 'Without our trying to help these countries with their economic and social development, the world would rebel against the strong U.S. commercial presence,' " he said. (Liberation News Service, quoted in *Akwesasne Notes,* September 1977, p. 31.)

[8]See *Isis* International Bulletin no. 2, "Breast-Feeding: A Political Issue"; also "Baby Food Politics" in *Isis* no. 7; and Jane Cottingham, ed., *Bottle Babies: A Guide to the Baby Foods Issue,* published by *Isis,* December 1976.

long as women have real psychological and economic choices. It is the *uses* of technology for both genocidal and gynecidal purposes which more and more women now view as a major emergency.

Another example: the sudden rise of 50 percent in the number of Cae-   18
sarean operations performed in U.S. hospitals has attracted the attention of feminists in health work and childbirth education, as well as of some male physicians. Here again low-income women stand a higher chance of being viewed as "poor risks" in pregnancy and given Caesareans—using Medicaid money to pay the higher costs of this kind of delivery.[9] It is increasingly clear that medical technology has, in U.S. hospitals, but also in other parts of the world, become a means of alienating women from the act of giving birth, hence from their own bodies, their own procreative powers, and of keeping birth itself so far as possible in male control. It has also become a major industry. The story of this male "theft of childbirth" has been told and documented by Ehrenreich and English, by Suzanne Arms, and by myself;[10] and there is an active feminist health and home-birth movement dedicated to the project of "taking our bodies back." But the effort to seize the process of birth from women is now abetted by a technology far more developed than when in the seventeenth century the Chamberlen family hid the secret of the forceps for three generations. This new level of technology and medical research can create female genitals in a male-to-female transsexual; it can offer "restructured vaginas" as a solution for heterosexual sex problems; it can project mammal cloning as a realistic possibility; yet it has been unable to produce a truly safe and effective contraceptive device. The enormous complexity of sex-change surgery, as Janice Raymond has exhaustively shown, is now a major medical industry, aimed at solving the problems of gender-suffering through technology rather than through profound societal changes which would do away with sex roles altogether.[11]

Finally, while a powerful corporate state works to remove the right of mother-   19
hood from thousands of poor and Third World women, a powerful Church and other corporate interests agitate as "friends of the fetus." As Alice Rossi has pointed out,

> There are now far more fetuses in the American work-place than there ever were children in our mines and factories in the whole history of American child labor; yet there have been no large-scale investigations of the potential influence on the fetus of the vast array of new chemicals and synthetic substances in the environments in which employed women work. In one of the few studies in this area, [Vilma] Hunt found a

---

[9]Maritza Arrastia, "Epidemic of Caesareans," *Seven Days*, May 5, 1978.

[10]B. Ehrenreich and D. English, *Witches, Midwives, and Nurses: A History of Women Healers* (Old Westbury, N.Y.: Feminist Press, 1973); Suzanne Arms, *Immaculate Deception* (Boston: Houghton Mifflin, 1975); Adrienne Rich, *Of Woman Born: Motherhood as Experience and Institution* (New York: Norton, 1976).

[11]Raymond, op cit.

significant correlation between severe air pollution and the incidence of fetal distress, prematurity, and stillbirths.[12]

Both the Right-to-Life and the Population Control movements are obsessed with direct control of women's bodies—not with discovering and creating conditions which would make life more livable for the living. In the middle-class United States, a veneer of "alternate life-styles" disguises the reality that, here as everywhere, women's apparent "choices" whether to have or not have children are still dependent on the far from neutral will of male legislators, jurists, a male medical and pharmaceutical profession, well-financed lobbies, including the prelates of the Catholic Church, and the political reality that women do not as yet have self-determination over our bodies, and still live mostly in ignorance of our authentic physicality, our possible choices, our eroticism itself.

We are undermined and subverted, not simply by precarious and whimsical   20
abortion laws, precarious and fallible birth-control devices; but also by laws and conventions protecting a husband's right to rape and batter his wife or kidnap his children; by pornographic advertising which tells us we love to submit to sexual violence; by the victim-imagery of the Christian Church, which extols passive motherhood in the person of the Virgin Mary; by the very manner in which we give birth in hospitals, surrounded by male experts, supinely drugged or stirruped against our will, our babies taken from us at birth by other experts who will tell us how often to feed, when we may hold, our newborns. And, finally, by the whispering voice of the culture, internalized in us, that says *we* are forever guilty; guilty of living in a woman's body, guilty of getting pregnant, guilty of refusing the mother-role altogether. A male-dominated technological establishment and a male-dominated population-control network view both the planet and women's bodies as resources to be seized, exploited, milked, excavated, and controlled. Somehow, in the nightmare image of an earth overrun with starving people because feckless, antisocial women refuse to stop breeding, we can perceive contempt for women, for the children of women, and for the earth herself.

I have often asked myself whether the experience of motherhood under patri-   21
archy is finally radicalizing or conservatizing. In attempting to give our children the security, the stability, we know they need, do we become more obedient to a social order we know is morally bankrupt; do we give in to the pressures of convention, of schools, of jobs; are our children our hostages to the State, its real safeguard—and escape-valve—against the anger of women? Or do we discover, in motherhood, the coarse, bitter, bedrock truth of the way things are, the callousness of patriarchy, its hatred of women, its indifference to new life, even to youth itself, that supposed idolatry of American life? In motherhood we are often separated from

---

[12]Alice Rossi, "Children and Work in the Lives of Women," paper delivered at the University of Arizona, Tucson, February 7, 1976. See Chapter IV, "Work, Reproduction and Health," in Jeanne Mager Stellman, *Women's Work, Women's Health, Myths and Realities* (New York: Pantheon, 1977).

other women, enclosed in the home, and like paid domestic workers, we find it difficult to organize. Yet mothers *do* organize: to start cooperative childcare, to get broken glass cleaned off a playground, to keep schools open. In Brooklyn there is a Sisterhood of Black Single Mothers, surely one of the most beleaguered of all groups between the twin grindstones of gynephobia and racism. The Lesbian Mothers' National Defense Fund, based in Seattle, has helped a number of women to fight for and win custody of their children. The Welfare Mothers' Movement is a growing force across the country. These groups and others like them consist of women considered marginal to society, women who through color, poverty, and sexual preference already have reason to be politicized, in addition to their status as mothers. If they have organized under the daily, hourly emergency of their situations, mothers everywhere can organize. But we will need to disabuse ourselves of the myths of motherhood, of the idea of its sacredness, its protected status, its automatic validation of us as women.

The right to have or not have children; the right to have both children and a   22
selfhood not dependent on them; these are still being fought for, and this fight threatens every part of the patriarchal system. We cannot afford to settle for individual solutions. The myth that motherhood is "private and personal" is the deadliest myth we have to destroy, and we have to begin by destroying it in ourselves. The institution of motherhood—which is maintained by the law, by patriarchal technology and religion, by all forms of education—including pornography—has, by the most savage of ironies, alienated women from our bodies by incarcerating us in them.

The "quantum leap" of my title is of course a leap of the imagination. When I   23
chose that title, I was thinking a great deal about time. I am a woman of forty-nine, a lesbian/feminist, mother of three adult sons who still sometimes appear as young children in my dreams. The feminist movement of this half-century surfaced "just in time" for me; I had been a solitary feminist for too long. I know that the rest of my life will be spent working for transformations I shall not live to see realized. I feel daily, hourly impatience, and am pledged to the active and tenacious patience that a lifetime commitment requires: there can be no resignation in the face of backlash, setback, or temporary defeat; there can be no limits on what we allow ourselves to imagine. Because the past ten years of feminist thinking and action have been so full, so charged with revelations, challenges, as well as with anger and pain, we sometimes think of that decade as if it had been fifty years, not ten. *Why haven't we come further?* But in the great evolution of woman that this century's radical feminism envisions, we have only begun. And yet this longer historical view seems unbearable to me when I consider the urgency of each woman's life that may be lost, poured away like dishwater, because history does not move fast enough for her.

So the "quantum leap" implies that even as we try to deal with backlash and   24
emergency, we are imagining the new: a future in which women are powerful, full of our own power, not the old patriarchal power-over but the power-to-create, power-to-think, power-to-articulate and concretize our visions and transform our

lives and those of our children. I believe still, as I wrote in the afterword to *Of Woman Born,* that this power will begin to speak in us more and more as we repossess our own bodies, including the decision to mother or not to mother, and how, and with whom, and when. For the struggle of women to become self-determining is rooted in our bodies, and it is an indication of this that the token woman artist or intellectual or professional has so often been constrained to deny her female physicality in order to enter realms designated as male domain.

It has never been my belief that mothering could, under different circumstances, become easy. As I wrote at the end of my book: 25

> To destroy the institution is not to abolish motherhood. It is to release the creation and sustenance of life into the same realm of decision, struggle, surprise, imagination, and conscious intelligence, as any other difficult, but freely chosen, work.

This means, among other things, that a woman could choose motherhood   26
freely, not just because safe and effective birth control was universally available, but because she would have no need to prove her adequacy as a woman by getting pregnant; that a woman need not look for economic security to a man, getting pregnant as a by-product; that no false necessity would dictate a choice between a woman's uterus and her brain; that the woman mothering her child was a being with dignity in the world, who respected her body, who had as much power as any other individual person to act upon and shape her society, and who possessed the wherewithal to meet her own needs and those of her children, whether she chose to live with a man, with a woman, with other parents and children, or in a separate household with her children. These are minimal conditions; but implied in them are enormous social and political changes.

What would it mean to mother in a society where women were deeply valued   27
and respected, in a culture which was woman-affirming? What would it mean to bear and raise children in the fullness of our power to care for them, provide for them, in dignity and pride? What would it mean to mother in a society which had truly addressed the issues of racism and hunger? What would it mean to mother in a society which was making full use of the spiritual, intellectual, emotional, physical gifts of women, in all our difference and diversity? What would it mean to mother in a society which laid no stigma upon lesbians, so that women grew up with real emotional and erotic options in the choice of life companions and lovers? What would it mean to live and die in a culture which affirmed both life and death, in which both the living world and the bodies of women were released at last from centuries of violation and control? This is the quantum leap of the radical feminist vision.

I believe we must cope courageously and practically, as women have always   28
done, with the here and now, our feet on this ground where we now live. But nothing less than the most radical imagination will carry us beyond this place, beyond the mere struggle for survival, to that lucid recognition of our possibilities which will keep us impatient, and unresigned to mere survival.

Rhetorical Focus

1. Rich's essay was originally a speech. What features of her text make this evident? How would the essay be different if it were originally intended to be read rather than heard?
2. Why do you think Rich chose the image of a weaving to illustrate the sensation of "elemental exploration" and "complex discovery" associated with motherhood?
3. Identify structures in the essay that are parallel. Analyze their rhetorical effect.

Thematic Focus

1. Compare and contrast Rich's perspective on mothering with Osborne's.
2. What distinction does Rich make between gynephobia and sexism? What connection does she make between gynephobia and maternal guilt?
3. Rich delivered her speech in 1978. Do you think it is dated? Why or why not?

Suggestions for Writing

1. Observe a mother interacting with a child. Describe and analyze the nature of the relationship.
2. Write an essay in which you make connections between Myrna in "Spilled Salt" and the Rich essay.
3. Rich claims that "a male-dominated technological establishment and a male-dominated population-control network view both the planet and women's bodies as resources to be seized, exploited, milked, excavated, and controlled" (paragraph 20). Support or refute her claim.

Chapter
6

Relations Among Races and Cultures

Throughout *Constellations*, we feature writers from various races and cultures, inviting you to compare their experiences and insights. Here, though, we exclusively focus on relations among races and cultures. As American society becomes more diverse, its citizens will increasingly have to acknowledge its multicultural nature. Indeed, for our society to progress, all of us must understand how our various cultures can best relate—both to each other and to the larger world. The constellations in this unit are intended to help you understand that you proceed from a particular cultural background when you write. Indeed, if you can bear in mind when you write that not all races or cultures share your beliefs, you can grow more able to address diverse audiences' possible concerns.

We begin with two essays that demonstrate just how challenging it can be for a majority group to grasp the perspective of an oppressed one. The white authors, Jane Tompkins and Diana Hume George, struggle to understand the past and present experience of Native Americans. Next, from an opposite point of view, Brent Staples, Arturo Madrid, and Mitsuye Yamada write about what it feels like for them to be a minority in this country. Although they write as an African-American, a Hispanic-American, and an Asian-American, respectively, their perspectives show interesting similarities. In particular, they all suggest that their real identities are in a crucial sense not visible to the majority. We then expand the scope of this unit by presenting two essays that bring up relations between America and other cultures, specifically Caribbean/South Atlantic ones. Jamaica Kincaid exposes the naïveté of American and European visitors to the island of Antigua, her poverty-stricken homeland, whereas June Jordan ponders her own visit to the Bahamas as an African-American woman. Finally, we turn to three African-American writers who, in effect, debate the best way of combating discrimination in their society. By presenting different views of affirmative action, Shelby Steele,

Roger Wilkins, and William Raspberry suggest that even its potential beneficiaries can disagree about it. Together, their essays also suggest the ongoing complexity of racial issues in America.

Several of the essays in *Constellations* may strike you as offering strong views with which you disagree, at least on a first reading. Yet, even if some of these texts initially trouble you, take them as an opportunity to consider perspectives other than your own. A composition classroom can be an excellent laboratory for exploring differences that unfortunately often provoke social conflict elsewhere. Throughout your reading, writing, and class discussions, use these texts to enhance your sense not only of the constellations that make up this book, but also of the constellations of people that make up America and the world.

TRYING TO VIEW ANOTHER RACE OR CULTURE REALISTICALLY

What sorts of knowledge, if any, can people gain about races or cultures not their own? In what ways should their claims about another race or culture be evaluated? What are the particular challenges that dominant groups confront when they seek to develop appropriate conceptions of minorities? Here Jane Tompkins and Diana Hume George grapple with such important questions, as they consider the difficulties that white Americans such as them face in perceiving Native Americans accurately. Although both writers have gained reputations for their academic scholarship rather than for their autobiographical essays, they use their essays here to reflect on their personal encounters with Native American culture. Tompkins weighs the implications of her visit to the Museum of the American Indian in New York City, whereas George explains how her visit to the Pine Ridge Sioux Reservation in South Dakota helped her understand her earlier experiences as the wife of a Native American.

Both authors point out that whites may fail to counteract their historical mistreatment of Native Americans if they simply romanticize them. Of course, as Louise Erdrich suggests in her poem about John Wayne (see the first constellation in the unit, "Mass Culture"), white culture has more often depicted Native Americans in an extremely negative light. Tompkins and George call our attention, however, to the fact that at various times in history, whites have also stereotyped Native Americans by associating them with a primitive nobility. In effect, these essays contribute to an ongoing debate about what constitutes a truly realistic view of Native Americans. You may know that while many people acclaimed the 1990 film *Dances With Wolves* for resisting the villainous image of Native Americans promoted by John Wayne Westerns, some accused the film of leaning too far in the other direction by glorifying them as mystical, gentle prophets in harmony with the land.

The two essays here will certainly not settle quarrels over depictions of Native Americans. Nor will they resolve once and for all the more general debate of how outsiders to a race or culture should approach it. Instead, take your reading of them as an opportunity to study by means of particular examples the complex issues we have mentioned. Can only Native Americans judge the statements that Tompkins and George make about them? Does George necessarily write with more authority than Tompkins because she once lived with Native Americans? What evidence do these authors use to support their theories about them? Do these authors demonstrate the kind of thinking process you hope that whites will show as they try to understand a minority group? Consider, finally, the experiences, ideas, and attitudes you may need to have if, as writer and citizen, you are to avoid stereotyping other peoples.

A Visit to the Museum

Jane Tompkins

Jane Tompkins (b. 1940) is Professor of English at Duke University in Durham, North Carolina. She graduated from Bryn Mawr College and earned both master's and doctoral degrees from Yale University. Besides editing an influential collection of essays on the role of the reader in literary interpretation, she has written *Sensational Designs: The Cultural Work of American Fiction 1790–1860,* which examines how the modern literary curriculum left out novels by women that were bestsellers during the nineteenth century. In the past few years, Tompkins has repeatedly analyzed the genre of the Western, as well as other texts and institutions depicting the American West. She is especially interested in the ways these works present distorted images of women and Native Americans.

Lately, Tompkins has also tried to inject the concerns of her everyday life into her writing, even when she deals with academic subjects. As she explains in a 1987 essay, "The criticism I would like to write would always take off from personal experience. Would always be in some way a chronicle of my hours and days." Yet in the same essay, she suggests that writers should continually ponder the relationship of their experience to the situations of other people and to larger cultural frameworks: "How can we speak personally to one another and yet not be self-centered? How can we be part of the great world and yet loyal to ourselves?" This blend of autobiography and cultural context appears not only in what you are about to read, but also in an account that Tompkins wrote of her visit to the Buffalo Bill Museum in Wyoming (see the Summer 1990 issue of *South Atlantic Quarterly*). The following essay, which concerns her visit to the Museum of the American Indian in New York City, appeared in the Fall 1989 issue of *The Georgia Review.*

Reflections Before Reading

What do you associate with museums? Think of ones you have visited or heard about. What do you think the purpose of a museum usually is? Tompkins writes about her visit to the Museum of the American Indian in New York City. What would you want such a museum to do? What, if anything, do you fear it might do?

On impulse, during a recent trip across the country, I turned off the interstate at   1 Oklahoma City to follow the signs to the National Cowboy Hall of Fame. I had taken to visiting museums lately, not only because I was interested in their contents, but also because I wanted to see how the contents had been selected, with what aim and what results. I knew that anthropologists and cultural historians had been writing about the politics of museums, and I shared their concerns, but I was interested too in the kinds of experience one has in a museum: the feelings and thoughts they arouse, the physical sensations they provide. I had started to reflect, in particular, on how museums devoted to the American West educated people to see the country's past in a certain way.

As befits a museum that celebrates the grandeur of the West, everything in the   2 National Cowboy Hall of Fame is on a large scale. A long colonnade leads to the broad entranceway; the lobby is open and inviting. An attractive older woman greeted me after I had paid admission, handed me a brochure, and asked if I had any questions. All this opulence and graciousness made me feel well-launched, if a little guilty. I had gone in prepared to analyze and find fault (a previous experience at a Western museum had alerted me to the bloodthirsty, conquistador character of some commemorations of the West), but the generosity and sophistication of this environment disarmed me almost completely. So what if the paintings showed stereotyped Indian chiefs and idealized cowboys; so what if the Indian art was displayed as if it were in an apartment featured by *Architectural Digest;* I was lulled by the soothing colors, the luminous spaces, the hushed admiration of the visitors, and the excellent air-conditioning. Even the enormous hall devoted to busts of the museum's donors wasn't enough to mar the experience.

Exiting along the stone path that curves across a pond dotted by fountains, I   3 found it impossible to cavil. It no longer mattered if a hundred pictures of rodeo stars, shown next to a hundred saddles and a hundred lassos, had been boring (never mind that it celebrated an American tradition of cruelty to animals). The museum itself had been beautiful, comfortable, and serene. I had enjoyed looking at the contemporary paintings; the portraits of western movie stars were a particular treat for me—and so was the John Wayne alcove, which offered a video full of wonderful clips from his films and a display of his collection of Chinese art and Western Americana. The hour had been a pleasure—exactly right as a respite from the long, hot drive between Amarillo and Tulsa.

This benign episode made me wonder. If I, a professional critic blooded for   4
the kill, had come away from the Cowboy Hall of Fame grateful for the pleasant interlude, maybe museum-going wasn't the serious business I had long considered it. Maybe it was more like going to the ballpark and eating a hot dog than attending a lecture or reading a book. Maybe, on the model of TV news programs like *60 Minutes* and *20/20*, it was information as entertainment. The product was no longer "culture" in the standard sense but a total experience—gorgeous gift shop, great snack bar, fantastic lighting, terrific videos—all of these making up the package. I had to admit that I liked visiting a really luxurious rest room, browsing through expensive art books, looking at some curious paintings, and listening to the plash of fountains. Under these conditions, questions of cultural indoctrination—of racism, male-worship, and ethnocentrism—just couldn't get any purchase in my brain. I felt refreshed.

In the history of my experiences with museums this one was uncharacteristi-   5
cally mild. I have an indelible memory of the children's lunchroom in the Museum of Natural History in New York: the little, olive-drab lockers where we deposited our brown paper bags reeking of bananas and mayonnaise, cheese, and oranges and bologna. The huge dinosaurs made of bones, the great canoe filled with terrifying warriors, the dioramas of Indians in their villages—these are among the most vivid impressions of my childhood. From a later period, I remember the Museum of the Works of the Duomo in Florence—an austere, light-filled space, all stone and air—with its Donatello statues of the prophets, radiating moral purpose.

These and other museums became for me touchstones, summarizing eras of   6
experience, my cultural capital, homes away from home. I had a love affair once with the De Young Museum in Golden Gate Park in San Francisco. Its jade collection and fierce Chinese bronzes drew me again and again; it was a temple where I came to worship something I now cannot describe. Museums always seemed to me to hold the key to higher realms. They stood for knowledge, skill, treasure, and ungraspable values, things for which a person ought to strive. They were like secular churches where people could come to reverence what they loved—baseball, Thomas Jefferson, the French Impressionists—and their teaching had been influential in my life.

What museums didn't say, however, turned out to be more important than   7
what they did. For I have recently learned that museums can teach one much amiss. Their power to distort history and to frustrate learning, as well as to inspire emulation, was brought home to me a few months ago when, on a sunny December afternoon, I made a visit to the Museum of the American Indian in New York.

After a half-hour delay on the 7th Avenue subway, I emerged blinking into the   8
sunlight of Spanish Harlem, feeling unsure of myself. Should I be frightened? Everything looked seedy, normal, and unthreatening. Instead of feeling I was in a war zone, which was what people had led me to expect, it was more like having left the capital for the provinces. No downtown bustle and importance here, just old people pulling grocery carts. I made my way across Broadway to the sidewalk at 155th St., the old-fashioned kind made of hexagonal pieces of stone, to where the

museum stands. It occupies the left wing of a large gray building that surrounds three sides of a disused courtyard, most of which is shut off from the public by an iron fence. The whole thing looked as if it had been built a hundred years ago and then forgotten. And inside, the Museum of the American Indian also has the air of a place that hasn't changed in a long time. It's the lighting that contributes to this impression most. A dim light spreads itself evenly over everything, giving all the spaces and the objects in them an indescribable tinge of sickly yellow-gray, the color of old train-station lavatories and ancient public-school buildings.

For here, indeed, is the museum of one's childhood. Here were cases   9
crammed with unfamiliar objects, glutting the eye and mind before one had even begun to look. The burden of so many things made me desperate for information, anything to stay mentally afloat. But in the Museum of the American Indian, aids to reflection are few. There's a mimeographed pamphlet available in the bookshop whose title sums up the situation nicely: "On Your Own with Great North American Indians." The information the museum does provide comes on placards, hand-lettered, a little shakily, in a vaguely gothic script, conveying an impression of old age all by themselves. The first one I read, propped in the corner of an overstuffed case, had two misspelled words, "enviornment" and "develope." Maybe it's just that I've been an English teacher all my life, but those misspelled words—and the thought of generations of schoolchildren reading them—filled me with despair and foreboding. These mistakes, along with the studied penmanship, prepared me for the prose, which had the character of labored student compositions: monotonous sentence structure, everything in the passive voice, no concrete details.

After a while, still reading to get my bearings, I began to notice a certain turn   10
these descriptions took. It often seemed that the clothing or decorative style or implement under discussion wasn't, in some subtle way, all that it could have been. What the case contained would be secondary to, or less important than, or not so brilliant as what had been produced by some other tribe, or in some other period, or at some different location. It was as if whoever had been responsible for the descriptions was unconsciously sabotaging an already doomed operation, unable to help himself. I felt rage mounting in me, and frustration. Why couldn't these objects have been displayed better, with imagination and flair, not to mention adequate lighting? Why couldn't the museum have provided lively, engaging accounts of the life these objects stood for? Why, for heaven's sake, couldn't they even get the *spelling* right? Why did they (whoever "they" were) have to be so *negative* about the things they had? And why, after all, was it the remains of the American Indians that were being treated in this shabby way? I had seen, two days before, Sienese paintings at the Metropolitan Museum of Art treated as holy treasures, magnificently offered for our veneration. Why were fourteenth-century Italians so much more important to us than the inhabitants of our own continent?

The sense of failure hit me strongest when I heard a metallic voice emanating   11
from behind some cases on the first floor. Wending my way back I discovered the Indian Museum's excuse for a video: a box with some colored slides of Indian artifacts that changed every few seconds, while a voiceover recited facts about the museum. These, too, were tinged by the air of defeat. The museum displayed 11,000 items; *however*, these were only a fraction of the one million items it owned, which were stored in a warehouse in the Bronx. The man who had amassed

the collection, George Gustav Heye, had established the museum early in the century; *however,* the opening was delayed by World War I. Why include this fact in a two-minute description?

There were other depressing features: on the walls of the dark stairwell hung 12 small hand-colored pictures of, I think, Indian costumes: it was hard to tell because they were unidentified. Stylistically flat, amateurishly mounted, brightly colored, they seemed more appropriate for a kindergarten than for a major collection. As I stood on the landing, deciding whether to look at the exhibit of contemporary Indian painting on my left, I heard someone urinating, long and heavy. I was standing outside the men's room. When I reflected on why I'd never had this experience before—hearing what I was hearing while staring into a roomful of paintings—I realized it was because in most museums the rest rooms are located at some distance from the exhibits.

Leaving the second floor, I went up to the third where, in a special exhibit of 13 artifacts from Central America, the museum seemed to be putting its best foot forward. Here, what my colleague Marianna Torgovnick calls "the jewelry-store method" of display had been adopted with a vengeance. Small cases with dark interiors housed a small number of items, spotlit from unexpected angles. Each case was visually stunning, a striking composition in light and shade. But most of the objects were lit only on one side or not illuminated at all, and this, coupled with the scarcity of information, made it hard to know what you were looking at and harder to remember what you had seen.

By this time I was so aggravated I couldn't look at anything without getting 14 angry. I realized that if I were going to get something out of this visit I would have to change my frame of mind. I would have to stop imagining the way it should have been—lustrous marble, elegant spaces, brilliant illumination, sophisticated aids to comprehension—and start looking for what *was* there. So, determined to get what I had come for, some experience or insight to treasure, I went back downstairs and began to look at the cases again, carefully, state by state—Oklahoma, Nebraska, Kentucky. And little by little I began to notice that what was in them was much richer, more varied, and more beautiful than any collection of American Indian artifacts I had ever seen.

There was statuary: I hadn't known that North American Indians made stat- 15 ues, if you except the totem carvings of the Northwest. Yet here were wooden figures of men and women, squat, square, austere, enigmatic, and powerful as any African carvings I had ever seen. There was an incredible variety of clothing, of different styles, in different materials, intricately and beautifully decorated. There were gorgeous cloaks, vests, leggings, shawls, headdresses, slippers, boots. Explosions of jewelry, amulets, necklaces, armbands, legbands. Every kind of implement, bowls, baskets, sieves, carving tools, weapons, pipes, cooking utensils, blankets, toys, carrying bags, dolls, masks, fetishes, drawings. And all of it made from so many kinds of skins, furs, hides, bones, teeth, claws, horns, stones, woods, clays, and grasses.

One reads about the intense spiritual lives of the North American Indians, but 16 their physical existence, it is always implied, was nasty, brutish, and short. The display cases in the Museum of the American Indian contradict these notions. What came through to me in a way it never had before was the richness of the material lives of these peoples, the reality of the Indians' contact with things. Things they had held in their hands, things they had protected and adorned their bodies with, things they had used, things they had simply seen. The beauty, stylistic coherence, workmanship, and utility of the objects in each case, and the way they fit together into a kind of whole made me think, involuntarily, the word "culture." I knew of course that North American Indians had a culture, or rather, individual cultures. All "peoples" had "cultures," no matter how technologically unlike our culture theirs may have been. I had known this, but until now, I had known it only as a piety of cultural relativism, not as an immediate experience. *That* was what the Museum of the American Indian gave me. The immediate visual and tactile experience, the sensory evidence, abundant, amassed, incontrovertible, of the textural life-world of Native American people.

But this was not just an impression of material shapes. For as the objects of a given tribe reflected those of others stylistically, the labor that went into them, the knowledge and skill, the time and care, the consistency with which motifs were repeated, and the talismanic power that certain objects obviously possessed, combined to hint at what must have been the density and force of the cultural stories that gave the objects meaning. And yet their stillness now, cheek by cheek with one another, under glass where they had lain for so many years, was the stillness of death. Testaments of life, of the vibrancy, cohesion, and viability of a particular way of life, now they were testaments of extinction. 17

It was odd. Something about the way the objects were displayed—too many, too close together, not really explained, in depressing surroundings—or something in the objects themselves, or something in me, allowed them to speak in a way they had never spoken to me before. I didn't know what to feel. The objects had given me a glimpse of an independent life, glorious and untouchable, an integrity of action and being that had existed once in Oklahoma, in Kentucky, and perhaps existed somewhere still, on another plane, like music. That was cause for celebration. But at the same time and all around me was evidence of failure—whose failure was hard to say—the museum's failure to honor what it possessed, the failure of the society that had produced Spanish Harlem, the failure of the nation that had destroyed the civilizations whose remnants it now half-heartedly preserved? 18

Museums are halls of fame, meant to honor those whose works they preserve, not to superintend their slide into oblivion. In our culture—and who, exactly, were "we"?—honor meant space, light, opulence, being up-to-date; it meant pride of place, prominence, visibility. The Museum of the American Indian had been accorded none of these. The feelings of secondariness and disappointment I had felt creeping into even the most impersonal information did not come out of nowhere: they were a response to neglect. I felt neglected myself as I stood there, and at the same time, responsible. I looked at the meager offerings of the gift shop and went home. 19

Three days later I came back to learn more about the museum (it was my last day in New York), and to verify some of the observations I had made. It was Friday of the week after Christmas and New York was full of tourists; I had twice fought my way through crowds at the Met. But the Indian Museum seemed even more deserted than it had before. It was only early afternoon, and a weekday, but on reaching the entrance I found a pair of great brass doors—depicting, in bas-relief, 20 scenes from American Indian life—swung tightly shut. There was no sign telling when the Museum would be open or when it would be closed, only the doors, and from their surface, staring back at me, indecipherable, some patches of brilliant white graffiti.

I wasn't surprised. The day before I had imagined the museum staff working   21
in crowded back rooms, ill lit, with old oak desks (or if you were lower in the pecking order, old metal ones), ancient filing cabinets, partitions made of wood or pebbled glass, linoleum floors, and vintage watercoolers. The people who staffed the museum, I thought as I stood by the closed doors, probably didn't want to work. They were too demoralized. They would jump at a holiday, I thought. But of course this couldn't be the real reason the museum was closed. The real reason, as someone suggested later, was probably that there wasn't enough money to keep it open. Not enough to pay the heat and electricity. Still, it came to the same thing: no one had cared enough.

There was a certain logic in this. The main traditions of this country grow out   22
of Europe. The masters of fourteenth-century Sienese painting currently being honored at the Met had been Christian and urban, they had spoken an Indo-European language, they had the alphabet, the printing press, gunpowder, the stirrup; their institutions, their technology, their worldviews were the grandfathers of ours. Some of their kinsmen would "discover" this continent a century or so later. Culturally, they were more "American" than the Iroquois and the Chippewa, so it made sense that we should honor their works.

But there was another logic which spoke more plainly still. The line that led   23
from the European "discovery" of the continent led also to the near extinction of Native Americans and to the massive destruction of animals, even of entire species. It led to cancer, unbreathable air, dead lakes, dying forests, toxic-waste dumps, chemical disasters, and the possible annihilation of all living creatures through nuclear war. There was a connection, I thought, between these dusty trophies and the dying continent. Whatever ferocities the Indian peoples might have practiced, their traditions had a reverence for the whole web of creation that could have served us as a model for understanding the planet we inhabited, that could have helped us to live less destructively.

Books I had read about the native peoples of North America—*Black Elk*   24
Speaks, Paula Gunn Allen's *The Sacred Hoop*, Calvin Martin's *Keepers of the Game*, Anthony F. C. Wallace's *The Death and Rebirth of the Seneca*, James Axtell's *The European and the Indian*, Vine Deloria's *God Is Red*—these books and others had taught me that Indians did not behave as if the human species were infinitely more important and valuable than all other species, or even more important than plants and stones, rivers and mountains. A person could become a wolf or an owl without loss of status. The instrumental relationship people of "our" culture have to the material world, treating nonhuman existents as if they had no value except their utility for us, allowed for a dazzling manipulation of the external environment. But the price seemed to be a loss of mutuality. If you treat a person as a slave, naturally that person will hate you. If you treat things as if they have no intrinsic worth, they will turn against you, too.

I had scarcely any right to these speculations, knowing so little about Indian   25
cultures. But I couldn't help thinking that the neglect of their treasures, and what

that neglect stood for in terms of our ignorance, was correlated with the dungeon of the subway I had ridden, the trash I had seen on Broadway, and the graffiti glaring back from the doors. The subway that had gotten me to the museum and the airplane that had brought me to New York and that I was about to board again in a few hours belonged to the same machinery that had made these items into relics. I saw that, being a creature of modern technology, my coming to the museum on a subway, reading some placards, and then going home in an airplane guaranteed that I would never know what the objects in the museum meant in any thoroughgoing, tangible sense. And it occurred to me that the way to find out about them would not be to read more books about Indians.

Studying had its place, but studying was what *we* did—collecting, in the process, so many dry bones. (I subsequently learned that there were tens of thousands of Indian skeletons being held in American museums for purposes of "study.") Studying was part of the machinery, which is to say, of the instrumentalism that destroyed the environment that had made Indian life possible. Study was what had motivated collections such as this. Later on, I read about the controversy surrounding the Museum of the American Indian—where it should be housed, who should control it, who should pay, how much—and discovered that the founder, George Gustav Heye, had cared nothing for the public, nothing for what Native Americans themselves felt about his disposition of their treasures, but only for "solving the great mystery of the origin of the prehistoric races of the Western Hemisphere." I wanted to distance myself from this way of relating to the objects in the cases, I wanted to see the world as the people who made the objects saw it, I wanted to get into their bodies and feel what they had felt, and I saw that to do this, it would be necessary to live differently. 26

What would have to happen was this: a rattle in one of the cases would have to begin to shake, a headdress start to tremble, an amulet to levitate and hurtle through the glass and into my hand. I would have to walk onto a reservation somewhere and start living without books or TV. I would have to get to the other plane. It didn't matter that the Museum of the American Indian was on 155th Street instead of further downtown. It didn't matter that the lighting was dim. A better address and glitzier surroundings wouldn't have made the difference, as far as learning was concerned. In fact, the opulent, high pressure, visually exciting, marble-and-mirrors display I'd imagined as an alternative to the museum's dinginess might have been the worst thing of all. Such an exhibition would have sent me home satisfied, having created the illusion of "being there." The dim light and dull paint let me know I wasn't anywhere but in an underfunded, dispirited, bureaucratic institution. Maybe that was why the objects spoke. It was the contrast that had allowed them to appear. 27

So my visit was a success after all. The museum had done its work. I had received my instruction. 28

Or so I thought—until I sent this description of my museum visit to my friend Annette Kolodny, who had recently become Dean of Humanities at the University of Arizona in Tucson. Her reply was hard to take, like some good medicines that in the end will make you better. For though deeply appreciative of the essay, she begged me to consider the following: 29

. . . the awakening you describe . . . leaves you open to charges of "romanticizing" the Indian yourself. For example: except for a small enclave of rabid traditionalists on a very few reservations, you would have great difficulty "walking onto a reservation somewhere and starting to live without books or TV." TV is ubiquitous on the reservations. Books less so.

The essay also has an insistently nostalgic tone which assumes the "vanishing Red Man" motif. In fact, Native Americans continue to have and practice a viable, meaningful culture; some of the native people I have come to know here would bridle at your suggestion that all is vanished; or that the adaptations made to the modern world (and to white conquest) are somehow inauthentic. For many native people, the white tendency nowadays to sing the praises of the Indian as having lived in harmony with nature is a species of white self-delusion. Whites make the Indian the new pastoral locus; but whites don't do a damned thing to help reverse the appalling statistics of infant mortality or TB on the reservations. What I'm saying, Jane, is that you need to monitor the essay to make certain you're not inadvertently singing another hymn to some version of the Noble Savage (in harmony with nature, freed of the constraints of modern society, unfettered by the complications of technology, etc.). The rugs now being woven by Navajo, Hopi, etc.—but which don't sell to the tourists—show reservation scenes, representationally, with broken-down cars behind a shack, in the front yard of a hogan, and various animals scattered around. Tourists don't buy these rugs, of course, because the rugs are true; and we still want our Indians living in some kind of pure rural splendor. No place in the image for abandoned cars.

I love what you're trying to do and say in that essay. Just try to read it as a Pascua Yaqui living on a reservation in the middle of Tucson, where whites repeatedly come to "watch" the seasonal dances but never stay to help teach the children or provide medicine for the ill. And imagine the Yaqui's seething resentment of those whites who believe that, because they attend the public dances, they "know" or "understand" or have experienced something authentic about Yaqui culture. And also imagine the rage of some other native person who *knows* that contained within the walls of that museum are precious religious artifacts belonging to the tribe, indeed, without which the tribe can no longer prosper. That Indian doesn't want a better museum to display the artifacts; s/he wants the thing(s) returned to the tribe!

Everything Annette had said rang true. I knew that white people like me used Indian culture as a way of dreaming about what their own culture couldn't give them while ignoring the present realities of Native American life, behaving as if there weren't any Indians any more or as if those who survived were somehow less real than those who had lived in the seventeenth century. I had even written, in an essay published three years ago: "The relationship most non-Indians have to the people who first populated this continent . . . [is] characterized by narcissistic fantasies of freedom and adventure, of a life lived closer to nature and to spirit than the life we lead now. . . . The American Indian Movement in the early seventies couldn't get people to pay attention to what was happening to Indians who were alive in the present, so powerful was this country's infatuation with people who wore loincloths, lived in tepees, and roamed the plains and forests long ago." Knowing this, why had I fallen into the trap? For it was true that I had been "romanticizing" for my own purposes.

It was worse than that. I had recently read an entire book manuscript by Marianna Torgovnick, *Gone Primitive* (forthcoming from the University of Chicago Press), about the way modern anthropologists, art critics, novelists, psychologists,   30 explorers, and ordinary citizens use primitive peoples as the site for elaborating their dreams—of power, sexual conquest, racial superiority, belonging. How had I forgotten all this? And finally: was my dream of another life—away from TV and airplanes and worry over spelling mistakes—just an ignorant fantasy? Or did it represent some legitimate impulse to deepen and intensify my contact with the world, to get closer to reality, and to my self?

I don't have an answer to such questions, but they, in turn, raise others that are   31
worth considering. It is one thing to think and write in the abstract about the politics of museums. It is another to make a visit: to take the subway uptown on Christmas vacation, or to turn off the highway on a cross-country trip and walk into a real place, have real sensations, react to spaces, lighting, information (or the lack thereof); to see actual objects—feathers, bones, paintings; and then to browse in a gift shop, have a cup of coffee, sit down to rest your feet.

Something about the immediacy of the experience makes museum-going not   32
the purely intellectual encounter it becomes when one is writing professional crit-icism about it. The real-life context of a visit—time pressures, physical needs, the desire to be lifted out of oneself momentarily—push other considerations aside. In the event, one tries to get some enjoyment out of what is there, and to learn some-thing from it, no matter how inadequately presented or overproduced the exhibits may be. For one does feel educated, however minimally, by the information that typically accompanies a Native American artifact displayed in a glass case; one learns what it was made from and how, what it was used for, and by what kind of person. The trouble is, the placards never say how, and by what right, this particu-lar object got to the museum, who took it away from whom, under what circum-stances, and for what reason. Museum information provides a kind of false contex-tualization. One learns more than enough about decorative styles and methods of production, but nothing about the historical and political conditions that put the objects there—nothing that would interrupt one's dream of another life.

Could there be an Indian museum that represented the totality of Native   33
American experience to which people would want to come on their vacations? Should such a museum provoke utopian desires as well as a sense of tragedy and the need for present help?

I once visited a small museum in Cherokee, North Carolina—the "Cyclo-   34
rama"—that was controlled by Indians themselves. It was modest: a few dioramas that told the story of the Trail of Tears, a few artifacts exhibited so that you could really see how they had been used, and a sound-and-light show (made of practi-cally nothing) that dramatized the Cherokees' loss of territory and the diminution of their numbers over the years.

The visit took little more than a half hour (my husband was waiting for me in   35
the parking lot). Everything in the place looked homemade and more than a little worn. But this museum had achieved its purpose fully: it had taught me some things about the Cherokee Nation in a straightforward and consistently interesting way. Whoever had put it together had brought to it two elements that most such enterprises lack: a sense of what works and what doesn't when it comes to educat-ing the public—and the Cherokee point of view.

I learned recently that museum curators are beginning to respond to critiques   36
of their policies and practices. Stanford University and the University of Minnesota
are returning their entire collections to local tribes, and the Smithsonian itself has
agreed to return burial artifacts and skeletal remains, on request, to contemporary
tribes that can prove with "reasonable certainty" that the objects in question belong to them. Signs, perhaps, that museums of the future may be differently conceived and organized. I hope so. The Cherokee museum suggests to me that what
will be needed, however, is not a great deal of money, nor a great deal of space, nor
a lot of high-tech video equipment, nor even hundreds of objects to put on display,
but rather—in the case of Indian museums—the Native American perspective and
some good pedagogical sense.

One month ago, it was announced that the long and bitter controversy over   37
where to house the extensive collection of the Museum of the American Indian
had at long last been resolved, and that, ironically, it was to be given the last available space on the Mall in Washington. At one time, I would have been overjoyed at
the news. Now, I am not so sure.

Rhetorical Focus

1. Given that Tompkins focuses on her visit to the Museum of the American
   Indian, why do you think she chooses to begin with an account of her visit
   to the National Cowboy Hall of Fame?
2. The rest of this essay is organized into stages, each marked by a change in
   Tompkins's thinking. What changes of mind does she record, and where?
3. Tompkins makes a risky rhetorical move here: Near the end of her essay,
   she includes a letter from Annette Kolodny that significantly criticizes what
   she has written so far. Does Kolodny's letter invalidate all that Tompkins
   has written up to that point? Why or why not? What, if anything, does
   Tompkins *gain* by including the letter?

Thematic Focus

1. Before reading this essay, did you share Tompkins's skepticism toward museums? If so, why? If not, does she succeed in making you suspicious of
   them?
2. Look again at the quotations from Tompkins in our headnote to her essay.
   Do you think she succeeds here in speaking personally without being self-
   centered? Do you get the impression that her visit to the museum has
   ultimately enabled her to improve her understanding of Native Americans? Support your answers with references to her text.
3. How much can a museum reasonably tell about a particular tribe, or about
   Native Americans in general? If other people are to achieve a truly informed understanding of Native Americans, what do you think they should
   do besides visit museums?

Wounded Chevy At Wounded Knee

Diana Hume George

Diana Hume George (b. 1948) is Professor of English at Pennsylvania State at Erie, The Behrend College. Over the years, her interests have been markedly interdisciplinary, ranging from literary criticism and creative writing to psychoanalytic theory, feminist theory, art history, and American studies. Especially interested in the late poet Anne Sexton, George has published a biography of Sexton, entitled *Oedipus Anne,* has edited a volume of essays about her, and has co-edited a collection of her poems. George's books also include two volumes of her own poetry *(The Evolution of Love, The Resurrection of the Body), Blake and Freud,* and *Epitaph and Icon: A Guide to Eighteenth-Century Burying Grounds* (with Malcom A. Nelson). Like Tompkins, George has recently begun writing essays that mix personal experience with cultural analysis. The following essay, which appeared in a 1990 issue of *The Missouri Review,* is part of a work-in-progress entitled *The Lonely Other: A Woman Watching America.*

Reflections Before Reading

George visits not a museum but an actual Indian reservation: Pine Ridge in South Dakota. What do you think she might encounter? George also recalls her former marriage as a white woman to a Native American. Do you assume that this personal experience will enable her to speak more authoritatively about Native Americans than Tompkins can? Why or why not?

—Pine Ridge Sioux Reservation, July 1989

"If you break down on that reservation, your car belongs to the Indians. They don't like white people out there." This was our amiable motel proprietor in Custer, South Dakota, who asked where we were headed and then propped a conspiratorial white elbow on the counter and said we'd better make sure our vehicle was in good shape. To get to Wounded Knee, site of the last cavalry massacre of the Lakota in 1890 and of more recent confrontations between the FBI and

1

the American Indian Movement, you take a road out of Pine Ridge on the Lakota Reservation and go about eight miles. If you weren't watching for it you could miss it, because nothing is there but a hill, a painted board explaining what happened, a tiny church, and a cemetery.

The motel man told us stories about his trucking times, when by day his gas stops were friendly, but by night groups of Indian men who'd been drinking used to circle his truck looking for something to steal—or so he assumed. He began carrying a .357 Magnum with him "just in case." Once he took his wife out to Pine Ridge. "She broke out in hives before we even got there." And when they were stopped on the roadside and a reservation policeman asked if they needed help, she was sure he was going to order her out of the car, steal it, and, I suppose, rape and scalp her while he was at it. As he told us these contradictory stories, he seemed to be unaware of the irony of warning us that the Indians would steal our car if they got a chance, and following with a story about an Indian who tried to help them just in case they might be having trouble.

He did make a distinction between the reservation toughs and the police. He wasn't a racist creep, but rather a basically decent fellow whose view of the world was narrowly white. I briefly entertained the notion of staying a while, pouring another cup of coffee, and asking him a few questions that would make him address the assumptions behind his little sermon, but I really wanted to get on my way, and I knew he wasn't going to change his mind about Indians here in the middle of his life in the middle of the Black Hills.

Mac and I exchanged a few rueful remarks about it while we drove. But we both knew that the real resistance to dealing with Indian culture on these trips that have taken us through both Pueblo and Plains Indian territories hasn't come from outside of our car or our minds, but rather from within them. More specifically, from within me. For years Mac has read about the Plains Indians with real attentiveness, and with an openness to learning what he can about the indigenous peoples of North America. He reads histories, biographies, novels, and essays, thinks carefully about the issues involved, remembers what he has read, informs himself with curiosity and respect about tribes that have occupied the areas we visit. For a couple of years he urged me toward these materials, many of which have been visible around our home for years: *Black Elk Speaks, In a Sacred Manner We Live, Bury My Heart at Wounded Knee,* studies of Indian spiritual and cultural life. While we were in Lakota country this time, he was reading Mari Sandoz' biography of Crazy Horse. But he has long since given up on getting me to pay sustained attention to these rich materials, because my resistance has been firm and long-standing. I am probably better informed about Indian life than most Americans ever thought of being, but not informed enough for a thoughtful reader and writer. My resistance has taken the form of a mixture of pride and contempt: pride that I already know more than these books can tell me, and contempt for the white liberal-intellectual's romance with all things Indian. But my position has been very strange perhaps, given that I was married to an American Indian for five years, lived on a reservation, and am the mother of a half-Indian son.

I've been mostly wrong in my attitudes, but it's taken me years to understand that. Wounded Knee is where I came to terms with my confusion, rejection, and ambivalence, and it happened in a direct confrontation with past events that are now twenty years old. My resistance broke down because of an encounter with a young Lakota named Mark, who is just about my own son's age.

I grew up in the 1950s and 1960s in a small white community on the edge of   6
the Cattaraugus Seneca Indian Reservation in western New York State. Relations between Indians and whites in my world were bitter, and in many respects replicated the dynamics between whites and blacks in the South, with many exceptions due to the very different functions and circumstances of these two groups of people of color in white America. The school system had recently been integrated after the closing of the Thomas Indian School on the reservation. The middle class whites wanted nothing to do with the Indians, whom they saw as drunkards and degenerates, in many cases subhuman. When I rebelled against the restraints of my white upbringing, the medium for asserting myself against my parents and my world was ready-made, and I grabbed it.

I began hanging out on the reserve with young Indians and shifted my social   7
and sexual arena entirely to the Indian world. I fell in love with an idea of noble darkness in the form of an Indian carnival worker, got pregnant by him, married him, left the white world completely, and moved into his. Despite the fact that this was the sixties, my actions weren't politically motivated; or, rather, my politics were entirely personal at that point. While my more aware counterparts might have done some of the same things as conscious political and spiritual statements, I was fifteen when I started my romance with Indians, and I only knew that I was in love with life outside the constricting white mainstream, and with all the energy that vibrates on the outer reaches of cultural stability. My heart, and what would later become my politics, were definitely in the right place, and I have never regretted where I went or what I came to know. But for twenty years that knowledge spoiled me for another kind of knowing.

Whatever my romantic notions were about the ideal forms of American Indian   8
wisdom—closeness to the land, respect for other living creatures, a sense of harmony with natural cycles, a way of walking lightly in the world, a manner of living that could make the ordinary and profane into the sacred—I learned that on the reservation I was inhabiting a world that was contrary to all these values. American Indian culture at the end of the road has virtually none of these qualities. White America has destroyed them. Any culture in its death throes is a grim spectacle, and there can be no grimmer reality than that endured by people on their way to annihilation.

I did not live among the scattered wise people or political activists of the Seneca Nation. I did not marry a nominal American Indian from a middleclass family.   9
I married an illiterate man who dropped out of school in the seventh grade and was in school only intermittently before that. He traveled around the east with carnivals running a ferris wheel during the summer months, and logged wood on the reservation during the winter—when he could get work. Home base was an old trailer without plumbing, in the woods, where his mother lived. He drank sporadically but heavily, and his weekends, often his weekdays, were full of pool tables, bar brawls, the endlessness of hanging out with little to do. He didn't talk much. How I built this dismal life into a romanticized myth about still waters running

deep gives me an enduring respect for the mythopoeic, self-deluding power of desire, wish, will.

When I was married to him my world was a blur of old cars driven by drunk   10
men in the middle of the night, of honky-tonk bars, country music, late night fights with furniture flying, food stamps and welfare lines, stories of injury and death. The smell of beer still sickens me slightly. I was sober as a saint through all of this, so I didn't have the insulation of liquor, only of love. I lived the contrary of every white myth about Indian life, both the myths of the small town white racists and those of the smitten hippies. When I finally left that life behind, extricating myself and my child in the certain knowledge that to stay would mean something very like death for both of us, I removed myself in every respect. I knew how stupid white prejudice was, understood the real story about why Indians drank and wasted their lives, felt the complexities so keenly that I couldn't even try to explain them to anyone white. But similarly, I knew how bird-brained the lovechild generation's romance with Indian culture was.

My husband went on to a career of raping white women that had begun dur-   11
ing—or maybe before—our marriage. When he was finally caught, convicted and sent to Attica, I was long since done with that part of my life. My son pulled me back toward it with his own love for his father, and I still keep in touch with my husband's mother on the reservation, sometimes helping her to handle white bu-reaucracy, but that's all. I heard at a remove of miles, of eons, it seemed, about the early deaths of young men I'd known well—deaths due to diabetes, to lost limbs, or to car wrecks at high speed—and I felt something, but I didn't have to deal with it. When I tried to think about that past life in order to put it into some kind of perspective, no whole picture emerged. When I tried to write about it, no words would come. And when I tried to be open to learning something new about Indi-ans in America on my trips, my heart closed up tight, and with it my mind. When I went to Wounded Knee, the wounds of these other Indians half a continent and half a lifetime away were a part of the landscape.

We pull off the side of the road to read the billboard that tells what happened   12
here. "MASSACRE OF WOUNDED KNEE" is the header, but upon close in-spection you see that "Massacre" is a new addition, painted over something else. "Battle," perhaps? What did it used to say, I wonder, and hope I'll run into a local who can tell me. While I'm puzzling over this, an old Chevy sputters into the pull-off and shakes to a stop. It's loaded with dark faces, a young man and an older woman with many small children. The man gets out and walks slowly to the front of the car, rolling up his T-shirt over his stomach to get air on his skin. As he raises the hood, a Comanche truck pulls in beside him with one woman inside. It's very hot, and I weave a little in the glare of sun. Suddenly I see the past, superimposed on this hot moment. I've seen it before, again and again, cars full of little Indian kids in the heat of summer on the sides of roads. I glance again, see the woman in the front seat, know that she's their mother or their aunt. She looks weary and re-signed, not really sad. She expects this.

And then in another blink it's not only that I have seen this woman; I have   13
been this woman, my old car or someone else's packed with little kids who are

almost preternaturally quiet, wide-eyed and dark skinned and already knowing that this is a big part of what life is about, sitting in boiling back seats, their arms jammed against the arms of their brother, their sister, their cousin. There is no use asking when they'll get there, wherever "there" is. It will happen when it happens, when the adults as helpless as they figure out what to do. In the meantime they sweat and stare. But I am not this woman any more, not responsible for these children, some of whose intelligent faces will blank into a permanent sheen of resignation before they're five. I am a tourist in a new Plymouth Voyager, my luggage rack packed with fine camping equipment, my Minolta in my hand to snap pictures of the places I can afford to go.

When Mac suggests that we offer to help them, I am not surprised at my flat   14
negative feeling. He doesn't know what that means, I surmise, and I don't have any way to tell him. Help them? Do you want to get anywhere today, do you have the whole afternoon? The young man's shoulders bend over the motor. He is fit and beautiful, his good torso moves knowingly but powerlessly over the heat rising from beneath the hood. I recognize him, as well as the woman. He has no job. He talks about getting off the reservation, finding work, living the dreams he still has. He'll talk this way for a few more years, then give up entirely. He drinks too much. He has nothing to do. Drinking is the only thing that makes him really laugh, and his only way to release rage. I also know that whatever else is wrong with it the car is out of gas, and that these people have no money. Okay, sure, I say to Mac, standing to one side while he asks how we can help. Close to the car now, I see that the woman is the young man's mother. These kids are his brothers and sisters.

The car is out of gas and it needs a jump. The battery is bad. The woman in the   15
other car is the young man's aunt, who can give him a jump but has no money to give him for gas—or so she says. I know her, too. She is more prosperous than her relatives, and has learned the hard way never to give them any money, because she needs it herself and if she gives it to them she'll never see it again. She made her policy years ago, and makes it stick no matter what. She has to.

Well, then, we'll take them to the nearest gas station. Do they have a gas can?   16
No, just a plastic washer fluid jug with no top. Okay, that will have to do. How far is the nearest gas? Just up the road a couple of miles. But they don't have any money because they were on their way to cash his mother's unemployment check when they ran out of gas, and the town where they can do that is many miles away. So can we loan them some money for gas? We can. He gets in the front seat. I get in the back, and as we pull away from the windy parking area, I look at the woman and the kids who will be sitting in the car waiting until we return. She knows she can't figure out how soon that will be. She stares straight ahead. I don't want to catch her eye, nor will she catch mine.

Right here up this road. Mark is in his early twenties. Mac asks him questions.   17
He is careful and restrained in his answers at first, then begins to open up. No, there's no work around here. Sometimes he does a little horse-breaking or fence-mending for the ranchers. All the ranches here are run by whites who had the money to make the grim land yield a living. They lease it from the Lakota. Mark went away to a Job Corps camp last year, but he had to come back because his twenty-one year old brother died last winter, leaving his mother alone with the

little ones. He froze to death. He was drinking at a party, and went outside to take a leak. Mark said they figured he must have just stopped for a minute to rest, and then he fell asleep. They found him frozen in the morning. Mark had to come back home to bury his brother and help his mother with the kids.

As we bounce over the dirt road, I stare at the back of Mark's head and at his good Indian profile when he turns toward Mac to speak. He is so familiar to me that I could almost reach out to touch his black straight hair, his brown shoulder. He is my husband, he is my son. I want to give him hope. He speaks about getting out of here, going to "Rapid"—Lakota shorthand for Rapid City—and making a life. He is sick of having nothing to do, he wants work, wants an apartment. But he can't leave yet; he has to stay to help his mother. But things are going to be okay, because he has just won a hundred thousand dollars and is waiting for them to send the check.   18

What?   19

"You know the Baja Sweepstakes?" He pronounces it Bay-jah. "Well, I won it, I think I won it, I got a letter. My little brother sent in the entry form we got with my CD club and he put my name on it, and it came back saying that I'm one of a select few chosen people who've won a hundred thousand dollars. That's what it said, it said that, and I had to scratch out the letters and if three of them matched it means I win, and they matched, and so I sent it back in and now I'm just waiting for my money. It should come pretty soon and then everything will be okay." He repeats it over and over again in the next few minutes: he's one of a select few chosen people.   20

As he speaks of this, his flat voice becomes animated. Slowly I begin to believe that he believes this. Whatever part of him knows better is firmly shelved for now. This hope, this belief that hundreds of thousands of dollars are on the way is what keeps him going, what keeps him from walking out into the sky—or to the outhouse in the winter to take a leak and a nap in the snow. What will you do with the money, I ask. Well, first he is going to buy his mother and the kids a house.   21

The first gas stop is a little shack that's closed when we finally get there. Sandy wind and no sign of life. Miles on down the road is a small Lakota grocery store with only a few items on the shelves and a sign that reads "Stealing is not the Lakota way." Mac hands Mark a five dollar bill. You can kiss that five bucks goodbye, I say to Mac. I know, he nods. When Mark comes back out he has the gas, and also a big cup of Seven-Up and a bag of Nachos. You want some, he asks me? He hands Mac a buck fifty in change. On the way back I hold the gas can in the back seat, placing my hand over the opening. Despite the open windows, the van fills with fumes. My head begins to ache. I am riding in a dream of flatness, ranch fences, Mark's dark head in front of me wishing away his life, waiting for the break that takes him to Rapid. Later I learn that we are in Manderson, and this is the road where Black Elk lived.   22

Mark is talking about white people now. Yes, they get along okay. For "yes" he has an expression of affirmation that sounds sort of like "huh." Mari Sandoz spells it "hou" in her books on the Lakota. The Lakota are infiltrated in every way by whites, according to Mark. Lots of people in charge are white, the ranchers are white. And there's a place in Rapid called Lakota Hills, fancy houses meant for   23

Lakotas, but whites live in them. Later it occurs to us that this is probably a development named Lakota Hills that has nothing at all to do with the Indians, but it has
their name and so Mark thinks it belongs to them. I am angry for him that we
borrow their name this way and paste it on our air-conditioned prosperity. I don't
have anything to say to him. I lean back and close my eyes. It would be easy to be
one of them again. I remember now how it's done. You just let everything flatten
inside.

And when we return to Wounded Knee, the pull-off is empty. Mother, chil-   24
dren, car, aunt, all are gone. There's nothing but wind and dust. This doesn't surprise me. Mark's mother knows better than to wait for her son's return if other help
comes along. Mark means well, but maybe she has learned that sometimes it's
hours before he gets back with gas—hours and a couple of six-packs if he has the
chance. Now we face the prospect of driving Mark around the reservation until we
can find them. I have just resigned myself to this when his aunt pulls back in and
says they're broken down again a couple of miles up. We can leave now. Mark
thanks us, smiles, and shyly allows us the liberty of having his aunt take a picture of
all three of us. I am feeling a strange kind of shame, as though I had seen him
naked, because he told us his secret and I knew it was a lie.

Unemployment, high rates of suicide and infant mortality, fetal alcohol syn-   25
drome, death by accident and drinking-related diseases such as diabetes: these are
now the ways that American Indians are approaching their collective demise. Over
a century ago, American whites began this destruction by displacing and killing the
pte, the Indian name for the buffalo the plains Indians depended upon. We herded
them together in far crueler ways than they had herded the bison, whose sacredness the Indians respected even as they killed them for food and shelter. The
history of our genocide is available in many historical and imaginative sources.
What is still elusive, still amazingly misunderstood, is how and why the Indians
seem to have participated in their own destruction by their failure to adapt to
changed circumstances.

Whites can point to the phenomenal adjustments of other non-Caucasian   26
groups in America, most recently the Asians, who were badly mistreated and who
have nevertheless not only adapted but excelled. Indians even come off badly in
comparison to the group in some respects most parallel to them, American blacks,
whose slowness in adapting seems at first glance to have more justification. Blacks
were, after all, our slaves, brought here against their will, without close cultural ties
to keep them bound together in a tradition of strength; and on the whole blacks are
doing better than Indians. However slowly, a black middle class is emerging in
America. What's the matter with Indians? Why haven't they adjusted better as a
group?

The American Indian Movement is of course strong in some areas, and Indi-   27
ans have articulate, tough leaders and savvy representatives of their cause who are
fighting hard against the tide of despair gripping the heart of their race. But they're
still losing, and they know it. Estimates of unemployment on the Pine Ridge and
Rosebud reservations run as high as 85%. Health officials at Pine Ridge estimate
that as many as 25% of babies born on the reservation now have fetal alcohol

syndrome. This culturally lethal condition cannot be overemphasized, since it means that the next generation of Lakota are genetically as well as socioeconomically crippled; one of the consequences of fetal alcohol syndrome is not only physical disability, but mental retardation. The prospects are phenomenally depressing for Lakota leaders whose traditional values are associated with mental acuity and imaginative wisdom. Mark is vastly ignorant and gullible, but he is intelligent enough. Many of his younger brothers and sisters are not only underprivileged and without educational advantages, but also—let the word be spoken—stupid. When the light of inquiry, curiosity, mental energy, dies out in the eyes of young Indians early in their stunted lives because they have nowhere to go and nothing to do, it is one kind of tragedy. When it is never present to die out in the first place, the magnitude of the waste and devastation is exponentially increased. Indian leaders who are now concentrating on anti-alcohol campaigns among their people are doing so for good reasons.

Indian leaders disagree about culpability at this point. Essentially the arguments become theories of genocide or suicide. On one end of the spectrum of blame is the theory that it is all the fault of white America. The evidence that can be marshalled for this point of view is massive: broken treaties, complete destruction of the Indian ways of life, welfare dependency established as the cheapest and easiest form of guilt payment, continued undermining of Indian autonomy and rights. The problem with this perspective, say others, is that it perpetuates Indian desperation and permits the easy way out—spend your life complaining that white America put you here, and drink yourself into the oblivion of martyrdom instead of taking responsibility for your own life. Some Indians say they've heard enough about white America's culpability, and prefer to transfer responsibility—not blame, but responsibility—to the shoulders of their own people. "White people aren't doing this to us—we're doing it to ourselves," said one Pine Ridge health official on National Public Radio's Morning Edition recently. She sees the victim stance as the lethal enemy now.   28

The situation is as nearly hopeless as it is possible to be. Assimilation failed the first time and would fail if tried concertedly again, because Indian culture is rural and tribal, and tied to open land, not urban airlessness. The Indian model is the encampment or village—the latter more recently and under duress—and not the city. Even the more stationary pueblo model is by definition not urban. The only real hope for Indian prosperity would be connected to vast tracts of land—not wasteland, but rich land. Nor are most Indians farmers in the sense that white America defines the farm. Though they might be, and have been, successful farmers under pressure, this is not their traditional milieu. Supposing that many tribes could adapt to the farming model over hunting and gathering, they would need large tracts of fine land to farm—and there are none left to grant them.   29

When the American government gave the Lakota 160 acres apiece and said "Farm this," they misunderstood the Indians completely; and even if Indians had been able to adapt readily—a change approximately as difficult as asking an urban yuppie to become a nomad moving from encampment to encampment—the land they were given was inadequate to the purpose. Grubbing a living out of the land we have given them—in what John Wesley Powell called "the arid region" west of   30 the one hundredth meridian—takes a kind of know-how developed and perfected by white Americans, and it also takes capital. It is no coincidence that the large ranches on Pine Ridge are almost entirely leased by whites who had the initial wherewithal to make the land yield.

The Sioux were a people whose lives were shaped by a sense of seeking and   31 vision that white America could barely understand, even if we were to try—and we do not try. The life of a Sioux of a century and a half ago was framed by the Vision Quest, a search for goals, identity, purpose. One primary means of fulfillment was self-sacrifice. Now, as Royal Hassrick has written, "No longer is there anything which they can deny themselves, and so they have sacrificed themselves in pity." Whereas they were once people whose idea of being human was bound to creative self-expression, their faces now reflect what Hassrick calls "apathy and psychic emaciation." Collectively and individually they have become a people without a vision.

Why do they drink themselves into obliteration and erasure? Why not? When   32 white America approaches the problem from within our own ethnocentric biases, we can't see why people would allow themselves to be wasted in this way, why they would not take the initiative to better themselves, to save themselves through the capitalist individuality that says "*I* will make it out of this." But in fact part of their problem is that they have tried to do this, as have most Indian peoples. They've bought the American dream in part, and become greedy for money and material goods. Life on an Indian reservation—almost any reservation—is a despairing imitation of white middle class values. In this respect Indians are like all other minority groups in ghettos in America, and this explains why Mark has a CD player instead of the more modest possessions we would not have begrudged him. If he is anything like the Indians I lived with, he also has a color TV, though he may well live in a shack or trailer without plumbing and without siding.

Their own dreams have evaded them, and so have ours. Mark and his brothers   33 and sisters have been nourished on memories of a culture that vanished long before they were born, and on the promises of a different one, from whose advantages they are forever excluded. Does Mark really believe he has won the sweepstakes? What he received was obviously one of those computer letters that invites the recipient to believe that he has won something. Without the education that could teach him to read its language critically—or to read it adequately at all—he has been deceived into believing that a *deus ex machina* in the form of the Baja Sweepstakes will take him out of his despair.

In 1890, the year of the final defeat of the Sioux at Wounded Knee, the Ghost   34 Dance was sweeping the plains. Begun by a few leaders, especially the Paiute seer Wovoka, the Ghost Dance promised its practitioners among the warriors that the buffalo would return and the white man would be defeated. Ghost Dancers believed that their ceremonial dancing and the shirts they wore would make them proof against the white man's bullets. Among the Sioux warriors at Wounded Knee, the willing suspension of disbelief was complete. It made the warriors reckless and abandoned, throwing normal caution and survival strategy to the wind.

A tragically inverted form of the self-delusion embodied in the Ghost Dance is   35 practiced today on Pine Ridge and other Sioux reservations. The original Ghost

Dance has beauty and vitality, as well as desperation, as its sources. Now many Sioux men who would have been warriors in another time behave as though liquor and passivity will not kill them. Mark chooses to suspend his disbelief in white promises, and to wait for a hundred thousand dollars to arrive in the mail.

Hank Doctor was my husband's best friend on the Seneca reservation. He was 36 raunchy, hard-drinking, outrageous in behavior and looks. His hair was long and scraggly, his nearly black eyes were genuinely wild, and his blue jeans were always caked with dust and falling down his hips. His wit was wicked, his laugh raucous, dangerous, infectious. Hank was merciless toward me, always making white-girl jokes, telling me maybe I better go home to my mama where I'd be safe from all these dark men. He wanted me to feel a little afraid in his world, told me horrible stories about ghost-dogs that would get me on the reservation if I ventured out at night—and then he'd laugh in a way that said hey, white girl, just joking, but not entirely. He alternated his affection toward me with edgy threats; made fun of the too-white way I talked or walked; took every opportunity to make me feel foolish and out of place. He was suspicious that I was just slumming it as a temporary rebellion—maybe taking notes in my head—and that I'd probably run for home when the going got too tough. Of course he was right, even though I didn't know it at the time. I liked him a lot.

A few years ago, my son Bernie went through a period when he chose to 37 remove himself from my world and go live in his father's, from which I'd taken him when he was three. I didn't try to stop him, even though I knew he was hanging out with people who lived dangerously. I used to lie in bed unable to go to sleep because I was wondering what tree he'd end up wrapped around with his dad. He was a minor, but I was essentially helpless to prevent this. If I'd forced the issue, it would only have made his desire to know a forbidden world more intense. He lived there for months, and I slowly learned to get to sleep at night. Mothers can't save their children. And he had a right.

The day I knew he'd ultimately be okay was when he came home and told me 38 about Hank. He wondered if I'd known Hank? He'd never met him before because Hank had been out west for years. Now he was back home, living in a shack way out in the country, terribly crippled with diabetes and other ailments from drinking, barely able to walk. Hank would have been in his midforties at this time. Bernie and his dad took rabbits to Hank when they went hunting so that Hank would have something to eat. During these visits, Hank talked non-stop about the old days, reminding big Bernard of all their bar brawls, crowing to young Bernie that the two of them could beat anyone then they fought as a team, recounting the times they'd dismantled the insides of buildings at four in the morning. He told his stories in vivid, loving detail. His gift for metaphor was precise and fine, his memory perfect even if hyperbolic. He recalled the conversations leading up to fights; the way a person had leaned over the bar; and who had said what to whom just before the furniture flew.

Bernie was impressed with him, but mostly he thought it was pathetic, this 39 not-yet-old man, who looked like he was in his seventies, with nothing to remember but brawls. I told Bernie to value Hank for the way he remembered, the way he could make a night from twenty years ago intensely present again, his gift for swagger and characterization, his poetry, his laughter. In another time Hank would have been a tribal narrator, a story-catcher with better exploits to recount. He would have occupied a special place in Seneca life because of his gifts.

My son left the reservation valuing and understanding important things about   40
his father's world, but not interested in living in its grip. He lives in Florida where he's a chef in a resort, and he's going to college. A month ago his daughter, my granddaughter, was born. She is named Sequoia, after the Cherokee chief who gave his people an alphabet and a written language. Bernie took her to the reservation on his recent visit north and introduced the infant Sequoia to her great-grandmother. My husband's mother says that big Bernard is drinking again, using up her money, and she doesn't know how much more she can take. I know she'll take as much as she has to. I hope I'll see Bernard some day soon to say hello, and maybe we can bend together over our granddaughter, for whom I know we both have many hopes.

Just before we leave Wounded Knee, I walk over to Aunt Lena's Comanche   41
and point to the tribal sign that tells the story. "It says 'Massacre' there, but it used to say something else." I ask her if she knows what it said before. She looks over my shoulder and laughs. "That's funny," she says, "I've lived here all my life, but you know, I never did read that sign." We're miles down the road before I realize that I never finished reading it myself.

Rhetorical Focus

1. Why do you think George begins with three paragraphs about her conversation with the motel proprietor?
2. George shifts to the present tense when she describes her encounter with Mark and his family at Wounded Knee. Does this strategy make sense to you? Why or why not?
3. Both Tompkins and George use a personal narrative of a specific occasion to make their points about whites and Native Americans. What if they had just stated these points outright, without describing their personal visits to the museum and Wounded Knee? Would anything significant be lost?

Thematic Focus

1. What did George's visit to Wounded Knee apparently enable her to understand? What, if anything, did her essay about it help *you* understand?
2. What advantages does George's personal history seem to give her as she builds a context for Mark and his family? In what ways, if any, might her personal history limit her perspective? To what extent, do you think, does George's and Tompkins's whiteness limit the authority of each in writing about Native Americans?
3. According to George, how much control do contemporary Native Americans have over their own destiny? Do you sense that Tompkins would agree with her? Why or why not?

Suggestions for Writing

1. Compare Tompkins and George as white students of Native American culture. Are their thinking processes similar? Do they show the same amount of self-reflection? Do you believe they demonstrate equal sensitivity toward Native Americans as they try to perceive them accurately? Support your analysis with detailed references to the texts.

2. Describe a personal experience in which you either learned something new about another cultural group or became newly aware of your limited ability to understand it. Your thesis will be what you concluded from the experience, but use most of your essay to re-create it for your readers.

3. A committee is currently soliciting contributions for the new Museum of the American Indian, to be built in Washington, D.C. at a cost of $106 million. If you share Tompkins's concerns about the museum or have other concerns about it, write the committee a letter identifying what about the museum you would need to be sure of before you contributed any money for it. If you think people should not worry about supporting the museum, write Tompkins a letter explaining why.

ACKNOWLEDGING MINORITY PERSPECTIVES

In the previous constellation, members of a dominant group struggled to understand the historical experiences of a subjugated one. When you analyze how races or cultures relate, however, you also should consider what various minorities themselves think of those in power. Even if you yourself are a member of a minority group, you should try determining the extent to which other minorities share your perceptions. In particular, everyone ought to acknowledge what various minorities see as oppressive practices of the majority. Oral and written testimonies by members of minority groups indicate that these practices include not only discriminatory behavior toward them, but also excessive and unfair generalizations about them.

Here, Brent Staples, Arturo Madrid, and Mitsuye Yamada register the impact of white America on them by pointing out the ways they have had to counteract its images of their respective minority groups. Staples discusses his attempts at coping with white women's tendency to fear him as an African-American man when they encounter him on the street. Madrid recalls the stereotypical images that he as an Hispanic-American has had to combat all his life. Yamada describes her efforts to overcome the typical association of Asian-American women with polite silence. Given that these authors are African-American, Hispanic-American, and Asian-American, their perspectives differ to some extent. Also, gender differences clearly matter: Staples has to deal with a certain image of African-American males, while Yamada confronts a harmful image of Asian-American women even as she notes the ways that her whole ethnic group has been stereotyped. Nevertheless, the three essays do address certain common themes. For one thing, they all address the visibility and invisibility of minorities—the ways they are seen by the majority as merely "other," or not really seen by it at all. Interestingly, both Madrid and Yamada refer to Ralph Ellison's 1952 novel *Invisible Man,* which had an African-American protagonist but whose title obviously resonates for various minorities as they urge white America to see them more realistically. (Paule Marshall also refers to this book in the first constellation of "Places and Communities.") All three essays also detail the practical consequences for minorities of the majority's stereotypes. For example, they point out ways that these stereotypes have led to restrictions on minorities' freedom of space. All three, in effect, raise another important issue: What steps are needed to ensure appropriate treatment of minorities, and who must take them? Staples, Madrid, and Yamada work toward this goal partly by writing their essays. They press us to consider, though, what are the responsibilities of all of us in ensuring that races and cultures truly acknowledge one another.

Just Walk On By

Brent Staples

Brent Staples (b. 1951) graduated from Widener University in his home town of Chester, Pennsylvania. Subsequently, he earned master's and doctoral degrees in psychology at the University of Chicago, where he was also an instructor of statistics. He served, too, as a consultant for Ebony Management Associates and as a reporter for *The Chicago Sun-Times* before becoming an editor of *The New York Times Book Review* in 1985. In 1987, he became first assistant metropolitan editor of the *Times,* and in 1990 joined its editorial board to write about politics and culture. His book *Parallel Time: A Memoir* is scheduled to be published in 1991. The following essay first appeared in the September 1986 issue of *Ms.* magazine, as part of a special section on men's perspectives.

Reflections Before Reading

In his essay, Staples recalls his experiences as an African-American man walking by white women on the street. Specifically, he discusses the ways he has had to cope with their automatic fear of him. Are you personally

familiar with such an encounter, or have you heard of other people going
through it? What do you expect an African-American man's attitude toward
such encounters will be? What emotions do you think he will show in
recalling them? In what way(s) might the possible tensions of such
encounters be alleviated?

My first victim was a woman—white, well dressed, probably in her early twenties. I   1
came upon her late one evening on a deserted street in Hyde Park, a relatively
affluent neighborhood in an otherwise mean, impoverished section of Chicago. As
I swung onto the avenue behind her, there seemed to be a discreet, uninflamma-
tory distance between us. Not so. She cast back a worried glance. To her, the
youngish black man—a broad six feet two inches with a beard and billowing hair,
both hands shoved into the pockets of a bulky military jacket—seemed menacingly
close. After a few more quick glimpses, she picked up her pace and was soon
running in earnest. Within seconds she disappeared into a cross street.

That was more than a decade ago. I was 22 years old, a graduate student newly   2
arrived at the University of Chicago. It was in the echo of that terrified woman's
footfalls that I first began to know the unwieldy inheritance I'd come into—the
ability to alter public space in ugly ways. It was clear that she thought herself the
quarry of a mugger, a rapist, or worse. Suffering a bout of insomnia, however, I was
stalking sleep, not defenseless wayfarers. As a softy who is scarcely able to take a
knife to a raw chicken—let alone hold it to a person's throat—I was surprised,
embarrassed, and dismayed all at once. Her flight made me feel like an accomplice
in tyranny. It also made it clear that I was indistinguishable from the muggers who
occasionally seeped into the area from the surrounding ghetto. That first encounter, and those that followed, signified that a vast, unnerving gulf lay between nighttime pedestrians—particularly women—and me. And I soon gathered that being
perceived as dangerous is a hazard in itself. I only needed to turn a corner into a
dicey situation, or crowd some frightened, armed person in a foyer somewhere, or
make an errant move after being pulled over by a policeman. Where fear and
weapons meet—and they often do in urban America—there is always the possibility of death.

In that first year, my first away from my hometown, I was to become thor-   3
oughly familiar with the language of fear. At dark, shadowy intersections in Chicago, I could cross in front of a car stopped at a traffic light and elicit the *thunk,
thunk, thunk, thunk* of the driver—black, white, male, or female—hammering
down the door locks. On less traveled streets after dark, I grew accustomed to but
never comfortable with people who crossed to the other side of the street rather
than pass me. Then there were the standard unpleasantries with police, doormen,
bouncers, cab drivers, and others whose business it is to screen out troublesome
individuals *before* there is any nastiness.

I moved to New York nearly two years ago and I have remained an avid night   4
walker. In central Manhattan, the near-constant crowd cover minimizes tense one-
on-one street encounters. Elsewhere—visiting friends in SoHo, where sidewalks

are narrow and tightly spaced buildings shut out the sky—things can get very taut indeed.

Black men have a firm place in New York mugging literature. Norman Pod- 5
horetz in his famed (or infamous) 1963 essay, "My Negro Problem—And Ours," recalls growing up in terror of black males; they "were tougher than we were, more ruthless," he writes—and as an adult on the Upper West Side of Manhattan, he continues, he cannot constrain his nervousness when he meets black men on certain streets. Similarly, a decade later, the essayist and novelist Edward Hoagland extols a New York where once "Negro bitterness bore down mainly on other Negroes." Where some see mere panhandlers, Hoagland sees "a mugger who is clearly screwing up his nerve to do more than just *ask* for money." But Hoagland has "the New Yorker's quick-hunch posture for broken-field maneuvering," and the bad guy swerves away.

I often witness that "hunch posture," from women after dark on the warren- 6
like streets of Brooklyn where I live. They seem to set their faces on neutral and, with their purse straps strung across their chests bandolier style, they forge ahead as though bracing themselves against being tackled. I understand, of course, that the danger they perceive is not a hallucination. Women are particularly vulnerable to street violence, and young black males are drastically overrepresented among the perpetrators of that violence. Yet these truths are no solace against the kind of alienation that comes of being ever the suspect, against being set apart, a fearsome entity with whom pedestrians avoid making eye contact.

It is not altogether clear to me how I reached the ripe old age of 22 without 7
being conscious of the lethality nighttime pedestrians attributed to me. Perhaps it was because in Chester, Pennsylvania, the small, angry industrial town where I came of age in the 1960s, I was scarcely noticeable against a backdrop of gang warfare, street knifings, and murders. I grew up one of the good boys, had perhaps a half-dozen fist fights. In retrospect, my shyness of combat has clear sources.

Many things go into the making of a young thug. One of those things is the 8
consummation of the male romance with the power to intimidate. An infant discovers that random flailings send the baby bottle flying out of the crib and crashing to the floor. Delighted, the joyful babe repeats those motions again and again, seeking to duplicate the feat. Just so, I recall the points at which some of my boyhood friends were finally seduced by the perception of themselves as tough guys. When a mark cowered and surrendered his money without resistance, myth and reality merged—and paid off. It is, after all, only manly to embrace the power to frighten and intimidate. We, as men, are not supposed to give an inch of our lane on the highway; we are to seize the fighter's edge in work and in play and even in love; we are to be valiant in the face of hostile forces.

Unfortunately, poor and powerless young men seem to take all this nonsense 9
literally. As a boy, I saw countless tough guys locked away; I have since buried several, too. They were babies, really—a teenage cousin, a brother of 22, a childhood friend in his mid-twenties—all gone down in episodes of bravado played out in the streets. I came to doubt the virtues of intimidation early on. I chose, perhaps even unconsciously, to remain a shadow—timid, but a survivor.

The fearsomeness mistakenly attributed to me in public places often has a 10
perilous flavor. The most frightening of these confusions occurred in the late 1970s

and early 1980s when I worked as a journalist in Chicago. One day, rushing into the office of a magazine I was writing for with a deadline story in hand, I was mistaken for a burglar. The office manager called security and, with an ad hoc posse, pursued me through the labyrinthine halls, nearly to my editor's door. I had no way of proving who I was. I could only move briskly toward the company of someone who knew me.

Another time I was on assignment for a local paper and killing time before an   11
interview. I entered a jewelry store on the city's affluent Near North Side. The proprietor excused herself and returned with an enormous red Doberman pinscher straining at the end of a leash. She stood, the dog extended toward me, silent to my questions, her eyes bulging nearly out of her head. I took a cursory look around, nodded, and bade her good night. Relatively speaking, however, I never fared as badly as another black male journalist. He went to nearby Waukegan, Illinois, a couple of summers ago to work on a story about a murderer who was born there. Mistaking the reporter for the killer, police hauled him from his car at gunpoint and but for his press credentials would probably have tried to book him. Such episodes are not uncommon. Black men trade tales like this all the time.

In "My Negro Problem—And Ours," Podhoretz writes that the hatred he feels   12
for blacks makes itself known to him through a variety of avenues—one being his discomfort with that "special brand of paranoid touchiness" to which he says blacks are prone. No doubt he is speaking here of black men. In time, I learned to smother the rage I felt at so often being taken for a criminal. Not to do so would surely have led to madness—via that special "paranoid touchiness" that so annoyed Podhoretz at the time he wrote the essay.

I began to take precautions to make myself less threatening. I move about with   13
care, particularly late in the evening. I give a wide berth to nervous people on subway platforms during the wee hours, particularly when I have exchanged business clothes for jeans. If I happen to be entering a building behind some people who appear skittish, I may walk by, letting them clear the lobby before I return, so as not to seem to be following them. I have been calm and extremely congenial on those rare occasions when I've been pulled over by the police.

And on late-evening constitutionals along streets less traveled by, I employ   14
what has proved to be an excellent tension-reducing measure: I whistle melodies from Beethoven and Vivaldi and the more popular classical composers. Even steely New Yorkers hunching toward nighttime destinations seem to relax, and occasionally they even join in the tune. Virtually everybody seems to sense that a mugger wouldn't be warbling bright, sunny selections from Vivaldi's *Four Seasons*. It is my equivalent of the cowbell that hikers wear when they know they are in bear country.

Rhetorical Focus

1. Why do you think Staples begins his essay the way he does, given that his first sentence is misleading?
2. Trace how Staples organizes his essay through various references to fear, right up to the last sentence about hikers versus bears. For each reference, identify who is experiencing fear.

3. Recall that Staples wrote this essay for *Ms.*, whose audience is mostly women. What might he have wanted this group of readers to get out of it?

Thematic Focus

1. Identify places in the essay where Staples reports his emotions. Are his feelings consistent? Are there any places where you think his feelings may be other than what he states?
2. Judging by this essay, what would a reasonable perspective on African-American men have to take into account?
3. How do you think the situation described by Staples can best be addressed? Who do you think should address it?

Missing People and Others

Arturo Madrid

Arturo Madrid (b. 1939) is President of the Tomas Rivera Center, which he founded in 1985. Located in Claremont, California, the Center researches educational, social, and economic issues affecting Hispanic-Americans. Madrid graduated from the University of New Mexico, his home state, and later received a doctorate in Spanish literature from the University of California at Los Angeles. He has taught at Dartmouth College, the University of California at San Diego, and the University of Minnesota, where he served as Associate Dean of Humanities and Fine Arts. He has also directed the Fund for the Improvement of Post-Secondary Education and the Ford Foundation Graduate Fellowship Program. The following essay first appeared in the May/June 1988 issue of *Change: The Magazine of Higher Education*, as part of a special section on Hispanic-Americans.

Reflections Before Reading

What races and cultures are absent from your campus? What kinds of people who *are* on your campus does the majority treat as "others"—that is, as people not in the mainstream and not worth paying careful attention to? Think not only of students, but also of faculty and support staff (Madrid refers to groundskeepers and food-service personnel, for instance). Madrid focuses on what it is like for Hispanic-Americans to be "missing people" and "others," especially in the educational system. What do you associate with this particular group? How did you come to make these associations?

I am a citizen of the United States, as are my parents and as were their parents, grandparents, and great-grandparents. My ancestors' presence in what is now the United States antedates Plymouth Rock, even without taking into account any American Indian heritage I might have.

I do not, however, fit those mental sets that define America and Americans. My physical appearance, my speech patterns, my name, my profession (a professor of Spanish) create a text that confuses the reader. My normal experience is to be asked, "And where are *you* from?"

My response depends on my mood. Passive-aggressive, I answer, "From here." Aggressive-passive, I ask, "Do you mean where am I originally from?" But ultimately my answer to those follow-up questions that ask about origins will be that we have always been from here.

Overcoming my resentment I will try to educate, knowing that nine times out of ten my words fall on inattentive ears. I have spent most of my adult life explaining who I am not. I am exotic, but—as Richard Rodriguez of *Hunger of Memory* fame so painfully found out—not exotic enough . . . not Peruvian, or Pakistani, or Persian, or whatever.

I am, however, very clearly *the other*, if only your everyday, garden-variety, domestic *other*. I've always known that I was *the other*, even before I knew the vocabulary or understood the significance of being *the other*.

I grew up in an isolated and historically marginal part of the United States, a small mountain village in the state of New Mexico, the eldest child of parents native to that region and whose ancestors had always lived there. In those vast and empty spaces, people who look like me, speak as I do, and have names like mine predominate. But the *americanos* lived among us: the descendants of those nineteenth-century immigrants who dispossessed us of our lands; missionaries who came to convert us and stayed to live among us; artists who became enchanted with our land and humanscape and went native; refugees from unhealthy climes, crowded spaces, unpleasant circumstances; and, of course, the inhabitants of Los Alamos, whose socio-cultural distance from us was moreover accentuated by the fact that they occupied a space removed from and proscribed to us. More importantly, however, they—*los americanos*—were omnipresent (and almost exclusively so) in newspapers, newsmagazines, books, on radio, in movies and, ultimately, on television.

Despite the operating myth of the day, school did not erase my otherness. It   7
did try to deny it, and in doing so only accentuated it. To this day, schooling is more
socialization than education, but when I was in elementary school—and given
where I was—socialization was everything. School was where one became an
American. Because there was a pervasive and systematic denial by the society that
surrounded us that we were Americans. That denial was both explicit and implicit.
My earliest memory of the former was that there were two kinds of churches:
theirs and ours. The more usual was the implicit denial, our absence from the
larger cultural, economic, political and social spaces—the one that reminded us
constantly that we were *the other*. And school was where we felt it most acutely.

Quite beyond saluting the flag and pledging allegiance to it (a very intense and   8
meaningful action, given that the U.S. was involved in a war and our brothers,
cousins, uncles, and fathers were on the front lines) becoming American was learning English and its corollary—not speaking Spanish. Until very recently ours was a
proscribed language—either *de jure* (by rule, by policy, by law) or *de facto* (by
practice, implicitly if not explicitly; through social and political and economic pressure). I do not argue that learning English was not appropriate. On the contrary.
Like it or not, and we had no basis to make any judgments on that matter, we were
Americans by virtue of having been born Americans, and English was the common
language of Americans. And there was a myth, a pervasive myth, that said that if we
only learned to speak English well—and particularly without an accent—we would
be welcomed into the American fellowship.

Senator Sam Hayakawa notwithstanding, the true text was not our speech, but   9
rather our names and our appearance, for we would always have an accent, however perfect our pronunciation, however excellent our enunciation, however divine our diction. That accent would be heard in our pigmentation, our physiog-
nomy, our names. We were, in short, *the other*.

Being *the other* means feeling different; is awareness of being distinct; is con-   10
sciousness of being dissimilar. It means being outside the game, outside the circle,
outside the set. It means being on the edges, on the margins, on the periphery.
Otherness means feeling excluded, closed out, precluded, even disdained and
scorned. It produces a sense of isolation, of apartness, of disconnectedness, of
alienation.

Being *the other* involves a contradictory phenomenon. On the one hand being   11
the other frequently means being invisible. Ralph Ellison wrote eloquently about
that experience in his magisterial novel *The Invisible Man*. On the other hand,
being *the other* sometimes involves sticking out like a sore thumb. What is she/he
doing here?

If one is *the other*, one will inevitably be perceived unidimensionally; will be   12
seen stereotypically; will be defined and delimited by mental sets that may not
bear much relation to existing realities. There is a darker side to otherness as well.
The other disturbs, disquiets, discomforts. It provokes distrust and suspicion. *The
other* makes people feel anxious, nervous, apprehensive, even fearful. *The other*
frightens, scares.

For some of us being *the other* is only annoying; for others it is debilitating; for   13
still others it is damning. Many try to flee otherness by taking on protective color-

ations that provide invisibility, whether of dress or speech or manner or name. Only a fortunate few succeed. For the majority, otherness is permanently sealed by physical appearance. For the rest, otherness is betrayed by ways of being, speaking or of doing.

I spent the first half of my life downplaying the significance and consequences   14
of otherness. The second half has seen me wrestling to understand its complex and deeply ingrained realities; striving to fathom why otherness denies us a voice or visibility or validity in American society and its institutions; struggling to make otherness familiar, reasonable, even normal to my fellow Americans.

I am also a missing person. Growing up in northern New Mexico I had only a   15
slight sense of our being missing persons. *Hispanos,* as we called (and call) our-selves in New Mexico, were very much a part of the fabric of the society and there were Hispano professionals everywhere about me: doctors, lawyers, school teach-ers, and administrators. My people owned businesses, ran organizations and were both appointed and elected public officials.

To be sure, we did not own the larger businesses, nor at the time were we   16
permitted to be part of the banking world. Other than that, however, people who looked like me, spoke like me, and had names like mine, predominated. There was, to be sure, Los Alamos, but as I have said, it was removed from our realities.

My awareness of our absence from the larger institutional life of society be-   17
came sharper when I went off to college, but even then it was attenuated by the circumstances of history and geography. The demography of Albuquerque still strongly reflected its historical and cultural origins, despite the influx of Midwest-erners and Easterners. Moreover, many of my classmates at the University of New Mexico in Albuquerque were Hispanos, and even some of my professors were.

I thought that would obtain at UCLA, where I began graduate studies in 1960.   18
Los Angeles already had a very large Mexican population, and that population was visible even in and around Westwood and on the campus. Many of the grounds-keepers and food-service personnel at UCLA were Mexican. But Mexican-Ameri-can students were few and mostly invisible, and I do not recall seeing or knowing a single Mexican-American (or, for that matter, black, Asian, or American Indian) professional on the staff or faculty of that institution during the five years I was there.

Needless to say, persons like me were not present in any capacity at Dart-   19
mouth College—the site of my first teaching appointment—and, of course, were not even part of the institutional or individual mind-set. I knew then that we—a "we" that had come to encompass American Indians, Asian-Americans, black Americans, Puerto Ricans, and women—were truly missing persons in American institutional life.

Over the past three decades, the *de jure* and *de facto* segregations that have   20
historically characterized American institutions have been under assault. As a con-sequence, minorities and women have become part of American institutional life, and although there are still many areas where we are not to be found, the missing persons phenomenon is not as pervasive as it once was.

However, the presence of *the other,* particularly minorities, in institutions and   21
in institutional life, is, as we say in Spanish, *a flor de tierra;* spare plants whose
roots do not go deep, a surface phenomenon, vulnerable to inclemencies of an
economic, political, or social nature.

Our entrance into and our status in institutional life is not unlike a scenario set   22
forth by my grandmother's pastor when she informed him that she and her family
were leaving their mountain village to relocate in the Rio Grande Valley. When he
asked her to promise that she would remain true to the faith and continue to involve herself in the life of the church, she assured him that she would and asked
him why he thought she would do otherwise.

"Doña Trinidad," he told her, "in the Valley there is no Spanish church. There   23
is only an American church." "But," she protested, "I read and speak English and
would be able to worship there." Her pastor's response was: "It is possible that they
will not admit you, and even if they do, they might not accept you. And that is why
I want you to promise me that you are going to go to church. Because if they don't
let you in through the front door, I want you to go in through the back door. And if
you can't get in through the back door, go in the side door. And if you are unable to
enter through the side door I want you to go in through the window. What is
important is that you enter and that you stay."

Some of us entered institutional life through the front door; others through   24
the back door; and still others through side doors. Many, if not most of us, came in
through windows and continue to come in through windows. Of those who entered
through the front door, some never made it past the lobby; others were ushered
into corners and niches. Those who entered through back and side doors inevitably
have remained in back and side rooms. And those who entered through windows
found enclosures built around them. For despite the lip service given to the goal of
the integration of minorities into institutional life, what has occurred instead is
ghettoization, marginalization, isolation.

Not only have the entry points been limited: in addition, the dynamics have   25
been singularly conflictive. Gaining entry and its corollary—gaining space—have
frequently come as a consequence of demands made on institutions and institutional officers. Rather than entering institutions more or less passively, minorities
have, of necessity, entered them actively, even aggressively. Rather than taking,
they have demanded. Institutional relations have thus been adversarial, infused
with specific and generalized tensions.

The nature of the entrance and the nature of the space occupied have greatly   26
influenced the view and attitudes of the majority population within those institutions. All of us are put into the same box; that is, no matter what the individual
reality, the assessment of the individual is inevitably conditioned by a perception
that is held of the class. Whatever our history, whatever our record, whatever our
validations, whatever our accomplishments, by and large we are perceived unidimensionally and are dealt with accordingly.

My most recent experience in this regard is atypical only in its explicitness. A   27
few years ago I allowed myself to be persuaded to seek the presidency of a large
and prestigious state university. I was invited for an interview and presented myself before the selection committee, which included members of the board of

trustees. The opening question of the brief but memorable interview was directed at me by a member of that august body. "Dr. Madrid," he asked, "why does a one-dimensional person like you think he can be the president of a multi-dimensional institution like ours?"

If, as I happen to believe, the well-being of a society is directly related to the degree and extent to which all of its citizens participate in its institutions, we have a challenge before us. One of the strengths of our society—perhaps its main strength—has been a tradition of struggle against clubbishness, exclusivity, and restriction.   28

Today, more than ever, given the extraordinary changes that are taking place in our society, we need to take up that struggle again—irritating, grating, troublesome, unfashionable, unpleasant as it is. As educated and educator members of this society, we have a special responsibility for leading the struggle against marginalization, exclusion, and alienation.   29

Let us work together to assure that all American institutions, not just its precollegiate educational and penal institutions, reflect the diversity of our society. Not to do so is to risk greater alienation on the part of a growing segment of our society. It is to risk increased social tension in an already conflictive world. And ultimately it is to risk the survival of a range of institutions that, for all their defects and deficiencies, permit us the space, the opportunity, and the freedom to improve our individual and collective lot; to guide the course of our government, and to redress whatever grievances we have. Let us join together to expand, not to close the circle.   30

Rhetorical Focus

1. What assumptions does Madrid seem to make about his audience? For example, what does he seem to think his readers have yet to know or realize? What does he seem to think they are or are not capable of doing?
2. How does Madrid use the two terms in his title to organize his essay? What is the relationship between them?
3. Both Madrid and Staples make points through anecdotes. Are they equally effective in resorting to them? Are the points of their anecdotes similar?

Thematic Focus

1. Madrid gives several reasons for boosting the status of "missing people" in higher education. What are they? Do you agree with them?
2. How might Madrid's discussion of "otherness" apply to Staples's situation? Note also the ways that these authors refer to "space." Do they express similar notions of who controls it?
3. Staples ends by emphasizing personal strategies he has used to reassure white people about African-Americans. Madrid ends on a collective note, asking his audience to join him in working on behalf of Hispanic-Americans. If these two authors met, do you think they would therefore disagree over how minority groups can best gain status? Why or why not?

Invisibility Is an Unnatural Disaster: Reflections of an Asian American Woman

Mitsuye Yamada

Mitsuye Yamada (b. 1923) is a second-generation Japanese-American poet and teacher. She grew up in Seattle, Washington. During World War II, she was interned along with other Japanese-Americans at the Minidoka Relocation Center in Idaho. Besides publishing *Camp Notes and Other Poems* and *Desert Run: Poems and Stories,* she has taught creative writing, as well as children's literature, at Cypress College in Orange County, California. Founder of Multi-Cultural Women Writers of Orange County, she is presently co-editing a volume entitled *Sowing Ti Leaves: Writings by Multicultural Women.* The following essay appeared in a 1979 issue of the journal *Bridge: An Asian American Perspective.*

Reflections Before Reading

What might Yamada's title mean? Have you ever felt treated as "invisible"? If so, what were the circumstances and consequences? Who or what was at fault? Yamada's essay deals specifically with Asian-American women. What images of them do you think American culture emphasizes?

Last year for the Asian segment of the Ethnic American Literature course I was teaching, I selected a new anthology entitled *Aiiieeeee!* compiled by a group of outspoken Asian American writers. During the discussion of the long but thought-provoking introduction to this anthology, one of my students blurted out that she was offended by its militant tone and that as a white person she was tired of always being blamed for the oppression of all the minorities. I noticed several of her classmates eyes nodding in tacit agreement. A discussion of the "militant" voices in some of the other writings we had read in the course ensued. Surely, I pointed out, some of these other writings have been just as, if not more, militant as the words in this introduction? Had they been offended by those also but failed to express their feelings about them? To my surprise, they said they were not offended by any of the Black American, Chicano or American Indian writings, but were hard-pressed to explain why when I asked for an explanation. A little further discussion revealed that they "understood" the anger expressed by the Blacks and Chicanos and they "empathized" with the frustrations and sorrow expressed by the American Indian. But the Asian Americans??

Then finally, one student said it for all of them: "It made me angry. *Their* anger made *me* angry, because I didn't even know the Asian Americans felt oppressed. I didn't expect their anger." 2

At this time I was involved in an academic due process procedure begun as a result of a grievance I had filed the previous semester against the administrators at my college. I had filed a grievance for violation of my rights as a teacher who had worked in the district for almost eleven years. My student's remark "Their anger made me angry . . . I didn't expect their anger," explained for me the reactions of some of my own colleagues as well as the reactions of the administrators during those previous months. The grievance procedure was a time-consuming and emotionally draining process, but the basic principle was too important for me to ignore. That basic principle was that I, an individual teacher, do have certain rights which are given and my superiors cannot, should not, violate them with impunity. When this was pointed out to them, however, they responded with shocked surprise that I, of all people, would take them to task for violation of what was clearly written policy in our college district. They all seemed to exclaim, "We don't understand this; this is so uncharacteristic of her; she seemed such a nice person, so polite, so obedient, so non-trouble-making." What was even more surprising was once they were forced to acknowledge that I was determined to start the due process action, they assumed I was not doing it on my own. One of the administrators suggested someone must have pushed me into this, undoubtedly some of "those feminists" on our campus, he said wryly. 3

In this age when women are clearly making themselves visible on all fronts, I, an Asian American woman, am still functioning as a "front for those feminists" and therefore invisible. The realization of this sinks in slowly. Asian Americans as a whole are finally coming to claim their own, demanding that they be included in the multicultural history of our country. I like to think, in spite of my administrator's myopia, that the most stereotyped minority of them all, the Asian American woman, is just now emerging to become part of that group. It took forever. Perhaps it is important to ask ourselves why it took so long. We should ask ourselves this question just when we think we are emerging as a viable minority in the fabric of our society. I should add to my student's words, "because I didn't even know they felt oppressed," that it took this long because we Asian American women have not admitted to ourselves that we *were* oppressed. We, the visible minority that is invisible. 4

I say this because until a few years ago I have been an Asian American woman working among non-Asians in an educational institution where most of the deci- 5 sion-makers were men;° an Asian American woman thriving under the smug illusion that I was *not* the stereotypic image of the Asian woman because I had a career teaching English in a community college. I did not think anything assertive was necessary to make my point. People who know me, I reasoned, the ones who count, know who I am and what I think. Thus, even when what I considered a veiled racist remark was made in a casual social setting, I would "let it go" because it was pointless to argue with people who didn't even know their remark was racist. I had supposed that I was practicing passive resistance while being stereotyped, but it was so passive no one noticed I was resisting; it was so much my expected role that it ultimately rendered me invisible.

My experience leads me to believe that contrary to what I thought, I had actu-   6
ally been contributing to my own stereotyping. Like the hero in Ralph Ellison's novel *The Invisible Man,* I had become invisible to white Americans, and it clung to me like a bad habit. Like most bad habits, this one crept up on me because I took it in minute doses like Mithradates' poison and my mind and body adapted so well to it I hardly noticed it was there.

For the past eleven years I have busied myself with the usual chores of an   7
English teacher, a wife of a research chemist, and a mother of four rapidly growing children. I hadn't even done much to shatter this particular stereotype: the middle class woman happy to be bringing home the extra income and quietly fitting into the man's world of work. When the Asian American woman is lulled into believing that people perceive her as being different from other Asian women (the submissive, subservient, ready-to-please, easy-to-get-along-with Asian woman), she is kept comfortably content with the state of things. She becomes ineffectual in the milieu in which she moves. The seemingly apolitical middle class woman and the apolitical Asian woman constituted a double invisibility.

I had created an underground culture of survival for myself and had become   8
in the eyes of others the person I was trying not to be. Because I was permitted to go to college, permitted to take a stab at a career or two along the way, given "free choice" to marry and have a family, given a "choice" to eventually do both, I had assumed I was more or less free, not realizing that those who are free make and take choices; they do not choose from options proffered by "those out there."

I, personally, had not "emerged" until I was almost fifty years old. Apparently   9
through a long conditioning process, I had learned how *not* to be seen for what I am. A long history of ineffectual activities had been, I realize now, initiation rites toward my eventual invisibility. The training begins in childhood; and for women and minorities, whatever is started in childhood is continued throughout their adult lives. I first recognized just how invisible I was in my first real confrontation with my parents a few years after the outbreak of World War II.

During the early years of the war, my older brother, Mike, and I left the con-   10
centration camp in Idaho to work and study at the University of Cincinnati. My parents came to Cincinnati soon after my father's release from Internment Camp

---

°It is hoped this will change now that a black woman is Chancellor of our college district.

(these were POW camps to which many of the Issei° men, leaders in their communities, were sent by the FBI), and worked as domestics in the suburbs. I did not see them too often because by this time I had met and was much influenced by a pacifist who was out on a "furlough" from a conscientious objectors' camp in Trenton, North Dakota. When my parents learned about my "boy friend" they were appalled and frightened. After all, this was the period when everyone in the country was expected to be one-hundred percent behind the war effort, and the Nisei° boys who had volunteered for the Armed Forces were out there fighting and dying to prove how American we really were. However, during interminable arguments with my father and overheard arguments between my parents, I was devastated to learn they were not so much concerned about my having become a pacifist, but they were more concerned about the possibility of my marrying one. They were understandably frightened (my father's prison years of course were still fresh on his mind) about repercussions on the rest of the family. In an attempt to make my father understand me, I argued that even if I didn't marry him, I'd still be a pacifist; but my father reassured me that it was "all right" for me to be a pacifist because as a Japanese national and a *"girl" it didn't make any difference to anyone.* In frustration I remember shouting, "But can't you see, *I'm* philosophically committed to the pacifist cause," but he dismissed this with "In my college days we used to call philosophy, foolosophy," and that was the end of that. When they were finally convinced I was not going to marry "my pacifist," the subject was dropped and we never discussed it again.

As if to confirm my father's assessment of the harmlessness of my opinions, my   11
brother Mike, an American citizen, was suddenly expelled from the University of Cincinnati while I, "an enemy alien," was permitted to stay. We assumed that his stand as a pacifist, although he was classified a 4-F because of his health, contributed to his expulsion. We were told the Air Force was conducting sensitive wartime research on campus and requested his removal, but they apparently felt my presence on campus was not as threatening.

I left Cincinnati in 1945, hoping to leave behind this and other unpleasant   12
memories gathered there during the war years, and plunged right into the politically active atmosphere at New York University where students, many of them returning veterans, were continuously promoting one cause or other by making speeches in Washington Square, passing out petitions, or staging demonstrations. On one occasion, I tagged along with a group of students who took a train to Albany to demonstrate on the steps of the State Capitol. I think I was the only Asian in this group of predominantly Jewish students from NYU. People who passed us were amused and shouted "Go home and grow up." I suppose Governor Dewey, who refused to see us, assumed we were a group of adolescents without a cause as most college students were considered to be during those days. It appears they weren't expecting any results from our demonstration. There were no newspersons, no security persons, no police. No one tried to stop us from doing what we

---

°Issei—Immigrant Japanese, living in the U.S.
°Nisei—Second generation Japanese, born in the U.S.

were doing. We simply did "our thing" and went back to our studies until next time, and my father's words were again confirmed: it made no difference to anyone, being a young student demonstrator in peacetime, 1947.

Not only the young, but those who feel powerless over their own lives know   13
what it is like not to make a difference on anyone or anything. The poor know it only too well, and we women have known it since we were little girls. The most insidious part of this conditioning process, I realize now, was that we have been trained not to expect a response in ways that mattered. We may be listened to and responded to with placating words and gestures, but our psychological mind set has already told us time and again that we were born into a ready-made world into which we must fit ourselves, and that many of us do it very well.

This mind set is the result of not believing that the political and social forces   14
affecting our lives are determined by some person, or a group of persons, probably sitting behind a desk or around a conference table.

Just recently I read an article about "the remarkable track record of success"   15
of the Nisei in the United States. One Nisei was quoted as saying he attributed our stamina and endurance to our ancestors whose characters had been shaped, he said, by their living in a country which has been constantly besieged by all manner of natural disasters, such as earthquakes and hurricanes. He said the Nisei has inherited a steely will, a will to endure and hence, to survive.

This evolutionary explanation disturbs me, because it equates the "act of God"   16
(i.e. natural disasters) to the "act of man" (i.e., the war, the evacuation). The former is not within our power to alter, but the latter, I should think, is. By putting the "acts of God" on par with the acts of man, we shrug off personal responsibilities.

I have, for too long a period of time accepted the opinion of others (even   17
though they were directly affecting my life) as if they were objective events totally out of my control. Because I separated such opinions from the persons who were making them, I accepted them the way I accepted natural disasters; and I endured them as inevitable. I have tried to cope with people whose points of view alarmed me in the same way that I had adjusted to natural phenomena, such as hurricanes, which plowed into my life from time to time. I would readjust my dismantled feelings in the same way that we repaired the broken shutters after the storm. The Japanese have an all-purpose expression in their language for this attitude of resigned acceptance: "Shikataganan." "It can't be helped." "There's nothing I can do about it." It is said with the shrug of the shoulders and tone of finality, perhaps not unlike the "those-were-my-orders" tone that was used at the Nuremberg trials. With all the sociological studies that have been made about the causes of the evacuations of the Japanese Americans during World War II, we should know by now that "they" knew that the West Coast Japanese Americans would go without too much protest, and of course, "they" were right, for most of us (with the exception of those notable few), resigned to our fate, albeit bewildered and not willingly. We were not perceived by our government as responsive Americans; we were objects that happened to be standing in the path of the storm.

Perhaps this kind of acceptance is a way of coping with the "real" world. One   18
stands against the wind for a time, and then succumbs eventually because there is

no point to being stubborn against all odds. The wind will not respond to entreaties anyway, one reasons; one should have sense enough to know that. I'm not ready to accept this evolutionary reasoning. It is too rigid for me; I would like to think that my new awareness is going to make me more visible than ever, and to allow me to make some changes in the "man made disaster" I live in at the present time. Part of being visible is refusing to separate the actors from their actions, and demanding that they be responsible for them.

By now, riding along with the minorities' and women's movements, I think we   19
are making a wedge into the main body of American life, but people are still look- ing right through and around us, assuming we are simply tagging along. Asian American women still remain in the background and we are heard but not really listened to. Like Musak, they think we are piped into the airwaves by someone else. We must remember that one of the most insidious ways of keeping women and minorities powerless is to let them only talk about harmless and inconsequen- tial subjects, or let them speak freely and not listen to them with serious intent.

We need to raise our voices a little more, even as they say to us "This is so   20
uncharacteristic of you." To finally recognize our own invisibility is to finally be on the path toward visibility. Invisibility is not a natural state for anyone.

Rhetorical Focus

1. What does Yamada accomplish with her opening paragraphs about her class? Is its reaction familiar to you?
2. Yamada does not give specific details of her grievance against the college. Does this omission matter, or do you think her purpose in writing the essay is still served?
3. Does Yamada blend generalization and anecdote effectively? Does she use each to the same degree that Staples and Madrid do?

Thematic Focus

1. What does Yamada suggest here were the important stages in her life? How would you describe her present thinking?
2. What about Asian-American history matters in this essay? In what ways does it matter that Yamada is a woman as well as an Asian-American?
3. Yamada suggests that to at least some extent, her problems as an Asian- American woman are her own fault. Where in the text does she blame herself? Where does she suggest that American society is to blame as well? Do you think Staples and Madrid would agree with her? Why or why not?

Suggestions for Writing

1. Explain how each of these three essays could be said to develop the idea that "invisibility is an unnatural disaster." You will need to identify how

each author's real identity has been "invisible," how the situations each has faced can be considered "unnatural," and how these situations have been, or could have been, a "disaster" for them.

2. Describe an occasion when other people held a stereotyped image of you that thwarted your ambitions or limited your freedom. In your description, explain what about you these people were unwilling to recognize, whether you could have asserted yourself more, and whether the stereotyping had lasting effects on you.

3. The essays you have read deal with African-Americans, Hispanic-Americans, and Asian-Americans. From these three groups, choose one whose history has not been all that "visible" to you. Research an aspect of the group's history by reading at least two additional articles. Then write an essay in which you report your findings to your class. Be sure to provide documentation for the articles you consult.

CROSS-CULTURAL RELATIONS

Races and cultures do not interact simply within the borders of the United States, of course. The next two texts expand the geographical context of this unit by looking at the relations between tourist and native in the Caribbean/South Atlantic region. At the same time, each text draws from this setting larger implications for American society. In the first selection, Jamaica Kincaid directly addresses a hypothetical North American or European visitor arriving on her native island of Antigua. As she contrasts the comfortable, sheltered life of the tourist with the Antiguans' poverty, she also points to a larger history of slavery and colonialism that implicates several Western nations, including the United States.

In the second selection, June Jordan describes the day that she concluded her own visit to the Bahamas, still self-conscious as an African-American about the deference given her by black hotel staff. Reflecting on the privileges she enjoyed over the natives, she acknowledges, like Kincaid, the history of Western domination. She also ponders social barriers that persist back home, including ones based on gender and class. When you read this pair of texts, therefore, you will see how they use roughly the same foreign setting to critique American values, and you will need to decide whether you agree with them. Probably, you will be struck as well, though, by a difference in their perspectives: Kincaid writes as a native speaking to a tourist, while Jordan writes as the latter. Compare these perspectives as rhetorical strategies. What effects does each achieve? Compare them, too, as vantage points on relations among races and cultures. Kincaid observes that most of the world's natives are too poor to become tourists. What insights, then, can the native provide into this situation? What must the tourist think about if the situation is to be improved?

Antigua

Jamaica Kincaid

Jamaica Kincaid (b. 1949) grew up on the island of St. John's, Antigua, West
Indies, before emigrating to the United States at the age of 17. Kincaid
now lives and writes in Bennington, Vermont. She is mostly known for her
short stories in *The New Yorker,* as well as for three books of fiction: *At
The Bottom of the River, Annie John,* and *Lucy.* Much of this work reflects
her own childhood on Antigua and her subsequent life in America. In 1988,
she published a nonfiction work about her native island, entitled *A Small
Place.* The following is the first section of three in this book.

Reflections Before Reading

Did you ever visit some place as a tourist and sense that you had a certain
power over the natives there? If so, when? What implications did you draw
from the experience? Have you ever lived in a place frequently visited by
tourists? If so, how did your community view them? Kincaid's text is about
tourists visiting her native island of Antigua. What do you associate with this
place? How do you explain your amount of knowledge about it?

If you go to Antigua as a tourist, this is what you will see. If you come by aeroplane, 1
you will land at the V. C. Bird International Airport. Vere Cornwall (V. C.) Bird is
the Prime Minister of Antigua. You may be the sort of tourist who would wonder
why a Prime Minister would want an airport named after him—why not a school,
why not a hospital, why not some great public monument? You are a tourist and
you have not yet seen a school in Antigua, you have not yet seen the hospital in
Antigua, you have not yet seen a public monument in Antigua. As your plane de-
scends to land, you might say, What a beautiful island Antigua is—more beautiful
than any of the other islands you have seen, and they were very beautiful, in their
way, but they were much too green, much too lush with vegetation, which indicated to you, the tourist, that they got quite a bit of rainfall, and rain is the very
thing that you, just now, do not want, for you are thinking of the hard and cold and
dark and long days you spent working in North America (or, worse, Europe), earning some money so that you could stay in this place (Antigua) where the sun always
shines and where the climate is deliciously hot and dry for the four to ten days you

are going to be staying there; and since you are on your holiday, since you are a
tourist, the thought of what it might be like for someone who had to live day in, day
out in a place that suffers constantly from drought, and so has to watch carefully
every drop of fresh water used (while at the same time surrounded by a sea and an
ocean—the Caribbean Sea on one side, the Atlantic Ocean on the other), must
never cross your mind.

You disembark from your plane. You go through customs. Since you are a
tourist, a North American or European—to be frank, white—and not an Antiguan
black returning to Antigua from Europe or North America with cardboard boxes of
much needed cheap clothes and food for relatives, you move through customs
swiftly, you move through customs with ease. Your bags are not searched. You
emerge from customs into the hot, clean air: immediately you feel cleansed, immediately you feel blessed (which is to say special); you feel free. You see a man, a taxi
driver; you ask him to take you to your destination; he quotes you a price. You
immediately think that the price is in the local currency, for you are a tourist and
you are familiar with these things (rates of exchange) and you feel even more free,
for things seem so cheap, but then your driver ends by saying, "In U.S. currency."
You may say, "Hmmmm, do you have a formal sheet that lists official prices and
destinations?" Your driver obeys the law and shows you the sheet, and he apolo-
gises for the incredible mistake he has made in quoting you a price off the top of
his head which is so vastly different (favouring him) from the one listed. You are
driven to your hotel by this taxi driver in his taxi, a brand-new Japanese-made
vehicle. The road on which you are travelling is a very bad road, very much in need
of repair. You are feeling wonderful, so you say, "Oh, what a marvellous change
these bad roads are from the splendid highways I am used to in North America."
(Or, worse, Europe.) Your driver is reckless; he is a dangerous man who drives in
the middle of the road when he thinks no other cars are coming in the opposite
direction, passes other cars on blind curves that run uphill, drives at sixty miles an
hour on narrow, curving roads when the road sign, a rusting, beat-up thing left
over from colonial days, says 40 MPH. This might frighten you (you are on your
holiday; you are a tourist); this might excite you (you are on your holiday; you are a
tourist), though if you are from New York and take taxis you are used to this style of
driving: most of the taxi drivers in New York are from places in the world like this.
You are looking out the window (because you want to get your money's worth); you
notice that all the cars you see are brand-new, or almost brand-new, and that they
are all Japanese-made. There are no American cars in Antigua—no new ones, at
any rate; none that were manufactured in the last ten years. You continue to look at
the cars and you say to yourself, Why, they look brand-new, but they have an awful
sound, like an old car—a very old, dilapidated car. How to account for that? Well,
possibly it's because they use leaded gasoline in these brand-new cars whose engines were built to use non-leaded gasoline, but you musn't ask the person driving
the car if this is so, because he or she has never heard of unleaded gasoline. You
look closely at the car; you see that it's a model of a Japanese car that you might
hesitate to buy; it's a model that's very expensive; it's a model that's quite impractical for a person who has to work as hard as you do and who watches every penny
you earn so that you can afford this holiday you are on. How do they afford such a

car? And do they live in a luxurious house to match such a car? Well, no. You will be surprised, then, to see that most likely the person driving this brand-new car filled with the wrong gas lives in a house that, in comparison, is far beneath the status of the car; and if you were to ask why you would be told that the banks are encouraged by the government to make loans available for cars, but loans for houses not so easily available; and if you ask again why, you will be told that the two main car dealerships in Antigua are owned in part or outright by ministers in government. Oh, but you are on holiday and the sight of these brand-new cars driven by people who may or may not have really passed their driving test (there was once a scandal about driving licences for sale) would not really stir up these thoughts in you. You pass a building sitting in a sea of dust and you think, It's some latrines for people just passing by, but when you look again you see the building has written on it PIGOTT'S SCHOOL. You pass the hospital, the Holberton Hospital, and how wrong you are not to think about this, for though you are a tourist on your holiday, what if your heart should miss a few beats? What if a blood vessel in your neck should break? What if one of those people driving those brand-new cars filled with the wrong gas fails to pass safely while going uphill on a curve and you are in the car going in the opposite direction? Will you be comforted to know that the hospital is staffed with doctors that no actual Antiguan trusts; that Antiguans always say about the doctors, "I don't want them near me"; that Antiguans refer to them not as doctors but as "the three men" (there are three of them); that when the Minister of Health himself doesn't feel well he takes the first plane to New York to see a real doctor; that if any one of the ministers in government needs medical care he flies to New York to get it?

It's a good thing that you brought your own books with you, for you couldn't just go to the library and borrow some. Antigua used to have a splendid library, but in The Earthquake (everyone talks about it that way—The Earthquake; we Antiguans, for I am one, have a great sense of things, and the more meaningful the thing, the more meaningless we make it) the library building was damaged. This was in 1974, and soon after that a sign was placed on the front of the building saying, THIS BUILDING WAS DAMAGED IN THE EARTHQUAKE OF 1974. REPAIRS ARE PENDING. The sign hangs there, and hangs there more than a decade later, with its unfulfilled promise of repair, and you might see this as a sort of quaintness on the part of these islanders, these people descended from slaves—what a strange, unusual perception of time they have. REPAIRS ARE PENDING, and here it is many years later, but perhaps in a world that is twelve miles long and nine miles wide (the size of Antigua) twelve years and twelve minutes and twelve days are all the same. The library is one of those splendid old buildings from colonial times, and the sign telling of the repairs is a splendid old sign from colonial times. Not very long after The Earthquake Antigua got its independence from Britain, making Antigua a state in its own right, and Antiguans are so proud of this that each year, to mark the day, they go to church and thank God, a British God, for this. But you should not think of the confusion that must lie in all that and you must not think of the damaged library. You have brought your own books with you, and among them is one of those new books about economic history, one of those books explaining how the West (meaning Europe and North America after its conquest and settlement by

Europeans) got rich: the West got rich not from the free (free—in this case meaning got-for-nothing) and then undervalued labour, for generations, of the people
like me you see walking around you in Antigua but from the ingenuity of small
shopkeepers in Sheffield and Yorkshire and Lancashire, or wherever; and what a
great part the invention of the wristwatch played in it, for there was nothing noble-
minded men could not do when they discovered they could slap time on their
wrists just like that (isn't that the last straw; for not only did we have to suffer the
unspeakableness of slavery, but the satisfaction to be had from "We made you
bastards rich" is taken away, too), and so you needn't let that slightly funny feeling
you have from time to time about exploitation, oppression, domination develop
into full-fledged unease, discomfort; you could ruin your holiday. They are not
responsible for what you have; you owe them nothing; in fact, you did them a big
favour, and you can provide one hundred examples. For here you are now, passing
by Government House. And here you are now, passing by the Prime Minister's
Office and the Parliament Building, and overlooking these, with a splendid view of
St. John's Harbour, the American Embassy. If it were not for you, they would not
have Government House, and Prime Minister's Office, and Parliament Building
and embassy of powerful country. Now you are passing a mansion, an extraordinary house painted the colour of old cow dung, with more aerials and antennas
attached to it than you will see even at the American Embassy. The people who live
in this house are a merchant family who came to Antigua from the Middle East less
than twenty years ago. When this family first came to Antigua, they sold dry goods
door to door from suitcases they carried on their backs. Now they own a lot of
Antigua; they regularly lend money to the government, they build enormous (for
Antigua), ugly (for Antigua), concrete buildings in Antigua's capital, St. John's,
which the government then rents for huge sums of money; a member of their
family is the Antiguan Ambassador to Syria; Antiguans hate them. Not far from this
mansion is another mansion, the home of a drug smuggler. Everybody knows he's a
drug smuggler, and if just as you were driving by he stepped out of his door your
driver might point him out to you as the notorious person that he is, for this drug
smuggler is so rich people say he buys cars in tens—ten of this one, ten of that
one—and that he bought a house (another mansion) near Five Islands, contents
included, with cash he carried in a suitcase: three hundred and fifty thousand
American dollars, and, to the surprise of the seller of the house, lots of American
dollars were left over. Overlooking the drug smuggler's mansion is yet another
mansion, and leading up to it is the best paved road in all of Antigua—even better
than the road that was paved for the Queen's visit in 1985 (when the Queen came,
all the roads that she would travel on were paved anew, so that the Queen might
have been left with the impression that riding in a car in Antigua was a pleasant
experience). In this mansion lives a woman sophisticated people in Antigua call
Evita. She is a notorious woman. She's young and beautiful and the girlfriend of
somebody very high up in the government. Evita is notorious because her relationship with this high government official has made her the owner of boutiques and
property and given her a say in cabinet meetings, and all sorts of other privileges
such a relationship would bring a beautiful young woman.

Oh, but by now you are tired of all this looking, and you want to reach your   4
destination—your hotel, your room. You long to refresh yourself; you long to eat
some nice lobster, some nice local food. You take a bath, you brush your teeth. You
get dressed again; as you get dressed, you look out the window. That water—have
you ever seen anything like it? Far out, to the horizon, the colour of the water is
navy-blue; nearer, the water is the colour of the North American sky. From there
to the shore, the water is pale, silvery, clear, so clear that you can see its pinkish-
white sand bottom. Oh, what beauty! Oh, what beauty! You have never seen anything like this. You are so excited. You breathe shallow. You breathe deep. You see
a beautiful boy skimming the water, godlike, on a Windsurfer. You see an incredibly unattractive, fat, pastrylike-fleshed woman enjoying a walk on the beautiful
sand, with a man, an incredibly unattractive, fat, pastrylike-fleshed man; you see
the pleasure they're taking in their surroundings. Still standing, looking out the
window, you see yourself lying on the beach, enjoying the amazing sun (a sun so
powerful and yet so beautiful, the way it is always overhead as if on permanent
guard, ready to stamp out any cloud that dares to darken and so empty rain on you
and ruin your holiday; a sun that is your personal friend). You see yourself taking a
walk on that beach, you see yourself meeting new people (only they are new in a
very limited way, for they are people just like you). You see yourself eating some
delicious, locally grown food. You see yourself, you see yourself . . . You must not
wonder what exactly happened to the contents of your lavatory when you flushed
it. You must not wonder where your bathwater went when you pulled out the
stopper. You must not wonder what happened when you brushed your teeth. Oh,
it might all end up in the water you are thinking of taking a swim in; the contents of
your lavatory might, just might, graze gently against your ankle as you wade care-
free in the water, for you see, in Antigua, there is no proper sewage-disposal system. But the Caribbean Sea is very big and the Atlantic Ocean is even bigger; it
would amaze even you to know the number of black slaves this ocean has swallowed up. When you sit down to eat your delicious meal, it's better that you don't
know that most of what you are eating came off a plane from Miami. And before it
got on a plane in Miami, who knows where it came from? A good guess is that it
came from a place like Antigua first, where it was grown dirt-cheap, went to Miami, and came back. There is a world of something in this, but I can't go into it
right now.

The thing you have always suspected about yourself the minute you become a   5
tourist is true: A tourist is an ugly human being. You are not an ugly person all the
time; you are not an ugly person ordinarily; you are not an ugly person day to day.
From day to day, you are a nice person. From day to day, all the people who are
supposed to love you on the whole do. From day to day, as you walk down a busy
street in the large and modern and prosperous city in which you work and live,
dismayed, puzzled (a cliché, but only a cliché can explain you) at how alone you
feel in this crowd, how awful it is to go unnoticed, how awful it is to go unloved,
even as you are surrounded by more people than you could possibly get to know in
a lifetime that lasted for millennia, and then out of the corner of your eye you see

someone looking at you and absolute pleasure is written all over that person's face, and then you realise that you are not as revolting a presence as you think you are (for that look just told you so). And so, ordinarily, you are a nice person, an attractive person, a person capable of drawing to yourself the affection of other people (people just like you), a person at home in your own skin (sort of; I mean, in a way; I mean, your dismay and puzzlement are natural to you, because people like you just seem to be like that, and so many of the things people like you find admirable about yourselves—the things you think about, the things you think really define you—seem rooted in these feelings): a person at home in your own house (and all its nice house things), with its nice back yard (and its nice back-yard things), at home on your street, your church, in community activities, your job, at home with your family, your relatives, your friends—you are a whole person. But one day, when you are sitting somewhere, alone in that crowd, and that awful feeling of displacedness comes over you, and really, as an ordinary person you are not well equipped to look too far inward and set yourself aright, because being ordinary is already so taxing, and being ordinary takes all you have out of you, and though the words "I must get away" do not actually pass across your lips, you make a leap from being that nice blob just sitting like a boob in your amniotic sac of the modern experience to being a person visiting heaps of death and ruin and feeling alive and inspired at the sight of it; to being a person lying on some faraway beach, your stilled body stinking and glistening in the sand, looking like something first forgotten, then remembered, then not important enough to go back for; to being a person marvelling at the harmony (ordinarily, what you would say is the backwardness) and the union these other people (and they are other people) have with nature. And you look at the things they can do with a piece of ordinary cloth, the things they fashion out of cheap, vulgarly colored (to you) twine, the way they squat down over a hole they have made in the ground, the hole itself is something to marvel at, and since you are being an ugly person this ugly but joyful thought will swell inside you: their ancestors were not clever in the way yours were and not ruthless in the way yours were, for then would it not be you who would be in harmony with nature and backwards in that charming way? An ugly thing, that is what you are when you become a tourist, an ugly, empty thing, a stupid thing, a piece of rubbish pausing here and there to gaze at this and taste that, and it will never occur to you that the people who inhabit the place in which you have just paused cannot stand you, that behind their closed doors they laugh at your strangeness (you do not look the way they look); the physical sight of you does not please them; you have bad manners (it is their custom to eat their food with their hands; you try eating their way, you look silly; you try eating the way you always eat, you look silly); they do not like the way you speak (you have an accent); they collapse helpless from laughter, mimicking the way they imagine you must look as you carry out some everyday bodily function. They do not like you. *They do not like me!* That thought never actually occurs to you. Still, you feel a little uneasy. Still, you feel a little foolish. Still, you feel a little out of place. But the banality of your own life is very real to you; it drove you to this extreme, spending your days and your nights in the company of people who despise you, people you do not like really, people you would not want to have as your actual neighbour. And so you must devote yourself to puzzling out how much of what you are told is really, really true (Is ground-up bottle glass in peanut sauce really a delicacy around here, or will it do just what you think ground-up bottle glass will do? Is this rare, multicoloured, snout-mouthed fish really an aphrodisiac, or will it cause you to fall asleep permanently?). Oh, the hard work all of this is, and is it any wonder, then, that on your return home you feel the need of a long rest, so that you can recover from your life as a tourist?

That the native does not like the tourist is not hard to explain. For every native   6
of every place is a potential tourist, and every tourist is a native of somewhere. Every native everywhere lives a life of overwhelming and crushing banality and boredom and desperation and depression, and every deed, good and bad, is an attempt to forget this. Every native would like to find a way out, every native would like a rest, every native would like a tour. But some natives—most natives in the world—cannot go anywhere. They are too poor. They are too poor to go anywhere. They are too poor to escape the reality of their lives; and they are too poor to live properly in the place where they live, which is the very place you, the tourist, want to go—so when the natives see you, the tourist, they envy you, they envy your ability to leave your own banality and boredom, they envy your ability to turn their own banality and boredom into a source of pleasure for yourself.

Rhetorical Focus

1. Kincaid's most striking rhetorical device here is her use of the second person. That is, she addresses the tourist as "you." Is this technique effective? Why or why not? Cite particular sentences in the text.
2. Kincaid organizes most of her text by following the tourist's movements on the island. What are the advantages of this strategy? What, if any, are the disadvantages?
3. Identify some places where Kincaid describes the tourist's thoughts with words that the tourist might indeed use. Then identify some places where she describes the tourist's thoughts with words that the tourist would probably *not* use. Should Kincaid have stayed with one or the other technique? Why or why not?

Thematic Focus

1. Did Kincaid make you laugh? Why or why not?
2. Throughout her text, Kincaid contrasts the perspectives of tourist and native. Do her criticisms of the tourist seem fair to you? To what extent does she criticize Antiguans?
3. On the basis of Kincaid's text, how would you characterize the relationship between America and Antigua?

Report from the Bahamas

June Jordan

Born in Harlem in 1936, June Jordan was trained as a city planner. One of her mentors was Buckminster Fuller, inventor of the geodesic dome. Currently, she is a professor of Afro-American studies and women's studies at the University of California at Berkeley. Previously she taught at City College of the City University of New York, Sarah Lawrence College, Yale University, and the State University of New York at Stony Brook. Chiefly known for her volumes of poetry, she has also written plays, biographies, and two volumes of essays, *Civil Wars* (1981) and *On Call* (1985). "Report from the Bahamas" appears in *On Call*. The essay originated as a keynote address to the New England Women's Studies Association Conference in 1982, and it also appeared in the November 1982 issue of *Ms.* magazine. As in many of her essays, Jordan here intensely describes her personal experiences while addressing issues not only of race and culture but also of gender and class.

Reflections Before Reading

Here, as her title indicates, the African-American writer June Jordan describes her visit to the Bahamas. Have you seen commercials and print advertisements for this area, or for roughly similar tourist places such as Jamaica and Antigua? If so, what images are used to advertise them? Now that you have read Kincaid's text about Antigua, what do you hope tourists visiting a similar place will be sensitive to? Do you think an African-American tourist there would pay attention to things that a white tourist would not? If so, what sorts of things?

I am staying in a hotel that calls itself The Sheraton British Colonial. One of the photographs advertising the place displays a middle-aged Black man in a waiter's tuxedo, smiling. What intrigues me most about the picture is just this: while the Black man bears a tray full of "colorful" drinks above his left shoulder, both of his feet, shoes and trouserlegs, up to ten inches above his ankles, stand in the also "colorful" Caribbean salt water. He is so delighted to serve you he will wade into the water to bring you Banana Daquiris while you float! More precisely, he will wade into the water, fully clothed, oblivious to the ruin of his shoes, his trousers, his health, and he will do it with a smile.

I am in the Bahamas. On the phone in my room, a spinning complement of plastic pages offers handy index clues such as CAR RENTAL and CASINOS. A message from the Ministry of Tourism appears among these travellers tips. Opening with a paragraph of "WELCOME," the message then proceeds to "A PAGE OF HISTORY," which reads as follows:

> New World History begins on the same day that modern Bahamian history begins—October 12, 1492. That's when Columbus stepped ashore—British influence came first with the Eleutherian Adventurers of 1647—After the Revolutions, American Loyalists fled from the newly independent states and settled in the Bahamas. Confederate blockade-runners used the island as a haven during the War between the States, and after the War, a number of Southerners moved to the Bahamas . . .

There it is again. Something proclaims itself a legitimate history and all it does is track white Mr. Columbus to the British Eleutherians through the Confederate Southerners as they barge into New World surf, land on New World turf, and nobody saying one word about the Bahamian people, the Black peoples, to whom the only thing new in their island world was this weird succession of crude intruders and its colonial consequences.

This is my consciousness of race as I unpack my bathing suit in the Sheraton British Colonial. Neither this hotel nor the British nor the long ago Italians nor the white Delta airline pilots belong here, of course. And every time I look at the photograph of that fool standing in the water with his shoes on I'm about to have a West Indian fit, even though I know he's no fool; he's a middle-aged Black man who needs a job and this is his job—pretending himself a servile ancillary to the pleasures of the rich. (Compared to his options in life, I am a rich woman. Compared to most of the Black Americans arriving for this Easter weekend on a three nights four days' deal of bargain rates, the middleaged waiter is a poor Black man.)

We will jostle along with the other (white) visitors and join them in the tee shirt shops or, laughing together, learn ruthless rules of negotiation as we, Black Americans as well as white, argue down the price of handwoven goods at the nearby straw market while the merchants, frequently toothless Black women seated on the concrete in their only presentable dress, humble themselves to our careless games:

"Yes? You like it? Eight dollar."

"Five."

"I give it to you. Seven."

And so it continues, this weird succession of crude intruders that, now, includes me and my brothers and my sisters from the North.

This is my consciousness of class as I try to decide how much money I can spend on Bahamian gifts for my family back in Brooklyn. No matter that these other Black women incessantly weave words and flowers into the straw hats and bags piled beside them on the burning dusty street. No matter that these other Black women must work their sense of beauty into these things that we will take away as cheaply as we dare, or they will do without food.

We are not white, after all. The budget is limited. And we are harmlessly   10 killing time between the poolside rum punch and "The Native Show on the Patio" that will play tonight outside the hotel restaurant.

This is my consciousness of race and class and gender identity as I notice the   11 fixed relations between these other Black women and myself. They sell and I buy or I don't. They risk not eating. I risk going broke on my first vacation afternoon.

We are not particularly women anymore; we are parties to a transaction de-   12 signed to set us against each other.

"Olive" is the name of the Black woman who cleans my hotel room. On my   13 way to the beach I am wondering what "Olive" would say if I told her why I chose The Sheraton British Colonial; if I told her I wanted to swim. I wanted to sleep. I did not want to be harassed by the middleaged waiter, or his nephew. I did not want to be raped by anybody (white or Black) at all and I calculated that my safety as a Black woman alone would best be assured by a multinational hotel corpora-tion. In my experience, the big guys take customer complaints more seriously than the little ones. I would suppose that's one reason why they're big; they don't like to lose money anymore than I like to be bothered when I'm trying to read a god-damned book underneath a palm tree I paid $264 to get next to. A Black woman seeking refuge in a multinational corporation may seem like a contradiction to some, but there you are. In this case it's a coincidence of entirely different self-interests: Sheraton/cash = June Jordan's short run safety.

Anyway, I'm pretty sure "Olive" would look at me as though I came from   14 someplace as far away as Brooklyn. Then she'd probably allow herself one indig-nant query before righteously removing her vacuum cleaner from my room; "and why in the first place you come down you without your husband?"

I cannot imagine how I would begin to answer her.   15

My "rights" and my "freedom" and my "desire" and a slew of other New World   16 values; what would they sound like to this Black woman described on the card atop my hotel bureau as "Olive the Maid"? "Olive" is older than I am and I may smoke a cigarette while she changes the sheets on my bed. Whose rights? Whose freedom? Whose desire?

And why should she give a shit about mine unless I do something, for real,   17 about hers?

It happens that the book that I finished reading under a palm tree earlier   18 today was the novel, *The Bread Givers,* by Anzia Yezierska. Definitely autobio-graphical, Yezierska lays out the difficulties of being both female and "a person" inside a traditional Jewish family at the start of the 20th century. That any Jewish woman became anything more than the abused servant of her father or her hus-band is really an improbable piece of news. Yet Yezierska managed such an un-likely outcome for her own life. In *The Bread Givers,* the heroine also manages an important, although partial, escape from traditional Jewish female destiny. And in the unpardonable, despotic father, the Talmudic scholar of that Jewish family, did I not see my own and hate him twice, again? When the heroine, the young Jewish child, wanders the streets with a filthy pail she borrows to sell herring in order to raise the ghetto rent and when she cries, "Nothing was before me but the hunger in our house, and no bread for the next meal if I didn't sell the herring. No longer like a fire engine, but like a houseful of hungry mouths my heart cried, 'herring— herring! Two cents apiece!' " who would doubt the ease, the sisterhood of conversation possible between that white girl and the Black women selling straw bags on the streets of paradise because they do not want to die? And is it not obvious that the wife of that Talmudic scholar and "Olive," who cleans my room here at the hotel, have more in common than I can claim with either one of them?

This is my consciousness of race and class and gender identity as I collect wet   19
towels, sunglasses, wristwatch, and head towards a shower.

I am thinking about the boy who loaned this novel to me. He's white and he's   20
Jewish and he's pursuing an independent study project with me, at the State University where I teach whether or not I feel like it, where I teach without stint because, like the waiter, I am no fool. It's my job and either I work or I do without everything you need money to buy. The boy loaned me the novel because he thought I'd be interested to know how a Jewish-American writer used English so that the syntax, and therefore the cultural habits of mind expressed by the Yiddish language, could survive translation. He did this because he wanted to create another connection between us on the basis of language, between his knowledge/his love of Yiddish and my knowledge/my love of Black English.

He has been right about the forceful survival of the Yiddish. And I had be-   21
come excited by this further evidence of the written voice of spoken language protected from the monodrone of "standard" English, and so we had grown closer on this account. But then our talk shifted to student affairs more generally, and I had learned that this student does not care one way or the other about currently jeopardized Federal Student Loan Programs because, as he explained it to me, they do not affect him. He does not need financial help outside his family. My own son, however, is Black. And I am the only family help available to him and that means, if Reagan succeeds in eliminating Federal programs to aid minority students, he will have to forget about furthering his studies, or he or I or both of us will have to hit the numbers pretty big. For these reasons of difference, the student and I had moved away from each other, even while we continued to talk.

My consciousness turned to race, again, and class.   22

Sitting in the same chair as the boy, several weeks ago, a graduate student   23
came to discuss her grade. I praised the excellence of her final paper; indeed it had seemed to me an extraordinary pulling together of recent left brain/right brain research with the themes of transcendental poetry.

She told me that, for her part, she'd completed her reading of my political   24
essays. "You are so lucky!" she exclaimed.

"What do you mean by that?"   25
"You have a cause. You have a purpose to your life."   26
I looked carefully at this white woman; what was she really saying to me?   27
"What do you mean?" I repeated.   28
"Poverty. Police violence. Discrimination in general."   29
(Jesus Christ, I thought: Is that her idea of lucky?)   30

"And how about you?" I asked.   31

"Me?"   32

"Yeah, you. Don't you have a cause?"   33

"Me? I'm just a middle aged woman: a housewife and a mother. I'm a no-   34
body."

For a while, I made no response.   35

First of all, speaking of race and class and gender in one breath, what she said   36
meant that those lucky preoccupations of mine, from police violence to nuclear
wipe-out, were not shared. They were mine and not hers. But here she sat, friendly
as an old stuffed animal, beaming good will or more "luck" in my direction.

In the second place, what this white woman said to me meant that she did not   37
believe she was "a person" precisely because she had fulfilled the traditional female functions revered by the father of that Jewish immigrant, Anzia Yezierska.
And the woman in front of me was not a Jew. That was not the connection. The link
was strictly female. Nevertheless, how should that woman and I, another female
connect, beyond this bizarre exchange?

If she believed me lucky to have regular hurdles of discrimination then why   38
shouldn't I insist that she's lucky to be a middle class white Wasp female who lives
in such well-sanctioned and normative comfort that she even has the luxury to
deny the power of the privileges that paralyze her life?

If she deserts me and "my cause" where we differ, if, for example, she aban-   39
dons me to "my" problems of race, then why should I support her in "her" problems of housewifely oblivion?

Recollection of this peculiar moment brings me to the shower in the bathroom   40
cleaned by "Olive." She reminds me of the usual Women's Studies curriculum
because it has nothing to do with her or her job: you won't find "Olive" listed
anywhere on the reading list. You will likewise seldom hear of Anzia Yezierska. But
yes, you will find, from Florence Nightingale to Adrienne Rich, a white procession
of independently well-to-do women writers. (Gertrude Stein/Virginia Woolf/Hilda
Doolittle are standard names among the "essential" women writers).

In other words, most of the women of the world—Black and First World and   41
white who work because we must—most of the women of the world persist far
from the heart of the usual Women's Studies syllabus.

Similarly, the typical Black History course will slide by the majority experience   42
it pretends to represent. For example, Mary McLeod Bethune will scarcely receive
as much attention as Nat Turner, even though Black women who bravely and effi-
ciently provided for the education of Black people hugely outnumber those few
Black men who led successful or doomed rebellions against slavery. In fact, Mary
McLeod Bethune may not receive even honorable mention because Black History
too often apes those ridiculous white history courses which produce such dangerous gibberish as The Sheraton British Colonial "history" of the Bahamas. Both
Black and white history courses exclude from their central consideration those
people who neither killed nor conquered anyone as the means to new identity,
those people who took care of every one of the people who wanted to become "a
person," those people who still take care of the life at issue: the ones who wash and
who feed and who teach and who diligently decorate straw hats and bags with all of
their historically unrequired gentle love: the women.

Oh the old rugged cross
on a hill far away
Well I cherish the old rugged cross

It's Good Friday in the Bahamas. Seventy-eight degrees in the shade. Except for
Sheraton territory, everything's closed.

It so happens that for truly secular reasons I've been fasting for three days. My   43
hunger has now reached nearly violent proportions. In the hotel sandwich shop,
the Black woman handling the counter complains about the tourists; why isn't the
shop closed and why don't the tourists stop eating for once in their lives. I'm fam-
ished and I order chicken salad and cottage cheese and lettuce and tomato and a
hard boiled egg and a hot cross bun and apple juice.

She eyes me with disgust.   44

To be sure, the timing of my stomach offends her serious religious practices.   45
Neither one of us apologizes to the other. She seasons the chicken salad to the
peppery max while I listen to the loud radio gospel she plays to console herself. It's
a country Black version of "The Old Rugged Cross."

As I heave much chicken into my mouth tears start. It's not the pepper. I am,   46
after all, a West Indian daughter. It's the Good Friday music that dominates the
humid atmosphere.

Well I cherish the old rugged cross

And I am back, faster than a 747, in Brooklyn, in the home of my parents where we
are wondering, as we do every year, if the sky will darken until Christ has been
buried in the tomb. The sky should darken if God is in His heavens. And then,
around 3 P.M., at the conclusion of our mournful church service at the neighborhood St. Phillips, and even while we dumbly stare at the black cloth covering the
gold altar and the slender unlit candles, the sun should return through the high
gothic windows and vindicate our waiting faith that the Lord will rise again, on
Easter.

How I used to bow my head at the very name of Jesus: ecstatic to abase myself   47
in deference to His majesty.

My mouth is full of salad. I can't seem to eat quickly enough. I can't think how   48
I should lessen the offense of my appetite. The other Black woman on the prem-
ises, the one who disapprovingly prepared this very tasty break from my fast,
makes no remark. She is no fool. This is a job that she needs. I suppose she notices
that at least I included a hot cross bun among my edibles. That's something in my
favor. I decide that's enough.

I am suddenly eager to walk off the food. Up a fairly steep hill I walk without   49
hurrying. Through the pastel desolation of the little town, the road brings me to a
confectionary pink and white plantation house. At the gates, an unnecessarily large
statue of Christopher Columbus faces me down, or tries to. His hand is fisted to
one hip. I look back at him, laugh without deference, and turn left.

It's time to pack it up. Catch my plane. I scan the hotel room for things not to   50
forget. There's that white report card on the bureau.

"Dear Guests:" it says, under the name "Olive." I am your maid for the day.   51
Please rate me: Excellent. Good. Average. Poor. Thank you."

I tuck this momento from the Sheraton British Colonial into my notebook.   52
How would "Olive" rate *me?* What would it mean for us to seem "good" to each
other? What would that rating require?

But I am hastening to leave. Neither turtle soup nor kidney pie nor any conch   53
shell delight shall delay my departure. I have rested, here, in the Bahamas, and I'm
ready to return to my usual job, my usual work. But the skin on my body has
changed and so has my mind. On the Delta flight home I realize I am burning up,
indeed.

So far as I can see, the usual race and class concepts of connection, or gender   54
assumptions of unity, do not apply very well. I doubt that they ever did. Otherwise
why would Black folks forever bemoan our lack of solidarity when the deal turns
real. And if unity on the basis of sexual oppression is something natural, then why
do we women, the majority people on the planet, still have a problem?

The plane's ready for takeoff. I fasten my seatbelt and let the tumult inside my   55
head run free. Yes: race and class and gender remain as real as the weather. But
what they must mean about the contact between two individuals is less obvious
and, like the weather, not predictable.

And when these factors of race and class and gender absolutely collapse is   56
whenever you try to use them as automatic concepts of connection. They may
serve well as indicators of commonly felt conflict, but as elements of connection
they seem about as reliable as precipitation probability for the day after the night
before the day.

It occurs to me that much organizational grief could be avoided if people un-   57
derstood that partnership in misery does not necessarily provide for partnership
for change: *When we get the monsters off our backs all of us may want to run in
very different directions.*

And not only that: even though both "Olive" and "I" live inside a conflict nei-   58
ther one of us created, and even though both of us therefore hurt inside that conflict, I may be one of the monsters she needs to eliminate from her universe and, in
a sense, she may be one of the monsters in mine.

I am reaching for the words to describe the difference between a common   59
identity that has been imposed and the individual identity any one of us will
choose, once she gains that chance.

That difference is the one that keeps us stupid in the face of new, specific   60
information about somebody else with whom we are supposed to have a connection because a third party, hostile to both of us, has worked it so that the two of us,
like it or not, share a common enemy. *What happens beyond the idea of that enemy
and beyond the consequences of that enemy?*

I am saying that the ultimate connection cannot be the enemy. The ultimate   61
connection must be the need that we find between us. It is not only who you are, in
other words, but what we can do for each other that will determine the connection.

I am flying back to my job. I have been teaching contemporary women's po-   62
etry this semester. One quandary I have set myself to explore with my students is
the one of taking responsibility without power. We had been wrestling ideas to the
floor for several sessions when a young Black woman, a South African, asked me
for help, after class.

Sokutu told me she was "in a trance" and that she'd been unable to eat for two weeks.   63

"What's going on?" I asked her, even as my eyes startled at her trembling and emaciated appearance.   64

"My husband. He drinks all the time. He beats me up. I go to the hospital. I can't eat. I don't know what/anything."   65

In my office, she described her situation. I did not dare to let her sense my fear and horror. She was dragging about, hour by hour, in dread. Her husband, a young Black South African, was drinking himself into more and more deadly violence against her.   66

Sokutu told me how she could keep nothing down. She weighed 90 lbs. at the outside, as she spoke to me. She'd already been hospitalized as a result of her husband's battering rage.   67

I knew both of them because I had organized a campus group to aid the liberation struggles of Southern Africa.   68

Nausea rose in my throat. What about this presumable connection: this husband and this wife fled from that homeland of hatred against them, and now what? He was destroying himself. If not stopped, he would certainly murder his wife.   69

She needed a doctor, right away. It was a medical emergency. She needed protection. It was a security crisis. She needed refuge for battered wives and personal therapy and legal counsel. She needed a friend.   70

I got on the phone and called every number in the campus directory that I could imagine might prove helpful. Nothing worked. There were no institutional resources designed to meet her enormous, multifaceted, and ordinary woman's need.   71

I called various students. I asked the Chairperson of the English Department for advice. I asked everyone for help.   72

Finally, another one of my students, Cathy, a young Irish woman active in campus IRA activities, responded. She asked for further details. I gave them to her.   73

"Her husband," Cathy told me, "is an alcoholic. You have to understand about alcoholics. It's not the same as anything else. And it's a disease you can't treat any old way.   74

I listened, fearfully. Did this mean there was nothing we could do?   75

"That's not what I'm saying," she said. "But you have to keep the alcoholic part of the thing central in everybody's mind, otherwise her husband will kill her. Or he'll kill himself."   76

She spoke calmly, I felt there was nothing to do but to assume she knew what she was talking about.   77

"Will you come with me?" I asked her, after a silence. "Will you come with me and help us figure out what to do next?"   78

Cathy said she would but that she felt shy: Sokutu comes from South Africa. What would she think about Cathy?   79

"I don't know," I said. "But let's go."   80

We left to find a dormitory room for the young battered wife.   81

It was late, now, and dark outside.   82

On Cathy's VW that I followed behind with my own car, was the sticker that   83
reads BOBBY SANDS FREE AT LAST. My eyes blurred as I read and reread the
words. This was another connection: Bobby Sands and Martin Luther King Jr. and
who would believe it? I would not have believed it; I grew up terrorized by Irish
kids who introduced me to the word "nigga."

And here I was following an Irish woman to the room of a Black South African.   84
We were going to that room to try to save a life together.

When we reached the little room, we found ourselves awkward and large.   85
Sokutu attempted to treat us with utmost courtesy, as though we were honored
guests. She seemed surprised by Cathy, but mostly Sokutu was flushed with relief
and joy because we were there, with her.

I did not know how we should ever terminate her heartfelt courtesies and   86
address, directly, the reason for our visit: her starvation and her extreme physical
danger.

Finally, Cathy sat on the floor and reached out her hands to Sokutu.   87

"I'm here," she said quietly, "Because June has told me what has happened to   88
you. And I know what it is. Your husband is an alcoholic. He has a disease. I know
what it is. My father was an alcoholic. He killed himself. He almost killed my
mother. I want to be your friend."

"Oh," was the only small sound that escaped from Sokutu's mouth. And then   89
she embraced the other student. And then everything changed and I watched all of
this happen so I know that this happened: this connection.

And after we called the police and exchanged phone numbers and plans were   90
made for the night and for the next morning, the young South African woman
walked down the dormitory hallway, saying goodbye and saying thank you to us.

I walked behind them, the young Irish woman and the young South African,   91
and I saw them walking as sisters walk, hugging each other, and whispering and
sure of each other and I felt how it was not who they were but what they both know
and what they were both preparing to do about what they know that was going to
make them both free at last.

And I look out the windows of the plane and I see clouds that will not kill me   92
and I know that someday soon other clouds may erupt to kill us all.

And I tell the stewardess No thanks to the cocktails she offers me. But I look   93
about the cabin at the hundred strangers drinking as they fly and I think even here
and even now I must make the connection real between me and these strangers
everywhere before those other clouds unify this ragged bunch of us, too late.

Rhetorical Focus

1. Recall that even though this essay deals with relations among races and
   cultures, Jordan first presented it as an address to a conference of scholars
   in women's studies. In what ways, if any, might this audience have influenced her overall purpose? Where in the text do you think she might be
   taking this audience especially into account?
2. Jordan extensively uses repetition in this essay. Select a few examples and
   explain whether they are effective.

3. This essay does not follow strict chronological order; it goes back and forth in time. For instance, it climaxes with the meeting between the South African and Irish women, even though the incident occurred before Jordan left for the Bahamas. Given that the incident did occur earlier, why do you think Jordan chooses to place it near the end of her essay? Do you find her text and Kincaid's equally coherent in structure, or is one text's organization easier to follow? Explain.

Thematic Focus

1. Jordan's "report from the Bahamas" also reports situations in the United States. What connections does Jordan draw between her experiences in the two countries? Do these connections seem plausible to you? Why or why not?
2. What do you infer from Jordan's practice of capitalizing the word "Black" and putting the word "white" in lower case? Taken together, what are Jordan's and Kincaid's criticisms of the way that white people see history?
3. Does this essay leave you optimistic or pessimistic about the ability of people to connect with each other across social barriers? Compare it to Kincaid's text in this respect. Support your answer by referring to details of each.

Suggestions for Writing

1. Kincaid's hypothetical tourist does not worry much about the Antiguans' lives. As a tourist in the Bahamas, Jordan does feel guilty at times. Choose one of these tourists and explain whether you think the person's attitude makes sense. Give reasons for your belief, referring to specific details in the text you are examining.
2. Describe an experience you had in which you recognized the power that tourists can have over inhabitants of a place. With whom did your sympathies lie? Why did you feel this way?
3. Look again at the scene in Jordan's essay where the South African and Irish women connected with each other; then, describe a specific occasion when you saw very different people manage to connect in some sense. Explain how these people seemed different, what you think enabled them to connect, and what form their connection took.

THE DEBATE OVER AFFIRMATIVE ACTION

Trying to promote satisfactory relations among races and cultures, Americans have more and more found themselves arguing over just what laws and policies to implement. In particular, they increasingly debate the wisdom of affirmative action. Obviously, government should ensure that historically oppressed groups no longer suffer discrimination, but less obvious is what employers, schools, and other organizations should now do to affirm civil rights. Many people have called for hiring and admissions procedures that redress past injustices against minorities and white women by giving them special consideration. Many other people have insisted that such procedures cannot take race and gender into account if they are to be truly fair. Even groups who apparently stand to gain from affirmative action disagree over aspects of it. Indeed, you can learn a great deal about the complexities of this topic by examining the ways that intended beneficiaries of affirmative action have debated its merits.

We end this unit by featuring three African-American writers with different views on affirmative action. First, Shelby Steele questions its current forms, claiming that it does little to help minorities progress and even threatens their self-image. Next, Roger Wilkins defends affirmative action, suggesting that minorities still need it to prosper in a society still dominated by whites. Finally, William Raspberry seeks to distinguish the various uses and abuses of affirmative action, trying to determine when it is fair and when it is not. As you work through the arguments of these authors, you will undoubtedly find yourself agreeing with some statements and disagreeing with others. Try, however, to determine the range of issues that any argument about affirmative action must acknowledge if it is ultimately to persuade the range of audiences that make up American society.

Affirmative Action: The Price of Preference

Shelby Steele

A native of Chicago, Shelby Steele (b. 1946) earned an undergraduate degree in political science at Coe College in Cedar Rapids, Iowa, a master's degree in sociology at Southern Illinois University, and a doctorate in English at the University of Utah. Presently, he teaches English at San José State University in California. Recently, Steele has emerged as a major commentator on American race relations, not only because of his eloquence but also because his stance is distinctly conservative among African-Americans who have written on this subject. Besides hosting a public broadcasting television documentary on the Bensonhurst incident (see the essays by Marianna De Marco Torgovnick and Barbara Grizzuti Harrison in "Places and Communities"), he has contributed to such journals as *The American Scholar, Harper's,* and *The New York Times Magazine,* where the following essay appeared on May 13, 1990. It is collected along with others of his essays in his best-selling 1990 book *The Content of Our Character,* which won the National Book Critics Circle Award.

Reflections Before Reading

Have you had any experience with affirmative action? If so, what? What issues, events, and social trends do you think people debating affirmative action might bring up? Do you have a position on anything to do with affirmative action? If so, what? Note Steele's subtitle. What might he mean by that?

In a few short years, when my two children will be applying to college, the affirma-   1
tive action policies by which most universities offer black students some form of preferential treatment will present me with a dilemma. I am a middle-class black, a college professor, far from wealthy, but also well-removed from the kind of deprivation that would qualify my children for the label "disadvantaged." Both of them have endured racial insensitivity from whites. They have been called names, have suffered slights, and have experienced firsthand the peculiar malevolence that racism brings out in people. Yet, they have never experienced racial discrimination, have never been stopped by their race on any path they have chosen to follow. Still, their society now tells them that if they will only designate themselves as black on their college applications, they will likely do better in the college lottery than if they conceal this fact. I think there is something of a Faustian bargain in this.

Of course, many blacks and a considerable number of whites would say that I   2
was sanctimoniously making affirmative action into a test of character. They would say that this small preference is the meagerest recompense for centuries of unrelieved oppression. And to these arguments other very obvious facts must be added. In America, many marginally competent or flatly incompetent whites are hired everyday—some because their white skin suits the conscious or unconscious racial preference of their employer. The white children of alumni are often grandfathered into elite universities in what can only be seen as a residual benefit of historic white privilege. Worse, white incompetence is always an individual matter, while for blacks it is often confirmation of ugly stereotypes. The Peter Principle was not conceived with only blacks in mind. Given that unfairness cuts both ways, doesn't it only balance the scales of history that my children now receive a slight preference over whites? Doesn't this repay, in a small way, the systematic denial under which their grandfather lived out his days?

So, in theory, affirmative action certainly has all the moral symmetry that fair-   3
ness requires—the injustice of historical and even contemporary white advantage

is offset with black advantage; preference replaces prejudice, inclusion answers exclusion. It is reformist and corrective, even repentent and redemptive. And I would never sneer at these good intentions. Born in the late forties in Chicago, I started my education (a charitable term in this case) in a segregated school and suffered all the indignities that come to blacks in a segregated society. My father, born in the South, only made it to the third grade before the white man's fields took permanent priority over his formal education. And though he educated himself into an advanced reader with an almost professional authority, he could only drive a truck for a living and never earned more than ninety dollars a week in his entire life. So yes, it is crucial to my sense of citizenship, to my ability to identify with the spirit and the interests of America, to know that this country, however imperfectly, recognizes its past sins and wishes to correct them.

Yet good intentions, because of the opportunity for innocence they offer us,   4
are very seductive and can blind us to the effects they generate when implemented. In our society, affirmative action is, among other things, a testament to white goodwill and to black power, and in the midst of these heavy investments, its effects can be hard to see. But after twenty years of implementation, I think affirmative action has shown itself to be more bad than good and that blacks—whom I will focus on in this essay—now stand to lose more from it than they gain.

In talking with affirmative action administrators and with blacks and whites in   5
general, it is clear that supporters of affirmative action focus on its good intentions while detractors emphasize its negative effects. Proponents talk about "diversity" and "pluralism"; opponents speak of "reverse discrimination," the unfairness of quotas and set-asides. It was virtually impossible to find people outside either camp. The closest I came was a white male manager at a large computer company who said, "I think it amounts to reverse discrimination, but I'll put up with a little of that for a little more diversity." I'll live with a little of the effect to gain a little of the intention, he seemed to be saying. But this only makes him a halfhearted supporter of affirmative action. I think many people who don't really like affirmative action support it to one degree or another anyway.

I believe they do this because of what happened to white and black Americans   6
in the crucible of the sixties when whites were confronted with their racial guilt and blacks tasted their first real power. In this stormy time white absolution and black power coalesced into virtual mandates for society. Affirmative action became a meeting ground for these mandates in the law, and in the late sixties and early seventies it underwent a remarkable escalation of its mission from simple anti-discrimination enforcement to social engineering by means of quotas, goals, time-tables, set-asides and other forms of preferential treatment.

Legally, this was achieved through a series of executive orders and EEOC   7
guidelines that allowed racial imbalances in the workplace to stand as proof of racial discrimination. Once it could be assumed that discrimination explained racial imbalances, it became easy to justify group remedies to presumed discrimination, rather than the normal case-by-case redress for proven discrimination. Preferential treatment through quotas, goals, and so on is designed to correct imbalances based on the assumption that they always indicate discrimination. This expansion of what constitutes discrimination allowed affirmative action to escalate

into the business of social engineering in the name of anti-discrimination, to push society toward statistically proportionate racial representation, without any obligation of proving actual discrimination.

What accounted for this shift, I believe, was the white mandate to achieve a   8 new racial innocence and the black mandate to gain power. Even though blacks had made great advances during the sixties without quotas, these mandates, which came to a head in the very late sixties, could no longer be satisfied by anything less than racial preferences. I don't think these mandates in themselves were wrong, since whites clearly needed to do better by blacks and blacks needed more real power in society. But, as they came together in affirmative action, their effect was to distort our understanding of racial discrimination in a way that allowed us to offer the remediation of preference on the basis of mere color rather than actual injury. By making black the color of preference, these mandates have reburdened society with the very marriage of color and preference (in reverse) that we set out to eradicate. The old sin is reaffirmed in a new guise.

But the essential problem with this form of affirmative action is the way it   9 leaps over the hard business of developing a formerly oppressed people to the point where they can achieve proportionate representation on their own (given equal opportunity) and goes straight for the proportionate representation. This may satisfy some whites of their innocence and some blacks of their power, but it does very little to truly uplift blacks.

A white female affirmative action officer at an Ivy League university told me   10 what many supporters of affirmative action now say: "We're after diversity. We ideally want a student body where racial and ethnic groups are represented according to their proportion in society." When affirmative action escalated into social engineering, diversity became a golden word. It grants whites an egalitarian fairness (innocence) and blacks an entitlement to proportionate representation (power). *Diversity* is a term that applies democratic principles to races and cultures rather than to citizens, despite the fact that there is nothing to indicate that real diversity is the same thing as proportionate representation. Too often the result of this on campuses (for example) has been a democracy of colors rather than of people, an artificial diversity that gives the appearance of an educational parity between black and white students that has not yet been achieved in reality. Here again, racial preferences allow society to leapfrog over the difficult problem of developing blacks to parity with whites and into a cosmetic diversity that covers the blemish of disparity—a full six years after admission, only about 26 percent of black students graduate from college.

Racial representation is not the same thing as racial development, yet affirma-   11 tive action fosters a confusion of these very different needs. Representation can be manufactured; development is always hard-earned. However, it is the music of innocence and power that we hear in affirmative action that causes us to cling to it and to its distracting emphasis on representation. The fact is that after twenty years of racial preferences, the gap between white and black median income is greater than it was in the seventies. None of this is to say that blacks don't need policies that ensure our right to equal opportunity, but what we need more is the development that will let us take advantage of society's efforts to include us.

I think that one of the most troubling effects of racial preferences for blacks is   12
a kind of demoralization, or put another way, an enlargement of self-doubt. Under
affirmative action the quality that earns us preferential treatment is an implied
inferiority. However this inferiority is explained—and it is easily enough explained
by the myriad deprivations that grew out of our oppression—it is still inferiority.
There are explanations, and then there is the fact. And the fact must be borne by
the individual as a condition apart from the explanation, apart even from the fact
that others like himself also bear this condition. In integrated situations where
blacks must compete with whites who may be better prepared, these explanations
may quickly wear thin and expose the individual to racial as well as personal self-
doubt.

All of this is compounded by the cultural myth of black inferiority that blacks   13
have always lived with. What this means in practical terms is that when blacks
deliver themselves into integrated situations, they encounter a nasty little reflex in
whites, a mindless, atavistic reflex that responds to the color black with alarm.
Attributions may follow this alarm if the white cares to indulge them, and if they
do, they will most likely be negative—one such attribution is intellectual ineptness.
I think this reflex and the attributions that may follow it embarrass most whites
today, therefore, it is usually quickly repressed. Nevertheless, on an equally atavistic level, the black will be aware of the reflex his color triggers and will feel a stab of
horror at seeing himself reflected in this way. He, too, will do a quick repression,
but a lifetime of such stabbings is what constitutes his inner realm of racial doubt.

The effects of this may be a subject for another essay. The point here is that   14
the implication of inferiority that racial preferences engender in both the white
and black mind expands rather than contracts this doubt. Even when the black
sees no implication of inferiority in racial preferences, he knows that whites do, so
that—consciously or unconsciously—the result is virtually the same. The effect of
preferential treatment—the lowering of normal standards to increase black representation—puts blacks at war with an expanded realm of debilitating doubt, so that
the doubt itself becomes an unrecognized preoccupation that undermines their
ability to perform, especially in integrated situations. On largely white campuses,
blacks are five times more likely to drop out than whites. Preferential treatment,
no matter how it is justified in the light of day, subjects blacks to a midnight of
self-doubt, and so often transforms their advantage into a revolving door.

Another liability of affirmative action comes from the fact that it indirectly   15
encourages blacks to exploit their own past victimization as a source of power and
privilege. Victimization, like implied inferiority, is what justifies preference, so that
to receive the benefits of preferential treatment one must, to some extent, become
invested in the view of one's self as a victim. In this way, affirmative action nurtures
a victim-focused identity in blacks. The obvious irony here is that we become inadvertently invested in the very condition we are trying to overcome. Racial preferences send us the message that there is more power in our past suffering than our
present achievements—none of which could bring us a *preference* over others.

When power itself grows out of suffering, then blacks are encouraged to ex-   16
pand the boundaries of what qualifies as racial oppression, a situation that can lead
us to paint our victimization in vivid colors, even as we receive the benefits of

preference. The same corporations and institutions that give us preference are also seen as our oppressors. At Stanford University minority students—some of whom enjoy as much as $15,000 a year in financial aid—recently took over the president's office demanding, among other things, more financial aid. The power to be found in victimization, like any power, is intoxicating and can lend itself to the creation of a new class of super-victims who can feel the pea of victimization under twenty mattresses. Preferential treatment rewards us for being underdogs rather than for moving beyond that status—a misplacement of incentives that, along with its deepening of our doubt, is more a yoke than a spur.

But, I think, one of the worst prices that blacks pay for preference has to do   17 with an illusion. I saw this illusion at work recently in the mother of a middle-class black student who was going off to his first semester of college. "They owe us this, so don't think for a minute that you don't belong there." This is the logic by which many blacks, and some whites, justify affirmative action—it is something "owed," a form of reparation. But this logic overlooks a much harder and less digestible reality, that it is impossible to repay blacks living today for the historic suffering of the race. If all blacks were given a million dollars tomorrow morning it would not amount to a dime on the dollar of three centuries of oppression, nor would it obviate the residues of that oppression that we still carry today. The concept of historic reparation grows out of man's need to impose a degree of justice on the world that simply does not exist. Suffering can be endured and overcome, it cannot be repaid. Blacks cannot be repaid for the injustice done to the race, but we can be corrupted by society's guilty gestures of repayment.

Affirmative action is such a gesture. It tells us that racial preferences can do   18 for us what we cannot do for ourselves. The corruption here is in the hidden incentive *not* to do what we believe preferences will do. This is an incentive to be reliant on others just as we are struggling for self-reliance. And it keeps alive the illusion that we can find some deliverance in repayment. The hardest thing for any sufferer to accept is that his suffering excuses him from very little and never has enough currency to restore him. To think otherwise is to prolong the suffering.

Several blacks I spoke with said they were still in favor of affirmative action   19 because of the "subtle" discrimination blacks were subject to once on the job. One photojournalist said, "They have ways of ignoring you." A black female television producer said, "You can't file a lawsuit when your boss doesn't invite you to the insider meetings without ruining your career. So we still need affirmative action." Others mentioned the infamous "glass ceiling" through which blacks can see the top positions of authority but never reach them. But I don't think racial preferences are a protection against this subtle discrimination; I think they contribute to it.

In any workplace, racial preferences will always create two-tiered populations   20 composed of preferreds and unpreferreds. This division makes automatic a perception of enhanced competence for the unpreferreds and of questionable competence for the preferreds—the former earned his way, even though others were given preference, while the latter made it by color as much as by competence. Racial preferences implicitly mark whites with an exaggerated superiority just as they mark/blacks with an exaggerated inferiority. They not only reinforce America's oldest racial myth but, for blacks, they have the effect of stigmatizing the already stigmatized.

I think that much of the "subtle" discrimination that blacks talk about is often   21
(not always) discrimination against the stigma of questionable competence that affirmative action delivers to blacks. In this sense, preferences scapegoat the very people they seek to help. And it may be that at a certain level employers impose a glass ceiling, but this may not be against the race so much as against the race's reputation for having advanced by color as much as by competence. Affirmative action makes a glass ceiling virtually necessary as a protection against the corruptions of preferential treatment. This ceiling is the point at which corporations shift the emphasis from color to competency and stop playing the affirmative action game. Here preference backfires for blacks and becomes a taint that holds them back. Of course, one could argue that this taint, which is, after all, in the minds of whites, becomes nothing more than an excuse to discriminate against blacks. And certainly the result is the same in either case—blacks don't get past the glass ceiling. But this argument does not get around the fact that racial preferences now taint this color with a new theme of suspicion that makes it even more vulnerable to the impulse in others to discriminate. In this crucial yet gray area of perceived competence, preferences make whites look better than they are and blacks worse, while doing nothing whatever to stop the very real discrimination that blacks may encounter. I don't wish to justify the glass ceiling here, but only to suggest the very subtle ways that affirmative action revives rather than extinguishes the old rationalizations for racial discrimination.

In education, a revolving door; in employment, a glass ceiling.   22

I believe affirmative action is problematic in our society because it tries to   23
function like a social program. Rather than ask it to ensure equal opportunity we have demanded that it create parity between the races. But preferential treatment does not teach skills, or educate, or instill motivation. It only passes out entitlement by color, a situation that in my profession has created an unrealistically high demand for black professors. The social engineer's assumption is that this high demand will inspire more blacks to earn Ph.D.'s and join the profession. In fact, the number of blacks earning Ph.D.'s has declined in recent years. A Ph.D. must be developed from preschool on. He requires family and community support. He must acquire an entire system of values that enables him to work hard while delaying gratification. There are social programs, I believe, that can (and should) help blacks *develop* in all these areas, but entitlement by color is not a social program; it is a dubious reward for being black.

It now seems clear that the Supreme Court, in a series of recent decisions, is   24
moving away from racial preferences. It has disallowed preferences except in instances of "identified discrimination," eroded the precedent that statistical racial imbalances are *prima facie* evidence of discrimination, and in effect granted white males the right to challenge consent decrees that use preference to achieve racial balances in the workplace. One civil rights leader said, "Night has fallen on civil rights." But I am not so sure. The effect of these decisions is to protect the constitutional rights of everyone rather than take rights away from blacks. What they do take away from blacks is the special entitlement to more rights than others that

preferences always grant. Night has fallen on racial preferences, not on the fundamental rights of black Americans. The reason for this shift, I believe, is that the white mandate for absolution from past racial sins has weakened considerably during the eighties. Whites are now less willing to endure unfairness to themselves in order to grant special entitlements to blacks, even when these entitlements are justified in the name of past suffering. Yet the black mandate for more power in society has remained unchanged. And I think part of the anxiety that many blacks feel over these decisions has to do with the loss of black power they may signal. We had won a certain specialness and now we are losing it.

But the power we've lost by these decisions is really only the power that grows   25
out of our victimization—the power to claim special entitlements under the law because of past oppression. This is not a very substantial or reliable power, and it is important that we know this so we can focus more exclusively on the kind of development that will bring enduring power. There is talk now that Congress will pass new legislation to compensate for these new limits on affirmative action. If this happens, I hope that their focus will be on development and anti-discrimination rather than entitlement, on achieving racial parity rather than jerry-building racial diversity.

I would also like to see affirmative action go back to its original purpose of   26
enforcing equal opportunity—a purpose that in itself disallows racial preferences. We cannot be sure that the discriminatory impulse in America has yet been shamed into extinction, and I believe affirmative action can make its greatest contribution by providing a rigorous vigilance in this area. It can guard constitutional rather than racial rights, and help institutions evolve standards of merit and selection that are appropriate to the institution's needs yet as free of racial bias as possible (again, with the understanding that racial imbalances are not always an indication of racial bias). One of the most important things affirmative action can do is to define exactly what racial discrimination is and how it might manifest itself within a specific institution. The impulse to discriminate *is* subtle and cannot be ferreted out unless its many guises are made clear to people. Along with this there should be monitoring of institutions and heavy sanctions brought to bear when actual discrimination is found. This is the sort of affirmative action that America owes to blacks and to itself. It goes after the evil of discrimination itself, while preferences only sidestep the evil and grant entitlement to its *presumed* victims.

But if not preferences, then what? I think we need social policies that are   27
committed to two goals: the educational and economic development of disadvantaged people, regardless of race, and the eradication from our society—through close monitoring and severe sanctions—of racial, ethnic, or gender discrimination. Preferences will not deliver us to either of these goals, since they tend to benefit those who are not disadvantaged—middle-class white women and middle-class blacks—and attack one form of discrimination with another. Preferences are inexpensive and carry the glamour of good intentions—change the numbers and the good deed is done. To be against them is to be unkind. But I think the unkindest cut is to bestow on children like my own an undeserved advantage while neglecting the development of those disadvantaged children on the East Side of my city who will likely never be in a position to benefit from a preference. Give my children

fairness; give disadvantaged children a better shot at development—better elementary and secondary schools, job training, safer neighborhoods, better financial assistance for college, and so on. Fewer blacks go to college today than ten years ago; more black males of college age are in prison or under the control of the criminal justice system than in college. This despite racial preferences.

The mandates of black power and white absolution out of which preferences   28
emerged were not wrong in themselves. What was wrong was that both races focused more on the goals of these mandates than on the means to the goals. Blacks can have no real power without taking responsibility for their own educational and economic development. Whites can have no racial innocence without earning it by eradicating discrimination and helping the disadvantaged to develop. Because we ignored the means, the goals have not been reached, and the real work remains to be done.

Rhetorical Focus

1. Steele announces that his essay will focus on blacks. If he had focused on whites and mostly addressed himself to them, do you think he would have made different points? Why or why not?
2. What concessions does Steele make to advocates of affirmative action? Was it a bad rhetorical decision for him to make such concessions, or do they ultimately serve his argument? Explain.
3. Note where Steele refers to his own life, and where he quotes people with whom he has talked. Does this sort of material help his argument? Should he have brought it in more? Less? Explain.

Thematic Focus

1. Now that you have read Steele's essay, how do you explain his subtitle? What does he think *is* the price of preference, and who does he think pays the price?
2. What are the various reasons Steele gives for opposing current forms of affirmative action? What does he want American society to do instead of relying on it? Do you agree with him? Why or why not?
3. What criticisms does Steele make of white America? Do you these seem appropriate to you? Why or why not?

In Ivory Towers

Roger Wilkins

A long-time civil rights activist and commentator on American race relations, Roger Wilkins (b. 1932) earned undergraduate and law degrees at the University of Michigan. His many career activities have included serving as assistant attorney general of the United States (1966–1969), as program director at the Ford Foundation (1969–1972), as a member of *The Washington Post* editorial board (1972–1974), as urban affairs columnist and editorial board member for *The New York Times* (1974–1979), and currently as a professor of history and American culture at George Mason University in Fairfax, Virginia. Wilkins published his autobiography *A Man's Life* in 1982. He still contributes op-ed pieces to newspapers such as *The Washington Post* and writes a regular column for *Mother Jones,* a magazine with a leftist slant. "In Ivory Towers" appeared in its July/August 1990 issue.

Reflections Before Reading

What might an African-American writer defending affirmative action say? Think of how Steele's kind of argument might be challenged. What do you think people usually mean when they refer to colleges and universities as "ivory towers"? What might Wilkins mean? Do you think of your own school as in any sense an "ivory tower"? Why or why not?

Blacks are among those expressing second thoughts about affirmative action in college and university life these days. The first concern is expressed by a brilliant young black friend, who laments that despite his formidable intellectual accomplishments, people still judge him not as a splendid scholar, but only as a smart black. The second is a concern expressed by some black educators that students admitted under affirmative action programs may come to doubt their own capacities as a result. 1

These complaints proceed from the same idea: that the main thing to think about when considering affirmative action is the damage it does to black self-esteem—either because whites will doubt blacks' capacities, or because the remedy itself makes blacks doubt their own capacities. I understand this burden, having 2

"In Ivory Towers" by Roger Wilkins, MOTHER JONES, July/August 1990—Volume 15 Number 5. Reprinted with permission from MOTHER JONES magazine, © 1990, Foundation for National Progress.

carried part of it all my adult life, but the simple colloquial response I give to black faculty members and black students who express similar concerns to me is: "You're upset because you think *affirmative action* makes white folks look at you funny. Hell, white folks were looking at black folks funny long before affirmative action was invented. They been lookin' at black folks funny since 1619."

The founding tenet of racism is that blacks are inferior, particularly when it comes to intellectual capability. And an underpinning of racism has been an all-out cultural onslaught on the self-esteem of blacks, to transform them from assertive and self-sufficient human beings into dependents, mere extensions of the will of the whites who choose to use them. 3

Affirmative action, even weakly and spottily deployed, opens doors of opportunity that would otherwise be slammed tight. As a result, the country is better and stronger. It surely is one of the most effective antidotes to the widespread habit of undervaluing the capacities of minorities and women. It also serves as a counterbalance to the tendency to overvalue, as a recruitment tool, the effectiveness and fairness of old-boy networks. 4

But affirmative action did not magically erase racism. It simply pushed back the boundaries of the struggle a little bit, giving some of us better opportunities to fulfill our capacities, and higher perches from which to conduct our battles. Anyone who thinks there are no more battles to be fought, even on the highest battlements of the ivoriest of the ivory towers, simply doesn't understand America. 5

Whatever confusion I've had about such things was knocked out of me a long time ago. Almost everything that has happened to me since I was twenty-one has resulted from one sort of affirmative action or another. Thirty-seven years as the object of affirmative action in such places as the Department of Justice, the Ford Foundation, the *Washington Post* and the *New York Times* have given me a rich understanding of the endurance of U.S. racism. I have done battle and emerged with enough self-confidence to assert that all of the places that hired me because of affirmative action were better for having done so. 6

Nevertheless, I am sympathetic to the desire of my young black friend for the excellence of his mind to wash the color off his accomplishments. Unfortunately, even in 1990, color is not irrelevant in the United States at any level—and perhaps that is fortunate, for it maintains some fragmentary bond between my friend and poor black people who need his concern and strength. I am reminded, in this regard, of the wisdom embedded in an old joke that comes from deep in African-American culture. In this story, two old white men are rocking on a porch in a Southern town. Says the first, "Zeke, what do you call a black man with a Ph.D. who has just won the Nobel Prize in physics?" Replies Zeke, after a long pause and much contemplative rocking, "I calls him nigger." 7

Not all white people are as deeply racist as Zeke, of course, but enough are to make it wise for young black people to follow what our mothers and fathers have taught us over the generations: that white people's judgments of us are to be viewed with great skepticism, and that accepting those judgments whole is apt to be hazardous to our mental health. Thus, mental toughness and an independent sense of our own worth are elements as essential to the black survival kit in 1990 as they ever were. 8

Not only do black professors need to know this, but black students entering   9
predominantly white campuses have to be taught it, as well. Such campuses are
products of white-American culture, and most black youngsters, particularly those
from the inner cities, find them to be alien places. Moreover, they sometimes get
mixed messages. Often recruited assiduously, they frequently find pockets of hostility and seas of indifference.

That is not a reason for less affirmative action, but for more—at the faculty,   10
staff level. There should be many black adults on those campuses to make them
feel less foreign to black students and more like places of opportunity, full of challenges that can be overcome with excellence and effort. If the number of knowledgeable and sympathetic adults is minuscule, the youngsters will see that the
commitment to an atmosphere where everyone can learn is crimped and limited.

In this imperfect world, racism remains a major affliction that burdens all   11
Americans—and it hits black Americans right in the self-esteem. But it must surely
be easier to firm up your self-regard when you are employed with tenure than
when working as an itinerant researcher. Similarly, the task is undoubtedly easier
for a college graduate—even one who had to struggle with self-doubt during college years because of affirmative action—than for someone who has never gone to
college.

It would be nice to think that in the academy we could escape cultural habits   12
wrought during more than three centuries of legal racial oppression. But that won't
happen in this century. So black people—even those who are privileged—just have
to suck it in and keep on pushing, breaking their own paths and making a way for
those still struggling behind.

Rhetorical Focus

1. Whom does Wilkins apparently regard as his primary audience?
2. Like Steele, Wilkins brings in personal experience to support his claims.
   Does one of these authors use it more persuasively than the other? Use
   examples to support your answer.
3. Wilkins has to write within the limited space of a magazine column. Do you
   think it affects his ability to be as persuasive as Steele? Why or why not?
   Should he have used his limited space to make his argument differently? If
   so, how?

Thematic Focus

1. How much faith does Wilkins put in affirmative action as a way of helping
   African-Americans?
2. Do you agree with Wilkins that "color is not irrelevant in the United States
   at any level" (paragraph 7)? Give reasons for your position.
3. How might Wilkins's essay be considered a response to Steele's?

Affirmative Action and Fairness

William Raspberry

A native of Mississippi, William Raspberry (b. 1935) received a B.A. degree in history from Indiana Central College in 1958. In 1962, he joined the staff of *The Washington Post* as a reporter. Since 1966, he has written an editorial column for the newspaper. Besides appearing three times a week in the *Post*, Raspberry's column is now syndicated nationwide twice a week. Usually, he addresses social, political, economic, and educational issues affecting other African-Americans. Often, he takes a determinedly independent, middle-of-the-road position on such topics. The following piece appeared as Raspberry's *Post* column on December 7, 1990.

Reflections Before Reading

What do you think someone taking a "middle" position on affirmative action might say—in other words, someone who does not fully agree or fully disagree with Steele or Wilkins? Note Raspberry's title. Do you think the previous two essays have been concerned with "fairness"? Why or why not? Do you think hiring and college admissions procedures can be "fair" if they pay attention to an applicant's race? Why or why not?

Affirmative action is arguably the single most divisive racial issue in American politics today. Blacks (and not merely the self-serving) see it as an indisputable necessity for translating racial equality from empty theory to fact. Whites (and not just the followers of Jesse Helms) see it as just another name for racial quotas, an abrogation of the idea of equal opportunity. 1

And yet, the argument between us, recently underscored by President Bush's veto of the Civil Rights Act of 1990 (which he persisted in calling a "quota bill"), may have more to do with how the issue is stated than with what we believe. 2

Ask us whether we favor affirmative action, and blacks are overwhelmingly likely to answer yes. We simply don't trust whites, who make most of the critical decisions as to hiring and promotion, to be fair about it in the absence of any requirement that they take into account the actual results of their decisions: numbers. 3

But put the question differently. Ask blacks to establish reasonable criteria for   4
a job and then ask us whether we believe that a minority or a woman should be
hired in preference to a white man who better meets those criteria, and the answer
is likely to be a resounding no.

Only those who imagine that affirmative action and race preference are the   5
same thing would see the responses as contradictory. They aren't. They are both
calls for racial fairness. The first insists that fairness have real consequences, the
second that qualifications matter.

The debate, really, is over the validity of qualifications which too often find   6
merit in attributes that tell too little of what we need to know about an applicant
and that tend to favor those who already enjoy race-based advantage.

Take, for instance, the case of two applicants for law school: one the black son   7
of a husbandless cleaning woman, a graduate of a dreadful inner-city high school
and an open-enrollment state college; the other the child of two white professionals and the graduate of an elite academy and an Ivy League University. If the first
scored 32 (out of a possible 48) on the Law School Admission Tests and the second
scored 34—and the two were dead even on other admissions criteria—who would
get the single available seat in your law school?

In point of fact, the parents of the white applicant would likely have sufficient   8
pull to get their child into a decent law school, perhaps their own alma mater, even
with lower test scores. But taking the scores alone, hardly any admissions officer
would count it "reverse discrimination" to favor the black applicant. The purpose
of the test is to predict law school success, and the charwoman's son, having overcome handicaps that might have derailed a less determined youngster, would be
rated a "can't miss."

I don't know people who would refuse to apply a little judicious affirmative   9
action in such a case, or in the case of any applicant whose record disclosed both
the minimum academic qualifications and extraordinary success in overcoming
disadvantage.

I don't know people who wouldn't want some assurance that racially skewed   10
hiring or promotion numbers are the result of something other than discrimination: the more skewed the numbers, the greater the insistence that they be justified.

I don't know people who don't believe that employers have a duty both to   11
assemble a competent work force and to take pains to be racially fair about it.

And I don't know people who wouldn't be troubled by the experience of a   12
young colleague of mine who was all but offered a job by the editor of a Midwest-
ern newspaper, only to be told that the paper had a hiring freeze when it was
learned that my colleague was white.

The paper may have needed a black reporter for any number of reasons, rang-   13
ing from a lawsuit settlement to a wish to improve its coverage of minorities to a
need to repair relations with its black readership. But the way the situation was
handled raises the specter of the sort of affirmative action that makes decent people uneasy. It doesn't seem fair.

And since fairness is the most effective claim blacks (or any other disadvan-   14
taged minority) have on the society, it is in our interest to insist on fairness. There

won't always be agreement as to what is fair, but it makes sense to avoid policies that magnify the appearance of unfairness.

Affirmative action to ensure nondiscrimination, or to equalize opportunity, will nearly always seem fair. Affirmative action to make up for past societal unfairness is trickier. Affirmative action that benefits well-off blacks at the expense of poor whites, or that gives lesser qualified blacks preference over better qualified whites, or that merely replaces white pigs at the public trough with black ones, will hardly ever seem fair—even to those who advocate it.

15

Rhetorical Focus

1. Do you find Raspberry's use of repetition effective?
2. Does Raspberry bring in the story of his white colleague at an appropriate place in his argument? Given his apparent purpose, should he have left it out or inserted it elsewhere? Explain.
3. Unlike the other two authors in this constellation, Raspberry is writing a column for a newspaper. Judging by his piece, what are the features of this genre?

Thematic Focus

1. Raspberry focuses on *fairness*. Does he adequately convey what he means by this term? Support your answers with examples from his text.
2. Do you agree with what Raspberry says about the case of the two law school applicants? Why or why not? What do you think Steele and Wilkins would say about this case? In general, are you persuaded by Raspberry's attempt to stake out a middle-of-the-road position on affirmative action? Why or why not?
3. The affirmative action policies of many institutions are designed to help white women, too. Do you think taking them into account would necessitate changes in any of these authors' statements? If so, what are some of the statements that would have to be changed?

Suggestions for Writing

1. Write an essay in which you rank these essays from most to least convincing, and explain why you rank them the way you do. Be sure to refer to specific passages in each text as you defend your reasoning.
2. Explain what you would say to (1) the white female affirmative action officer who Steele reports wanted "diversity" at her Ivy League school, or (2) the young black friend of Wilkins who worries about self-esteem, or (3) one of the people mentioned by Raspberry. Concentrate on developing and supporting the main point you would want to make to your chosen person. If you prefer, put your essay in the form of a letter to the person.
3. All three of these essays deal with college and university admission standards. In deciding whom to admit, many colleges and universities pres-

ently think it fair to consider not only test scores and previous grades but also such factors as race, sex, geographic region, athletic ability, extracurricular activities, and ties to alumni. Identify which of these factors, if any, you think it fair for your school to consider. Be sure to give reasons for your stand.

Chapter
7

Mass Culture

A s you use this book in your composition class, and as you navigate other courses, you will find yourself asked to write responses to other people's texts. *Texts* are not limited to written material of the academic world, though. One set of texts you have already encountered and probably reacted to may be called "mass culture." By this term, we basically mean texts such as films, television shows, best-selling books, widely circulated magazines, and popular songs. The increasing use of this term throughout the twentieth century points to historical circumstances that you should also bear in mind. For one thing, it indicates that the modern age has seen individual artisans, artists, and performers overshadowed by large cultural enterprises, including corporations that produce culture mainly because they seek huge profits. Analysts of mass culture often debate, therefore, whether its vast commercial interests lead it merely to reinforce the existing social order.

This issue grows even more important as *culture* reaches an increasing "mass" of people. Contrary to earlier centuries, the electronic media now enable texts to circulate over vast distances to millions of human beings, sometimes in a manner of seconds. For example, you may recall that during the 1990 Persian Gulf War, American television viewers learned of Iraqi SCUD attacks on Tel Aviv at almost the same time its inhabitants did (and Americans could call friends in Tel Aviv to urge that they take cover!). Because the images and messages of the media have become a constant presence in our lives, we need to probe their background, meanings, and effects. Otherwise, *mass culture* takes on still another sense: It turns its audience into one mechanical mass, submitting mindlessly to whatever the media transmit. In fact, some analysts of mass culture argue that this state of affairs now exists. Others argue that at least some audiences resist or reinterpret the texts that mass culture presents, and that the rest can be helped to understand its power so that it does not overwhelm them.

Certainly, we hope our constellations here will help you sharply analyze mass culture. First, we present Joan Didion's and Louise Erdrich's portrayals of the legendary Western star John Wayne, to suggest how you can examine mass culture by studying its icons—performers whose very image takes on mythic stature for their audiences. The next pair of texts encourages you to consider what constitutes *realism* for film and television, taking as an example their depictions of socioeconomic status. Benjamin DeMott faults several recent films for failing to acknowledge class divisions in America, while Barbara Ehrenreich praises the image of the working class in the television series *Roseanne*.

Next, we pursue the issue of realism by presenting two essays on whether and how television news sacrifices too much in order to entertain its audiences. This particular topic has, of course, grown more important as increasing numbers of people come to rely on television alone for news about their world. Although the two authors, Neil Postman and John Fiske, are both concerned about the effects of television news, Postman concentrates on pointing out the dangers of its becoming more like show business, while Fiske suggests that it needs to be entertaining as well as enlightening.

Finally, we present you with a contemporary, mass culture version of what is actually a centuries-old debate over how culture should relate to morality. More specifically, we present the differing views of Jon Pareles, Charles Krauthammer, David Mills, and Michele Wallace on the morality of rap music, while encouraging you to argue your own position. Overall, whether or not you agree with the particular texts you read here, enlist them in an effort to understand better the texts of mass culture surrounding us all. You may not be used to analyzing such texts as intensely as these authors do; you may even prefer to dismiss mass culture simply as entertainment. However, the more you are willing to ponder it through your reading and your writing, the more you ensure that it can never turn you and others into an uncritical mass.

ICONS OF MASS CULTURE: THE EXAMPLE OF JOHN WAYNE

A good way to begin analyzing mass culture is to study some performers' appeal. Throughout the development of mass media such as radio, television, film, video, and the recording industry, various performers have achieved the stature of cultural icons. You may know that in earlier times, icons were images of saints or other sacred figures. Several religions, especially Eastern Orthodox ones, still maintain them in churches and worship them as much as the people they represent. In the twentieth century, however, various secular performers have also acquired a virtually sacred or mythic aura. How and why do certain representatives of mass culture gain this power over their audiences? More precisely, what ideologies and historical forces are at work when these performers become icons of mass culture? Of course, their success may be due in part to their sheer talent. Usually, however, they also must fit or transform their audiences' values. In other words, their success can tell you something about what much of a society esteems or believes. Their reputations usually depend as well on the public relations machinery of mass culture—its ways of advertising and selling their images. What, for example, would various rock stars do without the vast marketing power of MTV? Of course, even the most idolized performers are not acclaimed by everyone; indeed, a segment of society may actively criticize particular performers because they endorse values that have oppressed that group. You can, in fact, better understand icons of mass culture if you try to determine how, why, and for whom their appeal has limits.

The following constellation presents two authors' perspectives on a Hollywood icon of several decades, the Western star John Wayne. Joan Didion begins her essay about him by recalling the ways that his image shaped her childhood dreams of romance; then, she reports how Wayne and his friends idealized the world of men when she visited his film set years later as an adult. Louise Erdrich's poem depicts the complex feelings of Native Americans watching a John Wayne Western, offering you the opportunity to see how a group different from Didion regards him. Because he is now deceased, with other film heroes and heroines succeeding him, use these texts to speculate as well on the relationship between his popularity and his particular historical period. Take them as an invitation, too, to consider the values and processes reinforcing the popularity of current stars in various fields. As you think about their impact, though, keep in mind that various people may view even widely loved stars differently. Doing so will help you analyze not only the nature of these performers, but also the possible attitudes of your own readers.

John Wayne: A Love Song

Joan Didion

One of America's most distinguished contemporary writers, Joan Didion
was born in Sacramento, California in 1934 and graduated from the
University of California at Berkeley. After moving to New York, she began
her career as a writer for *Vogue* in 1956. Subsequently, she returned to
California. Although today she is well-known for novels such as *Play It As It
Lays, A Book of Common Prayer,* and *Democracy,* she is perhaps even
more highly regarded for her ironic nonfiction commentaries on people,
places, and trends in America. "John Wayne: A Love Song" first appeared
in *The Saturday Evening Post* in 1965. The essay served partly as a report
on the making of Wayne's latest film, *The Sons of Katie Elder,* and in fact, it
was accompanied by photographs of him and his family on the movie set.
At the same time, Didion offers her personal reflections on Wayne's career
and what he has meant to her as a celebrity icon. Didion included this piece
in her first collection of essays, *Slouching Towards Bethlehem* (1968). There,
she generally ponders the disorienting changes in America's cultural images,
referring especially to Hollywood, San Francisco, and other parts of
California. Didion continued to explore this theme in her second collection,
The White Album (1979). Note that Didion herself has been directly involved
with the film industry, writing with her husband John Gregory Dunne the
screenplays for such films as *The Panic in Needle Park* and the Barbra
Streisand version of *A Star is Born.* She has also written two other books of
reportage on places of social turmoil, *Salvador* (1983) and *Miami* (1987). In
recent years, Didion has lived in both Los Angeles and New York and has
written magazine profiles of turbulent events in both cities.

Reflections Before Reading

List some current performers who are wildly popular, along with the physical
images you associate with them. Why do you think their fans like them?
Think not only of their intrinsic appeal, but also of the ways they are
promoted and the values they seem to represent. In the following texts,
Joan Didion and Louise Erdrich examine the image of John Wayne. What, if
anything, do you associate with him? Do you encounter many people who
are still fans of him? Why or why not?

In the summer of 1943 I was eight, and my father and mother and small brother   1
and I were at Peterson Field in Colorado Springs. A hot wind blew through that
summer, blew until it seemed that before August broke, all the dust in Kansas
would be in Colorado, would have drifted over the tar-paper barracks and the
temporary strip and stopped only when it hit Pikes Peak. There was not much to
do, a summer like that: there was the day they brought in the first B-29, an event to
remember but scarcely a vacation program. There was an Officers' Club, but no
swimming pool; all the Officers' Club had of interest was artificial blue rain behind
the bar. The rain interested me a good deal, but I could not spend the summer
watching it, and so we went, my brother and I, to the movies.

We went three and four afternoons a week, sat on folding chairs in the dark-   2
ened Quonset hut which served as a theater, and it was there, that summer of 1943
while the hot wind blew outside, that I first saw John Wayne. Saw the walk, heard
the voice. Heard him tell the girl in a picture called *War of the Wildcats* that he
would build her a house, "at the bend in the river where the cottonwoods grow." As
it happened I did not grow up to be the kind of woman who is the heroine in a
Western, and although the men I have known have had many virtues and have
taken me to live in many places I have come to love, they have never been John
Wayne, and they have never taken me to that bend in the river where the cottonwoods grow. Deep in that part of my heart where the artificial rain forever falls,
that is still the line I wait to hear.

I tell you this neither in a spirit of self-revelation nor as an exercise in total   3
recall, but simply to demonstrate that when John Wayne rode through my childhood, and perhaps through yours, he determined forever the shape of certain of
our dreams. It did not seem possible that such a man could fall ill, could carry
within him that most inexplicable and ungovernable of diseases. The rumor struck
some obscure anxiety, threw our very childhoods into question. In John Wayne's
world, John Wayne was supposed to give the orders. "Let's ride," he said, and
"Saddle up." "Forward *ho*," and "A man's gotta do what he's got to do." "Hello,
there," he said when he first saw the girl, in a construction camp or on a train or
just standing around on the front porch waiting for somebody to ride up through
the tall grass. When John Wayne spoke, there was no mistaking his intentions; he
had a sexual authority so strong that even a child could perceive it. And in a world
we understood early to be characterized by venality and doubt and paralyzing ambiguities, he suggested another world, one which may or may not have existed ever
but in any case existed no more: a place where a man could move free, could make
his own code and live by it; a world in which, if a man did what he had to do, he
could one day take the girl and go riding through the draw and find himself home
free, not in a hospital with something going wrong inside, not in a high bed with
the flowers and the drugs and the forced smiles, but there at the bend in the bright
river, the cottonwoods shimmering in the early morning sun.

"Hello, there." Where did he come from, before the tall grass? Even his his-   4
tory seemed right, for it was no history at all, nothing to intrude upon the dream.
Born Marion Morrison in Winterset, Iowa, the son of a druggist. Moved as a child
to Lancaster, California, part of the migration to that promised land sometimes
called "the west coast of Iowa." Not that Lancaster was the promise fulfilled; Lan-

caster was a town on the Mojave where the dust blew through. But Lancaster was still California, and it was only a year from there to Glendale, where desolation had a different flavor: antimacassars among the orange groves, a middle-class prelude to Forest Lawn. Imagine Marion Morrison in Glendale. A Boy Scout, then a student at Glendale High. A tackle for U.S.C., a Sigma Chi. Summer vacations, a job moving props on the old Fox lot. There, a meeting with John Ford, one of the several directors who were to sense that into this perfect mold might be poured the inarticulate longings of a nation wondering at just what pass the trail had been lost. "Dammit," said Raoul Walsh later, "the son of a bitch looked like a man." And so after a while the boy from Glendale became a star. He did not become an actor, as he has always been careful to point out to interviewers ("How many times do I gotta tell you, I don't act at all, I *re*-act"), but a star, and the star called John Wayne would spend most of the rest of his life with one or another of those directors, out on some forsaken location, in search of the dream.

> *Out where the skies are a trifle bluer*
> *Out where friendship's a little truer*
> *That's where the West begins.*

Nothing very bad could happen in the dream, nothing a man could not face   5
down. But something did. There it was, the rumor, and after a while the headlines. "I licked the Big C," John Wayne announced, as John Wayne would, reducing those outlaw cells to the level of any other outlaws, but even so we all sensed that this would be the one unpredictable confrontation, the one shoot-out Wayne could lose. I have as much trouble as the next person with illusion and reality, and I did not much want to see John Wayne when he must be (or so I thought) having some trouble with it himself, but I did, and it was down in Mexico when he was making the picture his illness had so long delayed, down in the very country of the dream.

It was John Wayne's 165th picture. It was Henry Hathaway's 84th. It was   6
number 34 for Dean Martin, who was working off an old contract to Hal Wallis, for whom it was independent production number 65. It was called *The Sons of Katie Elder,* and it was a Western, and after the three-month delay they had finally shot the exteriors up in Durango, and now they were in the waning days of interior shooting at Estudio Churubusco outside Mexico·City, and the sun was hot and the air was clear and it was lunchtime. Out under the pepper trees the boys from the Mexican crew sat around sucking caramels, and down the road some of the technical men sat around a place which served a stuffed lobster and a glass of tequila for one dollar American, but it was inside the cavernous empty commissary where the talent sat around, the reasons for the exercise, all sitting around the big table picking at *huevos con queso* and Carta Blanca beer. Dean Martin, unshaven. Mack Gray, who goes where Martin goes. Bob Goodfried, who was in charge of Paramount publicity and who had flown down to arrange for a trailer and who had a delicate stomach. "Tea and toast," he warned repeatedly. "That's the ticket. You can't trust the lettuce." And Henry Hathaway, the director, who did not seem to be listening to Goodfried. And John Wayne, who did not seem to be listening to anyone.

"This week's gone slow," Dean Martin said, for the third time.   7

"How can you say that?" Mack Gray demanded.   8

"*This . . . week's . . . gone . . . slow*, that's how I can say it."   9

"You don't mean you want it to end."   10

"I'll say it right out, Mack, I want it to *end*. Tomorrow night I shave this beard,   11
I head for the airport, I say *adiós amigos!* Bye-bye *muchachos!*"

Henry Hathaway lit a cigar and patted Martin's arm fondly. "Not tomorrow,   12
Dino."

"Henry, what are you planning to add? A World War?"   13

Hathaway patted Martin's arm again and gazed into the middle distance. At   14
the end of the table someone mentioned a man who, some years before, had tried
unsuccessfully to blow up an airplane.

"He's still in jail," Hathaway said suddenly.   15

"In jail?" Martin was momentarily distracted from the question whether to   16
send his golf clubs back with Bob Goodfried or consign them to Mack Gray.
"What's he in jail for if nobody got killed?"

"Attempted murder, Dino," Hathaway said gently. "A felony."   17

"You mean some guy just *tried* to kill me he'd end up in jail?"   18

Hathaway removed the cigar from his mouth and looked across the table.   19
"Some guy just tried to kill *me* he wouldn't end up in jail. How about you, Duke?"

Very slowly, the object of Hathaway's query wiped his mouth, pushed back his   20
chair, and stood up. It was the real thing, the authentic article, the move which had
climaxed a thousand scenes on 165 flickering frontiers and phantasmagoric battle-
fields before, and it was about to climax this one, in the commissary at Estudio
Churubusco outside Mexico City. "Right," John Wayne drawled. "I'd kill him."

Almost all the cast of *Katie Elder* had gone home, that last week; only the   21
principals were left, Wayne, and Martin, and Earl Holliman, and Michael Anderson, Jr., and Martha Hyer. Martha Hyer was not around much, but every now and
then someone referred to her, usually as "the girl." They had all been together nine
weeks, six of them in Durango. Mexico City was not quite Durango; wives like to
come along to places like Mexico City, like to shop for handbags, go to parties at
Merle Oberon Pagliai's, like to look at her paintings. But Durango. The very name
hallucinates. Man's country. Out where the West begins. There had been ahue-
huete trees in Durango; a waterfall, rattlesnakes. There had been weather, nights
so cold that they had postponed one or two exteriors until they could shoot inside
at Churubusco. "It was the girl," they explained. "You couldn't keep the girl out in
cold like that." Henry Hathaway had cooked in Durango, *gazpacho* and ribs and
the steaks that Dean Martin had ordered flown down from the Sands; he had
wanted to cook in Mexico City, but the management of the Hotel Bamer refused to
let him set up a brick barbecue in his room. "You really missed something, *Durango*," they would say, sometimes joking and sometimes not, until it became a
refrain, Eden lost.

But if Mexico City was not Durango, neither was it Beverly Hills. No one else   22
was using Churubusco that week, and there inside the big sound stage that said LOS
HIJOS DE KATIE ELDER on the door, there with the pepper trees and the bright sun
outside, they could still, for just so long as the picture lasted, maintain a world

peculiar to men who like to make Westerns, a world of loyalties and fond raillery, of sentiment and shared cigars, of interminable desultory recollections; campfire talk, its only point to keep a human voice raised against the night, the wind, the rustlings in the brush.

"Stuntman got hit accidentally on a picture of mine once," Hathaway would   23
say between takes of an elaborately choreographed fight scene. "What was his name, married Estelle Taylor, met her down in Arizona."

The circle would close around him, the cigars would be fingered. The delicate   24
art of the staged fight was to be contemplated.

"I only hit one guy in my life," Wayne would say. "Accidentally, I mean. That   25
was Mike Mazurki."

"Some guy. Hey, Duke says he only hit one guy in his life, Mike Mazurki."   26

"Some choice." Murmurings, assent.   27

"It wasn't a choice, it was an accident."   28

"I can believe it."   29

"You bet."   30

"Oh boy. Mike Mazurki."   31

And so it would go. There was Web Overlander, Wayne's makeup man for   32
twenty years, hunched in a blue Windbreaker, passing out sticks of Juicy Fruit. "*Insect* spray," he would say. "Don't tell us about insect spray. We saw insect spray in Africa, all right. Remember Africa?" Or, "*Steamer* clams. Don't tell us about steamer clams. We got our fill of steamer clams all right, on the *Hatari!* appearance tour. Remember Bookbinder's?" There was Ralph Volkie, Wayne's trainer for eleven years, wearing a red baseball cap and carrying around a clipping from Hedda Hopper, a tribute to Wayne. "This Hopper's some lady," he would say again and again. "Not like some of these guys, all they write is sick, sick, sick, how can you call that guy *sick*, when he's got pains, coughs, works all day, *never complains*. That guy's got the best hook since Dempsey, not *sick*."

And there was Wayne himself, fighting through number 165. There was   33
Wayne, in his thirty-three-year-old spurs, his dusty neckerchief, his blue shirt. "You don't have too many worries about what to wear in these things," he said. "You can wear a blue shirt, or, if you're down in Monument Valley, you can wear a yellow shirt." There was Wayne, in a relatively new hat, a hat which made him look curiously like William S. Hart. "I had this old cavalry hat I loved, but I lent it to Sammy Davis. I got it back, it was unwearable. I think they all pushed it down on his head and said *O.K., John Wayne*—you know, a joke."

There was Wayne, working too soon, finishing the picture with a bad cold and   34
a racking cough, so tired by late afternoon that he kept an oxygen inhalator on the set. And still nothing mattered but the Code. "That guy," he muttered of a reporter who had incurred his displeasure. "I admit I'm balding. I admit I got a tire around my middle. What man fifty-seven doesn't? Big news. Anyway, that guy."

He paused, about to expose the heart of the matter, the root of the distaste,   35
the fracture of the rules that bothered him more than the alleged misquotations, more than the intimation that he was no longer the Ringo Kid. "He comes down, uninvited, but I ask him over anyway. So we're sitting around drinking mescal out of a water jug."

He paused again and looked meaningfully at Hathaway, readying him for the   36
unthinkable denouement. "He had to be *assisted* to his room."

They argued about the virtues of various prizefighters, they argued about the   37
price of J & B in pesos. They argued about dialogue.

"As rough a guy as he is, Henry, I still don't think he'd raffle off his mother's   38
Bible."

"I like a shocker, Duke."   39

They exchanged endless training-table jokes. "You know why they call this   40
memory sauce?" Martin asked, holding up a bowl of chili.

"Why?"   41

"Because you *remember it in the morning.*"   42

"Hear that, Duke? Hear why they call this memory sauce?"   43

They delighted one another by blocking out minute variations in the free-for-   44
all fight which is a set piece in Wayne pictures; motivated or totally gratuitous, the
fight sequence has to be in the picture, because they so enjoy making it. "Listen—
this'll really be funny. Duke picks up the kid, see, and then it takes both Dino and
Earl to throw him out the door—*how's that?*"

They communicated by sharing old jokes; they sealed their camaraderie by   45
making gentle, old-fashioned fun of wives, those civilizers, those tamers. "So Se-
ñora Wayne takes it into her head to stay up and have one brandy. So for the rest of
the night it's 'Yes, Pilar, you're right, dear. I'm a bully, Pilar, you're right, I'm
impossible.' "

"You hear that? Duke says Pilar threw a table at him."   46

"Hey, Duke, here's something funny. That finger you hurt today, get the Doc   47
to bandage it up, go home tonight, show it to Pilar, tell her she did it when she
threw the table. You know, make her think she was really cutting up."

They treated the oldest among them respectfully; they treated the youngest   48
fondly. "You see that kid?" they said of Michael Anderson, Jr. "What a kid."

"He don't act, it's right from the heart," said Hathaway, patting his heart.   49

"Hey kid," Martin said. "You're gonna be in my next picture. We'll have the   50
whole thing, no beards. The striped shirts, the girls, the hi-fi, the eye lights."

They ordered Michael Anderson his own chair, with "BIG MIKE" tooled on the   51
back. When it arrived on the set, Hathaway hugged him. "You see that?" Anderson
asked Wayne, suddenly too shy to look him in the eye. Wayne gave him the smile,
the nod, the final accolade. "I saw it, kid."

On the morning of the day they were to finish *Katie Elder,* Web Overlander   52
showed up not in his Windbreaker but in a blue blazer. "Home, Mama," he said,
passing out the last of his Juicy Fruit. "I got on my getaway clothes." But he was
subdued. At noon, Henry Hathaway's wife dropped by the commissary to tell him
that she might fly over to Acapulco. "Go ahead," he told her. "I get through here,
all I'm gonna do is take Seconal to a point just this side of suicide." They were all
subdued. After Mrs. Hathaway left, there were desultory attempts at reminiscing,
but man's country was receding fast; they were already halfway home, and all they
could call up was the 1961 Bel Air fire, during which Henry Hathaway had ordered
the Los Angeles Fire Department off his property and saved the place himself by,

among other measures, throwing everything flammable into the swimming pool. "Those fire guys might've just given it up," Wayne said. "Just let it burn." In fact this was a good story, and one incorporating several of their favorite themes, but a Bel Air story was still not a Durango story.

In the early afternoon they began the last scene, and although they spent as much time as possible setting it up, the moment finally came when there was nothing to do but shoot it. "Second team out, first team in, *doors closed*," the assistant director shouted one last time. The stand-ins walked off the set, John Wayne and Martha Hyer walked on. "All right, boys, *silencio,* this is a picture." They took it twice. Twice the girl offered John Wayne the tattered Bible. Twice John Wayne told her that "there's a lot of places I go where that wouldn't fit in." Everyone was very still. And at 2:30 that Friday afternoon Henry Hathaway turned away from the camera, and in the hush that followed he ground out his cigar in a sand bucket. "O.K.," he said. "That's it." 53

Since that summer of 1943 I had thought of John Wayne in a number of ways. I had thought of him driving cattle up from Texas, and bringing airplanes in on a single engine, thought of him telling the girl at the Alamo that "Republic is a beautiful word." I had never thought of him having dinner with his family and with me and my husband in an expensive restaurant in Chapultepec Park, but time brings odd mutations, and there we were, one night that last week in Mexico. For a while it was only a nice evening, an evening anywhere. We had a lot of drinks and I lost the sense that the face across the table was in certain ways more familiar than my husband's. 54

And then something happened. Suddenly the room seemed suffused with the dream, and I could not think why. Three men appeared out of nowhere, playing guitars. Pilar Wayne leaned slightly forward, and John Wayne lifted his glass almost imperceptibly toward her. "We'll need some Pouilly-Fuissé for the rest of the table," he said, "and some red Bordeaux for the Duke." We all smiled, and drank the Pouilly-Fuissé for the rest of the table and the red Bordeaux for the Duke, and all the while the men with the guitars kept playing, until finally I realized what they were playing, what they had been playing all along: "The Red River Valley" and the theme from *The High and the Mighty.* They did not quite get the beat right, but even now I can hear them, in another country and a long time later, even as I tell you this. 55

Rhetorical Focus

1. Note how Didion refers to "dreams" throughout her essay. Obviously, such references help unify its various sections. Does the meaning of "the dream" change, however, or does it remain basically the same?
2. Didion begins and ends by referring to herself. When reporting on the making of the film, however, she leaves herself out. Can you guess what she is feeling anyway? Should she have stated her views more plainly?

3. At the beginning of her third paragraph and then at the end, Didion directly addresses the reader. Does this strategy make sense to you? Should she have used it throughout the essay?

Thematic Focus

1. What do you think about John Wayne after reading this essay? What do you think about Didion as an observer of him?
2. Identify three particular groups who would view John Wayne differently from one another. How would each interpret what Didion reports about him and his friends?
3. Early in her essay, Didion asserts that John Wayne "determined forever the shape of certain of our dreams." Near the end, in recalling her dinner with Wayne, Didion suggests that initially she felt "that the face across the table was in certain ways more familiar than my husband's." Can the images of film stars really be so powerful? What does your answer imply about mass culture?

Dear John Wayne
Louise Erdrich

Of German-American and Chippewa descent, Louise Erdrich (b. 1954) grew up in Wahpeton, North Dakota. Her parents both worked for the Bureau of Indian Affairs, her father as a teacher. Erdrich graduated from the then-new Native American Studies program at Dartmouth College in 1976, and went on to earn a master's degree in creative writing from Johns Hopkins University in 1977. In her subsequent writing career, she has frequently collaborated as editor or co-author with her husband, the anthropologist and novelist Michael Dorris. Together they wrote the 1991 novel *The Crown of Columbus*. Primarily known today as a fiction writer, Erdrich has examined the lives of Native Americans through short stories and three novels: *Love Medicine* (which won the National Book Critics Circle Award in 1984), *Beet Queen* (1986), and *Tracks* (1989). Erdrich has also written poetry, however, examining through it various myths and images that have affected Native Americans. This poem on the image of John Wayne comes from her 1984 volume *Jacklight*.

Reflections Before Reading

Erdrich's poem describes Native Americans watching a John Wayne Western at a drive-in movie theater. What typical features of such a film might they especially react to? What do you think their reaction(s) will be? In what ways, if any, do you suspect that this text will differ from Didion's?

> August and the drive-in picture is packed.
> We lounge on the hood of the Pontiac
> surrounded by the slow-burning spirals they sell
> at the window, to vanquish the hordes of mosquitoes.
> Nothing works. They break through the smoke screen for blood.

1

> Always the lookout spots the Indians first,
> spread north to south, barring progress.
> The Sioux or some other Plains bunch
> in spectacular columns, ICBM missiles,
> feathers bristling in the meaningful sunset.

2

> The drum breaks. There will be no parlance.
> Only the arrows whining, a death-cloud of nerves
> swarming down on the settlers
> who die beautifully, tumbling like dust weeds
> into the history that brought us all here
> together: this wide screen beneath the sign of the bear.

3

> The sky fills, acres of blue squint and eye
> that the crowd cheers. His face moves over us,
> a thick cloud of vengeance, pitted
> like the land that was once flesh. Each rut,
> each scar makes a promise: *It is*
> *not over, this fight, not as long as you resist.*

4

> *Everything we see belongs to us.*

5

> A few laughing Indians fall over the hood
> slipping in the hot spilled butter.
> *The eye sees a lot, John, but the heart is so blind.*
> *Death makes us owners of nothing.*
> He smiles, a horizon of teeth
> the credits reel over, and then the white fields

6

> again blowing in the true-to-life dark.
> The dark films over everything.
> We get into the car
> scratching our mosquito bites, speechless and small
> as people are when the movie is done.
> We are back in our skins.

7

How can we help but keep hearing his voice,   8
the flip side of the sound track, still playing:
Come on, boys, we got them
where we want them, drunk, running.
They'll give us what we want, what we need.
Even his disease was the idea of taking everything.
Those cells, burning, doubling, splitting out of their skins.

Rhetorical Focus

1. Erdrich describes an audience of Native Americans watching a John Wayne film at a drive-in movie theater. How does she develop the poem by noting changes in them as they watch?
2. What are the different voices in the poem? Whom do they address? What do you think of each?
3. Erdrich has written a page and a half poem, whereas Didion has written an essay of several pages. Does the difference in genre and length matter as you look to both texts for an understanding of John Wayne as cultural icon? Explain.

Thematic Focus

1. According to the poem, what interpretation of Native American history did John Wayne's films present? What does the poem suggest would be a more accurate interpretation?
2. Although Erdrich focuses on Wayne's screen image, she does end by referring to his real-life cancer. Didion refers to his illness, too. Do the two authors give it the same meaning and significance?
3. Compare the vision of John Wayne held by the Native Americans in Erdrich's poem with Didion's childhood vision of him. Do these two visions strike you as equally valid? Why or why not? Does the gender of either author seem to influence her attitude toward John Wayne as a male hero? Explain.

Suggestions for Writing

1. Explain the extent to which Didion's perceptions of John Wayne are challenged by Erdrich's poem about him. In what respects, if any, do these two authors seem very much at odds about him? In what respects, if any, might Didion be able to agree with what Erdrich's poem says about him? Support your generalizations with specific references to the texts.
2. Explain how, when you were younger, a particular performer "shaped certain of your dreams" for better or worse. Give concrete details of this person's typical performances and their effect on you. Why were you attracted to this performer? What does your being attracted say about the values you

had at the time? Have you changed in significant ways from the younger self who was attracted to this performer? Are you still attracted?

3. When Didion and Erdrich write about John Wayne, they analyze someone long esteemed as an American film hero. At the same time, they suggest that his heroic image may have grown outdated. Analyze a character from a recent film or television show who is evidently being put forth as a hero or heroine. More specifically, identify the particular aspects of this character's purported heroism, explain what it implies for you about current American values, and explain whether you yourself welcome such an image of heroism. You may find it useful to compare this hero or heroine with the type played by John Wayne.

REALISM IN FILM AND TELEVISION: DEPICTING SOCIAL CLASS

Analysts of mass culture have often pondered just how realistic its depictions of life are and should be. Most people expect mass culture to entertain them, and usually it complies with significant amounts of fantasy. Almost all of us can fondly recall films, television shows, recordings, and other works of mass culture that offered us pleasantly unreal visions of life. Is entertainment incompatible with realism, however? Should we, in fact, demand from mass culture a significant amount of unvarnished truth? What constitutes *realism,* anyway?

This constellation emphasizes such issues by presenting two essays that examine how particular works of mass culture treat divisions of social class in this country. In the first essay, Benjamin DeMott criticizes several recent American films for failing to admit that American class barriers are strong. Because they imply that poor and working-class people can easily triumph over people who are better off, DeMott feels that these films encourage Americans to evade our society's continuing problem of inequality. In the second essay, Barbara Ehrenreich also calls for sensitivity to class, suggesting that the mass media should especially acknowledge the spirit, struggles, and complexity of working-class people. Although she criticizes some television shows, she basically celebrates the depiction of class in Roseanne Barr's series. Taken together, then, DeMott and Ehrenreich not only demonstrate ways of analyzing class in two mass media, but also suggest what unrealistic and realistic treatments of class may be like. Of course, you will have to decide whether their arguments are convincing—whether, that is, film and television ought to treat class realistically, as well as whether these authors' particular notions of class make sense.

Admittedly, the very meaning of the term *class* can get fuzzy. Sociologists have debated for years over precisely how to define it. While many of us associate the term simply with degrees of wealth, others of us also define a class as a set of particular experiences, values, and peers. Another issue is whether and how classes should be analyzed in relation to one another. Certainly, DeMott and Ehrenreich want mass culture to probe not just each class alone, but also the ways that classes do and do not react to one another in the social hierarchy. As you read these essays, review your own thoughts about the classes that exist in America, the barriers that separate them, and what mass culture should say about the effect of class on people's lives.

In Hollywood, Class Doesn't Put Up Much of a Struggle

Benjamin DeMott

Benjamin DeMott (b. 1924) is the Mellon Professor of Humanities at Amherst College in Amherst, Massachusetts. He has written columns on literature, higher education, and cultural affairs for a wide range of periodicals, including *The Atlantic, Harper's, The American Scholar, Change, New England Monthly,* and *Entertainment Weekly.* Besides his novels *The Body's Cage* and *A Married Man,* he has published several books of cultural criticism, including *Hells & Benefits, You Don't Say, Supergrow,* and *Surviving the Seventies,* as well as *The Imperial Middle: Why Americans Can't Think Straight About Class,* a 1990 book related to the following selection. In the book, DeMott argues that Americans generally refuse to acknowledge class differences, thereby perpetuating the inequality that really exists. He accuses American films and television shows in particular of reinforcing what he takes to be this country's "mythology of classlessness." DeMott was prompted to write the book when the National Endowment of the Humanities and the Public Broadcasting System criticized his daughter for using her grants from them to produce an unusually candid documentary on working-class high school students in Muncie, Indiana. DeMott's essay here originally appeared in *The New York Times* Sunday Arts and Leisure section on January 20, 1991. It applies the themes of his book to several recent American films.

Reflections Before Reading

What do you associate with the concept of social class? Is this a concept that you are relatively familiar with, or is it one that you have not thought much about at all? Would you say that your social class has been an important factor in your life? Why or why not? The following essay analyzes depictions of social class in recent American films. What details, if any, from films you have seen come to mind when you hear the term *social class?*

Increasingly in recent years movies have been dealing with power issues and class   1
relationships—interactions between masters and servants, executives and underlings, yuppies and waitresses, millionaires and hookers, rich aristocrats and social-
nobody lawyers. Think of "Reversal of Fortune" and "The Bonfire of the Vanities."
Think of "White Palace" and "Pretty Woman." Think of Michael Corleone's struggle for social acceptance in "The Godfather Part III." Think of "Working Girl," or
"Driving Miss Daisy," or "Dirty Dancing." Script after script links up clout and
cloutlessness, often to stunning box-office effect.

Not every movie version of the power theme speaks specifically about class   2
relationships, and some versions are only loosely linked to social reality. The two
worlds of "Edward Scissorhands," for example—hilltop mansion and tract house;
solitary helpless artist versus artist-baiting mob—are derived less from everyday
experience than from fairy tales, allegory and satire.

Usually, though, conventional realism is the chosen mode, and class skir-   3
mishes are sketched. The camera in "White Palace," a popular film released a few
months ago, studies St. Louis's fancier suburbs and its rundown Dog Town; class
conflict erupts at the movie's crisis point. Nora, the waitress–heroine (Susan Sa-
randon), listens smolderingly to her yuppie lover's upper-middle friends and relations uttering their hypocritical socio-political pieties, and explodes. Storming her
way out, she cries: "*I'm* working class!"

At first glance the angry explicitness of her outcry and the movie's declaration   4
of difference look promising. They could signify that Hollywood is reaching toward
maturity, trying to teach itself and the nation how to think straight about social
hierarchy—the realities of class and class power. The need for such instruction is
patent. This country has an ignoble tradition of evading social facts—pretending
that individual episodes of upward mobility obviate grappling with the hardening
socio-economic differences in our midst. Movies that deal responsibly with class
relationships could, in theory, moderate the national evasiveness.

But, regrettably, contemporary "class movies" don't deal responsibly with   5
class. The tone of their treatment of rich and poor is new; it is harsher and meaner
than that of Frank Capra's "little guy" sagas or George Cukor's social comedies or
John Ford's populism that were pleasing to our parents and grandparents in the
30's, 40's and 50's.

The harsher tone, however, doesn't bespeak fundamental change. At their   6
best, Hollywood's new-style "class movies" nod at realities of social difference—

and then go on to obfuscate them. At their worst, these films are driven by near-total dedication to a scam—the maddening, dangerous deceit that there are no classes in America.

One favorite story line stresses discovery: people who think firm class lines   7
exist come to discover, by the end of the tale, that they're mistaken; everybody's really the same.

In the 1988 blockbuster "Working Girl," Tess McGill (Melanie Griffith), ini-   8
tially a bottom-dog secretary–gofer, is positive she can make it to the top. But her peers in the word-processing pool regard her aspirations as foolish. They tell her, flat out, that the real world has lines and distinctions and that her daydreams of glory and business power are foolish. "I sing and dance in my underwear," says one pal, "but I'm not Madonna." The implicit message: Get real, Tess. Accept the reality of levels.

But Tess, of course, accepts no such thing. She reads W, takes classes to im-   9
prove her accent, seizes her boss's office when the latter breaks her leg skiing—and winds up not only doing deals but ordering the boss (Sigourney Weaver) to get her bony bottom out of sight. What does it take to get to the top? Desire, period. Tess's desire flies her straight up to a managerial perch, allowing her to become, almost effortlessly, all she can be: no problem, few barriers, class dismissed. In the final frame the doubters in the secretarial pool acknowledge their error; they rise to applaud the heroine who proved them wrong.

A second familiar story line involves upendings: characters theoretically on the   10
social bottom shake the cages of characters who try to use their position to humil-iate those below. The top dogs are so stupid they don't realize that socioeconomic power only lasts for a second and that they can be overcome by any intrepid under-ling.

Consider "Pretty Woman," the 1990 film that became one of the highest-   11
grossing movies ever and is now near the top of video best-seller and rental charts. The would-be humiliators in this movie are snobbish salespeople on chic Rodeo Drive. Vivian (Julia Roberts), a hooker, runs afoul of them when she is sent on a shopping spree by the corporate raider (Richard Gere) who has hired her for a week. The raider wants elegance and the hooker aims to oblige. . . . but on her first pass at the drive she's suited up in hooker garb, and the salespeople are offended. "I don't think we have anything for you. *Please leave.*"

Quickly the snobs are undone. The corporate raider flashes plastic and tells a   12
shop manager that they'll be spending big and need appropriate cosseting. In min-utes—through instruction in fork-tine-counting, for instance—the raider effects the few alterations of manners required to transform Vivian the street hooker into grandeur.

Regally togged, her arms filled with sleek clothes boxes, Vivian returns to the   13
salespeople who were mean to her and sticks it to them in economic not moral terms. If they had been nice to her, they would have made a killing. ("You work on commission, don't you?")

Power is temporary and snobs are dopes—so goes the message. Ostracize a   14
hooker in midmorning and she'll ruin you before tea. *Class dismissed.*

Comparable dismissals occur in movies drawing huge audiences of high school   15
students. They usually have plot lines showing bottom dogs gliding smoothly and

painlessly to the top. In "Dirty Dancing" (1987), Patrick Swayze, playing a talented working-class dancer (he has a card in the "housepainters and plasterers union"), competes for esteem with a Yale medical school student—and wins in a breeze.

In John Hughes's "Some Kind of Wonderful" (1987) and "Pretty in Pink"   16
(1986), working-class heroes or heroines become romantically interested in class-mates who rank above them, in terms of money and status, in the school society. As the attachments develop, the poor students commence to display gifts and talents that prove them equal to or intrinsically superior to the arrogant, insecure charac-ters in whom they've become interested.

Once the nonclass, merit-based order or hierarchy has been established, and   17
superficial, class-based gradations have been eliminated, the poor boy or girl chooses whether to continue the relationship with the pseudo-superior as an equal or to end it. Either way, the experience bolsters the belief that, in school and out, social strata are evanescent and meaningless.

It's hardly surprising that the myth of America as a classless society emerges at   18
its most schematic in movies aimed at relatively youthful, unsophisticated audi-ences. But the same impulse to paper over social differences surfaces in many more ambitious films purporting to raise subjects considered controversial by Hol-lywood standards (social injustice, war, the treatment of minorities).

And not infrequently that impulse drives film makers—such as Francis Ford   19
Coppola in "The Godfather Part III" and Barry Levinson in "Avalon"—to overplay ethnic influence and underplay class influence on character.

But what is truly striking is the array of ploys and devices by which movie   20
makers bring off escapes from significant confrontation with class realities. The Vietnam War film "Platoon" (1986), for example, lets on at the beginning that it will show us an upper-middle white soldier learning about differences between himself and the sons of the working class who compose the majority of his com-rades in arms.

But in place of the experience of learning, we're offered liberal platitudes and   21
star turns. The hero writes his grandmother that his fellow soldiers are the salt of the earth (little corroboration supplied); the soldiers themselves—particularly the blacks among them—are brought on for a succession of amusing monologues, fol-lowing which they disappear, shipped out dead or alive; at no point is the gritty stuff of class difference even momentarily engaged.

In the much-acclaimed "Driving Miss Daisy" (1989), the early intimation is   22
that the focus will be on relations between white employers and black servants. But almost immediately the outlines of that social difference are blurred. The white employer is Jewish and her synagogue is bombed; poor black and rich white become one, joint victims of discriminatory violence. ("You're my best friend, Hoke.") Class dismissed once more.

The story is nearly the same even in those unusual movies that focus solely   23
on minority communities. Social difference is glanced at, defined in a few snippets of dialogue—and then trashed, often by means of a joke. In "House Party," Reginald Hudlin's 1990 film about teen-age life, the joke is about sex. Through establishing shots and talk, two girlfriends are placed at a social distance from each other. One lives in "the projects," the other in an expensively middle-class subur-ban home.

The film offers a single moment of reflection on the social difference in ques-   24
tion; a young man points out that there is plenty of space for making out in the rich
girl's house, none where the projects girl lives. Yet once more, class dismissed.

The reason all this matters is simple. Treating class differences as totally in-   25
consequential strengthens the national delusion that class power and position are
insignificant. It encourages the middle-class—those with the clearest shot at upward mobility—to assume, wrongly, that all citizens enjoy the same freedom of
movement that they enjoy. And it makes it easier for political leaders to speak as
though class power had nothing to do with the inequities of life in America. ("Class
is for European democracies or something else," says George Bush. "It isn't for the
United States of America. We are not going to be divided by class.")

Movies that deal responsibly with class relationships might help to embolden   26
leaders to begin talking candidly about real as opposed to phony issues of "fairness." But movies obviously can't do this as long as their makers are in terror of
allowing class permanently out of the closet.

It's true that occasional moments occur when movie audiences can grasp the   27
substantive dimensions of social difference. A person reached toward from above
or below is seen to possess inner, mysterious resources (or limits) about which
someone differently placed on the social scale can have no inkling, and can't conceivably lay claim.

There is one such moment in "Working Girl." Following orders, Tess, as sec-   28
retarial underling, books her boss, Katharine Parker (Ms. Weaver), into a chalet
for a ski weekend. She is helping Katharine fasten her new ski boots in the office
when she is asked where in the chalet the room is located. Tess doesn't know;
Katharine dials the resort and at once a flood of flawless German fills the room.

The camera angle shows us Tess's awe; we gaze up with her (from the glossy   29
white boots that she, as footman, is buckling) to this animated, magical, Ivy-
educated mistress of the world, self-transformed into Europe, performing in another language. Katharine is demonstrating quite casually that bottom dogs have
no exact knowledge of what lies between them and their ideal, that top dogs
possess secret skills nobody learns overnight, as in charm class, or by changing
hairstyles—skills traceable to uncounted indulgent hours of tutoring, study and
travel.

The bottom dog's eyes widen, a frightening truth dawns. If a talent so mes-   30
merizing—this poured-forth foreign self—can be invisible until now, must there
not be others equally well concealed? Maybe this dream to be her *is* foolish. What
unimaginable barriers stand between me and my desire?

In the movie culture the answer to such questions is, of course: no real barri-   31
ers, none. "Be all you can be" means, at the bottom as at the top, "Be whatever you
wish," fear no obstacle, see no obstacle, there are no obstacles. "Working Girl" is,
finally, a story about how ambitious working girls just can't lose—one more movie
that obliterates class.

"White Palace," for all its initial explicitness about the reality of social differ-   32
ences, is, finally, a story asserting that such differences simply don't matter; pure
passion erases them every time.

The other week Senator Daniel Patrick Moynihan told a Wall Street Journal   33 reporter that the fundamental issue in this country is "class, not race." It's essential, he said, "to at least start thinking about it, start talking about it. Let's be honest. We're not doing that."

One reason we're not is that movies remain firmly resolved against letting us.   34

Rhetorical Focus

1. How does DeMott organize his essay? Does he present his major points in an order that makes sense to you? Would the impact of his argument be changed if he altered the sequence of his examples?
2. Does DeMott provide enough examples to support his points? How much does the success of his argument depend on his readers' having seen all or almost all of the films he mentions?
3. DeMott uses the phrase "class dismissed" several times as a refrain (see paragraphs 9, 14, 22, and 24). Is this an effective rhetorical device? Why or why not?

Thematic Focus

1. Do you find yourself agreeing with DeMott that Hollywood can and should be "trying to teach itself and the nation how to think straight about social hierarchy—the realities of class and class power" (paragraph 4)? Does the immense popularity of certain films he criticizes weaken his argument? Why or why not?
2. What are the specific types of plots that DeMott identifies? Have you seen these scenarios in other films, or on television? If so, where?
3. What kind of plot does DeMott seem to want? Think of a film you have seen that you believe he might like, or consider how one of the scenes that he mentions could be rewritten so he would approve of it. Why do you think the film industry does not produce films with this kind of plot more often?

The Wretched of the Hearth

Barbara Ehrenreich

Barbara Ehrenreich (b. 1941) graduated from Reed College and earned a doctorate in biology from Rockefeller University. A prolific full-time writer for several years now, she is primarily known for her witty but sharply pointed essays and books on issues of class and gender. She often analyzes how these issues are treated by the mass media and experts in various professions. Ehrenreich has co-authored *Witches, Midwives, and Nurses: A History of Women Healers, Complaints and Disorders: The Sexual Politics of Sickness, For Her Own Good: 150 Years of Advice to Women, Re-Making Love: The Femininization of Sex,* and *The Mean Season: The Attack on the Welfare State.* On her own, she has written *The Hearts of Men: American Dreams and the Flight From Commitment, Fear of Falling: The Inner Life of the Middle Class,* and *The Worst Years of Our Lives,* a collection of her essays. Recently, she has been a columnist for *Ms.* and *Mother Jones.* The following essay is her review of Roseanne Barr's autobiography in the April 2, 1990 issue of *The New Republic.*

Reflections Before Reading

What social class or classes have you seen depicted in television series? If possible, give a few specific examples from shows you have seen. The following essay deals specifically with the depiction of working-class people in the television series *Roseanne.* If you have seen this series, what do you think might reasonably be said about its portrayal of the working class? Is it fair to expect at least some television series to note that America has different social classes? Why or why not?

In the second half of the eighties when American conservatism had reached its   1
masochistic zenith with the re-election of Ronald Reagan, when women's liberation had been replaced by the more delicate sensibility known as post-feminism, when everyone was a yuppie and the heartiest word of endorsement in our vocabulary was "appropriate," there was yet this one paradox: our favorite TV personages were a liberal black man and a left-wing white feminist. Cosby could be explained

"The Wretched of the Hearth" by Barbara Ehrenreich, THE NEW REPUBLIC, April 2, 1990, Vol. 202, Number 14. Reprinted by permission of the author.

as a representative of America's officially pro-family mood, but Roseanne is a trickier case. Her idea of humor is to look down on her sleeping family in the eponymous sitcom and muse, "Mmmm, I wonder where we could find an all-night taxidermist."

If zeitgeist were destiny, Roseanne would never have happened. Only a few years ago, we learn from her autobiography, Roseanne Barr was just your run-of-the-mill radical feminist mother-of-three, writing poems involving the Great Goddess, denouncing all known feminist leaders as sellout trash, and praying for the sixties to be born again in a female body. Since the entertainment media do not normally cast about for fat, loud-mouthed feminists to promote to superstardom, we must assume that Roseanne has something to say that many millions of people have been waiting to hear. Like this, upon being told of a woman who stabbed her husband thirty-seven times: "I admire her restraint." [2]

Roseanne is the neglected underside of the eighties, bringing together its great themes of poverty, obesity, and defiance. The overside is handled well enough by Candice Bergen ("Murphy Brown") and Madonna, who exist to remind us that talented women who work out are bound to become fabulously successful. Roseanne works a whole different beat, both in her sitcom and in the movie *She-Devil,* portraying the hopeless underclass of the female sex: polyester-clad, overweight occupants of the slow track; fast-food waitresses, factory workers, housewives, members of the invisible pink-collar army; the despised, the jilted, the underpaid. [3]

But Barr—and this may be her most appealing feature—is never a victim. In the sitcom, she is an overworked mother who is tormented by her bosses at such locales as Wellman Plastics (where she works the assembly line) and Chicken Divine (a fast-food spot). But Roseanne Connor, her sitcom character, has, as we say in the blue-collar suburbs, a mouth on her. When the cute but obnoxious boss at Wellman calls the workers together and announces, "I have something to tell you," Roseanne yells out, "What? That you feel you're a woman trapped in a man's body?" In *She-Devil,* where Barr is unfortunately shorn of her trademark deadpan snarl, revenge must take more concrete forms: she organizes an army of the wretched of the earth—nursing home patients and clerical workers—to destroy her errant husband and drive the slender, beautiful, rich-and-famous Other Woman dotty. [4]

At some point, the women's studies profession is bound to look up from its deconstructions and "re-thinkings" and notice Roseanne. They will then observe, in article and lecture form, that Barr's radicalism is distributed over the two axes of gender and class. This is probably as good an approach as any. Barr's identity is first of all female—her autobiography is titled *My Life As a Woman*—but her female struggles are located in the least telegenic and most frequently overlooked of social strata—the white, blue-collar working class. In anticipation of Roseannology, let us begin with Barr's contribution to the sociology of social class, and then take up her impressive achievements in the area of what could be called feminist theory. [5]

"Roseanne" the sitcom, which was inspired by Barr the stand-up comic, is a radical departure simply for featuring blue-collar Americans—and for depicting them as something other than half-witted greasers and low-life louts. The working [6] class does not usually get much of a role in the American entertainment spectacle. In the seventies mumbling, muscular blue-collar males (*Rocky, The Deer Hunter, Saturday Night Fever*) enjoyed a brief modishness on the screen, while Archie Bunker, the consummate blue-collar bigot, raved away on the tube. But even these grossly stereotyped images vanished in the eighties, as the spectacle narrowed in on the brie-and-chardonnay class. Other than "Roseanne," I can find only one sitcom that deals consistently with the sub-yuppie condition: "Married . . . With Children," a relentlessly nasty portrayal of a shoe salesman and his cognitively disabled family members. There may even be others, but sociological zeal has not sufficed to get me past the opening sequences of "Major Dad," "Full House," or "Doogie Howser."

Not that "Roseanne" is free of class stereotyping. The Connors must bear part of the psychic burden imposed on all working-class people by their economic and occupational betters: they inhabit a zone of glad-handed gemeinschaft,° evocative, now and then, of the stock wedding scene (*The Godfather, The Deer Hunter, Working Girl*) that routinely signifies lost old-world values. They indulge in a manic physicality that would be unthinkable among the more controlled and genteel Huxtables. They maintain a traditional, low-fiber diet of white bread and macaroni. They are not above a fart joke.   7

Still, in "Roseanne" I am willing to forgive the stereotypes as markers designed to remind us of where we are: in the home of a construction worker and his minimum-wage wife. Without the reminders, we might not be aware of how thoroughly the deeper prejudices of the professional class are being challenged. Roseanne's fictional husband Dan (played by the irresistibly cuddly John Goodman) drinks domestic beer and dedicates Sundays to football; but far from being a Bunkeresque boor, he looks to this feminist like the fabled "sensitive man" we have all been pining for. He treats his rotund wife like a sex goddess. He picks up on small cues signaling emotional distress. He helps with homework. And when Roseanne works overtime, he cooks, cleans, and rides herd on the kids without any of the piteous whining we have come to expect from upscale males in their rare, and lavishly documented, encounters with soiled Pampers.   8

Roseanne Connor has her own way of defying the stereotypes. Variously employed as a fast-food operative, a factory worker, a bartender, and a telephone salesperson, her real dream is to be a writer. When her twelve-year-old daughter Darlene (brilliantly played by Sara Gilbert) balks at a poetry-writing assignment, Roseanne gives her a little talking-to involving Sylvia Plath: "She inspired quite a few women, including *moi.*" In another episode, a middle-aged friend thanks Roseanne for inspiring her to dump her chauvinist husband and go to college. We have come a long way from the dithering, cowering Edith Bunker.   9

Most of the time the Connors do the usual sitcom things. They have the little domestic misunderstandings that can be patched up in twenty-four minutes with wisecracks and a round of hugs. But "Roseanne" carries working-class verisimili-   10

°Community ties.

tude into a new and previously taboo dimension—the workplace. In the world of employment, Roseanne knows exactly where she stands: "All the good power jobs are taken. Vanna turns the letters. Leona's got hotels. Margaret's running England . . . 'Course she's not doing a very good job. . . ."

And in the workplace as well as the kitchen, Roseanne knows how to dish it   11 out. A friend of mine, herself a denizen of the low-wage end of the work force, claims to have seen an episode in which Roseanne led an occupational health and safety battle at Wellman Plastics. I missed that one, but I have seen her, on more than one occasion, reduce the boss's ego to rubble. At Chicken Divine, for example, she is ordered to work weekends—an impossibility for a working mother—by an officious teenage boss who confides that he doesn't like working weekends either. In a sequence that could have been crafted by Michael Moore,° Roseanne responds: "Well, that's real good 'cause you never do. You sit in your office like a little Napoleon, making up schedules and screwing up people's lives." To which he says, "That's what they pay me for. And you are paid to follow my orders." Blah blah blah. To which she says, staring at him for a long time and then observing with an evil smile: "You know, you got a little prize hanging out of your nose there."

The class conflict continues on other fronts. In one episode, Roseanne arrives   12 late for an appointment with Darlene's history teacher, because she has been forced to work overtime at Wellman. The teacher, who is leaning against her desk stretching her quadriceps when Roseanne arrives, wants to postpone the appointment because she has a date to play squash. When Roseanne insists, the teacher tells her that Darlene has been barking in class, "like a dog." This she follows with some psychobabble—on emotional problems and dysfunctional families—that would leave most mothers, whatever their social class, clutched with guilt. Not Roseanne, who calmly informs the yuppie snit that, in the Connor household, everybody barks like dogs.

Now this is the kind of class-militant populism that the Democrats, most of   13 them anyway, never seem to get right: up with the little gal; down with the snotty, the pretentious, and the overly paid. At least part of the appeal of "Roseanne" is that it ratifies the resentments of the underdog majority. But this being a sitcom, and Barr being a pacifist, the class-anger never gets too nasty. Even the most loathsome bosses turn out to be human, and in some cases pathetically needy. Rather than hating the bad guys, we end up feeling better about ourselves, which is the function of all good and humanistic humor anyway.

According to high conservative theory, the leftish cast to a show like "Rose-   14 anne" must reflect the media manipulations of the alleged "liberal elite." But the politics of "Roseanne"—including its feminist side, which we will get to in a minute—reflects nothing so much as the decidedly un-elite politics of Barr herself. On the Larry King show a few weeks ago, Barr said that she prefers the term "working class" to "blue collar" because (and I paraphrase) it reminds us of the existence of class, a reality that Americans are all too disposed to forget. In her

---

°Writer–director of *Roger and Me*, a 1989 documentary that satirized the management of General Motors.

autobiography, right up front in the preface, she tells us that it is a "book about the women's movement . . . a book about the left."

   Roseanne: My Life As a Woman traces her journey from alienation to political   15
commitment. It must stand as another one of Barr's commanding oddities. Where you would expect a standard rags-to-riches story, you find a sort of rags-to-revolution tale: more an intellectual and spiritual memoir than the usual chronicle of fearsome obstacles and lucky breaks. She was born the paradigmatic outsider, a Jew in Mormon Utah, and a low-income Jew at that. Within the Mormon culture, she was the "Other" (her own term), the "designated Heathen" in school Christmas pageants, always being reminded that "had we been in a Communist country, I would never have been allowed to express my religion, because 'dissent' is not tolerated there." At home she was loved and encouraged, but the emotional density of the Holocaust-haunted Barr family eventually proved too much for her. After a breakdown and several months of hospitalization, she ran away, at nineteen, to find the sixties, or what was left of them in 1971.

   Her hippie phase left Barr with some proto-politics of the peace-and-love va-   16
riety, three children, and an erratic wage-earner for a husband. It was in this condition that she wandered into the Woman to Woman bookstore on Colfax Avenue in Denver, where she discovered the Movement. Barr seems to have required very little in the way of consciousness-raising. With one gigantic "click," she jumped right in, joined the collective, and was soon occupied giving "seminars on racism, classism, anti-Semitism, pornography, and taking power." If this seems like a rather sudden leap to political leadership, I can attest from my own experience with venues like Woman to Woman that it happens every day.

   But even within the ecumenical embrace of feminism, Barr remained the   17
Outsider. "We did not agree anymore," she tells us of her collective, "with Betty Friedan, Gloria Steinem, or party politics within the women's movement," which she believes has turned into "a professional, careerist women's thing." When she found her "voice," it spoke in a new tone of working-class existentialism: "I began to speak as a working-class woman who is a mother, a woman who no longer believed in change, progress, growth, or hope." It was this special brand of proletarian feminism that inspired her stand-up comic routine. "I am talking about organizing working-class women and mothers," she tells us, and her comic persona was her way of going about it.

   Middle-class feminism has long admitted the possibility of a working-class   18
variant, but the general expectation has been that it would be a diluted version of the "real," or middle-class, thing. According to the conventional wisdom, working-class women would have no truck with the more anti-male aspects of feminism, and would be repelled by the least insult to the nuclear family. They would be comfortable only with the bread-and-butter issues of pay equity, child care, and parental leave. They would be culturally conservative, sensible, dull.

   But we had not met Barr. Her stand-up routine was at first almost too vulgar   19
and castrating for Denver's Comedy Works. In her autobiography, Barr offers an example. Heckled by a drunk for not being "feminine," she turned around, stared at her assailant, and said, "Suck my dick." I wish *Roseanne: My Life As a Woman* gave more examples of her early, Denver-era, stand-up style, but the recently released videotape "Roseanne" (made later in a Los Angeles club) may be a fair

representation. On it she promotes a product called "Fem-Rage," designed to overcome female conditioning during that "one day of the month when you're free to be yourself," and leaves her female fans with the memorable question: "Ever put those maxi-pads on adhesive side up?"

In "Roseanne," the sitcom, however, Barr has been considerably tamed. No longer standing bravely, and one must admit massively, alone with the microphone, she comes to us now embedded in the family; overwhelmed by domestic detail, surrounded by children too young for R-rated language, padding back and forth between stove, refrigerator, and kitchen table. Some of the edge is off here. There are no four-letter words, no menstruation jokes; and Roseanne's male-baiting barbs just bounce off her lovable Dan. Still, what better place for the feminist comic than in a family sitcom? Feminist theory, after all, cut its teeth on the critique of the family. Barr continues the process—leaving huge gaping holes where there was sweetness and piety.

All family sitcoms, of course, teach us that wisecracks and swift put-downs are the preferred modes of affectionate discourse. But Roseanne takes the genre a step further—over the edge, some may say. In the era of big weddings and sudden man shortages, she describes marriage as "a life sentence, without parole." And in the era of the biological time clock and the petted yuppie midlife baby, she can tell Darlene to get a fork out of the drawer and "stick it through your tongue." Or she can say, when Dan asks "Are we missing an offspring?" at breakfast, "Yeah. Where do you think I got the bacon?"

It is Barr's narrow-eyed cynicism about the family, even more than her class consciousness, that gives "Roseanne" its special frisson. Archie Bunker got our attention by telling us that we (blacks, Jews, "ethnics," WASPs, etc.) don't really like each other. Barr's message is that even within the family we don't much like each other. We love each other (who else do we have?); but The Family, with its impacted emotions, its lopsided division of labor, and its ancient system of age-graded humiliations, just doesn't work. Or rather, it doesn't work unless the contradictions are smoothed out with irony and the hostilities are periodically blown off as humor. Coming from mom, rather than from a jaded teenager or a bystander dad, this is scary news indeed.

So Barr's theoretical outlook is, in the best left–feminist tradition, dialectical. On the one hand, she presents the family as a zone of intimacy and support, well worth defending against the forces of capitalism, which drive both mothers and fathers out of the home, scratching around for paychecks. On the other hand, the family is hardly a haven, especially for its grown-up females. It is marred from within by—among other things—the patriarchal division of leisure, which makes dad and the kids the "consumers" of mom's cooking, cleaning, nurturing, and (increasingly) her earnings. Mom's job is to keep the whole thing together—to see that the mortgage payments are made, to fend off the viperish teenagers, to find the missing green sock—but mom is no longer interested in being a human sacrifice on the altar of "pro-family values." She's been down to the feminist bookstore; she's been reading Sylvia Plath.

This is a bleak and radical vision. Not given to didacticism, Barr offers no programmatic ways out. Surely, we are led to conclude, pay equity would help, along with child care, and so on. But Barr leaves us hankering for a quality of change that goes beyond mere reform: for a world in which even the lowliest among us—the hash-slinger, the sock-finder, the factory hand—will be recognized as the poet she truly is.

Maybe this is just too radical. The tabloids have taken to stalking Barr as if she   25 were an unsightly blot on the electronic landscape of our collective dreams. *The New York Times* just devoted a quarter of a page to some upscale writer's prissy musings on Roseanne. "Was I just being squeamish" for disliking Barr, she asks herself: "a goody-two-shoes suburban feminist who was used to her icons being chic and sugar-coated instead of this gum-chewing, male-bashing . . . working-class mama with a big mouth?" No, apparently she is not squeamish. Barr is just too, well, unfeminine.

We know what Barr would say to that, and exactly how she would say it. Yeah,   26 she's crude, but so are the realities of pain and exploitation she seeks to remind us of. If middle-class feminism can't claim Roseanne, maybe it's gotten a little too dainty for its own good. We have a long tradition of tough-talking females behind us, after all, including that other great working-class spokesperson, Mary "Mother" Jones, who once advised the troops, "Whatever you do, *don't* be ladylike."

Rhetorical Focus

1. What audience(s) does Ehrenreich seem interested in reaching here as she discusses the class consciousness of *Roseanne* and its star? In other words, whose assumptions does she apparently want to address and correct?
2. How does Ehrenreich bring in other depictions of class in mass culture to make her point about *Roseanne*'s distinct achievement?
3. Because her official purpose is to review Roseanne Barr's autobiography, Ehrenreich necessarily refers to the star's life. If her assignment had been to help us understand the role of class on Barr's television show, would Ehrenreich still have needed the biographical details? Should DeMott have considered filmmakers' personal history and circumstances in criticizing Hollywood's depiction of class? Explain.

Thematic Focus

1. Why does Ehrenreich like *Roseanne?* Does her analysis of the series' appeal make sense to you? Do you agree, for example, with her remarks about the show's treatment of the family as an institution? If viewers of the series have not had Ehrenreich's thoughts about it, is her argument invalidated?
2. To what extent does Ehrenreich deal with images of men and women, as well as images of class? Identify places in her text where these concerns intersect.
3. Do you find Ehrenreich and DeMott equally convincing? Why or why not?

Suggestions for Writing

1. Both Ehrenreich and DeMott want mass culture to acknowledge more of the realities of social class in America. Write an essay explaining whether they appear to have similar notions of how mass culture should depict class. Do they seem to want the same sorts of plots? Refer to examples in each of their texts.
2. Describe a personal experience that made you very conscious of class differences. What were the signs of these differences? Were they overcome? Why or why not? What, ultimately, did you learn from this experience?
3. Explain the social-class background of the characters in a recent film or television show. Be sure to identify what about the characters makes you think they belong to one or more particular classes. You may want to consider, for example, the characters' living conditions, jobs, possessions, worries, and hopes. As part of your analysis, indicate whether you accept this depiction of class, and give reasons for your judgment.

THE RELATION BETWEEN NEWS AND ENTERTAINMENT

The previous constellation examined the question of realism in mass culture, focusing in particular on depictions of social class in films and television shows. Here we continue to pursue the subject of realism, this time focusing on television news. A common charge leveled against television is that it presents the news superficially in order to keep viewers entertained. The issue has even grown hotter as more and more people depend solely on television for news. For example, during the Persian Gulf War of 1990, many people appreciated the exciting, fastbreaking coverage of television networks such as CNN, but others pointed out that newspapers often wound up providing more accurate and in-depth reports.

Here we offer two ways of looking at the relation between entertainment and news on television. Neil Postman basically lambastes the medium for turning news into show business, while John Fiske suggests how to make television news entertaining as well as informative. Underlying their arguments are two rather different theories of mass culture. These theories are not firmly opposed, but there is some tension between them. In fact, versions of these theories have competed with each other throughout the twentieth-century history of cultural analysis. One is a deterministic view. Postman considers television a dangerously mind-numbing medium and its audiences mostly victims of the brief, disconnected images with which it depicts the world. The selection in this chapter comes from a book in which he relentlessly bemoans the power of television, and he even gave it the ominous title, *Amusing Ourselves to Death.* Although Postman would not bother to criticize television in the first place if he did not hope to some extent that it could be reformed, he clearly believes that it may overwhelm American society's powers of critical thinking. The other theory is more optimistic. While Fiske believes, too, that television can dominate people by emphasizing passive forms of entertainment, he also thinks television can combine entertainment with enlightenment. Furthermore, he thinks people have the capacity to resist television images and even reinterpret them for admirably creative purposes. Note that often in his articles and books, Fiske speaks more of "popular culture" than of "mass culture." In fact, the following excerpt comes from a book of his entitled *Reading Popular Culture*. For him, the term *popular culture* implies that people can develop a genuinely active, communal, and realistic understanding of their world, whereas the term *mass culture* suggests for him that they simply acquiesce to the media.

As you weigh the particular details of these two authors' arguments, consider the basic assumptions about mass culture that each makes. Do you share Postman's fear of television's effects? Do you like Fiske's proposed solutions? Does the vision that one has of the mass audience make more sense than the other's? In comparison with these authors, what have you assumed about television audiences? What do you think should be the relation between television news and entertainment?

"Now . . . This"

Neil Postman

Neil Postman (b. 1931) is a professor of communication arts and sciences at New York University. He has long specialized in media ecology, the study of how mass media interact with the larger society. Postman has written by himself or collaborated on many books about the relations of media, education, and language. He and Charles Weingartner provoked much debate with their 1969 book *Teaching as a Subversive Activity,* which attacked the schools for not doing more to encourage active, critical thinking. Postman also gained attention when, ten years later, he wrote a sequel, entitled *Teaching as a Conserving Activity.* There, he called for a rigorous, structured, authoritative curriculum, believing that schools now had to counteract television and other forces that increasingly fragmented students' minds. Postman continued to warn against the power of television in his 1985 book *Amusing Ourselves to Death: Public Discourse in the Age of Show Business,* from which the following is an excerpt.

Reflections Before Reading

Do you consider yourself reasonably well-informed about current events? Why or why not? How do you explain your degree of knowledge about the news? Do you think your amount of knowledge is typical of your generation? Where and when do you try to find out local, national, and international news? In the following selection, Neil Postman analyzes the ways that television presents news. What images, if any, come to mind when you think of television news programs? Do you believe they can present the news well? Why or why not?

The American humorist H. Allen Smith once suggested that of all the worrisome   1
words in the English language, the scariest is "uh oh," as when a physician looks at
your X-rays, and with knitted brow says, "Uh oh." I should like to suggest that the
words which are the title of this chapter are as ominous as any, all the more so
because they are spoken without knitted brow—indeed, with a kind of idiot's delight. The phrase, if that's what it may be called, adds to our grammar a new part of
speech, a conjunction that does not connect anything to anything but does the
opposite: separates everything from everything. As such, it serves as a compact
metaphor for the discontinuities in so much that passes for public discourse in
present-day America.

"Now . . . this" is commonly used on radio and television newscasts to indicate   2
that what one has just heard or seen has no relevance to what one is about to hear
or see, or possibly to anything one is ever likely to hear or see. The phrase is a
means of acknowledging the fact that the world as mapped by the speeded-up
electronic media has no order or meaning and is not to be taken seriously. There is
no murder so brutal, no earthquake so devastating, no political blunder so costly—
for that matter, no ball score so tantalizing or weather report so threatening—that
it cannot be erased from our minds by a newscaster saying, "Now . . . this." The
newscaster means that you have thought long enough on the previous matter (approximately forty-five seconds), that you must not be morbidly preoccupied with it
(let us say, for ninety seconds), and that you must now give your attention to another fragment of news or a commercial.

Television did not invent the "Now . . . this" world view. As I have tried to   3
show, it is the offspring of the intercourse between telegraphy and photography.
But it is through television that it has been nurtured and brought to a perverse
maturity. For on television, nearly every half hour is a discrete event, separated in
content, context, and emotional texture from what precedes and follows it. In part
because television sells its time in seconds and minutes, in part because television
must use images rather than words, in part because its audience can move freely to
and from the television set, programs are structured so that almost each eight-
minute segment may stand as a complete event in itself. Viewers are rarely required to carry over any thought or feeling from one parcel of time to another.

Of course, in television's presentation of the "news of the day," we may see the   4
"Now . . . this" mode of discourse in its boldest and most embarrassing form. For

there, we are presented not only with fragmented news but news without context, without consequences, without value, and therefore without essential seriousness; that is to say, news as pure entertainment.

Consider, for example, how you would proceed if you were given the opportunity to produce a television news show for any station concerned to attract the largest possible audience. You would, first, choose a cast of players, each of whom has a face that is both "likable" and "credible." Those who apply would, in fact, submit to you their eight-by-ten glossies, from which you would eliminate those whose countenances are not suitable for nightly display. This means that you will exclude women who are not beautiful or who are over the age of fifty, men who are bald, all people who are overweight or whose noses are too long or whose eyes are too close together. You will try, in other words, to assemble a cast of talking hair-do's. At the very least, you will want those whose faces would not be unwelcome on a magazine cover.

Christine Craft has just such a face, and so she applied for a co-anchor position on KMBC-TV in Kansas City. According to a lawyer who represented her in a sexism suit she later brought against the station, the management of KMBC-TV "loved Christine's look." She was accordingly hired in January 1981. She was fired in August 1981 because research indicated that her appearance "hampered viewer acceptance." What exactly does "hampered viewer acceptance" mean? And what does it have to do with the news? Hampered viewer acceptance means the same thing for television news as it does for any television show: Viewers do not like looking at the performer. It also means that viewers do not believe the performer, that she lacks credibility. In the case of a theatrical performance, we have a sense of what that implies: The actor does not persuade the audience that he or she is the character being portrayed. But what does lack of credibility imply in the case of a news show? What character is a co-anchor playing? And how do we decide that the performance lacks verisimilitude? Does the audience believe that the newscaster is lying, that what is reported did not in fact happen, that something important is being concealed?

It is frightening to think that this may be so, that the perception of the truth of a report rests heavily on the acceptability of the newscaster. In the ancient world, there was a tradition of banishing or killing the bearer of bad tidings. Does the television news show restore, in a curious form, this tradition? Do we banish those who tell us the news when we do not care for the face of the teller? Does television countermand the warnings we once received about the fallacy of the ad hominem argument?

If the answer to any of these questions is even a qualified "Yes," then here is an issue worthy of the attention of epistemologists. Stated in its simplest form, it is that television provides a new (or, possibly, restores an old) definition of truth: The credibility of the teller is the ultimate test of the truth of a proposition. "Credibility" here does not refer to the past record of the teller for making statements that have survived the rigors of reality-testing. It refers only to the impression of sincerity, authenticity, vulnerability or attractiveness (choose one or more) conveyed by the actor/reporter.

This is a matter of considerable importance, for it goes beyond the question of   9
how truth is perceived on television news shows. If on television, credibility replaces reality as the decisive test of truth-telling, political leaders need not trouble
themselves very much with reality provided that their performances consistently
generate a sense of verisimilitude. I suspect, for example, that the dishonor that
now shrouds Richard Nixon results not from the fact that he lied but that on television he looked like a liar. Which, if true, should bring no comfort to anyone, not
even veteran Nixon-haters. For the alternative possibilities are that one may look
like a liar but be telling the truth; or even worse, look like a truth-teller but in fact
be lying.

As a producer of a television news show, you would be well aware of these   10
matters and would be careful to choose your cast on the basis of criteria used by
David Merrick and other successful impresarios. Like them, you would then turn
your attention to staging the show on principles that maximize entertainment
value. You would, for example, select a musical theme for the show. All television
news programs begin, end, and are somewhere in between punctuated with music.
I have found very few Americans who regard this custom as peculiar, which fact I
have taken as evidence for the dissolution of lines of demarcation between serious
public discourse and entertainment. What has music to do with the news? Why is it
there? It is there, I assume, for the same reason music is used in the theater and
films—to create a mood and provide a leitmotif for the entertainment. If there
were no music—as is the case when any television program is interrupted for a
news flash—viewers would expect something truly alarming, possibly life-altering.
But as long as the music is there as a frame for the program, the viewer is comforted to believe that there is nothing to be greatly alarmed about; that, in fact, the
events that are reported have as much relation to reality as do scenes in a play.

This perception of a news show as a stylized dramatic performance whose   11
content has been staged largely to entertain is reinforced by several other features,
including the fact that the average length of any story is forty-five seconds. While
brevity does not always suggest triviality, in this case it clearly does. It is simply not
possible to convey a sense of seriousness about any event if its implications are
exhausted in less than one minute's time. In fact, it is quite obvious that TV news
has no intention of suggesting that any story *has* any implications, for that would
require viewers to continue to think about it when it is done and therefore obstruct
their attending to the next story that waits panting in the wings. In any case, viewers are not provided with much opportunity to be distracted from the next story
since in all likelihood it will consist of some film footage. Pictures have little difficulty in overwhelming words, and short-circuiting introspection. As a television
producer, you would be certain to give both prominence and precedence to any
event for which there is some sort of visual documentation. A suspected killer
being brought into a police station, the angry face of a cheated consumer, a barrel
going over Niagara Falls (with a person alleged to be in it), the President disem-
barking from a helicopter on the White House lawn—these are always fascinating
or amusing, and easily satisfy the requirements of an entertaining show. It is, of
course, not necessary that the visuals actually document the point of a story. Nei-

ther is it necessary to explain why such images are intruding themselves on public consciousness. Film footage justifies itself, as every television producer well knows.

It is also of considerable help in maintaining a high level of unreality that the   12
newscasters do not pause to grimace or shiver when they speak their prefaces or epilogs to the film clips. Indeed, many newscasters do not appear to grasp the meaning of what they are saying, and some hold to a fixed and ingratiating enthusiasm as they report on earthquakes, mass killings and other disasters. Viewers would be quite disconcerted by any show of concern or terror on the part of newscasters. Viewers, after all, are partners with the newscasters in the "Now . . . this" culture, and they expect the newscaster to play out his or her role as a character who is marginally serious but who stays well clear of authentic understanding. The viewers, for their part, will not be caught contaminating their responses with a sense of reality, any more than an audience at a play would go scurrying to call home because a character on stage has said that a murderer is loose in the neighborhood.

The viewers also know that no matter how grave any fragment of news may   13
appear (for example, on the day I write a Marine Corps general has declared that nuclear war between the United States and Russia is inevitable), it will shortly be followed by a series of commercials that will, in an instant, defuse the import of the news, in fact render it largely banal. This is a key element in the structure of a news program and all by itself refutes any claim that television news is designed as a serious form of public discourse. Imagine what you would think of me, and this book, if I were to pause here, tell you that I will return to my discussion in a moment, and then proceed to write a few words in behalf of United Airlines or the Chase Manhattan Bank. You would rightly think that I had no respect for you and, certainly, no respect for the subject. And if I did this not once but several times in each chapter, you would think the whole enterprise unworthy of your attention. Why, then, do we not think a news show similarly unworthy? The reason, I believe, is that whereas we expect books and even other media (such as film) to maintain a consistency of tone and a continuity of content, we have no such expectation of television, and especially television news. We have become so accustomed to its discontinuities that we are no longer struck dumb, as any sane person would be, by a newscaster who having just reported that a nuclear war is inevitable goes on to say that he will be right back after this word from Burger King; who says, in other words, "Now . . . this." One can hardly overestimate the damage that such juxtapositions do to our sense of the world as a serious place. The damage is especially massive to youthful viewers who depend so much on television for their clues as to how to respond to the world. In watching television news, they, more than any other segment of the audience, are drawn into an epistemology based on the assumption that all reports of cruelty and death are greatly exaggerated and, in any case, not to be taken seriously or responded to sanely.

I should go so far as to say that embedded in the surrealistic frame of a televi-   14
sion news show is a theory of anticommunication, featuring a type of discourse that abandons logic, reason, sequence and rules of contradiction. In aesthetics, I be-

lieve the name given to this theory is Dadaism; in philosophy, nihilism; in psychiatry, schizophrenia. In the parlance of the theater, it is known as vaudeville.

For those who think I am here guilty of hyperbole, I offer the following de-   15
scription of television news by Robert MacNeil, executive editor and co-anchor of
the "MacNeil-Lehrer Newshour." The idea, he writes, "is to keep everything brief,
not to strain the attention of anyone but instead to provide constant stimulation
through variety, novelty, action, and movement. You are required . . . to pay attention to no concept, no character, and no problem for more than a few seconds at a
time." He goes on to say that the assumptions controlling a news show are "that
bite-sized is best, that complexity must be avoided, that nuances are dispensable,
that qualifications impede the simple message, that visual stimulation is a substitute for thought, and that verbal precision is an anachronism."

Robert MacNeil has more reason than most to give testimony about the tele-   16
vision news show as vaudeville act. The "MacNeil-Lehrer Newshour" is an unusual
and gracious attempt to bring to television some of the elements of typographic
discourse. The program abjures visual stimulation, consists largely of extended explanations of events and in-depth interviews (which even there means only five to
ten minutes), limits the number of stories covered, and emphasizes background
and coherence. But television has exacted its price for MacNeil's rejection of a
show business format. By television's standards, the audience is minuscule, the
program is confined to public-television stations, and it is a good guess that the
combined salary of MacNeil and Lehrer is one-fifth of Dan Rather's or Tom
Brokaw's.

If you were a producer of a television news show for a commercial station, you   17
would not have the option of defying television's requirements. It would be demanded of you that you strive for the largest possible audience, and, as a consequence and in spite of your best intentions, you would arrive at a production very
nearly resembling MacNeil's description. Moreover, you would include some
things MacNeil does not mention. You would try to make celebrities of your newscasters. You would advertise the show, both in the press and on television itself.
You would do "news briefs," to serve as an inducement to viewers. You would have
a weatherman as comic relief, and a sportscaster whose language is a touch uncouth (as a way of his relating to the beer-drinking common man). You would, in
short, package the whole event as any producer might who is in the entertainment
business.

The result of all this is that Americans are the best entertained and quite likely   18
the least well-informed people in the Western world. I say this in the face of the
popular conceit that television, as a window to the world, has made Americans
exceedingly well informed. Much depends here, of course, on what is meant by
being informed. I will pass over the now tiresome polls that tell us that, at any given
moment, 70 percent of our citizens do not know who is the Secretary of State or
the Chief Justice of the Supreme Court. Let us consider, instead, the case of Iran
during the drama that was called the "Iranian Hostage Crisis." I don't suppose
there has been a story in years that received more continuous attention from television. We may assume, then, that Americans know most of what there is to know

about this unhappy event. And now, I put these questions to you: Would it be an exaggeration to say that not one American in a hundred knows what language the Iranians speak? Or what the word "Ayatollah" means or implies? Or knows any details of the tenets of Iranian religious beliefs? Or the main outlines of their political history? Or knows who the Shah was, and where he came from?

Nonetheless, everyone had an opinion about this event, for in America everyone is entitled to an opinion, and it is certainly useful to have a few when a pollster shows up. But these are opinions of a quite different order from eighteenth- or nineteenth-century opinions. It is probably more accurate to call them emotions rather than opinions, which would account for the fact that they change from week to week, as the pollsters tell us. What is happening here is that television is altering the meaning of "being informed" by creating a species of information that might properly be called *disinformation*. I am using this word almost in the precise sense in which it is used by spies in the CIA or KGB. Disinformation does not mean false information. It means misleading information—misplaced, irrelevant, fragmented or superficial information—information that creates the illusion of knowing something but which in fact leads one away from knowing. In saying this, I do not mean to imply that television news deliberately aims to deprive Americans of a coherent, contextual understanding of their world. I mean to say that when news is packaged as entertainment, that is the inevitable result. And in saying that the television news show entertains but does not inform, I am saying something far more serious than that we are being deprived of authentic information. I am saying we are losing our sense of what it means to be well informed. Ignorance is always correctable. But what shall we do if we take ignorance to be knowledge?

Rhetorical Focus

1. Why does Postman choose the title he does for this chapter? Is it an effective device for calling attention to his recurring theme? What other titles are possible?
2. Postman directly addresses his readers throughout the chapter. In particular, he has them imagine what they would do if they produced a newscast. Considering that most will not, in fact, become television news producers, is this technique effective?
3. In what places, if any, does Postman directly acknowledge what his reader may be thinking about his claims? Should he have acknowledged the reader's possible disagreement more than he does?

Thematic Focus

1. Postman develops his argument about television news by comparing it to various other show business productions. What specific analogies does he make? Do they seem fair? Why or why not?
2. Postman worries that "the perception of the truth of a report rests heavily on the acceptability of the newscaster" (paragraph 7). Do you think he is right to be concerned? Why or why not?

3. Postman makes a number of other specific points while generally criticizing television news. For example, do you agree with him that television
   news stories need to be longer? Do you think the frequency of commercials "all by itself refutes any claim that television news is designed as a
   serious form of public discourse" (paragraph 13)? What do you think of his
   assertion "that Americans are the best entertained and quite likely the least
   well-informed people in the Western world" (paragraph 18)?

Popular News
John Fiske

A native of Great Britain, John Fiske (b. 1939) has taught there as well as in
Australia and the United States. At present, he is a professor of
communication arts at the University of Wisconsin—Madison. Fiske likes to
analyze a wide range of cultural phenomena. In his book *Reading the
Popular*, from which the following is an excerpt, he studies not only
television news but also rock videos, Madonna as cultural icon, television
quiz shows, the Sears Tower in Chicago, shopping malls, and even life at
the beach. Other books that Fiske has written or co-authored include
*Understanding Popular Culture, Myths of Oz: Reading Australian Popular
Culture, Television Culture, Introduction to Communication Studies,* and
Reading Television.

Reflections Before Reading

In the following selection, Fiske argues that television news should try to
boost its popularity. He suggests that we know broadcast news is popular
when people talk later about what it reported. What news items do you
recall people talking about recently? Do any of these items have something
in common? If so, what? Do you think television, radio, and newspapers can
do more to increase people's interest in the news? If so, what? What do
you think Postman would want the mass media to keep in mind as they
tried to make the news more appealing?

The familiar division of television's programming into information and entertain-   1
ment carries with it the implication that information is objective, true, educational,
and important, whereas entertainment, by opposition, is subjective, fictional, es-
capist, trivial, and, frequently, harmful. Ultimately, information is judged to provide "good" television and entertainment "bad," so to be entertaining comes to
mean to compromise standards, to pander to the low. The logical extension of this
simplistic opposition is that the final choice facing us is between good, accurate,
responsible television that may be unpopular, and bad, compromised, irresponsible television that people actually want to watch.

TV news is the terrain over which such cultural struggles are waged—open to   2
attack from one flank for compromising standards of accuracy and social responsibility in order to attract audiences, and from the other for being boring, irrelevant,
and eminently forgettable. It would be better for TV news if it confidently asserted
that its position in the repertoire of news media is one that makes its popularity its
defining characteristic. It should, therefore, be evaluated less by informational criteria and more by those of popular appeal. We should demand of our television
news that it make the events of the world *popular,* that it subject them to popular
taste and attempt to make them part of the popular consciousness of society. To
encourage a wide diversity of people to want to watch it, and to remember and
think about its events, TV news must meet the key criteria of popular taste, those
of relevance and pleasurable productivity.

❖   ❖   ❖

If the function of broadcast news is to encourage the popular circulation of   3
information about the nation and the world, then our criteria for evaluating it must
include those of entertainment. We should not criticize it for "pandering" to entertainment, but rather should evaluate *how* entertaining it is, and *what* information
it makes entertaining. In other words, we need to evaluate it according to the
criteria of popular culture.

Broadcast news should aim to stimulate its audiences to take up its informa-   4
tion and insert it into the culture of their everyday lives. It should aim to be talked
about, which means it must discard its role of privileged information-giver, with its
clear distinction between the one who knows (the author) and those who do not
(the audience), for that gives it the place and the tone of the author-god and discourages popular productivity. Rather, it should aim to involve its viewers in making sense of the world around them, it should encourage them to be participants in
the process, not recipients of its products: it should, in [Michel] de Certeau's
terms, aim to make them readers rather than decipherers. Instead of promoting a
final truth, then, it should provoke discussion (like soap opera) or disagreement
(like sportscasting).

Ironically, TV news is ideally suited to this—it is the professional practices of   5
journalism and their ideology of objectivity that militate against it. News has, potentially at least, all the elements of popularity built into it, and it fights against
them in order to conform to a professional ideology that is essentially literate, ho-
mogenizing, and textually authoritarian—and therefore inappropriate. Central to
this ideology is objectivity. Objectivity is authority in disguise: "objective" facts

always support particular points of view and their "objectivity" can exist only as part of the play of power. But, more important, objective facts cannot be challenged: objectivity discourages audience activity and participation. Rather than being "objective," therefore, TV news should present multiple perspectives that, like those of soap opera, have as unclear a hierarchy as possible: the more complex the events it describes, the more the contradictions among the different social positions from which to make sense of them should be left open and raw. The anchor and reporters should be less concerned about telling the final truth of what has happened, and should present, instead, different ways of understanding it and the different points of view inscribed in those different ways. So, too, they should not disguise their processes of selection and editing, but should open them up to reveal news as a production, not as transparent reportage.

The people cope well with contradictions; popular culture in industrial socie-   6
ties is largely constructed out of them, for the social experience of the subordinate is contradictory to its core—the social system that nurtures and rewards them also oppresses them; they simultaneously play along with it and oppose it in a form of constant lived irony. The abrasive faces of the contradictory spark meanings that escape the control of the dominant, that become available to be made into the popular. It is contradictions, the unresolved relationships among different social experiences, that provoke discussion and encourage the oral reproduction of meanings that is so central to popular culture. This is not a mere recirculation of meanings already presented, it is a reworking of the stuff from which meanings are made, a restructuring of social relations and discursive relations that is the responsibility and creativity of the reader and not of the producer of the text.

This, of course, is risky business, for the meanings that people make will often   7
evade social control—they may be offensive, oppositional, embarrassing. But it is this that will make them popular, active meanings, and will make the events of which they make sense seem to *matter*. News's constant attempt to close down contradictions and resolve them into a final objective meaning (the "true facts") actually kills those events, distances them from the viewers and makes them easily forgettable and, as many a survey has shown, frequently forgotten.

News should eschew not only objectivity, but also narrative closure. Instead of   8
attempting to find a narrative end-point from which to look back and understand what has gone before (and all journalists are trained to do this), it should, like soap opera, leave its multiple narratives open, unresolved. Instead of saying, "This is what happened today," it should say, "These are the events we are in the middle of." It should not present itself as the record of what has occurred, for that is the literate narrative of books and films, but rather as the ongoing, unresolved narrative of soap opera, for that is television's equivalent of the oral narratives through which we make sense of our daily lives. Soap opera is so readily incorporated into everyday life because its formal structures represent the liveness, the nowness, the unwrittenness of oral culture.

When news stresses its immediacy, it is actually stressing its recency, not its   9
liveness: any liveness it may have had has been closed off into the past tense, so the best it can do is to stress how recently past (but not live) its events are. Soap opera, like oral culture, like the events that news is actually dealing with, draws no firm

line between past and present and therefore suggests the continuity of this past–present with the unwritten future, a continuity that is broken by news's concern with telling us the final truth of what *has* happened. The journalistic search for a point of narrative closure is a search for a point from which the only view is backward.

This is a legacy from print journalism, with its roots in literate culture, but the electronic media become popular to the extent that they distance themselves from the literate and approximate the oral. It may be appropriate for newspapers or journals to speak of current affairs with a voice of authority, to narrativize them so that they make coherent sense—even, perhaps, to present that sense as the objective truth. In so doing they are aligning themselves, appropriately enough, with literate, disciplined, controlled culture. They invite educated, disciplined readers who will read *with* them, not mindlessly agreeing with what they say, but cooperating with the discursive strategies by which they say it. 10

But the popular reader is undisciplined. He or she dips into and out of the text, selecting fragments to pay attention to because they fit his or her criteria of relevance, not because they are preferred by the textual structure. So [J.] Lewis found that some of the viewers of a political news story in the United Kingdom gave their attention to a live film insert and ignored the narrative framing and explanation given it by the rest of the text. From a literate point of view, they "got it wrong." But such a "misunderstanding" of the textually preferred meaning of an event is a typical reading practice of the popular, for it frees that event from the meanings of those with textual power, and opens it up to meanings that are relevant to the various formations of the people. A "misreading" of this sort is a necessary practice of the popular. It is part of the popular disrespect for the text, a way of treating the text as a resource, not as a revered object or as an authoritative message-bearer. 11

Frequently the events that news covers will be distant from the everyday lives of its viewers, and it will not be able to construct, in the way that soap opera does, multiple points of pertinence from which viewer-specific relevances can be made. But if its content is to be dictated more by educational than popular criteria, then its form should reverse these priorities. It should aim to make those events deemed by educational criteria to be of national significance as popular as possible. To achieve this it must not preach or teach; rather, it must invite participatory readings and lay itself open to viewer-selected, viewer-produced, viewer-circulated meanings of its content—for only this viewer productivity can make those events part of the micro-level culture of the everyday. 12

When the events of the news become woven orally into the fabric of everyday life they are made to *matter*. It is more important in a democracy to stimulate people into making national and international events matter in their daily lives than it is to teach them about the "truth" of those events. Popular news must escape the control of those who wish to promote a certain set of meanings of the world. Popular news must not be propaganda, even in its original sense of the propagation of the (Christian) truth; it must not serve the sociopolitical interests of any set of social forces because, in so doing, it risks failing to meet the two criteria of the popular—relevance and productivity. 13

Currently, there are many complaints about the quality of TV news. There are   14
similar complaints about the low level of participation in political life, and about
low levels of knowledge about politics and national history. It is all too tempting to
make a commonsense truth out of this—that poor television news is responsible
for the low levels of political participation and knowledge. Of course, there must
be some connection between the two; TV news is one of the sources of political
knowledge and one of the potential motivators of political activity. But the relationship between the political life of a nation and its television news, particularly in
the realm of the popular, is never one of cause and effect—in either direction—
nor is it self-evident that the criteria by which the news is judged to be "poor"
would, if applied rigorously, make it popular. Indeed, many of the criticisms of
television news criticize those of its characteristics that make it more readily accessible to popular cultural uses.

The more valid criticism of television news is that it is not popular enough. Far   15
from wishing to improve its objectivity, its depth, or its authority, I would wish to
increase its openness, its contradictions, the multiplicity of its voices and points of
view. Television news is already like soap opera, but it needs to extend these similarities if it is to engage its topics relevantly and importantly with the everyday lives
of the people.

Rhetorical Focus

1. What does Fiske accomplish with his first two paragraphs?
2. When explaining what he wants television newscasts to do, Fiske suggests
   that they should be more like soap operas. Is his resorting to such an analogy a wise rhetorical move, given that Postman, for example, feels television news is becoming too *much* like show business?
3. How would you characterize Fiske's emotional tone, especially in comparison with Postman's? Does Fiske's tone affect the power of his argument
   for you? Why or why not?

Thematic Focus

1. Fiske asserts that "The anchor and reporters should be less concerned
   about telling the final truth of what has happened, and should present,
   instead, different ways of understanding it and the different points of view
   inscribed in those different ways" (paragraph 5). He even suggests that
   television news present contradictory accounts. Do you believe such a
   newscast can indeed be popular? Do you think you would enjoy it, or
   would you simply be irritated by it?
2. Fiske cites the case of British television viewers who focused on a piece of
   news film "and ignored the narrative framing and explanation given it by
   the rest of the text" (paragraph 11). Evidently, he approves of their "misreading." Does his attitude make sense? Why or why not?

3. How does Fiske define *objectivity*? What does he have against it? Would his argument encourage or discourage what Postman calls "disinformation"? Explain.

Suggestions for Writing

1. Explain whether you agree with Fiske's last sentence: "Television news is already like soap opera, but it needs to extend these similarities if it is to engage its topics relevantly and importantly with the everyday lives of the people." As part of your explanation, indicate the specific qualities of soap opera that Fiske has in mind. Indicate, too, what you think Postman would say about Fiske's proposal. Give details from both texts, as well as reasons for your own opinion of the proposal.
2. Ask four students how often they try to learn about the news and what their source of news usually is. Then, write an essay in which you report and evaluate what you heard. Do you think any of your interview subjects should be doing anything differently? Why or why not? Refer to specific statements they made.
3. Watch a television newscast, and then write an essay explaining whether you think it appropriately balanced serious news with entertainment. Be sure to refer to specific details of the show. If you prefer, your essay can take the form of a letter to the producer.

DEBATING MASS CULTURE AND MORALITY: THE CASE OF RAP MUSIC

This unit has considered several issues in film and television. We conclude by plunging into an issue that has actually preoccupied many writers over the course of centuries: the debate over how culture and morality should relate. Does culture have to be moral? If it is not, should it be censored? How should *culture* and *morality* be defined, anyway? In contemporary mass culture, numerous events have prompted these questions. You may already be familiar with debates over community antipornography legislation, film ratings, warning stickers on record albums, the influence on young people of heavy-metal music groups, and the National Endowment for the Arts' funding of the Robert Mapplethorpe photography exhibition.

Here, we present a controversy over rap music. In 1990, an album by the rap group 2 Live Crew was banned in three counties in Florida. The group itself was charged with giving an obscene performance there, although it was later found innocent of that charge. With the following essays, we have set up a forum on these events and the general topic of rap music's validity. Jon Pareles gives a background for rap music in general and of the 2 Live Crew case in particular. He also points out what he considers the acceptable and the troublesome aspects of rap. Next, Charles Krauthammer launches an all-out attack on 2 Live Crew and rap, associating this kind of music with other cultural events that he believes genuinely damage society. In the essay that follows, however, David Mills defends 2 Live Crew and rap music, insisting that both must be understood and tolerated as elements of African-American culture. Finally, writing from a black feminist point of view, Michele Wallace accuses 2 Live Crew and other rap artists of sexism. She concludes by suggesting that female rappers may counteract it. As you encounter the shifting perspectives of these authors, consider your own position on their concerns and how you would try to persuade others of it. Note in particular how they put rap in different cultural contexts as they evaluate its nature, background, and effects. Think, too, about the ways you would challenge or defend the ethics of various art forms you know.

Rap: Slick, Violent, Nasty and, Maybe, Hopeful

Jon Pareles

Jon Pareles (b. 1953) is a music critic for *The New York Times*. He studied piano and flute at Yale University, where he also wrote music criticism for the student newspaper, played in the concert band, and participated in rock, jazz, and classical ensembles. After graduating in 1974, he worked as a free-lance writer before becoming music editor for *Crawdaddy* magazine in 1977. In 1979, he became associate editor for *Rolling Stone,* and in 1980 a senior editor for *The Village Voice.* Having occasionally written pop and jazz criticism for *The New York Times* since 1982, he joined the newspaper's staff in 1985. Pareles has also co-edited *Rolling Stone Encyclopedia of Rock & Roll.* The following article by him appeared in the *Times* on June 17, 1990.

Reflections Before Reading

List three examples of mass culture that you find extremely offensive or that someone you know has found so. Think of particular films, television shows, books, magazines, concert or stage performances, album covers, and song lyrics. Why might someone find these examples offensive? Would you favor warning people about them? Limiting access to them? Banning them outright? Why or why not? The essays in this constellation deal with rap music, specifically addressing the 1990 controversy over the rap group 2 Live Crew. What, if anything, do you associate with this controversy and with rap in general?

Rap music now has a criminal record. On June 6, United States District Court Judge Jose Gonzalez of Fort Lauderdale, Fla., declared that "As Nasty as They Wanna Be," an album by the 2 Live Crew, a rap group that is based in Miami, was obscene in the three counties under his jurisdiction, making it the first recording to be declared obscene by a Federal court. In the next few days, a record-store owner who had continued to sell the album was arrested; two members of the group were also arrested for performing one of the album's songs before an adults-only audience. 1

It was only the latest, if potentially the most far-reaching, of rap's skirmishes with mainstream culture. As the voice of the young black male, rap has become a vivid, contentious cultural symbol. From its beginnings in the mid-1970's—when rap was part of New York's emerging hip-hop subculture, which also included break dancing and graffiti art—rap has been met by condescension, rejection and outright fear from those outside its domain. 2

Although rappers have made a point of denouncing black-on-black crime, many promoters refuse to book rap concerts fearing the audience would include violent members of a troubled community already plagued by crime. Some radio stations chose not to play rap music because their research shows that the music alienates many listeners. People who monitor rock lyrics—from pop critics to the Parents' Music Resource Center (a group that advocates voluntary warning stickers on potentially offensive albums) to the Gay and Lesbian Alliance Against Defamation—worry about some rappers' overt homophobia, sexism and other bigotry along with their descriptions of violence. 3

To many listeners, white and black, rap is the sound of a threatening underclass—although, increasingly, suburbanites as well as urban teen-agers are embracing rap, which includes tall tales, jokes, ethical advice, political statements and baroquely exuberant metaphorical flights. Like the punk rock that appeared almost simultaneously in the 1970's, rap has as much to do with attitude as with conventionally defined musical skills. Rappers live by their wit—their ability to rhyme, the speed of their articulation—and by their ability to create outsized personas through words alone. 4

"The skills you need to be a good rapper are the same skills you need to get ahead in mainstream society," said Philippe Bourgois, an assistant professor of anthropology at San Francisco State University who is writing a book, "Scrambling," about street culture. "You have to write well and speak well in a creative manner, which are exactly the skills you need in an information-processing city like New York. And rap is about making something of yourself—it's the American dream." 5

Put simply, rap is an affirmation of self. It might define that self as successful,   6
well paid, flaunting status symbols like jewelry and cars. And often, it defines that
self as a sexually insatiable guy with a touch of the outlaw—an exaggerated version
of the demeaning stereotypes young black men have grown up with.

"When you're faced with a stereotype, you can disavow it or you can embrace   7
it and exaggerate it to the nth degree," said Henry Louis Gates, the John Spencer
Bassett professor of English at Duke University. "The rappers take the white
Western culture's worst fear of black men and make a game out of it."

With the furor over the 2 Live Crew, rap machismo has undergone ever closer   8
scrutiny. The 2 Live Crew has been accused of misogyny and glorifying abuse of
women. Yet while their rhymes on "As Nasty as They Wanna Be" are openly, lout-
ishly sexist, treating women entirely as objects, the lyrics are so single-mindedly
concerned with self-gratification that the consequences for women don't seem to
enter their minds.

Taken literally, the bulk of rap songs (like much heavy-metal rock) reveal ad-   9
olescent attitudes toward women, who are often presented as either materialistic
and cold or easy sexual conquests. But not all rap machismo should be taken entirely at face value. Like other black literary and oral traditions, rap lyrics also
involve double-entendre, allegory and parody. Some rap machismo can be a metaphor for pride or political empowerment; it can be a shared joke, as it often is in 2
Live Crew's wildly hyperbolic rhymes. And while machismo has been a convention
during rap's first decade, it is now under fire from female rappers like Queen
Latifah and Roxanne Shanté.

By bringing the fractured rhythms and unlikely juxtapositions of the television   10
age to the dance floor, rap revolutionized popular music and became the commercial success story of the 1980's. The recent No. 1 album on the Billboard pop charts
was "Please Hammer Don't Hurt 'Em" by the Oakland rapper M. C. Hammer.

Over the last decade, while major record companies waited for the supposed   11
fad to run its course, street-level independent labels made fortunes from rap hits.
Now all the major companies have signed rap groups, and rap has its own daily
show on MTV, where "Yo! MTV Raps" garners some of the cable channel's highest
ratings. Rap is out of the ghetto.

While there are a few female rappers, and a handful of white rappers, rap is   12
still an overwhelmingly black male style. Rap emerged when disk jockeys at clubs
and parties in the South Bronx began improvising rhymes over the instrumentals
of dance records, perhaps inspired by Jamaican disk jockeys or "toasters" who had
been doing the same thing. It spread and diversified. Soon there were specialists in
rhyming, or M.C.'s, and virtuosic disk jockeys, who created a musical backdrop by
intercutting shorter and shorter pieces of more and more records, often "scratching" the records—twitching them backward and forward under the needle—to
create percussive sounds.

Early rap mixed party chants with the braggadocio of the blues, jailhouse   13
chants and the dozens, a primarily male game of escalating insults. But soon after
the first rap recordings appeared, at the end of the 1970's, some songs took on
deeper content. With "The Breaks" by Kurtis Blow in 1980 and "The Message" by
Grandmaster Flash and the Furious Five featuring Melle Mel in 1982, rap began
to talk about ghetto life, often with humorous or belligerent candor.

Rap evolved fast. Using turntables and drum machines, rap groups could cut a   14
single in a basement, and rap entrepreneurs could press records quickly and sell
them from the trunks of their cars. As the music changed, stars and styles rose and
fell within months. In its constantly changing slang and shifting concerns—no
other pop has so many antidrug songs—rap's flood of words presents a fictional-
ized oral history of a brutalized generation.

A Liberating Moment

"The difference between public culture and private culture has disappeared," Mr.   15
Gates said, "There was material that was exclusively the province of the black oral
tradition and race-record tradition, but now people have decided to cross the line.
People like Keenan Ivory Wayans and Spike Lee and Eddie Murphy, along with
the rappers, they're saying all the things that we couldn't say even in the 1960's
about our own excesses, things we could only whisper in dark rooms. They're saying we're going to explode all these sacred cows. It's fascinating, and it's upsetting
everybody—not just white people but black people. But it's a liberating moment."

Where the old style was mostly bragging—and went with a fashion statement   16
of fat gold chains and other showy possessions—current rap embraces jokers, nice
guys, bawdy fantasists, storytellers, romantics and political activists. Public Enemy
brings black nationalist and Black Muslim ideas of self-determination to rap's most
advanced sonic collages, sometimes with divisive effect. Public Enemy was
branded anti-Semitic because of statements by a member who has since left the
group.

The controversy was revived when Public Enemy's "Welcome to the Terror-   17
dome" alluded to the incident with these cryptic lines: "Crucifixion ain't no
fiction/So called chosen frozen/Apology made to whoever pleases/Still they got me
like Jesus." Some listeners interpreted the lyrics as blaming the Jews for crucifying
Christ.

A Review from the F.B.I.

N. W. A. and Ice-T chant stylized, calmly observed tales of ghetto violence, includ-   18
ing N. W. A.'s infamous (and widely misread) "__Tha Police," which starts with a
scene of police brutality and ends with what a band member has called a "revenge
fantasy" about shooting policemen. In an unusual response to an artistic work, the
Federal Bureau of Investigation wrote a letter to the band's record company complaining that the song advocated violence against police officers.

"I see rap as reflective," Mr. Bourgois said, "and what people should be scared   19
about is the extent to which the songs reflect reality. That there is such unbelievable violence in these communities is a national tragedy, while the fact that people
express themselves in terms of violence is a part of American culture, a way of
thinking that goes back to the Wild West. I wouldn't worry about rap music leading
to violence. On the contrary, rap music leads to a productive expression of alienation and oppression, and it's good that it gets channeled into creative outlets

rather than drug addiction or physical violence. I see people, high-school dropouts, who carry around notebooks in their back pockets so they can compare their latest rhymes."

Of all the complaints against rap, the one that seems most unequivocal is about homophobia. Too few rappers can resist making some sort of swipe at gays, often taking a detour in a song to do so and rarely suggesting any double meaning. It seems an unexamined prejudice.   20

Rap's remarkable rate of change may make some complaints quickly obsolete. In a short time, simple boasts have given way to multileveled storytelling and political comment; when some rappers made a connection between gold chains and the South African gold industry, many rappers' neckwear of choice became leather Africa medallions instead of gold "dooky ropes." It's conceivable that a newer generation will not take sexism and homophobia so lightly. Rap will no doubt continue to reveal the tensions of the communities it speaks to. But with its humor, intelligence and fast-talking grace, it may also represent a way to transcend those tensions.   21

Rhetorical Focus

1. Where does Pareles evidently consider his purpose to be summarizing issues and events for his audience? Where does he evidently feel free to take a position of his own?
2. Note the authorities that Pareles quotes in explaining rap. How might his choices of them have been affected by his article's being for *The New York Times*? Where, if anywhere, do you agree with his choice of authority? Where, if anywhere, do you wish he had quoted other kinds of authorities than he did?
3. In several paragraphs, Pareles makes a statement about rap in his first sentence and then develops it. Identify three paragraphs in which he does this and explain precisely how they develop.

Thematic Focus

1. What context does Pareles establish for "rap machismo" (paragraph 8)? Do you think he is too harsh toward it? Too easy?
2. Pareles alludes to homophobia and possible anti-Semitism in rap music. Why might someone who is not necessarily gay or Jewish be concerned about these things? Do you think it is indeed fair for someone to take the presence or absence of them into account when judging the cultural worth of songs?
3. In his concluding paragraph, Pareles suggests that "Rap's remarkable rate of change may make some complaints quickly obsolete." How might strong critics of rap respond to this statement? Would you agree with their view of it? Why or why not?

Culture Has Consequences

Charles Krauthammer

Charles Krauthammer (b. 1950) graduated from McGill University in 1970
and studied at Balliol College, Oxford the following year. At both institutions,
his main interest was political science. Then he dramatically switched fields,
graduating from Harvard Medical School in 1975. After practicing psychiatry
for five years, however, Krauthammer returned to writing about politics. First
serving as a speechwriter for Vice President Walter Mondale, he then
became senior editor of *The New Republic* and started writing columns for
various magazines and newspapers. In 1985, he published a collection of his
essays entitled *Cutting Edges: Making Sense of the Eighties,* and in 1987,
he won the Pulitzer Prize for his commentary. Today, Krauthammer regularly
contributes not only to *The New Republic* but also *Time* and *The
Washington Post,* where the following appeared on October 26,
1990—shortly after a Florida jury found 2 Live Crew innocent of giving an
obscene performance.

Reflections Before Reading

Krauthammer criticizes the jury that found 2 Live Crew innocent of giving an
obscene performance. Going by your own knowledge of the group and/or
Pareles's description of it, why might someone be displeased with the jury's
verdict? What other cultural phenomena might such a person be disturbed
by? Note Krauthammer's title. Do you think cultural forms such as music,
film, television, and books can have serious consequences for people? Why
or why not?

According to a jury of its peers, 2 Live Crew meets the community standards of   1
Broward County, Fla. After listening to "He'll tear the [expletive for vagina] open
'cause it's satisfaction" and "Grabbed one by the hair, threw her on the floor/
opened up her thighs and guess what I saw," jury foreman David Garsow, of the
Key Biscayne Presbyterian Church choir, was unfazed. "Representing a cross section of the community as we do," he declared, "we did not feel it was obscene."

Broward County has thus confirmed what most of us know. Community stan- 2
dards, having adjusted to fit the culture, have reached a new low. Standards in
publishing, for example, have hit so low that at Simon & Schuster, reports *Time*,
the publication of "American Psycho," Bret Easton Ellis's new novel, has left some
editorial staff outraged. It is filled with such degrading violence and torture, particularly of women, that Ellis's past cover artist has refused to design this one. "I
felt disgusted with myself for reading it," he said. Simon & Schuster, unfazed,
plans to "market it aggressively."°

Of course, that American popular culture is drenched in sex and violence, and 3
a degrading combination of the two is a truism. But it is then hard to understand
the surprise that greets the resulting degradation and depravity of real life: a qua-
drupling of rapes in 30 years, random shootings of children (four in one eight-day
period in New York), a doubling of the number of youths shot to death in the last
six years alone.

What happened to innocence? The number of 14-to-17-year-olds arrested to- 4
day is 30 times what it was in 1950. Every year, one in 10 teenage girls gets pregnant. Teen suicides, now the second leading cause of death among adolescents, are
double what they were 20 years ago.

These signs of decay produce a general puzzlement. How did we get to such a 5
pass? How? Well, life imitates art. Culture has consequences. Is it so hard to make
a connection between culture and society? Most people, and in particular 2 Live
Crew's intellectual defenders, fervently believe in the connection between good
art and the good society. If they did not think that good art is elevating, artists
would not make it and the people would not support it. And yet the corollary—if
good art can elevate then bad art can degrade—is a proposition they refuse to
grasp.

Kids see 10,000 killings on TV by age 18. Is it any wonder that a growing 6
number might like to commit just one? Sexual aggression and misogyny are celebrated in rap. Is it any wonder that kids arrested for rape and murder are utterly
conscienceless and uncomprehending? MTV is a nonstop masturbation fantasy. Is
it any wonder that a generation of teens raised on it produces a million pregnancies
every year?

In order to deny the obvious, however, the social pathologies of American life 7
are ascribed not to culture but to government: to cuts in spending, lack of health
care, insufficient sex education. As Bill Bennett said recently of a report cataloging
the growing agony of American adolescents, "The Code Blue report says the problem is behavior, not health. . . . Yet its major recommendations are health-service
related (guaranteed access to health services and health instruction for teenage
students, for example). In other words, Code Blue identifies a crisis of the spirit, a
sickness in the soul, and it recommends (in effect) aspirin, Band-Aids, and a hall
pass to see the nurse."

°Simon & Schuster ultimately decided not to publish *American Psycho*, but Vintage did publish it in
March 1991.

As a psychiatrist, I used to see psychotic patients who, urged on by voices   8
inside their heads, did crazy and terrible things, like immolating themselves. Now
we have legions of kids walking around with the technological equivalent: 2 Live
Crew wired by Walkman directly into their brains, proposing to "bust your [same
expletive again] then break your backbone. . . . I wanna see you bleed." Surprised
that a whole generation is busting and breaking and bleeding? Culture has consequences.

But hasn't mass culture always settled on the lowest common denominator?   9
Yes, but the lowest common denominator is not what it used to be. It has been
sinking rapidly. There is no comparing the brutality and cynicism of today's pop
culture to that of 40 years ago. From "High Noon" to "Robocop" is a long descent.

And it is not just that we have never had a denominator so low. We have never   10
had a culture so mass. In the past, a libertarianism that permitted everything to be
said and done could at worst corrupt the intellectuals, a rather dispensable class.
Today no child escapes the assault of an omnivorous, omnipresent culture.

Until now, no society had combined total liberty with mass culture, let alone   11
with technology that hard wires the stuff into the brain. History is therefore no
guide as to what happens next. The mayhem in the streets, however, tells the story.

Rhetorical Focus

1. Where, if anywhere, does Krauthammer seem to assume that his audience
   shares his perceptions? Where, if anywhere, does he apparently feel that
   he has to make his audience aware of things it has not fully realized?
2. Note Krauthammer's frequent use of questions. Are they effective, or
   should he have confined himself to statements?
3. Both Krauthammer and Pareles start off by reporting court actions regarding 2 Live Crew. Compare their first paragraphs as strategies for introduc-
   ing their articles. In what ways does Krauthammer suggest that his rhetorical purpose differs from Pareles's? Do you approve of both first
   paragraphs as strategies for getting the reader's interest? Why or why not?

Thematic Focus

1. Do you agree with Krauthammer that "culture has consequences"—or,
   more precisely, that the examples of culture he finds bad can lead to the
   consequences he describes?
2. Krauthammer makes a number of other strong statements in this article.
   Which do you find yourself agreeing with or disagreeing with? Why?
3. Choose a particular passage from Pareles's article that you think would
   bother Krauthammer. What might he say about it? Would he be right?
   Why or why not?

The Obscenity Case: Criminalizing Black Culture

David Mills

David Mills (b. 1961) grew up in Washington, D.C., where he is now a staff writer for *The Washington Post*. He holds a Bachelor of Science degree in journalism from the University of Maryland. Mills was a reporter for *The Baltimore Sun, The Wall Street Journal,* and *The Washington Times* before joining the *Post* in 1990. There he mostly contributes articles and interviews on issues in American cultural life. Mills is especially interested in music of the 1970s and African-American popular culture. The following article appeared in the *Post* on June 17, 1990, the same day Pareles's article did. As Mills explained in an interview with us, he differs from Krauthammer in arguing here that culture *is* a consequence—in other words, that rap music must be understand and accepted as a response to earlier African-American cultural history.

Reflections Before Reading

Note Mills's title. Do you suspect the charges against 2 Live Crew risked "criminalizing black culture"? Why or why not? What do you think Mills will have to do to justify his use of this phrase?

A rap fan in Tennessee sent me a letter last month, before a U.S. district judge in Florida declared the 2 Live Crew's latest album obscene, and before the Crew's leader, Luther Campbell, was arrested and manacled because of words uttered during a nightclub performance, words uttered to an audience of paying adults. 1

"I do not think that 2 Live Crew is actually on trial," the young man wrote. "I believe that black expression as a whole is on trial. . . . And if 2 Live Crew are found to be obscene, other forms of black expression will be targeted. This could act as the catalyst for anti-black censorship of a much greater scale." 2

Paranoia? Or does the banning of "As Nasty as They Wanna Be" in southern Florida indeed represent an immediate threat to free speech, especially the speech of African American young men? 3

Consider the experience of other popular—and foulmouthed—rappers. Be- 4
fore a 1988 concert in Columbus, Ga., police officers warned Ice-T that he'd be
arrested if he uttered certain profane words onstage, he says. Ice-T performed one
song and canceled the rest of his show. Last summer, members of N.W.A. (Niggers With Attitudes) were chased out of Detroit's Joe Louis Arena by the police
after the rappers, egged on by a chanting crowd, began performing their master-
piece of vituperation, "[Expletive] tha Police." And in Cincinnati, the town that so
dutifully tried to protect its citizens from the photographs of Robert Mapplethorpe, a judge fined members of N.W.A. $100 apiece for "offensively coarse
utterances" between songs during a Riverfront Coliseum show.

The criminalization of a challenging form of black expressiveness raises some 5
urgent questions. Should federal courts be determining the artistic worth of products of the African American culture? Just what artistic worth can there be in a
collection of songs as violently raunchy and mean-spirited as 2 Live Crew's "As
Nasty as They Wanna Be"?

Where are the black scholars and intellectuals who should be able to place the 6
2 Live Crew in its cultural context and who, regardless of whatever distaste they
may have for the album, must act as the first line of defense when black artists
come under attack? And where are the 1.7 million people who have bought "As
Nasty as They Wanna Be"? Where is their outrage? It is now a crime in Florida's
Broward, Dade and Palm Beach counties to own this album. Anyone—young or
old, black or white—who has "Nasty" lying around the house or in the automobile
tape deck, is breaking the law. In Florida, possession of obscene material is pun-
ishable by up to 60 days in jail and a $500 fine.

E. Ethelbert Miller, director of Howard University's Afro-American Resource 7
Center, says the masses of black people tend to get alarmed only over the issue of
racism, and tend to sit out public debates on such "abstract" matters as artistic
freedom. He doesn't think that officials who attack "Nasty" are necessarily "sin-
gling out African American art. It's a whole climate out there . . . the right-wing
social agenda. And this is where I respect the right wing—they're organized."

Miller hasn't heard the 2 Live Crew's album, nor is he much of a rap fan. But 8
as a poet and an opponent of censorship, he defends the group. "At this particular
point, because people are politicizing art, what you have to always be protecting is
the ability to create. That's the struggle."

"Neither the 'rap' or 'hip-hop' musical genres are on trial," writes U.S. District 9
Judge Jose A. Gonzales Jr. of Fort Lauderdale in the opinion he rendered 11 days
ago. "The narrow issue before this court is whether the recording entitled 'As
Nasty as They Wanna Be' is legally obscene," and therefore unprotected by the
First Amendment. "This court's role is not to serve as a censor or an art and music
critic."

Despite this declamation, the judge displays a crucial lack of understanding of 10
rap music and its cultural context when he applies the Supreme Court's three tests
for obscenity to "As Nasty as They Wanna Be."

Let us accept Gonzales's conclusion that the album meets the first two tests— 11
that it "appeals to the prurient interest" and that, "measured by contemporary
community standards, the work depicts or describes, in a patently offensive way,
sexual conduct" as defined by state law.

Gonzales writes that the 2 Live Crew's lyrics "are replete with references to   12
female and male genitalia, human sexual excretion, oral–anal contact, fellatio, group
sex, specific sexual positions, sado-masochism, the turgid state of the male sexual
organ, masturbation, cunnilingus, sexual intercourse, and the sounds of moaning."

Indeed they are. Luther Campbell has purposefully explored the farthest   13
fringes of comic vulgarity and overblown phallicism. Thus has the 2 Live Crew
carved out a niche in the highly competitive rap market.

Yet all those lascivious lyrics are perfectly permissible under the First Amend-   14
ment, unless the album, "taken as a whole, lacks serious literary, artistic, political
or scientific value." That is the Supreme Court's third test for obscenity. And it gets
to the heart of things: What qualifies U.S. District Judge Jose Gonzales to assess
the artistic value of a rap album?

In the words of Henry Louis Gates, a Duke University English professor and   15
an expert on African American "vernacular culture": "I don't see how people can
jump into somebody else's culture, with completely no knowledge of that culture,
and then decide what's obscene and what's not."

The Supreme Court says a work must be judged "as a whole." But Gonzales   16
goes to great lengths to justify focusing almost exclusively on the dirty words. The
judge, citing "expert testimony," writes that "a central characteristic of 'rap' music
is its emphasis on the *verbal* message." He goes on to conclude that "it does not
significantly alter the message of the 'Nasty' recording to reduce it to a written
transcription."

He is absolutely wrong. Apart from the fact that rap is an outgrowth of funk—   17
that it is fundamentally a dance music—rap is not about the words per se. It's
about the rendition of the words. The emphasis is not verbal, it is *oral.* The rappers
call it "flow." To misunderstand this is to miss the essence of rap as a vibrant man-
ifestation of the black oral tradition.

Only by listening to the 2 Live Crew, not by reading its lyrics on a sheet of   18
paper, do you realize that their sexual rants aren't to be taken literally. (Just as that
bawdy old limerick about a guy named Dave, "who kept a dead whore in his cave,"
shouldn't be interpreted as a celebration of necrophilia.) Anyone who thinks the
song "Put Her in the Buck" is intended as a sex manual—or that rap fans perceive
it as such—hasn't heard the goofy way one of the Crew barks out the title.

The 2 Live Crew engages in a style of African American ribaldry that is rooted   19
in the inner-city BS heard on street corners and in schoolyards. It's the kind of
humor found throughout the '70s on the adults-only "party records" of comedians
such as Richard Pryor, Richard and Willie and Rudy Ray Moore. (Snippets of their
material, not coincidentally, can be found on "As Nasty as They Wanna Be"). The
"adults-only" designation didn't keep those records out of the hands of teenage
fellas back then, who, after all, enjoyed a dirty joke as much as anyone.

In court, the group's main argument was that "Nasty" has artistic value as   20
comedy and satire. Gonzales did not agree: "It cannot be reasonably argued that
the violence, perversion, abuse of women, graphic depictions of all forms of sexual
conduct, and microscopic descriptions of human genitalia contained on this recording are comedic art."

This again demonstrates the danger of a cultural outsider passing judgment on   21
something he doesn't understand. Just as you cannot appreciate a rap song by

merely reading its lyrics—disregarding its rhythm tracks, disregarding the nuances of its vocalization—you cannot fully understand this profane style of rapping if you disregard the larger folklore of the streets.

There are fascinating echoes in today's hard-edged rap music not only of black comedy but of the low-budget "black exploitation" action movies of the early '70s and the stylized folk performance-poems, called "toasts," that emanated from the world of pimps and hustlers. "As Nasty as They Wanna Be" has real cultural underpinnings. 22

Comedian Rudy Ray Moore, the spiritual godfather of the 2 Live Crew, made a career of recording versions of vulgar, sometimes violent, often sexually exaggerated toasts such as "Dolemite" and "Pimpin' Sam." A member of 2 Live Crew drops a nasty couplet about lesbians rubbing belly to belly in "[Expletive] Almighty"; the same couplet can be found in Moore's version of the ultra-scatological toast "Dance of the Freaks," recorded more than 15 years earlier, and in one written collection of toasts, you can find a version of "Dance of the Freaks" recited by a Sing Sing inmate in 1954. 23

Perhaps the most famous of toasts, the metaphorical jungle tale "The Signifying Monkey," was adapted by tough-guy rapper Schoolly D in 1988. During the '70s, Moore recorded a couple of versions, one in his blaxploitation movie debut, "Dolemite." And Henry Louis Gates, in his scholarly study "The Signifying Monkey: A Theory of African-American Literary Criticism," traces the monkey tale to a trickster figure in West African mythology. 24

Toasts can be so compelling that one of the legendary, radical Last Poets adopted the style (and the name Lightnin' Rod) for his LP "Hustler's Convention" in 1973. Over funky background music from the likes of Kool and the Gang, a criminal flamboyantly spins his underworld tale. "I was a down stud's dream, a hustler supreme. There wasn't no game that I couldn't play. And if I caught a dude cheatin', I would give him a beatin', and I might even blow him away!" By the end of the record, after being beaten and shot by the cops and spending years on death row, this "nickel-and-dime" hustler has become politicized. Some 15 years later, Ice-T released his first album, "Rhyme Pays," a virtual homage to "Hustler's Convention." 25

Between 1972 and 1976, independent film producers and distributors churned out countless action movies with titles such as "Black Gunn," "Black Caesar," "Black Samson," "Black Fist," "The Black Godfather," "Black Samurai" and "Boss Nigger." Designed to appeal, obviously, to the fantasies of young black males, these films were often set in the criminal world. 26

"In the black community of past decades, the old-style pimp had sometimes been viewed as a folk hero of sorts: a smooth-talking, sexy, hip, moneyed man in control of his destiny," writes film historian Donald Bogle in "Blacks in American Films and Television." Describing the 1973 pimp's saga "The Mack," he continues: "By the 1970s, one might have assumed the pimp would be seen for other things he represented, primarily as an exploiter of women. Instead, young black moviegoers seemed to delight in [the hero's] pretty looks, his firm control over his women, his striking array of material comforts . . . and his tenacious grip on survival." 27

Although whites usually held financial and creative control over these films, it   28
was the performances of black actors that often resonated.

Rappers in their late 20s, such as Luther Campbell, probably have fond mem-   29
ories of watching movies like "The Mack" and "Super Fly" on the big screen. At the
end of Public Enemy's "Burn, Hollywood, Burn"—an indictment of the movie
industry's depiction of African Americans, from Stepin Fetchit to "Driving Miss
Daisy"—guest rapper Big Daddy Kane says, "Yo, check it out, man, I got 'Black
Caesar' at the crib. Y'all want to go check that out?"

Indeed, with many of those old blaxploitation films now on videocassette,   30
younger rappers have a smorgasbord of macho fantasies to build upon. Take Poison Clan, two 19-year-olds billed as "The Baby 2 Live Crew" and signed to Campbell's Miami-based label, Luke Records (formerly Luke Skyywalker Records, until
"Star Wars" producer George Lucas sued Campbell). On the upcoming album "2
Low Life Muthas," the Clan's JT boasts that being a pimp is how he can afford
"eatin' shrimp."

To understand the 2 Live Crew is to realize the difference between being a   31
lowlife and pretending to be a lowlife, the difference between sick, mean humor
and true sickness and meanness. "A lot of people fail to see that music is acting,"
says Debbie Bennett, spokeswoman for Luke Records. Of 2 Live Crew, she says,
"You won't find four nicer guys."

But it's their pretense, in all its outrageous sexual explicitness, that fits   32
squarely into the tradition of comedy albums and films that draw upon the rich
black folklore of the streets. That is the "artistic value" of "As Nasty as They Wanna
Be," which entitles it to protection under the First Amendment. That is the context
in which the 2 Live Crew must be judged. And that is why U.S. District Judge Jose
Gonzales was wrong to declare the album "utterly without any redeeming social
value," and why anyone who is serious about the African American popular culture
should be disturbed by his ruling.

Of course, "just because something comes out of the black culture, just be-   33
cause it has black cultural authenticity, doesn't make it good," says Stanley Crouch,
noted jazz critic and essayist. Rap in general is "an expression of a lower aspect of
the culture," in his view. The members of 2 Live Crew specifically are "some vulgar street-corner-type clowns," "spiritual cretins," "slime."

"We're so defensive about ourselves that we feel that we always have to come   34
forward and defend anything that says it represents black authenticity," Crouch
says. "We do not have to celebrate the lowest elements in our society. . . . I look at
those people—pimps and hustlers—as parasites. We cannot make a powerful
Afro-American culture if we're going to base it on what hustlers and pimps think
about the world."

No doubt. But "As Nasty as They Wanna Be" is a piece of entertainment, not a   35
blueprint for living. Personally, I don't find the album very entertaining. I am bothered by the meanness of the humor regarding women, just as I am bothered by the
jokes of Andrew Dice Clay. But the 2 Live Crew has sold 1.7 million copies of this
album, and Clay is packing arenas. Are they driving the culture, or simply reflecting it?

Janine McAdams, the black-music columnist for Billboard magazine, says, "I   36
am tired of seeing Luke kicked around the way he has been in a purely political
game to quash freedom of expression." On the other hand, after listening to
"Nasty" once last year, she says, "I will never pick it up again. I hate it. It disgusts
me."

"I wish Luther Campbell could demonstrate more respect for women," Mc-   37
Adams says. "I think he thinks it's humorous, and in certain respects I guess it
is. . . . I have mixed feelings about it. If people had derogatory thoughts about
women, if they had perverted sexual fantasies, they had those thoughts, I'm sure,
before Luther came along."

Stanley Crouch, by the way, confesses to owning "three or four" raunchy Rudy   38
Ray Moore LPs. "I've had those records for 15 years. I bought 'em because they
reminded me of stuff guys said on the street corners when I was growing up. I
haven't listened to them in a while." Does Crouch recall finding those records
funny? "Yeah, I thought they were kind of comical," he says. But "I have evolved
far beyond that."

Rhetorical Focus

1. Why do you think Mills chooses to begin with a letter from someone else?
    Does his article then manage to convince you that the letter makes sense?
2. What concessions does Mills make to critics of 2 Live Crew? Is making
    such concessions rhetorically effective, or do they wind up weakening his
    argument?
3. Mills, Pareles, and Krauthammer each establish a "cultural context" for the
    development of rap music, but Mills goes back farther into the past. Do his
    historical details indeed strike you as relevant? What about the authorities
    he quotes?

Thematic Focus

1. What reasons does Mills give in arguing that Judge Gonzalez's decision was
    wrong? Do these reasons make sense to you? Why or why not?
2. Mills describes various developments in African-American cultural history.
    What general points is he making as he does? Does his sense of this history
    differ from Pareles's in significant respects? Explain.
3. Mills asserts that the "sexual rants" of the band "aren't to be taken literally"
    (paragraph 18). Look again at the lyrics that Krauthammer quotes in his
    opening paragraph. If, in fact, the band did not really mean them, do you
    think listeners have no right to be bothered by them? Why or why not?

When Black Feminism Faces the Music, and the Music Is Rap

Michele Wallace

Born in Harlem in 1952, Michele Wallace was educated at City College of
the City University of New York, where she now teaches English and
women's studies. She has also taught creative writing and African-American
literature at the University of California at San Diego, the University of
Oklahoma, and the State University of New York at Buffalo. Wallace gained
national attention when, at the age of 26, she wrote *Black Macho and the
Myth of the Superwoman,* a book that accused African-American men of
responding to white oppression by negatively stereotyping women of their
own race. More recently, Wallace has published *Invisibility Blues: From Pop
to Theory* (1991), a collection of essays on the culture of African-Americans
and the mass media's general depiction of them. The following article on rap
music appeared in *The New York Times* on July 29, 1990.

Reflections Before Reading

As her title suggests, Wallace is an African-American feminist. What sorts of
things do you think she will focus on in discussing rap music? On what
issues raised by the previous writers would you especially like to see her
point of view? Do you expect that she will utterly condemn rap music? Why
or why not?

Like many black feminists, I look on sexism in rap as a necessary evil. In a society 1
plagued by poverty and illiteracy, where young black men are as likely to be in
prison as in college, rap is a welcome articulation of the economic and social frustrations of black youth.

In response to disappointments faced by poor urban blacks negotiating their 2
future, rap offers the release of creative expression and historical continuity: It
draws on precedents as diverse as jazz, reggae, calypso, Afro-Cuban, African and

heavy-metal, and its lyrics include rudimentary forms of political, economic and social analysis.

But with the failure of our urban public schools, rappers have taken education   3
into their own hands; these are oral lessons (reading and writing being low priorities). And it should come as no surprise that the end result emphasizes innovations in style and rhythm over ethics and morality. Although there are exceptions, like raps advocating world peace (the W.I.S.E. Guyz's "Time for Peace") and opposing drug use (Ice-T's "I'm Your Pusher"), rap lyrics can be brutal, raw and, where women are the subject, glaringly sexist.

Given the genre's current crossover popularity and success in the market-   4
place, including television commercials, rap's impact on young people is growing. A large part of the appeal of pop culture is that it can offer symbolic resolutions to life's contradictions. But when it comes to gender, rap has not resolved a thing.

Though styles vary—from that of the X-rated Ice-T to the sybaritic Kwaneé to   5
the hyperpolitics of Public Enemy—what seems universal is how little male rappers respect sexual intimacy and how little regard they have for the humanity of the black woman. Witness the striking contrast within rap videos: for men, standard attire is baggy outsize pants; for women, spike heels and short skirts. Videos often feature the ostentatious and fetishistic display of women's bodies. In Kool Moe Dee's "How Ya Like Me Now," women gyrate in tight leather with large revealing holes. In Digital Underground's video "Doowutchyalike," set poolside at what looks like a fraternity house party, a rapper in a clown costume pretends to bite the backside of a woman in a bikini.

As Trisha Rose, a black feminist studying rap, puts it, "Rap is basically a locker   6
room with a beat."

The recent banning of the sale of 2 Live Crew's album "As Nasty as They   7
Wanna Be" by local governments in Florida and elsewhere has publicized rap's treatment of women as sex objects, but it also made a hit of a record that contains some of the bawdiest lyrics in rap. Though such sexual explicitness in lyrics is rare, the assumptions about women—that they manipulate men with their bodies—are typical.

In an era when the idea that women want to be raped should be obsolete, rap   8
lyrics and videos presuppose that women always desire sex, whether they know it or not. In Bell Biv DeVoe's rap-influenced pop hit single "Poison," for instance, a beautiful girl is considered poison because she does not respond affirmatively and automatically to a sexual proposition.

Bell Hooks, author of "Yearning: Race, Gender, Cultural Politics" (South End,   9
1990), sees the roots of rap as a youth rebellion against all attempts to control black masculinity, both in the streets and in the home. "That rap would be anti-domesticity and in the process anti-female should come as no surprise," Ms. Hooks says.

At present there is only a small platform for black women to address the prob-   10
lems of sexism in rap and in their community. Feminist criticism, like many other forms of social analysis, is widely considered part of a hostile white culture. For a black feminist to chastise misogyny in rap publicly would be viewed as divisive and counterproductive. There is a widespread perception in the black community that public criticism of black men constitutes collaborating with a racist society.

The charge is hardly new. Such a reaction greeted Ntozake Shange's play "For   11
Colored Girls Who Have Considered Suicide When the Rainbow Is Enuf," my
own essays, "Black Macho and the Myth of the Superwoman," and Alice Walker's
novel "The Color Purple," all of which were perceived as critical of black men.
After the release of the film version of "The Color Purple," feminists were lam-
basted in the press for their supposed lack of support for black men; such critical
analysis by black women has all but disappeared. In its place is "A Black Man's
Guide to the Black Women," a vanity-press book by Shahrazad Ali, which has sold
more than 80,000 copies by insisting that black women are neurotic, insecure and
competitive with black men.

Though misogynist lyrics seem to represent the opposite of Ms. Ali's world   12
view, these are, in fact, just two extremes on the same theme: Ms. Ali's prescription for what ails the black community is that women should not question men
about their sexual philandering, and should be firmly slapped across the mouth
when they do. Rap lyrics suggest just about the same: women should be silent and
prone.

There are those who have wrongly advocated censorship of rap's more sexually   13
explicit lyrics, and those who have excused the misogyny because of its basis in
black oral traditions.

Rap is rooted not only in the blaxploitation films of the 60's but also in an   14
equally sexist tradition of black comedy. In the use of four-letter words and explicit
sexual references, both Richard Pryor and Eddie Murphy, who themselves drew
upon the earlier examples of Redd Foxx, Pigmeat Markham and Moms Mabley,
are conscious reference points for the 2 Live Crew. Black comedy, in turn, draws
on an oral tradition in which black men trade "toasts," stories in which dangerous
bagmen and trickster figures like Stackolee and Dolomite sexually exploit women
and promote violence among men. The popular rapper Ice Cube, in the album
"Amerikkka's Most Wanted," is Stackolee come to life. In "The Nigga Ya Love to
Hate," he projects an image of himself as a criminal as dangerous to women as to
the straight white world.

Rap remains almost completely dominated by black males and this mind-set.   15
Although women have been involved in rap since at least the mid-80's, record
companies have only recently begun to promote them. And as women rappers like
Salt-n-Pepa, Monie Love, M. C. Lyte, L. A. Star and Queen Latifah slowly gain
more visibility, rap's sexism may emerge as a subject for scrutiny. Indeed, the answer may lie with women, expressing in lyrics and videos the tensions between the
sexes in the black community.

Today's women rappers range from a high ground that doesn't challenge male   16
rap on its own level (Queen Latifah) to those who subscribe to the same sexual
high jinks as male rappers (Oaktown's 3.5.7). M. C. Hammer launched Oaktown's
3.5.7., made up of his former backup dancers. These female rappers manifest the
worst-case scenario: their skimpy, skintight leopard costumes in the video of "Wild
and Loose (We Like It)" suggest an exotic animalistic sexuality. Their clothes fall to
their ankles. They take bubble baths. Clearly, their bodies are more important
than rapping. And in a field in which writing one's own rap is crucial, their lyrics
are written by their former boss, M. C. Hammer.

Most women rappers constitute the middle ground: they talk of romance, nar-   17
cissism and parties. On the other hand, Salt-n-Pepa on "Shake Your Thang" uses
the structure of the 1969 Isley Brothers song "It's Your Thing" to insert a pro-
tofeminist rap response: "Don't try to tell me how to party. It's my dance and it's my
body." M. C. Lyte, in a dialogue with Positive K on "I'm Not Havin' It," comes
down hard on the notion that women can't say no and criticizes the shallowness of
the male rap.

Queen Latifah introduces her video, "Ladies First," performed with the En-   18
glish rapper Monie Love, with photographs of black political heroines like Winnie
Mandela, Sojourner Truth, Harriet Tubman and Angela Davis. With a sound that
resembles scat as much as rap, Queen Latifah chants "Stereotypes they got to go"
against a backdrop of newsreel footage of the apartheid struggle in South Africa.
The politically sophisticated Queen Latifah seems worlds apart from the adolescent, buffoonish sex orientation of most rap. In general, women rappers seem so
much more grown up.

Can they inspire a more beneficent attitude toward sex in rap?   19

What won't subvert rap's sexism is the actions of men; what will is women   20
speaking in their own voice, not just in artificial female ghettos, but with and to
men.

Rhetorical Focus

1. Trace the stages of Wallace's essay—the parts into which it can be divided.
   Do all these stages seem necessary for her argument? Why or why not?
2. In discussing sexism in rap music, Wallace refers to images of men and
   women in rap videos as well as statements about them in song lyrics. Is this
   a fair rhetorical move? Why or why not?
3. As you read Wallace on sexism in rap, do you find yourself tending to give
   her more rhetorical authority than the other writers because she is an African-American woman and they are not? What does your answer imply
   about the role of authors' race and gender when they write about subjects
   such as rap?

Thematic Focus

1. Wallace makes important points in her first and last sentences, but these
   points are not quite the same. Indeed, someone might even find the sentences contradictory, given that the first declares sexism in rap "a necessary
   evil" and the last indicates that female rappers will "subvert" it. How might
   the presence of both sentences be explained? Do you think Wallace was
   right to include both in her essay? Why or why not?
2. What does Wallace think her readers should acknowledge about African-
   American history as they evaluate sexism in rap? Does she succeed in convincing you that the historical trends she points out are indeed important
   to consider?

3. To what extent might each of the three preceding writers agree with Wallace? Might any of them significantly disagree with her? If so, who? In what respects?

Suggestions for Writing

1. Write an essay in which you respond to the writer in this constellation with whom you disagree most. Concentrate on why you disagree, referring to specific statements that the writer makes. Also indicate, however, whether there are any areas of agreement between you. If you wish, you can put your essay in the form of a letter to this person. You can also refer to one or more of the other writers if you find statements of theirs relevant to your own argument.

2. Choose a particular kind of film, television show, book, music, or visual art that you have come to enjoy even though you know many other people do not care for it. Write an essay in which you try to persuade them to experience this art form more than they have. Indicate the kinds of experiences and information you think they will need to have in order to share your enjoyment of the art form. Also indicate any prejudices they will need to suspend if they are to give it a chance.

3. Research another case where the relation between mass culture and morality became an issue. Then, write an essay in which you summarize and evaluate the views of two articles that took opposite sides in this case. Possible cases include debates over ways of restricting access (for example, album warning labels, film ratings, the outright banning of pornography, the censorship of certain books in schools), the 1990 controversy over the National Endowment of the Arts' funding of artists such as Robert Mapplethorpe and Andres Serrano, and debates further back in history over particular works, such as *Ulysses* and *Lady Chatterley's Lover*.

Chapter

8

Language

*L*anguage surrounds us so completely that we rarely feel the need to examine it carefully. As children, we found it a useful and natural tool; it got us what we needed. As adults, we are often judged by how we speak and write, how we pronounce our words and shape our sentences. Often, language behavior that seems so obvious proves to be more complex than we imagine. In school, most of us studied language, but this study probably did not involve much more than grammar or usage. We learned a lot of rules about punctuation and memorized a lot of information about compound sentences. Few of us were encouraged to look seriously at language behavior, to investigate, for example, whether language is as neutral and fair as people think, or to explore the power of language to shape our thought, our vision of who we are.

Although language seems fresh to young children learning it for the first time, we are all born into the conventions and vocabulary of a language already centuries old. It is true that new words are created or coined every day, but most of the basic structures and words we use to both shape and reflect the world are very old. Although they were probably useful 500 years ago, are the rules of syntax and grammar still useful? Do these ancient patterns reflect our values or those of people from another era, whose ideas about race, gender, and class we may not feel comfortable with? One of our oldest philosophical problems, whether language creates or reflects reality, is still considered an open question. This chapter should help to give you a perspective on this and similar debates on language.

In linguistics, the scientific study of language, the notion that some ways of speaking are inherently better or more correct than others is discouraged. Linguists are more interested in describing and explaining than in passing judgment. Those outside linguistics, however, often see a particular way of using English as morally proper; variations are criticized. In our first section, John Simon, a theater critic and journalist, is quite upset by the "decline" of correct English, while Jim Quinn sees no cause for alarm. In our second constellation of readings, Robin Lakoff, Casey Miller, and Kate Swift are all concerned that some outdated language habits might perpetuate sexist attitudes. James Baldwin and Geneva Smitherman argue for the validity of Black English in our third constellation, and the controversy over obscenity is taken up by Dan Rothwell and Barbara Lawrence in the last constellation. Rothwell, a linguist, seems content to explain and describe Americans' use of forbidden words, while Lawrence sees danger in their casual acceptance. These conflicting viewpoints remind us that we can take nothing for granted in the highly charged study of language. Throughout these readings, we hope you will be strong readers, testing your ideas, your experiences, and your intuitions as expert users of English against these assembled writers. We hope that you will also come to your own conclusions about the influence of language on your life.

CORRECT ENGLISH

Some writers feel so protective about the English language that they want to purify it of what they consider bad grammar, sloppy syntax, and misused words. Then they want to preserve it in this correct state against change, against the uncultivated, the permissive, and the ignorant. Others encourage change and think correct English is mostly the opinion of those in power at the moment.

Pronunciation, syntax, and so on should probably not be judged on absolute standards, for all language and dialects have their own rules, their own internal consistency and logic. To many educated speakers of English, aristocrats in England sound better than dock workers in Brooklyn, but that is probably more a matter of social status, taste, and bias than grammatical correctness.

John Simon, a language purist, would be appalled by this last claim. To him, the dock worker simply does not know how to speak correctly; the educated English speaker does. Jim Quinn, however, thinks it is Simon who is ignorant; he takes a more democratic stance, welcoming change and growth. Read each perspective with an open mind. Who is in charge of English? Who determines what is correct? On what grounds are their decisions made? Are the powerful trying to impose their views of language on others?

Why Good English Is Good for You

John Simon

John Simon (b. 1925) taught humanities at M.I.T. (Massachusetts Institute of Technology) and at Harvard University for a few years before turning to film and drama reviewing. He is presently a theater critic for *New York* magazine and is best known as an outspoken defender of what he calls "good" English. His book, *Paradigms Lost* (1980), from which the following essay is taken, contains essays on language and the decline of literacy that Simon wrote during his years as a language columnist for *Esquire* magazine.

Reflections Before Reading

How do you think words get the "definitions" we read in the dictionary? Can definitions of words change? How might this happen? Language conservatives claim that *Webster's Third International Dictionary* is too permissive. What do you think this means? Are you sometimes self-conscious about pronouncing words incorrectly or using bad grammar? Do you think most people are? Why?

What's good English to you that . . . you should grieve for it? What good is correct speech and writing, you may ask, in an age in which hardly anyone seems to know, and no one seems to care? Why shouldn't you just fling bloopers, bloopers riotously with the throng, and not stick out from the rest like a sore thumb by using the language correctly? Isn't grammar really a thing of the past, and isn't the new idea to communicate in *any* way as long as you can make yourself understood? 1

The usual, basic defense of good English (and here, again, let us not worry about nomenclature—for all I care, you may call it "Standard English," "correct American," or anything else) is that it helps communication, that it is perhaps even a *sine qua non* of mutual understanding. Although this is a crude truth of sorts, it strikes me as, in some ways, both more and less than the truth. Suppose you say, "Everyone in their right mind would cross on the green light" or "Hopefully, it won't rain tomorrow," chances are very good that the person you say this to will 2 understand you, even though you are committing obvious solecisms or creating needless ambiguities. Similarly, if you write in a letter, "The baby has finally ceased it's howling" (spelling *its* as *it's*), the recipient will be able to figure out what was meant. But "figuring out" is precisely what a listener or reader should not have to do. There is, of course, the fundamental matter of courtesy to the other person, but it goes beyond that: why waste time on unscrambling simple meaning when there are more complex questions that should receive our undivided attention? If the many cooks had to worry first about which out of a large number of pots had no leak in it, the broth, whether spoiled or not, would take forever to be ready.

It is, I repeat, only initially a matter of clarity. It is also a matter of concision.   3
Space today is as limited as time. If you have only a thousand words in which to convey an important message it helps to know that "overcomplicated" is correct and "overly complicated" is incorrect. Never mind the grammatical explanations; the two extra characters and one space between words are reason enough. But what about the more advanced forms of word-mongering that hold sway nowadays? Take redundancy, like the "hopes and aspirations" of Jimmy Carter, quoted by Edwin Newman as having "a deeply profound religious experience"; or elaborate jargon, as when Charles G. Walcutt, a graduate professor of English at CUNY, writes (again as quoted by Newman): "The colleges, trying to remediate increasing numbers of . . . illiterates up to college levels, are being highschoolized"; or just obfuscatory verbiage of the pretentious sort, such as this fragment from a letter I received: "It is my impression that effective int*er*personal verbal communication depends on prior effective int*ra*-personal verbal communication." What this means is that if you think clearly, you can speak and write clearly—except if you are a "certified speech and language pathologist," like the writer of the letter I quote. (By the way, she adds the letters Ph.D. after her name, though she is not even from Germany, where *Herr* and *Frau Doktor* are in common, not to say vulgar, use.)

But except for her ghastly verbiage, our certified language pathologist (what-   4
ever that means) is perfectly right: there is a close connection between the ability to think and the ability to use English correctly. After all, we think in words, we conceptualize in words, we work out our problems inwardly with words, and using them correctly is comparable to a craftsman's treating his tools with care, keeping his materials in good shape. Would you trust a weaver who hangs her wet laundry on her loom, or lets her cats bed down in her yarn? The person who does not respect words and their proper relationships cannot have much respect for ideas— very possibly cannot have ideas at all. My quarrel is not so much with minor errors that we all fall into from time to time even if we know better as it is with basic sloppiness or ignorance or defiance of good English.

Training yourself to speak and write correctly—and I say "training yourself"   5
because nowadays, unfortunately, you cannot depend on other people or on institutions to give you the proper training, for reasons I shall discuss later—training yourself, then, in language, means developing at the very least two extremely useful faculties: your sense of discipline and your memory. Discipline because language is with us always, as nothing else is: it follows us much as, in the old morality play, Good Deeds followed Everyman, all the way to the grave; and, if the language is written, even beyond. Let me explain: if you can keep an orderly apart-

ment, if you can see to it that your correspondence and bill-paying are attended to regularly, if your diet and wardrobe are maintained with the necessary care—good enough; you are a disciplined person.

But the preliminary discipline underlying all others is nevertheless your   6 speech: the words that come out of you almost as frequently and—if you are tidy—as regularly as your breath. I would go so far as to say that, immediately after your bodily functions, language is first, unless you happen to be an ascetic, an anchorite, or a stylite; but unless you are a sty*lite*, you had better be a sty*list*.

Most of us—almost all—must take in and give out language as we do breath,   7 and we had better consider the seriousness of language pollution as second only to air pollution. For the linguistically disciplined, to misuse or mispronounce a word is an unnecessary and unhealthy contribution to the surrounding smog. To have taught ourselves not to do this, or—being human and thus also imperfect—to do it as little as possible, means deriving from every speaking moment the satisfaction we get from a cap that snaps on to a container perfectly, an elevator that stops flush with the landing, a roulette ball that comes to rest exactly on the number on which we have placed our bet. It gives us the pleasure of hearing or seeing our words— because they are abiding by the rules—snapping, sliding, falling precisely into place, expressing with perfect lucidity and symmetry just what we wanted them to express. This is comparable to the satisfaction of the athlete or ballet dancer or pianist finding his body or legs or fingers doing his bidding with unimpeachable accuracy.

And if someone now says that "in George Eliot's lesser novels, she is not com-   8 pletely in command" is perfectly comprehensible even if it is ungrammatical, the "she" having no antecedent in the nominative (*Eliot's* is a genitive), I say, "Comprehensible, perhaps, but lopsided," for the civilized and orderly mind does not feel comfortable with that "she"—does not hear that desired and satisfying click of correctness—unless the sentence is restructured as "George Eliot, in her lesser novels, is not . . ." or in some similar way. In fact, the fully literate ear can be thrown by this error in syntax; it may look for the antecedent of that "she" elsewhere than in the preceding possessive case. Be that as it may, playing without rules and winning—in this instance, managing to communicate without using good English—is no more satisfactory than winning in a sport or game by accident or by disregarding the rules: which is really cheating.

The second faculty good speech develops is, as I have mentioned before, our   9 memory. Grammar and syntax are partly logical—and to that extent they are also good exercisers and developers of our logical faculty—but they are also partly arbitrary, conventional, irrational. For example, the correct "compared to" and "contrasted with" could, from the logical point of view, just as well be "contrasted to" and "compared with" ("compared with," of course, is correct, but in a different sense from the one that concerns us here, namely, the antithesis of "contrasted with"). And, apropos *different,* logic would have to strain desperately to explain the exclusive correctness of "different from," given the exclusive correctness of "other than," which would seem to justify "different than," jarring though that is to the cultivated ear.

But there it is: some things are so because tradition, usage, the best speakers   10 and writers, the grammar books and dictionaries have made them so. There may even exist some hidden historical explanation: something, perhaps, in the Sanskrit, Greek, Latin, or other origins of a word or construction that you and I may very easily never know. We can, however, memorize; and memorization can be a wonderfully useful thing—surely the Greeks were right to consider Mnemosyne (memory) the mother of the Muses, for without her there would be no art and no science. And what better place to practice one's mnemonic skills than in the study of one's language?

There is something particularly useful about speaking correctly and precisely   11
because language is always there as a foundation—or, if you prefer a more fluid image, an undercurrent—beneath what is going on. Now, it seems to me that the great difficulty of life lies in the fact that we must almost always do two things at a time. If, for example, we are walking and conversing, we must keep our mouths as well as feet from stumbling. If we are driving while listening to music, we must not allow the siren song of the cassette to prevent us from watching the road and the speedometer (otherwise the less endearing siren of the police car or the ambulance will follow apace). Well, it is just this sort of bifurcation of attention that care for precise, clear expression fosters in us. By learning early in life to pay attention both to what we are saying and to how we are saying it, we develop the much-needed life skill of doing two things simultaneously.

Put another way, we foster our awareness of, and ability to deal with, form and   12
content. If there is any verity that modern criticism has fought for, it is the recognition of the indissolubility of content and form. Criticism won the battle, won it so resoundingly that this oneness has become a contemporary commonplace. And shall the fact that form *is* content be a platitude in all the arts but go unrecognized in the art of self-expression, whether in conversation or correspondence, or whatever form of spoken or written utterance a human being resorts to? Accordingly, you are going to be judged, whether you like it or not, by the correctness of your English as much as by the correctness of your thinking; there are some people to whose ear bad English is as offensive as gibberish, or as your picking your nose in public would be to their eyes and stomachs. The fact that people of linguistic sensibilities may be a dying breed does not mean that they are wholly extinct, and it is best not to take any unnecessary chances.

To be sure, if you are a member of a currently favored minority, many of your   13
linguistic failings may be forgiven you—whether rightly or wrongly is not my concern here. But if you cannot change your sex or color to the one that is getting preferential treatment—Bakke case or no Bakke case—you might as well learn good English and profit by it in your career, your social relations, perhaps even in your basic self-confidence. That, if you will, is the ultimate practical application of good English; but now let me tell you about the ultimate impractical one, which strikes me as being possibly even more important.

Somewhere in the prose writings of Charles Péguy, who was a very fine poet   14
and prose writer—and, what is perhaps even more remarkable, as good a human being as he was an artist—somewhere in those writings is a passage about the decline of pride in workmanship among French artisans, which, as you can deduce, set in even before World War I, wherein Péguy was killed. In the passage I refer to, Péguy bemoans the fact that cabinetmakers no longer finish the backs of furniture—the sides that go against the wall—in the same way as they do the ex-

posed sides. What is not seen was just as important to the old artisans as what is seen—it was a moral issue with them. And so, I think, it ought to be with language. Even if no one else notices the niceties, the precision, the impeccable sense of grammar and syntax you deploy in your utterances, you yourself should be aware of them and take pride in them as in pieces of work well done.

Now, I realize that there are two possible reactions among you to what I have said up to this point. Some of you will say to yourselves: what utter nonsense! Language is a flexible, changing, living organism that belongs to the people who speak it. It has always been changed according to the ways in which people chose to speak it, and the dictionaries and books on grammar had to, and will have to, adjust themselves to the people and not the other way around. For isn't it the glory of language that it keeps throwing up new inventions as surf tosses out differently polished pebbles and bits of bottle glass onto the shore, and that in this inexhaustible variety, in this refusal to kowtow to dry-as-dust scholars, lies its vitality, its beauty? 15

Others among you, perhaps fewer in number, will say to yourselves: quite so, there is such a thing as Standard English, or purity of speech, or correctness of expression—something worth safeguarding and fostering; but how the devil is one to accomplish that under the prevailing conditions: in a democratic society full of minorities that have their own dialects or linguistic preferences, and in a world in which television, advertising, and other mass media manage daily to corrupt the language a little further? Let me try to answer the first group first, and then come back to the questions of the second. 16

Of course language is, and must be, a living organism to the extent that new inventions, discoveries, ideas enter the scene and clamor rightfully for designations. Political, social, and psychological changes may also affect our mode of expression, and new words or phrases may have to be found to reflect what we might call historical changes. It is also quite natural for slang terms to be invented, become popular, and, in some cases, remain permanently in the language. It is perhaps equally inevitable (though here we are on more speculative ground) for certain words to become obsolescent and obsolete, and drop out of the language. But does that mean that grammar and syntax have to keep changing, that pronunciations and meanings of words must shift, that more complex or elegant forms are obliged to yield to simpler or cruder ones that often are not fully synonymous with them and not capable of expressing certain fine distinctions? Should, for instance, "terrestrial" disappear entirely in favor of "earthly," or are there shades of meaning involved that need to remain available to us? Must we sacrifice "notwithstanding" because we have "in spite of" or "despite"? Need we forfeit "jettison" just because we have "throw overboard"? And what about "disinterested," which is becoming a synonym for "uninterested," even though that means something else, and though we have no other word for "disinterested"? 17

"Language has *always* changed," say these people, and they might with equal justice say that there has always been war or sickness or insanity. But the truth is that some sicknesses that formerly killed millions have been eliminated, that some so-called insanity can today be treated, and that just because there have always been wars does not mean that someday a cure cannot be found even for that 18 scourge. And if it cannot, it is only by striving to put an absolute end to war, by pretending that it can be licked, that we can at least partly control it. Without such assumptions and efforts, the evil would be so widespread that, given our current weaponry, we would no longer be here to worry about the future of language.

But we are here, and having evolved linguistically this far, and having the   19
means—books of grammar, dictionaries, education for all—to arrest unnecessary change, why not endeavor with might and mind to arrest it? Certain cataclysms cannot be prevented: earthquakes and droughts, for example, can scarcely, if at all, be controlled; but we can prevent floods, for which purpose we have invented dams. And dams are precisely what we can construct to prevent floods of ignorance from eroding our language, and, beyond that, to provide irrigation for areas that would otherwise remain linguistically arid.

For consider that what some people are pleased to call linguistic evolution was   20
almost always a matter of ignorance prevailing over knowledge. There is no valid reason, for example, for the word *nice* to have changed its meaning so many times—except ignorance of its exact definition. Had the change never occurred, or had it been stopped at any intermediate stage, we would have had just as good a word as we have now and saved some people a heap of confusion along the way. But if *nice* means what it does today—and it has two principal meanings, one of them, as in "nice distinction," alas, obsolescent—let us, for heaven's sake, keep it where it is, now that we have the means with which to hold it there.

If, for instance, we lose the accusative case *whom*—and we are in great danger   21
of losing it—our language will be the poorer for it. Obviously, "The man, whom I had never known, was a thief" means something other than "The man who I had never known was a thief." Now, you can object that it would be just as easy in the first instance to use some other construction; but what happens if *this* one is used incorrectly? Ambiguity and confusion. And why should we lose this useful distinction? Just because a million or ten million or a billion people less educated than we are cannot master the difference? Surely it behooves us to try to educate the ignorant up to our level rather than to stultify ourselves down to theirs. Yes, you say, but suppose they refuse to or are unable to learn? In that case, I say, there is a doubly good reason for not going along with them. Ah, you reply, but they are the majority, and we must accept their way or, if the revolution is merely linguistic, lose our "credibility" (as the current parlance, rather confusingly, has it) or, if the revolution is political, lose our heads. Well, I consider a sufficient number of people to be educable enough to be capable of using *who* and *whom* correctly, and to derive satisfaction from this capability—a sufficient number, I mean, to enable us to preserve *whom,* and not to have to ask "for who the bell tolls."

The main problem with education, actually, is not those who need it and can-   22
not get it, but those who should impart it and, for various reasons, do not. In short, the enemies of education are the educators themselves: miseducated, underpaid, overburdened, and intimidated teachers (frightened because, though the pen is supposed to be mightier than the sword, the switchblade is surely more powerful than the ferrule), and professors who—because they are structural linguists, democratic respecters of alleged minority rights, or otherwise misguided folk—believe in the sacrosanct privilege of any culturally underprivileged minority or majority to

dictate its ignorance to the rest of the world. For, I submit, an English improvised by slaves and other strangers to the culture—to whom my heart goes out in every human way—under dreadfully deprived conditions can nowise equal an English that the best literary and linguistic talents have, over the centuries, perceptively and painstakingly brought to a high level of excellence.

So my answer to the scoffers in this or any audience is, in simplest terms, the   23
following: contrary to popular misconception, language does not belong to the people, or at least not in the sense in which *belong* is usually construed. For things can rightfully belong only to those who invent or earn them. But we do not know who invented language: is it the people who first made up the words for *father* and *mother*, for *I* and *thou*, for *hand* and *foot;* or is it the people who evolved the subtler shadings of language, its poetic variety and suggestiveness, but also its un-ambiguousness, its accurate and telling details? Those are two very different groups of people and two very different languages, and I, as you must have guessed by now, consider the latter group at least as important as the former. As for *earning* language, it has surely been earned by those who have striven to learn it properly, and here even economic and social circumstances are but an imperfect excuse for bad usage; history is full of examples of people rising from humble origins to learn, against all kinds of odds, to speak and write correctly—even brilliantly.

Belong, then, should be construed in the sense that parks, national forests,   24
monuments, and public utilities are said to belong to the people: available for properly respectful use but not for defacement and destruction. And all that we propose to teach is how to use and enjoy the gardens of language to their utmost aesthetic and salubrious potential. Still, I must now address myself to the group that, while agreeing with my aims, despairs of finding practical methods for their implementation.

True enough, after a certain age speakers not aware of Standard English or not   25
exceptionally gifted will find it hard or impossible to change their ways. Neverthe-less, if there were available funds for advanced methods in teaching; if teachers themselves were better trained and paid, and had smaller classes and more assis-tants; if, furthermore, college entrance requirements were heightened and the motivation of students accordingly strengthened; if there were no structural lin-guists and National Councils of Teachers of English filling instructors' heads with notions about "Students' Rights to Their Own Language" (they have every right to it as a *second* language, but none as a *first*); if teachers in all disciplines, including the sciences and social sciences, graded on English usage as well as on specific proficiencies; if aptitude tests for various jobs stressed good English more than they do; and, above all, if parents were better educated and more aware of the need to set a good example to their children, and to encourage them to learn correct usage, the situation could improve enormously.

Clearly, to expect all this to come to pass is utopian; some of it, however, is   26
well within the realm of possibility. For example, even if parents do not speak very good English, many of them at least can manage an English that is good enough to correct a very young child's mistakes; in other words, most adults can speak a good enough four-year-old's idiom. They would thus start kids out on the right path; the rest could be done by the schools.

But the problem is what to do in the most underprivileged homes: those of   27
blacks, Hispanics, immigrants from various Asian and European countries. This is
where day-care centers could come in. If the fathers and mothers could be gain-
fully employed, their small children would be looked after by day-care centers
where—is this asking too much?—good English could be inculcated in them. The
difficulty, of course, is what to do about the discrepancy the little ones would note
between the speech of the day-care people and that of their parents. Now, it seems
to me that small children have a far greater ability to learn things, including languages, than some people give them credit for. Much of it is indeed rote learning,
but, where languages are concerned, that is one of the basic learning methods even
for adults. There is no reason for not teaching kids another language, to wit, Standard English, and turning this, if desirable, into a game: "At home you speak one
way; here we have another language," at which point the instructor can make up
names and explanations for Standard English that would appeal to pupils of that
particular place, time, and background.

At this stage of the game, as well as later on in school, care should be exercised   28
to avoid insulting the language spoken in the youngsters' homes. There must be
ways to convey that both home and school languages have their validity and uses
and that knowing both enables one to accomplish more in life. This would be hard
to achieve if the children's parents were, say, militant blacks of the Geneva Smitherman sort, who execrate Standard English as a weapon of capitalist oppression
against the poor of all races, colors, and religions. But, happily, there is evidence
that most black, Hispanic, and other non–Standard English–speaking parents want
their children to learn correct English so as to get ahead in the world.

Yet how do we defend ourselves against the charge that we are old fogeys who   29
cannot emotionally adjust to the new directions an ever-living and changing language must inevitably take? Here I would want to redefine or, at any rate, clarify,
what "living and changing" means, and also explain where we old fogeys stand.
Misinformed attacks on Old Fogeydom, I have noticed, invariably represent us as
people who shudder at a split infinitive and would sooner kill or be killed than
tolerate a sentence that ends with a preposition. Actually, despite all my travels
through Old Fogeydom, I have yet to meet one inhabitant who would not stick a
preposition onto the tail of a sentence; as for splitting infinitives, most of us O.F.'s
are perfectly willing to do that, too, but tactfully and sparingly, where it feels right.
There is no earthly reason, for example, for saying "to dangerously live," when "to
live dangerously" sounds so much better; but it does seem right to say (and write)
"What a delight to sweetly breathe in your sleeping lover's breath"; that sounds
smoother, indeed sweeter, than "to breathe in sweetly" or "sweetly to breathe in."
But infinitives begging to be split are relatively rare; a sensitive ear, a good eye for
shades of meaning will alert you whenever the need to split arises; without that ear
and eye, you had better stick to the rules.

About the sense in which language is, and must be, alive, let me speak while   30
donning another of my several hats—actually it is not a hat but a cap, for there
exists in Greenwich Village an inscription on a factory that reads "CRITIC CAPS."
So with my drama critic's cap on, let me present you with an analogy. The world
theater today is full of directors who wreak havoc on classic plays to demonstrate

their own ingenuity, their superiority, as it were, to the author. These directors—aborted playwrights, for the most part—will stage productions of *Hamlet* in which the prince is a woman, a flaming homosexual, or a one-eyed hunchback.

Well, it seems to me that the same spirit prevails in our approach to linguistics, with every newfangled, ill-informed, know-nothing construction, definition, pronunciation enshrined by the joint efforts of structural linguists, permissive dictionaries, and allegedly democratic but actually demagogic educators. What really makes a production of, say, *Hamlet* different, and therefore alive, is that the director, while trying to get as faithfully as possible at Shakespeare's meanings, nevertheless ends up stressing things in the play that strike him most forcefully; and the same individuality in production design and performances (the Hamlet of Gielgud versus the Hamlet of Olivier, for instance—what a world of difference!) further differentiates one production from another, and bestows on each its particular vitality. So, too, language remains alive because each speaker (or writer) can and must, *within the framework of accepted grammar, syntax, and pronunciation,* produce a style that is his very own, that is as personal as his posture, way of walking, mode of dress, and so on. It is such stylistic differences that make a person's—or a nation's—language flavorous, pungent, alive, and all this without having to play fast and loose with the existing rules. **31**

But to have this, we need, among other things, good teachers and, beyond them, enlightened educators. I shudder when I read in the *Birmingham* (Alabama) *Post-Herald* of October 6, 1978, an account of a talk given to eight hundred English teachers by Dr. Alan C. Purves, vice-president of the National Council of Teachers of English. Dr. Purves is quoted as saying things like "We are in a situation with respect to reading where . . . ," and culminating in the following truly horrifying sentence: "I am going to suggest that when we go back to the basics, I think what we should be dealing with is our charge to help students to be more proficient in producing meaningful language—language that says what it means." Notice all the deadwood, the tautology, the anacoluthon in the first part of that sentence; but notice especially the absurdity of the latter part, in which the dubious word "meaningful"—a poor relation of "significant"—is thought to require explaining to an audience of English teachers. **32**

Given such leadership from the N.C.T.E., the time must be at hand when we shall hear—not just "Don't ask for who the bell rings" (*ask not* and *tolls* being, of course, archaic, elitist language), but also "It rings for you and I." **33**

Rhetorical Focus

1. Simon begins his argument with a question and then answers it with several examples. Where does his argument go after that? What, for example, is the purpose of the "language pathologist" anecdote?
2. Simon seems to misuse "like" for "such as." Can you find other examples of conservative "errors"? Does this damage his argument?
3. One important aspect of writing arguments is to anticipate and to deal with the objections intelligent opponents might have to your main point. Simon seems to do this in the paragraphs beginning, "Now, I realize that there are

two possible reactions among you. . . ." How fairly do you think he answers the objections? Make a list of the objections and his rebuttal.

Thematic Focus

1. John Simon claims there is pleasure and pride in speaking and writing correctly. Does he suggest other consequences?
2. Simon uses the words *cultivated, civilized, orderly,* and *educated* to describe those who use language correctly. What are some terms he uses for those who disagree with him?
3. Simon suggests that certain minority groups speak the way they do out of ignorance. What criteria is Simon using here? Do you think the issue is more complicated than he asserts? In what ways?

Who Changes Language

Jim Quinn

Jim Quinn, a poet, satirist, and columnist for various publications, takes a more liberal position on language than Simon. His book *American Tongue and Cheek* (1980) from which the following excerpt is taken, is a criticism of the linguistic conservatives who dedicate their energies to "protecting" the language from change. Such "pop grammarians," according to Quinn, fail to see that language is an outgrowth and a reflection of culture. Because our culture is constantly changing, our language will and should inevitably evolve as well.

Reflections Before Reading

Is the dialect you speak, with its particular pronunciation, words, and phrases, the "correct" one in this country? Do the newscasters on local television stations speak the same dialect as you do? Are they "correct"? How does one judge these matters? Can you remember being corrected for using bad English? Do you remember the specific details? How did you feel?

A Primer of Language Politics

The proper pop grammarian attitude to change is to see it as ugly, unnecessary,   1
illiterate, obscurantist, illogical, alien, ignorant, and threatening not only to the
language but to the maintenance of the social order.

In almost all cases, there is an unpleasant edge to the pop grammar com-   2
plaint—it sounds a little like the way realist painters used to refer to modernists,
and the way modernist painters now refer to the young realists. It is as if the pop
grammarian was saying, "I learned this new and difficult dialect. I changed the way
I spoke, lost my accent, submitted myself to all sorts of humiliation by my wonderful English teachers. Now I've made it—and I'm going to make sure that nobody
else makes it without going through the same thing." Language is seen as a skill
anyone can acquire (like painting in perspective, or painting in broad abstract
brush strokes), if they care enough.

Not to care is to attack the pop grammarians' whole life, and their hard-won   3
position in the writing business.

This helps to explain why pop grammarians frequently say that they have a   4
vested interest in correcting errors—after all, they are writers, and they feel that
television (from above) and careless ignorance (from below) are combining to destroy their wonderful, supple, eloquent medium, the standard dialect of English.
After all, what is thinking but making distinctions—and every time the word *flaunt*
is used to mean *flout,* or *hopefully* to mean *it is to be hoped,* or *disinterested* for
uninterested, a distinction dies, and with it a possible thought in English.

Let's try to answer this by talking about language change—who does it, and   5
how is it done. It is easiest, perhaps, to separate the changers from the defenders
by means of a political metaphor: the Left, and the Right:

The Left (Language Changers)   1. Illiterates, semiliterates, occupiers of ethnic   6
or cultural ghettos. Most speech by the very poor or very isolated (by geography or
by prejudice) is not adventurous *in form.* Grammatical structures are essentially
old-fashioned, unchanged sometimes for centuries. Donald J. Lloyd, in *Snobs,
Slobs and the English Language,* has this to say:

> *Them things* was once standard, so were *he don't, guv, clumb* and *riz.* The common
> speech of the uneducated is comparatively static, though it varies from place to place it
> is everywhere conservative.
>   The changes made by the poor are likely to be in vocabulary—slang. Seldom writ-
> ten because its users seldom write, it is capable of great literary beauties, uncompli-
> cated force, compact suggestion and moving sentiment.

2. The new educated class. Lloyd points out that in the nineteenth century the   7
concentration of schools, colleges, publishing houses, and print shops in New England and New York helped establish a written standard, "native only to those who
grew up near the Hudson River or east of it. Elsewhere in America this written
standard has been a learned class dialect—learned in the schools as the property
and distinguishing mark of an educated class . . . an heirloom handed down from

the days when the whole nation looked to the school masters of New England for its book learning."

One interesting example of this is the spelling of *uh,* that little pause we all make in our speech from time to time. *Uh* is frequently spelled *er*—because *uh* is the way *er* is pronounced in the *r*-less standard New England dialect. If you speak a dialect where the *r*'s are pronounced, as I do, you may also remember how odd it sounded when you read the word *er*—and pronounced it to rhyme with *her.* Slowly, as standard pronunciation in the United States is demanding that *r*'s be pronounced—largely because it is pronounced in radio and TV announcer standard—the word is being spelled in the new dialect, *uh,* a fact that would have horrified Henry James, who insisted in an address to the graduating class of Harvard that the United States would never be capable of a real literature or a beautiful speech until it stopped pronouncing its *r*'s, an "ugly sound" that James insisted was "a morose grinding of the back teeth." 8

The domination of the East was a long one; as recently as 1959, according to *The New York Times* (July 23, 1979), 75 percent of the Ph.D.'s in America came from the East Coast. The educational explosion of the past twenty years has changed all that: in 1979, only 20 percent of the Ph.D.'s came from the East. 9

The new educated class is large, self-sufficient, and writes the language it knows. "Most," says Lloyd, 10

> *take their diplomas and go to work among their own people. They form a literate class greater in numbers and in proportion to the total population than ever before. Speaking the speech of their region, they mingle naturally and easily with its people. When they write, they write the language they know, and they print it, for the most part, in presses close at hand. Everywhere they speak a standard literate English—but with differences: a regional speech derived from the usages of the early settlers.*

Many of these people invent new words—out of their own experience. Nowhere is this more apparent than in contemporary physics—a science that seems always to be inventing new words for almost invisible phenomena. In the nineteenth century, scientists made up new words—out of Latin and Greek. Fowler complains that scientists could never be convinced to keep these two languages separate, and thus produced "barbarisms" like *Pleistocene, pliocene, miocene*—in each case the prefix is Greek and the suffix Latin. Fowler mourned that it was impossible to stop these words. "A barbarism is like a lie; it has got the start of us before we have found it out, and we cannot catch it; it is in possession, and our offers of other versions come too late. . . . It is worthwhile to mention this . . . on the chance that the men of science may some day wake up to their duties to the language—duties much less simple than they are apt to suppose." 11

That day has arrived. The newest words do not come from mixed Latin and Greek—because Latin and Greek are no longer studied by scientists. *Quark* is the name given newly discovered subatomic particles, and quarks come in colors; among the colors is *beauty.* Thinking of beauty as a color is a little odd—but apparently attractive to physicists who seem to enjoy the fact that their discipline requires them to think about things in an odd way. *Quark* as a word first appeared in *Finnegans Wake,* but the inventor of the scientific term, Murray Gell-Mann, is 12 frequently quoted as saying that he did not know that at the time. He just wanted a funny-sounding word for a funny-acting particle. The newest particle or substance that physicists claim to have discovered is the stuff that holds the atom together, and it is called *gluon,* from the word *glue,* and the suffix *-on.*

This delightful kind of invention is responsible for the use of words like *finalize, input, unsave* (in computer terminology, this does not mean the same thing as *destroy,* rather, it means not actually to throw something away but simply refuse to collect it—a fine and subtle distinction that should delight pop grammarians), *gigo* (garbage in, garbage out—give a machine nonsense instead of true data and you get only nonsense back), *mego* (*my eyes glaze over*—indicating boredom, and in combination with *garbage in garbage out—as, what is all this gigo and mego?*—the strongest possible condemnation). 13

3. Linguists. Frequently accused of being "anything goes" linguists. Or destroyers of Standard. Actually, linguists frequently insist that anything does not go—that in certain situations the Standard of the grammar books is wrong because it is alien and alienating. 14

This comes down to saying, in effect, *whatever is is right,* which is not usually considered a leftist statement (and resembles Hegel's conservative dictum—The *real is the returned*)—but in language, even conservatives are to the Left. 15

The Right (Language Preservers)   1. Real conservatives. This book is in favor of true conservatives. People who still say *icebox,* and who still use old-fashioned constructions. Conservatives are walking history books of the language, and they keep to old words and old ways out of a kind of instinct of preservation. 16

Titles of organizations frequently stay the same, and act as a way of dating the organization. For example, certain kinds of word chains are relatively new in modern English. So, simply from the titles of the two groups, we could tell that the National Council *of* Teachers *of* English is an older organization than the National Educational Association, or the Modern Language Association. 17

In "The Possessive Apostrophe in Names" (*American Speech,* October 1958), Robert L. Cord points out that "not one of the teachers colleges in the United States takes an apostrophe in its name. . . . Years ago, the apostrophe seems to have been employed in the form. . . . Old editions of the Encyclopaedia Britannica write of the *Teachers' College* of Columbia University." 18

A conservative almost never corrects others, however. For example, your aunt who still says *icebox* does not have a sign on her door that says, "The word fridge must not be used in this house. Violators will be humiliated." 19

And a language conservative is not necessarily conservative in any other matters. For example, as Lounsbury points out, Browning as a poet used many new words and new constructions in his work—he was what linguists today call an advanced speaker. Tennyson used almost none—a language conservative. That says something about them as poets—and nothing wrong about either of them. It is interesting that Tennyson, the language conservative, was interested in the newest scientific thought of his day—and was extremely modern in ideas; while Browning seems not to have bothered too much with scientific discovery, or worried about dealing with the new problems science presented to educated nineteenth-century 20 readers. But however interesting that is as literary criticism (any graduate student will see the essay staring him in the face: "Advanced Thought and Advanced Language in the Nineteenth Century—A Study of Contrasts in Browning and Tennyson"), it is important here only to help point out that we are all conservatives in some matters. I really can never bring myself to say *film* for *movie*.

The Far Right   Editors and teachers of English who are, or consider themselves,   21
masters of that school-mastered dialect called Standard. They frequently consider themselves guardians of the Standard—without the good sense of Fowler, who points out that trying to stamp out barbarisms is impossible.

For example, take the apostrophe. The state of Colorado by declaration of a   22
joint session of its congress decided in 1978 to drop the apostrophe from its motto. *Pike's Peak or Bust* became *Pikes Peak or Bust*. *The New York Times* deplored that decision in an editorial, declaring that this was just one more instance of permissive grammar, and praising the apostrophe in general as an outstanding felicity of English typesetting.

Of course, the state of Colorado was only following—belatedly—the advice of   23
the American Cartographic Association, which recommended in the early 1950s that the apostrophe be dropped in place names because it made maps extremely hard to read. That advice is followed by all modern atlases I have checked, by all dictionaries that print a gazetteer—and by *The New York Times* itself, which has, for at least fifteen years, been printing towns like Harpers Ferry, Virginia, and Toms River, New Jersey, without the apostrophe.

When Webster's Third International first appeared, it frightened the Far   24
Right out of its collective mind—and many publications, *Life* and *The New York Times* included, declared that they would not use Webster's Third, since it was too permissive. They would insist on Webster's Second as the dictionary of record. Bergen Evans, in the *Atlantic Monthly* (May 1962), had a little fun doing a word count of both publications:

> In the issue in which *Life* stated editorially that it would follow the Second International, there were over forty words, constructions and meanings which are in the Third International, but not in the Second. The issue of *The New York Times* which hailed the Second as the authority to which it would adhere . . . used one hundred and fifty-three separate words, phrases and constructions which are listed in the Third but not in the Second and nineteen others which are condemned in the Second. . . . *The Washington Post*, in an editorial captioned "Keep Your Old Webster's," says in the first sentence, "don't throw it away," and in the second, "hang on to it." But the old Webster's labels *don't* colloquial and doesn't include *hang on to* in this sense at all.

One example of Far Right language attitudes can be found in the stylebooks   25
published by leading papers, like *The New York Times* and *The Washington Post*. Certainly, there is a value to the paper in always printing the box scores of baseball games in a simple and rigorous way. The spelling of words transliterated from languages that do not have our alphabet is also a problem, and stylebooks choose for the harried reporter and copy editor an arbitrary "correct" form: *succoth* or

succah or *sukkah* from the Hebrew; *kif* or *kef* or *kief* from the Arabic; *Kruschev* or *Chruschev* or *Khrushchev* from the Russian—the list is long and the decisions are usually made without fuss or *hutzpah* (or *chutzpa*).

Most stylebooks are as innocuous, and as ineffective, as the pronouncements   26
of editors in editorials—like declarations that only Webster's Second will be used, they represent policy. The reporters and writers represent practice; and practice ultimately wins.

The Yahoo Right   The yahoos are, of course, the pop grammarians—who offer   27
the same strictures that the Far Right do, but with even less intelligence and understanding—without mastering the standard dialect themselves in many cases— and who publish interminable death of English despairs and private lists of language peeves. Professional busybodies and righters of imaginary wrongs, they are the Sunday visitors of language, dropping in weekly on the local poor to make sure that everything is up to their own idea of Standard, not because they care about the poor, of course, but because the diseases the poor contract from inadequate sanitation can be catching.

The Center   The Center is made up of those people who are the doers and   28
achievers of the world—hard workers, worried about the impression they make, and determined to rise in life.

They don't have the assurance of the taxi driver, the ghetto Black, or the teen-   29
ager speaking his high school slang. They care what people think about the language they use.

They do not have the power of print that the indigenous Ph.D. does—or the   30
same capacity to delight in their own invention and their own dialect.

They don't have the mastery of Standard that comes to people who have spent   31
years and years in the classroom—years that members of the Center have spent out on the streets humping for a living.

So they are the victims of the yahoos who frighten them with words like *illit-*   32
erate (back to the factory) and *ignoramus* (you'll never make it in the middle class, no matter how much money you earn). Randolph Quirk, in *The Use of English*, points out that at both ends of the social scale, the upper and lower classes, no one worries about language.

People of position and status do not need to worry about their language—"no   33
fear of being criticised or corrected is likely to cross their minds, and this gives their speech that characteristically unself-conscious and easy flow which is often envied. Their nonchalant attitude to language was epitomised in the nineteenth century in the words of Bulwer Lytton: 'I am free to confess that I don't know grammar. Lady Blessington, do *you* know grammar?' "

The very poor, or the isolated, or speakers of nonstandard dialects also speak   34
with "a similar degree of careless ease." They know their speech is condemned, and don't care.

In between is the Center.   35

They live their lives . . . in some degree of nervousness over their grammar, their pronunciation and their choice of words; sensitive and fearful of betraying themselves. . . . It is all too easy to raise an unworthy laugh at the anxious. The people thus uncomfortably stilted on linguistic high heels so often form part of what is, in many ways, the most admirable section of any society; the ambitious, tense, inner-driven people, who are bent on going places and doing things. The greater pity then if a disproportionate amount of their energy goes into . . . this shabby obsession with variant forms of English—especially if the net result is (as so often) merely to sound affected and ridiculous.

One of the purposes of this book is to try to get everybody, especially the anxious Centrists, to relax about language, and not to listen to the yahoo pop grammarians. But this book is not likely to accomplish that. This is a sad thing for the people in the Center who will endure lots of suffering and worry.   36

But not so sad for the language. As Quirk points out, the people in the Center, by trying to follow the unreasonable and silly dictates of the yahoo pop grammarians, sound affected and silly—and as a result, ironically, they are changing the language. In fact, as many studies by William Labov have shown, changes in pronunciation are most frequent in members of the upper working class and lower middle class—exactly those highly motivated movers and doers who are likely to change the way they talk. They may be searching for a new and more elegant way to disguise their origins, but they are changing the language nonetheless. Labov has found that the *r* is coming back into New York speech—among the anxious Center, of course. The poor do not attempt it, and the rich never bother to try. Nelson Rockefeller, for example, spoke in a rich r-less accent all of his life. In Philadelphia, where Labov has been working for years, he has found a truly amazing kind of shift in white speakers: 37

baby	becomes	*beebee*
me	becomes	*may*
Ann	becomes	*Ian*
fight	becomes	*foit*

and the sentence *City streets are often straight* is pronounced *Shitty shtreets are often shtraight.*

The more the person is a climber and doer and the wider their circle of acquaintances, the more they are likely to join in these shifts. Older working-class speakers, or middle-class speakers, do not participate.   38

So we look back over our list of people grouped by language attitudes, and we find the ones who change language and the ones who do not.   39

The poor and speakers of nonstandard dialects are likely to hold onto old grammatical forms—and introduce new slang.   40

The members of the new educated class are likely to hold onto varieties of Standard grammar but introduce new words from their professions, or make up new words for their professions.   41

The editors and writers and other media people are likely to be sure that they are holding onto the good old ways of Standard English grammar—and to use new words and new constructions from both the poor and the new educated class without realizing it.   42

The yahoo pop grammarians insist on logic and grammar and etymology and   43
actually introduce change themselves. Edwin Newman insists, despite everything
we know about the history of the word, that *culprit* means "guilty culprit," and the
word *guilty* is therefore a redundancy. John Simon takes him at his word, and a
new citation is added to the list that will eventually change the word to mean
"guilty culprit." Theodore Bernstein, in an excess of zeal about a language he knew
all too little about, insisted that *the hoi polloi* is redundant, since *hoi* means *the* in
Greek. Bernstein admits that *hoi polloi* without *the* sounds awkward and advises
everyone to simply avoid the construction. Every citation in every dictionary I am
able to find lists *the hoi polloi*—but John Simon, once again, takes Bernstein at half
his word, and drops *the* from *hoi polloi,* a phrase he loves to use: another new
citation—eventually, perhaps, *hoi polloi* will need no *the* in English.

The anxious workers in the center of language listen to all the fuss raised by   44
the pop grammarians and strain to bring their language under conscious control,
producing sounds never heard before: more change comes from anxiety than from
complacency.

And change is life. The slang of the poor, the new technical terms and jargon   45
of the professionals, the cant of journalism, the simplistic language notions of pop
grammarians—all keep language from going stale.

Samuel Johnson, in the preface to his dictionary, put the case for change very   46
strongly:

> . . . The language most likely to continue long without alteration, would be that of a
> nation raised a little, and but a little, above barbarity, secluded from strangers, and
> totally employed in procuring the conveniences of life; either without books, or, like
> some of the Mahometan countries, with very few: men thus busied and unlearned,
> having only such words as common use requires, would perhaps long continue to ex-
> press the same notions by the same signs. But no such constancy can be expected in a
> people polished by arts, and classed by subordination, where one part of the commu-
> nity is sustained and accommodated by the labour of the other. Those who have much
> leisure to think, will always be enlarging the stock of ideas, and every increase of knowl-
> edge, whether real or fancied, will produce new words, or combinations of words.
> . . . As any custom is disused, the words that expressed it must perish with it; as any
> opinion grows popular, it will innovate speech in the same proportion as it alters prac-
> tice.

You want language stability, says Johnson—primitive communism is the best   47
way to guarantee it. There seems to be nothing to add to that as far as the politics of
language attitudes goes—but there is still another justification for language
change, and it is an important one: language change is a product of language instinct, and it comes about because it is based on the same attitudes to language that
produce poetry. This idea was advanced by Kittredge and Greenough in *Words
and Their Ways in English Speech.*

The ordinary processes by which words change their meanings are essentially   48
the devices of poetry, say Kittredge and Greenough, and those processes go on as
long as the language is alive:

. . . There is no device we are accustomed to call poetical, no similitude so slight, no metaphor so strained or so commonplace, that language has not seized upon it to make new forms of expression as the needs of advancing thought have required them. Even when the resultant words appear intensely prosaic [*stonewalling, plumbers, laundering cash,* for example], the processes which created them are identical with those of artistic poetry.

The richness of our speech was not produced merely by the capacity of the   49
English to borrow words from other languages, say Kittredge and Greenough— "such a result was achieved only when this great mass of variously derived material had been subjected for centuries to the language-making instinct; that is, to the poetic faculty of man."

This last theory, a very old one (*Words and Their Ways* was first published in   50
1901), is especially attractive because it helps explain why people like new words so much, and not only new words, but new ways of making sentences, new sounds, new combinations—it is because "All language is poetry."

Rhetorical Focus

1. Quinn begins with a direct attack on the pop grammarians. Is this a successful rhetorical strategy? Quinn's essay seems to be more expository than argumentative. Describe how he chooses to write about language change. Is this technique effective?
2. Has Quinn prepared the reader for his conclusion? How?
3. How would you compare the organizational strategy of both Simon and Quinn. Do you think they achieve their objectives?

Thematic Focus

1. Quinn clearly thinks Simon is one of the "yahoo right." Which one of Simon's ideas would Quinn object to most? Which one of Quinn's ideas would Simon object to most?
2. Quinn embraces language change, while Simon urges us to resist. Do you think either of these attitudes would actually influence language behavior?
3. Some countries, such as France, have an academy that decides what is correct language usage and what is not. Do you think America should adopt this strategy? Explain.

Suggestions for Writing

1. Take a passage from John Simon's essay and write it in "bad English." What makes what you did "bad"?
2. Write a narrative about your experiences with some specific aspect of language learning. Include what you remember concerning the issues raised in these two essays.

3. Do you remember an English teacher who was especially conservative (far right or yahoo) or liberal? Write that person a letter explaining how you felt then and what you think now about your experience in that class.

GENDERED LANGUAGE

Because we use it so naturally, we often assume that language is a neutral communicative tool, serving us at our command. However, language is also part of our social reality and has been since long before we came on the scene. Although we do create new words, we mostly inherit our vocabulary, syntax, structures, and so forth from our past and present cultural environment, from the values, myths, biases, and dreams of our society.

If we live in an unjust society, or even if our culture was once biased, language will probably still reflect those values. However, because we also think and plan about the future with language, we should be able to influence culture with the language we choose. Language can both create and reproduce values, good and bad. Economic differences among people as well as differences of race, gender, and class will be reflected in language; therefore, those in power will have language behaviors different from those without influence. Also, because cultures tend to reproduce themselves, power or the lack of it will become evident in the language being taught at school. Robin Lakoff in the following essay is suggesting that women have been taught to speak in certain ways because they are "out of power," while men learn to speak in other ways because they expect to be in charge. Casey Miller and Kate Swift, in their essay, offer a number of concrete examples to support their thesis that language treats women unfairly. They argue that sexist language perpetuates false stereotypes and degrades both the victim and the user. As you read these essays, think of your own language use and compare it to the language you hear everyday. Start to notice the differences and consider whether your language might be a tool that helps you or a hindrance to social justice.

Talking Like a Lady

Robin Lakoff

Robin Lakoff (b. 1942) is a professor of linguistics at the University of California, Berkeley. A pioneer in the study of gender-related patterns in language, she is the author of many books and essays, among them *Language and Woman's Place* (1975), and co-author of *Face Value: The Politics of Beauty* (1984). The following excerpt from the July 1974 issue of *Ms.* considers the vocabulary and syntax unique to women's language in American culture and the problems that result.

Reflections Before Reading

Some people think women talk and write differently than men do. Is that your experience? Could you give specific examples of differences in vocabulary, syntax, or tone? Do males, for example, talk more in class? What connotations come to your mind when *lady* is used? What does it mean to act like a *lady?* How about acting like a *man?* When you talk to someone who has power over you, how do you change your speech? How about when you write a paper for a chemistry professor or for an English composition instructor? When you write a letter to an old friend?

"Women's language" is that pleasant (dainty?), euphemistic, never-aggressive way 1 of talking we learned as little girls. Cultural bias was built into the language we were allowed to speak, the subjects we were allowed to speak about, and the ways we were spoken of. Having learned our linguistic lesson well, we go out in the world, only to discover that we are communicative cripples—damned if we do, and damned if we don't.

If we refuse to talk "like a lady," we are ridiculed and criticized for being 2 unfeminine. ("She thinks like a man" is, at best, a left-handed compliment.) If we do learn all the fuzzy-headed, unassertive language of our sex, we are ridiculed for being unable to think clearly, unable to take part in a serious discussion, and therefore unfit to hold a position of power.

It doesn't take much of this for a woman to begin feeling she deserves such 3 treatment because of inadequacies in her own intelligence and education.

"Women's language" shows up in all levels of English. For example, women 4 are encouraged and allowed to make far more precise discriminations in naming

"You Are What You Say" by Robin Lakoff, MS magazine, July, 1974. Reprinted by permission.

colors than men do. Words like *mauve, beige, ecru, aquamarine, lavender,* and so on, are unremarkable in a woman's active vocabulary, but largely absent from that of most men. I know of no evidence suggesting that women actually *see* a wider range of colors than men do. It is simply that fine discriminations of this sort are relevant to women's vocabularies, but not to men's; to men, who control most of the interesting affairs of the world, such distinctions are trivial—irrelevant.

In the area of syntax, we find similar gender-related peculiarities of speech.   5
There is one construction, in particular, that women use conversationally far more than men: the tag-question. A tag is midway between an outright statement and a yes–no question; it is less assertive than the former, but more confident than the later.

A *flat statement* indicates confidence in the speaker's knowledge and is fairly   6
certain to be believed; a *question* indicates a lack of knowledge on some point and implies that the gap in the speaker's knowledge can and will be remedied by an answer. For example, if, at a Little League game, I have had my glasses off, I can legitimately ask someone else: "Was the player out at third?" A *tag question,* being intermediate between statement and question, is used when the speaker is stating a claim, but lacks full confidence in the truth of that claim. So if I say, "Is Joan here?" I will probably not be surprised if my respondent answers "no"; but if I say, "Joan is here, isn't she?" instead, chances are I am already biased in favor of a positive answer, wanting only confirmation. I still want a response, but I have enough knowledge (or think I have) to predict that response. A tag question, then, might be thought of as a statement that doesn't demand to be believed by anyone but the speaker, a way of giving leeway, of not forcing the addressee to go along with the views of the speaker.

Another common use of the tag question is in small talk when the speaker is   7
trying to elicit conversation: "Sure is hot here, isn't it?"

But in discussing personal feelings or opinions, only the speaker normally has   8
any way of knowing the correct answer. Sentences such as "I have a headache, don't I?" are clearly ridiculous. But there are other examples where it is the speaker's opinions, rather than perceptions, for which corroboration is sought, as in "The situation in Southeast Asia is terrible, isn't it?"

While there are, of course, other possible interpretations of a sentence like   9
this, one possibility is that the speaker has a particular answer in mind—"yes" or "no"—but is reluctant to state it baldly. This sort of tag question is much more apt to be used by women than by men in conversation. Why is this the case?

The tag question allows a speaker to avoid commitment, and thereby avoid   10
conflict with the addressee. The problem is that, by so doing, speakers may also give the impression of not really being sure of themselves, or looking to the addressee for confirmation of their views. This uncertainty is reinforced in more subliminal ways, too. There is a peculiar sentence intonation-pattern, used almost exclusively by women, as far as I know, which changes a declarative answer into a question. The effect of using the rising inflection typical of a yes–no question is to imply that the speaker is seeking confirmation, even though the speaker is clearly

the only one who has the requisite information, which is why the question was put to her in the first place:

(Q) When will dinner be ready?
(A) Oh . . . around six o'clock . . . ?

It is as though the second speaker were saying, "Six o'clock—if that's okay with you, if you agree." The person being addressed is put in the position of having to provide confirmation. One likely consequence of this sort of speech-pattern in a woman is that, often unbeknownst to herself, the speaker builds a reputation of tentativeness, and others will refrain from taking her seriously or trusting her with any real responsibilities, since she "can't make up her mind," and "isn't sure of herself."

Such idiosyncrasies may explain why women's language sounds much more   11
"polite" than men's. It is polite to leave a decision open, not impose your mind, or views, or claims, on anyone else. So a tag question is a kind of polite statement, in that it does not force agreement or belief on the addressee. In the same way a request is a polite command, in that it does not force obedience on the addressee, but rather suggests something be done as a favor to the speaker. A clearly stated order implies a threat of certain consequences if it is not followed, and—even more impolite—implies that the speaker is in a superior position and able to enforce the order. By couching wishes in the form of a request, on the other hand, a speaker implies that if the request is not carried out, only the speaker will suffer; noncompliance cannot harm the addressee. So the decision is really left up to addressee. The distinction becomes clear in these examples:

Close the door.
Please close the door.
Will you close the door?
Will you please close the door?
Won't you close the door?

In the same ways as words and speech patterns used *by* women undermine   12
her image, those used *to describe* women make matters even worse. Often a word may be used of both men and women (and perhaps of things as well); but when it is applied to women, it assumes a special meaning that, by implication rather than outright assertion, is derogatory to women as a group.

The use of euphemisms has this effect. A euphemism is a substitute for a word   13
that has acquired a bad connotation by association with something unpleasant or embarrassing. But almost as soon as the new word comes into common usage, it takes on the same old bad connotations, since feelings about the things or people referred to are not altered by a change of name; thus new euphemisms must be constantly found.

There is one euphemism for *woman* still very much alive. The word, of course,   14
is *lady. Lady* has a masculine counterpart, namely *gentleman*, occasionally shortened to *gent*. But for some reason *lady* is very much commoner than *gent(leman)*.

The decision to use *lady* rather than *woman,* or vice versa, may considerably   15
alter the sense of a sentence, as the following examples show:

(a) A woman (lady) I know is a dean at Berkeley.
(b) A woman (lady) I know makes amazing things out of shoelaces and old
     boxes.

The use of *lady* in (a) imparts a frivolous, or nonserious, tone to the sentence: 16
the matter under discussion is not one of great moment. Similarly, in (b), using
lady here would suggest that the speaker considered the "amazing things" not to
be serious art, but merely a hobby or an aberration. If *woman* is used, she might be
a serious sculptor. To say *lady doctor* is very condescending, since no one ever says
gentleman doctor or even *man doctor.* For example, mention in the San Francisco
Chronicle of January 31, 1972, of Madalyn Murray O'Hair as the *lady atheist* reduces her position to that of scatter-brained eccentric. Even *woman atheist* is
scarcely defensible: sex is irrelevant to her philosophical position.

Many women argue that, on the other hand, *lady* carries with it overtones   17
recalling the age of chivalry: conferring exalted stature on the person so referred
to. This makes the term seem polite at first, but we must also remember that these
implications are perilous: they suggest that a "lady" is helpless, and cannot do
things by herself.

Lady can also be used to infer frivolousness, as in titles of organizations. Those   18
that have a serious purpose (not merely that of enabling "the ladies" to spend time
with one another) cannot use the word *lady* in their titles, but less serious ones
may. Compare the *Ladies' Auxiliary* of a men's group, or the *Thursday Evening
Ladies' Browning and Garden Society* with *Ladies' Liberation* or *Ladies' Strike for
Peace.*

What is curious about this split is that *lady* is in origin a euphemism—a substi-   19
tute that puts a better face on something people find uncomfortable—for *woman.*
What kind of euphemism is it that subtly denigrates the people to whom it refers?
Perhaps *lady* functions as a euphemism for *woman* because it does not contain the
sexual implications present in *woman:* it is not "embarrassing" in that way. If this is
so, we may expect that, in the future, *lady* will replace woman as the primary word
for the human female, since *woman* will have become too blatantly sexual. That
this distinction is already made in some contexts at least is shown in the following
examples, where you can try replacing *woman* with *lady:*

(a) She's only twelve, but she's already a woman.
(b) After ten years in jail, Harry wanted to find a woman.
(c) She's my woman, see, so don't mess around with her.

Another common substitute for *woman* is *girl.* One seldom hears a man past   20
the age of adolescence referred to as a boy, save in expressions like "going out with
the boys," which are meant to suggest an air of adolescent frivolity and irresponsibility. But women of all ages are "girls": one can have a man—not a boy—Friday,
but only a girl—never a woman or even a lady—Friday; women have girlfriends,
but men do not—in a nonsexual sense—have boyfriends. It may be that this use of

girl is euphemistic in the same way the use of *lady* is: in stressing the idea of immaturity, it removes the sexual connotations lurking in *woman*. *Girl* brings to mind irresponsibility: you don't send a girl to do a woman's errand (or even, for that matter, a boy's errand). She is a person who is both too immature and too far from real life to be entrusted with responsibilities or with decisions of any serious or important nature.

Now let's take a pair of words which, in terms of the possible relationships in   21
an earlier society, were simple male–female equivalents, analogous to *bull: cow*. Suppose we find that, for independent reasons, society has changed in such a way that the original meanings now are irrelevant. Yet the words have not been discarded, but have acquired new meanings, metaphorically related to their original senses. But suppose these new metaphorical uses are no longer parallel to each other. By seeing where the parallelism breaks down, we discover something about the different roles played by men and women in this culture. One good example of such a divergence through time is found in the pair, *master: mistress*. Once used with reference to one's power over servants, these words have become unusable today in their original master–servant sense as the relationship has become less prevalent in our society. But the words are still common.

Unless used with reference to animals, *master* now generally refers to a man   22
who has acquired consummate ability in some field, normally nonsexual. But its feminine counterpart cannot be used this way. It is practically restricted to its sexual sense of "paramour." We start out with two terms, both roughly paraphrasable as "one who has power over another." But the masculine form, once one person is no longer able to have absolute power over another, becomes usable metaphorically in the sense of "having power over *something*." *Master* requires as its object only the name of some activity, something inanimate and abstract. But *mistress* requires a masculine noun in the possessive to precede it. One cannot say: "Rhonda is a mistress." One must be *someone's* mistress. A man is defined by what he does, a woman by her sexuality, that is, in terms of one particular aspect of her relationship to men. It is one thing to be an *old master* like Hans Holbein, and another to be an *old mistress*.

The same is true of the words *spinster* and *bachelor*—gender words for "one   23
who is not married." The resemblance ends with the definition. While *bachelor* is a neuter term, often used as a compliment, *spinster* normally is used pejoratively, with connotations of prissiness, fussiness, and so on. To be a bachelor implies that one has the choice of marrying or not, and this is what makes the idea of a bachelor existence attractive in the popular literature. He has been pursued and has successfully eluded his pursuers. But a spinster is one who has not been pursued, or at last not seriously. She is old, unwanted goods. The metaphorical connotations of *bachelor* generally suggests sexual freedom; of *spinster*, puritanism or celibacy.

These examples could be multiplied. It is generally considered a *faux pas*, in   24
society, to congratulate a woman on her engagement, while it is correct to congratulate her fiancé. Why is this? The reason seems to be that it is impolite to remind people of things that may be uncomfortable to them. To congratulate a woman on her engagement is really to say, "Thank goodness! You had a close call!" For the

man, on the other hand, there was no such danger. His choosing to marry is viewed as a good thing, but not something essential.

The linguistic double standard holds throughout the life of the relationship.   25
After marriage, bachelor and spinster become man and wife, not man and woman. The woman whose husband dies remains "John's widow"; John, however, is never "Mary's widower."

Finally, why is it that salesclerks and others are so quick to call women custom-   26
ers "dear," "honey," and other terms of endearment they really have no business using? A male customer would never put up with it. But women, like children, are supposed to enjoy these endearments, rather than being offended by them.

In more ways than one, it's time to speak up.   27

Rhetorical Focus

1. Lakoff begins in a no-nonsense fashion. She announces her point in the first two sentences and then follows with her organizational plan: She will give concrete examples of "damned if we do, and damned if we don't." What kinds of examples does she give—That is, how does she group them?
2. Most arguments are directed at a specific audience, for a specific purpose. Is it clear how Lakoff conceives of her audience and what she wants them to do?
3. How would you describe Lakoff's tone? Cite specific places where her tone seems clear.

Thematic Focus

1. How could you prove or disprove the notion that our language is sexist?
2. Can you give more examples of "women's vocabulary"? Can you think of counterexamples—that is, words that might give women authority?
3. Are women socialized to be more polite than men? Why? Do you agree with Lakoff's implication that power is behind our decisions (consciously made or not) to talk and write a certain way?

One Small Step for Genkind

Casey Miller and Kate Swift

Casey Miller (b. 1919) and Kate Swift (b. 1923) have been leaders in the
protest against sexist language for nearly 20 years. Miller and Swift are
free-lance editors who form an editorial partnership focusing on the effects
of language on women. They have written many books and articles on this
subject, including *Words and Women: New Language in New Times* (1977)
and *The Handbook of Nonsexist Writing for Writers, Editors and Speakers*
(1980). Their now-classic essay, "One Small Step for Genkind," appeared
first in *The New York Times Magazine* in 1972 and opened a dialogue on the
subject of sexist bias in language, which continues unabated today.

Reflections Before Reading

Does the word *genkind* make sense to you? Is it more inclusive than
mankind? When someone mentions a doctor, lawyer, scientist, or writer do
you assume they are talking about a man? Why? Make a list of words you
consider sexist. Are there realistic alternatives? Should publishers require
writers to use nonsexist language?

A riddle is making the rounds that goes like this: A man and his young son were in 1
an automobile accident. The father was killed and the son, who was critically injured, was rushed to a hospital. As attendants wheeled the unconscious boy into
the emergency room, the doctor on duty looked down at him and said, "My God,
it's my son!" What was the relationship of the doctor to the injured boy?

If the answer doesn't jump to your mind, another riddle that has been around 2
a lot longer might help: The blind beggar had a brother. The blind beggar's
brother died. The brother who died had no brother. What relation was the blind
beggar to the blind beggar's brother?

As with all riddles, the answers are obvious once you see them: The doctor was 3
the boy's mother and the beggar was her brother's sister. Then why doesn't everyone solve them immediately? Mainly because our language, like the culture it re-

"One Small Step for Genkind" by Casey Miller and Kate Swift, THE NEW YORK TIMES Magazine,
April 16, 1972. Copyright (c) Casey Miller and Kate Swift 1974. Reprinted by permission of the authors.

flects, is male oriented. To say that a woman in medicine is an exception is simply to confirm that statement. Thousands of doctors are women, but in order to be seen in the mind's eye, they must be called women doctors.

Except for words that refer to females by definition (mother, actress, Con- 4 gresswoman), and words for occupations traditionally held by females (nurse, secretary, prostitute), the English language defines everyone as male. The hypothetical person ("If a man can walk 10 miles in two hours . . ."), the average person ("the man in the street") and the active person ("the man on the move") are male. The assumption is that unless otherwise identified, people in general—including doctors and beggars—are men. It is a semantic mechanism that operates to keep women invisible: *man* and *mankind* represent everyone; *he* in generalized use refers to either sex; the "land where our fathers died" is also the land of our mothers—although they go unsung. As the beetle-browed and mustachioed man in a Steig cartoon says to his two male drinking companions, "When I speak of mankind, one thing I *don't* mean is womankind."

Semantically speaking, woman is not one with the species of man, but a dis- 5 tinct subspecies. "Man," says the 1971 edition of the Britannica Junior Encyclopedia, "is the highest form of life on earth. His superior intelligence, combined with certain physical characteristics, have enabled man to achieve things that are impossible for other animals." (The prose style has something in common with the report of a research team describing its studies on "the development of the uterus in rats, guinea pigs and men.") As though quoting the Steig character, still speaking to his friends in McSorley's, the Junior Encyclopedia continues: "Man must invent most of his behavior, because he lacks the instincts of lower animals. . . . Most of the things he learns have been handed down from his ancestors by language and symbols rather than by biological inheritance."

Considering that for the last 5,000 years society has been patriarchal, that 6 statement explains a lot. It explains why Eve was made from Adam's rib instead of the other way around, and who invented all those Adam-rib words like *fe*male and *wo*man in the first place. It also explains why, when it is necessary to mention woman, the language makes her a lower caste, a class separate from the rest of man; why it works to "keep her in her place."

This inheritance through language and other symbols begins in the home (also 7 called a man's castle) where man and wife (not husband and wife, or man and woman) live for a while with their children. It is reinforced by religious training, the educational system, the press, government, commerce and the law. As Andrew Greeley wrote not long ago in his magazine, "Man is a symbol-creating animal. He orders and interprets his reality by his symbols, and he uses the symbols to reconstruct that reality."

Consider some of the reconstructed realities of American history. When 8 school children learn from their textbooks that the early colonists gained valuable experience in governing themselves, they are not told that the early colonists who were women were denied the privilege of self-government; when they learn that in the 18th century the average man had to manufacture many of the things he and his family needed, they are not told that this "average man" was often a woman who manufactured much of what she and her family needed. Young people learn that intrepid pioneers crossed the country in covered wagons with their wives, children and cattle; they do not learn that women themselves were intrepid pioneers rather than part of the baggage.

In a paper published this year in Los Angeles as a guide for authors and editors of social-studies textbooks, Elizabeth Burr, Susan Dunn and Norma Farquhar document unintentional skewings of this kind that occur either because women are not specifically mentioned as affecting or being affected by historical events, or because they are discussed in terms of outdated assumptions. "One never sees a picture of women captioned simply 'farmers' or 'pioneers,'" they point out. The subspecies nomenclature that requires a caption to read "women farmers" or "women pioneers" is extended to impose certain jobs on women by definition. The textbook guide gives as an example the word *housewife*, which it says not only "suggests that domestic chores are the exclusive burden of females," but gives "female students the idea that they were born to keep house and teaches male students that they are automatically entitled to laundry, cooking and housecleaning services from the women in their families."

Sexist language is any language that expresses such stereotyped attitudes and expectations, or that assumes the inherent superiority of one sex over the other. When a woman says of her husband, who has drawn up plans for a new bedroom wing and left out closets, "Just like a man," her language is as sexist as the man's who says, after his wife has changed her mind about needing the new wing after all, "Just like a woman."

Male and female are not sexist words, but masculine and feminine almost always are. Male and female can be applied objectively to individual people and animals and, by extension, to things. When electricians and plumbers talk about male and female couplings, everyone knows or can figure out what they mean. The terms are graphic and culture free.

Masculine and feminine, however, are as sexist as any words can be, since it is almost impossible to use them without invoking cultural stereotypes. When people construct lists of "masculine" and "feminine" traits they almost always end up making assumptions that have nothing to do with innate differences between the sexes. We have a friend who happens to be going through the process of pinning down this very phenomenon. He is 7 years old and his question concerns why his coats and shirts button left over right while his sister's button the other way. He assumes it must have something to do with the differences between boys and girls, but he can't see how.

What our friend has yet to grasp is that the way you button your coat, like most sex-differentiated customs, has nothing to do with real differences but much to do with what society wants you to feel about yourself as a male or female person. Society decrees that it is appropriate for girls to dress differently from boys, to act differently, and to think differently. Boys must be masculine, whatever that means, and girls must be feminine.

Unabridged dictionaries are a good source for finding out what society decrees   14
to be appropriate, though less by definition than by their choice of associations and
illustrations. Words associated with males—*manly, virile* and *masculine,* for example—are defined through a broad range of positive attributes like strength, courage, directness and independence, and they are illustrated through such examples
of contemporary usage as "a manly determination to face what comes," "a virile
literary style," "a masculine love of sports." Corresponding words associated with
females are defined with fewer attributes (though weakness is often one of them)
and the examples given are generally negative if not clearly pejorative: "feminine
wiles," "womanish tears," "a womanlike lack of promptness," "convinced that
drawing was a waste of time, if not downright womanly."

Male-associated words are frequently applied to females to describe some-   15
thing that is either incongruous ("a mannish voice") or presumably commendable
("a masculine mind," "she took it like a man"), but female-associated words are
unreservedly derogatory when applied to males, and are sometimes abusive to females as well. The opposite of "masculine" is "effeminate," although the opposite
of "feminine" is simply "unfeminine."

One dictionary, after defining the word *womanish* as "suitable to or resem-   16
bling a woman," further defines it as "unsuitable to a man or to a strong character
of either sex." Words derived from "sister" and "brother" provide another apt example, for whereas "sissy," applied either to a male or female, conveys the message
that sisters are expected to be timid and cowardly, "buddy" makes clear that brothers are friends.

The subtle disparagement of females and corresponding approbation of males   17
wrapped up in many English words is painfully illustrated by "tomboy." Here is an
instance where a girl who likes sports and the out-of-doors, who is curious about
how things work, who is adventurous and bold instead of passive, is defined in
terms of something she is not—a boy. By denying that she can be the person she is
and still be a girl, the word surreptitiously undermines her sense of identity: it says
she is unnatural. A "tomboy," as defined by one dictionary, is a "girl, especially a
young girl, who behaves like a spirited boy." But who makes the judgment that she
is acting like a spirited boy, not a spirited girl? Can it be a coincidence that in the
case of the dictionary just quoted the editor, executive editor, managing editor,
general manager, all six members of the Board of Linguists, the usage editor, science editor, all six general editors of definitions, and 94 out of the 104 distinguished experts consulted on usage—are men?

It isn't enough to say that any invidious comparisons and stereotypes lexicog-   18
raphers perpetuate are already present in the culture. There are ways to define
words like womanly and tomboy that don't put women down, though the tradition
has been otherwise. Samuel Johnson, the lexicographer, was the same Dr. Johnson
who said, "A woman preaching is like a dog's walking on his hind legs. It is not done
well; but you are surprised to find it done at all."

Possibly because of the negative images associated with womanish and wom-   19
anlike, and with expressions like "woman driver" and "woman of the street," the
word woman dropped out of fashion for a time. The women at the office and the
women on the assembly line and the women one first knew in school all became

ladies or girls or gals. Now a countermovement, supported by the very term women's liberation, is putting back into words like woman and sister and sisterhood the meaning they were losing by default. It is as though, in the nick of time, women had seen that the language itself could destroy them.

Some long-standing conventions of the news media add insult to injury. When   20
a woman or girl makes news, her sex is identified at the beginning of a story, if possible in the headline or its equivalent. The assumption, apparently, is that whatever event or action is being reported, a woman's involvement is less common and therefore more newsworthy than a man's. If the story is about achievement, the implication is: "pretty good for a woman." And because people are assumed to be male unless otherwise identified, the media have developed a special and extensive vocabulary to avoid the constant repetition of "woman." The results, "Grandmother Wins Nobel Prize," "Blonde Hijacks Airliner," "Housewife to Run for Congress," convey the kind of information that would be ludicrous in comparable headlines if the subjects were men. Why, if "Unsalaried Husband to Run for Congress" is unacceptable to editors, do women have to keep explaining that to describe them through external or superficial concerns reflects a sexist view of women as decorative objects, breeding machines and extensions of men, not real people?

Members of the Chicago chapter of the National Organization for Women   21
recently studied the newspapers in their area and drew up a set of guidelines for the press. These include cutting out descriptions of the "clothes, physical features, dating life and marital status of women where such references would be considered inappropriate if about men"; using language in such a way as to include women in copy that refers to homeowners, scientists and business people where "newspaper descriptions often convey the idea that all such persons are male"; and displaying the same discretion in printing generalizations about women as would be shown toward racial, religious and ethnic groups. "Our concern with what we are called may seem trivial to some people," the women said, "but we regard the old usages as symbolic of women's position within this society."

The assumption that an adult woman is flattered by being called a girl is   22
matched by the notion that a woman in a menial or poorly paid job finds compensation in being called a lady. Ethel Strainchamps has pointed out that since lady is used as an adjective with nouns designating both high and low occupations (lady wrestler, lady barber, lady doctor, lady judge), some writers assume they can use the noun form without betraying value judgments. Not so, Strainchamps says, rolling the issue into a spitball: "You may write, 'He addressed the Republican ladies,' or 'The Democratic ladies convened' . . . but I have never seen 'the Communist ladies' or 'the Black Panther ladies' in print."

Thoughtful writers and editors have begun to repudiate some of the old us-   23
ages. "Divorcée," "grandmother" and "blonde," along with "vivacious," "pert," "dimpled" and "cute," were dumped by the Washington Post in the spring of 1970 by the executive editor, Benjamin Bradlee. In a memo to his staff, Bradlee wrote, "The meaningful equality and dignity of women is properly under scrutiny today

. . . because this equality has been less than meaningful and the dignity not always free of stereotype and condescension."

What women have been called in the press—or at least the part that operates   24
above ground—is only a fraction of the infinite variety of alternatives to "women" used in the subcultures of the English-speaking world. Beyond "chicks," "dolls," "dames," "babes," "skirts" and "broads" are the words and phrases in which women are reduced to their sexuality and nothing more. It would be hard to think of another area of language in which the human mind has been so fertile in devising and borrowing abusive terms. In "The Female Eunuch," Germaine Greer devotes four pages to anatomical terms and words for animals, vegetables, fruits, baked goods, implements and receptacles, all of which are used to dehumanize the female person. Jean Faust, in an article aptly called "Words That Oppress," suggests that the effort to diminish women through language is rooted in a male fear of sexual inadequacy. "Woman is made to feel guilty for and akin to natural disasters," she writes; "hurricanes and typhoons are named after her. Any negative or threatening force is given a feminine name. If a man runs into bad luck climbing up the ladder of success (a male-invented game), he refers to the 'bitch goddess' success."

The sexual overtones in the ancient and no doubt honorable custom of calling   25
ships "she" have become more explicit and less honorable in an age of air travel: "I'm Karen. Fly me." Attitudes of ridicule, contempt and disgust toward female sexuality have spawned a rich glossary of insults and epithets not found in dictionaries. And the usage in which four-letter words meaning copulate are interchangeable with cheat, attack and destroy can scarcely be unrelated to the savagery of rape.

In her updating of Ibsen's "A Doll's House," Clare Booth Luce has Nora tell   26
her husband she is pregnant—"In the way only men are supposed to get pregnant." "Men, pregnant?" he says, and she nods; "With ideas. Pregnancies there *[she taps his head]* are masculine. And a very superior form of labor. Pregnancies here *[taps her tummy]* are feminine—a very inferior form of labor."

Public outcry followed a revised translation of the New Testament describing   27
Mary as "pregnant" instead of "great with child." The objections were made in part on esthetic grounds: there is no attractive adjective in modern English for a woman who is about to give birth. A less obvious reason was that replacing the euphemism with a biological term undermined religious teaching. The initiative and generative power in the conception of Jesus are understood to be God's; Mary, the mother, was a vessel only.

Whether influenced by this teaching or not, the language of human reproduc-   28
tion lags several centuries behind scientific understanding. The male's contribution to procreation is still described as though it were the entire seed from which a new life grows: the initiative and generative power involved in the process are thought of as masculine, receptivity and nurturance as feminine. "Seminal" remains a synonym for "highly original," and there is no comparable word to describe the female's equivalent contribution.

An entire mythology has grown from this biological misunderstanding and its   29
semantic legacy; its embodiment in laws that for centuries made women nonpersons was a key target of the 19th-century feminist movement. Today, more than 50 years after women finally won the basic democratic right to vote, the word "libera-

tion" itself, when applied to women, means something less than when used of other groups of people. An advertisement for the N.B.C. news department listed Women's Liberation along with crime in the streets and the Vietnam war as "bad news." Asked for his views on Women's Liberation, a highly placed politician was quoted as saying, "Let me make one thing perfectly clear. I wouldn't want to wake up next to a lady pipe-fitter."

One of the most surprising challenges to our male-dominated culture is com-   30
ing from within organized religion, where the issues are being stated, in part, by confronting the implications of traditional language. What a growing number of theologians and scholars are saying is that the myths of the Judeo-Christian tradition, being the products of patriarchy, must be reexamined, and that the concept of an exclusively male ministry and the image of a male god have become idolatrous.

Women are naturally in the forefront of this movement, both in their efforts to   31
gain ordination and full equality and through their contributions to theological reform, although both these efforts are often subtly diminished. When the Rev. Barbara Anderson was ordained by the American Lutheran Church, one newspaper printed her picture over a caption headed "Happy Girl." *Newsweek*'s report of a protest staged last December by women divinity students at Harvard was jocular ("another tilt at the windmill") and sarcastic: "Every time anyone in the room lapsed into what [the students] regarded as male chauvinism—such as using the word 'mankind' to describe the human race in general—the outraged women . . . drowned out the offender with earpiercing blasts from party-favor kazoos. . . . What annoyed the women most was the universal custom of referring to God as 'He.' "

The tone of the report was not merely unfunny; it missed the connection be-   32
tween increasingly outmoded theological language and the accelerating number of women (and men) who are dropping out of organized religion, both Jewish and Christian. For language, including pronouns, can be used to construct a reality that simply mirrors society's assumptions. To women who are committed to the reality of religious faith, the effect is doubly painful. Professor Harvey Cox, in whose classroom the protest took place, stated the issue directly: The women, he said, were raising the "basic theological question of whether God is more adequately thought of in personal or suprapersonal terms."

Toward the end of Don McLean's remarkable ballad "American Pie," a song   33
filled with the imagery of abandonment and disillusion, there is a stanza that must strike many women to the quick. The church bells are broken, the music has died; then:

> And the three men I admire most,
> The Father, Son and the Holy Ghost,
> They caught the last train for the Coast—
> The day the music died.

Three men I admired most. There they go, briefcases in hand and topcoats   34
buttoned left over right, walking down the long cold platform under the city, past the baggage wagons and the hissing steam onto the Pullman. Bye, bye God—all

three of you—made in the image of male supremacy. Maybe out there in L.A. where the weather is warmer, someone can believe in you again.

The Roman Catholic theologian Elizabeth Farians says "the bad theology of   35 an overmasculinized church continues to be one of the root causes of women's oppression." The definition of oppression is "to crush or burden by abuse of power or authority; burden spiritually or mentally as if by pressure."

When language oppresses, it does so by any means that disparage and belittle.   36 Until well into the 20th century, one of the ways English was manipulated to disparage women was through the addition of feminine endings to nonsexual words. Thus a woman who aspired to be a poet was excluded from the company of real poets by the label poetess, and a woman who piloted an airplane was denied full status as an aviator by being called an aviatrix. At about the time poetess, aviatrix, and similar Adam-ribbisms were dropping out of use, H. W. Fowler was urging that they be revived. "With the coming expansion of women's vocations," he wrote in the first edition (1926) of "Modern English Usage," "feminines for vocation-words are a special need of the future." There can be no doubt he subconsciously recognized the relative status implied in the -ess designations. His criticism of a woman who wished to be known as an author rather than an authoress was that she had no need "to raise herself to the level of the male author by asserting her right to his name."

Who has the prior right to a name? The question has an interesting bearing on   37 words that were once applied to men alone, or to both men and women, but now, having acquired abusive associations, are assigned to women exclusively. Spinster is a gentle case in point. Prostitute and many of its synonyms illustrate the phenomenon better. If Fowler had chosen to record the changing usage of harlot from hired man (in Chaucer's time) through rascal and entertainer to its present definition, would he have maintained that the female harlot is trying to raise herself to the level of the male harlot by asserting her right to his name? Or would he have plugged for harlotress?

The demise of most -ess endings came about before the start of the new fem-   38 inist movement. In the second edition of "Modern English Usage," published in 1965, Sir Ernest Gowers frankly admitted what his predecessors had been up to. "Feminine designations," he wrote, "seem now to be falling into disuse. Perhaps the explanation of this paradox is that it symbolizes the victory of women in their struggle for equal rights; it reflects the abandonment by men of those ideas about women in the professions that moved Dr. Johnson to his rude remark about women preachers."

If Sir Ernest's optimism can be justified, why is there a movement back to   39 feminine endings in such words as chairwoman, councilwoman and congress-woman? Betty Hudson, of Madison, Conn., is campaigning for the adoption of "selectwoman" as the legal title for a female member of that town's executive body. To have to address a woman as "Selectman," she maintains, "is not only bad grammar and bad biology, but it implies that politics is still, or should be, a man's business." A valid argument, and one that was, predictably, countered by ridicule, the surefire weapon for undercutting achievement. When the head of the Federal

Maritime Commission, Helen D. Bentley, was named "Man of the Year" by an association of shipping interests, she wisely refused to be drawn into light-hearted debate with interviewers who wanted to make the award's name a humorous issue. Some women, of course, have yet to learn they are invisible. An 8-year-old who visited the American Museum of Natural History with her Brownie scout troop went through the impressive exhibit on pollution and overpopulation called "Can Man Survive?" Asked afterward, "Well, can he?" she answered, "I don't know about him, but we're working on it in Brownies."

Nowhere are women rendered more invisible by language than in politics.   40
The United States Constitution, in describing the qualifications for Representative, Senator and President, refers to each as *he*. No wonder Shirley Chisholm, the first woman since 1888 to make a try for the Presidential nomination of a major party, has found it difficult to be taken seriously.

The observation by Andrew Greeley already quoted—that "man" uses "his   41
symbols" to reconstruct "his reality"—was not made in reference to the symbols of language but to the symbolic impact the "nomination of a black man for the Vice-Presidency" would have on race relations in the United States. Did the author assume the generic term "man" would of course be construed to include "woman"? Or did he deliberately use a semantic device to exclude Shirley Chisholm without having to be explicit?

Either way, his words construct a reality in which women are ignored. As   42
much as any other factor in our language, the ambiguous meaning of *man* serves to deny women recognition as people. In a recent magazine article, we discussed the similar effect on women of the generic pronoun *he*, which we proposed to replace by a new common gender pronoun *tey*. We were immediately told, by a number of authorities, that we were dabbling in the serious business of linguistics, and the message that reached us from these scholars was loud and clear: It - is - absolutely - impossible - for - anyone - to - introduce - a - new - word - into - the - language - just - because - there - is - a - need - for - it, so - stop - wasting - your - time.

When words are suggested like "herstory" (for history), "sportsoneship" (for   43
sportsmanship) and "mistresspiece" (for the work of a Virginia Woolf) one suspects a not-too-subtle attempt to make the whole language problem look silly. But unless Alexander Pope, when he wrote "The proper study of mankind is man," meant that women should be relegated to the footnotes (or, as George Orwell might have put it, "All men are equal, but men are more equal than women"), viable new words will surely someday supersede the old.

Without apologies to Freud, the great majority of women do not wish in their   44
hearts that they were men. If having grown up with a language that tells them they are at the same time men and not men raises psychic doubts for women, the doubts are not of their sexual identity but of their human identity. Perhaps the present unrest surfacing in the Women's Movement is part of an evolutionary change in our particular form of life—the one form of all in the animal and plant kingdoms that orders and interprets its reality by symbols. The achievements of the species called man have brought us to the brink of self-destruction. If the species survives into the next century with the expectation of going on, it may only

be because we have become part of what Harlow Shapley calls the psychozoic kingdom, where brain overshadows brawn and rationality has replaced superstition.

Searching the roots of Western civilization for a word to call this new species of man and woman, someone might come up with *gen,* as in genesis and generic. With such a word, *man* could be used exclusively for males as *woman* is used for females, for gen would include both sexes. Like the words deer and bison, gen would be both plural and singular. Like progenitor, progeny, and generation, it would convey continuity. Gen would express the warmth and generalized sexuality of generous, gentle, and genuine; the specific sexuality of genital and genetic. In the new family of gen, girls and boys would grow to genhood, and to speak of genkind would be to include all the people of the earth.

45

Rhetorical Focus

1. The authors begin with a riddle. Is this an effective device? Which essay seems more focused, this one or "Talking Like a Lady?" Why?
2. How does this essay support its thesis? Compare the conclusion to that of the previous essay. What is the goal of each?
3. Compare the tone of this essay with Lakoff's. Give examples to support your opinion.

Thematic Focus

1. The authors claim that our society forces us to think of men and women as different, so it creates arbitrary differences, for example, bikes for boys and girls or different hair length and clothing. Do you agree? Why would cultures do this?
2. Does language mirror a culture's biases or does language create and perpetuate these attitudes? Will changing language habits change a person's ideas?
3. Which of the authors' examples made the most sense to you, which the least? Are you surprised by the responses of your classmates?

Suggestions for Writing

1. Write a letter to a friend in high school focusing on the idea that women have to talk more like men in college if they are to be taken seriously.
2. Choose a specific situation in school, perhaps a discussion class, or a club or sports meeting, or a lunch table or social event of any kind. Take notes on the language (vocabulary, tone, amount, and so forth) used by males and females. Write a brief report about your findings.
3. Try to remember experiences you have had that involved the appropriate or inappropriate use of language (in its broadest sense). Write a brief essay that draws some conclusion from these concrete examples.

BLACK ENGLISH

Linguists tell us that all languages are equally effective in fulfilling their purposes. Yet many people have a hard time accepting such an assertion. The language and the specific dialect that we speak sounds so natural to us and so obviously understandable that we often cannot help but smile at the language of those born in other regions of the country. The New England farmer and the Southern banker are never self-conscious about their dialects at home, but their grammar, syntax, and vocabulary must seem odd indeed to the Manhattanite.

This natural affection for our own way of speaking turns quite serious when racial, class, and gender bias allows some speakers to make claims of absolute correctness and superiority for their own way of speaking. It often follows that those who speak otherwise, especially if they are on the wrong end of the economic ladder, are thought to do so out of ignorance and laziness. This attitude has often caused pain, both financial and emotional, to those who are not white and upper-class because the language allowed in universities, in business, and in other institutions is limited to standard English, the dialect spoken by upper middle class whites. In the following two essays, Geneva Smitherman and James Baldwin raise issues that are important for all of us in our attempts to understand how language can be used to exclude those who are different.

If Black English Isn't a Language, Then Tell Me, What Is?

James Baldwin

James Baldwin was born in Harlem in 1924 and died in 1987. Determined from an early age that he would be a writer, Baldwin received many grants and fellowships and spent nine years in Paris as part of a colony of African-American artists. He has written prolifically, though not exclusively, about the experience of being a black in America. His most famous works include *Go Tell It on the Mountain* (1953), *Notes of a Native Son* (1955) and *The Fire Next Time* (1963). In the following essay, which first appeared in The *New York Times,* he recognizes the power of language as a political and social tool and comments on the ways in which that tool has been used in the struggle between blacks and whites throughout American history.

Reflections Before Reading

Do you feel your language is connected directly to your identity? How? When you speak, do you think your class, age, race, gender, and place of birth are revealed? Do you think black English is a language? Should students be allowed to speak it in schools? How about in writing? Should white teachers in predominantly nonwhite schools be required to know the dialect spoken by their students?

The argument concerning the use, or the status, or the reality, of black English is rooted in American history and has absolutely nothing to do with the question the argument supposes itself to be posing. The argument has nothing to do with language itself but with the *role* of language. Language, incontestably, reveals the speaker. Language, also, far more dubiously, is meant to define the other—and, in this case, the other is refusing to be defined by a language that has never been able to recognize him. 1

People evolve a language in order to describe and thus control their circumstances, or in order not to be submerged by a reality that they cannot articulate. (And, if they cannot articulate it, they *are* submerged.) A Frenchman living in Paris 2 speaks a subtly and crucially different language from that of the man living in Marseilles; neither sounds very much like a man living in Quebec; and they would all have great difficulty in apprehending what the man from Guadeloupe, or Martinique, is saying, to say nothing of the man from Senegal—although the "common" language of all these areas is French. But each has paid, and is paying, a different price for this "common" language, in which, as it turns out, they are not saying, and cannot be saying, the same things: They each have very different realities to articulate, or control.

What joins all languages, and all men, is the necessity to confront life, in   3
order, not inconceivably, to outwit death: The price for this is the acceptance, and achievement, of one's temporal identity. So that, for example, though it is not taught in the schools (and this has the potential of becoming a political issue) the south of France still clings to its ancient and musical Provençal, which resists being described as a "dialect." And much of the tension in the Basque countries, and in Wales, is due to the Basque and Welsh determination not to allow their languages to be destroyed. This determination also feeds the flames in Ireland for among the many indignities the Irish have been forced to undergo at English hands is the English contempt for their language.

It goes without saying, then, that language is also a political instrument,   4
means, and proof of power. It is the most vivid and crucial key to identity: it reveals the private identity, and connects one with, or divorces one from, the larger, public, or communal identity. There have been, and are, times, and places, when to speak a certain language could be dangerous, even fatal. Or, one may speak the same language, but in such a way that one's antecedents are revealed, or (one hopes) hidden. This is true in France, and is absolutely true in England: The range (and reign) of accents on that damp little island make England coherent for the English and totally incomprehensible for everyone else. To open your mouth in England is (if I may use black English) to "put your business in the street": You have confessed your parents, your youth, your school, your salary, your self-esteem, and, alas, your future.

Now, I do not know what white Americans would sound like if there had never   5
been any black people in the United States, but they would not sound the way they sound. *Jazz,* for example, is a very specific sexual term, as in *jazz me, baby,* but white people purified it into the Jazz Age. *Sock it to me,* which means, roughly, the same thing, has been adopted by Nathaniel Hawthorne's descendants with no qualms or hesitations at all, along with *let it all hang out* and *right on! Beat to his socks,* which was once the black's most total and despairing image of poverty, was transformed into a thing called the Beat Generation, which phenomenon was, largely, composed of *uptight,* middle-class white people, imitating poverty, trying to *get down,* to get *with it,* doing their *thing,* doing their despairing best to be *funky,* which we, the blacks, never dreamed of doing—we *were* funky, baby, like *funk* was going out of style.

Now, no one can eat his cake, and have it, too, and it is late in the day to   6
attempt to penalize black people for having created a language that permits the nation its only glimpse of reality, a language without which the nation would be even more *whipped* than it is.

I say that this present skirmish is rooted in American history, and it is. Black   7
English is the creation of the black diaspora. Blacks came to the United States
chained to each other, but from different tribes: Neither could speak the other's
language. If two black people, at that bitter hour of the world's history, had been
able to speak to each other, the institution of chattel slavery could never have
lasted as long as it did. Subsequently, the slave was given, under the eye, and the
gun, of his master, Congo Square, and the Bible—or, in other words, and under
these conditions, the slave began the formation of the black church, and it is within
this unprecedented tabernacle that black English began to be formed. This was
not, merely, as in the European example, the adoption of a foreign tongue, but an
alchemy that transformed ancient elements into a new language: *A language comes
into existence by means of brutal necessity, and the rules of the language are dictated by what the language must convey.*

There was a moment, in time, and in this place, when my brother, or my   8
mother, or my father, or my sister, had to convey to me, for example, the danger in
which I was standing from the white man standing just behind me, and to convey
this with a speed, and in a language, that the white man could not possibly understand, and that, indeed, he cannot understand, until today. He cannot afford to
understand it. This understanding would reveal to him too much about himself,
and smash that mirror before which he has been frozen for so long.

Now, if this passion, this skill, this (to quote Toni Morrison) "sheer intelli-   9
gence," this incredible music, the mighty achievement of having brought a people
utterly unknown to, or despised by "history"—to have brought this people to their
present, troubled, troubling, and unassailable and unanswerable place—if this absolutely unprecedented journey does not indicate that black English is a language,
I am curious to know what definition of language is to be trusted.

A people at the center of the Western world, and in the midst of so hostile a   10
population, has not endured and transcended by means of what is patronizingly
called a "dialect." We, the blacks, are in trouble, certainly, but we are not doomed,
and we are not inarticulate because we are not compelled to defend a morality that
we know to be a lie.

The brutal truth is that the bulk of the white people in America never had any   11
interest in educating black people, except as this could serve white purposes. It is
not the black child's language that is in question, it is not his language that is despised: It is his experience. A child cannot be taught by anyone who despises him,
and a child cannot afford to be fooled. A child cannot be taught by anyone whose
demand, essentially, is that the child repudiate his experience, and all that gives
him sustenance, and enter a limbo in which he will no longer be black, and in
which he knows that he can never become white. Black people have lost too many
black children that way.

And, after all, finally, in a country with standards so untrustworthy, a country   12
that makes heroes of so many criminal mediocrities, a country unable to face why
so many of the nonwhite are in prison, or on the needle, or standing, futureless, in
the streets—it may very well be that both the child, and his elder, have concluded
that they have nothing whatever to learn from the people of a country that has
managed to learn so little.

Rhetorical Focus

1. Most writing handbooks suggest that supporting paragraphs be specific, that concrete details be used. Baldwin seems to write this way but also at a more general level. Pick two specific paragraphs and explain how he writes about the purposes of language using both concrete details and abstractions.
2. Baldwin uses "finally" in the last paragraph as a sign of his conclusion but also as a last point in his argument for black English. Where does he begin his points and how would you describe the sequence he arranges them in?
3. Baldwin is fond of the colon. How does he use it in paragraphs 2, 3, 4, and 7?

Thematic Focus

1. If black children hear white (Standard) English on television and in movies, why do they not adopt its features?
2. Baldwin says that the bulk of whites in America "never had any interest in educating black people." Do you think he has a point?
3. Baldwin tries to explain why black English is a language. What do you think of his reasons?

White English in Blackface, or Who Do I Be?

Geneva Smitherman

Geneva Smitherman is a professor of communications and the Director of Black Studies at Wayne State University. Her writings on the subject of black language include *Black Language and Culture: Sounds of Soul* (1975) and *Talkin and Testifyin: The Language of Black America* (1977). The following essay points out that American blacks are forced to confront not only a linguistic discrepancy between Standard English and black English, but also a concomitant crisis of social and cultural identity.

Reflections Before Reading

If you spoke another dialect, do you think you would think differently or act differently? Do you think Standard English should be the only language allowed in American schools? It is often claimed that some politicians speak Standard English in Congress and their local dialect when campaigning back home. Do you have different languages for different situations? Explain.

Ain nothin in a long time lit up the English teaching profession like the current hassle over Black English. One finds beaucoup sociolinguistic research studies and language projects for the "disadvantaged" on the scene in nearly every sizable black community in the country.[1] And educators from K-Grad. School bees debating whether: (1) blacks should learn and use only standard white English (hereafter referred to as WE); (2) blacks should command both dialects, i.e., be bi-dialectal (hereafter BD); (3) blacks should be allowed (??????) to use standard Black English (hereafter BE or BI). The appropriate choice having everything to do with American political reality, which is usually ignored, and nothing to do with the educational process, which is usually claimed. I say without qualification that we cannot talk about the Black Idiom apart from Black Culture and the Black Experience. Nor can we specify educational goals for blacks apart from considerations about the structure of (white) American society.

"White English in Blackface, or Who Do I Be?" by Geneva Smitherman, THE BLACK SCHOLAR (May-June 1973). Reprinted by permission.

And we black folks is not gon take all that weight, for no one has empirically 2 demonstrated that linguistic/stylistic features of BE impede educational progress in communication skills, or any other area of cognitive learning. Take reading. It's don been charged, but not actually verified, that BE interferes with mastery of reading skills.[2] Yet beyond pointing out the gap between the young brother/ sistuh's phonological and syntactical patterns and those of the usually-middle-class-WE-speaking-teacher, this claim has not been validated. The distance between the two systems is, after all, short and is illuminated only by the fact that reading is taught *orally*. (Also get to the fact that preceding generations of BE-speaking folks learned to read, despite the many classrooms in which the teacher spoke a dialect different from that of her students.)

For example, a student who reads *den* for *then* probably pronounces initial /th/ 3 as /d/ in most words. Or the one who reads *doing* for *during* probably deletes intervocalic and final /r/ in most words. So it is not that such students can't read, they is simply employing the black phonological system. In the reading classrooms of today, what we bees needin is teachers with the proper attitudinal orientation who thus can distinguish actual reading problems from mere dialect differences. Or take the writing of an essay. The only percentage in writing a paper with WE spelling, punctuation, and usage is in maybe eliciting a positive *attitudinal* response from a prescriptivist middle-class-aspirant-teacher. Dig on the fact that sheer "correctness" does not a good writer make. And is it any point in dealing with the charge of BE speakers being "non-verbal" or "linguistically deficient" in oral communication skills—behind our many Raps who done disproved that in living, vibrant color?[3]

What linguists and educators need to do at this juncture is to take serious 4 cognizance of the Oral Tradition in Black Culture. The uniqueness of this verbal style requires a language competence/performance model to fit the black scheme of things. Clearly BI speakers possess rich communication skills (i.e., are highly *competent* in using language), but as yet there bees no criteria (evaluative, testing, or other instrument of measurement), based on black communication patterns, wherein BI speakers can demonstrate they competence (i.e., *performance*). Hence brothers and sisters fail on language performance tests and in English classrooms. Like, to amplify on what Nikki said, that's why we always lose, not only cause we don't know the rules, but it ain't even our game.

We can devise a performance model only after an analysis of the components 5 of BI. Now there do be linguists who supposedly done did this categorization and definition of BE.[4] But the descriptions are generally confining, limited as they are to discrete linguistic units. One finds simply ten to fifteen patterns cited, as for example, the most frequently listed one, the use of *be* as finite verb, contrasting with its deletion: (a) *The coffee be cold* contrasts with (b) *The coffee is cold*, the former statement denoting a continuing state of affairs, the latter applying to the present moment only. (Like if you the cook, (a) probably get you fired, and (b) only get you talked about.) In WE no comparable grammatical distinction exists and *The coffee is cold* would be used to indicate both meanings. However, rarely does one find an investigation of the total vitality of black expressive style, a style inextricable from the Black Cultural Universe, for after all, BI connects with Black Soul and niggers is more than deleted copulas.[5]

The Black Idiom should be viewed from two important perspectives: linguistic and stylistic. The linguistic dimension is comprised of the so-called nonstandard features of phonology and syntax (patterns like *dis heah* and *The coffee be cold*), and a lexicon generally equated with "slang" or hip talk. The stylistic dimension has to do with *rapping, capping, jiving,* etc., and with features such as cadence, rhythm, resonance, gestures, and all those other elusive, difficult-to-objectify elements that make up what is considered a writer or speaker's "style." While I am separating linguistic and stylistic features, I have done so only for the purpose of simplifying the discussion since the BI speaker runs the full gamut of both dimensions in any given speech event. 6

I acknowledge from the bell that we's dealing with a dialect structure which is a subsystem of the English language; thus BE and WE may not appear fundamentally different. Yet, though black folks speak English, it do seem to be an entirely different lingo altogether. But wherein lies the uniqueness? Essentially in language, as in other areas of Black Culture, we have the problem of isolating those elements indigenous to black folks from those cultural aspects shared with white folks. Anthropologist Johnnetta Cole suggests that Black Culture has three dimensions: (1) those elements shared with mainstream America; (2) those elements shared with all oppressed peoples; (3) those elements peculiar to the black condition in America.[6] Applying her concepts to language, I propose the accompanying schematic representation. 7

Referring to the first column, contemporary BE is simply one of the many dialects of contemporary American English, and it is most likely the case that the linguistic patterns of BE differ from those of WE in surface structure only. There's no essential linguistic difference between *dis heah* and *this here*, and from a strictly linguistic point of view, *God don't never change* can be written *God doesn't ever change* (though definitely not from a socio-cultural/political perspective, as Baraka quite rightly notes).[7] Perhaps we could make a case for deep structure difference in the BE use of *be* as finite verb (refer to *The coffee be cold* example above), but we be hard pressed to find any other examples, and even in this case, we could posit that the copula exists in the deep structure, and is simply deleted by some low-level phonological deletion rule, dig: The coffee is cold . . . The coffee's cold- . . . The coffee cold. My conclusion at this point is that despite the claims of some highly respected Creole linguists (with special propers to bad Sistuh Beryl Bailey),[8] the argument for deep structure differences between contemporary BE and WE syntax can not pass the test of rigorous transformational analysis. 8

Referring to the second column, we note the psychological tendency of oppressed people to adopt the modes of behavior and expression of their oppressors (also, during the African slave trade, the functional necessity of pidginized forms of European language). Not only does the conqueror force his victims into political subjugation, he also coerces them into adopting his language and doles out special rewards to those among the oppressed who best mimic his language and cultural style. In the initial language contact stage, the victims attempt to assemble the new language into their native linguistic mold, producing a linguistic mixture that is 9

Features shared with mainstream America	Features shared with all oppressed peoples	Features unique to black Americans
Linguistic 1. British/American English lexicon 2. Most aspects of British/American English phonology and syntax	*Linguistic* 1. Superimposition of dominant culture's language on native language, yielding 2. Pidginized form of dominant culture's language, subject to becoming extinct, due to 3. Historical evolution, linguistic leveling out in direction of dominant culture's dialect	*Linguistic* Unique meanings attributed to certain English lexical items *Stylistic* Unique communication patterns and rhetorical flourishes

termed *pidgin.* In the next stage, the pidgin may develop into a Creole, a highly systematic, widely used mode of communication among the oppressed, characterized by a substratum of patterns from the victim's language with an overlay of forms from the oppressor's language. As the oppressed people's identification with the victor's culture intensifies, the pidgin/Creole begins to lose its linguistic currency and naturally evolves in the direction of the victor's language. Reconstructing the linguistic history of BE, we theorize that it followed a similar pattern, but due to the radically different condition of black oppression in America, the process of *de-creolization* is nearly complete and has been for perhaps over a hundred years.

The most important features of BI are, of course, those referred to in column three, for they point us toward the linguistic uniqueness and cultural significance of the Oral Tradition in the Black Experience. It should be clear that all along I been talkin bout that Black Experience associated with the grass-roots folks, the masses, the sho-nuff niggers—in short, all those black folks who do not aspire to white middle-class American standards.

Within this tradition, language is used as a teaching/socializing force and as a means of establishing one's reputation via his verbal competence. Black talk is never meaningless cocktail chit-chat but a functional dynamic that is simultaneously a mechanism for acculturation and information-passing and a vehicle for achieving group recognition. Black communication is highly verbal and highly stylized; it is a performance before a black audience who become both observers and participants in the speech event. Whether it be through slapping of hands ("giving five" or "giving skin"), Amen's, or Right on's, the audience influences the direction of a given rap and at the same time acknowledges or withholds its approval, depending on the linguistic skill and stylistic ingenuity of the speaker. I mean like a Brother is only as bad as his rap bees.

TOWARD A BLACK LANGUAGE MODEL: LINGUISTIC

While we concede that black people use the vocabulary of the English lan-   12
guage, certain words are always selected out of that lexicon and given a special
black semantic slant. So though we rappin bout the same language, the reality
referents are different.

To give you a most vivid illustration, consider the use of what WE labels "ob-   13
scenities." From the streets of Detroit: (a) "That's a bad *muthafucka*." Referring to
a Cadillac Eldorado, obviously indicating approval. (b) "He's a no-good *muthafucka*." Referring to a person who has just "put some game" on the speaker,
obviously indicating disapproval. (c) "You *muthafuckin* right I wasn't gon let him
do that." Emphasizing how correct the listener's assessment is, obviously using the
term as a grammatical intensifier, modifying "right." (d) "We wasn't doin nothing,
just messin round and *shit*." Though a different "obscenity," the point is nonetheless illustrated, "shit" being used neutrally, as an expletive (filler) to complete the
sentence pattern; semantically speaking, it is an empty word in this contextual
environment.

Where I'm comin from is that the lexicon of BI, consisting of certain specially   14
selected words, requires a unique scheme of analysis to account for the diverse
range and multiplicity of meanings attributed to these words. While there do be
some dictionaries of Afro-American "slang," they fail to get at the important question: what are the psycho-cultural processes that guide our selection of certain
words out of the thousands of possible words in the Anglo-Saxon vocabulary? Like,
for instance, Kochman[9] has suggested that we value action in the black community, and so those words that have action implied in them, we take and give positive
meanings to, such as *swing, game, hip, hustle*, etc.; whereas words of implied stasis
are taken and given negative connotations, such as *lame, square, hung-up, stiffin
and jivin*, etc. At any rate, what I've tried to lay here are some suggestions in this
particular linguistic dimension; the definitive word on black lexicon is yet to be
given.

I shall go on to discuss the stylistic dimension of black communication pat-   15
terns, where I have worked out a more definitive model.

TOWARD A BLACK LANGUAGE MODEL: STYLISTIC

Black verbal style exists on a sacred–secular continuum, as represented by the   16
accompanying scheme. The model allows us to account for the many individual
variations in black speech, which can all be located at some point along the continuum.

The sacred style is rural and Southern. It is the style of the black preacher and   17
that associated with the black church tradition. It tends to be more emotive and
highly charged than the secular style. It is also older in time. However, though I've
called it "sacred," it abounds in secularisms. Black church service tends to be
highly informal, and it ain nothin for a preacher to get up in the pulpit and, say,

show off what he's wearing: "Y'all didn't notice the new suit I got on today, did y'all? Ain the Lord good to us. . . ."

The secular style is urban and Northern, but since it probably had its begin-   18
nings in black folk tales and proverbs, its *roots* are Southern and rural. This is the street culture style; the style found in barbershops and on street corners in the black ghettos of American cities. It tends to be more cool, more emotionally re-strained than the sacred style. It is newer and younger in time and only fully evolved as a distinct style with the massive wave of black migration to the cities.

Both sacred and secular styles share the following characteristics: 19

1. Call and response. This is basic to black oral tradition. The speaker's solo   20
voice alternates or is intermingled with the audience's response. In the sacred style, the minister is urged on by the congregation's Amen's, That's right, Rever-end's, or Preach Reverend's. One also hears occasional Take your time's when the preacher is initiating his sermon, the congregation desiring to savor every little bit of this good message they bout to hear. (In both sacred and secular political rap styles, the "Preach Reverend" is transposed to "Teach Brother.") In the secular style, the response can take the form of a back-and-forth banter between the speaker and various members of the audience. Or the audience might manifest its response in giving skin (fives) when a really down verbal point is scored. Other approval responses include laughter and phrases like "Oh, you mean, nigger," "Get back, nigger," "Git down, baby," etc.

2. Rhythmic pattern. I refer to cadence, tone, and musical quality. This is a   21
pattern that is lyrical, sonorous, and generally emphasizing sound apart from sense. It is often established through repetition, either of certain sounds or words. The preacher will get a rhythm going, conveying his message through sound rather than depending on sheer semantic import. "I-I-I-I-I-Oh-I-I-Oh, yeah, Lord-I-I-heard the voice of Jesus saying. . . ." Even though the secular style is characterized by rapidity, as in the toasts (narrative tales of bad niggers and they exploits, like Stag-O-Lee, or bad animals and they trickeration, like the Signifying Monkey), the speaker's voice tone still has that rhythmic, musical quality, just with a faster tempo.

3. Spontaneity. Generally, the speaker's performance is improvisational, with   22
the rich interaction between speaker and audience dictating and/or directing the

Sacred	Secular
Political rap style	*Political rap style*
Examples: Jesse Jackson	Examples: Malcolm X
Martin Luther King	Rap Brown
Political literary style	*Political literary style*
Examples: Barbara Ann Teer's	Examples: Don Lee
National Black Theatre	Last Poets
Nikki Giovanni's	
"Truth Is on Its Way"	

course and outcome of the speech event. Since the speaker does not prepare a formal document, his delivery is casual, nondeliberate, and uncontrived. He speaks in a lively, conversational tone, and with an ever-present quality of immediacy. All emphasis is on process, movement, and creativity of the moment. The preacher says "Y'all don wont to hear dat, so I'm gon leave it lone," and his audience shouts, "Naw, tell it Reverend, tell it!," and he does. Or, like, once Malcolm mentioned the fact of his being in prison, and sensing the surprise of his audience, he took advantage of the opportunity to note that all black people were in prison: "That's what America means: prison."

4. *Concreteness.* The speaker's imagery and ideas center around the empirical world, the world of reality, and the contemporary Here and Now. Rarely does he drift off into esoteric abstractions; his metaphors and illustrations are commonplace and grounded in everyday experience. Perhaps because of this concreteness, there is a sense of identification with the event being described or narrated, as in the secular style where the toast-teller's identity merges with that of the protagonist of his tale, and he becomes Stag-O-Lee or Shine; or when the preacher assumes the voice of God or the personality of a Biblical character. Even the experience of being saved takes on a presentness and rootedness in everyday life: "I first met God in 1925. . . ."   23

5. *Signifying.* This is a technique of talking about the entire audience or some member of the audience either to initiate verbal "war" or to make a point hit home. The interesting thang bout this rhetorical device is that the audience is not offended and realizes—naw, expects—the speaker to launch this offensive to achieve his desired effect. "Pimp, punk, prostitute, Ph.D.—all the P's—you still in slavery!" announces the Reverend Jesse Jackson. Malcolm puts down the nonviolent movement with: "In a revolution, you swinging, not singing." (Notice the characteristic rhythmic pattern in the above examples—the alliterative poetic effect of Jackson's statement and the rhyming device in Malcolm's.)   24

An analysis of black expressive style, such as presented here, should facilitate the construction of a performance instrument to measure the degree of command of the style of any given BI speaker. Linguists and educators sincerely interested in black education might be about the difficult, complex business of devising such a "test," rather than establishing linguistic remediation programs to correct a nonexistent remediation. Like in any other area of human activity, some BI rappers are better than others, and today's most effective black preachers, leaders, politicians, writers are those who rap in the black expressive style, appropriating the ritual framework of the Oral Tradition as vehicle for the conveyance of they political ideologies. Which brings me back to what I said from Jump Street. The real heart of this language controversy relates to/is the underlying political nature of the American educational system. Brother Frantz Fanon is highly instructive at this point. From his "Negro and Language," in *Black Skins, White Masks:*   25

> I ascribe a basic importance to the phenomenon of language. . . . To speak means . . . above all to assume a culture, to support the weight of a civilization. . . . Every dialect is a way of thinking. . . . And the fact that the newly returned [i.e., from white

schools] Negro adopts a language different from that of the group into which he was born is evidence of a dislocation, a separation. . . .

In showing why the "Negro adopts such a position . . . with respect to European languages," Fanon continues:

> It is because he wants to emphasize the rupture that has now occurred. He is incarnating a new type of man that he imposes on his associates and his family. And so his old mother can no longer understand him when he talks to her about his *duds*, the family's *crummy joint*, the *dump* . . . all of it, of course, tricked out with the appropriate accent.
>   In every country of the world, there are climbers, 'the ones who forget who they are,' and in contrast to them, 'the ones who remember where they came from.' The Antilles Negro who goes home from France expresses himself in the dialect if he wants to make it plain that nothing has changed.[10]

As black people go moving on up toward separation and cultural nationalism, the question of the moment is not which dialect, but which culture, not whose vocabulary but whose values, not *I am* vs. *I be*, but WHO DO I BE?   26

NOTES

1. For examples of such programs, see *Non-Standard Dialect*, Board of Education of the city of New York (National Council of Teachers of English, 1968); San-Su C. Lin, *Pattern Practices in the Teaching of Standard English to Students with a Non-Standard Dialect* (USOE Project 1339, 1965); Arno Jewett, Joseph Mersand, Doris Gunderson, *Improving English Skills of Culturally Different Youth in Large Cities* (U.S. Department of Health, Education and Welfare, 1964); *Language Programs for the Disadvantaged* (NCTE, 1965).
2. See, for example, Joan Baratz and Roger Shuy, ed., *Teaching Black Children to Read* (Center for Applied Linguistics, 1969); A. L. Davis, ed., *On the Dialects of Children* (NCTE, 1968); Eldonna L. Evertts, ed., *Dimensions of Dialect* (NCTE, 1967).
3. For the most racist and glaring of these charges, see Fred Hechinger, ed., *Pre-School Education Today* (Doubleday, 1966); for an excellent rebuttal, see William Labov, *Nonstandard English* (NCTE 1970); for a complete overview of the controversy and issues involved as well as historical perspective and rebuttal to the non-verbal claim, see my "Black Idiom and White Institutions," *Negro American Literature Forum*, Fall 1971.
4. The most thorough and scholarly of these, though a bit overly technical, is Walter Wolfram, *Detroit Negro Speech* (Center for Applied Linguistics, 1969).
5. Kochman is one linguist who done gone this route; see for instance his "Rapping in the Black Ghetto," *Trans-action*, February 1969. However, he makes some black folks mad because of what one of my students called his "superfluity," and others shame cause of his exposure of our "bad" street elements. Kochman's data: jam up with muthafuckas and pussy-copping raps collected from Southside Chicago.
6. Johnnetta B. Cole, "Culture: Negro, Black and Nigger," *The Black Scholar,* June 1970.
7. Imamu Baraka, "Expressive Language," *Home*, pp. 166–172.
8. See her "Toward a New Perspective in Negro English Dialectology," *American Speech* (1965) and "Language and Communicative Styles of Afro-American Children in the United States," *Florida FL Reporter* 7 (Spring/Summer 1969).

9. See Thomas Kochman, "The Kinetic Element in Black Idiom," paper read at the American Anthropological Association Convention, Seattle, Washington, 1968; also his *Rappin' and Stylin' Out: Communication in Urban Black America.*
10. Frantz Fanon, *Black Skin, White Masks,* trans. Charles Lamm Markmann (New York, 1967), pp. 17–40.

Rhetorical Focus

1. If we take the first sentence of the second paragraph as her theme, list some of the ways Smitherman supports this idea.
2. In the second part of this essay, Smitherman seems more interested in classifying than in arguing a point. Is this true or is there a "point" to her examples of sacred and secular characteristics? Use examples to support your answer.
3. Compare Smitherman's opening paragraph with Baldwin's. How would you compare the tone, the purpose, the structure of each?

Thematic Focus

1. Did you have trouble understanding Smitherman's use of black English? Were you annoyed? Was this an effective device to make her point?
2. Does Smitherman's essay suggest that black students should be taught to read and write differently from others?
3. Smitherman makes the same point Baldwin does about the important connection between the black idiom and black culture. Explain what they are getting at.

Suggestions for Writing

1. Take a brief passage from Baldwin and write it in black English. Do the reverse for Smitherman. Write a short paragraph analyzing the impact of these changes.
2. Take a position on *bidialectalism*—the use of two dialects—in the schools. Should students have to learn Standard English if they do not wish to? Should they be able to use both dialects? Write a one-page report on the issue of black English, which would be appropriate for submission to a school board.
3. Do research on any of the topics raised in these essays. Write a report that contains about 600 words (with one-inch margins and ten-pitch typing, about 250 words fit on a page). You might want to do library work, or field research interviewing people, recording brief examples of their speech.

VERBAL TABOOS

We can probably all remember getting into hot water as children for using some word our parents or teachers felt was bad or obscene or dirty. We quickly discovered that certain words had real power. Linguists have studied such taboo or forbidden words for a long time, but that does not seem to have diminished their allure, their magic, or their ability to shock. One strange insight about taboo words is that we know that words are not forbidden in polite company because they refer to things we disapprove of. We can use *feces,* but not *shit;* we can use *bottom* but not *ass.* Why? That is not entirely clear, even to those who examine these matters carefully.

It seems as if our society uses more taboo words and more often than any other. This phenomenon can perhaps be explained by the lure of doing or saying the forbidden; cursing does have a certain mystique. Adolescents become, they assume, more adult or more powerful by using obscenity. Interestingly, women have usually been socialized not to use taboo words perhaps because there can be power and intensity associated with crude talk. That might explain why many people in our society are still upset at women who talk aggressively or who flout society's verbal taboos. Men have been allowed more leeway in the use of obscenity. Is that because they have more power, or does obscenity give you power?

In the following essay, J. Dan Rothwell suggests that it does depend on the context. It matters who is using what word where. Age matters, as do social status, class, and gender. Rothwell thinks a study of taboo words and their side-kicks, euphemisms (polite words used to cover-up), unmasks society's values, the relative status of men and women, as well as its hidden fears. Barbara Lawrence is also impressed with the power of taboos but is angry that this power is often used against women. As you read these two pieces, notice your own response to taboo words. What does your reaction tell you about your cultural socialization or about your own tastes and values?

Verbal Taboos

J. Dan Rothwell

J. Dan Rothwell (1946–) was a professor of communications at Western Washington University. He now teaches communications at Cabrillo College in California. He has written widely on language topics, especially on verbal obscenity and semantics. His latest book is *In Mixed Company: Small Group Communications* (1991). The following article, taken from *Tell It Like It Isn't*, an analysis of sexism, violence, and racism in language, explores verbal taboos by placing them in a social context.

Reflections Before Reading

Do you think, as Rothwell asserts, "obscenity is in the mind of the beholder"—That is, are some words inherently "obscene"? Taboo words are usually turned into euphemisms that clean them up. In England, for example, "water closet" was once a euphemism for "bathroom." Eventually that term became taboo, so "W.C." was invented as a new euphemism. Try to make a list of taboo words and parallel euphemisms that you can recall from your childhood and adolescence.

Verbal taboos of one kind or another have existed among every human culture and 1 probably originated with the development of language. The history of English-speaking peoples, especially the more recent chronicles, attests to the prevalence of and attention paid by such cultures to verbal taboos. Lexicographer Noah Webster in 1833, offended by the coarse phrasing of the Bible, proceeded to "cleanse" it of its offensive terminology, thereby improving the divine rhetoric. He replaced *teat* with *breast* (a word soon to fall into disrepute), *to give suck* with *nourish*, *to go awhoring* with *to go astray*, *whoredom* with *carnal connection*, and references to the male genitals with *secrets* (certainly the world's most poorly kept).

Victorian prudery produced what must seem to many present day observers 2 supremely silly verbal taboos. One's lower extremities were not called *legs* but rather *limbs*. Children were not *born* but *sent* and never *breast-fed* but rather *nursed*. If you look at Victorian language as an accurate reflection of life as it was lived, then sex and elimination did not exist as human functions.

World War I temporarily diminished the strict Victorian taboos regarding ver-   3
bal propriety. In the 1930s, however, Hollywood stepped into the breach. American moviemakers, under threats of censorship, issued a list of banned words never
to be uttered in any motion picture. Some of the culprits included *virgin, harlot,
slut, tart, whore, son-of-a-bitch, sex, asexual, virtuous,* and *bum.*

Although such censorship of words can be easily mocked as the foolish prud-   4
ery of previous generations, the significance of verbal taboos in our culture has real
currency. Virtually all states have laws that restrict certain language from being
used in public places. The United States Criminal Code forbids "obscene, inde-
cent, or profane language" on the radio. Radio, television, print media, and the
movie industry all have established codes dealing with taboo language, although
these codes are vaguely worded and not always followed.

Verbal obscenity became an issue of no small consequence during the political   5
and social protests of the 1960s and '70s. Ultimately the U.S. Supreme Court was
drawn into the controversy and issued numerous decisions dealing with the use of
offensive language. Richard Nixon, doomed to resign as President, created a national incident when his private language was found to be more preoccupied with
the sexual and excretory side of life than many would have imagined.

Despite this long history of linguistic trepidation, verbal taboos are gradually   6
eroding. Cameron determined that several tabooed terms are among the seventy-
five most frequently used words in the English language. Many people pay lip
service to the verbal taboos but privately ignore sanctions placed on language.
Restrictions on printing offensive language have loosened considerably in the last
decade or so.

Nevertheless, as the restrictions on taboo language usage erode, pressures to   7
revive and preserve such taboos on language seem to increase. The National Council of Teachers of English (NCTE) conducted a "censorship survey" in 1966 and
1977. It found that there was a greater reported incidence of attempts to censor
educational materials in secondary schools in the 1977 survey compared with the
1966 survey. The most common objection noted by the teachers answering the
survey was to the language in the books in question. While the more explicit "obscenities" and "profanities" were cause for objection, some dictionaries that do not
include such terms came under fire. *The American Heritage Dictionary, Webster's
New World Dictionary of the American Language,* and the *Random House College
Dictionary* were some of the works singled out by members of various American
communities both large and small, rural and urban. These dictionaries carried
such words as *bed, fag, horny, hot, knock, queer, rubber, shack,* and *slut* with their
appropriate sexual definitions.

Increasing attempts to censor materials containing language deemed objec-   8
tionable (even "bad grammar" is a target of censorship attempts) comes from a
variety of sources. Concerned parents, nervous librarians, school board members,
administrators, the clergy, and perhaps most publicized, the efforts of Mel and
Norma Gabler, founders of the Educational Research Analysts, Inc., in Longview,
Texas, are the principal sources of such censorship pressure.

Interestingly, 75 percent of the objections from such groups reported in the   9
NCTE 1977 survey concern language and sex (which often overlap) but only 4

percent concern violence as the grounds of complaint. Clearly, taboo language remains a highly charged issue of no small consequence.

Some guardians of the public morals herald the maintenance of verbal taboos   10 as a sign of an advanced civilization, while at the same time decrying the erosion of these taboos as a sign of moral and social decay. Such a view equates words with things. No word is intrinsically dirty, however. Obscenity is in the mind of the beholder. Words become tabooed by social convention largely divorced from logic. A friend related a story to me a few years ago that illustrates this point. His two-year-old daughter was playing in their backyard with a neighbor's son who was about the same age. Apparently the little boy did something quite irksome to this usually even-tempered, cheerful little girl. She expressed her anger by turning to the little boy and proclaiming, "I'm going to shit on your head." She was immediately admonished by her mother, "Janie, we don't talk like that," whereupon Janie turned to the little boy and said: "I'm going to shit on your arm." The "logic" of arbitrary social convention that brands a word taboo must be learned. Relegating a few words to the dirty linen closet where they are scrubbed clean and transformed into euphemisms, circumlocutions, or babytalk hardly stands as one of human-kind's crowning achievements.

To carry this a bit further, consider the two terms *sexual intercourse* and *fuck*.   11 Both terms can denote copulation or sexual connection between two people, yet the connotations attached to the latter are often so powerful that only obscenity is perceived.

I have queried students concerning the difference between these two terms.   12 Common answers include: *fuck* is more aggressive, harsher, more shocking, and it's dirty. Once I posed this question to a group of more than 200 students in a large lecture hall. When I asked what the difference was between *fuck* and *sexual intercourse,* a male voice from the back of the room echoed forth, "Technique!"

Some words are designated obscene, coarse, or vulgar, not because of their   13 denotative meanings, but primarily because of the associations, experiences, and conditioning that produce such connotations as the ones above. Of the three elements of connotative meaning isolated by Osgood, Suci, and Tannebaum, a word such as *fuck* might conjure very negative evaluations inside our heads, generate great intensity on the potency dimension, and summon an image of fierce activity. Thus, the connotative meaning of the word *fuck* would be negative, strong, and active. When such connotations come to mind, denotations are obscured and we signally react to the word. (Have you already demonstrated such a signal reaction to my inclusion of "obscenities" in the last few paragraphs?)

Muriel Schultz points out the illogic produced by such signal reactions. She   14 observes that the word *rape* is an acceptable "four-letter word," yet it denotes a vicious, violent act that many would label *obscene.* The word *fuck,* however, can denote sexual intercourse, a universal human act proscribed only in certain instances. It can also have a nonsexual referent, as in "I'm all fucked up," which, of course, does not mean "I'm all sexual intercoursed up." Yet *fuck* is taboo no matter how it is used. Obviously it is not the act nor the way in which the word is used that brands certain words taboo. This brings to mind a statement attributed to D.H.

Lawrence, "Tell me what's wrong with words or with you, that the thing is all right but the word is taboo."

Verbal taboos are not hallmarks of a civilized society but rather a primitive confusion of words with things. Logic does not dictate which words should be proscribed. If that were the case *rape* would be the penultimate verbal obscenity. Filth does not exist as a characteristic intrinsic to any word. Montagu explains that *fuck* was an acceptable word in sixteenth century Scotland although it became "obscene" soon after. *Cunt* was a Standard English word for the female pudenda during the Middle Ages, and *shit* was Standard English from the sixteenth to the nineteenth century and then fell into disrepute. The words themselves, then, are not dirty, but we have attached such a label to certain words quite apart from logic and the arbitrary nature of word symbols. Characterizing some words as obscene, profane, dirty, and the like reifies them, makes these words things unto themselves apart from their contextual meaning. There is no clear yardstick, no empirical foundation for making such designations.   15

Nevertheless, verbal taboos exist and although they are slowly eroding in this country, they remain powerful controllers of verbal behavior in many circles, under various conditions. Understanding the verbal taboo phenomenon is significant for several reasons.   16

First, reaction to taboo language manifests in a very tangible way a central theme of this book, namely, that language is not a neutral vehicle of communication. Rather, language is a powerful instrument of communication that has an enormous influence on our perception and behavior. Gaining insight into the dynamics of the taboo language phenomenon can help us understand and respect the power of language and encourage us to nurture a rational, prudent attitude regarding language usage.   17

Second, the taboo language phenomenon is very probably the best example of reification in action. While we may recognize immediately the elementary truth in the statement, "Words are not things anymore than maps are territories," we often forget our general semantics when it comes to taboo language. We forget it at our own peril. Treating words as things can be a very dangerous practice.   18

Third, taboo language graphically illustrates how context determines meanings of words. Language is a dynamic process not a static entity. The meaning of a word, therefore, is not static but rather subject to alteration depending on the context in which the word is used. Failure to appreciate the complexity of this language process and the importance of responding intelligently to symbols of our own creation, can make us prisoners of our language, victims of our own invention.   19

Thus, a detailed discussion of taboo language—why we have verbal taboos, the several elements of context that affect our view of the degree of offensiveness of taboo terminology, and the kinds of response we have to such terminology—serves as a kind of case study that illustrates, amplifies, and explains in greater detail and depth, much of what was introduced in the first three chapters.   20

One final note of preamble should be mentioned here. While I am not insensitive to those who harbor religious scruples concerning "dirty words" and "profanity," and while I realize some people find this subject shocking, embarrassing, and   21 offensive, nevertheless, as you have already gathered by now, no effort will be made to employ circumlocution or to expurgate the taboo words. It would be hypocritical to argue on the one hand that designations of some words as dirty, profane, and obscene are a misuse of language and then on the other hand proceed to lend credence to this reification by avoiding the offending terms, substituting quaint little phrases, applying asterisks, or engaging in other forms of semantic camouflage. A psychiatrist who refuses to listen to a client's problems because he or she finds them "dirty," offensive, "obscene," or embarrassing would be labeled unprofessional at best. Language is the business of those who study and write about improving communication. To pursue it properly requires an intelligent, mature, and frank discussion of language in all forms, not a closed mind and a closed mouth.

✿   ✿   ✿

WHO: The Taboo Transgressors

Offensive language does not exist in isolation. It makes a difference who uses such language. There are at least three factors concerning who uses prohibited language that seem to strongly influence our perception of taboo words. They are sex, age, and degree of status. 22

It has long been a tenet of folk wisdom that women are the gentler sex. Consequently, they refrain from offensive, aggressive language and choose instead the more polite forms of speech. Jesperson was one of the first to comment on this generally accepted observation of female speech patterns. He asserted: 23

> There can be no doubt that women exercise a great and universal influence on linguistic development through their instinctive shrinking from coarse and gross expressions and their preference for refined (and in certain spheres) veiled and indirect expression.

Wolfram and Fasold update this view by pointing out that recent studies of linguistic change in the United States indicate that females are frequently responsible for the initial adoption of new prestige forms of language and primarily responsible for perpetuating the prestige norms of language for future generations.

Jesperson's claim that women instinctively shrink from stigmatized forms of language, however, is certainly subject to serious question. Society's definition of women relegates taboo language to the ranks of the "unfeminine"—coarse and offensive expression more properly suited to males. Women who use taboo language are speaking like men and are consequently stigmatized for departing from the societal definition of the female role. It has been taboo for women to use such nonstandard language because it threatens to disrupt the social order. Men have greater freedom to use language flexibly whereas women have greater restraints placed on their language usage. In a male dominated society women are expected to shrink from "coarse and gross expressions" because that is the role they have been delegated. The double standard whereby men can more freely employ taboo language than women reflects an unequal distribution of power. Women do not 24 control men's language (except in respect to observing the rules of propriety of expression when "ladies" are present), but men control the language of women in regards to stigmatized verbal discourse. Failure to observe the "proper" linguistic etiquette marks a woman as rebellious, a threat to the power of men to dominate women. It is small wonder that swearing by women elicits strong reproach.

There are close to a dozen studies that substantiate the strength of this double   25 standard. As a generalization it seems evident that men use taboo language more often than women as a consequence of social mores. Recent recognition of male chauvinism even in terms of language, however, has apparently begun to loosen the restraints on some of the use of taboo language by women. There are other factors that restrict usage of taboo language by various individuals, but being a woman is one that seems to be losing some of its relevance.

Age is another factor that influences our perception of taboo language. People   26 have basically two reactions to the use of taboo language by young children. Some think it is "cute" and openly laugh when a three-year-old calls them a "shithead." Such a response to a child's using "adults only" language merely encourages further forays into the forbidden realm of offensive language. Others respond with shock and outrage, viewing such words "out of the mouths of babes" as a demonstration of poor parental discipline and guidance.

Another double standard sometimes operates in regard to taboo terminology   27 and age. Those who severely punish young children for using taboo language may quite openly employ taboo terminology themselves. Parents are often surprised and shocked when, upon asking their children where they learned certain "nasty" terms, are informed that their children are only imitating their parents' speech. Again, the issue of power arises. Parents can dominate their children and restrict their language usage because it is the parents who establish the social conventions of behavior. Taboo language, then, becomes an instrument of rebellion against parental control and authority.

Parental patterns of discipline appear to affect children's use of taboo lan-   28 guage. In reference to pathological use of obscenity by children, Harrison and Hinshaw note that extremes at both ends of the discipline scale may result in excessive verbalization of obscenities. Ostensibly a rigid interdiction on taboo language encourages rebellion against such restrictions on freedom, and a seemingly unconcerned and uncaring attitude allows the use of such language to flourish unrestrainedly. In the former case, the child may be striking out against the bonds of conformity in hopes of developing individuality. In the latter case, the child may be trying to shock inattentive parents into noticing his or her very existence. Taboos foster invisibility. Violating societal taboos can produce visibility.

An additional element of this relationship between age and taboo language is   29 that older people tend to respond less favorably to taboo language in general than do young people, owing perhaps to changing social mores. Lewis found that individuals under thirty years old were much less likely to respond with disgust or anger when obscenities were used at college protest demonstrations than were older age groups—those thirty to forty-nine and those over fifty. Lodle discovered that subjects over thirty expressed "concern for others" as a major controlling element in a decision to use "dirty words." No other age group exhibited such a concern. How old the speaker is and the age of the receiver influence the perception of taboo language as either offensive or relatively innocuous.

The degree of status an individual possesses is a third factor that affects our view of taboo language. Status is the prestige position or rank one has in relation to others. Traditional "wisdom" assumes that the upper echelons of society, principally because of their exposure to education and "culture," are supposed to develop "refined" attitudes and employ dignified language, whereas the lower-class poor characteristically stoop to coarse and obscene nonstandard language variants. Linguistic research supports this commonly accepted view. Bernstein and Labov have demonstrated that a direct relationship exists between socioeconomic status and linguistic choice of speakers. Wolfram and Fasold cite research which clearly shows that stigmatized forms of speech and language usage are associated with low status groups while socially prestigious variants are adopted by high status groups as linguistic indicators of such status. Verbal obscenity thus becomes associated with "gutter talk," the stigmatized language of the uncouth, the uneducated, and the unwashed.   30

Those who make claim to high-status positions are expected to speak in dignified language, avoiding stigmatized forms of expression. Many Americans were upset by Harry Truman's penchant for salty language. "Bad language" became an issue during the 1960 Kennedy–Nixon debates, when Richard Nixon piously asserted that Eisenhower had "restored dignity and decency and, frankly, good language to the conduct of the Presidency of the United States."   31

Two incidents during the Watergate era provide insight into the relationship between status and the reaction to taboo language. It was revealed that two individuals of high status were guilty of verbal taboo violation. Earl Butz, Secretary of Agriculture during the Nixon Administration, reportedly made the following statement in reference to what "coloreds" supposedly want in life: "I'll tell you what coloreds want. It's three things: first, a tight pussy, second, loose shoes; and third, a warm place to shit. That's all." Richard Nixon was also guilty of utilizing proscribed language. "Expletive deleted" became a national joke when the Watergate tapes were the subject of public scrutiny. One particular statement, because of its incriminating features, stood out. Nixon's statement, "I don't give a shit what happens. I want you all to stonewall it. . . ." became national news. It is instructive to see how the people reacted to these two statements by high-status individuals.   32

Generally, there was a mixture of shock and outrage when it was revealed that Earl Butz and Richard Nixon talked like longshoremen. Butz, probably partly because his "joke" was a racial slur as well as a violation of language taboos, was forced to resign his post while under fire from an incensed public. Nixon was forced to resign for other reasons, but the public reaction to the revelation that he liberally sprinkled his private conversations with obscene and profane language was highly negative and hardly dispassionate. It was looked upon as a debasement of his high office. Presidents and members of the Cabinet are not supposed to speak gutter language.   33

Thus, age, sex, and status of the individual using taboo language play an important role in influencing perceptions of proscribed words. Who uses such language does make a difference.   34

Rhetorical Focus

1. Notice the structure of the section beginning with paragraph 22. It seems to conform to the traditional pattern of announcing a thesis in the first paragraph, dividing it into three parts (sex, age, status) that are then developed with reasons, examples, and facts in the following paragraphs, and ending with a summary conclusion. Describe how Rothwell moves from one section to the next.
2. Do you think he had a similar organizational plan in the opening section? Where is the thesis announced here? Which plan do you think is better? Why?
3. Describe Rothwell's tone or voice. Can you point to places where he might give away his opinion.

Thematic Focus

1. Rothwell draws a strong connection between taboo language and culture. Some cultures, the Japanese for example, do not have taboo words. What might that say about their culture and about ours?
2. Because many subcultures in American society use taboo words as a matter of course, does that suggest that our public morality is only a mask? What does your own experience with taboo words indicate about your relationship to the norms of the dominant culture?
3. In your experience, do taboo words give power to people? Does the use of euphemisms mean that we are afraid to face reality?

Four-Letter Words Can Hurt You

Barbara Lawrence

Barbara Lawrence is a professor of humanities at the State University of
New York at Old Westbury. In this essay, published in *The New York Times*
(1963), she considers both the meaning of obscenity and the frequency with
which obscene words specifically demean women. Instead of taking a
detached stance common in the university, Lawrence is clearly upset by
obscenity.

Reflections Before Reading

Were any taboo words or obscenities allowed in your home when you were
growing up? Were there limits? How did you learn them? Does your use of
"forbidden" words increase or decrease, depending on the group you are
with? Can you think of taboo words that annoy you, that you wish people
would not use? Why?

Why should any words be called obscene? Don't they all describe natural hu- 1
man functions? Am I trying to tell them, my students demand, that the "strong,
earthy, gut-honest"—or, if they are fans of Norman Mailer, the "rich, liberating,
existential"—language they use to describe sexual activity isn't preferable to
"phony-sounding, middle-class words like 'intercourse' and 'copulate'?" "Cop
You Late!" they say with fancy inflections and gagging grimaces. "Now, what is
that supposed to mean?"

Well, what is it supposed to mean? And why indeed should one group of words 2
describing human functions and human organs be acceptable in ordinary conversation and another, describing presumably the same organs and functions, be tabooed—so much so, in fact, that some of these words still cannot appear in print in
many parts of the English-speaking world?

The argument that these taboos exist only because of "sexual hangups" (mid- 3
dle-class, middle-age, feminist), or even that they are a result of class oppression
(the contempt of the Norman conquerors for the language of their Anglo-Saxon

serfs), ignores a much more likely explanation, it seems to me, and that is the sources and functions of the words themselves.

The best known of the tabooed sexual verbs, for example, comes from the German *ficken*, meaning "to strike"; combined, according to Partridge's etymological dictionary *Origins*, with the Latin sexual verb *futuere*; associated in turn with the Latin *fustis*, "a staff or cudgel"; the Celtic *buc*, "a point, hence to pierce"; the Irish *bot*, "the male member"; the Latin *battuere*, "to beat"; the Gaelic *batair*, "a cudgeller"; the Early Irish *bualaim*, "I strike"; and so forth. It is one of what etymologists sometimes call "the sadistic group of words for the man's part in copulation."

The brutality of this word, then, and its equivalents ("screw," "bang," etc.), is not an illusion of the middle class or a crotchet of Women's Liberation. In their origins and imagery these words carry undeniably painful, if not sadistic, implications, the object of which is almost always female. Consider, for example, what a "screw" actually does to the wood it penetrates; what a painful, even mutilating, activity this kind of analogy suggests. "Screw" is particularly interesting in this context, since the noun, according to Partridge, comes from words meaning "groove," "nut," "ditch," "breeding sow," "scrofula" and "swelling," while the verb, besides its explicit imagery, has antecedent associations to "write on," "scratch," "scarify," and so forth—a revealing fusion of a mechanical or painful action with an obviously denigrated object.

Not all obscene words, of course, are as implicitly sadistic or denigrating to women as these, but all that I know seem to serve a similar purpose: to reduce the human organism (especially the female organism) and human functions (especially sexual and procreative) to their least organic, most mechanical dimension; to substitute a trivializing or deforming resemblance for the complex human reality of what is being described.

Tabooed male descriptives, when they are not openly denigrating to women, often serve to divorce a male organ or function from any significant interaction with the female. Take the word "testes," for example, suggesting "witnesses" (from the Latin *testis*) to the sexual and procreative strengths of the male organ; and the obscene counterpart of this word, which suggests little more than a mechanical shape. Or compare almost any of the "rich," "liberating" sexual verbs, so fashionable today among male writers, with that much-derided Latin word "copulate" ("to bind or join together") or even that Anglo-Saxon phrase (which seems to have had no trouble surviving the Norman Conquest) "make love."

How arrogantly self-involved the tabooed words seem in comparison to either of the other terms, and how contemptuous of the female partner. Understandably so, of course, if she is only a "skirt," a "broad," a "chick," a "pussycat" or a "piece." If she is, in other words, no more than her skirt, or what her skirt conceals; no more than a breeder, or the broadest part of her; no more than a piece of a human being or a "piece of tail."

The most severely tabooed of all the female descriptives, incidentally, are those like a "piece of tail," which suggest (either explicitly or through antecedents) that there is no significant difference between the female channel through which we are all conceived and born and the anal outlet common to both sexes—a distinction that pornographers have always enjoyed obscuring.

This effort to deny women their biological identity, their individuality, their   10
humanness, is such an important aspect of obscene language that one can only
marvel at how seldom, in an era preoccupied with definitions of obscenity, this fact
is brought to our attention. One problem, of course, is that many of the people in
the best position to do this (critics, teachers, writers) are so reluctant today to
admit that they are angered or shocked by obscenity. Bored, maybe, unimpressed,
aesthetically displeased, but—no matter how brutal or denigrating the material—
never angered, never shocked.

And yet how eloquently angered, how piously shocked many of these same   11
people become if denigrating language is used about any minority group other
than women; if the obscenities are racial or ethnic, that is, rather than sexual.
Words like "coon," "kike," "spic," "wop," after all, deform identity, deny individuality and humanness in almost exactly the same way that sexual vulgarisms and
obscenities do.

No one that I know, least of all my students, would fail to question the values   12
of a society whose literature and entertainment rested heavily on racial or ethnic
pejoratives. Are the values of a society whose literature and entertainment rest as
heavily as ours on sexual pejoratives any less questionable?

Rhetorical Focus

1. Both Rothwell's and Lawrence's essay might be thought of as arguments.
   Rothwell seems to excuse or explain away taboo words with examples demonstrating context. What is Lawrence's strategy in making her point about
   obscenity?
2. Do you think it is effective to begin and end an essay with a question?
   Why?
3. How would you describe Lawrence's tone? Point to specific language that
   suggests her attitude.

Thematic Focus

1. Do you agree that sexual taboo words should be put on the same offensive
   level as racial slurs?
2. Make a list of all the taboo words you can think of having to do with love-
   making. Is Lawrence correct in saying that they carry painful implications
   for women?
3. Lawrence seems to be making quite a different point than Rothwell. What
   are their views on taboo words? How do you explain their different perceptions?

Suggestions for Writing

1. As a research project, listen carefully to how your friends and acquaintances use (or do not use) taboo words and euphemisms. Keep a journal for a

week, recording as much of the context as you can. Write a report of about 600 words that confirms or disproves any of Rothwell's or Lawrence's conclusions.

2. Should children be allowed to use taboo words? Should writers, filmmakers, television producers, college students, police officers, teachers? Explain your reasoning in a brief, focused essay of about 600–750 words.

3. Write a narrative that focuses on your own childhood and adolescent experiences with taboo words. Try to build a context for the ways you were socialized by such factors as parents, peers, movies, television and so forth. In your conclusion make some generalizations that touch on issues raised by Rothwell and Lawrence.

Chapter
9

Science and
Cultural Values

S cience is popularly thought of as a rigorous search for the truth, as an activity that gets to the heart of the matter, that digs deep to find what is really there. Consequently, it must be free from the usual biases and subjective judgments that plague other intellectual pursuits. For example, film criticism, the literary assessments of famous writers as well as history, political science, and philosophy seem to many knowledgeable observers to reflect not only unconscious cultural values but also rather individual likes and dislikes. On the other hand, most people think that biology, physics, and medicine are objective sciences, carefully designed to remove personal and societal bias. Scientists themselves will claim that good biology is good biology, whether practiced in America or the Sudan: Culture does not interfere.

We do not think this is an absurd concept: Chemistry certainly does seem less affected by politics than a historian's view of the Persian Gulf War or a critic's estimate of Bob Dylan's worth as a poet. Even so, we think there is an important connection between the questions scientists ask, the priorities they establish, and the historical moment in which they are working. Scientists in the same field usually have similar ideas because the language or the discourse they are required to use channels their thinking, which helps them to communicate more effectively but makes it difficult for them to see alternatives to the dominant perspective in their disciplines. Loren Eiseley, for example, was a famous anthropologist who followed his profession's thinking when analyzing bones, but in his heart, he doubted the certainty of the scientific method in his pursuit. He could never shake the belief that there was more to reality than meets scientists' eyes, more to the world than our culture can admit.

All the essays in this section revolve around this interaction between science and cultural values, between technology and ideology. Eiseley's haunting piece is paired with a mainstream, skeptical scientific view of the mystical and supernatural; the essays of two leading animal rights advocates offer interesting and passionate perspectives on how scientific, technological, and cultural morality can clash; William Buckley and Susan Sontag approach AIDS from opposing political and ideological viewpoints; and, finally, the objectivity of science is put in some jeopardy—first by Stephen Jay Gould, one of the world's leading evolutionists, and then by Elaine Morgan, who offers a provocative alternative to a male-centered view of evolution.

SCIENCE AND THE UNKNOWN

Before the great scientific discoveries of the past 300 years, the unexplainable was left to religion, superstition, and magic. Mysterious deaths, strange storms, and prophetic dreams puzzled the minds of even the most intellectual members of society. For many, the unknown was feared, and consequently, elaborate explanations were constructed to offer at least some sense of certainty for the confused mind. After the rise of the scientific method in the eighteenth century and the great medical discoveries of this century, however, most educated people thought that science could explain everything or soon would. As a result, there is today, among many people, an unquestioned trust in science that is comparable to the widespread belief in religion in the Middle Ages.

Yet, some thinkers feel that the pendulum has swung too far, that we expect too much of a discipline created by fallible minds. Perhaps this can explain a growing backlash against the absolutes of science. Why is astrology still around? Why is a belief in ghosts not uncommon? Loren Eiseley, the author of "The Dance of the Frogs," bemoans the loss of mystery and wonder that followed in science's wake. He is also a skeptic and wonders whether the scientist is not in danger of becoming too arrogant, too certain that the supernatural belonged in the Middle Ages rather than in the Age of the Atom.

As a counterpoint to Eiseley's tale, we have selected a brief statement against astrology by several scientists who might, in fact, be closely related in temper and outlook to the confident young narrator of "The Dance of the Frogs." There seems to be a fuzzy line between certainty and arrogance, between open-mindedness and gullibility.

The Dance of the Frogs

Loren Eiseley

Loren Eiseley (1907–1977), for many years a professor of anthropology at the University of Pennsylvania, was a highly acclaimed American anthropologist, archaeologist, naturalist, poet, essayist, and autobiographer. His writings are remarkable for their presentation of scientific concepts in a lyrical, sometimes mystical style. A fine example of Eiseley's mysticism can be found in the essay included here, "The Dance of the Frogs," which is taken from a collection, *The Star Throwers,* published a year after he died.

Reflections Before Reading

Do you think science has the potential to solve all the world's problems? Can science explain the supernatural? Are there supernatural phenomena, or are there just phenomena in the world we cannot explain? Are you open-minded about the validity of religions other than your own?

I

He was a member of the Explorers Club, and he had never been outside the state of Pennsylvania. Some of us who were world travelers used to smile a little about that, even though we knew his scientific reputation had been, at one time, great. It is always the way of youth to smile. I used to think of myself as something of an adventurer, but the time came when I realized that old Albert Dreyer, huddling with his drink in the shadows close to the fire, had journeyed farther into the Country of Terror than any of us would ever go, God willing, and emerge alive.   1

He was a morose and aging man, without family and without intimates. His membership in the club dated back into the decades when he was a zoologist famous for his remarkable experiments upon amphibians—he had recovered and actually produced the adult stage of the Mexican axolotl, as well as achieving remarkable tissue transplants in salamanders. The club had been flattered to have him then, travel or no travel, but the end was not fortunate. The brilliant scientist had become the misanthrope; the achievement lay all in the past, and Albert Dreyer kept to his solitary room, his solitary drink, and his accustomed spot by the fire.   2

The reason I came to hear his story was an odd one. I had been north that year, 3
and the club had asked me to give a little talk on the religious beliefs of the Indians
of the northern forest, the Naskapi of Labrador. I had long been a student of the
strange mélange of superstition and woodland wisdom that makes up the religious
life of the nature peoples. Moreover, I had come to know something of the strange
similarities of the "shaking tent rite" to the phenomena of the modern medium's
cabinet.

"The special tent with its entranced occupant is no different from the cabinet," 4
I contended. "The only difference is the type of voices that emerge. Many of the
physical phenomena are identical—the movement of powerful forces shaking the
conical hut, objects thrown, all this is familiar to Western psychical science. What
is different are the voices projected. Here they are the cries of animals, the voices
from the swamp and the mountain—the solitary elementals before whom the
primitive man stands in awe, and from whom he begs sustenance. Here the game
lords reign supreme; man himself is voiceless."

A low, halting query reached me from the back of the room. I was startled, 5
even in the midst of my discussion, to note that it was Dreyer.

"And the game lords, what are they?" 6

"Each species of animal is supposed to have gigantic leaders of more than 7
normal size," I explained. "These beings are the immaterial controllers of that particular type of animal. Legend about them is confused. Sometimes they partake of
human qualities, will and intelligence, but they are of animal shape. They control
the movements of game, and thus their favor may mean life or death to man."

"Are they visible?" Again Dreyer's low, troubled voice came from the back of 8
the room.

"Native belief has it that they can be seen on rare occasions," I answered. "In a 9
sense they remind one of the concept of the archetypes, the originals behind the
petty show of our small, transitory existence. They are the immortal renewers of
substance—the force behind and above animate nature."

"Do they dance?" persisted Dreyer. 10

At this I grew nettled. Old Dreyer in a heckling mood was something new. "I 11
cannot answer that question," I said acidly. "My informants failed to elaborate
upon it. But they believe implicitly in these monstrous beings, talk to and propiti-
ate them. It is their voices that emerge from the shaking tent."

"The Indians believe it," pursued old Dreyer relentlessly, "but do *you* believe 12
it?"

"My dear fellow—I shrugged and glanced at the smiling audience—"I have 13
seen many strange things, many puzzling things, but I am a scientist." Dreyer
made a contemptuous sound in his throat and went back to the shadow out of
which he had crept in his interest. The talk was over. I headed for the bar.

II

The evening passed. Men drifted homeward or went to their rooms. I had been a 14
year in the woods and hungered for voices and companionship. Finally, however, I
sat alone with my glass, a little mellow, perhaps, enjoying the warmth of the fire

and remembering the blue snowfields of the North as they should be remembered—in the comfort of warm rooms.

I think an hour must have passed. The club was silent except for the ticking of   15
an antiquated clock on the mantel and small night noises from the street. I must
have drowsed. At all events it was some time before I grew aware that a chair had
been drawn up opposite me. I started.

"A damp night," I said.   16

"Foggy," said the man in the shadow musingly. "But not too foggy. They like it   17
that way."

"Eh?" I said. I knew immediately it was Dreyer speaking. Maybe I had missed   18
something; on second thought, maybe not.

"And spring," he said. "Spring. That's part of it. God knows why, of course, but   19
we feel it, why shouldn't they? And more intensely."

"Look—" I said. "I guess—" The old man was more human than I thought. He   20
reached out and touched my knee with the hand that he always kept a glove over—
burn, we used to speculate—and smiled softly.

"You don't know what I'm talking about," he finished for me. "And, besides, I   21
ruffled your feelings earlier in the evening. You must forgive me. You touched on
an interest of mine, and I was perhaps overeager. I did not intend to give the
appearance of heckling. It was only that . . ."

"Of course," I said. "Of course." Such a confession from Dreyer was astound-   22
ing. The man might be ill. I rang for a drink and decided to shift the conversation
to a safer topic, more appropriate to a scholar.

"Frogs," I said desperately, like any young ass in a china shop. "Always ad-   23
mired your experiments. Frogs. Yes."

I give the old man credit. He took the drink and held it up and looked at me   24
across the rim. There was a faint stir of sardonic humor in his eyes.

"Frogs, no," he said, "or maybe yes. I've never been quite sure. Maybe yes.   25
But there was no time to decide properly." The humor faded out of his eyes. "Maybe I should have let go," he said. "It was what they wanted. There's no doubting
that at all, but it came too quick for me. What would you have done?"

"I don't know," I said honestly enough and pinched myself.   26

"You had better know," said Albert Dreyer severely, "if you're planning to   27
become an investigator of primitive religions. Or even not. I wasn't, you know, and
the things came to me just when I least suspected—But I forget, you don't believe
in them."

He shrugged and half rose, and for the first time, really, I saw the black-gloved   28
hand and the haunted face of Albert Dreyer and knew in my heart the things he
had stood for in science. I got up then, as a young man in the presence of his
betters should get up, and I said, and I meant it, every word: "Please, Dr. Dreyer,
sit down and tell me. I'm too young to be saying what I believe or don't believe in at
all. I'd be obliged if you'd tell me."

Just at that moment a strange, wonderful dignity shone out of the countenance   29
of Albert Dreyer, and I knew the man he was. He bowed and sat down, and there
were no longer the barriers of age and youthful ego between us. There were just
two men under a lamp, and around them a great waiting silence. Out to the ends of

the universe, I thought fleetingly, that's the way with man and his lamps. One has to huddle in, there's so little light and so much space. One—

III

"It could happen to anyone," said Albert Dreyer. "And especially in the spring.   30
Remember that. And all I did was to skip. Just a few feet, mark you, but I skipped. Remember that, too.

"You wouldn't remember the place at all. At least not as it was then." He   31
paused and shook the ice in his glass and spoke more easily.

"It was a road that came out finally in a marsh along the Schuykill River. Prob-   32
ably all industrial now. But I had a little house out there with a laboratory thrown in. It was convenient to the marsh, and that helped me with my studies of am-phibia. Moreover, it was a wild, lonely road, and I wanted solitude. It is always the demand of the naturalist. You understand that?"

"Of course," I said. I knew he had gone there, after the death of his young   33
wife, in grief and loneliness and despair. He was not a man to mention such things. "It is best for the naturalist," I agreed.

"Exactly. My best work was done there." He held up his black-gloved hand   34
and glanced at it meditatively. "The work on the axolotl, newt neoteny. I worked hard. I had—" he hesitated—"things to forget. There were times when I worked all night. Or diverted myself, while waiting the result of an experiment, by mid-night walks. It was a strange road. Wild all right, but paved and close enough to the city that there were occasional street lamps. All uphill and downhill, with bits of forest leaning in over it, till you walked in a tunnel of trees. Then suddenly you were in the marsh, and the road ended at an old, unused wharf.

"A place to be alone. A place to walk and think. A place for shadows to stretch   35
ahead of you from one dim lamp to another and spring back as you reached the next. I have seen them get tall, tall, but never like that night. It was like a road into space."

"Cold?" I asked.   36

"No. I shouldn't have said 'space.' It gives the wrong effect. Not cold. Spring.   37
Frog time. The first warmth, and the leaves coming. A little fog in the hollows. The way they like it then in the wet leaves and bogs. No moon, though; secretive and dark, with just those street lamps wandered out from the town. I often wondered what graft had brought them there. They shone on nothing—except my walks at midnight and the journeys of toads, but still . . ."

"Yes?" I prompted, as he paused.   38

"I was just thinking. The web of things. A politician in town gets a rake-off for   39
selling useless lights on a useless road. If it hadn't been for that, I might not have seen them. I might not even have skipped. Or, if I had, the effect—How can you tell about such things afterwards? Was the effect heightened? Did it magnify their power? Who is to say?"

"The skip?" I said, trying to keep things casual. "I don't understand. You mean,   40
just skipping? Jumping?"

Something like a twinkle came into his eyes for a moment. "Just that," he said.   41
"No more. You are a young man. Impulsive? You should understand."

"I'm afraid—" I began to counter.   42

"But of course," he cried pleasantly. "I forget. You were not there. So how   43
could I expect you to feel or know about this skipping. Look, look at me now. A
sober man, eh?"

I nodded. "Dignified," I said cautiously.   44

"Very well. But, young man, there is a time to skip. On country roads in the   45
spring. It is not necessary that there be girls. You will skip without them. You will
skip because something within you knows the time—frog time. Then you will
skip."

"Then I will skip," I repeated, hypnotized. Mad or not, there was a force in   46
Albert Dreyer. Even there under the club lights, the night damp of an unused road
began to gather.

IV

"It was a late spring," he said. "Fog and mist in those hollows in a way I had   47
never seen before. And frogs, of course. Thousands of them, and twenty species,
trilling, gurgling, and grunting in as many keys. The beautiful keen silver piping of
spring peepers arousing as the last ice leaves the ponds—if you have heard that
after a long winter alone, you will never forget it." He paused and leaned forward,
listening with such an intent inner ear that one could almost hear that far-off silver
piping from the wet meadows of the man's forgotten years.

I rattled my glass uneasily, and his eyes came back to me.   48

"They come out then," he said more calmly. "All amphibia have to return to   49
the water for mating and egg laying. Even toads will hop miles across country to
streams and waterways. You don't see them unless you go out at night in the right
places as I did, but that night—

"Well, it was unusual, put it that way, as an understatement. It was late, and   50
the creatures seemed to know it. You could feel the forces of mighty and archaic
life welling up from the very ground. The water was pulling them—not water as we
know it, but the mother, the ancient life force, the thing that made us in the days of
creation, and that lurks around us still, unnoticed in our sterile cities.

"I was no different from any other young fool coming home on a spring night,   51
except that as a student of life, and of amphibia in particular, I was, shall we say,
more aware of the creatures. I had performed experiments"—the black glove ges-
tured before my eyes. "I was, as it proved, susceptible.

"It began on that lost stretch of roadway leading to the river, and it began   52
simply enough. All around, under the street lamps, I saw little frogs and big frogs
hopping steadily toward the river. They were going in my direction.

"At that time I had my whimsies, and I was spry enough to feel the tug of that   53
great movement. I joined them. There was no mystery about it. I simply began to
skip, to skip gaily, and enjoy the great bobbing shadow I created as I passed onward with that leaping host all headed for the river.

"Now skipping along a wet pavement in spring is infectious, particularly going   54
downhill, as we were. The impulse to take mightier leaps, to soar farther, increases
progressively. The madness worked into me. I bounded till my lungs labored, and
my shadow, at first my own shadow, bounded and labored with me.

"It was only midway in my flight that I began to grow conscious that I was not   55
alone. The feeling was not strong at first. Normally a sober pedestrian, I was ecstat-
ically preoccupied with the discovery of latent stores of energy and agility which I
had not suspected in my subdued existence.

"It was only as we passed under a street lamp that I noticed, beside my own bob-   56
bing shadow, another great, leaping grotesquerie that had an uncanny suggestion
of the frog world about it. The shocking aspect of the thing lay in its size, and the fact
that, judging from the shadow, it was soaring higher and more gaily than myself.

" 'Very well,' you will say"—and here Dreyer paused and looked at me toler-   57
antly—" 'Why didn't you turn around? That would be the scientific thing to do.'

"It would be the scientific thing to do, young man, but let me tell you it is not   58
done—not on an empty road at midnight—not when the shadow is already beside
your shadow and is joined by another, and then another.

"No, you do not pause. You look neither to left nor right, for fear of what you   59
might see there. Instead, you dance on madly, hopelessly. Plunging higher, higher,
in the hope the shadows will be left behind, or prove to be only leaves dancing,
when you reach the next street light. Or that whatever had joined you in this midnight bacchanal will take some other pathway and depart.

"You do not look—you cannot look—because to do so is to destroy the uni-   60
verse in which we move and exist and have our transient being. You dare not look,
because, beside the shadows, there now comes to your ears the loose-limbed slap
of giant batrachian feet, not loud, not loud at all, but there, definitely there, behind
you at your shoulder, plunging with the utter madness of spring, their rhythm
entering your bones until you too are hurtling upward in some gigantic ecstasy that
it is not given to mere flesh and blood to long endure.

"I was part of it, part of some mad dance of the elementals behind the show of   61
things. Perhaps in that night of archaic and elemental passion, that festival of the
wetlands, my careless hopping passage under the street lights had called them,
attracted their attention, brought them leaping down some fourth-dimensional
roadway into the world of time.

"Do not suppose for a single moment I thought so coherently then. My lungs   62
were bursting, my physical self exhausted, but I sprang, I hurtled, I flung myself
onward in a company I could not see, that never outpaced me, but that swept me
with the mighty ecstasies of a thousand springs, and that bore me onward exult-
antly past my own doorstep, toward the river, toward some pathway long forgotten,
toward some unforgettable destination in the wetlands and the spring.

"Even as I leaped, I was changing. It was this, I think, that stirred the last   63
remnants of human fear and human caution that I still possessed. My will was in
abeyance; I could not stop. Furthermore, certain sensations, hypnotic or otherwise, suggested to me that my own physical shape was modifying, or about to
change. I was leaping with a growing ease. I was—

"It was just then that the wharf lights began to show. We were approaching the   64
end of the road, and the road, as I have said, ended in the river. It was this, I
suppose, that startled me back into some semblance of human terror. Man is a land
animal. He does not willingly plunge off wharfs at midnight in the monstrous company of amphibious shadows.

"Nevertheless their power held me. We pounded madly toward the wharf, and   65
under the light that hung above it, and the beam that made a cross. Part of me
struggled to stop, and part of me hurtled on. But in that final frenzy of terror
before the water below engulfed me I shrieked, '*Help! In the name of God, help
me! In the name of Jesus, stop!*' "

Dreyer paused and drew in his chair a little closer under the light. Then he   66
went on steadily.

"I was not, I suppose, a particularly religious man, and the cries merely re-   67
vealed the extremity of my terror. Nevertheless this is a strange thing, and whether
it involves the crossed beam, or the appeal to a Christian deity, I will not attempt to
answer.

"In one electric instant, however, I was free. It was like the release from de-   68
moniac possession. One moment I was leaping in an inhuman company of elder
things, and the next moment I was a badly shaken human being on a wharf. Strang-
est of all, perhaps, was the sudden silence of that midnight hour. I looked down in
the circle of the arc light, and there by my feet hopped feebly some tiny froglets of
the great migration. There was nothing impressive about them, but you will understand that I drew back in revulsion. I have never been able to handle them for
research since. My work is in the past."

He paused and drank, and then, seeing perhaps some lingering doubt and   69
confusion in my eyes, held up his black-gloved hand and deliberately pinched off
the glove.

A man should not do that to another man without warning, but I suppose he   70
felt I demanded some proof. I turned my eyes away. One does not like a webbed
batrachian hand on a human being.

As I rose embarrassedly, his voice came up to me from the depths of the chair.   71

"It is not the hand," Dreyer said. "It is the question of choice. Perhaps I was a   72
coward, and ill prepared. Perhaps"—his voice searched uneasily among his memories—"perhaps I should have taken them and that springtime without question.
Perhaps I should have trusted them and hopped onward. Who knows? They were
gay enough, at least."

He sighed and set down his glass and stared so intently into empty space that,   73
seeing I was forgotten, I tiptoed quietly away.

Rhetorical Focus:

1. Eiseley introduces this essay with a realistic scene in which he is giving a
   lecture on Indian superstitions and is asked a question by the mysterious
   Dreyer: "The Indians believe it, but do *you* believe it?" Why does Eiseley
   include this episode in the essay?
2. Why is it important that the tale of the dancing frogs is told by someone
   other than Eiseley himself?
3. Is this a nonfiction sketch, an essay, or a short story? Be specific about how
   you defend your choice, considering, for example, organization, theme,
   point of view, characterization, dialogue.

Thematic Focus:

1. The opposition of the scientific and the unscientific recurs throughout Eiseley's essay. Do you think it is incompatible for a scientist to believe in supernatural phenomena? Why or why not? Does the narrator end up a believer? Do you? If not, how might you explain what happens?
2. Eiseley remarks on the fact that Dreyer had gone to an isolated house to study amphibia in the wake of his young wife's death, "in grief, loneliness and despair." How does this information bear on the rest of the essay? What other information about Dreyer does Eiseley give us, which might affect our reading of the story?
3. In describing his frenzied midnight dance, Dreyer describes enormous shadows of creatures that were dancing beside him. He never actually looked at them, however: "You do not look—you cannot look—because to do so is to destroy the universe in which we move and exist and have our transient being." What are the implications of this sentence for scientists?

Objections to Astrology
Bart J. Bok

Bart J. Bok (1906–1983) was born in the Netherlands and was for years a professor of astronomy at Harvard and the University of Arizona. He was a world-famous authority on the age of the galaxy. With his wife, Priscilla, he wrote *The Milky Way* (5th edition, 1981), which is still considered a classic. He is the principal author of the following essay which he wrote with L. Jerome and P. Kurtz. It was then signed by almost 200 scientists.

Reflections Before Reading

Do you read the horoscopes in the daily newspaper? If not, do you think there is something wrong with people who do? Do you think there is any validity to the notion that your destiny and personality are determined by the position of the stars on the day you were born?

"Objections to Astrology" by Bart J. Bok, Lawrence E. Jerome, Paul Kurtz, THE HUMANIST, September/October, 1975. Copyright (c) 1975 by THE HUMANIST. Reprinted by permission.

Scientists in a variety of fields have become concerned about the increased accep-   1
tance of astrology in many parts of the world. We, the undersigned—astronomers,
astrophysicists, and scientists in other fields—wish to caution the public against
the unquestioning acceptance of the predictions and advice given privately and
publicly by astrologers. Those who wish to believe in astrology should realize that
there is no scientific foundation for its tenets.

In ancient times people believed in the predictions and advice of astrologers   2
because astrology was part and parcel of their magical world view. They looked
upon celestial objects as abodes or omens of the Gods and, thus, intimately connected with events here on earth; they had no concept of the vast distances from
the earth to the planets and stars. Now that these distances can and have been
calculated, we can see how infinitesimally small are the gravitational and other
effects produced by the distant planets and the far more distant stars. It is simply a
mistake to imagine that the forces exerted by stars and planets at the moment of
birth can in any way shape our futures. Neither is it true that the position of distant
heavenly bodies make certain days or periods more favorable to particular kinds of
action, or that the sign under which one was born determines one's compatibility
or incompatibility with other people.

Why do people believe in astrology? In these uncertain times many long for   3
the comfort of having guidance in making decisions. They would like to believe in a
destiny predetermined by astral forces beyond their control. However, we must all
face the world, and we must realize that our futures lie in ourselves, and not in the
stars.

One would imagine, in this day of widespread enlightenment and education,   4
that it would be unnecessary to debunk beliefs based on magic and superstition.
Yet, acceptance of astrology pervades modern society. We are especially disturbed
by the continued uncritical dissemination of astrological charts, forecasts, and
horoscopes by the media and by otherwise reputable newspapers, magazines, and
book publishers. This can only contribute to the growth of irrationalism and obscu-
rantism. We believe that the time has come to challenge directly, and forcefully,
the pretentious claims of astrological charlatans.

It should be apparent that these individuals who continue to have faith in   5
astrology do so in spite of the fact that there is no verified scientific basis for their
beliefs, and indeed that there is strong evidence to the contrary.

Rhetorical Focus

1. What is the assertion made here about astrology? Does the writer give
   good reasons why we should believe this assertion?
2. Is the opposition treated fairly here? What is your response to this approach?
3. If you were giving advice to Bok and his fellow scientists on how to improve
   the credibility of the persona, what words would you suggest be changed?

Thematic Focus

1. Does everything you believe about the world have a scientific foundation? Should it?
2. Would these scientists ask why people believe in religion? Is there a scientific basis for religions?
3. Why do you think intelligent people believe in astrology?

Suggestions for Writing

1. Write an explanation for what happens in "The Dance of the Frogs" from the point of view of Professor Bok and his fellow scientists.
2. Write a brief rebuttal to "Objections to Astrology" from the point of view of the narrator in Eiseley's essay/story.
3. Can you remember some event in your life that you cannot fully explain, something not easily affirmed or denied by reason and science? Write a narrative using that event as a focus.

ANIMAL RIGHTS

From all appearances, Americans love their pets. Dogs and cats live comfortably in our houses, sleep in our beds, receive medical care at our expense. They are often considered members of the family, entitled to affection and consideration, even privacy. In some cases they go to school, to psychologists, to motels for animals. When they die, they are buried with solemn rituals. Later, we grieve for them, miss them. On the other hand, millions of mammals, including cats and dogs, are routinely used in experiments for the pet industry, zoos, pharmaceutical manufacturers, and university researchers. We seem to give animals a special place in our lives, yet we also seem not to notice the numerous ways they are abused and exploited.

Our culture has conflicting attitudes toward animals. We have societies that protect them, yet we also eat them. Most people, however, make a sharp distinction between dogs and chickens, between pets and food. Ever since the Middle Ages, there has been a hierarchy of animals in the minds of humans: mammals at the top; fish in the middle; insects and other invertebrates, perhaps, at the bottom. The reasons for these distinctions and contradictions are difficult to grasp. Until recently, such musings were not thought to be serious concerns for intellectuals. That has now changed.

Philosophers have, in fact, turned their attention to the ways our culture thinks of animals and the ways science treats not only monkeys and cats, but all species. The essays in this section review some of that thinking, forcing us to consider what rights, if any, animals should have in our society. Tom Regan takes the position that we have no right to harm other animals, while David Quammen wonders whether Regan himself is not caught up in the centuries-old belief that humans must always come first.

Animal Rights, Human Wrongs

Tom Regan

Tom Regan (1938–   ) is a professor at North Carolina State University. He is an animal rights activist best known for his 1983 publication *The Case for Animal Rights*. The following excerpt is taken from his 1982 book *All That Dwell Therein*. It was originally a lecture given by Regan at a conference at Muhlenberg College in 1979.

Reflections Before Reading

Are animals treated fairly in our culture? Do we have any responsibility to see that all animals are treated equally? Do insects have any rights? rodents? plants? oysters? Would you equate animal abuse with racism or sexism?

At this moment workers on board the mother ship of a whaling fleet are disassembling the carcass of a whale. Though the species is officially protected by agreement of the member nations of the International Whaling Commission, it is not too fanciful to imagine the crew butchering a great blue whale, the largest creature ever known to have lived on the earth—larger than thirty elephants, larger even than three of the largest dinosaurs laid end to end. A good catch, this leviathan of the deep. And, increasingly, a rare one. For the great blue, like hundreds of other animal species, is endangered, may, in fact, already be beyond the point of recovery. 1

But the crew has other things on their mind. It will take hours of hard work to butcher the huge carcass, a process now carried out at sea. Nor is butchering at sea the only thing in whaling that has changed. The fabled days of a real hunt, of an individual Ahab pitted against a treacherous whale, must remain the work of fiction now. Whaling is applied technology, from the use of the most sophisticated sonar to on-board refrigeration, from tracking helicopters to explosive harpoons, the latter a technological advance that expedites a whale's death. Average time to 2 die: sometimes as long as twenty minutes; usually three to five. Here is one man's account of a whale's demise:

> The gun roars. The harpoon hurls through the air and the whale-line follows. There is a momentary silence, and then the muffled explosion as the time fuse functions and fragments the grenade. . . . There is now a fight between the mammal and the crew of the catching vessel—a fight to the death. It is a struggle that can have only one result. . . . Deep in the whale's vast body is the mortal wound, and even if it could shake off the harpoon it would be doomed. . . . A second harpoon buries itself just behind the dorsal fin . . . There is another dull explosion in the whale's vitals. Then comes a series of convulsions—a last despairing struggle. The whale spouts blood, keels slowly over and floats belly upward. It is dead.

For what? To what end? Why is this being done to the last remaining members of an irreplaceable species, certainly until recently, possibly at this very moment, by supposedly civilized men? For candle wax. For soap and oil. For pet food, margarine, fertilizer. For perfume.

In Thailand, at this moment, another sort of hunt, less technologically advanced, is in progress. The Thai hunter has hiked two miles through thick vegetation and now, with his keen vision, spots a female gibbon and her infant, sleeping high in a tree. Jean-Yves Domalain describes what follows: 3

> Down below, the hunter rams the double charge of gun-powder down the barrel with a thin iron rod, then the lead shot. The spark flashes from two flints, and the gun goes off in a cloud of white smoke. . . . Overhead there is an uproar. The female gibbon, mortally wounded, clings to life. She still has enough strength to make two gigantic leaps, her baby still clinging to the long hair of her left thigh. At the third leap she misses the branch she was aiming for, and in a final desperate effort manages to grasp a lower one; but her strength is ebbing away and she is unable to pull herself up. Slowly her fingers begin to loosen her grip. Death is there, staining her pale fur. The youngster flattens himself in terror against her bloodstained flank. Then comes the giddy plunge of a hundred feet or more, broken by a terrible rebound off a tree trunk.

The object of this hunt is not to kill the female gibbon, but to capture the baby. Unfortunately, in this case the infant's neck is broken by the fall, so the shots were wasted. The hunter will have to move on, seeking other prospects.

We are not dealing in fantasies when we consider the day's work of the Thai   4 hunter. Domalain makes it clear that both the method of capture (killing the mother to get the infant) and the results just seen (the death of both) are the rule rather than the exception in the case of gibbons. And chimpanzees. And tigers. And orangutans. And lions. Some estimate that for every one animal captured alive, ten have been killed. Domalain further states that for every ten captured only two will live on beyond a few months. The mortality rate stemming from hunts that aim to bring animals back alive thus is considerable.

Nor do we romanticize when we regard the female gibbon's weakening grip,   5 the infant's alarmed clutching, the bonds of surprise and terror that unite them as they begin their final descent. And for what? To what end? Why is this scene played out again and again? So that pet stores might sell "exotic animals." So that roadside zoos might offer "new attractions." So that the world's scientists might have "subjects" for their experiments.

Not far from here, perhaps at this moment, a rabbit makes a futile effort to 6 escape from a restraining device, called a stock, which holds the creature in place by clamping down around its neck. Immediately the reader thinks of trapping in the wild—that the stock must be a sort of trap, like the infamous leg-hold trap— but this is not so. The stock is a handmaiden of science, and the rabbit confined by it is not in the wild but in a research laboratory. If we look closely, we will see that one of the rabbit's eyes is ulcerated. It is badly inflamed, an open, running sore. After some hours the sore increases in size until barely half the eye is visible. In a few days the eye will become permanently blind. Sometimes the eye is literally burned out of its socket.

This rabbit is a research subject in what is known as the Draize test, named 7 after its inventor. This rabbit, and hundreds like it, is being used because rabbits happen not to have tear ducts and so cannot flush irritants from their eyes. Nor can they dilute them. The Draize test proceeds routinely as follows: concentrated so- lutions of a substance are made to drip into one of the rabbit's eyes; the other eye, a sort of control, is left untroubled. Swelling, redness, destruction of iris or cornea, loss of vision are measured and the substance's eye-irritancy is thereby scientifi- cally established.

What is this substance which in concentrated form invades the rabbit's eye? 8 Probably a cosmetic, a new variety of toothpaste, shampoo, mouthwash, talcum, hand lotion, eye cosmetic, face cream, hair conditioner, perfume, cologne. Why? To what end? In the name of what purpose does this unanesthetized rabbit endure the slow burning destruction of its eye? So that a researcher might establish the eye-irritancy of mouthwash and talc, toothpaste and cologne.

A final individual bids for our attention at this moment. A bobbie calf is a male 9 calf born in a dairy herd. Since the calf cannot give milk, something must be done with it. A common practice is to sell it as a source of veal, as in veal Parmigi- ana. To make this commercially profitable the calf must be raised in highly un- natural conditions. Otherwise the youngster would romp and play, as is its wont; equally bad, it would forage and consume roughage. From a businessman's point of view, this is detrimental to the product. The romping produces muscle, which makes for tough meat, and the roughage will contain natural sources of iron, which will turn the calf's flesh red. But studies show that consumers have a de- cided preference for pale veal. So the calf is kept permanently indoors, in a stall too narrow for it to turn around, frequently tethered to confine it further, its short life lived mostly in the dark on a floor of wood slats, its only contact with other living beings coming when it is fed and when, at the end, it is transported to the slaugh- terhouse.

Envision then the tethered calf, unable to turn around, unable to sit down 10 without hunching up, devoid of companionship, its natural urges to romp and for- age denied, fed a wholly liquid diet deliberately deficient in iron so as not to com- promise its pale flesh but to keep it anemic. For what? To what end? In the name of what purpose does the calf live so? So that humans might have pale veal!

          ◦   ◦   ◦

It would be grotesque to suggest that the whale, the rabbit, the gibbon, the   11
bobbie calf, the millions of animals brought so much pain and death at the hands of
humans are not harmed, for harm is not restricted to human beings. They are
harmed, harmed in a literal, not a metaphorical sense. They are made to endure
what is detrimental to their welfare, even death. Those who would harm them,
therefore, must justify doing so. Thus, members of the whaling industry, the cosmetics industry, the farming industry, the network of hunters–exporters–import-
ers must justify the harm they bring animals in a way that is consistent with recognizing the animals' right not to be harmed. To produce such a justification it is not
enough to argue that people profit, satisfy their curiosity, or derive pleasure from
allowing animals to be treated in these ways. These facts are not the morally relevant ones. Rather, what must be shown is that overriding the right of animals not to
be harmed is justified because of further facts. For example, because we have very
good reason to believe that overriding the individual's right prevents, and is the
only realistic way to prevent, vastly greater harm to other innocent individuals.

Let us ask the whaling industry whether they have so justified their trade.   12
Have they made their case in terms of the morally relevant facts? Our answer must
be: No! And the cosmetic industry? No! The farmers who raise veal calves? No!
The retailer of exotic animals? No! A thousand times we must say: No! I do not say
that they cannot possibly justify what they do. The individual's right not to be
harmed, we have argued, almost always trumps the interests of the group, but it is
possible that such a right must sometimes give way. Possibly the rights of animals
must sometimes give way to human interests. It would be a mistake to rule this
possibility out. Nevertheless, the onus of justification must be borne by those who
cause the harm to show that they do not violate the rights of the individuals involved.

We allow then that it is *possible* that harming animals might be justified; but   13
we also maintain that those harming animals typically fail to show that the harm
caused is *actually* justified. A further question we must ask ourselves is what, morally speaking, we ought to do in such a situation? Reflection on comparable situations involving human beings will help make the answer clear.

Consider racism and sexism. Imagine that slavery is an institution of the day   14
and that it is built on racist or sexist lines. Blacks or women are assigned the rank of
slave. Suppose we are told that in extreme circumstances even slavery might conceivably be justified, and that we ought not to object to it or try to bring it down,
even though no one has shown that it is actually justified in the present case. Well,
I do not believe for a moment that we would accept such an attempt to dissuade us
from toppling the institution of slavery. Not for a moment would we accept the
general principle involved here, that an institution actually is justified because it
might conceivably be justified. We would accept the quite different principle that
we are morally obligated to oppose any practice that appears to violate rights unless we are shown that it really does not do so. To be satisfied with anything less is
to cheapen the value attributable to the victims of the practice.

Exactly the same line of reasoning applies in the case where animals are re-   15
garded as so many dispensable commodities, models, subjects, and the like. We

ought not to back away from bringing these industries and related practices to a halt just because it is *possible* that the harm caused to the animals *might* be justified. If we do, we fail to mean it when we say that animals are not mere things, that they are the subjects of a life that is better or worse for them, that they have inherent value. As in the comparable case involving harm to human beings, our duty is to act, to do all that we can to put an end to the harm animals are made to endure. That the animals themselves cannot speak out on their own behalf, that they cannot organize, petition, march, exert political pressure, or raise our level of consciousness—all this does not weaken our obligation to act on their behalf. If anything, their impotence makes our obligation the greater.

We can hear, if we will but listen, the muffled detonation of the explosive   16
harpoon, the sharp crack of the Thai hunter's rifle, the drip of the liquid as it strikes the rabbit's eye, the bobbie calf's forlorn sigh. We can see, if we will but look, the last convulsive gasps of the great blue whale, the dazed terror of the gibbons' eyes, the frenzied activity of the rabbit's feet, the stark immobility of the bobbie calf. But not at this moment only. Tomorrow, other whales, other rabbits will be made to suffer; tomorrow, other gibbons, other calves will be killed, and others the day after. And others, stretching into the future. All this we know with certainty. All this and more, incalculably more, *will* go on, if we do not act today, as act we must. Our respect for the value and rights of the animals cannot be satisfied with anything less.

Rhetorical Focus

1. Regan begins his essay with a rhetorical strategy calculated to persuade. What is that strategy, and do you think it is effective?
2. Regan's essay is filled with questions to which he provides the answers. Find three examples of such questions. How does Regan use these questions and responses to mold his audience's attitude? Does it work? How did you respond?
3. Some might argue that Regan's essay is an appeal to the emotions, especially the last paragraph. Do you agree? Do you think this is a valid method of persuasion? Are there more effective strategies?

Thematic Focus

1. Regan acknowledges the possibility that animal rights must sometimes yield to human interests, but he argues that "the onus of justification must be borne by those who cause the harm." What sort of justifications might there be for violating animal rights?
2. One of the basic issues underlying the animal rights movement seems to be the definition of the word *harm*. How does Regan define harm? Do you think he is right? Why or why not?

3. Regan illustrates the animal rights issue by comparing it to the questions of slavery and sexism. Do you find this comparison compelling? Are the rights of minorities such as blacks and women on a par with the rights of animals? Explain.

Animal Rights and Beyond

David Quammen

David Quammen (b. 1948–   ) makes it quite clear that he is *not* a scientist. He is, however, a writer with a bent for science and nature, and it is his mission to write about these subjects in a lively, readable style. He writes a monthly column called "Natural Acts" for *Outside* magazine, and it is from a collection of these essays (also entitled *Natural Acts*) that the following selection on animal rights is drawn.

Reflections Before Reading

Are animals on earth for our own use? Do humans have responsibility for the living conditions of animals or of plants? If you think animals do have some rights, such as freedom from torture, how far are you willing to extend those rights? Does everything that is alive have some claim to exist? How can humans decide which animals (or plants) to value?

Do non-human animals have rights? Should we humans feel morally bound to   1 exercise consideration for the lives and well-being of individual members of other animal species? If so, how much consideration, and by what logic? Is it permissible to torture and kill? Is it permissible to kill cleanly, without prolonged pain? To abuse or exploit without killing? For a moment, don't think about whales or wolves or the California condor; don't think about the cat or the golden retriever with whom you share your house. Think about chickens. Think about laboratory monkeys and then think about lab rats and then also think about lab frogs. Think about scallops. Think about mosquitoes.

It's a Gordian question, by my lights, but one not very well suited to Alexandrian answers. Some people would disagree, judging the matter simply enough settled, one way or the other. *Of course they have rights. Of course they don't.* I say beware any such snappy, steel-trap thinking. Some folk would even—this late in the evolution of human sensibility—call it a frivolous question, a time-filling diversion for emotional hemophiliacs and cranks. *Women's rights, gay rights, now for Christ sake they want ANIMAL rights.* Notwithstanding the ridicule, the strong biases toward each side, it is certainly a serious philosophical issue, important and tricky, with almost endless implications for the way we humans live and should live on this planet.

Philosophers of earlier ages, if they touched the subject at all, were likely to be dismissive. Thomas Aquinas announced emphatically that animals "are intended for man's use in the natural order. Hence it is no wrong for man to make use of them, either by killing or in any other way whatever." Descartes held that animals are merely machines. As late as 1901, a moral logician named Joseph Rickaby (who happened to be a Jesuit, but don't necessarily hold that against him) declared: "Brute beasts, not having understanding and therefore not being persons, cannot have any rights. The conclusion is clear." Maybe not quite so clear. Recently, just during the past decade, professional academic philosophers have at last begun to address the matter more open-mindedly.

Two thinkers in particular have been influential: an Australian named Peter Singer, an American named Tom Regan. In 1975 Singer published a book titled *Animal Liberation*, which stirred up the debate among his colleagues and is still treated as a landmark. Eight years later Tom Regan published *The Case for Animal Rights*, a more thorough and ponderous opus that stands now as a sort of companion piece to the Singer book. In between there came a number of other discussions of animal rights—including a collection of essays edited jointly by Singer and Regan. Despite the one-time collaboration, Peter Singer and Tom Regan represent two distinct schools of thought: They reach similar conclusions about the obligations of humans to other animals, but the moral logic is very different, and possibly also the implications. Both men have produced some formidable work and both, to my simple mind, show some shocking limitations of vision.

I've spent the past week amid these books, Singer's and Regan's and the rest. It has been an edifying experience, and now I'm more puzzled than ever. I keep thinking about monkeys and frogs and mosquitoes and—sorry, but I'm quite serious—carrots.

Peter Singer's view is grounded upon the work of Jeremy Bentham, that eighteenth-century British philosopher generally known as the founder of utilitarianism. "The greatest good for the greatest number" is a familiar cartoon version of what, according to Bentham, should be achieved by the ethical ordering of society and behavior. A more precise summary is offered by Singer: "In other words, the interests of every being affected by an action are to be taken into account and given the same weight as the like interests of any other being." If this much is granted, the crucial next point is deciding what things constitute *interests* and who or what qualifies as a *being*. Evidently Bentham did not have just humans in mind. Back in 1789, optimistically and perhaps presciently, he wrote: "The day *may* come when the rest of the animal creation may acquire those rights which never could have been withholden from them but by the hand of tyranny." Most philosophers of his day were inclined (as most in our day are still inclined) to extend moral coverage only to humans, because only humans (supposedly) are rational and communicative. Jeremy Bentham took exception: "The question is not, Can they *reason?* nor, Can they *talk?* but, Can they *suffer?*" On this crucial point, Peter Singer follows Bentham.

The capacity to suffer, says Singer, is what separates a being with legitimate   7
interests from an entity without interests. A stone has no interests that must be respected, because it cannot suffer. A mouse can suffer; therefore it has interests and those interests must be weighed in the moral balance. Fine, that much seems simple enough. Certain people of sophistic or Skinnerian bent would argue that there is no proof a mouse can in fact suffer, that it's merely an anthropomorphic assumption; but since each of us has no proof that *anyone* else actually suffers besides ourselves, we are willing, most of us, to grant the assumption. More problematic is that very large gray area between stones and mice.

Peter Singer declares: "If a being suffers, there can be no moral justification   8
for disregarding that suffering, or for refusing to count it equally with the like suffering of any other being. But the converse of this is also true. If a being is not capable of suffering, or of enjoyment, there is nothing to take into account." Where is the boundary? Where falls the line between creatures who suffer and those that are incapable? Singer's cold philosophic eye travels across the pageant of living species—chickens suffer, mice suffer, fish suffer, um, lobsters most likely suffer, *look alive, you other creatures!*—and his damning stare lands on the oyster.

No I'm not making this up. The oyster, by Singer's best guess, doesn't suffer.   9
Its nervous system lacks the requisite complexity. Therefore, while lobsters and crawfish and shrimp possess inviolable moral status, the oyster has none. It is a difficult judgment, Singer admits, by no means an infallible one, but "somewhere between a shrimp and an oyster seems as good a place to draw the line as any, and better than most."

Moral philosophy, no one denies, is an imperfect science.   10

Tom Regan takes exception with Singer on two important points. First, he   11
disavows the utilitarian framework, with its logic that abuse or killing of animals by humans is wrong because it yields a net *overall* decrease in welfare, among all beings who qualify for moral status. No, argues Regan, that logic is false and pernicious. The abuse or killing is wrong in its *essence*—however the balance comes out on overall welfare—because it violates the rights of those individual animals. Individual rights, in other words, take precedence over the maximizing of the common good. Second, in Regan's opinion the capacity to suffer is not what marks the elect. Mere suffering is not sufficient. Instead he posits the concept of *inherent*

value, a complex and magical quality possessed by some living creatures but not others.

A large portion of Regan's book is devoted to arguing toward this concept. He   12
is more uncompromisingly protective of certain creatures—those with rights—
than Singer, but he is also more selective; the hull of his ark is sturdier, but the
gangplank is narrower. According to Regan, individual beings possess inherent
value (and therefore inviolable rights) if they "are able to perceive and remember;
if they have beliefs, desires, and preferences; if they are able to act intentionally in
pursuit of their desires or goals; if they are sentient and have an emotional life; if
they have a sense of the future, including a sense of their own future; if they have a
psychophysical identity over time; and if they have an individual experiential welfare that is logically independent of their utility for, and the interests of, others." So
Tom Regan is not handing rights around profligately, to every cute little beast that
crawls over his foot. In fact we all probably know a few humans who, at least on a
bad night, might have trouble meeting those standards. But how would Regan
himself apply them? Where does he see the line falling? Who qualifies for inherent
value, and what doesn't?

Like Singer, Regan has thought this point through. Based on his grasp of biol-   13
ogy and ethology, he is willing to grant rights to "mentally normal mammals of a
year or more."

Also like Singer, he admits that the judgment is not infallible: "Because we are   14
uncertain where the boundaries of consciousness lie, it is not unreasonable to advocate a policy that bespeaks moral caution." So chickens and frogs should be
given the benefit of the doubt, as should all other animals that bear a certain degree of anatomical and physiological resemblance to us mentally normal mammals.

But Regan does not specify just what degree.   15

The books by Singer and Regan leave me with two very separate reactions.   16
The first combines admiration and gratitude. These men are applying the methods
of systematic philosophy to an important and much-neglected question. Furthermore, they don't content themselves with just understanding and describing a pattern of gross injustice; they also emphatically say *Let's stop it!* They are fighting a
good fight. Peter Singer's book in particular has focused attention on the outrageous practices that are routine in American factory farms, in "psychological" ex-
perimentation, in research on the toxicity of cosmetics. Do you know how chickens
are dealt with on the large poultry operations? How veal is produced? How the
udders of dairy cows are kept flowing? Do you know the sorts of ingenious but
pointless torment that thousands of monkeys and millions of rats endure, each
year, to fill the time and the dissertations of uninspired graduate students? If you
don't, by all means read Singer's *Animal Liberation*.

The second reaction is negative. Peter Singer and Tom Regan, it seems to me,   17
share a breathtaking smugness and myopia not too dissimilar to the brand they so
forcefully condemn. Theirs is a righteous and vigorous smugness, not a passive and
unreflective one. But still.

Singer inveighs against a sin he labels *speciesism*—discrimination against cer-   18
tain creatures based solely upon the species to which they belong. Regan uses a

slightly less confused and less clumsy phrase, *human chauvinism,* to indicate roughly the same thing. Both of them arrive (supposedly by sheer logic) at the position that vegetarianism is morally obligatory: To kill and eat a "higher" animal represents absolute violation of one being's rights; to kill and eat a plant evidently violates nothing at all. Both Singer and Regan claim to disparage the notion—pervasive in Western philosophy since Protagoras—that "Man is the measure of all things." Both argue elaborately against anthropocentrism, while creating new moral frameworks that are also decidedly anthropocentric. Make no mistake: Man is still the measure, for Singer and Regan. The test for inherent value has changed only slightly. Instead of asking *Is the creature a human?,* they simply ask *How similar to human is similar enough?*

Peter Singer explains that shrimp deserve brotherly treatment but oysters, so different from us, are fair game for the gumbo. In Tom Regan's vocabulary, the redwood tree is an "inanimate natural object," sharing that category with clouds and rocks. But some simple minds would say: Life is life.   19

Rhetorical Focus

1. The essay opens with a series of questions. Does the essay answer these either directly or indirectly? Is there one thesis to this essay? Where is it? Could it be moved?
2. In his essay, Quammen summarizes the arguments of Pete Singer, an Australian animal rights activist. Singer claims that the important issue is whether a given species has the capacity to *suffer* and decides that while lobsters and shrimp do suffer, oysters do not. Does Quammen find this position to be reasonable? Explain. How does he make his opinion of Singer's argument clear to the reader? Is this effective?
3. Examine the way Quammen uses quotes in paragraphs 3 and 5. Can you make some generalizations?

Thematic Focus

1. Quammen notes that some people consider the question of animal rights to be a "frivolous question, a time-filling diversion for emotional hemophiliacs and cranks." Do you think these people have a point? Do you think animal rights is a legitimate political issue? Why or why not?
2. Quammen claims that the issue of animal rights is "a serious philosophical issue . . . with almost endless implications for the way we humans live and should live on this planet." In what way is this issue a philosophical one? What are some of the philosophical questions that arise in discussions about animal rights? Which of these questions do you feel is most important?
3. Quammen concludes his essay by pointing out what he considers an inconsistency in the arguments of both Singer and Regan. Each writer argues that vegetarianism is "morally obligatory." Quammen wonders, however, why the two authors feel it wrong to kill and eat animals yet have no diffi-

culty eating plants. "Life is life," says Quammen. What is the point he is making? What implications does it have?

Suggestions for Writing

1. Write a position paper on this issue of animal rights. So far, Singer, Regan, and Quammen have carved out positions and given reasons. Where do you stand and why?
2. Recall some specific instances where animals played a part in your childhood. Group these together and write a generalization about children and animals.
3. Interview some students or faculty members about their views on animal rights. Write a brief report about your findings.

AIDS AND POLITICS

Diseases have always been more than a medical problem, more than just an infection in the body. Ever since the biblical plagues and surely during the Black Death, societies have thought of disease as an indication that something was morally or spiritually wrong, perhaps that some religious or political principle was being violated. In *Oedipus Rex,* for example, the city of Thebes is suffering from a plague because their king has inadvertently married his mother. It was not uncommon then to think that the natural world and the moral universe were closely linked.

Even in the modern era, illness has often been seen as a form of punishment. This connection seems to intensify when sexual behavior is involved; consequently, syphilis and AIDS have clearly been associated with something immoral. They are not simply illnesses like a cold or the flu, but something more sinister, as if a particular group's idea of what a sin is could bring down upon a victim a terrible retribution from an angry god. Even the medical establishment, for all its apparent objectivity, has been greatly affected by our culture's inability to separate illness and sin, disease and morality. Some doctors, for example, refuse to treat AIDS patients.

Because recent discussions surrounding AIDS have often been irrational, William Buckley attempts to argue his rather extreme position in measured tones. Susan Sontag, politically the opposite of Buckley, tries to find cultural understanding in the language surrounding the AIDS controversy. Try to locate your own feelings in these two essays that demonstrate the powerful connection between disease and ideology.

Identify All the Carriers

William F. Buckley, Jr.

William F. Buckley, Jr. (b. 1925) is one of America's most influential essayists, well-known for his provocative opinions and politics. He founded and for years edited the conservative journal *The National Review;* he now writes a syndicated newspaper column called "On the Right." Although he is best known for his political books and essays, Buckley has also written books on sailing and numerous spy novels. Whatever one's view of Buckley's political orientation, it cannot be denied that he is usually a provocative and incisive thinker. The following editorial first appeared in *The New York Times* on March 18, 1986.

Reflections Before Reading

Do you think AIDS patients should be publicly identified in some way in order to protect other citizens? When you hear that someone has AIDS, what is your response? How do you think our culture has responded to AIDS? To cancer?

I have read and listened, and I think now that I can convincingly crystallize the 1 thoughts chasing about in the minds of, first, those whose concern with AIDS victims is based primarily on a concern for them and for the maintenance of the most rigid standards of civil liberties and personal privacy, and, second, those whose anxiety to protect the public impels them to give subordinate attention to the civil amenities of those who suffer from AIDS and primary attention to the safety of those who do not.

Arguments used by both sides are sometimes utilitarian, sometimes moral, 2 sometimes a little of each—and almost always a little elusive. Most readers will locate their own inclinations and priorities somewhere other than in the polar positions here put forward by design.

School A suspects, in the array of arguments of School B, a venture in ethical 3 opportunism. Look, they say, we have made enormous headway in the matter of civil rights for all, dislodging the straight-laced from mummified positions they inherited through eclectic superstitions ranging from the Bible's to Freud's. A generation ago, homosexuals lived mostly in the closet. Nowadays they take over cities and parade on Halloween and demand equal rights for themselves qua homosexuals, not merely as apparently disinterested civil libertarians.

Along comes AIDS, School A continues, and even though it is well known that   4
the virus can be communicated by infected needles, known also that heterosexuals can transmit the virus, still it is both a fact and the popular perception that AIDS is the special curse of the homosexual, transmitted through anal sex between males. And if you look hard, you will discern that little smirk on the face of the man oh-so-concerned about public health. He is looking for ways to safeguard the public, sure, but he is by no means reluctant, in the course of doing so, to sound an invidious tocsin whose clamor is a call to undo all the understanding so painfully cultivated over a generation by those who have fought for the privacy of their bedroom. What School B is really complaining about is the extension of civil rights to homosexuals.

School A will not say all that in words quite so jut-jawed, but it plainly feels   5
that no laws or regulations should be passed that have the effect of identifying the AIDS carrier. It isn't, School A concedes, as if AIDS were transmitted via public drinking fountains. But any attempt to segregate the AIDS carrier is primarily an act of moral ostracism.

School B does in fact tend to disapprove forcefully of homosexuality, but tends   6
to approach the problem of AIDS empirically. It argues that acquired immune deficiency syndrome is potentially the most serious epidemic to have shown its face in this century. Summarizing currently accepted statistics, the *Economist* recently raised the possibility "that the AIDS virus will have killed more than 250,000 Americans in eight years' time." Moreover, if the epidemic extended to that point, it would burst through existing boundaries. There would then be "no guarantee that the disease will remain largely confined to groups at special risk, such as homosexuals, hemophiliacs and people who inject drugs intravenously. If AIDS were to spread through the general population, it would become a catastrophe." Accordingly, School B says, we face a utilitarian imperative, and this requires absolutely nothing less than the identification of the million-odd people who, the doctors estimate, are carriers.

How?   7

Well, the military has taken the first concrete step. Two million soldiers will be   8
given the blood test, and those who have AIDS will be discreetly discharged.

Discreetly, you say!   9

Hold on. I'm coming to that. You have the military making the first massive   10
move designed to identify AIDS sufferers—and, bear in mind, an AIDS carrier today is an AIDS carrier on the day of his death, which day, depending on the viral strain, will be two years from now or when he is threescore and 10. The next logical step would be to require of anyone who seeks a marriage license that he present himself not only with a Wassermann test but also an AIDS test.

But if he has AIDS, should he then be free to marry?   11

Only after the intended spouse is advised that her intended husband has   12
AIDS, and agrees to sterilization. We know already of children born with the disease, transmitted by the mother, who contracted it from the father.

What then would School B suggest for those who are not in the military and   13
who do not set out to get a marriage license? Universal testing?

Yes, in stages. But in rapid stages. The next logical enforcer is the insurance   14
company. Blue Cross, for instance, can reasonably require of those who wish to
join it a physical examination that requires tests. Almost every American, making
his way from infancy to maturity, needs to pass by one or another institutional
turnstile. Here the lady will spring out, her right hand on a needle, her left on a
computer, to capture a blood specimen.

Is it then proposed by School B that AIDS carriers should be publicly identi-   15
fied as such?

The evidence is not completely in as to the communicability of the disease.   16
But while much has been said that is reassuring, the moment has not yet come
when men and women of science are unanimously agreed that AIDS cannot be
casually communicated. Let us be patient on that score, pending any tilt in the
evidence: If the news is progressively reassuring, public identification would not
be necessary. If it turns in the other direction and AIDS develops among, say,
children who have merely roughhoused with other children who suffer from
AIDS, then more drastic segregation measures would be called for.

But if the time has not come, and may never come, for public identification,   17
what then of private identification?

Everyone detected with AIDS should be tatooed in the upper forearm, to   18
protect common-needle users, and on the buttocks, to prevent the victimization of
other homosexuals.

You have got to be kidding! That's exactly what we suspected all along! You are   19
calling for the return of the Scarlet Letter, but only for homosexuals!

Answer: The Scarlet Letter was designed to stimulate public obloquy. The   20
AIDS tattoo is designed for private protection. And the whole point of this is that
we are not talking about a kidding matter. Our society is generally threatened, and
in order to fight AIDS, we need the civil equivalent of universal military training.

Rhetorical Focus:

1. Buckley begins his essay as if to present both sides of a controversial issue.
   Does he, in fact, give School A and School B equally objective treatment?
2. One element of argumentation is to try to anticipate and answer the objections of your opposition. Does Buckley do this? Be specific. Do you have
   other objections to his plan? Is it possible that this is a satire? How could
   we tell?
3. What differences can you discern in the language Buckley uses when he
   argues for School A and when he argues for School B?

Thematic Focus:

1. School A, according to Buckley, considers the idea of segregating AIDS
   carriers to be "an act of moral ostracism." Why might such segregation be
   considered a moral issue?

2. Do you agree with Buckley that our society is generally threatened by AIDS? If so, do you think it is logical that we institute "the civil equivalent of universal military training"? What does this phrase mean?

3. Do you think the private rights of individuals should take precedence over the safety of the general population? Do you think it is necessary to identify AIDS carriers in any way? Can you think of alternatives to Buckley's suggested method of identification?

The Language of AIDS

Susan Sontag

Susan Sontag, one of America's most prominent intellectuals, was born in New York City in 1933. At the age of 18 years, she earned her BA in philosophy from the University of Chicago. She subsequently earned two master's degrees from Harvard: one in English and one in philosophy. She has taught religion, philosophy, and writing at Columbia, Rutgers, and the City University of New York.

Sontag is a prolific author. Her articles and reviews have appeared in *Harper's, The Atlantic, Partisan Review,* and *The New York Review of Books.* Her collections of essays (most notably *Against Interpretation* (1966) have demonstrated the diversity of her interests and have established her as a cultural critic. She is also a film critic and has written and directed several films.

The following excerpt is a chapter from a book-length essay titled *AIDS and Its Metaphors,* published in 1989. This book is Sontag's second consideration of disease; she wrote first about cancer in *Illness as Metaphor* in 1978.

Reflections Before Reading

Do you think some people believe disease to be a kind of retribution for some wrong committed by the victim? Do you think people who get AIDS in some way "deserve it"? Is this true for syphilis, heart attacks, obesity, lung cancer, depression?

The emergence of a new catastrophic epidemic, when for several decades it had   1
been confidently assumed that such calamities belonged to the past, would not be
enough to revive the moralistic inflation of an epidemic into a "plague." It was
necessary that the epidemic be one whose most common means of transmission is
sexual.

Cotton Mather called syphilis a punishment "which the Just Judgment of God   2
has reserved for our Late Ages." Recalling this and other nonsense uttered about
syphilis from the end of the fifteenth to the early twentieth centuries, one should
hardly be surprised that many want to view AIDS metaphorically—as, plaguelike,
a moral judgment on society. Professional fulminators can't resist the rhetorical
opportunity offered by a sexually transmitted disease that is lethal. Thus, the fact
that AIDS is predominantly a heterosexually transmitted illness in the countries
where it first emerged in epidemic form has not prevented such guardians of public morals as Jesse Helms and Norman Podhoretz from depicting it as a visitation
specially aimed at (and deservedly incurred by) Western homosexuals, while another Reagan-era celebrity, Pat Buchanan, orates about "AIDS and Moral Bank-
ruptcy," and Jerry Falwell offers the generic diagnosis that "AIDS is God's judgment on a society that does not live by His rules." What is surprising is not that the
AIDS epidemic has been exploited in this way but that such cant has been confined to so predictable a sector of bigots; the official discourse about AIDS invariably includes admonitions against bigotry.

The pronouncements of those who claim to speak for God can mostly be dis-   3
counted as the rhetoric regularly prompted by sexually transmitted illness—from
Cotton Mather's judgment to recent statements by two leading Brazilian clerics,
Bishop Falcão of Brasilia, who declares AIDS to be "the consequence of moral
decadence," and the Cardinal of Rio de Janeiro, Eugenio Sales, who wants it both
ways, describing AIDS as "God's punishment" and as "the revenge of nature."
More interesting, because their purposes are more complex, are the secular sponsors of this sort of invective. Authoritarian political ideologies have a vested interest in promoting fear, a sense of the imminence of takeover by aliens—and real
diseases are useful material. Epidemic diseases usually elicit a call to ban the entry
of foreigners, immigrants. And xenophobic propaganda has always depicted immigrants as bearers of disease (in the late nineteenth century: cholera, yellow fever,
typhoid fever, tuberculosis). It seems logical that the political figure in France who
represents the most extreme nativist, racist views, Jean-Marie Le Pen, has attempted a strategy of fomenting fear of this new alien peril, insisting that AIDS is
not just infectious but contagious, and calling for mandatory nationwide testing
and the quarantine of everyone carrying the virus. And AIDS is a gift to the present
regime in South Africa, whose Foreign Minister declared recently, evoking the
incidence of the illness among the mine workers imported from neighboring all-
black countries: "The terrorists are now coming to us with a weapon more terrible
than Marxism: AIDS."

The AIDS epidemic serves as an ideal projection for First World political   4
paranoia. Not only is the so-called AIDS virus the quintessential invader from the
Third World. It can stand for any mythological menace. In this country, AIDS has
so far evoked less pointedly racist reactions than in Europe, including the Soviet

Union, where the African origin of the disease is stressed. Here it is as much a reminder of feelings associated with the menace of the Second World as it is an image of being overrun by the Third. Predictably, the public voices in this country most committed to drawing moral lessons from the AIDS epidemic, such as Norman Podhoretz, are those whose main theme is worry about America's will to maintain its bellicosity, its expenditures on armaments, its firm anti-communist stance, and who find everywhere evidence of the decline of American political and imperial authority. Denunciations of "the gay plague" are part of a much larger complaint, common among antiliberals in the West and many exiles from the Russian bloc, about contemporary permissiveness of all kinds: a now-familiar diatribe against the "soft" West, with its hedonism, its vulgar sexy music, its indulgence in drugs, its disabled family life, which have sapped the will to stand up to communism. AIDS is a favorite concern of those who translate their political agenda into questions of group psychology: of national self-esteem and self-confidence. Although these specialists in ugly feelings insist that AIDS is a punishment for deviant sex, what moves them is not just, or even principally, homophobia. Even more important is the utility of AIDS in pursuing one of the main activities of the so-called neoconservatives, the Kulturkampf against all that is called, for short (and inaccurately), the 1960s. A whole politics of "the will"—of intolerance, of paranoia, of fear of political weakness—has fastened on this disease.

AIDS is such an apt goad to familiar, consensus-building fears that have been 5 cultivated for several generations, like fear of "subversion"—and to fears that have surfaced more recently, of uncontrollable pollution and of unstoppable migration from the Third World—that it would seem inevitable that AIDS be envisaged in this society as something total, civilization-threatening. And raising the disease's metaphorical stature by keeping alive fears of its easy transmissibility, its imminent spread, does not diminish its status as, mainly, a consequence of illicit acts (or of economic and cultural backwardness). That it is a punishment for deviant behavior and that it threatens the innocent—these two notions about AIDS are hardly in contradiction. Such is the extraordinary potency and efficacy of the plague metaphor: it allows a disease to be regarded both as something incurred by vulnerable "others" and as (potentially) everyone's disease.

Still, it is one thing to emphasize how the disease menaces everybody (in order 6 to incite fear and confirm prejudice), quite another to argue (in order to defuse prejudice and reduce stigma) that eventually AIDS will, directly or indirectly, affect everybody. Recently these same mythologists who have been eager to use AIDS for ideological mobilization against deviance have backed away from the most panic-inspiring estimates of the illness. They are among the most vocal of those who insist that infection will *not* spread to "the general population" and have turned their attention to denouncing "hysteria" or "frenzy" about AIDS. Behind what they now consider the excessive publicity given the disease, they discern the desire to placate an all-powerful minority by agreeing to regard "their" disease as "ours"—further evidence of the sway of nefarious "liberal" values and of America's spiritual decline. Making AIDS everyone's problem and therefore a subject on which everyone needs to be educated, charge the antiliberal AIDS mythologists, subverts our understanding of the difference between "us" and "them"; indeed, exculpates or at least makes irrelevant moral judgments about "them." (In such rhetoric the disease continues to be identified almost exclusively with homosexuality, and specifically the practice of sodomy.) "Has America become a country where classroom discussion of the Ten Commandments is impermissible but teacher instructions in safe sodomy are to be mandatory?" inquires Pat Buchanan, protesting the "foolish" proposal made in the report of the recent Presidential Commission on the epidemic, chaired by Admiral Watkins, to outlaw discrimination against people with AIDS. Not the disease but the appeals heard from the most official quarters "to set aside prejudice and fear in favor of compassion" (the words of the Watkins Report) have become a principal target, suggesting as they do a weakening of this society's power (or willingness) to punish and segregate through judgments about sexual behavior.

More than cancer, but rather like syphilis, AIDS seems to foster ominous fantasies about a disease that is a marker of both individual and social vulnerabilities. The virus invades the body; the disease (or, in the newer version, the fear of the disease) is described as invading the whole society. In late 1986 President Reagan pronounced AIDS to be spreading—"insidiously" of course—"through the length and breadth of our society."* But AIDS, while the pretext for expressing dark intimations about the body politic, has yet to seem credible as a political metaphor for internal enemies, even in France, where AIDS—in French *le sida*—was quickly added to the store of political invective. Le Pen has dismissed some of his opponents as "AIDS-ish" (*sidatique*), and the antiliberal polemicist Louis Pauwels said that lycée students on strike last year were suffering from "mental AIDS" (*sont atteint d'un sida mental*). Neither has AIDS proved of much use as a metaphor for international political evil. True, Jeane Kirkpatrick once couldn't resist comparing international terrorism to AIDS, but such sallies are rare—perhaps because for that purpose the cancer metaphor has proved so fecund.   7

This doesn't mean that AIDS is not used, preposterously, as a metaphor, but only that AIDS has a metaphoric potential different from that of cancer. When the movie director in Alain Tanner's film *La Vallée Fantôme* (1987) muses, "Cinema is like a cancer," and then corrects himself, "No, it's infectious, it's more like AIDS," the comparison seems lumberingly self-conscious as well as a decided underuse of AIDS. Not its infectiousness but its characteristic latency offers a more distinctive use of AIDS as a metaphor. Thus, the Palestinian Israeli writer Anton Shammas in the Jerusalem weekly *Kol Háir,* in a fit of medical, sexual, and political fantasy, recently described Israel's Declaration of Independence of 1948 as   8

> the AIDS of "the Jewish State in the Land of Israel," whose long incubation has produced Gush Emunim and . . . [Rabbi Meir] Kahane. That is where it all began, and that is where it all will end. AIDS, I am sorry to say, despite my sympathy for homosex-

---

*Reagan's affirmation through cliché of the frightening reality of a disease of other people contrasts with his more original denial of the reality of his own illness. When asked how he felt after his cancer operation, he declared: "I didn't have cancer. I had something inside of me that had cancer in it and it was removed."

uals, affects mainly monoerotics, and a mononational Jewish State contains by definition the seeds of its own destruction: the collapse of the political immune system that we call democracy. . . . Rock Hudson, who once was as beautiful as a Palmachnik, now lies dying long after the dissolution of the Palmach. The State of Israel (for Jews, of course) was indeed once beautiful. . . .

And even more promising than its connection with latency is the potential of AIDS as a metaphor for contamination and mutation. Cancer is still common as a metaphor for what is feared or deplored, even if the illness is less dreaded than before. If AIDS can eventually be drafted for comparable use, it will be because AIDS is not only invasive (a trait it shares with cancer) or even because it is infectious, but because of the specific imagery that surrounds viruses.

Virology supplies a new set of medical metaphors independent of AIDS which   9
nevertheless reinforce the AIDS mythology. It was years before AIDS that William Burroughs oracularly declared, and Laurie Anderson echoed, "Language is a virus." And the viral explanation is invoked more and more often. Until recently, most of the infections recognized as viral were ones, like rabies and influenza, that have very rapid effects. But the category of slow-acting viral infections is growing. Many progressive and invariably fatal disorders of the central nervous system and some degenerative diseases of the brain that can appear in old age, as well as the so-called auto-immune diseases, are now suspected of being, in fact, slow virus diseases. (And evidence continues to accumulate for a viral cause of at least some human cancers.) Notions of conspiracy translate well into metaphors of implacable, insidious, infinitely patient viruses. In contrast to bacteria, which are relatively complex organisms, viruses are described as an extremely primitive form of life. At the same time, their activities are far more complex than those envisaged in the earlier germ models of infection. Viruses are not simply agents of infection, contamination. They transport genetic "information," they transform cells. And they themselves, many of them, evolve. While the smallpox virus appears to stay constant for centuries, influenza viruses evolve so rapidly that vaccines need to be modified every year to keep up with changes in the "surface coat" of the virus.° The virus or, more accurately, viruses thought to cause AIDS are at least as mutable as the influenza viruses. Indeed, "virus" is now a synonym for change. Linda Ronstadt, recently explaining why she prefers doing Mexican folk music to rock 'n' roll, observed: "We don't have any tradition in contemporary music except change. Mutate, like a virus."

So far as "plague" still has a future as a metaphor, it is through the ever more   10
familiar notion of the virus. (Perhaps no disease in the future caused by a bacillus will be considered as plague-like.) Information itself, now inextricably linked to the powers of computers, is threatened by something compared to a virus. Rogue or

---

°The reason that a vaccine is considered the optimal response to viruses has to do with what makes them "primitive." Bacteria have many metabolic differences from mammalian cells and can reproduce outside the cells of their host, which makes it possible to find substances that target them specifically. With viruses, which bond with their host cells, it is a much more difficult problem to distinguish viral functions from normal cellular ones. Hence, the main strategy for controlling viral infections has been the development of vaccines, which do not "attack" a virus directly (as penicillin attacks infectious bacteria) but "forestall" infection by stimulating the immune system in advance.

pirate programs, known as software viruses, are described as paralleling the behavior of biological viruses (which can capture the genetic code of parts of an organism and effect transfers of alien genetic material). These programs, deliberately planted onto a floppy disk meant to be used with the computer or introduced when the computer is communicating over telephone lines or data networks with other computers, copy themselves onto the computer's operating system. Like their biological namesakes, they won't produce immediate signs of damage to the computer's memory, which gives the newly "infected" program time to spread to other computers. Such metaphors drawn from virology, partly stimulated by the omnipresence of talk of AIDS, are turning up everywhere. (The virus that destroyed a considerable amount of data at the student computer center at Lehigh University in Bethlehem, Pennsylvania, in 1987, was given the name PC AIDS. In France, computer specialists already speak of the problem of *le sida informatique*.) And they reinforce the sense of the omnipresence of AIDS.

It is perhaps not surprising that the newest transforming element in the modern world, computers, should be borrowing metaphors drawn from our newest transforming illness. Nor is it surprising that descriptions of the course of viral infection now often echo the language of the computer age, as when it is said that a virus will normally produce "new copies of itself." In addition to the mechanistic descriptions, the way viruses are animistically characterized—as a menace in waiting, as mutable, as furtive, as biologically innovative—reinforces the sense that a disease can be something ingenious, unpredictable, novel. These metaphors are central to ideas about AIDS that distinguish this illness from others that have been regarded as plague-like. For though the fears AIDS represents are old, its status as that unexpected event, an entirely new disease—a new judgment, as it were—adds to the dread.

11

Rhetorical Focus

1. What sort of language does Sontag employ to make plain her own position about public figures such as Jesse Helms and Jerry Falwell? Does she avoid explicitly stating her position? Look at the third paragraph, for example, and write a topic sentence for it.

2. The title of the book from which this essay is taken is *AIDS and Its Metaphors*. What is the particular metaphor Sontag discusses in this essay? Do you find the comparison a convincing one?

3. In the second section of her essay, Sontag discusses the language that is used to describe the activities of the AIDS virus. What are some of the terms she mentions? What are their connotations?

Thematic Focus

1. Why does Sontag object so much to the use of AIDS as a metaphor for social and political phenomena? What connection does she make between AIDS and computers?

2. Why do you think that sexually transmitted diseases have been such a prime target for judgment in our society?
3. Sontag speaks of a distinct "us" and "them" mentality evident in the political and religious discussions of AIDS. Can you see any of this mentality in Buckley's essay? Are there factual differences between the two essays? Ideological? Moral? Political?

Suggestions for Writing

1. Assume you had originally read Buckley's essay in the *Times*. Write a letter to the editor responding to his proposal.
2. Do some library research on some specific disease or plague. Write a brief report on the cultural response to this disease.
3. What responsibility does a society have to care for ill or disabled citizens? Answer this question in an essay that argues for a specific policy.

SCIENCE AND GENDER

There is a folk expression that claims that you find whatever you are looking for. This seems to make good sense if we are talking about the ease with which we find fault with our enemies, or the extraordinary praise parents lavish on their ordinary children. Most people, however, would not extend the saying to biologists studying evolution or sociologists analyzing a group's behavior. In these cases, scientists find what is really there, or so goes the conventional wisdom. It might, however, be the case that scientists can find only what their cultural assumptions allow them to see. Although many people still believe that the scientific method is absolved of personal and societal prejudice, there are scientists who doubt that anyone can completely step outside their cultural values, their historical moment, or even their own subjective biases.

We are all familiar with the scorn now heaped upon Nazi scientists who proved that they were a superior race, but this "scientific conclusion" is more typical than we would like to admit. All of us at the university want to believe we are not captured by prevailing thought, unable to creatively examine alternatives. However, some times it is extremely difficult to go against all the experts; even the leading minds of other ages had trouble believing that the sun was the center of our solar system, that plagues were not caused by a bad alignment of the planets, that humans evolved from lower forms, and that homosexuality was not a disease. History indicates, in other words, that the dogma of today is likely to be the folly of tomorrow.

In the following two essays, Stephen Jay Gould and Elaine Morgan alert us to the ongoing interaction of science and ideology, in this case gender bias. Gould takes us to Victorian England to tell an amusing and important narrative, which warns us to be skeptical of expert claims dealing with race, gender, and class. In his last two paragraphs, however, Gould is also critical of Elaine Morgan's perspective in *The Descent of Woman*, the first chapter of which is included here. It will be interesting to see whether you think Morgan's account is "farcical," or whether you think Gould himself is a victim of the inability to objectively examine alternative explanations.

Women's Brains

Stephen Jay Gould

Stephen Jay Gould (b. 1941), a Harvard professor teaching geology, biology, and the history of science, has made his reputation as a scientist with a gift for communicating the complexities of science to a lay audience. He writes a monthly column for *Natural History* magazine entitled "This View of Life," and frequently contributes reviews to *The New York Review of Books*. His many essays, in which Gould considers a broad spectrum of scientific subjects, are collected in popular volumes such as *The Panda's Thumb* and *Hen's Teeth and Horse's Toes*.

Reflections Before Reading

Are men more intelligent than women? If science could prove that they are, would you agree? Do you think scientists are free from bias about race, gender, and class in their work? How might the culture in which scientists, professors, doctors, and lawyers work affect their professional judgments?

In the prelude to *Middlemarch*, George Eliot lamented the unfulfilled lives of   1
talented women:

> Some have felt that these blundering lives are due to the inconvenient indefiniteness with which the Supreme Power has fashioned the natures of women: if there were one level of feminine incompetence as strict as the ability to count three and no more, the social lot of women might be treated with scientific certitude.

Eliot goes on to discount the idea of innate limitation, but while she wrote in   2
1872, the leaders of European anthropometry were trying to measure "with scientific certitude" the inferiority of women. Anthropometry, or measurement of the
human body, is not so fashionable a field these days, but it dominated the human
sciences for much of the nineteenth century and remained popular until intelligence testing replaced skull measurement as a favored device for making invidious
comparisons among races, classes, and sexes. Craniometry, or measurement of the
skull, commanded the most attention and respect. Its unquestioned leader, Paul
Broca (1824–80), professor of clinical surgery at the Faculty of Medicine in Paris,
gathered a school of disciples and imitators around himself. Their work, so meticulous and apparently irrefutable, exerted great influence and won high esteem as a
jewel of nineteenth-century science.

Broca's work seemed particularly invulnerable to refutation. Had he not mea-   3
sured with the most scrupulous care and accuracy? (Indeed, he had. I have the
greatest respect for Broca's meticulous procedure. His numbers are sound. But
science is an inferential exercise, not a catalog of facts. Numbers, by themselves,
specify nothing. All depends upon what you do with them.) Broca depicted himself
as an apostle of objectivity, a man who bowed before facts and cast aside superstition and sentimentality. He declared that "there is no faith, however respectable,
no interest, however legitimate, which must not accommodate itself to the
progress of human knowledge and bend before truth." Women, like it or not, had
smaller brains than men and, therefore, could not equal them in intelligence. This
fact, Broca argued, may reinforce a common prejudice in male society, but it is also
a scientific truth. L. Manouvrier, a black sheep in Broca's fold, rejected the inferiority of women and wrote with feeling about the burden imposed upon them by
Broca's numbers:

> Women displayed their talents and their diplomas. They also invoked philosophical
> authorities. But they were opposed by *numbers* unknown to Condorcet or to John
> Stuart Mill. These numbers fell upon poor women like a sledge hammer, and they
> were accompanied by commentaries and sarcasms more ferocious than the most mi-
> sogynist imprecations of certain church fathers. The theologians had asked if women
> had a soul. Several centuries later, some scientists were ready to refuse them a human
> intelligence.

Broca's argument rested upon two sets of data: the larger brains of men in   4
modern societies, and a supposed increase in male superiority through time. His
most extensive data came from autopsies performed personally in four Parisian
hospitals. For 292 male brains, he calculated an average weight of 1,325 grams;
140 female brains averaged 1,144 grams for a difference of 181 grams, or 14 percent of the male weight. Broca understood, of course, that part of this difference
could be attributed to the greater height of males. Yet he made no attempt to
measure the effect of size alone and actually stated that it cannot account for the
entire difference because we know, a priori, that women are not as intelligent as
men (a premise that the data were supposed to test, not rest upon):

We might ask if the small size of the female brain depends exclusively upon the small size of her body. Tiedemann has proposed this explanation. But we must not forget that women are, on the average, a little less intelligent than men, a difference which we should not exaggerate but which is, nonetheless, real. We are therefore permitted to suppose that the relatively small size of the female brain depends in part upon her physical inferiority and in part upon her intellectual inferiority.

In 1873, the year after Eliot published *Middlemarch,* Broca measured the   5 cranial capacities of prehistoric skulls from L'Homme Mort cave. Here he found a difference of only 99.5 cubic centimeters between males and females, while modern populations range from 129.5 to 220.7. Topinard, Broca's chief disciple, explained the increasing discrepancy through time as a result of differing evolutionary pressures upon dominant men and passive women:

> The man who fights for two or more in the struggle for existence, who has all the responsibility and the cares of tomorrow, who is constantly active in combating the environment and human rivals, needs more brain than the woman whom he must protect and nourish, the sedentary woman, lacking any interior occupations, whose role is to raise children, love, and be passive.

In 1879, Gustave Le Bon, chief misogynist of Broca's school, used these data   6 to publish what must be the most vicious attack upon women in modern scientific literature (no one can top Aristotle). I do not claim his views were representative of Broca's school, but they were published in France's most respected anthropological journal. Le Bon concluded:

> In the most intelligent races, as among the Parisians, there are a large number of women whose brains are closer in size to those of gorillas than to the most developed male brains. This inferiority is so obvious that no one can contest it for a moment; only its degree is worth discussion. All psychologists who have studied the intelligence of women, as well as poets and novelists, recognize today that they represent the most inferior forms of human evolution and that they are closer to children and savages than to an adult, civilized man. They excel in fickleness, inconstancy, absence of thought and logic, and incapacity to reason. Without doubt there exist some distinguished women, very superior to the average man, but they are as exceptional as the birth of any monstrosity, as, for example, of a gorilla with two heads; consequently, we may neglect them entirely.

Nor did Le Bon shrink from the social implications of his views. He was horrified by the proposal of some American reformers to grant women higher education on the same basis as men: 7

> A desire to give them the same education, and, as a consequence, to propose the same goals for them, is a dangerous chimera. . . . The day when, misunderstanding the inferior occupations which nature has given her, women leave the home and take part in our battles; on this day a social revolution will begin, and everything that maintains the sacred ties of the family will disappear.

Sound familiar?[*]

I have reexamined Broca's data, the basis for all this derivative pronounce-   8
ment, and I find his numbers sound but his interpretation ill-founded, to say the
least. The data supporting his claim for increased difference through time can be
easily dismissed. Broca based his contention on the samples from L'Homme Mort
alone—only seven male and six female skulls in all. Never have so little data
yielded such far ranging conclusions.

In 1888, Topinard published Broca's more extensive data on the Parisian hos-   9
pitals. Since Broca recorded height and age as well as brain size, we may use modern statistics to remove their effect. Brain weight decreases with age, and Broca's
women were, on average, considerably older than his men. Brain weight increases
with height, and his average man was almost half a foot taller than his average
woman. I used multiple regression, a technique that allowed me to assess simultaneously the influence of height and age upon brain size. In an analysis of the data
for women, I found that, at average male height and age, a woman's brain would
weigh 1,212 grams. Correction for height and age reduces Broca's measured difference of 181 grams by more than a third, to 113 grams.

I don't know what to make of this remaining difference because I cannot as-   10
sess other factors known to influence brain size in a major way. Cause of death has
an important effect: degenerative disease often entails a substantial diminution of
brain size. (This effect is separate from the decrease attributed to age alone.) Eu-
gene Schreider, also working with Broca's data, found that men killed in accidents
had brains weighing, on average, 60 grams more than men dying of infectious
diseases. The best modern data I can find (from American hospitals) records a full
100-gram difference between death by degenerative arteriosclerosis and by violence or accident. Since so many of Broca's subjects were very elderly women, we
may assume that lengthy degenerative disease was more common among them
than among the men.

More importantly, modern students of brain size still have not agreed on a   11
proper measure for eliminating the powerful effect of body size. Height is partly
adequate, but men and women of the same height do not share the same body
build. Weight is even worse than height, because most of its variation reflects nu-
trition rather than intrinsic size—fat versus skinny exerts little influence upon the
brain. Manouvrier took up this subject in the 1880s and argued that muscular mass
and force should be used. He tried to measure this elusive property in various ways
and found a marked difference in favor of men, even in men and women of the
same height. When he corrected for what he called "sexual mass," women actually
came out slightly ahead in brain size.

---

[*]When I wrote this essay, I assumed that Le Bon was a marginal, if colorful, figure. I have since learned
that he was a leading scientist, one of the founders of social psychology, and best known for a seminal
study on crowd behavior, still cited today (*La psychologie des foules*, 1895), and for his work on unconscious motivation.

Thus, the corrected 113-gram difference is surely too large; the true figure is   12
probably close to zero and may as well favor women as men. And 113 grams, by the
way, is exactly the average difference between a 5 foot 4 inch and a 6 foot 4 inch
male in Broca's data. We would not (especially us short folks) want to ascribe
greater intelligence to tall men. In short, who knows what to do with Broca's data?
They certainly don't permit any confident claim that men have bigger brains than
women.

To appreciate the social role of Broca and his school, we must recognize that   13
his statements about the brains of women do not reflect an isolated prejudice toward a single disadvantaged group. They must be weighed in the context of a general theory that supported contemporary social distinctions as biologically ordained. Women, blacks, and poor people suffered the same disparagement, but
women bore the brunt of Broca's argument because he had easier access to data on
women's brains. Women were singularly denigrated but they also stood as surro-
gates for other disenfranchised groups. As one of Broca's disciples wrote in 1881:
"Men of the black races have a brain scarcely heavier than that of white women."
This juxtaposition extended into many other realms of anthropological argument,
particularly to claims that, anatomically and emotionally, both women and blacks
were like white children—and that white children, by the theory of recapitulation,
represented an ancestral (primitive) adult stage of human evolution. I do not regard as empty rhetoric the claim that women's battles are for all of us.

Maria Montessori did not confine her activities to educational reform for   14
young children. She lectured on anthropology for several years at the University of
Rome, and wrote an influential book entitled *Pedagogical Anthropology* (English
edition, 1913). Montessori was no egalitarian. She supported most of Broca's work
and the theory of innate criminality proposed by her compatriot Cesare Lombroso.
She measured the circumference of children's heads in her schools and inferred
that the best prospects had bigger brains. But she had no use for Broca's conclusions about women. She discussed Manouvrier's work at length and made much of
his tentative claim that women, after proper correction of the data, had slightly
larger brains than men. Women, she concluded, were intellectually superior, but
men had prevailed heretofore by dint of physical force. Since technology has abol-
ished force as an instrument of power, the era of women may soon be upon us: "In
such an epoch there will really be superior human beings, there will really be men
strong in morality and in sentiment. Perhaps in this way the reign of women is
approaching, when the enigma of her anthropological superiority will be deci-
phered. Woman was always the custodian of human sentiment, morality and hon-
or."

This represents one possible antidote to "scientific" claims for the constitu-   15
tional inferiority of certain groups. One may affirm the validity of biological distinctions but argue that the data have been misinterpreted by prejudiced men with
a stake in the outcome, and that disadvantaged groups are truly superior. In recent
years, Elaine Morgan has followed this strategy in her *Descent of Woman,* a speculative reconstruction of human prehistory from the woman's point of view—and
as farcical as more famous tall tales by and for men.

I prefer another strategy. Montessori and Morgan followed Broca's philoso- 16
phy to reach a more congenial conclusion. I would rather label the whole enterprise of setting a biological value upon groups for what it is; irrelevant and highly
injurious. George Eliot well appreciated the special tragedy that biological labeling
imposed upon members of disadvantaged groups. She expressed it for people like
herself—women of extraordinary talent. I would apply it more widely—not only to
those whose dreams are flouted but also to those who never realize that they may
dream—but I cannot match her prose. In conclusion, then, the rest of Eliot's prelude to *Middlemarch:*

> The limits of variation are really much wider than anyone would imagine from the
> sameness of women's coiffure and the favorite love stories in prose and verse. Here and
> there a cygnet is reared uneasily among the ducklings in the brown pond, and never
> finds the living stream in fellowship with its own oary-footed kind. Here and there is
> born a Saint Theresa, foundress of nothing, whose loving heartbeats and sobs after an
> unattained goodness tremble off and are dispersed among hindrances instead of cen-
> tering in some long-recognizable deed.

Rhetorical Focus:

1. Why does Gould include so many quotes from scientists such as Broca and
   Le Bon? What is the effect of these quotes on the modern reader?
2. Gould claims that Broca was a bad interpreter of data. Find two instances
   in the essay where Gould backs up that claim.
3. Toward the end of his essay, Gould considers different "antidotes" to the
   poison of quasi-scientific claims about the constitutional superiority of
   white males to other social groups. Name two of these antidotes. Which
   one do you think might be most effective?

Thematic Focus:

1. What does Gould mean when he writes that "science is an inferential exercise, not a catalog of facts. Numbers, by themselves, specify nothing. All
   depends upon what you do with them"?
2. Gould invokes the old phrase that "women's battles are for all of us." In
   what way is women's struggle against data such as Broca's relevant to other
   social groups?
3. Gould argues that any sort of biological values based on comparisons between groups of people is "irrelevant and highly injurious." Do you agree
   with him? Can such comparisons really be avoided? Have you ever made a
   decision based on such comparisons?

The Man-Made Myth

Elaine Morgan

Elaine Morgan was born in 1920 in Wales and later studied at Oxford University. Her first book, *The Descent of Woman* (from which this reading was excerpted), was a controversial main selection for the Book-of-the-Month Club. In the book, she held that because of the female's need for protection for herself and her young, she evolved into an aquatic primate for 12 million years. Her next book, *The Aquatic Ape,* was published in 1982.

Reflections Before Reading

Do you think the account of creation in the Bible has had an effect on our perception of the status of men and women in society? Is it possible that the male was not the most important figure in early primitive groups? Can male scientists objectively interpret scientific facts? Can women scientists? What would you say is the difference between a fact and a theory? Is evolution either?

According to the Book of Genesis, God first created man. Woman was not only an 1
afterthought, but an amenity. For close on two thousand years this holy scripture was believed to justify her subordination and explain her inferiority; for even as a copy she was not a very good copy. There were differences. She was not one of His best efforts.

There is a line in an old folk song that runs: "I called my donkey a horse gone 2
wonky." Throughout most of the literature dealing with the differences between the sexes there runs a subtle underlying assumption that woman is a man gone wonky; that woman is a distorted version of the original blueprint; that they are the norm, and we are the deviation.

It might have been expected that when Darwin came along and wrote an en- 3
tirely different account of *The Descent of Man,* this assumption would have been eradicated, for Darwin didn't believe she was an afterthought: he believed her origin was at least contemporaneous with man's. It should have led to some kind of breakthrough in the relationship between the sexes. But it didn't.

Almost at once men set about the congenial and fascinating task of working   4
out an entirely new set of reasons why woman was manifestly inferior and irreversibly subordinate, and they have been happily engaged on this ever since. Instead of
theology they use biology, and ethology, and primatology, but they use them to
reach the same conclusions.

They are now prepared to debate the most complex problems of economic   5
reform not in terms of the will of God, but in terms of the sexual behavior patterns
of the cichlid fish; so that if a woman claims equal pay or the right to promotion
there is usually an authoritative male thinker around to deliver a brief homily on
hormones, and point out that what she secretly intends by this, and what will inevitably result, is the "psychological castration" of the men in her life.

Now, that may look to us like a stock piece of emotional blackmail—like the   6
woman who whimpers that if Sonny doesn't do as she wants him to do, then Mother's going to have one of her nasty turns. It is not really surprising that most women
who are concerned to win themselves a new and better status in society tend to
sheer away from the whole subject of biology and origins, and hope that we can
ignore all that and concentrate on ensuring that in the future things will be different.

I believe this is a mistake. The legend of the jungle heritage and the evolution   7
of man as a hunting carnivore has taken root in man's mind as firmly as Genesis
ever did. He may even genuinely believe that equal pay will do something terrible
to his gonads. He has built a beautiful theoretical construction, with himself on the
top of it, buttressed with a formidable array of scientifically authenticated facts.
We cannot dispute the facts. We should not attempt to ignore the facts. What I
think we can do is to suggest that the currently accepted interpretation of the facts
is not the only possible one.

I have considerable admiration for scientists in general, and evolutionists and   8
ethologists in particular, and though I think they have sometimes gone astray, it
has not been purely through prejudice. Partly it is due to sheer semantic accident—the fact that "man" is an ambiguous term. It means the species; it also
means the male of the species. If you begin to write a book about man or conceive
a theory about man you cannot avoid using this word. You cannot avoid using a
pronoun as a substitute for the word, and you will use the pronoun "he" as a simple
matter of linguistic convenience. But before you are halfway through the first
chapter a mental image of this evolving creature begins to form in your mind. It
will be a male image, and he will be the hero of the story: everything and everyone
else in the story will relate to him.

All this may sound like a mere linguistic quibble or a piece of feminist petu-   9
lance. If you stay with me, I hope to convince you it's neither. I believe the deeply
rooted semantic confusion between "man" as a male and "man" as a species has
been fed back into and vitiated a great deal of the speculation that goes on about
the origins, development, and nature of the human race.

A very high proportion of the thinking on these topics is androcentric (male-   10
centered) in the same way as pre-Copernican thinking was geocentric. It's just as
hard for man to break the habit of thinking of himself as central to the species as it
was to break the habit of thinking of himself as central to the universe. He sees

himself quite unconsciously as the main line of evolution, with a female satellite revolving around him as the moon revolves around the earth. This not only causes him to overlook valuable clues to our ancestry, but sometimes leads him into making statements that are arrant and demonstrable nonsense.

The longer I went on reading his own books about himself, the more I longed   11
to find a volume that would begin: "When the first ancestor of the human race descended from the trees, she had not yet developed the mighty brain that was to distinguish her so sharply from all other species. . . ."

Of course, she was no more the first ancestor than he was—but she was no *less*   12
the first ancestor, either. She was there all along, contributing half the genes to each succeeding generation. Most of the books forget about her for most of the time. They drag her onstage rather suddenly for the obligatory chapter on Sex and Reproduction, and then say: "All right, love, you can go now," while they get on with the real meaty stuff about the Mighty Hunter with his lovely new weapons and his lovely new straight legs racing across the Pleistocene plains. Any modifications in her morphology are taken to be imitations of the Hunter's evolution, or else designed solely for his delectation.

Evolutionary thinking has been making great strides lately. Archeologists,   13
ethologists, paleontologists, geologists, chemists, biologists, and physicists are closing in from all points of the compass on the central area of mystery that remains. For despite the frequent triumph dances of researchers coming up with another jawbone or another statistic, some part of the miracle is still unaccounted for. Most of their books include some such phrase as: ". . . the early stages of man's evolutionary progress remain a total mystery." "Man is an accident, the culmination of a series of highly improbable coincidences. . . ." "Man is a product of circumstances special to the point of disbelief." They feel there is still something missing, and they don't know what.

The trouble with specialists is that they tend to think in grooves. From time to   14
time something happens to shake them out of that groove. Robert Ardrey tells how such enlightenment came to Dr. Kenneth Oakley when the first Australopithecus remains had been unearthed in Africa: "The answer flashed without warning in his own large-domed head: 'Of course we believed that the big brain came first! We assumed that the first man was an Englishman!' " Neither he, nor Ardrey in relating the incident, noticed that he was still making an equally unconscious, equally unwarrantable assumption. One of these days an evolutionist is going to strike a palm against his large-domed head and cry: "Of course! We assumed the first human being was a man!"

First, let's have a swift recap of the story as currently related, for despite all the   15
new evidence recently brought to light, the generally accepted picture of human evolution has changed very little.

Smack in the center of it remains the Tarzanlike figure of the prehominid   16
male who came down from the trees, saw a grassland teeming with game, picked up a weapon, and became a Mighty Hunter.

Almost everything about us is held to have derived from this. If we walk erect   17
it was because the Mighty Hunter had to stand tall to scan the distance for his prey.

If we lived in caves it was because hunters need a base to come home to. If we learned to speak it was because hunters need to plan the next safari and boast about the last. Desmond Morris, pondering on the shape of a woman's breasts, instantly deduces that they evolved because her mate became a Mighty Hunter, and defends this preposterous proposition with the greatest ingenuity. There's something about the Tarzan figure which has them all mesmerized.

I find the whole yarn pretty incredible. It is riddled with mysteries, and incon-   18
sistencies, and unanswered questions. Even more damning than the unanswered questions are the questions that are never even asked, because, as Professor Peter Medawar has pointed out, "scientists tend not to ask themselves questions until they can see the rudiments of an answer in their minds." I shall devote this chapter to pointing out some of these problems before outlining a new version of the Naked Ape story which will suggest at least possible answers to every one of them, and fifteen or twenty others besides.

The first mystery is, "What happened during the Pliocene?"   19

There is a wide acceptance now of the theory that the human story began in   20
Africa. Twenty million years ago in Kenya, there existed a flourishing population of apes of generalized body structure and of a profusion of types from the size of a small gibbon up to that of a large gorilla. Dr. L.S.B. Leakey has dug up their bones by the hundred in the region of Lake Victoria, and they were clearly doing very well there at the time. It was a period known as the Miocene. The weather was mild, the rainfall was heavier than today, and the forests were flourishing. So far, so good.

Then came the Pliocene drought. Robert Ardrey writes of it: "No mind can   21
apprehend in terms of any possible human experience the duration of the Pliocene. Ten desiccated years were enough, a quarter of a century ago, to produce in the American Southwest that maelstrom of misery, the dust bowl. To the inhabitant of the region the ten years must have seemed endless. But the African Pliocene lasted twelve million."

On the entire African continent no Pliocene fossil bed has ever been found.   22
During this period many promising Miocene ape species were, not surprisingly, wiped out altogether. A few were trapped in dwindling pockets of forest and when the Pliocene ended they reappeared as brachiating apes—specialized for swinging by their arms.

Something astonishing also reappeared—the Australopithecines, first discov-   23
ered by Professor Raymond Dart in 1925 and since unearthed in considerable numbers by Dr. Leakey and others.

Australopithecus emerged from his horrifying twelve-million-year ordeal   24
much refreshed and improved. The occipital condyles of his skull suggest a bodily posture approaching that of modern man, and the orbital region, according to Sir Wilfred le Gros Clark, has "a remarkably human appearance." He was clever, too. His remains have been found in the Olduvai Gorge in association with crude pebble tools that have been hailed as the earliest beginning of human culture. Robert Ardrey says: "We entered the [Pliocene] crucible a generalized creature bearing only the human potential. We emerged a being lacking only a proper brain and a chin. What happened to us along the way?" The sixty-four-thousand-dollar question: "What happened to them? Where did they go?"

Second question: "Why did they stand upright?" The popular versions skim   25
very lightly over this patch of thin ice. Desmond Morris says simply: "With strong
pressure on them to increase their prey-killing prowess, they became more upright—fast, better runners." Robert Ardrey says equally simply: "We learned to
stand erect in the first place as a necessity of the hunting life."

But wait a minute. We were quadrupeds. These statements imply that a quad-   26
ruped suddenly discovered that he could move faster on two legs than on four. Try
to imagine any other quadruped discovering that—a cat? a dog? a horse?—and
you'll see that it's totally nonsensical. Other things being equal, four legs are bound
to run faster than two. The bipedal development was violently unnatural.

Stoats, gophers, rabbits, chimpanzees, will sit or stand bipedally to gaze into   27
the distance, but when they want speed they have sense enough to use all the legs
they've got. The only quadrupeds I can think of that can move faster on two legs
than four are things like kangaroos—and a small lizard called the Texas boomer,
and he doesn't keep it up for long. The secret in these cases is a long heavy coun-
terbalancing tail which we certainly never had. You may say it was a natural development for a primate because primates sit erect in trees—but *was* it natural? Ba-
boons and macaques have been largely terrestrial for millions of years without any
sign of becoming bipedal.

George A. Bartholomew and Joseph B. Birdsell point out: ". . . the extreme   28
rarity of bipedalism among animals suggests that it is inefficient except under very
special circumstances. Even modern man's unique vertical locomotion when compared to that of quadrupedal mammals, is relatively ineffective. . . . A significant
nonlocomotor advantage must have resulted."

What was this advantage? The Tarzanists suggest that bipedalism enabled this   29
ape to race after game while carrying weapons—in the first instance, presumably
pebbles. But a chimp running off with a banana (or a pebble), if he can't put it in
his mouth, will carry it in one hand and gallop along on the others, because even
three legs are faster than two. So what was our ancestor supposed to be doing?
Shambling along with a rock in each hand? Throwing boulders that took two hands
to lift?

No. There must have been a pretty powerful reason why we were constrained   30
over a long period of time to walk about on our hind legs *even though it was slower*.
We need to find that reason.

Third question: How did the ape come to be using these weapons, anyway?   31
Again Desmond Morris clears this one lightly, at a bound: "With strong pressure
on them to increase their prey-killing prowess . . . their hands became strong efficient weapon-holders." Compared to Morris, Robert Ardrey is obsessed with
weapons, which he calls "mankind's most significant cultural endowment." Yet his
explanation of how it all started is as cursory as anyone else's: "In the first evolutionary hour of the human emergence we became sufficiently skilled in the use of
weapons to render redundant our natural primate daggers" (i.e., the large prehominid canine teeth).

But wait a minute—how? and why? Why did one, and only one, species of   32
those Miocene apes start using weapons? A cornered baboon will fight a leopard; a
hungry baboon will kill and eat a chicken. He could theoretically pick up a chunk of
flint and forget about his "natural primate daggers," and become a Mighty Hunter.

He doesn't do it, though. Why did we? Sarel Eimerl and Irven de Vore point out in their book *The Primates:*

"Actually, it takes quite a lot of explaining. For example, if an animal's normal   33
mode of defense is to flee from a predator, it flees. If its normal method of defense is to fight with its teeth, it fights with its teeth. It does not suddenly adopt a totally new course of action, such as picking up a stick or a rock and throwing it. The idea would simply not occur to it, and even if it did, the animal would have no reason to suppose that it would work."

Now primates do acquire useful tool-deploying habits. A chimpanzee will use   34
a stick to extract insects from their nests, and a crumpled leaf to sop up water. Wolfgang Köhler's apes used sticks to draw fruit toward the bars of their cage, and so on.

But this type of learning depends on three things. There must be leisure for   35
trial-and-error experiment. The tools must be either in unlimited supply (a forest is full of sticks and leaves) or else in *exactly the right place.* (Even Köhler's brilliant Sultan could be stumped if the fruit was in front of him and a new potential tool was behind him—he needed them both in view at the same time.) Thirdly, for the habit to stick, the same effect must result from the same action every time.

Now look at that ape. The timing is wrong—when he's faced with a bristling   36
rival or a charging cat or even an escaping prey, he won't fool around inventing fancy methods. A chimp sometimes brandishes a stick to convey menace to an adversary, but if his enemy keeps coming, he drops the stick and fights with hands and teeth. Even if we postulate a mutant ape cool enough to think, with the adrenalin surging through his veins, "There must be a better way than teeth," he still has to be lucky to notice that right in the middle of the primeval grassland there happens to be a stone of convenient size, precisely between him and his enemy. And when he throws it, he has to score a bull's-eye, first time and every time. Because if he failed to hit a leopard he wouldn't be there to tell his progeny that the trick only needed polishing up a bit; and if he failed to hit a springbok he'd think: "Ah well, that obviously doesn't work. Back to the old drawing board."

No. If it had taken all that much luck to turn man into a killer, we'd all be still   37
living on nut cutlets.

A lot of Tarzanists privately realize that their explanations of bipedalism and   38
weapon-wielding won't hold water. They have invented the doctrine of "feedback," which states that though these two theories are separately and individually nonsense, together they will just get by. It is alleged that the ape's bipedal gait, however unsteady, made him a better rock thrower (why?) and his rock throwing, however inaccurate, made him a better biped. (Why?) Eimerl and de Vore again put the awkward question: Since chimps can both walk erect and manipulate simple tools, "why was it only the hominids who benefited from the feed-back?" You may well ask.

Next question: Why did the naked ape become naked?   39

Desmond Morris claims that, unlike more specialized carnivores such as lions   40
and jackals, the ex-vegetarian ape was not physically equipped to "make lightning dashes after his prey." He would "experience considerable overheating during the hunt, and the loss of body hair would be of great value for the supreme moments of the chase."

This is a perfect example of androcentric thinking. There were two sexes   41
around at the time, and I don't believe it's ever been all that easy to part a woman
from a fur coat, just to save the old man from getting into a muck-sweat during his
supreme moments. What was supposed to be happening to the female during this
period of denudation?

Dr. Morris says: "This system would not work, of course, if the climate was too   42
intensely hot, because of damage to the exposed skin." So he is obviously dating the
loss of hair later than the Pliocene "inferno." But the next period was the turbulent
Pleistocene, punctuated by mammoth African "pluvials," corresponding to the Ice
Ages of the north. A pluvial was century after century of torrential rainfall; so we
have to picture our maternal ancestor sitting naked in the middle of the plain while
the heavens emptied, needing both hands to keep her muddy grip on a slippery,
squirming, equally naked infant. This is ludicrous. It's no advantage to the species
for the Mighty Hunter to return home safe and cool if he finds his son's been
dropped on his head and his wife is dead of hypothermia.

This problem could have been solved by dimorphism—the loss of hair could   43
have gone further in one sex than the other. So it did, of course. But unfortunately
for the Tarzanists it was the stay-at-home female who became nakedest, and the
overheated hunter who kept the hair on his chest.

Next question: Why has our sex life become so involved and confusing?   44

The given answer, I need hardly say, is that it all began when man became a   45
hunter. He had to travel long distances after his prey and he began worrying about
what the little woman might be up to. He was also anxious about other members of
the hunting pack, because, Desmond Morris explains, "if the weaker males were
going to be expected to cooperate on the hunt, they had to be given more sexual
rights. The females would have to be more shared out."

Thus it became necessary, so the story goes, to establish a system of "pair   46
bonding" to ensure that couples remained faithful for life. I quote: "The simplest
and most direct method of doing this was to make the shared activities of the pair
more complicated and more rewarding. In other words, to make sex sexier."

To this end, the Naked Apes sprouted ear lobes, fleshy nostrils, and everted   47
lips, all allegedly designed to stimulate one another to a frenzy. Mrs. A.'s nipples
became highly erogenous, she invented and patented the female orgasm, and she
learned to be sexually responsive at all times, even during pregnancy, "because
with a one-male–one-female system, it would be dangerous to frustrate the male
for too long a period. It might endanger the pair bond." He might go off in a huff,
or look for another woman. Or even refuse to cooperate on the hunt.

In addition, they decided to change over to face-to-face sex, instead of the   48
male mounting from behind as previously, because this new method led to "personalized sex." The frontal approach means that "the incoming sexual signals and
rewards are kept tightly linked with the identity signals from the partner." In simpler words, you know who you're doing it with.

This landed Mrs. Naked Ape in something of a quandary. Up till then, the   49
fashionable thing to flaunt in sexual approaches had been "a pair of fleshy, hemi-
spherical buttocks." Now all of a sudden they were getting her nowhere. She
would come up to her mate making full-frontal identity signals like mad with her
nice new earlobes and nostrils, but somehow he just didn't want to know. He

missed the fleshy hemispheres, you see. The position was parlous, Dr. Morris urges. "If the female of our species was going to successfully shift the interest of the male round to the front, evolution would have to do something to make the frontal region more stimulating." Guess what? Right the first time: she invested in a pair of fleshy hemispheres in the thoracic region and we were once more saved by the skin of our teeth.

All this is good stirring stuff, but hard to take seriously. Wolf packs manage to cooperate without all this erotic paraphernalia. Our near relatives the gibbons remain faithful for life without "personalized" frontal sex, without elaborate erogenous zones, without perennial female availability. Why couldn't we? 50

Above all, since when has increased sexiness been a guarantee of increased fidelity? If the naked ape could see all this added sexual potential in his own mate, how could he fail to see the same thing happening to all the other females around him? What effect was that supposed to have on him, especially in later life when he noticed Mrs. A.'s four hemispheres becoming a little less fleshy than they used to be? 51

We haven't yet begun on the unasked questions. Before ending this chapter I will mention just two out of many. 52

First: If female orgasm was evolved in our species for the first time to provide the woman with a "behavioral reward" for increased sexual activity, why in the name of Darwin has the job been so badly bungled that there have been whole tribes and whole generations of women hardly aware of its existence? Even in the sex-conscious U.S.A., according to Dr. Kinsey, it rarely gets into proper working order before the age of about thirty. How could natural selection ever have operated on such a rickety, unreliable, late-developing endowment when in the harsh conditions of prehistory a woman would be lucky to survive more than twenty-nine years, anyway? 53

Second: Why in our species has sex become so closely linked with aggression? In most of the higher primates sexual activity is the one thing in life which is totally incompatible with hostility. A female primate can immediately deflect male wrath by presenting her backside and offering sex. Even a male monkey can calm and appease a furious aggressor by imitating the gesture. Nor is the mechanism confined to mammals. Lorenz tells of an irate lizard charging down upon a female painted with male markings to deceive him. When he got close enough to realize his mistake, the taboo was so immediate and so absolute that his aggression went out like a light, and being too late to stop himself he shot straight up into the air and turned a back somersault. 54

Female primates admittedly are not among the species that can count on this absolute chivalry at all times. A female monkey may be physically chastised for obstreperous behavior; or a male may (on rare occasions) direct hostility against her when another male is copulating with her; but between the male and female engaged in it, sex is always the friendliest of interactions. There is no more hostility associated with it than with a session of mutual grooming. 55

How then have sex and aggression, the two irreconcilables of the animal kingdom, become in our species alone so closely interlinked that the words for sexual activity are spat out as insults and expletives? In what evolutionary terms are we to 56 explain the Marquis de Sade, and the subterranean echoes that his name evokes in so many human minds?

Not, I think, in terms of Tarzan. It is time to approach the whole thing again right from the beginning: this time from the distaff side, and along a totally different route. 57

Rhetorical Focus:

1. Many critics believe that in argument, how a writer sounds is as important as the evidence he or she presents. The writer's voice or persona may be ironic, authoritative, balanced, or insecure. What voice do you hear in Morgan's essay?
2. Another ingredient of argument is the writer's treatment of the opposing argument. Describe how Morgan organizes her refutation. Do you find her arguments against male scientists fair? Explain.
3. Point to specific examples of irony (or sarcasm) in the essay. What do you think the writer's intention is? Does it work for you?

Thematic Focus:

1. What is Morgan's general point about science and gender? What are some of her specific points about evolution and gender?
2. In Gould's essay, he is critical of Morgan. What do you think his objections are? Do you agree?
3. Is it possible to separate science and gender? Explain.

Suggestions for Writing

1. Interview a female scientist (social or physical) at your university about the place of gender in her specialty. Write a report on your findings.
2. Is Gould suggesting in the third sentence of the first paragraph ("Anthropometry . . . ") that IQ testing today is as biased as craniometry? Write a response to this sentence in which you explore the possibilities of such a claim.
3. Examine another aspect of American life, such as movies, TV and magazine ads, politics, sports, or education for ways gender is or is not a factor. Write a focused essay using concrete examples to support your point.

Chapter
10

Ethics

W hen we study ethics, we analyze our moral choices and the principles behind them. As the previous units in this book suggest, writers often explore ethical questions and express ethical beliefs, even if they think themselves engaged in purely objective description and judgment. The very word *ethics* bears a close relation to *ethos,* a term that classical rhetoric used for the particular moral image that a writer or speaker projects.

Of course, we may not be fully aware of the ethics that we endorse and the ethos that we convey when we write. We can gain insight into them through a composition class where we respond to one another's drafts. Furthermore, as this unit emphasizes, we can understand our morals better if we consider particular situations where ethical issues arise. The first pair of texts examines what interviews reveal about the languages that people use to express their moral principles. In a selection from the best-selling book *Habits of the Heart,* Robert Bellah and his co-authors analyze the moral vocabulary of a man they interviewed, whereas in an excerpt from her influential book *In a Different Voice,* Carol Gilligan explains the different moralities shown by a boy and a girl in interviews. The next two constellations each focus on a specific controversy that has led Americans to review their values. First, Richard Selzer, Sallie Tisdale, and Anna Quindlen present different views of abortion. Then come three perspectives on euthanasia: a piece from *The Journal of the American Medical Association* that dramatizes an instance of it, a critical response to that piece, and an article from *The New England Journal of Medicine* recounting how the physician author helped a terminally ill woman commit suicide. The final pair of texts shows how particular events can spur us to analyze the ethics of our society. Lewis Thomas considers what a book about a nasty tribe implies about nations like ours, and the prospect of war between America and Iraq leads Barbara Ehrenreich to consider the ways in which our country is a warrior culture.

People can get quite emotional about moral questions. Indeed, ethics often involves feeling as much as logic. The whole topic can, in fact, seem utterly subjective. When you read these texts, you may find yourself wondering whether and how we should try to evaluate rationally people's moral stands. Do the authors of *Habits of the Heart* have any right to judge Brian Palmer, their interview subject? Should Carol Gilligan distinguish Amy's morality from Jake's? Can the arguments over abortion and euthanasia ever be resolved? Is it fair to generalize about the ethics of a culture? Rather than being overwhelmed by such questions, however, take this unit as an opportunity to learn the possibilities as well as the limits of ethical inquiry. Using the selections here as a springboard for discussion, try to identify ways in which we can improve not only our readers' moral reasoning, but also perhaps our own.

LANGUAGES OF MORALITY

As other sections of this book suggest, words are not neutral; they carry implications. Among other things, writers often need to consider the ethical implications of the particular terms they use. In fact, at the beginning of her book *In a Different Voice: Psychological Theory and Women's Development,* Carol Gilligan wants us all to acknowledge "that the way people talk about their lives is of significance, that the language they use and the connections they make reveal the world that they see and in which they act." Because we cannot assume that we share the same values, we should be alert to the differences as well as the similarities that our moral languages reveal. These differences most clearly emerge, of course, when we actively disagree with one another over an issue such as abortion or euthanasia. Even when we appear to hold the same position, though, we may significantly differ in the ways we justify it. Two people may be alike in favoring capital punishment, but if one does so because "the present system of laws is always right" and the other because "sometimes we must do awful things for our safety," their moral philosophies actually diverge.

The following case studies come from two highly influential books on languages of morality. Since their publication in the 1980s, a wide range of academic fields have pondered their methods and conclusions. The first text is an excerpt from *Habits of the Heart: Individualism and Commitment in American Life,* by a team of authors who are mostly social scientists. The book as a whole calls for Americans to analyze their moral values—their "habits of the heart"—and especially to reconsider their endorsement of individualism over community feeling. Our excerpt here raises this theme by discussing an interview subject whom the authors call Brian Palmer. The second text is from Gilligan's book, which generally raises the issue of whether men and women differ in their moral languages and values. Concerned that psychological research traditionally uses the male as the norm when constructing models of human development, Gilligan emphasizes that women often define morality as caring for other people, while men often identify it with maintaining individual rights. She proposes and explores this distinction in the excerpt here, in which she analyzes how a particular boy and girl, Jake and Amy, respond differently to the same hypothetical dilemma.

As you read these selections, you will no doubt find yourself evaluating their particular claims. Try to determine, too, the variety of ways that people's vocabularies can reflect their moral values. Consider also the language you use when you take moral positions—and the overall philosophy your language reveals.

Brian Palmer

Robert N. Bellah, Richard Madsen, William M. Sullivan, Ann Swidler, and Steven M. Tipton

This selection comes from a 1987 best-selling book entitled *Habits of the Heart: Individualism and Commitment in American Life,* by a team of authors. The lead author is Robert N. Bellah (b. 1927), a professor of sociology at the University of California at Berkeley. Two others are sociologists: Robert W. Madsen from the University of California at San Diego and Ann Swidler from Stanford University. William M. Sullivan is a professor of philosophy at La Salle College, and Steven M. Tipton teaches in the Candler School of Theology at Emory University.

To prepare for their book, the authors spent five years interviewing more than 200 people in various parts of the country. As they state in their preface, they wanted to explore with their subjects such questions as, "How ought we to live? How do we think about how to live? Who are we, as Americans? What is our character?" Above all, they were concerned with the issue of "how to preserve or create a morally coherent life". Throughout the book, they draw on their interviews to suggest that Americans have failed to establish such a life, mainly because American culture emphasizes a language of individualism rather than one recognizing deep community ties.

After the preface, the selection here begins the book. "Brian Palmer" is the name the authors give for one of the people Ann Swidler interviewed in the area of San Jose, California, often known as Silicon Valley.

Reflections Before Reading

Do you think the typical American is too self-involved? Why or why not?
How much do you value individualism, and how much relations with others?
This selection focuses on a man who significantly changed his behavior
when he had to deal with an unexpected event in his life. What sorts of
turning-point experiences do you think can lead people to alter their lives
dramatically? Can you identify any turning points in your own life?
Ultimately, do you think people's moral beliefs can completely change?

Living well is a challenge. Brian Palmer, a successful businessman, lives in a com-   1
fortable San Jose suburb and works as a top-level manager in a large corporation.
He is justifiably proud of his rapid rise in the corporation, but he is even prouder of
the profound change he has made recently in his idea of success. "My value system," he says, "has changed a little bit as the result of a divorce and reexamining
life values. Two years ago, confronted with the work load I have right now, I would
stay in the office and work until midnight, come home, go to bed, get up at six, and
go back in and work until midnight, until such time as it got done. Now I just kind
of flip the bird and walk out. My family life is more important to me than that, and
the work will wait, I have learned." A new marriage and a houseful of children have
become the center of Brian's life. But such new values were won only after painful
difficulties.

Now forty-one, his tall, lean body bursting with restless energy, Brian recalls a   2
youth that included a fair amount of hell-raising, a lot of sex, and considerable
devotion to making money. At twenty-four, he married. Shouldering the adult responsibilities of marriage and children became the guiding purpose of his life for
the next few years.

Whether or not Brian felt his life was satisfying, he was deeply committed to   3
succeeding at his career and family responsibilities. He held two full-time jobs to
support his family, accepting apparently without complaint the loss of a youth in
which, he himself reports, "the vast majority of my time from, say, the age of fifteen to twenty-two or twenty-three was devoted toward giving myself pleasure of
one sort or another." Brian describes his reasons for working so hard after he married quite simply. "It seemed like the thing to do at the time," he says. "I couldn't
stand not having enough money to get by on, and with my wife unable to contribute to the family income, it seemed like the thing to do. I guess self reliance is one
of the characteristics I have pretty high up in my value system. It was second nature. I didn't even question the thing. I just went out and did it." Brian and his wife
came to share very little in their marriage, except, as he thought, good sex, children, and devotion to his career. With his wife's support, he decided to "test"
himself "in the Big League," and he made it, although at great cost to his marriage
and family life. "What was my concept of what constituted a reasonable relationship? I guess I felt an obligation to care for materially, provide for, a wife and my
children, in a style to which I'd like to see them become accustomed. Providing for
my family materially was important. Sharing wasn't important. Sharing of my time

wasn't important. I put in extremely long hours, probably averaging sixty to sixty-five hours a week. I'd work almost every Saturday. Always in the office by 7:30. Rarely out of the office before 6:30 at night. Sometimes I'd work until 10:30 or 11. That was numero uno. But I compensated for that by saying, I have this nice car, this nice house, joined the Country Club. Now you have a place you can go, sit on your butt, drink, go into the pool. I'll pay the bills and I'll do my thing at work."

For Brian's wife, the compensations apparently weren't enough. After almost   4
fifteen years of marriage, "One day I came home. In fact, our house was for sale, and we had an offer on the house. My wife said, 'Before you accept an offer, you should probably know that once we sell this house, we will live in different houses.' That was my official notification that she was planning to divorce me."

The divorce, "one of the two or three biggest surprises of my life," led Brian to   5
reassess his life in fundamental ways and to explore the limits of the kind of success he had been pursuing. "I live by establishing plans. I had no plan for being single, and it gave me a lot of opportunity to think, and in the course of thinking, I read for the first time in many, many years. Got back into classical music for the first time since my college years. I went out and bought my first Bach album and a stereo to play it on. Mostly the thinking process of being alone and relating to my children."

When his children chose to live with him, Brian found himself forced to shift   6
his sense of himself and his priorities in life. "I found that being a single parent is not all that it is cracked up to be. I found it an extremely humbling experience. Whereas I go into the office in the morning and I have a personal secretary and a staff of managers and a cast of hundreds working for me, I came home and just like every Tom, Dick, and Harry in the world, I'd clean up garbage after these three big boys of mine. I'd spend two hours preparing and cleaning up after dinner, doing laundry, folding clothes, sweeping the floor, and generally doing manual labor of the lowest form. But the fact that my boys chose to live with me was a very important thing to me. It made me feel that maybe I had been doing something right in the parenting department."

Although his wife had left him, and he later found out that she had been   7
having an affair, Brian's period of reflection led him to rethink his role in the relationship. "Being a compulsive problem solver, I analyzed the failure. I don't like failure. I'm very competitive. I like to win. So I went back and reexamined where the thing broke down and found that I had contributed at least 50 percent and, depending on the vantage point, maybe 99 percent of the ultimate demise of the institution. Mostly it was asking myself the question of why am I behaving in such and such a way. Why am I doing this at work? Why was I doing this at home? The answer was that I was operating as if a certain value was of the utmost importance to me. Perhaps it was success. Perhaps it was fear of failure, but I was extremely success-oriented, to the point where everything would be sacrificed for the job, the career, the company. I said bullshit. That ain't the way it should be."

The revolution in Brian's thinking came from a reexamination of the true   8
sources of joy and satisfaction in his life. And it is particularly in a marriage to a woman very different from his first wife that Brian has discovered a new sense of himself and a different understanding of what he wants out of life. He has a new sense of what love can be. "To be able to receive affection freely and give affection and to give of myself and know it is a totally reciprocal type of thing. There's just

almost a psychologically buoyant feeling of being able to be so much more involved and sharing. Sharing experiences of goals, sharing of feelings, working together to solve problems, etc. My viewpoint of a true love, husband-and-wife type of relationship is one that is founded on mutual respect, admiration, affection, the ability to give and receive freely." His new wife, a divorcée his own age, brings four children to their marriage, added to Brian's own three. They have five children still living at home, and a sense of energy, mutual devotion, and commitment sufficient to make their family life a joy.

In many ways, Brian's is an individual success story. He has succeeded materially, and he has also taken hold of the opportunity to reach out beyond material success to a fuller sense of what he wants from life. Yet despite the personal triumph Brian's life represents, despite the fulfillment he seems to experience, there is still something uncertain, something poignantly unresolved about his story.   9

The difficulty becomes most evident when Brian tries to explain why it is that his current life is, in fact, better than his earlier life built around single-minded devotion to his career. His description of his reasons for changing his life and of his current happiness seems to come down mainly to a shift in his notions of what would make him happy. His new goal—devotion to marriage and children—seems as arbitrary and unexamined as his earlier pursuit of material success. Both are justified as idiosyncratic preference rather than as representing a larger sense of the purpose of life. Brian sees himself as consistently pursuing a utilitarian calculus—devotion to his own self-interest—except that there has been an almost inexplicable change in his personal preferences. In describing the reasons for this change, he begins, "Well, I think I just reestablished my priorities." He sometimes seems to reject his past life as wrong; but at other times, he seems to say he simply got bored with it. "That exclusive pursuit of success now seems to me not a good way to live. That's not the most important thing to me. I have demonstrated to myself, to my own satisfaction, that I can achieve about what I want to achieve. So the challenge of goal realization does not contain that mystique that it held for me at one time. I just have found that I get a lot of personal reward from being involved in the lives of my children."   10

American cultural traditions define personality, achievement, and the purpose of human life in ways that leave the individual suspended in glorious, but terrifying, isolation. These are limitations of our culture, of the categories and ways of thinking we have inherited, not limitations of individuals such as Brian who inhabit this culture. People frequently live out a fuller sense of purpose in life than they can justify in rational terms, as we see in Brian's case and many others.   11

Brian's restless energy, love of challenges, and appreciation of the good life are characteristic of much that is most vital in American culture. They are all qualities particularly well-suited to the hard-driving corporate world in which he works. When Brian describes how he has chosen to live, however, he keeps referring to "values" and "priorities" not justified by any wider framework of purpose or belief. What is good is what one finds rewarding. If one's preferences change, so does the nature of the good. Even the deepest ethical virtues are justified as matters of personal preference. Indeed, the ultimate ethical rule is simply that individuals should be able to pursue whatever they find rewarding, constrained only by the requirement that they not interfere with the "value systems" of others. "I guess I   12 feel like everybody on this planet is entitled to have a little bit of space, and things that detract from other people's space are kind of bad," Brian observes. "One of the things that I use to characterize life in California, one of the things that makes California such a pleasant place to live, is people by and large aren't bothered by other people's value systems as long as they don't infringe upon your own. By and large, the rule of thumb out here is that if you've got the money, honey, you can do your thing as long as your thing doesn't destroy someone else's property, or interrupt their sleep, or bother their privacy, then that's fine. If you want to go in your house and smoke marijuana and shoot dope and get all screwed up, that's your business, but don't bring that out on the street, don't expose my children to it, just do your thing. That works out kind of neat."

In a world of potentially conflicting self-interests, no one can really say that one value system is better than another. Given such a world, Brian sets great store by one basic principle—the importance of honesty and communication. It is through communication that people have a chance to resolve their differences, since there is no larger moral ideal in terms of which conflicts can be resolved. "Communication is critical not only to a man-and-woman relationship, it is the essence of our being on this planet in my opinion. Given open communication and the ability to think problems out, most problems can be solved." Solving conflicts becomes a matter of technical problem solving, not moral decision. Lying, which would interfere in a critical way with the ability to communicate accurately and resolve interpersonal conflicts, is thus wrong, but, even here, wrongness is largely a matter of practicality—it doesn't pay. "The bottom line of my personal value system applies to the way I conduct business. My predecessor was characterized as a notorious, habitual, and compulsive liar, and that's a difficult act to follow. That's probably one of the reasons that led to his demise—that his lies were catching up with him and he left before the walls came tumbling down." 13

Not lying is one of the major things Brian wants to teach his children. "Why is integrity important and lying bad? I don't know. It just is. It's just so basic. I don't want to be bothered with challenging that. It's part of me. I don't know where it came from, but it's very important." Brian says "values" are important, and he stresses the importance of teaching them to his children. But apart from the injunction not to lie, he is vague about what those values are. "I guess a lot of them are Judeo-Christian ethics of modern society, that certain things are bad." Even the things that may be "absolutely wrong," such as killing, stealing, and lying, may just be matters of personal preference—or at least injunctions against them exist detached from any social or cultural base that could give them broader meaning. 14

Are there some things that are just absolutely wrong? "I don't think I would pontificate and say that I'm in a position to establish values for humanity in general, although I'm sufficiently conceited to say that if the rest of the world would live by my value system it would be a better place," Brian says. The justification he offers is simply, "I'm quite comfortable with my values." Yet values, in turn, continually slip back for Brian into a matter of personal preferences, and the only ethical problem is to make the decision that accords with one's preferences. His increased commitment to family and children rather than to material success seems strangely lacking in substantive justification. "I just find that I get more 15 personal satisfaction from choosing course B over course A. It makes me feel better about myself. To participate in this union of chaos to try and mold something, this family situation—and maybe it's because of this bringing two families together—is a challenge. Believe me, this is a challenge. Maybe that's why it fascinates me. Maybe that's why it's important to me."

Despite the combination of tenderness and admiration he expresses for his wife, the genuine devotion he seems to feel for his children, and his own resilient self-confidence, Brian's justification of his life thus rests on a fragile foundation. Morally, his life appears much more coherent than when he was dominated by careerism, but, to hear him talk, even his deepest impulses of attachment to others are without any more solid foundation than his momentary desires. He lacks a language to explain what seem to be the real commitments that define his life, and to that extent the commitments themselves are precarious.   16

Rhetorical Focus

1. Why do you think the authors chose the sentence they did to begin the first paragraph and the whole section on Brian Palmer? More precisely, how do the first paragraph and the whole section proceed to explore the different meanings that the words in this sentence can have?
2. Do you find the proportion of quotation and commentary appropriate? Should the authors have engaged in less analysis, or more? Do you see any differences between the authors' language and Brian Palmer's?
3. Brian Palmer's statements do not necessarily appear in the order in which he made them. In what ways do the authors strike you as organizing their interview material to have a certain effect on their readers? For example, where does the "turning point" in their own presentation come?

Thematic Focus

1. How do you feel toward Brian Palmer? Did your attitude shift as you read?
2. Do you agree with the authors' analysis of Brian Palmer? Consider in particular their last sentence.
3. In criticizing American individualism throughout their book, the authors do not build their case just on the remarks of Brian Palmer. They simply use him to begin their argument. What other kinds of people would they need to include in order for you to accept their generalizations about American culture?

Jake and Amy

Carol Gilligan

Carol Gilligan (b. 1936) is Professor of Education in the Harvard Graduate School of Education. She has co-edited two books on women's psychological development, *Mapping the Moral Domain* and *Making Connections: The Relational Worlds of Adolescent Girls at Emma Willard School.* The following comes from her own 1982 book *In a Different Voice: Psychological Theory and Women's Development.* It has influenced many areas of scholarship, especially women's studies, because it challenges the way that traditional models of psychological development focus just on men. In particular, Gilligan critiques the scale of moral development outlined by her own teacher, Lawrence Kohlberg. She argues that it values men's typical concern for individual rights, while it neglects the ethic of care that women often show. This second kind of moral language is for Gilligan a "different voice" that psychological theory must recognize. In this excerpt we call "Jake and Amy," Gilligan examines how a particular boy and girl respond to the same moral dilemma.

Reflections Before Reading

The media have used the term *gender gap* to describe the sometimes very different responses of men and women in public opinion surveys. Do you find evidence of a gender gap when you and your friends discuss moral issues? In other words, do you find that men and women talk about moral issues differently? This excerpt specifically concerns how an 11-year-old boy and girl responded to a hypothetical dilemma created by Lawrence Kohlberg. As Gilligan describes it, "a man named Heinz considers whether or not to steal a drug which he cannot afford to buy in order to save the life of his wife." The main question is, " 'Should Heinz steal the drug?' " (paragraph 2). Jot down your own immediate response to this question. Do you think men and women would tend to answer it differently? What about an 11-year-old boy and girl?

The two children were in the same sixth-grade class at school and were participants   1
in the rights and responsibilities study, designed to explore different conceptions
of morality and self. The sample selected for this study was chosen to focus

the variables of gender and age while maximizing developmental potential by holding constant, at a high level, the factors of intelligence, education, and social class that have been associated with moral development, at least as measured by existing scales. The two children in question, Amy and Jake, were both bright and articulate and, at least in their eleven-year-old aspirations, resisted easy categories of sex-role stereotyping, since Amy aspired to become a scientist while Jake preferred English to math. Yet their moral judgments seem initially to confirm familiar notions about differences between the sexes, suggesting that the edge girls have on moral development during the early school years gives way at puberty with the ascendance of formal logical thought in boys.

The dilemma that these eleven-year-olds were asked to resolve was one in the   2
series devised by Kohlberg to measure moral development in adolescence by presenting a conflict between moral norms and exploring the logic of its resolution. In this particular dilemma, a man named Heinz considers whether or not to steal a drug which he cannot afford to buy in order to save the life of his wife. In the standard format of Kohlberg's interviewing procedure, the description of the dilemma itself—Heinz's predicament, the wife's disease, the druggist's refusal to lower his price—is followed by the question, "Should Heinz steal the drug?" The reasons for and against stealing are then explored through a series of questions that vary and extend the parameters of the dilemma in a way designed to reveal the underlying structure of moral thought.

Jake, at eleven, is clear from the outset that Heinz should steal the drug. Con-   3
structing the dilemma, as Kohlberg did, as a conflict between the values of property and life, he discerns the logical priority of life and uses that logic to justify his choice:

> For one thing, a human life is worth more than money, and if the druggist only makes $1,000, he is still going to live, but if Heinz doesn't steal the drug, his wife is going to die. (*Why is life worth more than money?*) Because the druggist can get a thousand dollars later from rich people with cancer, but Heinz can't get his wife again. (*Why not?*) Because people are all different and so you couldn't get Heinz's wife again.

Asked whether Heinz should steal the drug if he does not love his wife, Jake replies that he should, saying that not only is there "a difference between hating and killing," but also, if Heinz were caught, "the judge would probably think it was the right thing to do." Asked about the fact that, in stealing, Heinz would be breaking the law, he says that "the laws have mistakes, and you can't go writing up a law for everything that you can imagine."

Thus, while taking the law into account and recognizing its function in main-   4
taining social order (the judge, Jake says, "should give Heinz the lightest possible sentence"), he also sees the law as man-made and therefore subject to error and change. Yet his judgment that Heinz should steal the drug, like his view of the law as having mistakes, rests on the assumption of agreement, a societal consensus around moral values that allows one to know and expect others to recognize what is "the right thing to do."

Fascinated by the power of logic, this eleven-year-old boy locates truth in   5
math, which, he says, is "the only thing that is totally logical." Considering the

moral dilemma to be "sort of like a math problem with humans," he sets it up as an equation and proceeds to work out the solution. Since his solution is rationally derived, he assumes that anyone following reason would arrive at the same conclusion and thus that a judge would also consider stealing to be the right thing for Heinz to do. Yet he is also aware of the limits of logic. Asked whether there is a right answer to moral problems, Jake replies that "there can only be right and wrong in judgment," since the parameters of action are variable and complex. Illustrating how actions undertaken with the best of intentions can eventuate in the most disastrous of consequences, he says, "like if you give an old lady your seat on the trolley, if you are in a trolley crash and that seat goes through the window, it might be that reason that the old lady dies."

Theories of developmental psychology illuminate well the position of this   6
child, standing at the juncture of childhood and adolescence, at what Piaget describes as the pinnacle of childhood intelligence, and beginning through thought to discover a wider universe of possibility. The moment of preadolescence is caught by the conjunction of formal operational thought with a description of self still anchored in the factual parameters of his childhood world—his age, his town, his father's occupation, the substance of his likes, dislikes, and beliefs. Yet as his self-description radiates the self-confidence of a child who has arrived, in Erikson's terms, at a favorable balance of industry over inferiority—competent, sure of himself, and knowing well the rules of the game—so his emergent capacity for formal thought, his ability to think about thinking and to reason things out in a logical way, frees him from dependence on authority and allows him to find solutions to problems by himself.

This emergent autonomy follows the trajectory that Kohlberg's six stages of   7
moral development trace, a three-level progression from an egocentric understanding of fairness based on individual need (stages one and two), to a conception of fairness anchored in the shared conventions of societal agreement (stages three and four), and finally to a principled understanding of fairness that rests on the free-standing logic of equality and reciprocity (stages five and six). While this boy's judgments at eleven are scored as conventional on Kohlberg's scale, a mixture of stages three and four, his ability to bring deductive logic to bear on the solution of moral dilemmas, to differentiate morality from law, and to see how laws can be considered to have mistakes points toward the principled conception of justice that Kohlberg equates with moral maturity.

In contrast, Amy's response to the dilemma conveys a very different impres-   8
sion, an image of development stunted by a failure of logic, an inability to think for herself. Asked if Heinz should steal the drug, she replies in a way that seems evasive and unsure:

> Well, I don't think so. I think there might be other ways besides stealing it, like if he could borrow the money or make a loan or something, but he really shouldn't steal the drug—but his wife shouldn't die either.

Asked why he should not steal the drug, she considers neither property nor law but rather the effect that theft could have on the relationship between Heinz and his wife:

If he stole the drug, he might save his wife then, but if he did, he might have to go to jail, and then his wife might get sicker again, and he couldn't get more of the drug, and it might not be good. So, they should really just talk it out and find some other way to make the money.

Seeing in the dilemma not a math problem with humans but a narrative of 9 relationships that extends over time, Amy envisions the wife's continuing need for her husband and the husband's continuing concern for his wife and seeks to respond to the druggist's need in a way that would sustain rather than sever connection. Just as she ties the wife's survival to the preservation of relationships, so she considers the value of the wife's life in a context of relationships, saying that it would be wrong to let her die because, "if she died, it hurts a lot of people and it hurts her." Since Amy's moral judgment is grounded in the belief that, "if somebody has something that would keep somebody alive, then it's not right not to give it to them," she considers the problem in the dilemma to arise not from the druggist's assertion of rights but from his failure of response.

As the interviewer proceeds with the series of questions that follow from Kohl- 10 berg's construction of the dilemma, Amy's answers remain essentially unchanged, the various probes serving neither to elucidate nor to modify her initial response. Whether or not Heinz loves his wife, he still shouldn't steal or let her die; if it were a stranger dying instead, Amy says that "if the stranger didn't have anybody near or anyone she knew," then Heinz should try to save her life, but he should not steal the drug. But as the interviewer conveys through the repetition of questions that the answers she gave were not heard or not right, Amy's confidence begins to diminish, and her replies become more constrained and unsure. Asked again why Heinz should not steal the drug, she simply repeats, "Because it's not right." Asked again to explain why, she states again that theft would not be a good solution, adding lamely, "if he took it, he might not know how to give it to his wife, and so his wife might still die." Failing to see the dilemma as a self-contained problem in moral logic, she does not discern the internal structure of its resolution; as she constructs the problem differently herself, Kohlberg's conception completely evades her.

Instead, seeing a world comprised of relationships rather than of people stand- 11 ing alone, a world that coheres through human connection rather than through systems of rules, she finds the puzzle in the dilemma to lie in the failure of the druggist to respond to the wife. Saying that "it is not right for someone to die when their life could be saved," she assumes that if the druggist were to see the consequences of his refusal to lower his price, he would realize that "he should just give it to the wife and then have the husband pay back the money later." Thus she considers the solution to the dilemma to lie in making the wife's condition more salient to the druggist or, that failing, in appealing to others who are in a position to help.

Just as Jake is confident the judge would agree that stealing is the right thing 12 for Heinz to do, so Amy is confident that, "if Heinz and the druggist had talked it out long enough, they could reach something besides stealing." As he considers the law to "have mistakes," so she sees this drama as a mistake, believing that "the world should just share things more and then people wouldn't have to steal." Both children thus recognize the need for agreement but see it as mediated in different ways—he impersonally through systems of logic and law, she personally through communication in relationship. Just as he relies on the conventions of logic to deduce the solution to this dilemma, assuming these conventions to be shared, so she relies on a process of communication, assuming connection and believing that her voice will be heard. Yet while his assumptions about agreement are confirmed by the convergence in logic between his answers and the questions posed, her assumptions are belied by the failure of communication, the interviewer's inability to understand her response.

Although the frustration of the interview with Amy is apparent in the repeti-   13
tion of questions and its ultimate circularity, the problem of interpretation is focused by the assessment of her response. When considered in the light of Kohlberg's definition of the stages and sequence of moral development, her moral judgments appear to be a full stage lower in maturity than those of the boy. Scored as a mixture of stages two and three, her responses seem to reveal a feeling of powerlessness in the world, an inability to think systematically about the concepts of morality or law, a reluctance to challenge authority or to examine the logic of received moral truths, a failure even to conceive of acting directly to save a life or to consider that such action, if taken, could possibly have an effect. As her reliance on relationships seems to reveal a continuing dependence and vulnerability, so her belief in communication as the mode through which to resolve moral dilemmas appears naive and cognitively immature.

Yet Amy's description of herself conveys a markedly different impression.   14
Once again, the hallmarks of the preadolescent child depict a child secure in her sense of herself, confident in the substance of her beliefs, and sure of her ability to do something of value in the world. Describing herself at eleven as "growing and changing," she says that she "sees some things differently now, just because I know myself really well now, and I know a lot more about the world." Yet the world she knows is a different world from that refracted by Kohlberg's construction of Heinz's dilemma. Her world is a world of relationships and psychological truths where an awareness of the connection between people gives rise to a recognition of responsibility for one another, a perception of the need for response. Seen in this light, her understanding of morality as arising from the recognition of relationship, her belief in communication as the mode of conflict resolution, and her conviction that the solution to the dilemma will follow from its compelling representation seem far from naive or cognitively immature. Instead, Amy's judgments contain the insights central to an ethic of care, just as Jake's judgments reflect the logic of the justice approach. Her incipient awareness of the "method of truth," the central tenet of nonviolent conflict resolution, and her belief in the restorative activity of care, lead her to see the actors in the dilemma arrayed not as opponents in a contest of rights but as members of a network of relationships on whose continuation they all depend. Consequently her solution to the dilemma lies in activating the network by communication, securing the inclusion of the wife by strengthening rather than severing connections.

But the different logic of Amy's response calls attention to the interpretation   15
of the interview itself. Conceived as an interrogation, it appears instead as a dia-

logue, which takes on moral dimensions of its own, pertaining to the interviewer's uses of power and to the manifestations of respect. With this shift in the conception of the interview, it immediately becomes clear that the interviewer's problem in understanding Amy's response stems from the fact that Amy is answering a different question from the one the interviewer thought had been posed. Amy is considering not *whether* Heinz should act in this situation ("*should* Heinz steal the drug?") but rather *how* Heinz should act in response to his awareness of his wife's need ("Should Heinz *steal* the drug?"). The interviewer takes the mode of action for granted, presuming it to be a matter of fact; Amy assumes the necessity for action and considers what form it should take. In the interviewer's failure to imagine a response not dreamt of in Kohlberg's moral philosophy lies the failure to hear Amy's question and to see the logic in her response, to discern that what appears, from one perspective, to be an evasion of the dilemma signifies in other terms a recognition of the problem and a search for a more adequate solution.

Thus in Heinz's dilemma these two children see two very different moral problems—Jake a conflict between life and property that can be resolved by logical deduction, Amy a fracture of human relationship that must be mended with its own thread. Asking different questions that arise from different conceptions of the moral domain, the children arrive at answers that fundamentally diverge, and the arrangement of these answers as successive stages on a scale of increasing moral maturity calibrated by the logic of the boy's response misses the different truth revealed in the judgment of the girl. To the question, "What does he see that she does not?" Kohlberg's theory provides a ready response, manifest in the scoring of Jake's judgments a full stage higher than Amy's in moral maturity; to the question, "What does she see that he does not?" Kohlberg's theory has nothing to say. Since most of her responses fall through the sieve of Kohlberg's scoring system, her responses appear from his perspective to lie outside the moral domain.

16

Rhetorical Focus

1. Why is Gilligan especially concerned to explain Amy's moral reasoning? Does Gilligan think it is better than Jake's?
2. Does Gilligan interpret Jake's and Amy's remarks as much as the *Habits of the Heart* authors interpret Brian Palmer's? If there is a difference in the amount of interpretation, how might it be explained?
3. The subtitle of Gilligan's book is "Psychological Theory and Women's Development." The subtitle of *Habits of the Heart* is "Individualism and Commitment in American Life." How do these different concerns lead the selections to emphasize different things, even if the books are both generally concerned with moral languages?

Thematic Focus

1. Are you convinced by Gilligan's explanations of the children's responses to the Heinz dilemma? What do you think are the advantages and disadvantages of using children as interview subjects in the first place? Can they tell us as much as Brian Palmer and other adults?

2. Both this selection and the excerpt from *Habits of the Heart* discuss "communication" (paragraphs 12-14 in Gilligan's text, paragraph 13 in the excerpt from *Habits*). Do they mean the same thing by it? Do they have the same views of it?

3. What might Carol Gilligan say about Brian Palmer? What might the *Habits of the Heart* authors say about Jake and Amy?

Suggestions for Writing

1. The texts in this constellation focus on the moral values of three people: Brian Palmer, Jake, and Amy. Write an essay in which you compare yourself to at least two of these people as you describe an occasion when you demonstrated your own moral values. What exactly was the occasion? What moral values did you reveal? As you revealed them, did your thinking resemble Brian Palmer's, Jake's, or Amy's? Refer to specific remarks by these people as you compare yourself to them.

2. Choose someone you know well who, like Brian Palmer, experienced a turning point—in other words, a situation that led the person to make what he or she considered significant changes. Write an essay describing this turning point from your point of view, identifying what about the person you think actually changed and what you think stayed the same. If the person's own interpretation of the turning point would differ from yours, indicate what the differences would be. If you wish, you can write about a turning point that you experienced. In that case, identify the degree of change you now think you went through as you look back on the experience.

3. Present the Heinz dilemma to at least six people of roughly the same age, with males and females equally represented. Try to have these people elaborate their responses enough so that you can sense their general patterns of moral reasoning. Then, write an essay in which you report your analysis of these responses to the members of your class. State in particular whether you discovered any gender differences. Include at least one direct quotation from each of your subjects to support your analysis.

THE DEBATE OVER ABORTION

The next two constellations deal with ethical matters that continue to generate heated debate: abortion and euthanasia. They provoke intense discussions partly because they force us to define when life itself begins and ends, as well as how much control government should have over our ethical decisions. These topics compel us to review what we believe about human existence, moral responsibilities, and the limits of individual choice. Often, they also require us to consider the ways that our ethical stands may be influenced by our personal experience, as well as aspects of our social position, such as our gender, occupation, and financial status.

This constellation focuses on the debate over abortion. Richard Selzer emphasizes what he takes to be the horrifying aspects of abortion, while Sallie Tisdale and Anna Quindlen suggest that society keep it legal despite mixed feelings they have about it. Besides indicating some of the different positions that people can take on abortion, these essays illustrate the ways in which personal experience and social position can figure in the debate over it. While both Selzer and Tisdale are medical professionals, they write from different perspectives. He is a doctor who ultimately focuses on his response to a single abortion he witnessed; she is a nurse who reflects on her day-to-day experience in an abortion clinic serving people from a range of social classes. Quindlen writes from the perspective of a woman who is outside the medical profession and has not personally had an abortion, but who nevertheless feels entitled and able to draw on her own life as she explores the topic's moral significance. These essays are not, then, straightforward and dryly objective statements on abortion. We chose them in part because they represent the human feelings as well as the moral reasoning that arguments over abortion have typically involved. Nevertheless, they review issues it has given rise to, they promote certain attitudes toward it, and they present reasons for their stands. When you read them, inevitably you will reflect on your own attitude toward abortion and determine how successful each essay is in reinforcing or changing it. As you study these texts, however, also consider the values and rhetorical strategies you would apply to other ethical controversies.

Abortion

Richard Selzer

Richard Selzer (b. 1928) was originally trained as a doctor. He is now retired
from his medical career, but for many years he taught at the Yale Medical
School and practiced surgery. He did not begin his career as a writer,
however, until he was almost 40 years old. Since then, he has gained
increasing renown for his essays and short stories on medical subjects. His
volumes of fiction include *Rituals of Surgery* and *Imagine a Woman and
Other Tales*. His essays are collected in *Confessions of a Knife, Letters to a
Young Doctor, Taking the World in for Repairs,* and *Mortal Lessons: Notes
on the Art of Surgery,* a 1976 book in which the following essay appears.

Reflections Before Reading

What is your own position on abortion? What issues do you think the topic
raises? What do you expect or hope an essay entitled "Abortion" will
include? What insights and experiences might a surgeon bring to the topic?

1 Horror, like bacteria, is everywhere. It blankets the earth, endlessly lapping to find
that one unguarded entryway. As though narcotized, we walk beneath, upon,
through it. Carelessly we touch the familiar infected linen, eat from the universal
dish; we disdain isolation. We are like the newborn that carry immunity from their
mothers' wombs. Exteriorized, we are wrapped in impermeable membranes that
cannot be seen. Then one day, the defense is gone. And we awaken to horror.

2 In our city, garbage is collected early in the morning. Sometimes the bang of
the cans and the grind of the truck awaken us before our time. We are resentful,
mutter into our pillows, then go back to sleep. On the morning of August 6, 1975,
the people of 73rd Street near Woodside Avenue do just that. When at last they
rise from their beds, dress, eat breakfast and leave their houses for work, they have
forgotten, if they had ever known, that the garbage truck had passed earlier that
morning. The event has slipped into unmemory, like a dream.

3 They close their doors and descend to the pavement. It is midsummer. You
measure the climate, decide how you feel in relation to the heat and the humidity.
You walk toward the bus stop. Others, your neighbors, are waiting there. It is all so

familiar. All at once you step on something soft. You feel it with your foot. Even through your shoe you have the sense of something unusual, something marked by a special "give." It is a foreignness upon the pavement. Instinct pulls your foot away in an awkward little movement. You look down, and you see . . . a tiny naked body, its arms and legs flung apart, its head thrown back, its mouth agape, its face serious. A bird, you think, fallen from its nest. But there is no nest here on 73rd Street, no bird so big. It is rubber, then. A model, a . . . joke. Yes, that's it, a joke. And you bend to see. Because you must. And it is no joke. Such a gray softness can be but one thing. It is a baby, and dead. You cover your mouth, your eyes. You are fixed. Horror has found its chink and crawled in, and you will never be the same as you were. Years later you will step from a sidewalk to a lawn, and you will start at its softness, and think of that upon which you have just trod.

Now you look about; another man has seen it too. "My God," he whispers.   4
Others come, people you have seen every day for years, and you hear them speak with strangely altered voices. "Look," they say, "it's a baby." There is a cry. "Here's another!" and "Another!" and "Another!" And you follow with your gaze the index fingers of your friends pointing from the huddle where you cluster. Yes, it is true! There *are* more of these . . . little carcasses upon the street. And for a moment you look up to see if all the unbaptized sinless are falling from Limbo.

Now the street is filling with people. There are police. They know what to do.   5
They rope off the area, then stand guard over the enclosed space. They are controlled, methodical, these young policemen. Servants, they do not reveal themselves to their public master; it would not be seemly. Yet I do see their pallor and the sweat that breaks upon the face of one, the way another bites the lining of his cheek and holds it thus. Ambulance attendants scoop up the bodies. They scan the street; none must be overlooked. What they place upon the litter amounts to little more than a dozen pounds of human flesh. They raise the litter, and slide it home inside the ambulance, and they drive away. You and your neighbors stand about in the street which is become for you a battlefield from which the newly slain have at last been bagged and tagged and dragged away. *But what shrapnel is this? By what explosion flung, these fragments that sink into the brain and fester there?* Whatever smell there is in this place becomes for you the stench of death. The people of 73rd Street do not then speak to each other. It is too soon for outrage, too late for blindness. It is the time of unresisted horror.

Later, at the police station, the investigation is brisk, conclusive. It is the hos-   6
pital director speaking: ". . . fetuses accidentally got mixed up with the hospital rubbish . . . were picked up at approximately eight fifteen A.M. by a sanitation truck. Somehow, the plastic lab bag, labeled HAZARDOUS MATERIAL, fell off the back of the truck and broke open. No, it is not known how the fetuses got in the orange plastic bag labeled HAZARDOUS MATERIAL. It is a freak accident." The hospital director wants you to know that it is not an everyday occurrence. Once in a lifetime, he says. But you have seen it, and what are his words to you now?

He grows affable, familiar, tells you that, by mistake, the fetuses got mixed up   7
with the other debris. (Yes, he says *other;* he says *debris.*) He has spent the entire day, he says, trying to figure out how it happened. He wants you to know that. Somehow it matters to him. He goes on:

Aborted fetuses that weigh one pound or less are incinerated. Those weighing   8
over one pound are buried at a city cemetery. He says this. Now you see. It *is*
orderly. It *is* sensible. The world is *not* mad. This is still a civilized society.

There is no more. You turn to leave. Outside on the street, men are talking   9
things over, reassuring each other that the right thing is being done. But just this
once, you know it isn't. You saw, and you know.

And you know, too, that the Street of the Dead Fetuses will be wherever you   10
go. You are part of its history now, its legend. It has laid claim upon you so that you
cannot entirely leave it—not ever.

I am a surgeon. I do not shrink from the particularities of sick flesh. Escaping   11
blood, all the outpourings of disease—phlegm, pus, vomitus, even those occult
meaty tumors that terrify—I see as blood, disease, phlegm, and so on. I touch
them to destroy them. But I do not make symbols of them. I have seen, and I am
used to seeing. Yet there are paths within the body that I have not taken, penetralia
where I do not go. Nor is it lack of technique, limitation of knowledge that forbids
me these ways.

It is the western wing of the fourth floor of a great university hospital. An   12
abortion is about to take place. I am present because I asked to be present. I
wanted to see what I had never seen.

The patient is Jamaican. She lies on the table submissively, and now and then   13
she smiles at one of the nurses as though acknowledging a secret.

A nurse draws down the sheet, lays bare the abdomen. The belly mounds   14
gently in the twenty-fourth week of pregnancy. The chief surgeon paints it with a
sponge soaked in red antiseptic. He does this three times, each time a fresh
sponge. He covers the area with a sterile sheet, an aperture in its center. He is a
kindly man who teaches as he works, who pauses to reassure the woman.

He begins.   15

A little pinprick, he says to the woman.   16

He inserts the point of a tiny needle at the midline of the lower portion of her   17
abdomen, on the downslope. He infiltrates local anesthetic into the skin, where it
forms a small white bubble.

The woman grimaces.   18

That is all you will feel, the doctor says. Except for a little pressure. But no   19
more pain.

She smiles again. She seems to relax. She settles comfortably on the table. The   20
worst is over.

The doctor selects a three-and-one-half-inch needle bearing a central stylet.   21
He places the point at the site of the previous injection. He aims it straight up and
down, perpendicular. Next he takes hold of her abdomen with his left hand, palm-
ing the womb, steadying it. He thrusts with his right hand. The needle sinks into
the abdominal wall.

Oh, says the woman quietly.   22

But I guess it is not pain that she feels. It is more a recognition that the deed is   23
being done.

Another thrust and he has speared the uterus.   24

We are in, he says.   25

He has felt the muscular wall of the organ gripping the shaft of his needle. A   26
further slight pressure on the needle advances it a bit more. He takes his left hand
from the woman's abdomen. He retracts the filament of the stylet from the barrel
of the needle. A small geyser of pale yellow fluid erupts.

We are in the right place, says the doctor. Are you feeling any pain? he asks.   27

She smiles, shakes her head. She gazes at the ceiling.   28

In the room we are six: two physicians, two nurses, the patient, and me. The   29
participants are busy, very attentive. I am not at all busy—but I am no less attentive. I want to see.

I see something! It is unexpected, utterly unexpected, like a disturbance in the   30
earth, a tumultuous jarring. I see a movement—a small one. But I have seen it.

And then I see it again. And now I see that it is the hub of the needle in the   31
woman's belly that has jerked. First to one side. Then to the other side. Once more
it wobbles, is *tugged,* like a fishing line nibbled by a sunfish.

Again! And I *know!*   32

It is the *fetus* that worries thus. It is the fetus struggling against the needle.   33
Struggling? How can that be? I think: *that cannot be.* I think: the fetus feels no
pain, cannot feel fear, has no *motivation.* It is merely reflex.

I point to the needle.   34

It is a reflex, says the doctor.   35

By the end of the fifth month, the fetus weighs about one pound, is about   36
twelve inches long. Hair is on the head. There are eyebrows, eyelashes. Pale pink
nipples show on the chest. Nails are present, at the fingertips, at the toes.

At the beginning of the sixth month, the fetus can cry, can suck, can make a   37
fist. He kicks, he punches. The mother can feel this, can *see* this. His eyelids, until
now closed, can open. He may look up, down, sideways. His grip is very strong. He
could support his weight by holding with one hand.

A reflex, the doctor says.   38

I hear him. But I saw something in that mass of cells *understand* that it must   39
bob and butt. And I see it again! I have an impulse to shove to the table—it is just a
step—seize that needle, pull it out.

We are not six, I think. We are *seven.*   40

Something strangles *there.* An effort, its effort, binds me to it.   41

I do not shove to the table. I take no little step. It would be . . . well, madness.   42
Everyone here wants the needle where it is. Six do. No, *five* do.

I close my eyes. I see the inside of the uterus. It is bathed in ruby gloom. I see   43
the creature curled upon itself. Its knees are flexed. Its head is bent upon its chest.
It is in fluid and gently rocks to the rhythm of the distant heartbeat.

It resembles . . . a sleeping infant.   44

Its place is entered by something. It is sudden. A point coming. A needle!   45

A spike of *daylight* pierces the chamber. Now the light is extinguished. The   46
needle comes closer in the pool. The point grazes the thigh, and I stir. Perhaps I

wake from dozing. The light is there again. I twist and straighten. My arms and legs *push.* My hand finds the shaft—grabs! I *grab.* I bend the needle this way and that. The point probes, touches on my belly. My mouth opens. Could I cry out? All is a commotion and a churning. There is a presence in the pool. An activity! The pool colors, reddens, darkens.

I open my eyes to see the doctor feeding a small plastic tube through the 47 barrel of the needle into the uterus. Drops of pink fluid overrun the rim and spill onto the sheet. He withdraws the needle from around the plastic tubing. Now only the little tube protrudes from the woman's body. A nurse hands the physician a syringe loaded with a colorless liquid. He attaches it to the end of the tubing and injects it.

Prostaglandin, he says. 48

Ah well, prostaglandin—a substance found normally in the body. When given 49 in concentrated dosage, it throws the uterus into vigorous contraction. In eight to twelve hours, the woman will expel the fetus.

The doctor detaches the syringe but does not remove the tubing. 50

In case we must do it over, he says. 51

He takes away the sheet. He places gauze pads over the tubing. Over all this 52 he applies adhesive tape.

I know. We cannot feed the great numbers. There is no more room. I know, I 53 know. It is a woman's right to refuse the risk, to decline the pain of childbirth. And an unwanted child is a very great burden. An unwanted child is a burden to himself. I know.

And yet . . . there is the flick of that needle. I *saw* it. I saw . . . I *felt*—in that 54 room, a pace away, life prodded, life fending off. I saw life avulsed—swept by flood, blackening—then *out.*

There, says the doctor. It's all over. It wasn't too bad, was it? he says to the 55 woman.

She smiles. It is all over. Oh, yes. 56

And who would care to imagine that from a moist and dark commencement six 57 months before there would ripen the cluster and globule, the sprout and pouch of man?

And who would care to imagine that trapped within the laked pearl and a 58 dowry of yoke would lie the earliest stuff of dream and memory?

It is a persona carried here as well as a person, I think. I think it is a signed 59 piece, engraved with a hieroglyph of human genes.

I did not think this until I saw. The flick. The fending off. 60

Later, in the corridor, the doctor explains that the law does not permit abor- 61 tion beyond the twenty-fourth week. That is when the fetus may be viable, he says. We stand together for a moment, and he tells of an abortion in which the fetus *cried* after it was passed.

What did you do? I ask him. 62

There was nothing *to* do but let it live, he says. It did very well, he says. A case   63
of mistaken dates.

Rhetorical Focus

1. Selzer begins with an incident of "unresisted horror" (paragraph 6) that, as the hospital director points out, "is not an everyday occurrence" (paragraph 7). Is Selzer justified in using it, then?
2. Selzer does not organize his essay in a conventional way. How might he justify the sections he breaks it into, and the order he puts them in? Note how he also shifts personal pronouns, alternately using "we," "they," "you," and "I." Do these changes make sense?
3. As Selzer describes the abortion, he provides many sensory details. What is the effect of these details on you? In many of his essays, Selzer has described in detail other kinds of operations. Do you think these descriptions would affect you in the same way, or does it matter here that you are reading about an abortion in particular? Explain. If someone wanted to defend a woman's right to an abortion, do you think he or she would describe the operation here differently? If so, what sorts of details might he or she focus on?

Thematic Focus

1. Do you find yourself agreeing with Selzer's perception of abortion? Why or why not?
2. Does Selzer fairly acknowledge what can be said in favor of legalizing abortion?
3. Selzer does not spell out what he would like the legal system to do about abortion. What legal policies do you think society would adopt if it agreed with Selzer's essay? Why do you think he did not identify these policies himself?

We Do Abortions Here

Sallie Tisdale

Sallie Tisdale (b. 1957) is a registered nurse who, like Selzer, has written on issues in modern medicine. She has been especially concerned with medical institutions. Her books include *The Sorcerer's Apprentice: Tales of the Modern Hospital, Harvest Moon: Portrait of a Nursing Home,* and *Lot's Wife: Salt and the Human Condition.* She has also written articles on the institutional treatment of mentally retarded people, technology fairs that offer simulations of reality, and her own childhood as the daughter of a firefighter. The following essay appeared in the October 1987 issue of *Harper's.* At the time she wrote it, Tisdale was working as a nurse in an abortion clinic.

Reflections Before Reading

What are you curious to know about daily life in an abortion clinic? What qualities do you think someone would need in order to work there? Would you respect such a person? Why or why not? What sorts of things might she notice and emphasize that Selzer does not?

We do abortions here; that is all we do. There are weary, grim moments when I think I cannot bear another basin of bloody remains, utter another kind phrase of reassurance. So I leave the procedure room in the back and reach for a new chart. Soon I am talking to an eighteen-year-old woman pregnant for the fourth time. I push up her sleeve to check her blood pressure and find row upon row of needle marks, neat and parallel and discolored. She has been so hungry for her drug for so long that she has taken to using the loose skin of her upper arms; her elbows are already a permanent ruin of bruises. She is surprised to find herself nearly four months pregnant. I suspect she is often surprised, in a mild way, by the blows she is dealt. I prepare myself for another basin, another brief and chafing loss. 1

"How can you stand it?" Even the clients ask. They see the machine, the strange instruments, the blood, the final stroke that wipes away the promise of pregnancy. Sometimes I see that too: I watch a woman's swollen abdomen sink to softness in a few stuttering moments and my own belly flip-flops with sorrow. But all it takes for me to catch my breath is another interview, one more story that sounds so much like the last one. There is a numbing sameness lurking in this job: 2

the same questions, the same answers, even the same trembling tone in the voices. The worst is the sameness of human failure, of inadequacy in the face of each day's dull demands.

In describing this work, I find it difficult to explain how much I enjoy it most of the time. We laugh a lot here, as friends and as professional peers. It's nice to be with women all day. I like the sudden, transient bonds I forge with some clients: moments when I am in my strength, remembering weakness, and a woman in weakness reaches out for my strength. What I offer is not power, but solidness, offered almost eagerly. Certain clients waken in me every tender urge I have— others make me wince and bite my tongue. Both challenge me to find a balance. It is a sweet brutality we practice here, a stark and loving dispassion. 3

I look at abortion as if I am standing on a cliff with a telescope, gazing at some great vista. I can sweep the horizon with both eyes, survey the scene in all its distance and size. Or I can put my eye to the lens and focus on the small details, suddenly so close. In abortion the absolute must always be tempered by the contextual, because both are real, both valid, both hard. How can we do this? How can we refuse? Each abortion is a measure of our failure to protect, to nourish our own. Each basin I empty is a promise—but a promise broken a long time ago. 4

I grew up on the great promise of birth control. Like many women my age, I took the pill as soon as I was sexually active. To risk pregnancy when it was so easy to avoid seemed stupid, and my contraceptive success, as it were, was part of the promise of social enlightenment. But birth control fails, far more frequently than laboratory trials predict. Many of our clients take the pill; its failure to protect them is a shocking realization. We have clients who have been sterilized, whose husbands have had vasectomies; each one is a statistical misfit, fine print come to life. The anger and shame of these women I hold in one hand, and the basin in the other. The distance between the two, the length I pace and try to measure, is the size of an abortion. 5

The procedure is disarmingly simple. Women are surprised, as though the mystery of conception, a dark and hidden genesis, requires an elaborate finale. In the first trimester of pregnancy, it's a mere few minutes of vacuuming, a neat tidying up. I give a woman a small yellow Valium, and when it has begun to relax her, I lead her into the back, into bareness, the stirrups. The doctor reaches in her, opening the narrow tunnel to the uterus with a succession of slim, smooth bars of steel. He inserts a plastic tube and hooks it to a hose on the machine. The woman is framed against white paper that crackles as she moves, the light bright in her eyes. Then the machine rumbles low and loud in the small windowless room; the doctor moves the tube back and forth with an efficient rhythm, and the long tail of it fills with blood that spurts and stumbles along into a jar. He is usually finished in a few minutes. They are long minutes for the woman; her uterus frequently reacts to its abrupt emptying with a powerful, unceasing cramp, which cuts off the blood vessels and enfolds the irritated, bleeding tissue. 6

I am learning to recognize the shadows that cross the faces of the women I hold. While the doctor works between her spread legs, the paper drape hiding his intent expression, I stand beside the table. I hold the woman's hands in mine, 7 resting them just below her ribs. I watch her eyes, finger her necklace, stroke her hair. I ask about her job, her family; in a haze she answers me; we chatter, faces close, eyes meeting and sliding apart.

I watch the shadows that creep up unnoticed and suddenly darken her face as   8
she screws up her features and pushes a tear out each side to slide down her cheeks. I have learned to anticipate the quiver of chin, the rapid intake of breath and the surprising sobs that rise soon after the machine starts to drum. I know this is when the cramp deepens, and the tears are partly the tears that follow pain—the sharp, childish crying when one bumps one's head on a cabinet door. But a well of woe seems to open beneath many women when they hear that thumping sound. The anticipation of the moment has finally come to fruit; the moment has arrived when the loss is no longer an imagined one. It has come true.

I am struck by the sameness and I am struck every day by the variety here—   9
how this commonplace dilemma can so display the differences of women. A twenty-one-year-old woman, unemployed, uneducated, without family, in the fifth month of her fifth pregnancy. A forty-two-year-old mother of teenagers, shocked by her condition, refusing to tell her husband. A twenty-three-year-old mother of two having her seventh abortion, and many women in their thirties having their first. Some are stoic, some hysterical, a few giggle uncontrollably, many cry.

I talk to a sixteen-year-old uneducated girl who was raped. She has gonorrhea.   10
She describes blinding headaches, attacks of breathlessness, nausea. "Sometimes I feel like two different people," she tells me with a calm smile, "and I talk to my-self."

I pull out my plastic models. She listens patiently for a time, and then holds   11
her hands wide in front of her stomach.

"When's the baby going to go up into my stomach?" she asks.   12

I blink. "What do you mean?"   13

"Well," she says, still smiling, "when women get so big, isn't the baby in your   14
stomach? Doesn't it hatch out of an egg there?"

My first question in an interview is always the same. As I walk down the hall   15
with the woman, as we get settled in chairs and I glance through her files, I am trying to gauge her, to get a sense of the words, and the tone, I should use. With some I joke, with others I chat, sometimes I fall into a brisk, business-like patter. But I ask every woman, "Are you sure you want to have an abortion?" Most nod with grim knowing smiles. "Oh, yes," they sigh. Some seek forgiveness, offer ex-cuses. Occasionally a woman will flinch and say, "Please don't use that word."

Later I describe the procedure to come, using care with my language. I don't   16
say "pain" any more than I would say "baby." So many are afraid to ask how much it will hurt. "My sister told me—" I hear. "A friend of mine said—" and the dire expectations unravel. I prick the index finger of a woman for a drop of blood to test, and as the tiny lancet approaches the skin she averts her eyes, holding her trembling hand out to me and jumping at my touch.

It is when I am holding a plastic uterus in one hand, a suction tube in the   17
other, moving them together in imitation of the scrubbing to come, that women ask the most secret question. I am speaking in a matter-of-fact voice about "the

tissue" and "the contents" when the woman suddenly catches my eye and asks, "How big is the baby now?" These words suggest a quiet need for a definition of the boundaries being drawn. It isn't so odd, after all, that she feels relief when I describe the growing bud's bulbous shape, its miniature nature. Again I gauge, and sometimes lie a little, weaseling around its infantile features until its clinging power slackens.

But when I look in the basin, among the curdlike blood clots, I see an elfin 18 thorax, attenuated, its pencilline ribs all in parallel rows with tiny knobs of spine rounding upwards. A translucent arm and hand swim beside.

A sleepy-eyed girl, just fourteen, watched me with a slight and goofy smile all 19 through her abortion. "Does it have little feet and little fingers and all?" she'd asked earlier. When the suction was over she sat up woozily at the end of the table and murmured, "Can I see it?" I shook my head firmly.

"It's not allowed," I told her sternly, because I knew she didn't really want to 20 see what was left. She accepted this statement of authority, and a shadow of confused relief crossed her plain, pale face.

Privately, even grudgingly, my colleagues might admit the power of abortion 21 to provoke emotion. But they seem to prefer the broad view and disdain the telescope. Abortion is a matter of choice, privacy, control. Its uncertainty lies in specific cases: retarded women and girls too young to give consent for surgery, women who are ill or hostile or psychotic. Such common dilemmas are met with both compassion and impatience: they slow things down. We are too busy to chew over ethics. One person might discuss certain concerns, behind closed doors, or describe a particularly disturbing dream. But generally there is to be no ambivalence.

Every day I take calls from women who are annoyed that we cannot see them, 22 cannot do their abortion today, this morning, now. They argue the price, demand that we stay after hours to accommodate their job or class schedule. Abortion is so routine that one expects it to be like a manicure: quick, cheap, and painless.

Still, I've cultivated a certain disregard. It isn't negligence, but I don't always 23 pay attention. I couldn't be here if I tried to judge each case on its merits; after all, we do over a hundred abortions a week. At some point each individual in this line of work draws a boundary and adheres to it. For one physician the boundary is a particular week of gestation; for another, it is a certain number of repeated abortions. But these boundaries can be fluid too: one physician overruled his own limit to abort a mature but severely malformed fetus. For me, the limit is allowing my clients to carry their own burden, shoulder the responsibility themselves. I shoulder the burden of trying not to judge them.

This city has several "crisis pregnancy centers" advertised in the Yellow Pages. 24 They are small offices staffed by volunteers, and they offer free pregnancy testing, glossy photos of dead fetuses, and movies. I had a client recently whose mother is active in the anti-abortion movement. The young woman went to the local crisis center and was told that the doctor would make her touch her dismembered baby, that the pain would be the most horrible she could imagine, and that she might, after an abortion, never be able to have children. All lies. They called her at home and at work, over and over and over, but she had been wise enough to give a false name. She came to us a fugitive. We who do abortions are marked, by some, as impure. It's dirty work.

When a deliveryman comes to the sliding glass window by the reception desk   25
and tilts a box toward me, I hesitate. I read the packing slip, assess the shape and weight of the box in light of its supposed contents. We request familiar faces. The doors are carefully locked; I have learned to half glance around at bags and boxes, looking for a telltale sign. I register with security when I arrive, and I am careful not to bang a door. We are all a little on edge here.

Concern about size and shape seem to be natural, and so is the relief that   26
follows. We make the powerful assumption that the fetus is different from us, and even when we admit the similarities, it is too simplistic to be seduced by form alone. But the form is enormously potent—humanoid, powerless, palm-sized, and pure, it evokes an almost fierce tenderness when viewed simply as what it appears to be. But appearance, and even potential, aren't enough. The fetus, in becoming itself, can ruin others; its utter dependence has a sinister side. When I am struck in the moment by the contents in the basin, I am careful to remember the context, to note the tearful teenager and the woman sighing with something more than relief. One kind of question, though, I find considerably trickier.

"Can you tell what it is?" I am asked, and this means gender. This question is   27
asked by couples, not women alone. Always couples would abort a girl and keep a boy. I have been asked about twins, and even if I could tell what race the father was.

An eighteen-year-old woman with three daughters brought her husband to   28
the interview. He glared first at me, then at his wife, as he sank lower and lower in the chair, picking his teeth with a toothpick. He interrupted a conversation with his wife to ask if I could tell whether the baby would be a boy or a girl. I told him I could not.

"Good," he replied in a slow and strangely malevolent voice, "'cause if it was a   29
boy I'd wring her neck."

In a literal sense, abortion exists because we are able to ask such questions,   30
able to assign a value to the fetus which can shift with changing circumstances. If the human bond to a child were as primitive and unflinchingly narrow as that of other animals, there would be no abortion. There would be no abortion because there would be nothing more important than caring for the young and perpetuating the species, no reason for sex but to make babies. I sense this sometimes, this wordless organic duty, when I do ultrasounds.

We do ultrasound, a sound-wave test that paints a faint, gray picture of the   31
fetus, whenever we're uncertain of gestation. Age is measured by the width of the skull and confirmed by the length of the femur or thighbone; we speak of a pregnancy as being a certain "femur length" in weeks. The usual concern is whether a pregnancy is within the legal limit for an abortion. Women this far along have

bellies which swell out round and tight like trim muscles. When they lie flat, the mound rises softly above the hips, pressing the umbilicus upward.

It takes practice to read an ultrasound picture, which is grainy and etched as 32 though in strokes of charcoal. But suddenly a rapid rhythmic motion appears—the beating heart. Nearby is a soft oval, scratched with lines—the skull. The leg is harder to find, and then suddenly the fetus moves, bobbing in the surf. The skull turns away, an arm slides across the screen, the torso rolls. I know the weight of a baby's head on my shoulder, the whisper of lips on ears, the delicate curve of a fragile spine in my hand. I know how heavy and correct a newborn cradled feels. The creature I watch in secret requires nothing from me but to be left alone, and that is precisely what won't be done.

These inadvertently made beings are caught in a twisting web of motive and 33 desire. They are at least inconvenient, sometimes quite literally dangerous in the womb, but most often they fall somewhere in between—consequences never quite believed in come to roost. Their virtue rises and falls outside their own nature: they become only what we make them. A fetus created by accident is the most absolute kind of surprise. Whether the blame lies in a failed IUD, a slipped condom, or a false impression of safety, that fetus is a thing whose creation has been actively worked against. Its existence is an error. I think this is why so few women, even late in a pregnancy, will consider giving a baby up for adoption. To do so means making the fetus real—imagining it as something whole and outside oneself. The decision to terminate a pregnancy is sometimes so difficult and confounding that it creates an enormous demand for immediate action. The decision is a rejection; the pregnancy has become something to be rid of, a condition to be ended. It is a burden, a weight, a thing separate.

Women have abortions because they are too old, and too young, too poor, and 34 too rich, too stupid, and too smart. I see women who berate themselves with violent emotions for their first and only abortion, and others who return three times, five times, hauling two or three children, who cannot remember to take a pill or where they put the diaphragm. We talk glibly about choice. But the choice for what? I see all the broken promises in lives lived like a series of impromptu obstacles. There are the sweet, light promises of love and intimacy, the glittering promise of education and progress, the warm promise of safe families, long years of innocence and community. And there is the promise of freedom: freedom from failure, from faithlessness. Freedom from biology. The early feminist defense of abortion asked many questions, but the one I remember is this: Is biology destiny? And the answer is yes, sometimes it is. Women who have the fewest choices of all exercise their right to abortion the most.

Oh, the ignorance. I take a woman to the back room and ask her to undress; a 35 few minutes later I return and find her positioned discreetly behind a drape, still wearing underpants. "Do I have to take these off too?" she asks, a little shocked. Some swear they have not had sex, many do not know what a uterus is, how sperm and egg meet, how sex makes babies. Some late seekers do not believe themselves pregnant; they believe themselves *impregnable.* I was chastised when I began this job for referring to some clients as girls: it is a feminist heresy. They come so young, snapping gum, sockless and sneakered, and their shakily applied eyeliner smears when they cry. I call them girls with maternal benignity. I cannot imagine them as mothers.

The doctor seats himself between the woman's thighs and reaches into the 36 dilated opening of a five-month pregnant uterus. Quickly he grabs and crushes the fetus in several places, and the room is filled with a low clatter and snap of forceps, the click of the tanaculum, and a pulling, sucking sound. The paper crinkles as the drugged and sleepy woman shifts, the nurse's low, honey-brown voice explains each step in delicate words.

I have fetus dreams, we all do here: dreams of abortions one after the other; of 37 buckets of blood splashed on the walls; trees full of crawling fetuses. I dreamed that two men grabbed me and began to drag me away. "Let's do an abortion," they said with a sickening leer, and I began to scream, plunged into a vision of sucking, scraping pain, of being spread and torn by impartial instruments that do only what they are bidden. I woke from this dream barely able to breathe and thought of kitchen tables and coat hangers, knitting needles striped with blood, and women all alone clutching a pillow in their teeth to keep the screams from piercing the apartment-house walls. Abortion is the narrowest edge between kindness and cruelty. Done as well as it can be, it is still violence—merciful violence, like putting a suffering animal to death.

Maggie, one of the nurses, received a call at midnight not long ago. It was a 38 woman in her twentieth week of pregnancy; the necessarily gradual process of cervical dilation begun the day before had stimulated labor, as it sometimes does. Maggie and one of the doctors met the woman at the office in the night. Maggie helped her onto the table, and as she lay down the fetus was delivered into Maggie's hands. When Maggie told me about it the next day, she cupped her hands into a small bowl— "It was just like a little kitten," she said softly, wonderingly. "Everything was still attached."

At the end of the day I clean out the suction jars, pouring blood into the sink, 39 splashing the sides with flecks of tissue. From the sink rises a rich and humid smell, hot, earthy, and moldering; it is the smell of something recently alive beginning to decay. I take care of the plastic tub on the floor, filled with pieces too big to be trusted to the trash. The law defines the contents of the bucket I hold protectively against my chest as "tissue." Some would say my complicity in filling that bucket gives me no right to call it anything else. I slip the tissue gently into a bag and place it in the freezer, to be burned at another time. Abortion requires of me an entirely new set of assumptions. It requires a willingness to live with conflict, fearlessness, and grief. As I close the freezer door, I imagine a world where this won't be necessary, and then return to the world where it is.

Rhetorical Focus

1. What image does Tisdale project of herself? Did she turn out to be the kind of person you thought a nurse in an abortion clinic might be like? As a

writer on abortion, does she have more authority than Selzer does because she has seen many more abortions and talked with many more abortion patients?

2. Choose a passage from this essay that for you has especially striking language. Why, specifically, does it affect you?

3. Both Selzer and Tisdale interweave personal emotions with clinical details. Do their reports of their emotions affect you in the same way? Why or why not?

Thematic Focus

1. Tisdale remarks that the staff members in the clinic "are too busy to chew over ethics" (paragraph 21), but obviously this essay does. Summarize in a sentence or two what you take her feelings about abortion to be. Do you share them more than you do Selzer's? Why or why not?

2. Tisdale states, "In abortion the absolute must always be tempered by the contextual, because both are real, both valid, both hard" (paragraph 4). What social circumstances does she apparently want us to consider when we make judgments about abortion? Do you agree that these circumstances should be considered? Why or why not? Is the context that Selzer establishes for abortion significantly different from Tisdale's? Explain.

3. Both Selzer and Tisdale rely on graphic, even brutal images as they register their points. To what extent do they mention similar details, even if they interpret them perhaps in different ways? Some people might argue that the clinical details of abortion are distasteful, and even detract from a proper discussion of the subject. What would you say to them?

Some Thoughts About Abortion

Anna Quindlen

After graduating from Barnard College in New York City, Anna Quindlen (b. 1952) served as a reporter for *The New York Post* and then for *The New York Times.* Subsequently, she became a columnist for *The Times,* and she is chiefly known today for her work in this capacity. Quindlen has actually written three *Times* columns. In the first, "About New York," she concentrated on aspects of the city. In 1986, she began a second column, "Life in the Thirties," in which she used her experiences as an individual, wife, and mother to reflect on her generation. This column became nationally syndicated, and Quindlen collected selections from it in a 1988 book entitled *Living Out Loud,* where the following essay appears. After taking time off to raise her children, Quindlen began a third column for *The Times* in 1990. In it, she gives explicitly personal responses to news events, thus continuing to link her own life with the larger world.

Reflections Before Reading

Are there any issues in the abortion debate that Selzer and Tisdale have failed to address and that you would like to see a third writer bring up? If so, what are they? Unlike Selzer and Tisdale, Quindlen is not a medical professional. Do you think that a layperson's stand on abortion deserves at least as much respect as a medical person's? Why or why not? Unlike Selzer, Tisdale and Quindlen write as women. Do you think women should have more power than men to decide what public policy toward abortion should be? Why or why not? Quindlen also writes as a mother. In what ways might this aspect of her own life figure in her thinking about abortion?

It was always the look on their faces that told me first. I was the freshman dormi- 1
tory counselor and they were the freshmen at a women's college where everyone was smart. One of them would come into my room, a golden girl, a valedictorian,

an 800 verbal score on the S.A.T.'s, and her eyes would be empty, seeing only a busted future, the devastation of her life as she knew it. She had failed biology, messed up the math; she was pregnant.

That was when I became pro-choice.   2

It was the look in his eyes that I will always remember, too. They were as black   3
as the bottom of a well, and in them for a few minutes I thought I saw myself the way I had always wished to be—clear, simple, elemental, at peace. My child looked at me and I looked back at him in the delivery room, and I realized that out of a sea of infinite possibilities it had come down to this: a specific person, born on the hottest day of the year, conceived on a Christmas Eve, made by his father and me miraculously from scratch.

Once I believed that there was a little blob of formless protoplasm in there and   4
a gynecologist went after it with a surgical instrument, and that was that. Then I got pregnant myself—eagerly, intentionally, by the right man, at the right time—and I began to doubt. My abdomen still flat, my stomach roiling with morning sickness, I felt not that I had protoplasm inside, but, instead, a complete human being in miniature to whom I could talk, sing, make promises. Neither of these views was accurate; instead, I think, the reality is something in the middle. And that is where I find myself now, in the middle—hating the idea of abortions, hating the idea of having them outlawed.

For I know it is the right thing in some times and places. I remember sitting in   5
a shabby clinic far uptown with one of those freshmen, only three months after the Supreme Court had made what we were doing possible, and watching with wonder as the lovely first love she had had with a nice boy unraveled over the space of an hour as they waited for her to be called, degenerated into sniping and silences. I remember a year or two later seeing them pass on campus and not even acknowledge each other because their conjoining had caused them so much pain, and I shuddered to think of them married, with a small psyche in their unready and unwilling hands.

I've met fourteen-year-olds who were pregnant and said they could not have   6
abortions because of their religion, and I see in their eyes the shadows of twenty-two-year-olds I've talked to who lost their kids to foster care because they hit them or used drugs or simply had no money for food and shelter. I read not long ago about a teenager who said she meant to have an abortion but she spent the money on clothes instead: now she has a baby who turns out to be a lot more trouble than a toy. The people who hand out those execrable little pictures of dismembered fetuses at abortion clinics seem to forget the extraordinary pain children may endure after they are born when they are unwanted, even hated, or simply tolerated.

I believe that in a contest between the living and the almost living, the latter   7
must, if necessary, give way to the will of the former. That is what the fetus is to me, the almost living. These questions began to plague me—and, I've discovered, a good many other women—after I became pregnant. But they became even more acute after I had my second child, mainly because he is so different from his brother. On two random nights eighteen months apart the same two people managed to conceive, and on one occasion the tumult within turned itself into a curly-haired brunet with merry black eyes who walked and talked late and loved the

whole world, and on another it became a blond with hazel Asian eyes and a pug nose who tried to conquer the world almost as soon as he entered it.

If we were to have an abortion next time for some reason or another, which 8 infinite possibility becomes, not a reality, but a nullity? The girl with the blue eyes? The improbable redhead? The natural athlete? The thinker? My husband, ever at the heart of the matter, put it another way. Knowing he is finding two children somewhat more overwhelming than he expected, I asked if he would want me to have an abortion if I accidentally became pregnant again right away. "And waste a perfectly good human being?" he said.

Coming to this quandary has been difficult for me. In fact, I believe the issue 9 of abortion is difficult for all thoughtful people. I don't know anyone who has had an abortion who has been casual about it. If there is one thing I find intolerable about most of the so-called right-to-lifers, it is that they try to portray abortion rights as something that feminists thought up on a slow Saturday over a light lunch. That is nonsense. I also know that some people who support abortion rights are most comfortable with a monolithic position because it seems the strongest front against the smug and sometimes violent opposition.

But I don't feel all one way about abortion anymore, and I don't think it serves 10 a just cause to pretend that many of us do. For years I believed that a woman's right to choose was absolute, but now I wonder. Do I, with a stable home and marriage and sufficient stamina and money, have the freedom to choose abortion because a pregnancy is inconvenient just now? Legally I do have the right; legally I want always to have that right. It is the morality of exercising it under those circumstances that makes me wonder.

Technology has foiled us. The second trimester has become a time of resur- 11 rection; a fetus at six months can be one woman's late abortion, another's premature, viable child. Photographers now have film of embryos the size of a grape, oddly human, flexing their fingers, sucking their thumbs. Women have amniocentesis to find out whether they are carrying a child with birth defects that they may choose to abort. Before the procedure, they must have a sonogram, one of those fuzzy black-and-white photos like a love song heard through static on the radio, which shows someone is in there.

I have taped on my VCR a public television program in which somehow, inex- 12 plicably, a film is shown of a fetus *in utero* scratching its face, seemingly putting up a tiny hand to shield itself from the camera's eye. It would make a potent weapon in the arsenal of the antiabortionists. I grow sentimental about it as it floats in the salt water, part fish, part human being. It is almost living, but not quite. It has almost turned my heart around, but not quite turned my head.

Rhetorical Focus

1. Quindlen begins her essay by juxtaposing two "looks" (see the first sentences of paragraphs 1 and 3). How does this rhetorical strategy help her establish the issues that she goes on to explore in the rest of her essay? Note the statement of belief she also makes at the beginning (paragraph 2).

Do you think readers should take this as a thesis statement? In other words, do you think her main purpose in this essay is to get readers to become prochoice? Explain.

2. Do you think Quindlen uses examples convincingly when she refers to other people in paragraphs 5 and 6? Why or why not? Like Selzer and Tisdale, Quindlen also supports her ideas by referring to her personal experience; however, she has neither observed an abortion nor had one herself. Does she succeed in convincing you anyway that a discussion of her own family life belongs in an essay about abortion? Why or why not?

3. Like Selzer and Tisdale, Quindlen refers to images of the developing fetus. She mostly does so in her last two paragraphs. What do you think the other two authors would say about her placing such images there? Support your speculations with references to all three texts.

Thematic Focus

1. Quindlen states that her position on abortion is "in the middle" (paragraph 4). Do you agree with this label? Why or why not? Do you think you take a middle position on abortion? Explain.

2. What is the distinction between legality and morality that Quindlen draws in paragraph 10? Does this distinction make sense to you? Why or why not?

3. Quindlen's last sentence indicates a conflict between her heart and her head. In what ways does the rest of the essay suggest this conflict? Does Quindlen strike you as experiencing more inner conflict about abortion than Selzer and Tisdale do? Support your answer by referring to passages in all three texts.

Suggestions for Writing

1. Write an essay in which you draw on the three essays you have read to identify what you think people should take into account when they formulate a position on abortion. Which of Selzer's observations and thoughts, if any, should people heed? Which of Tisdale's? Which of Quindlen's? Are there any issues that none of them raises, but that should be raised? If you find one or more of these texts not worth heeding at all, explain why.

2. Write an essay identifying how one of these authors might respond to each of the other two. Support your speculations about the author's responses by referring to specific passages in the essays. Indicate in your conclusion whether you agree with the responses you believe that the author you focus on would make.

3. Quindlen reminds us that a number of college students face the decision of whether to have an abortion. Imagine the following situation: Your college's administration does not want to be seen as condoning abortion. Student health clinic personnel are therefore not allowed to give students information about local abortion clinics. Write a letter to the dean of

students supporting this policy or advocating a new one, depending on the beliefs you actually hold. Give specific reasons why the college should hold your position.

THE DEBATE OVER EUTHANASIA

This constellation focuses on euthanasia, the act of ending someone's life because death seems more merciful. Medication and hospital technology keep more and more people minimally alive when in the past they would have died. Thus, increasingly, we need to decide when, if ever, a life gets so poor that someone has a right to end it. We must also decide who should have ultimate authority in such cases. Take the example of a brain-dead man kept barely alive by a respirator. If the members of his family want it disconnected, must they have evidence that he would agree with them? If so, what must the evidence be? Aside from the family, what role should the doctor or hospital board have in this decision? What should be the role of the legal system? Another issue arises over methods. You may tolerate certain acts of passive euthanasia, in which further treatment is simply withheld, but would you ever approve of active euthanasia, the deliberate killing of a patient? What about actively helping someone to end his or her own life?

Society continues to debate these questions, as the attention given to two recent texts indicates. The first appeared in *The Journal of the American Medical Association (JAMA)*. This periodical regularly features "A Piece of My Mind," where readers contribute anecdotes that raise professional concerns. The January 8, 1988 column provoked hundreds of responses in *The Journal* and elsewhere. Written anonymously, "It's Over, Debbie" related with approval a case in which a doctor committed active euthanasia or something close to it. While many agreed wholly or in part with the article, many others deplored it and even criticized *JAMA* for publishing it. We present both the article and a piece criticizing it, which appeared in the April 8, 1988 issue of *JAMA*. We also present an article that generated news when it appeared in the March 7, 1991 issue of *The New England Journal of Medicine*. In "Death and Dying—A Case of Individualized Decision Making," Dr. Timothy E. Quill openly acknowledges how he indirectly assisted a terminally ill patient when she decided to end her life before she suffered very much. Consider the issues that all three pieces here raise, how they raise them, and how you would approach the controversy over euthanasia, as well as other ethical challenges that society still faces.

It's Over, Debbie

Anonymous

The Journal of the American Medical Association has a regular column
entitled "A Piece of My Mind," in which readers tell anecdotes dealing with
general concerns of the medical profession. What follows was the column
for January 8, 1988. The author's name was withheld.

Reflections Before Reading

Under what circumstances would you think it all right to withhold further
treatment from a patient? Who do you think should make such decisions?
Do you think it is ever all right for doctors to administer a drug that they
know will hasten their patient's death? If you wanted to dramatize an act of
euthanasia that would make several points about the subject, what scenario
would you create?

The call came in the middle of the night. As a gynecology resident rotating through   1
a large, private hospital, I had come to detest telephone calls, because invariably I
would be up for several hours and would not feel good the next day. However, duty
called, so I answered the phone. A nurse informed me that a patient was having
difficulty getting rest, could I please see her. She was on 3 North. That was the
gynecologic-oncology unit, not my usual duty station. As I trudged along, bumping
sleepily against walls and corners and not believing I was up again, I tried to imagine what I might find at the end of my walk. Maybe an elderly woman with an
anxiety reaction, or perhaps something particularly horrible.

I grabbed the chart from the nurses' station on my way to the patient's room,   2
and the nurse gave me some hurried details: a 20-year-old girl named Debbie was
dying of ovarian cancer. She was having unrelenting vomiting apparently as the
result of an alcohol drip administered for sedation. Hmmm, I thought. Very sad.
As I approached the room I could hear loud, labored breathing. I entered and saw
an emaciated, dark-haired woman who appeared much older than 20. She was
receiving nasal oxygen, had an IV, and was sitting in bed suffering from what was
obviously severe air hunger. The chart noted her weight at 80 pounds. A second
woman, also dark-haired but of middle age, stood at her right, holding her hand.
Both looked up as I entered. The room seemed filled with the patient's desperate

effort to survive. Her eyes were hollow, and she had suprasternal and intercostal retractions with her rapid inspirations. She had not eaten or slept in two days. She had not responded to chemotherapy and was being given supportive care only. It was a gallows scene, a cruel mockery of her youth and unfulfilled potential. Her only words to me were, "Let's get this over with."

I retreated with my thoughts to the nurses' station. The patient was tired and needed rest. I could not give her health, but I could give her rest. I asked the nurse to draw 20 mg of morphine sulfate into a syringe. Enough, I thought, to do the job. I took the syringe into the room and told the two women I was going to give Debbie something that would let her rest and to say good-bye. Debbie looked at the syringe, then laid her head on the pillow with her eyes open, watching what was left of the world. I injected the morphine intravenously and watched to see if my calculations on its effects would be correct. Within seconds her breathing slowed to a normal rate, her eyes closed, and her features softened as she seemed restful at last. The older woman stroked the hair of the now-sleeping patient. I waited for the inevitable next effect of depressing the respiratory drive. With clocklike certainty, within four minutes the breathing rate slowed even more, then became irregular, then ceased. The dark-haired woman stood erect and seemed relieved.

3

It's over, Debbie.

4

Rhetorical Focus

1. In what ways does this text indicate that it was written for members of the medical profession? If you are not a member of this profession, what passages in the text, if any, are difficult for you to understand? Overall, do you consider this text basically accessible to a layperson? Why or why not?
2. How much of this text reveals the narrator's emotions? Did you find the amount of personal feeling expressed here sufficient? Explain.
3. Judging by this text, what seem to be the advantages and the disadvantages of examining the subject of euthanasia through a dramatized case?

Thematic Focus

1. If the narrator had ended by stating the moral of this story, what do you think it would have been?
2. Do you approve of what the doctor did? Should he or she have done anything differently?
3. How much do particular circumstances matter in this text? Would you have changed your mind about it if the circumstances it depicts were somewhat different? Explain.

"Doctors Must Not Kill"

Willard Gaylin, Leon R. Kass, Edmund D. Pellegrino, and Mark Siegler

This response to "It's Over, Debbie" appeared in the April 8, 1988 issue of *The Journal of the American Medical Association*. The authors are all medical doctors. Willard Gaylin heads the Hastings Center in Briarcliff Manor, New York, an institute for research in medical ethics. Leon R. Kass serves on the Committee on Social Thought at the University of Chicago, and Mark Siegler is a member of the Center for Clinical Medical Ethics there. Edmund D. Pellegrino is affiliated with the Kennedy Institute of Ethics at Georgetown University.

Reflections Before Reading

What are possible responses to "It's Over, Debbie"? In particular, what might doctors hostile to it say? What in the text do you hope they will pay attention to?

In the middle of the night, a sleepy gynecology resident is called to attend a young 1
woman, dying of cancer, whom he has never seen before. Horrified by her severe distress, and proceeding alone without consultation with anyone, he gives her a lethal injection of morphine, clearly intending the death that promptly ensues. The resident submits a first-person account of his killing to the *Journal of the American Medical Association*. Without any editorial comment, *JAMA* publishes the account, withholding the author's name at his request. What in the world is going on?

Before the sophisticated obscure our vision with clouds of arguments and sub- 2
tle qualifications, we must fix our gaze on the brute facts.

First, on his own admission, the resident appears to have committed a felony: 3
premeditated murder. Direct intentional homicide is a felony in all American ju-

risdictions, for which the plea of merciful motive is no excuse. That the homicide was clearly intentional is confirmed by the resident's act of unrepentant publication.

Second, law aside, the physician behaved altogether in a scandalously unprofessional and unethical manner. He did not know the patient: he had never seen her before, he did not study her chart, he did not converse with her or her family. He never spoke to *her* physician. He took as an unambiguous command her only words to him, "Let's get this over with": he did not bother finding out what precisely she meant or whether she meant it wholeheartedly. He did not consider alternative ways of bringing her relief or comfort; instead of comfort, he gave her death. This is no humane and thoughtful physician succumbing with fear and trembling to the pressures and well-considered wishes of a patient well known to him, for whom there was truly no other recourse. This is, by his own account, an impulsive yet cold technician, arrogantly masquerading as a knight of compassion and humanity. (Indeed, so cavalier is the report and so cold-blooded the behavior, it strains our credulity to think that the story is true.) 4

Third, law and professional manner both aside, the resident violated one of the first and most hallowed canons of the medical ethic: doctors must not kill. Generations of physicians and commentators on medical ethics have underscored and held fast to the distinction between ceasing useless treatments (or allowing to die) and active, willful taking of life; at least since the Oath of Hippocrates, Western medicine has regarded the killing of patients, even on request, as a profound violation of the deepest meaning of the medical vocation. As recently as 1986, the Judicial Council of the American Medical Association, in an opinion regarding treatment of dying patients, affirmed the principle that a physician "should not intentionally cause death." Neither legal tolerance nor the best bedside manner can ever make medical killing medically ethical. 5

The conduct of the physician is inexcusable. But the conduct of the editor of *JAMA* is incomprehensible. By publishing this report, he knowingly publicizes a felony and shields the felon. He deliberately publicizes the grossest medical malfeasance and shields the malefactor from professional scrutiny and judgment, presumably allowing him to continue his practices without possibility of rebuke and remonstrance, not even from the physician whose private patient he privately dispatched. Why? For what possible purpose central to *JAMA*'s professional mission? 6

According to newspaper reports, the editor of *JAMA* published the article "to promote discussion" of a timely and controversial topic. But is this a responsible way for the prestigious voice of our venerable profession to address the subject of medical killing? Is it morally responsible to promulgate challenges to our most fundamental moral principles without editorial rebuke or comment, "for the sake of discussion"? Decent folk do not deliberately stir discussion of outrageous practices, like slavery, incest, or killing those in our care. 7

What is to be done? Regarding the case at hand, the proper course is clear. *JAMA* should voluntarily turn all the information it has regarding the case over to the legal authorities in the pertinent jurisdictions. The physician's name should also be reported to his hospital directors and to his state and county medical societies for their scrutiny and action. The Council on Ethical and Judicial Affairs of 8 the American Medical Association should examine the case, as well as the decision to publish it. Justice requires nothing less.

But much more is at stake than punishing an offender. The very soul of medicine is on trial. For this is not one of those peripheral issues about which pluralism and relativism can be tolerated, about which a value-free stand on the substance can be hedged around with procedural safeguards to ensure informed consent or "sound decision-making." Nor is this an issue, like advertising, fee-splitting, or cooperation with chiropractors, that touches medicine only as a trade. This issue touches medicine at its very moral center; if this moral center collapses, if physicians become killers or are even merely licensed to kill, the profession—and, therewith, each physician—will never again be worthy of trust and respect as healer and comforter and protector of life in all its frailty. For if medicine's power over life may be used equally to heal or to kill, the doctor is no more a moral professional but rather a morally neutered technician.

These are perilous times for our profession. The Hemlock Society and others are in the courts and legislatures trying to legalize killing by physicians at patient request. Such a proposal is almost certainly going to be on the ballot in California next November. High costs of care for the old and incurable already tempt some physicians to regard as "dispensable" some patients who never express the wish to die. In the Netherlands, where the barriers to physician killing are gone, there are now many well-documented cases of such cryptic and "uninvited" killing by doctors.

Now is not the time for promoting neutral discussion. Rather, now is the time for the medical profession to rally in defense of its fundamental moral principles, to repudiate any and all acts of direct and intentional killing by physicians and their agents. We call on the profession and its leadership to obtain the best advice, regarding both theory and practice, about how to defend the profession's moral center and to resist growing pressures both from without and from within. We call on fellow physicians to say that we will not deliberately kill. We must say also to each of our fellow physicians that we will not tolerate killing of patients and that we shall take disciplinary action against doctors who kill. And we must say to the broader community that if it insists on tolerating or legalizing active euthanasia, it will have to find nonphysicians to do its killing.

Rhetorical Focus

1. Does the question that ends the opening paragraph strike you as a reasonable conclusion to it? Why or why not?
2. The authors believe it important first to list what they call "the brute facts." Do you agree with their use of this term, considering what they identify with it? Why or why not?
3. In the middle of their response, the authors shift to criticizing the editor of the journal. Do they thereby go off on a tangent, or is this move logical? Explain.

Thematic Focus

1. If you had to revise "It's Over, Debbie" so that these authors were comfortable with it, what changes would you make? Could any kind of euthanasia take place?
2. The authors declare, "Now is not the time for promoting neutral discussion" (paragraph 11). Why do they feel this way? Do you agree with them?
3. The authors suggest that "It's Over, Debbie" is a work of fiction. Would you be seriously bothered if it were? Why or why not?

Death and Dignity—A Case of Individualized Decision Making

Timothy E. Quill

Timothy E. Quill (b. 1949) attended Amherst College as an undergraduate and then earned a doctor of medicine degree at the University of Rochester in New York, where he is now an associate professor of medicine and psychiatry. Also a practicing internist, he serves as Associate Chief of Medicine at Gennessee Hospital in Rochester. The following essay appeared in the March 7, 1991 issue of *The New England Journal of Medicine*. After the essay was published, a grand jury considered indicting Quill, but ultimately decided not to charge him with a crime.

Reflections Before Reading

The case referred to in the title of this article is that of a terminally ill patient who ended her own life and solicited the author's indirect assistance in doing so. What sorts of things might Quill have considered in deciding whether and how to help his patient kill herself? Do you think a doctor can be justified in cooperating with a patient who did this? Why or why not? Do you think you might feel differently about this case than you did about Debbie's? Why or why not?

Diane was feeling tired and had a rash. A common scenario, though there was something subliminally worrisome that prompted me to check her blood count. Her hematocrit was 22, and the white-cell count was 4.3 with some metamyelocytes and unusual white cells. I wanted it to be viral, trying to deny what was staring me in the face. Perhaps in a repeated count it would disappear. I called Diane and told her it might be more serious than I had initially thought—that the test needed to be repeated and that if she felt worse, we might have to move quickly. When she pressed for the possibilities, I reluctantly opened the door to leukemia. Hearing the word seemed to make it exist. "Oh, shit!" she said. "Don't tell me that." Oh, shit! I thought, I wish I didn't have to.   1

Diane was no ordinary person (although no one I have ever come to know has been really ordinary). She was raised in an alcoholic family and had felt alone for much of her life. She had vaginal cancer as a young woman. Through much of her adult life, she had struggled with depression and her own alcoholism. I had come to know, respect, and admire her over the previous eight years as she confronted these problems and gradually overcame them. She was an incredibly clear, at times brutally honest, thinker and communicator. As she took control of her life, she developed a strong sense of independence and confidence. In the previous 3½ years, her hard work had paid off. She was completely abstinent from alcohol, she had established much deeper connections with her husband, college-age son, and several friends, and her business and her artistic work were blossoming. She felt she was really living fully for the first time.   2

Not surprisingly, the repeated blood count was abnormal, and detailed examination of the peripheral-blood smear showed myelocytes. I advised her to come into the hospital, explaining that we needed to do a bone marrow biopsy and make some decisions relatively rapidly. She came to the hospital knowing what we would find. She was terrified, angry, and sad. Although we knew the odds, we both clung to the thread of possibility that it might be something else.   3

The bone marrow confirmed the worst: acute myelomonocytic leukemia. In the face of this tragedy, we looked for signs of hope. This is an area of medicine in which technological intervention has been successful, with cures 25 percent of the time—long-term cures. As I probed the costs of these cures, I heard about induction chemotherapy (three weeks in the hospital, prolonged neutropenia, probable infectious complications, and hair loss; 75 percent of patients respond, 25 percent do not). For the survivors, this is followed by consolidation chemotherapy (with similar side effects; another 25 percent die, for a net survival of 50 percent). Those still alive, to have a reasonable chance of long-term survival, then need bone marrow transplantation (hospitalization for two months and whole-body irradiation, with complete killing of the bone marrow, infectious complications, and the possibility for graft-versus-host disease—with a survival of approximately 50 percent, or   4

25 percent of the original group). Though hematologists may argue over the exact percentages, they don't argue about the outcome of no treatment—certain death in days, weeks, or at most a few months.

Believing that delay was dangerous, our oncologist broke the news to Diane 5 and began making plans to insert a Hickman catheter and begin induction chemotherapy that afternoon. When I saw her shortly thereafter, she was enraged at his presumption that she would want treatment, and devastated by the finality of the diagnosis. All she wanted to do was go home and be with her family. She had no further questions about treatment and in fact had decided that she wanted none. Together we lamented her tragedy and the unfairness of life. Before she left, I felt the need to be sure that she and her husband understood that there was some risk in delay, that the problem was not going to go away, and that we needed to keep considering the options over the next several days. We agreed to meet in two days.

She returned in two days with her husband and son. They had talked exten- 6 sively about the problem and the options. She remained very clear about her wish not to undergo chemotherapy and to live whatever time she had left outside the hospital. As we explored her thinking further, it became clear that she was convinced she would die during the period of treatment and would suffer unspeakably in the process (from hospitalization, from lack of control over her body, from the side effects of chemotherapy, and from pain and anguish). Although I could offer support and my best effort to minimize her suffering if she chose treatment, there was no way I could say any of this would not occur. In fact, the last four patients with acute leukemia at our hospital had died very painful deaths in the hospital during various stages of treatment (a fact I did not share with her). Her family wished she would choose treatment but sadly accepted her decision. She articulated very clearly that it was she who would be experiencing all the side effects of treatment and that odds of 25 percent were not good enough for her to undergo so toxic a course of therapy, given her expectations of chemotherapy and hospitalization and the absence of a closely matched bone marrow donor. I had her repeat her understanding of the treatment, the odds, and what to expect if there were no treatment. I clarified a few misunderstandings, but she had a remarkable grasp of the options and implications.

I have been a longtime advocate of active, informed patient choice of treat- 7 ment or nontreatment, and of a patient's right to die with as much control and dignity as possible. Yet there was something about her giving up a 25 percent chance of long-term survival in favor of almost certain death that disturbed me. I had seen Diane fight and use her considerable inner resources to overcome alcoholism and depression, and I half expected her to change her mind over the next week. Since the window of time in which effective treatment can be initiated is rather narrow, we met several times that week. We obtained a second hematology consultation and talked at length about the meaning and implications of treatment and nontreatment. She talked to a psychologist she had seen in the past. I gradually understood the decision from her perspective and became convinced that it was the right decision for her. We arranged for home hospice care (although at that time Diane felt reasonably well, was active, and looked healthy), left the door open for her to change her mind, and tried to anticipate how to keep her comfortable in the time she had left.

Just as I was adjusting to her decision, she opened up another area that would   8
stretch me profoundly. It was extraordinarily important to Diane to maintain control of herself and her own dignity during the time remaining to her. When this was no longer possible, she clearly wanted to die. As a former director of a hospice program, I know how to use pain medicines to keep patients comfortable and lessen suffering. I explained the philosophy of comfort care, which I strongly believe in. Although Diane understood and appreciated this, she had known of people lingering in what was called relative comfort, and she wanted no part of it. When the time came, she wanted to take her life in the least painful way possible. Knowing of her desire for independence and her decision to stay in control, I thought this request made perfect sense. I acknowledged and explored this wish but also thought that it was out of the realm of currently accepted medical practice and that it was more than I could offer or promise. In our discussion, it became clear that preoccupation with her fear of a lingering death would interfere with Diane's getting the most out of the time she had left until she found a safe way to ensure her death. I feared the effects of a violent death on her family, the consequences of an ineffective suicide that would leave her lingering in precisely the state she dreaded so much, and the possibility that a family member would be forced to assist her, with all the legal and personal repercussions that would follow. She discussed this at length with her family. They believed that they should respect her choice. With this in mind, I told Diane that information was available from the Hemlock Society that might be helpful to her.

A week later she phoned me with a request for barbiturates for sleep. Since I   9
knew that this was an essential ingredient in a Hemlock Society suicide, I asked her to come to the office to talk things over. She was more than willing to protect me by participating in a superficial conversation about her insomnia, but it was important to me to know how she planned to use the drugs and to be sure that she was not in despair or overwhelmed in a way that might color her judgment. In our discussion, it was apparent that she was having trouble sleeping, but it was also evident that the security of having enough barbiturates available to commit suicide when and if the time came would leave her secure enough to live fully and concentrate on the present. It was clear that she was not despondent and that in fact she was making deep, personal connections with her family and close friends. I made sure that she knew how to use the barbiturates for sleep, and also that she knew the amount needed to commit suicide. We agreed to meet regularly, and she promised to meet with me before taking her life, to ensure that all other avenues had been exhausted. I wrote the prescription with an uneasy feeling about the boundaries I was exploring—spiritual, legal, professional, and personal. Yet I also felt strongly that I was setting her free to get the most out of the time she had left, and to maintain dignity and control on her own terms until her death.

The next several months were very intense and important for Diane. Her son   10
stayed home from college, and they were able to be with one another and say much that had not been said earlier. Her husband did his work at home so that he and Diane could spend more time together. She spent time with her closest friends. I

had her come into the hospital for a conference with our residents, at which she illustrated in a most profound and personal way the importance of informed decision making, the right to refuse treatment, and the extraordinarily personal effects of illness and interaction with the medical system. There were emotional and physical hardships as well. She had periods of intense sadness and anger. Several times she became very weak, but she received transfusions as an outpatient and responded with marked improvement of symptoms. She had two serious infections that responded surprisingly well to empirical courses of oral antibiotics. After three tumultuous months, there were two weeks of relative calm and well-being, and fantasies of a miracle began to surface.

Unfortunately, we had no miracle. Bone pain, weakness, fatigue, and fevers began to dominate her life. Although the hospice workers, family members, and I tried our best to minimize the suffering and promote comfort, it was clear that the end was approaching. Diane's immediate future held what she feared the most—increasing discomfort, dependence, and hard choices between pain and sedation. She called up her closest friends and asked them to come over to say goodbye, telling them that she would be leaving soon. As we had agreed, she let me know as well. When we met, it was clear that she knew what she was doing, that she was sad and frightened to be leaving, but that she would be even more terrified to stay and suffer. In our tearful goodbye, she promised a reunion in the future at her favorite spot on the edge of Lake Geneva, with dragons swimming in the sunset. 11

Two days later her husband called to say that Diane had died. She had said her final goodbyes to her husband and son that morning, and asked them to leave her alone for an hour. After an hour, which must have seemed an eternity, they found her on the couch, lying very still and covered by her favorite shawl. There was no sign of struggle. She seemed to be at peace. They called me for advice about how to proceed. When I arrived at their house, Diane indeed seemed peaceful. Her husband and son were quiet. We talked about what a remarkable person she had been. They seemed to have no doubts about the course she had chosen or about their cooperation, although the unfairness of her illness and the finality of her death were overwhelming to us all. 12

I called the medical examiner to inform him that a hospice patient had died. When asked about the cause of death, I said, "acute leukemia." He said that was fine and that we should call a funeral director. Although acute leukemia was the truth, it was not the whole story. Yet any mention of suicide would have given rise to a police investigation and probably brought the arrival of an ambulance crew for resuscitation. Diane would have become a "coroner's case," and the decision to perform an autopsy would have been made at the discretion of the medical examiner. The family or I could have been subject to criminal prosecution, and I to professional review, for our roles in support of Diane's choices. Although I truly believe that the family and I gave her the best care possible, allowing her to define her limits and directions as much as possible, I am not sure the law, society, or the medical profession would agree. So I said "acute leukemia" to protect all of us, to protect Diane from an invasion into her past and her body, and to continue to shield society from the knowledge of the degree of suffering that people often undergo in the process of dying. Suffering can be lessened to some extent, but in 13 no way eliminated or made benign, by the careful intervention of a competent, caring physician, given current social constraints.

Diane taught me about the range of help I can provide if I know people well   14
and if I allow them to say what they really want. She taught me about life, death, and honesty and about taking charge and facing tragedy squarely when it strikes. She taught me that I can take small risks for people that I really know and care about. Although I did not assist in her suicide directly, I helped indirectly to make it possible, successful, and relatively painless. Although I know we have measures to help control pain and lessen suffering, to think that people do not suffer in the process of dying is an illusion. Prolonged dying can occasionally be peaceful, but more often the role of the physician and family is limited to lessening but not eliminating severe suffering.

I wonder how many families and physicians secretly help patients over the   15
edge into death in the face of such severe suffering. I wonder how many severely ill or dying patients secretly take their lives, dying alone in despair. I wonder whether the image of Diane's final aloneness will persist in the minds of her family, or if they will remember more the intense, meaningful months they had together before she died. I wonder whether Diane struggled in that last hour, and whether the Hemlock Society's way of death by suicide is the most benign. I wonder why Diane, who gave so much to so many of us, had to be alone for the last hour of her life. I wonder whether I will see Diane again, on the shore of Lake Geneva at sunset, with dragons swimming on the horizon.

Rhetorical Focus

1. What do you take to be Quill's purpose(s) in writing this essay? Use specific passages to support your reasoning.
2. Where, if anywhere, does Quill indicate his personal feelings? Where, if anywhere, is his tone objective or matter of fact? Overall, do you consider his tone appropriate throughout his account of Diane's case? Why or why not? Consider, among other things, the medical audience for which he is writing. Do you think you represent a significantly different audience, with a different sense of what is appropriate? Explain.
3. Unlike the anonymous author of "It's Over, Debbie," Quill has decided to reveal who he is. Are you more sympathetic to him than to the author of "Debbie" because he reveals his identity?

Thematic Focus

1. What adjectives would you use to describe Diane, based on Quill's account of her? What adjectives would you use to describe the image that Quill presents of himself? What adjectives would you use to describe the relationship between doctor and patient depicted here? In general, do you accept what each of them did? Why or why not?

2. Which strike you more, the similarities or the differences between Quill's behavior and that of the doctor in "It's Over, Debbie"? Support your reasoning by referring to specific passages in each text.

3. What might the authors of " 'Doctors Must Not Kill' " say about Quill? Do you think they might tolerate his account more than they did "It's Over, Debbie"? Why or why not?

Suggestions for Writing

1. Acknowledging that you are a layperson, write an essay for *The Journal of the American Medical Association* in which you give your own response to "It's Over, Debbie," or an essay for *The New England Journal of Medicine* in which you respond to Quill's essay. Indicate in particular whether you tolerate the behavior described in the text you are discussing. In explaining your response, refer in some way to the other two texts that you have read.

2. Write a version of "It's Over, Debbie" that would clearly suggest to most readers that the doctor is wrong. Keep the first person narrator. You can change features of the plot, but try sticking to the original as much as possible.

3. As he recalls Diane's case, Quill notes that her decision to obtain fatal drugs "opened up another area that would stretch me profoundly" (paragraph 8). Describe an occasion when the behavior of someone you know stretched *you* profoundly, in the sense that it forced you to analyze and perhaps revise some of your deepest ethical beliefs and assumptions. What were the actions and issues involved? Did the situation have a lasting impact on you? If so, in what way? You might use the narrative form that Quill uses.

THE ETHICS OF A CULTURE

The preceding sections in this unit touch on society's moral character in general even as they deal with particular individuals and controversies. Throughout this book, we have presented essays that raise questions about the ethics of American culture. Now we conclude this unit, and this book, with two essays that focus on the subject. In an admittedly speculative piece from his *New England Journal of Medicine* column of the early 1970s, Lewis Thomas attempts to understand what the nasty behavior of a tribe called the Iks suggests about other civilizations, including ours. In a column for *Time* that appeared in October 1990, three months before America went to war against Iraq, Barbara Ehrenreich argues against its doing so by criticizing it as a warrior culture.

When undertaking cultural criticism such as this, writers face at least two questions. First, when are we justified in making any generalization about our own culture, or about any other? Some would say that the members of a culture are too diverse for them all to fit one large statement. Both Thomas and Ehrenreich would thus be unwise to characterize Americans and Iks in any way. Yet others would claim that cultures do show general patterns of behavior, and that consciously or unconsciously, we do, in fact, generalize about them all the time. A second question concerns the specific nature of generalizations about a culture's ethics. When, if ever, are we justified in morally judging the behavior of our culture or that of another? Some would call for a relativist position, arguing that we do not have a right to impose our personal standards on the rest of our own society or on another. Others would say that it is hard and actually unreasonable for us to accept everything that cultures do, even if our criticisms expose us in turn to accusations of self-righteousness or ethnocentrism. Perhaps the central issue then becomes what evidence cultural critics such as Thomas and Ehrenreich use to support their generalizations, and what particular effects they aim for when they make them. See whether you agree with them as they use tribal cultures to illuminate the moral values of our own. Think, too, of the methods and assumptions you would draw on to analyze the ethics of a culture.

The Iks

Lewis Thomas

Lewis Thomas (b. 1913) is a well-known cell biologist who has become just as famous for his work as an essayist. In the early 1970s, he began writing monthly columns for *The New England Journal of Medicine*. Three collections of these have been published: *The Lives of a Cell*, a 1974 volume that won the National Book Award, *The Medusa and the Snail*, and *Late Night Thoughts on Listening to Mahler's Ninth Symphony*. He has also published his autobiography, *The Youngest Science*, and a collection of essays on language, *Et Cetera, Et Cetera: Notes of a Word-Watcher*. For many years Chancellor of the Memorial Sloan-Kettering Cancer Center in New York, Thomas is now scholar-in-residence at Cornell University Medical College. The following essay appears in *The Lives of a Cell*. The book Thomas refers to is Colin M. Turnbull's *The Mountain People*.

Reflections Before Reading

Do you think there is a basic human nature? If so, what do you think humans have in common? Do you think that cultures often have very different moral standards? When, if ever, do Americans have a right to make generalizations about a tribe in another part of the world? What, if anything, might such a tribe enable Americans to learn about themselves?

The small tribe of Iks, formerly nomadic hunters and gatherers in the mountain   1
valleys of northern Uganda, have become celebrities, literary symbols for the ultimate fate of disheartened, heartless mankind at large. Two disastrously conclusive
things happened to them: the government decided to have a national park, so they
were compelled by law to give up hunting in the valleys and become farmers on
poor hillside soil, and then they were visited for two years by an anthropologist who
detested them and wrote a book about them.

The message of the book is that the Iks have transformed themselves into an   2
irreversibly disagreeable collection of unattached, brutish creatures, totally selfish
and loveless, in response to the dismantling of their traditional culture. Moreover,
this is what the rest of us are like in our inner selves, and we will all turn into Iks
when the structure of our society comes all unhinged.

The argument rests, of course, on certain assumptions about the core of hu-   3
man beings, and is necessarily speculative. You have to agree in advance that man
is fundamentally a bad lot, out for himself alone, displaying such graces as affection
and compassion only as learned habits. If you take this view, the story of the Iks can
be used to confirm it. These people seem to be living together, clustered in small,
dense villages, but they are really solitary, unrelated individuals with no evident
use for each other. They talk, but only to make ill-tempered demands and cold refus-
als. They share nothing. They never sing. They turn the children out to forage as soon
as they can walk, and desert the elders to starve whenever they can, and the foraging children snatch food from the mouths of the helpless elders. It is a mean society.

They breed without love or even casual regard. They defecate on each other's   4
doorsteps. They watch their neighbors for signs of misfortune, and only then do
they laugh. In the book they do a lot of laughing, having so much bad luck. Several
times they even laughed at the anthropologist, who found this especially repellent
(one senses, between the lines, that the scholar is not himself the world's luckiest
man). Worse, they took him into the family, snatched his food, defecated on his
doorstep, and hooted dislike at him. They gave him two bad years.

It is a depressing book. If, as he suggests, there is only Ikness at the center   5
of each of us, our sole hope for hanging on to the name of humanity will be in
endlessly mending the structure of our society, and it is changing so quickly and
completely that we may never find the threads in time. Meanwhile, left to ourselves alone, solitary, we will become the same joyless, zestless, untouching lone
animals.

But this may be too narrow a view. For one thing, the Iks are extraordinary.   6
They are absolutely astonishing, in fact. The anthropologist has never seen people

like them anywhere, nor have I. You'd think, if they were simply examples of the common essence of mankind, they'd seem more recognizable. Instead, they are bizarre, anomalous. I have known my share of peculiar, difficult, nervous, grabby people, but I've never encountered any genuinely, consistently detestable human beings in all my life. The Iks sound more like abnormalities, maladies.

I cannot accept it. I do not believe that the Iks are representative of isolated, revealed man, unobscured by social habits. I believe their behavior is something extra, something laid on. This unremitting, compulsive repellence is a kind of complicated ritual. They must have learned to act this way; they copied it, somehow.   7

I have a theory, then. The Iks have gone crazy.   8

The solitary Ik, isolated in the ruins of an exploded culture, has built a new defense for himself. If you live in an unworkable society you can make up one of your own, and this is what the Iks have done. Each Ik has become a group, a one-man tribe on its own, a constituency.   9

Now everything falls into place. This is why they do seem, after all, vaguely familiar to all of us. We've seen them before. This is precisely the way groups of one size or another, ranging from committees to nations, behave. It is, of course, this aspect of humanity that has lagged behind the rest of evolution, and this is why the Ik seems so primitive. In his absolute selfishness, his incapacity to give anything away, no matter what, he is a successful committee. When he stands at the door of his hut, shouting insults at his neighbors in a loud harangue, he is city addressing another city.   10

Cities have all the Ik characteristics. They defecate on doorsteps, in rivers and lakes, their own or anyone else's. They leave rubbish. They detest all neighboring cities, give nothing away. They even build institutions for deserting elders out of sight.   11

Nations are the most Iklike of all. No wonder the Iks seem familiar. For total greed, rapacity, heartlessness, and irresponsibility there is nothing to match a nation. Nations, by law, are solitary, self-centered, withdrawn into themselves. There is no such thing as affection between nations, and certainly no nation ever loved another. They bawl insults from their doorsteps, defecate into whole oceans, snatch all the food, survive by detestation, take joy in the bad luck of others, celebrate the death of others, live for the death of others.   12

That's it, and I shall stop worrying about the book. It does not signify that man is a sparse, inhuman thing at his center. He's all right. It only says what we've always known and never had enough time to worry about, that we haven't yet learned how to stay human when assembled in masses. The Ik, in his despair, is acting out this failure, and perhaps we should pay closer attention. Nations have themselves become too frightening to think about, but we might learn some things by watching these people.   13

Rhetorical Focus

1. How does this essay suggest that it is a narrative of Thomas's developing thought process? Why do you think he organizes his essay this way? Is it possible that he did not actually think about the Iks in the series of steps he presents here? If so, can he be accused of misleading us?

2. In what ways does Thomas use repetition to connect parts of his essay?
3. Describe Thomas's tone in the last paragraph. Should all his statements be taken straight? Refer to particular ones as you explain your reasoning.

Thematic Focus

1. In what ways does Thomas rely on the anthropologist's book? In what ways does he depart from it? In general, do you think Thomas is entitled to speculate about the Iks' significance even though he has not directly encountered them, let alone been one of them? Explain your reasoning.
2. Do you agree with Thomas's analysis of the Iks? Do they pose issues for you that Thomas does not discuss or sufficiently acknowledge? If so, what?
3. By the end of the essay, what does Thomas seem most concerned about? Do you share his concern? Why or why not?

The Warrior Culture

Barbara Ehrenreich

Barbara Ehrenreich (b. 1941) has frequently written on mass culture and politics. She has co-authored *Witches, Wives, and Nurses: A History of Women Healers, Complaints and Disorders: The Sexual Politics of Sickness, For Her Own Good: 150 Years of the Experts' Advice to Women, Re-Making Love: The Femininization of Sex,* and *The Mean Season: The Attack on the Welfare State.* On her own, she has written *The Hearts of Men: American Dreams and the Flight From Commitment, Fear of Falling: The Inner Life of the Middle Class,* and *The Worst Years of Our Lives,* a collection of her essays. She has written regular columns for *Ms.* and *Mother Jones.* The following essay appeared as the back-page column in the October 15, 1990 issue of *Time,* when Americans were debating whether to go to war against Iraq. War did begin three months later.

Reflections Before Reading

Do you think there are "warrior cultures"? What do you associate with this term? Does applying it to America make sense to you? Why or why not? What position did you take regarding America's decision to go to war against Iraq? Why did you hold this position?

In what we like to think of as "primitive" warrior cultures, the passage to manhood requires the blooding of a spear, the taking of a scalp or head. Among the Masai of eastern Africa, the North American Plains Indians and dozens of other pretechnological peoples, a man could not marry until he had demonstrated his capacity to kill in battle. Leadership too in a warrior culture is typically contingent on military prowess and wrapped in the mystique of death. In the Solomon Islands a chief's importance could be reckoned by the number of skulls posted around his door, and it was the duty of the Aztec kings to nourish the gods with the hearts of human captives.

All warrior peoples have fought for the same high-sounding reasons: honor, glory or revenge. The nature of their real and perhaps not conscious motivations is a subject of much debate. Some anthropologists postulate a murderous instinct, almost unique among living species, in human males. Others discern a materialistic motive behind every fray: a need for slaves, grazing land or even human flesh to eat. Still others point to the similarities between war and other male pastimes—the hunt and outdoor sports—and suggest that it is boredom, ultimately, that stirs men to fight.

But in a warrior culture it hardly matters which motive is most basic. Aggressive behavior is rewarded whether or not it is innate to the human psyche. Shortages of resources are habitually taken as occasions for armed offensives, rather than for hard thought and innovation. And war, to a warrior people, is of course the highest adventure, the surest antidote to malaise, the endlessly repeated theme of legend, song, religious myth and personal quest for meaning. It is how men die and what they find to live for.

"You must understand that Americans are a warrior nation," Senator Daniel Patrick Moynihan told a group of Arab leaders in early September, one month into the Middle East crisis. He said this proudly, and he may, without thinking through the ugly implications, have told the truth. In many ways, in outlook and behavior the U.S. has begun to act like a primitive warrior culture.

We seem to believe that leadership is expressed, in no small part, by a willingness to cause the deaths of others. After the U.S. invasion of Panama, President Bush exulted that no one could call him "timid"; he was at last a "macho man." The press, in even more primal language, hailed him for succeeding in an "initiation rite" by demonstrating his "willingness to shed blood."

For lesser offices too we apply the standards of a warrior culture. Female candidates are routinely advised to overcome the handicap of their gender by talking "tough." Thus, for example, Dianne Feinstein has embraced capital punishment, while Colorado senatorial candidate Josie Heath has found it necessary to announce that although she is the mother of an 18-year-old son, she is prepared to vote for war. Male candidates in some of the fall contests are finding their military records under scrutiny. No one expects them, as elected officials in a civilian government, to pick up a spear or a sling and fight. But they must state, at least, their willingness to have another human killed.

More tellingly, we are unnerved by peace and seem to find it boring. When the cold war ended, we found no reason to celebrate. Instead we heated up the "war on drugs." What should have been a public-health campaign, focused on the persistent shame of poverty, became a new occasion for martial rhetoric and muscle flexing. Months later, when the Berlin Wall fell and communism collapsed throughout Europe, we Americans did not dance in the streets. What we did, according to the networks, was change the channel to avoid the news. Nonviolent revolutions do not uplift us, and the loss of mortal enemies only seems to leave us empty and bereft.   7

Our collective fantasies center on mayhem, cruelty and violent death. Loving images of the human body—especially of bodies seeking pleasure or expressing love—inspire us with the urge to censor. Our preference is for warrior themes: the lone fighting man, bandoliers across his naked chest, mowing down lesser men in gusts of automatic-weapon fire. Only a real war seems to revive our interest in real events. With the Iraqi crisis, the networks report, ratings for news shows rose again—even higher than they were for Panama.   8

And as in any primitive warrior culture, our warrior elite takes pride of place. Social crises multiply numbingly—homelessness, illiteracy, epidemic disease— and our leaders tell us solemnly that nothing can be done. There is no money. We are poor, not rich, a debtor nation. Meanwhile, nearly a third of the federal budget flows, even in moments of peace, to the warriors and their weaponmakers. When those priorities are questioned, some new "crisis" dutifully arises to serve as another occasion for armed and often unilateral intervention.   9

Now, with Operation Desert Shield, our leaders are reduced to begging foreign powers for the means to support our warrior class. It does not seem to occur to us that the other great northern powers—Japan, Germany, the Soviet Union—might not have found the stakes so high or the crisis quite so threatening. It has not penetrated our imagination that in a world where the powerful, industrialized nation-states are at last at peace, there might be other ways to face down a pint-size Third World warrior state than with massive force of arms. Nor have we begun to see what an anachronism we are in danger of becoming: a warrior nation in a world that pines for peace, a high-tech state with the values of a warrior band.   10

A leftist might blame "imperialism"; a right-winger would call our problem "internationalism." But an anthropologist, taking the long view, might say this is just what warriors do. Intoxicated by their own drumbeats and war songs, fascinated by the glint of steel and the prospect of blood, they will go forth, time and again, to war.   11

Rhetorical Focus

1. Ehrenreich does not mention America until her fourth paragraph, and even then she does so only by quoting Daniel Moynihan. Why do you think she delays? Why do you think she relies on Moynihan's statement?
2. What do you think is Ehrenreich's overall purpose in writing this essay? What does she want her readers to do? Does Thomas's purpose seem similar, or different?
3. Thomas uses "I," but Ehrenreich does not. Should he have avoided it? Should she have used it? Explain.

Thematic Focus

1. What reasons does Ehrenreich give for considering America a "warrior culture"? Do you find yourself agreeing that this is at least one possible label for the country? Why or why not? Would you be disturbed if someone agreed with Ehrenreich that America is a "warrior culture" yet considered this label positive? Why or why not? In general, does America's victory in the war against Iraq affect your response to this essay? Explain.
2. Both Thomas and Ehrenreich draw analogies between tribal cultures and larger ones, including ours. Are these analogies equally justified? Why or why not?
3. As was common in the early 1970s, Thomas uses the generic male. Ehrenreich focuses more or less on specifically male behavior. Should gender distinctions matter in their essays? Explain.

Suggestions for Writing

1. Explain how Ehrenreich could have used Thomas's essay to back up her argument, or how Thomas could have used Ehrenreich's essay to back up his. As part of your explanation, refer to details of both texts, as well as to your overall opinions of them.
2. Whether or not it is fair for Ehrenreich to describe America in general as a "warrior culture," many people have observed that the specific worlds of business and sports often seem to call for their people to be warriorlike. Imagine either a corporation manager orienting new employees or a football coach welcoming back the team at the beginning of the season. Imagine further that this person is demanding that his or her group be warriors; then, write an essay in which you explain how you would feel about this person's demand. Would you be more inclined to worry about it or to accept it? Note that in explaining your attitude, you will need to identify what specific values and actions you think the manager or coach would probably have in mind when calling for warriors.

3. Like Ehrenreich, write an essay in which you point out some aspect of American life that you want your readers to notice more. Let the essay be called "The __ Culture," and you supply the missing word. Be sure to justify the particular word you choose by citing details of American life you have observed or read about.

Index